Fundamentals of Developmental Cognitive Neuroscience

An exciting introduction to the scientific interface between biological studies of the brain and behavioral studies of human development. The authors trace the field from its roots in developmental psychology and neuroscience, and highlight some of the most persuasive research findings before anticipating future directions the field may take. They begin with a brief orientation of the brain, along with genetics and epigenetics, and then summarize brain development and plasticity. Later chapters detail the neurodevelopmental basis of a wide variety of human competencies, including perception, language comprehension, socioemotional development, memory systems, literacy and numeracy, and self-regulation. Suitable for advanced undergraduate and graduate courses in developmental cognition or neuroscience, this textbook covers the prenatal period through to infancy, childhood, and adolescence. It is pedagogically rich, featuring interviews with leading researchers, learning objectives, review questions, further-reading recommendations, and numerous color figures. Instructor teaching is supported by lecture slides and a test bank.

Heather Bortfeld is Professor of Psychological Sciences and Cognitive and Information Sciences at the University of California, Merced. She has been a pioneer in the development of functional near-infrared spectroscopy (fNIRS) as a tool for measuring changes in brain activity in infants and toddlers as they engage with the world around them. She is currently the Emmett, Bernice, and Carlston Cunningham Endowed Chair in Cognitive Development at UC Merced, and an elected Fellow of the Association for Psychological Sciences.

Silvia A. Bunge is Professor of Psychology at the University of California, Berkeley, and directs the Building Blocks of Cognition Laboratory, which draws from the fields of cognitive neuroscience, developmental psychology, and education research. She studies the development of higher-level cognitive abilities, how they are shaped by experience, and how they support academic success. Professor Bunge is an elected Fellow of the Association for Psychological Sciences and the Humboldt Society of Experimental Psychologists.

Cambridge Fundamentals of Neuroscience in Psychology

Developed in response to a growing need to make neuroscience accessible to students and other non-specialist readers, the *Cambridge Fundamentals of Neuroscience in Psychology* series provides brief introductions to key areas of neuroscience research across major domains of psychology. Written by experts in cognitive, social, affective, developmental, clinical, and applied neuroscience, these books will serve as ideal primers for students and other readers seeking an entry point to the challenging world of neuroscience.

Books in the Series

Fundamentals of Developmental Cognitive Neuroscience

Heather Bortfeld
University of California, Merced

Silvia A. Bunge
University of California, Berkeley

Shaftesbury Road, Cambridge CB2 8EA, United Kingdom

One Liberty Plaza, 20th Floor, New York, NY 10006, USA

477 Williamstown Road, Port Melbourne, VIC 3207, Australia

314–321, 3rd Floor, Plot 3, Splendor Forum, Jasola District Centre, New Delhi – 110025, India

103 Penang Road, #05–06/07, Visioncrest Commercial, Singapore 238467

Cambridge University Press is part of Cambridge University Press & Assessment, a department of the University of Cambridge.

We share the University's mission to contribute to society through the pursuit of education, learning and research at the highest international levels of excellence.

www.cambridge.org
Information on this title: www.cambridge.org/highereducation/isbn/9781108498760

DOI: 10.1017/9781108595827

First published 2024

Printed in the United Kingdom by TJ Books Limited, Padstow Cornwall

A catalogue record for this publication is available from the British Library

Library of Congress Cataloging-in-Publication Data
Names: Bortfeld, Heather, 1969– author. | Bunge, Silvia A., author.
Title: Fundamentals of developmental cognitive neuroscience / Heather Bortfeld, University of California, Merced, Silvia A. Bunge, University of California, Berkeley.
Description: Cambridge, United Kingdom ; New York, NY : Cambridge University Press, 2024. | Series: Cambridge fundamentals of neuroscience in psychology | Includes bibliographical references.
Identifiers: LCCN 2023034039 | ISBN 9781108498760 (hardback) | ISBN 9781108595827 (ebook)
Subjects: LCSH: Cognitive neuroscience – Textbooks. | Developmental neurobiology – Textbooks. | Developmental psychology – Textbooks.
Classification: LCC QP360.5 .B67 2024 | DDC 612.8/233–dc23/eng/20231004
LC record available at https://lccn.loc.gov/2023034039

ISBN 978-1-108-49876-0 Hardback
ISBN 978-1-108-71256-9 Paperback

Additional resources for this publication at www.cambridge.org/FDCN

For Pamela Johnson, Mark Lieb, Gretchen Lieb, Robin Lieb, and Gabriel Lieb. You all helped me become who I am.

– H.B.

My deepest gratitude goes to Mario Bunge (1919–2020) and Marta Bunge (1938–2022) for their inspiration and unwavering support.

– S.A.B.

Contents

Preface

How do brains change from infancy through adolescence? How are they shaped by the interplay between different genotypes and environmental input? How do these brain changes manifest as changes in behavior? Our goal with this book is to introduce students to the field of Developmental Cognitive Neuroscience (DCN), the scientific interface between biological studies of the brain and behavioral studies of human development. Researchers in DCN study brain development and the corresponding cognitive, social, and emotional changes that take place beginning prenatally and continuing through childhood and adolescence. We study how a child's environment and experiences shape their developing brain.

Neuroscientific discoveries have been crucial to our understanding of psychological processes and their underlying brain basis. Nowhere is this more evident than in the field of cognitive development, a discipline focused on the perceptual and conceptual changes that emerge in concert with a brain that is growing and changing. Over the past several decades, behavioral psychologists have found new and better ways to look "under the hood" to understand the processes supporting developmental change, and neuroscientists have expanded their focus to include structural and functional mechanisms that help characterize human growth and development. Together, these efforts have had considerable impact on the way research on human development is conducted, culminating most recently in the founding of the field of DCN.

The DCN approach to research integrates measures of neural development and concomitant changes in cognitive, social, and affective processes in both typical and atypical populations. Critical to the melding of disciplines has been the application of a variety of techniques and technologies, including electrophysiology and functional neuroimaging, to the behavioral paradigms typically used in human development research. Together with insights from animal models, patient populations, and psychopharmacological and genetic assays, these approaches are providing a wider variety of data to help characterize developmental change. This book summarizes where the field currently stands, providing a much-needed integration of information from various and diverse methodological approaches, populations, and theoretical positions.

Motivation

What do we have to offer in writing a textbook on DCN? First, we teach courses about this field at both the undergraduate and graduate levels. Second, our complementary research interests span many of the topics covered in this book, as well as the full pediatric age range from infancy through adolescence. One of us (Bortfeld) focuses on language learning from infancy through early childhood and examines experience-dependent neural plasticity in the auditory system.

The other (Bunge) has studied executive functions, various forms of memory, reasoning, environmental influences on the developing brain, and applications to education. Third, both of us use techniques that range from the behavioral to neurophysiological: Bortfeld uses looking time techniques in conjunction with functional near-infrared spectroscopy; Bunge uses cognitive measures, eye-tracking, and structural and functional magnetic resonance imaging. Thus, our collective experience as researchers covers a broad age range and many of the developmental changes therein. We also can offer our experience in teaching these concepts to students at universities with very different student populations: three different University of California campuses (Berkeley, Davis, and Merced), Stony Brook University, Texas A&M, Brown, University of Connecticut, and Stanford. Our lives and our understanding of how to teach have been meaningfully changed by our interactions with the students at these schools. The irony is not lost on us that it is perhaps we who have learned the most from interactions with those who came to us for instruction.

Why did we write this book? In teaching, we have been hard pressed to find an up-to-date textbook that approaches the complex progression of brain changes that co-occur with the emergence of human abilities in an easily tractable way. Teaching a course on DCN requires a wide range of field-specific framing, including review of anatomical detail from developmental neuroscience, behavioral methods from developmental psychology, and technological innovations from cognitive neuroscience. After many years of culling and revising reading lists to cover those topics and address those needs, we realized that we ourselves would benefit from a coherent presentation of them all together and in one place – and we thought perhaps others would as well.

Our Approach

Our goal has been to characterize how the developing brain supports and interacts with the emergence of a diverse range of abilities. We believe that you can't begin to understand these complex capabilities without understanding the biology underlying them. Students often think of psychology in categories – cognitive, social, clinical – in large part because courses are designed to fit into specific psychological subdomains. When developmental psychology is the focus of a course, we have found that students assume biological details will not be part of the discussion. This bias is further reinforced by the superficial dichotomy of development as being influenced by nature *or* nurture, a tired framework that has stymied deeper understanding of human development. Our aim is to focus on and celebrate the interdependence of psychology and biology – of mind and brain.

For the most part, we cover research in humans from the vantage point of developmental psychology, cognitive neuroscience, and the intersection of these two fields. However, we do occasionally feature cellular and systems neuroscience research on laboratory animals that has provided important insights on a given topic. We also provide a high-level overview of genetics and epigenetics, but do not cover other areas of molecular neurobiology. As molecular, cellular, and systems neuroscience are large fields of research unto themselves, we cannot do them justice here. But in touching on these areas, we hope to spark students' curiosity about them.

To be clear, we also emphasize that understanding only the biology won't get us very far. That is, we believe that studying the biology of the brain is not an end in itself: DCN needs always to be informed and motivated by questions about actual behavior. Further, we don't think of behavior as being divided into the biological and the cognitive/social/emotional. The complex manifestation of the latter comes about through the mechanisms and developmental trajectories of the former. These aspects of behavior are intertwined in complex, interdependent ways. Our aim here is to explore how this comes to be.

We operate on the premise that a firm grasp of cognitive and brain changes in typically developing children is essential for understanding what goes awry in neurodevelopmental disorders that affect social, motoric, linguistic, and/or cognitive development. Most importantly, we think this understanding is essential for predicting the onset of a disorder in an individual child and providing insights relevant for early detection and treatment. Because there is so much ground to cover with regards to typical development, we cannot provide comprehensive coverage of these disorders, of which there are many. However, we do highlight several disorders in association with specific topics. When we teach this course, we encourage students who are interested in clinical psychology, neuropsychology, or medicine to pick a specific disorder to investigate for a class presentation or final paper.

The field of DCN is increasingly of interest not only in the clinical realm, but also in fields as far-flung as public health, education, the law, and more. Every day, policymakers, practitioners, and the public seek out information about the developing brain, and news headlines abound. We believe that a solid foundation in DCN is important for parsing these headlines, and for making informed decisions at both the personal and societal levels. We endeavor to provide a balanced discussion of a few hot-button issues and list many others in the concluding chapter. In our classes, we invite students who are interested in the broader societal implications of DCN to pick one of the issues highlighted in Chapter 14 for a presentation or final paper.

Organization

The book includes fourteen chapters, representing the arc of information necessary to understanding how someone progresses from a tiny cluster of cells to a sentient being. Thus, we devote the first four chapters to laying the groundwork for emerging human abilities. Chapter 2 provides an overview of the core methods used to examine development, including functional neuroimaging (fMRI/MEG), electrophysiology (EEG/ERP), functional near-infrared spectroscopy (fNIRS), and transcranial magnetic stimulation, as well as other basic neuroscience approaches based on cellular and animal models. Chapter 3 serves as a primer on genetics and epigenetics, while Chapter 4 summarizes the biological processes that underpin the emergence of a human from conception to birth and beyond, while also providing cursory orientation to the major divisions of the brain, and an introduction to the different cell types. Chapter 5 focuses on brain plasticity, providing a more nuanced examination of how nature and nurture interact continually to influence development. Chapters 6–8 provide foundational information about the emergence of basic processes – perception, attention, social awareness, and early language acquisition – that are necessary for a person to function in the world. Chapters 9–10 then focus on various forms of memory, and how we leverage memory in the service of goal-directed behavior, while Chapters 11–12 focus on the culturally constructed, educationally relevant skills of literacy and numeracy. Chapter 13 examines key drivers of behavior and the capacity for self-control.

Finally, we conclude with a chapter looking towards the future, anticipating new directions, including methods, in which the field is moving. This textbook is not intended to be a comprehensive treatment of all of DCN. For example, it does not provide extensive coverage of motor development and learning, social cognition in late childhood and adolescence, or computational research, all of which are exciting areas of research. Nonetheless, this book introduces students to DCN and a wide array of topics of active investigation in the field.

Pedagogical Features

Our approach is to tell a story about how research on a particular subtopic arrived at where it currently is. This necessarily includes having to make difficult decisions about what to include and what to leave out to ensure the story is a coherent one. We think we have achieved this, and have added several features to help students extract the bones of each story. These include:

- Learning objectives
- Chapter summaries
- Review questions
- Further readings, including influential empirical papers and reviews

We have also included in each chapter a "Scientist Spotlight": there are excerpts from an interview with a researcher whose focus of study relates to one of the topics under discussion in the text. The purpose of these spotlights is to personalize the science by providing the origin story of leading figures in the field. Each chapter also contains a box that provides a deeper dive into the details of an issue that is relevant to the main text.

Full citations for all references mentioned in the text are provided at the end of each chapter. Key terms are bolded and defined in each chapter, with more detailed definitions provided in an accompanying glossary; additional terms are italicized and defined in the text. Finally, we provide online resources to support instructors and students, including lecture slides and a test bank of additional questions.

Teaching with This Book

This book is intended for advanced undergraduates and early-stage graduate students who want to get into the meat of research on the brain basis for developmental change in behavior. It is ideally suited for a semester-long course (usually 14–16 weeks), but specific chapters can be selected in support of shorter course terms.

The book presupposes a high school-level biology background and an introductory psychology course. Before embarking on this journey through DCN, students should have a rough sense of the different parts of the brain and their functions. Instructors whose students have no background in neuroscience are encouraged to give an introductory lecture on gross neuroanatomy. However, students need not know neuroanatomy in depth from the outset of the course, as we introduce each brain region or network as it becomes relevant to a particular topic.

We have presented our interpretation of the story that has emerged from the body of DCN literature. We encourage instructors to add to that story with their own data points and interpretations, their own experiences, and when possible, current headlines that address the issues raised by recent findings. We include references to the original peer-reviewed scientific articles from which the data were sourced so that instructors can pursue more detailed information about any given study.

The book is designed to stand alone; a single chapter is sufficiently rich to serve as the assigned reading for one week's worth of lectures – or even two weeks, depending on the desired depth of coverage. For those wishing to take a deep dive on select topics rather than covering the entire textbook, each chapter lists empirical papers that can serve as the basis for discussion sections or student presentations. In whatever way an instructor approaches this course, we hope the excitement we experience as researchers in the field comes through in our writing.

Ultimately, our goal is for the book to help students think deeply and critically about human development, so that they can evaluate studies and formulate questions that are addressable through the methods and techniques of DCN. The mind–brain relationship has been the focus of inquiry for as long as humans have been thinking about thinking, and we happen to be passionate about understanding how the developing brain gives rise to the developing mind. Our hope is that we have adequately conveyed this passion, that it helps ignite similar excitement in students, and that it proves sufficiently intriguing to motivate many to enter this growing and continually developing field and join us in our search for the brain basis of human behavior.

Acknowledgments

We thank the many people who contributed to this book and associated materials. Jesse Gomez and Vaidehi Natu, Stephen Lomber, Tomás Ryan, and Ted Satterthwaite contributed text boxes providing a deeper dive into specific topics. Daniel Levitin provided extensive feedback on the full draft of the book, and unnamed experts solicited by Cambridge University Press each reviewed several chapters. Trainees in our labs and classes provided detailed input on specific chapters, along with helpful information and references; these include Haider Ali Bhatti, Monica Ellwood-Lowe, Aedan Enriquez, Lindsay Fleming, Elena Galeano Keiner, Leana King, Pradyumna Lanka, Elena Leib, Willa Voorhies, and the students in Heather's undergraduate course. Professor Janet Werker at the University of British Columbia provided extensive feedback on many chapters, incorporating comments from students in a graduate course: Erica Dharmawan, Denitza Dramkin, Raechel Drew, Jessica Flores de la Parra, Faith Jabs, Vivian Qi, Eloise West, and Francis Yuen. Additionally, Marta Bunge provided high-level input on several chapters. Graduate students Vinitha Rangarajan and Enitan Marcelle, along with research assistants Marisol Duran, Aedan Enriquez, and Dorsa Javaheri, assisted with figures and figure permissions. Mark Johnson, Michael Meaney, Damien Fair, Terry Jernigan, Takao Hensch, Janet Werker, Sally Rogers, Ghislaine Dehaine-Lambertz, Simona Ghetti, Beatriz Luna, Fumiko Hoeft, Daniel Ansari, and Eveline Crone participated in interviews for the scientist spotlight in each chapter, and Madison Lacanlale and Jaquelyn Borcea edited the videos of the interviews for online distribution.

1 Introduction to Developmental Cognitive Neuroscience

While out walking the dog this morning, one of us (Heather) encountered two very different parenting styles that exemplify the complex interaction of genes, brains, and environment that underlies the development of human cognition and behavior. Coming towards me was a young father on a walk in the neighborhood with his toddler. As the pair came nearer, I heard the child making the sounds of someone having difficulty learning to speak. He did not form any discernible words, although he clearly was trying to talk about – and with – my dog. I also could hear that the father was engrossed in a cell phone conversation, towering above the little boy, and all but ignoring us. Two blocks later, I found myself approaching another father with his toddler. This boy was commenting on everything around him in the way that children in the early throes of language learning do. The second father kneeled down to be at eye level with the boy, answering every question and commenting on each of the boy's observations. This father was engaged in conversation with his son, and the boy spoke in the manner typical of a three-year-old.

Unless these encounters were anomalous snapshots of these two young lives, these children living in the same place at the same moment in time are having very different experiences. How will their levels of achievement, happiness, and overall quality of life differ? What might be the relationship between those outcomes and their early experiences? Questions like these drive the research presented in this book.

In this introductory chapter, we provide an overview of Developmental Cognitive Neuroscience and how it came to be a field in its own right. We review its background concepts, such as historical approaches to understanding how the brain develops, how children learn, and the nature–nurture debate. This history is the basis for this exciting and novel approach to understanding human development. We outline key theoretical positions and contextualize them with data acquired across a range of methods, including many made possible by technological advances introduced in just the last several years. Our emphasis throughout this book will be on the three component parts of Developmental Cognitive Neuroscience, development, cognition, and neuroscience, whose theoretical perspectives, methodological approaches, and findings have contributed to the emergence of this entirely new field.

1.1 What Is Developmental Cognitive Neuroscience?

Developmental Cognitive Neuroscience (DCN) is an interdisciplinary field focused on the neural basis of cognitive and socioemotional development in typically and atypically developing populations, and how it underpins behavior. Most research in this field focuses on child development, from infancy through adolescence; however, there are also DCN researchers studying prenatal development, and others who study development across the entire lifespan. Findings from DCN inform our understanding of neurodevelopmental disorders and point to possible therapeutic approaches. So, too, do these findings help us explain individual differences: that is, why we have different traits and abilities from one another. DCN also elucidates brain organization and brain function more generally. After all, we understand a system far better if we know how it was assembled!

A thread throughout this book is the fact that your brain is not simply a product of your genes; rather, your genes participate in an ongoing, inherently noisy developmental process that is shaped by your experiences and your own behaviors in the world. The DNA contained in your cells is the starting point for how a brain region or neural network emerges via the developmental process to take on a particular function. DCN research aims to characterize how well-specified these networks are at birth, as well as how they are shaped by the particular inputs they receive throughout an organism's existence.

A key factor in the explosive growth of DCN in recent years has been a set of advances in how we study brain structure and function. Neuroscientific discoveries have been crucial to our understanding of psychological processes, and nowhere is this more evident than in the field of **cognitive development**, a discipline focused on the perceptual and conceptual changes that emerge in concert with a brain that is growing and changing. Over the past several decades, researchers have found new and better ways to look "under the hood" in humans to understand the processes supporting developmental change. These technologies have expanded the focus of cognitive development research to include structural and functional mechanisms that help characterize human growth and development. Collectively, these efforts have had considerable impact on the way research on human development is conducted, culminating most recently in the founding of the field of DCN.

Our understanding of human cognition has benefited enormously from major technological, methodological, and theoretical developments in how we study the human brain, and DCN has benefited from advances in applying them to pediatric populations. Prior to having access to these tools, researchers often focused on dysfunction to deduce normal function (i.e., trying to understand how the brain works by seeing what deficits occur when the brain is damaged or impaired through case studies). Thus, several of the book's chapters include stories of early research on dysfunction, serving to couch our understanding in historical terms. While these early descriptions were focused on adult patients, DCN researchers owe a great debt of gratitude to the pioneering neurosurgeons and neurologists who pursued the neural underpinnings of cognitive and behavioral disorders. Likewise, while our focus is on human development, animal work serves as a foundation for characterizing the lowest structural levels of the brain and understanding how they function. Correspondingly, we draw on a wide array of findings from animal research.

1.2   Levels of Analysis and Levels of Structure

A human brain is a **complex system**, composed of many components interacting with one another to varying degrees. Complex systems can be described at different levels, both in terms of their structure and how they can be analyzed. Structural levels of the brain range from individual neurons to neuronal networks to individual brain regions to large-scale brain networks (Figure 1.1). The phenomena of interest in DCN are not easily ascribed to one or another structural level. For example, some seemingly "high-level" cognitive phenomena originate in the properties of individual neurons; for example, a form of memory called behavioral priming is rooted in a decrease in neuronal firing in response to a repeated stimulus. Other phenomena, such as the ability to comprehend language, emerge as a product of activation of an entire neural network across a number of different brain areas. In short, as the philosopher Mario Bunge wrote, behavior arises from interactions within and across levels of the complex system that is the brain (Bunge, 1980).

The dominant approaches in DCN may appear biased towards larger-scale structural levels – that is, towards brain regions or large-scale networks over single neurons. This is a product of affordances of the tools available for use with human participants. Currently available techniques mean that we most often operate at the level of brain regions and large-scale networks, but interpretation of information obtained at these intermediate structural levels is increasingly

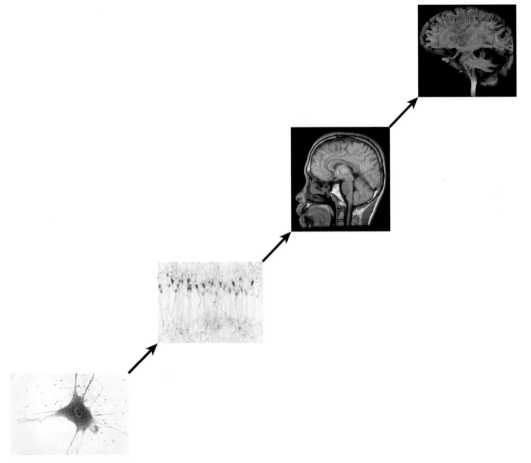

Figure 1.1 Levels of structural analysis include individual neurons, neuronal networks, individual brain regions, and large-scale brain networks.

Figure 1.2 Marr's levels of analysis.
(Adapted from Favela, 2020)

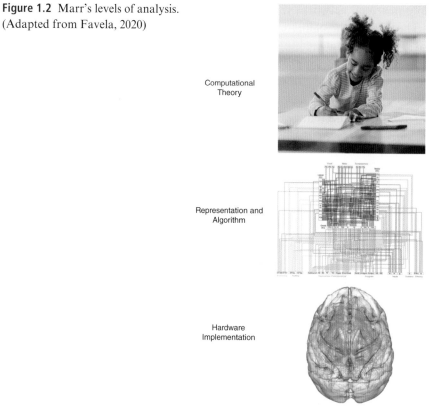

Computational
Theory

Representation and
Algorithm

Hardware
Implementation

informed by findings at the cellular and systems levels. In short, DCN research is – or should be – guided by the principle that no single structural level is superior to or takes precedence over another.

Structural levels should not be confused with **levels of analysis**. In his pioneering work on computational vision, David Marr (1982) provided an influential framework outlining the process of vision as the construction of representations, starting with the visual image itself. A central theme in Marr's approach – one that has had far-reaching influence in both neuroscience and cognitive science, as well as artificial intelligence – is levels of analysis. In **Marr's framework**, these levels consisted of computation, algorithm, and implementation (see Figure 1.2).

Overlap exists between structural levels of the brain and Marr's levels of analysis as they pertain to the characterization of cognition. For example, Marr's computational level is associated with the highest structural level (i.e., the behavior that arises from brain processes), while his implementation level better aligns with the brain's underlying biology. According to Marr, "an algorithm is likely to be understood more readily by understanding the nature of the problem [computation] being solved than by examining the mechanism (and the hardware) in which it is embodied" (Marr, 1982, p. 27). Unfortunately, because his framework reflected the dominant analogy in mid-to-late twentieth-century cognitive research – between the brain and a standard computer – the implementation level was often overlooked, or even dismissed as being "just" the underlying neurobiology. Cognitive scientists were encouraged by this to focus exclusively on the algorithmic and/or computational levels of the system without considering their relationship to the underlying implementation. Despite this limitation, Marr's levels-of-analysis framework is still useful today in establishing mechanistic accounts of how cognitive phenomena can be instantiated by a brain, particularly for researchers developing probabilistic models of cognitive or perceptual systems.

Fortunately for DCN, the quest to understand human development has embraced the importance of the hardware: the brain. In fact, DCN flips Marr's argument on its head, just as often examining the implementation to understand the algorithm as the other way around. Our perspective is that both frameworks – levels of structure and levels of analysis – are important to consider, as the processes and products of human development are **dynamic**, **multi-scaled**, and **emergent**. DCN as a field relies on researchers having access to data from different levels of structure (i.e., from single brain cells to whole brains) to address questions aimed at different levels of analysis (i.e., from implementation to computation). For example, on the structural side, whole-brain imaging can provide a network-level view that is critically informed by findings from other structural levels, whether those findings are from single-cell recordings from animals or from "lesioned" neural networks that are instantiated computationally.

1.3 What Do We Gain from Understanding How the Brain Develops?

The question of how a tiny clump of cells becomes a unique, thinking, feeling, and behaving person has long engaged scientists and non-scientists alike. For centuries, this question has been posed in terms of nature versus nurture, whereby researchers try to determine what portion of development is dictated by innate forces – such as our genes – versus the portion shaped by experience. In recent decades, new evidence has radically updated our understanding of genes and how they relate to the processes of individual development. The complexity of genetic impacts on fetal development, neuroplasticity, the functional organization of the brain, and cognition makes it clear that the nature–nurture debates are not just outdated; they are no longer helpful. To paraphrase an old saying about the difficulty of tracing a multi-level phenomenon back to its origin, "it's turtles all the way down," it's nature *and* nurture ... all the way down.

DCN embraces the perspective that, from conception onward, there are diverse and complex developmental processes impacting how you process information and solve problems, how well you concentrate, and whether you are eager to learn new things. These ways in which you engage with the world strongly influence your sense of self and agency: whether you feel that you have some control over your life, or whether you perceive your life to be a series of events caused by the capricious will of others. Ultimately, all of this informs the way you position yourself in relation to others. The research we review aims to delineate the developmental processes underlying these interrelated events, and this outcome in worldview.

Thus, a clear benefit of understanding how the brain develops is that it can provide a window onto what drives variability in human behavior, helping us better delineate different periods of time during which the brain remains plastic, when its structure and function can be molded in response to new inputs. DCN research provides important insights into the possible mechanisms that impact human cognition and behavior in long-lasting ways.

Finally, we'll state the obvious: it helps to have parents, other caregivers, and educators with the necessary time and resources to help navigate the developmental journey. Although they may buy any number of how-to books on the subject, even the most engaged parents don't have all the answers on how to raise a child. Research findings from DCN can provide important insights regarding how children's minds will develop, how they will change as they grow, and how the brain itself is changing in the process. Such findings can be integrated into a coherent perspective on child development that will help caregivers and educators navigate the tsunami of information about which aspects of biology, the environment, and their own behavior impact the developmental process.

1.4   Brief History of the Field

DCN is young, but substantial foundational research from multiple domains led to its recognition as a field in its own right. Critical to its emergence has been research conducted by Mark Johnson, Adele Diamond, Charles Nelson III, Uta Firth, Michael Posner, Helen Neville, Joan Stiles, and Annette Karmiloff-Smith, among many others. These pioneers were inspired by findings from a wide range of domains, while often operating in the margins of each.

As with the field of **cognitive neuroscience**, which emerged in the 1970s (and was given its name during a taxicab ride that Michael Gazzaniga shared with George Miller), DCN grew organically from converging research findings at different levels of analysis. The emergence of cognitive neuroscience, together with the combination of behavioral findings from developmental psychology and animal work in developmental neuroscience and developmental biology, came to a head, with a new perspective.

A number of distinguished scientists featured in our "Scientist Spotlight" sections describe the early days, when there was simply no field to identify with or to work within. Their mix of interests, for example, motivated them to draw on a range of research domains, including developmental psychology, evolution, cognition, neuroscience, and biology, to think about and study brain development. These researchers simply didn't fit neatly into any one of those domains. As a result, the origins of DCN as a field can be traced back to a handful of impromptu conference sessions and small workshops that took place in the late 1980s. The field has grown up around those early researchers who envisioned it as a possibility.

For the next 20 years, DCN-minded researchers presented their work at the annual conferences of a range of societies, including the International Society for Developmental Psychobiology, International Society of Infant Studies, Society for Research in Child Development, and various neuroscience conferences. At the tail end of the aughts, some of these researchers started organizing conferences devoted to DCN, drawing several hundred participants. In 2013, the Flux Society for Developmental Cognitive Neuroscience was established by Beatriz Luna, with help from several colleagues (Bradley Schlaggar, Bruce McCandliss, and one of us: Silvia). The annual

Flux Congress has expanded to 500 attendees in 2023, and is expected to continue to grow. (If you've ever wondered why your professors miss lectures to go to conferences, this is one of the reasons: lots can happen at a conference, including the development of an entirely new field!)

In 1997, Mark Johnson, featured in this chapter's Scientist Spotlight (Box 1.1), published the first DCN textbook with Blackwell Publishing (now Wiley-Blackwell). Together with co-author Michelle de Haan, Johnson has updated this textbook several times. The most recent edition – that book's fourth – was published in 2015. Another notable contribution was a book published in 2006 by Charles Nelson, Michelle de Haan, and Kathleen Thomas, titled *Neuroscience of Cognitive Development: The Role of Experience and the Developing Brain*. The first journal dedicated entirely to the field, *Developmental Cognitive Neuroscience*, was started in 2011 and is now thriving.

Box 1.1 Scientist Spotlight on Mark H. Johnson (University of Cambridge)

Mark H. Johnson [Box Figure 1.1] is Professor of Experimental Psychology and Head of the Department of Psychology at the University of Cambridge, UK. His prior posts include a Professorship at Carnegie Mellon University in the US, and Founding Director of the Centre for Brain & Cognitive Development at Birkbeck, University of London, UK. One of the pioneers in developmental cognitive neuroscience, Johnson wrote the first textbook in this field. His laboratory studies typical, at-risk, and atypical functional brain development in human infants and toddlers, using brain imaging, cognitive, behavioral, genetic, and computational modeling techniques.

I knew from childhood that I was interested in the intersection of psychology and biology, and also in key issues about development and evolution. Two questions motivated me. First, how can human thought arise from the gray jelly in our head that is our brain? And second, how is it that we develop from just a bunch of cells into a complex human being that talks, thinks, and acts? Over time it gradually dawned on me that that those two questions could be mutually informative if you studied how brain development relates to cognitive and behavioral changes during infancy and childhood. However, when I started out in science I found myself mid-way between two fields. Brain development was studied in animals and was primarily focused on the cellular level. With regard to living humans, structural MRI and PET scanning were only just starting to become available, but there was no functional MRI at that point. On the other hand, there was the field of cognitive and behavioral development, where the prevailing view was that questions about human cognition should not be "reduced down" to the level of brain processes. So when I started out trying to link behavioral and cognitive changes to changes in brain development

Box 1.1 (cont.)

nobody knew how to categorize what I did – for example, most people in cognitive development thought I was some kind of biologist, but they weren't really sure what sort!

Things began to change when I went to the very first McDonnell Pew summer school in the late 1980s, as that was around the time that I first met other people who actually had the same research interests as me: Chuck Nelson, Helen Neville, Adele Diamond, and a few others. It occurred to us collectively that there was a coherent new field of study here. Since then it's been amazing to watch the rapid emergence of a whole new branch of science: developmental cognitive neuroscience. In the ensuing years there have been several influential handbooks and a textbook; then conferences began – such as the Flux meeting – and we've gone from a handful of people to hundreds, or even thousands, of people specifically interested in the topic. I've been privileged to see the field grow up from the obscure interest of a handful of people to a proper discipline now taught at undergraduate and Master's level.

When the field was quite young we began to get several new methods – such as functional MRI – and a lot of great data started coming out. However, we had very little way to put all the bits of data together into a coherent framework, and to a certain extent this is still true today. From the neuroscience side, people would suggest that a particular structural or functional change caused changes in cognition or behavior, while from the cognitive development side investigators sought neural evidence to support their favorite cognitive theories. In contrast, what I wanted was a theory of human functional brain development. And I still do. "Interactive Specialization" is a first step towards this. I don't see it as a complete theory but think about it more as a set of assumptions that, when taken together, leads you to think about developmental cognitive neuroscience data in a certain way. According to the Interactive Specialization view it's not that parts of cortex get turned on at certain points in development, as was previously thought, but rather that they gradually become more specialized, or better tuned, for specific functions, stimuli, or task demands. This increased specialization or tuning up process results from the interaction between different areas of cortex and subcortical areas, cortico-cortico interactions, and from the child behaving in the world and selecting certain parts of the external world to interact with in certain ways. The Interactive Specialization view is rooted in a constructivist view of development, where we don't just see the brain in terms of a mosaic of isolated regions with independent developmental schedules, but rather each region developing within the context of all its neighboring connections including their hierarchical connectivity structure.

1.5   Why Study Developmental Cognitive Neuroscience? (*or* How Do I Tell Grandma What I'm Studying?)

We tell our own families that we study how the brain changes in the early years of a child's development, and how those changes influence the course of that child's life. As one example, consider learning and the ways it can change the brain. When we first learn something, whether it's a new idea or a new behavior (like learning to ride a two-wheel bicycle), it can seem impossibly complex, perhaps alien. Repeated thinking about a concept or practicing a behavior changes the neural context for that process; eventually, our learning is reflected in the very wiring of our brains. Ask yourself: What experiences do you remember from your own childhood that seemed to profoundly affect your understanding of the world, of other people, or of yourself?

We are interested in understanding all the factors and situations that affect brain development – and managing those factors is in the interest of individuals and society. Much of this book was written during the Covid-19 pandemic, amidst tremendous political and social upheaval both locally and globally. The events of that period – a worldwide pandemic, widespread protests over inequality and systemic racism, and unprecedented environmental change – have deeply affected society. The social isolation and remote schooling associated with the pandemic-driven shutdown led people to wonder about the long-term impact on toddlers, children, and teens. Will the effects on academic achievement, social development, and mental health be long-lasting? Does Covid affect the developing fetus? As scientists and students of science we need to recognize this and help others to recognize it.

More broadly, what we know, and will continue to learn, about brain development needs to be reflected in **evidence-based health and education policies**. This research also holds lessons for the treatment of adolescents in the criminal justice system, immigration policies that separate children from their parents, and housing and community development. Together, these situations create the cultural and societal environments in which the developmental trajectories of children are established.

1.6   What to Expect

An important point to keep in mind as we review individual studies throughout the following chapters is that each study – in any field of research – has its idiosyncrasies; we gain a clearer picture by considering a body of evidence, not a single experiment. The field of DCN moves rapidly, and our understanding of brain development continues to evolve. As a result, some of the findings presented here will undoubtedly need to be amended in the coming years. As we write, new papers come out every day, and we have had to restrain ourselves from trying to incorporate every exciting new finding. Suffice it to say that a literature search on any of the topics we feature will reveal a wealth of new citations. This continual growth is a strength of the **scientific method**: it is a cumulative and self-correcting process. As new findings continuously emerge, they will influence future theories – strengthening, modifying, or replacing them – in the context of the many results reviewed here. Ultimately, we are sensitive to the fact that DCN is young. The training wheels may be off, but only just. Great adventures lie ahead!

References

Bunge, M. (1980). *The mind-body problem: A psychobiological approach*. Pergamon Press.

Favela, L. H. (2020). Cognitive science as complexity science. *Wiley Interdisciplinary Reviews (WIREs) Cognitive Science*, 11(4), e1525. https://doi.org/10.1002/wcs.1525

Johnson, M. H. (1997). *Developmental cognitive neuroscience*. Blackwell.

Johnson, M. H., & de Haan, M. (2015). *Developmental cognitive neuroscience: An introduction*, 4th edition. Wiley-Blackwell.

Marr, D. (1982). *Vision: A computational investigation into the human representation and processing of visual information*. W. H. Freeman.

Nelson, C. A., de Haan, M., & Thomas, K. M. (2006). *Neuroscience of cognitive development: The role of experience and the developing brain*. John Wiley & Sons.

2   Methods and Populations

LEARNING OBJECTIVES

- Describe the main approaches used for studying behavior at different ages
- Explain how research on typically developing individuals can inform our understanding of atypical development, and vice versa
- Discuss which aspects of brain anatomy we can, and cannot, measure non-invasively with neuroimaging techniques (and which techniques those are)
- Specify the two main kinds of measures used to study brain function, and explain what they measure
- Present a high-level overview of each brain imaging method, and list their pros and cons
- Explain two main approaches to analyzing fMRI data, and outline considerations for age comparisons

How do we study cognitive and brain development in humans? This chapter will review how the application of behavioral techniques for testing infants, children, and adolescents merged with the broadening application of imaging technologies originating in neuroscientific research. With this as a background, in subsequent chapters we will be able to examine how genetic research informs our understanding of brain development and how brain changes underpin development of a range of abilities.

Today there are many ways to study the brain. We focus here predominantly on those most widely used in humans; however, our field is informed by animal research, which provides both constraints and an evolutionary context for the biology behind behavior. We'll highlight key findings from animal research in various chapters when they're relevant. But most of our work here will focus on those methods most commonly used with pediatric samples. We encourage interested readers to consult a cognitive neuroscience textbook to get a more complete picture of the methodologies used in adolescent, adult, and geriatric populations. Finally, this is a time of rapid advances in analysis techniques and the foundation we provide here will allow you to keep up with new developments (if you choose to). We also encourage you to seek out recent reviews on emerging methods. (This is actually a good rule of thumb for any science – don't assume that the field remains static, and search journals to find out what is new.)

While we introduce some commonly used methods in DCN research, this is not meant to be a complete inventory of all methods; new techniques, tools, and instruments are being introduced all the time, some of them conceptual, some statistical, some in the form of hardware (like fNIRS machines), some as software (like SPM, a software package for brain imaging). It's also important to recognize that there is no such thing as a single scientific method (because methods vary widely across the sciences, from physics, to chemistry, to psychological science, to neuroscience). What is common to all people who conduct science is an attitude. Scientists care about evidence (how it is collected, how it is interpreted) and most importantly, they are willing to change their theories based on evidence. As philosopher of science Lee McIntyre (2019, p. 7) writes, "it is not the subject or method of inquiry but the values and behavior of those who engage in it that makes science special." Scientists keep an open mind and update their beliefs based on new information.

We cover a lot of ground in this chapter so that it can serve as a reference for the rest of the book. It may feel overwhelming at first if it's all new to you. For a chapter like this, the science of learning suggests a strategy: go through it twice, skimming the first time and then actually reading it the second. On your first pass, don't get bogged down by the details; just focus on the big picture: What are the subheadings and what is the flow of the chapter going to be? What terms are new to you? After a preliminary pass like this, you should be aware of the main tools in a DCN researcher's toolkit, and what they measure. In your second pass you'll read it as you normally would and things you weren't sure about earlier should begin to gel. Starting with Chapter 3, and then through the rest of the book, you'll encounter these methods again to further reinforce your understanding. We invite you to return to this chapter now and then to think more deeply about how these methods work and what they can and can't tell us. We also provide information in the concluding chapter about several new and emerging methods.

2.1   Studying Behavior across Development

Ultimately, we want to understand how the developing brain gives rise to the developing mind. As such, good measures of behavior are of paramount importance. You may have heard the old phrase, *garbage in, garbage out*, an expression used by early computer scientists to describe the output of a program or algorithm that relied on bad data as input. The same is true here: if the measures are noisy, sloppy, biased, or don't actually measure what you think they do, no amount of expensive hardware will give you a clear and accurate answer to your experimental questions.

Here, we begin by outlining various pediatric populations studied in DCN, and then describe the main approaches used to study their behavior.

As lifespan psychologists rightly note, development doesn't have an endpoint: we continue to change throughout our lives. Some of these changes are well defined, often framed as stages: infancy, toddlerhood, childhood, pre-teen years, adolescence and young adulthood. In many people's minds, once a person becomes a young adult, the brain stops changing – other than growing old. Middle age or "the Golden Years" are just as much cultural or psychological stages as they are brain stages. But the reality is that all these life phases are characterized by changes in brains, gene expression, cognition, and behavior.

For mostly historical reasons, DCN research is typically defined as spanning the period of gestation through young adulthood. The cognitive neuroscientists who study older adults go by various names, such as lifespan psychologists or neuroscientists of aging, both of which seem like misnomers because they really don't focus on the initial decades of life, which are foundational to all that comes later. In this book, we are firmly focused on these early decades.

We focus on research conducted predominantly – but not exclusively – on typically developing children, as this provides a solid foundation on which to build our understanding of atypical development and of further lifespan development. To give you a flavor for problems of atypical development, we will discuss specific disorders such as Autism Spectrum Disorder and Attention Deficit Hyperactivity Disorder (topics that are typically covered in separate courses on psychopathology or developmental disorders), as well as unusual childhood contexts including early sensory deprivation and childhood poverty. Studying the neural basis of these forms of atypical development promises to provide insights for treatments, accommodations, and public health initiatives – and it has the added benefit of elucidating brain–behavior relations.

One important limitation of human research in general is the non-representativeness of children studied and reported on in journal articles (and in the textbooks that follow them). Most behavioral science research to date has been conducted on **WEIRD populations**: participants from **W**estern, **E**ducated, **I**ndustrialized, **R**ich, **D**emocratic nations (Henrich et al., 2010). This critique holds for DCN as well (Qu et al., 2021), with notable exceptions (Lloyd-Fox et al., 2014; Jensen et al., 2019; Wijeakumar et al., 2019). Layered on top of that is the challenge of recruiting a sample within a particular country that is representative of the socioeconomic and racial/ethnic diversity of the population. Unless researchers go out of their way to overcome this problem via widespread community outreach, samples are skewed towards families who live near research facilities and are available to participate in research, come across study advertisements, don't find it uncomfortable to visit a research facility or have their child undergo testing, and believe that science is on balance helpful (or at least not harmful) to society – and perhaps even think that the experience would be valuable for their children. As it stands, the extant body of research is undoubtedly biased towards Western samples and higher socioeconomic status individuals. In recent years, however, more and more researchers have been recruiting diverse samples – and there is a call to include details in publications regarding the racial/ethnic and socioeconomic backgrounds of sample participants (Qu et al., 2021). We still have a long way to go.

2.1.1 Study Designs

In an ideal world, how would you study development? There are two primary approaches. In one, we choose a phenomenon of interest – such as a child's concept of number, or their ability to read – and then test children of various ages. This is called a *cross-sectional* design, because we are looking across ages all at once in a single study. In the other approach, we would start with a group of children at one age and follow them around for many years – perhaps the rest of their lives – testing them at regular, prescribed intervals. This is called a *longitudinal* design, because it follows people across the length of some period of time. For both cross-sectional and longitudinal designs, you'd want to ensure that you recruit people from diverse backgrounds and experiences, and you'd use random sampling so that you're more likely to reduce the variability within each group being studied.

Take a minute and ask yourself: What might be the advantages and disadvantages of each approach?

One advantage of the longitudinal study design is that we are dealing with a cohort of individuals who have experienced many of the same world events that may shape their lives differently from people removed from them by just a few years; major wars, diseases, and natural disasters affect people differently depending on their age. Even technology does (as you know if you've ever tried to help your grandparents use their cell phone for something they haven't done with it before). If you are studying people born at different times it becomes difficult to distinguish those life events that were unique to their cohort from their own developmental trajectory.

One advantage of a cross-sectional study design is that we observe individuals of different ages at a single timepoint, and then combine them into a set of age-bracket categories, or we treat age as a continuous variable. Cross-sectional studies serve as a *proxy* for development: what is actually being examined with such a study design are age-related *differences* rather than *change*. Another advantage of cross-sectional studies is that they help science to advance more quickly: in the span of just a few years, we can observe a new phenomenon, report on it, and plan new experiments based on the results. With a long-duration longitudinal study, the results may not come in for one or more decades. Not to mention, brain imaging technology changes so rapidly that this approach isn't feasible in DCN.

Longitudinal studies are more sensitive to developmental change: that is, if an individual child changes over time on the variables we're watching, this may not be detected in cross-sectional studies. One possible reason is that there could exist pronounced variation across children at a given timepoint, and there may not be significant age differences between groups. Another potential reason (particularly in a small study) is that children sampled at different ages may not be well-matched: if it just so happens that the younger children in a study are particularly mature for their age, or had a better diet, they might not differ from older children. Thus, longitudinal studies are preferable from a theoretical standpoint; however, from a practical standpoint, they are more difficult to carry out and because of their increased cost and time to completion, they are less likely to receive support from funding agencies. Additionally, it is easier to sample a broad age range cross-sectionally, as following individual children for a decade or longer is no small feat! Invariably, some children will move, or drop out of the study for other reasons. Those who drop out may share something in common with one another, leaving the resulting sample skewed.

Thus, cross-sectional research is usually the first step when exploring a new line of research. If age differences are detected in a well-designed cross-sectional study, it is likely that there will also be longitudinal changes that can be investigated further.

An effective way to span a broad age range while also studying within-person change is through the use of a **cohort-sequential design** – also called an **accelerated longitudinal design** (Nesselroade & Baltes, 1979). In this type of study, researchers enroll children of different ages and follow each of them over time. For example, if one were to recruit 6-, 9-, and 12-year-olds and collect data from each of them three times, with roughly one year between timepoints, the resulting sample would span ages 6–14. In this way, researchers can have their developmental cake and eat it too: they can complete a study in three years that would take eight years given a pure longitudinal design, and they can model a **growth trajectory** that is informed by within-person change. This combined approach has gained popularity in DCN.

2.1.2 Converging Technologies and Methods

Developmental cognitive neuroscience in the twenty-first century primarily uses three broad methodological approaches: behavioral, neuroimaging, and genetic. Behavioral approaches include **observational and experimental behavioral studies** in which we observe how our participants spontaneously react, or behave, under circumstances that we control (to the extent possible); they also include **formal assessments** such as cognitive tests and questionnaires. The second type of study comprises a family of techniques that allow us to directly study brain structure and function under circumstances that we control; collectively these are called **neuroimaging** techniques. These methods include structural and functional MRI techniques, PET, EEG, fNIRS, and MEG (these abbreviations will be explained shortly). A third approach focuses on how genes influence behavior; it includes how gene expression changes over time in response to normal or atypical developmental trajectories, or in response to particular sorts of events in a person's life. (These genetic approaches are the topic of Chapter 3.)

Five other approaches that DCN researchers use are specialties and advanced topics beyond the scope of this book. (1) We study atypical populations with a variety of neurodevelopmental disorders; (2) we perform and reference animal studies that follow species through their own developmental trends, including mice, rats, and non-human primates (but not lions and tigers and bears – oh my!); (3) we study the effects of various pharmacological interventions on behavior, cognition, and developmental trajectories; (4) we build theories based on **meta-analytic** approaches, in which a large number of studies are examined statistically for trends and commonalities; (5) we use computational approaches, neural network modeling, and artificial intelligence (AI) models to better reveal the processes necessary to produce human-like (and infant-like) thoughts and behaviors.

The best of all worlds results when these various technologies and methodological approaches are brought together to create a complete picture of the topic we're interested in. That allows us to formulate stronger theories based on converging evidence. What happens when the evidence from these different approaches is contradictory, and fails to converge? This is one of the things that makes science so fun. When we get unexpected results, it very clearly shows us the gaps in our knowledge, and what experiments need to be performed next to resolve the contradictions. One of the most exciting findings for a scientist is this gap: that we *thought* we understood the phenomenon under study, and we were wrong. It is exciting because it gives us a chance to learn, and ultimately, to improve our understanding of human behavior.

2.2 Behavioral Studies

Behavioral experimentation involves designing tasks for adults or older children (outlined below and throughout this book), which often can't be used with infants or young children. Why not? We can't expect them to understand complex task instructions or provide the kinds of fine motor movements or verbal responses that are typically required. In response to this constraint, researchers have developed any number of creative ways to infer infants' and young children's cognitive abilities from their behavior. Moreover, behavioral testing techniques that work with young children won't work with infants, meaning behavioral measures are further tuned depending on children's specific ages.

2.2.1 Studying Infant Cognition

It is easy to underestimate what infants perceive or know or think about the world, because they can't tell us; they can't always show us, either, because they have limited control over their movements and an underdeveloped (or difficult-to-interpret) repertoire of gestures, sounds, and facial expressions. As a field, developmental psychology has advanced based on the design of increasingly clever techniques for finding out what children are capable of. One approach is to simplify what is required of the child while maintaining focus on the task or ability in question. When more carefully targeted tasks are designed, infants are able to demonstrate to us their abilities in a variety of targeted cognitive functions. Through this, the age at which infants first demonstrate a consistent ability to do something new, the **age-of-onset** for the task, has been revealed via increasingly clever experiments for abilities that include object permanence (Baillargeon, 1987), theory of mind (Kovacs et al., 2010), speech segmentation (Juscyzk & Aslin, 1995), and many others.

What are these clever techniques? How do we probe infant cognition? The most successful measurements take advantage of things that infants do naturally: they look, listen, suck, fuss, and otherwise do what they want to in response to the world around them. These behaviors have been harnessed by behavioral researchers as a means of tapping into infants' perceptual and conceptual experiences. Here we highlight the basis for the most commonly used measures, with the caveat that the devil is in the details: these infant behaviors are only as revealing about infants' internal processes as the experimental paradigms that elicit them – and the experimenters' attentiveness to the infant's behavior. (Many of these experiments are assisted by undergraduate student volunteers as a way to train them in scientific observation.) As in all research, careful experimental design is critical.

Early studies used **habituation** to measure learning in very young infants (e.g., Kagan & Lewis, 1965), which capitalizes on infants' tendency to disengage from things that have become overly familiar through repeated exposure. In an experiment, this involves exposing infants to repetitions of a single stimulus and measuring the amount of time needed before they stop reacting to it (i.e., their time to habituate). The most common form of habituation measure is infant looking behavior; however, in the youngest infants, habituation as indicated by a reduced sucking rate is likewise informative. We can also change a repeated, habituated stimulus to a novel one using a dishabituation paradigm that measures patterns in an infant's tendency to **dishabituate** following habituation. When infants reengage with a stimulus, whether by looking longer towards it or sucking faster in response to it, we can assume that they remember the repeated stimulus and distinguish it from the new stimulus. How much does a stimulus have to change before the infant notices it? That is one of the questions we ask to trace the development of perceptual abilities across time. And it's not just looking time; infants' heart rates change during habituation and dishabituation, and so heart rate can also be used as an indication of learning, even in a fetus that is still *in utero*!

Thus, habituation/dishabituation paradigms are research tools that have revealed that infants can discriminate between stimuli and sets of stimuli across a wide range of modalities (e.g., Fagan, 1970; Eimas et al., 1971; Wetherford & Cohen, 1973). Habituation paradigms opened up a new world of possibilities for research on infant perception. For example, Robert Fantz (1964) took advantage of infants' tendency to habituate to familiar stimuli by displaying two visual items at the same time (e.g., one to the infant's left and the other to its right) and compared infant looking times to each by tracking which of the two they looked at more (**paired comparison paradigms**). He found that infants tended to look longer at a new pattern relative to a previously seen one.

One issue that researchers have grappled with is that in both habituation and paired comparison paradigms, it is unclear whether infants' increased looking reflects a preference for the novel stimulus or avoidance of the repeated stimulus. In response, **preferential looking paradigms** emerged as a more nuanced form of measurement, in which infants' preference for stimuli, whether two new or two old stimuli, or a familiar versus novel stimulus, can be tracked as a function of their age, the amount of exposure they have received, and the complexity of the stimuli themselves. A so-called Goldilocks effect has been observed whereby infants respond to very specific combinations of features in a particular way (Kidd et al., 2014), as well as a function of their specific age. Our understanding of the impact of all these factors on infants' looking behavior has led to increasingly standardized testing procedures (Hunter & Ames, 1988; Sirois & Mareschal, 2002; Aslin, 2007).

The use of infant looking times was groundbreaking, and much of what we know about how infants perceive the world, and their sensitivity to changes in a stimulus, comes from these studies. In addition, the studies can tell us how infants form concepts and categories: if an infant treats two different stimuli as the same (habituating to one causes habituation to the other) it tells us that the infant cannot yet distinguish the parameter that we've varied (say color, or size). Figure 2.1 highlights three paradigms, all of which depend on how, and how long, infants respond (by looking or sucking) in response to experimental stimuli.

Because even minor experimental factors can influence infants' looking behavior, any theories we build or conclusions we draw must be based on the overall consistency of results across many experiments using the same paradigm and the same nuanced variations in stimuli. But looking behavior doesn't tell us everything. In DCN research, we couple infant behavioral paradigms with a wide range of multimodal measurements, including brain-based measures, providing important additional insights into our understanding of infants' perceptual and conceptual processing.

2.2.2 Studying Child and Adolescent Cognition

Standardized assessments, questionnaires, and other pen-and-paper instruments are an important part of research in DCN. These tools can establish a child's baseline general cognitive abilities, provide a diagnostic profile for developmental disorders, and serve as

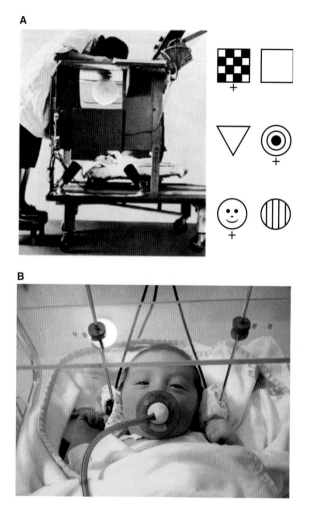

Figure 2.1 Infant testing methods. A. The Fantz Looking Chamber introduced a way to measure how long infants look at different visual stimuli. The infant is lying on its back, face-up, and viewing paired objects or images as the experimenter peers down through the top of the box to determine where the infant is looking. (Reprinted from Burbacher & Grant, 2012) B. The high amplitude sucking technique, during which sucking rate provides a measure of habituation/dishabituation. Here a newborn hears speech sounds through headphones that are contingent on sucks on a pacifier. (Reprinted from Moon et al., 2013) C. In looking time paradigms, where and for how long an infant attends to one of a set of objects or images is measured. This can be done via manual coding based on careful analysis of eye and head orientation or, as in this image, via eye-tracking technology. (Photo credit: Tobii AB)

screening devices. Many tools are available, each with a specific purpose and used with a particular age group; the tools include cognitive, developmental, neuropsychological, social, and psychiatric measures of function. Much of the research we highlight in this book includes standardized measures of specific cognitive, social, emotional, physical, and adaptive behaviors. Standardization provides some assurance to researchers that they are measuring the same ability across different laboratories. However, it is important to remember that there is tremendous variability in the quality of assessment instruments. Some lack the technical and/or psychometric qualities necessary for reliable and valid test scores. Others are not appropriate for diverse populations of children. Still others are limited in the measurement dimensions they cover. Nonetheless, there are plenty of psychometrically sound instruments available to researchers, and new ones are being developed all the time.

Assessments can take many forms; for example, a researcher may use paper-and-pencil or computerized tasks, interviews with the child, incidental observation of behavior, or the report of a caregiver, teacher, or clinician. The challenge for researchers is in selecting the instrument most appropriate for their specific research question. Many assessments can be fine-tuned to address specific questions or be made more general through the addition or elimination of items. Researchers should be trained in a specific assessment technique as, particularly for young children, the testing conditions – environmental, psychological, and physical, as well as a host of non-verbal cues given off by the experimenter – can impact a child's performance. Moreover, because a child's performance can vary from hour to hour or day to day, let alone year to year, it is critical to remember that evaluation results only provide a snapshot of a child's current level of functioning.

Many child assessment instruments with good psychometric properties were originally developed for instructional and/or diagnostic purposes, rather than for research. Thus, researchers often develop their own behavioral protocols for use alone or in combination with standardized assessments, as well as with the kinds of brain-based measures we outline in this chapter. We highlight research throughout this book that combines standardized assessments and/or custom lab-based measurements either alone or with a range of brain measures.

2.3   Probing Human Brain Structure

For thousands of years, human brain anatomy could only be studied *ex vivo*: that is, in the brains of deceased individuals, or patients with various brain insults, such as the famous cases of Broca and Wernicke's patients (Chapter 8), Henry Molaison, known as H.M. (Chapter 9), and Phineas Gage (Chapter 13). With the advent of non-invasive brain imaging techniques – particularly **magnetic resonance imaging (MRI)**, described below – we have the opportunity to safely measure both brain anatomy and the flow of blood through the brain, and thereby link it to brain structure, brain function, and behavior. In the next section, we discuss **structural**

MRI, as well as a specific class of anatomical MRI methods called **diffusion-weighted imaging**. As we shall see, many different ways of imaging brain anatomy (and the rest of the body) are possible with an MR scanner (Box 2.1). MR scanners are also used to measure brain *function*, as discussed in Section 2.4.

Box 2.1 Physics behind MRI Techniques

Magnetic resonance refers to the excitation of a system (e.g., atoms) by application of magnetic force. As shown in Box Figure 2.1A, an MRI scanner leverages this principle; it houses a powerful magnet (on the order of 3 Tesla), a radiofrequency head coil that emits RF pulses, and a gradient coil that assists with spatial localization of signal.

The human body, composed primarily of fat and water, is made up mostly of hydrogen atoms. As shown in Box Figure 2.1B, hydrogen ions (H+), called protons, typically spin in random orientations. In the presence of the strong magnetic field of an MRI scanner, protons align both in the direction of the magnetic field (parallel) and in the opposite direction (anti-parallel). However, a few more protons align in the direction of the magnetic field, thus producing a net magnetization in the direction of the magnetic field. The application of a radiofrequency (RF) pulse at the resonance frequency of the hydrogen atom knocks the small percentage of unmatched protons out of alignment with the main magnetic field. Once the RF pulse is stopped, the protons slowly return to their original state of alignment with the magnetic field, with a relaxation rate that differs based on tissue composition. An appropriately placed receiver coil (usually the same coil that emits the RF pulse, called a transmit-receive coil) detects the changes in the magnetic flux as the protons return back into alignment as an MR signal that can provide useful information about the underlying tissue.

Structural MRI: Protons (H+ ions) within different kinds of tissue relax at different rates, thereby generating signals of varying intensity. Variations in behavior of protons in gray matter, white matter, and cerebrospinal fluid show up as intensity differences that can be detected with structural MRI. In this way, it is possible to visualize brain anatomy at the macroscopic level.

Diffusion-weighted imaging: Water diffusion in the brain can also be tracked in an MRI scanner by applying a homogeneous magnetic field and measuring the signal emitted by protons in response to radiofrequency pulses. This signal is diminished when water molecules diffuse in the direction of the gradient; therefore, signal loss is greatest within brain structures that are oriented in this direction. Voxels within white matter tracts are highly anisotropic, and therefore appear as dark patches (areas of signal loss) in a DTI image. By changing the direction of the magnetic field gradient multiple times across the scan, we can measure water diffusion in all directions and model the tensor for each voxel.

fMRI: fMRI exploits the difference in relaxation rates between protons in oxygenated versus deoxygenated hemoglobin. Oxygen covers up the iron core of hemoglobin, dampening its distorting effect on the magnetic field of the scanner, and thereby boosting the BOLD signal.

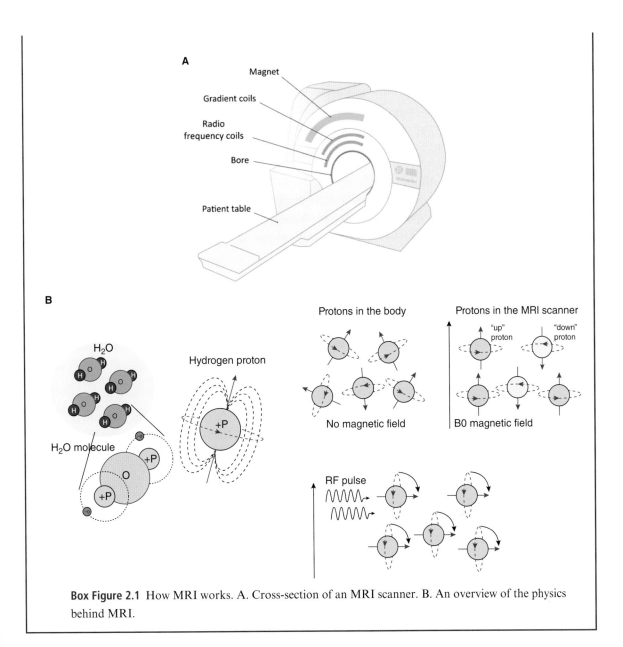

Box Figure 2.1 How MRI works. A. Cross-section of an MRI scanner. B. An overview of the physics behind MRI.

2.3.1 Structural MRI

With structural MRI, a series of two-dimensional images, or slices, are taken and assembled to build a three-dimensional image of the brain (Figure 2.2A). Shown here are three different views of the brain: an **axial (horizontal)** slice across the top, a **coronal** slice taken parallel to the face, and a **sagittal** slice taken from the side. With this method (Box 2.1), we can examine **gross anatomy**: that is, **macroscopic** features of the brain such as the folds in the brain (gyri and sulci), gray matter (functionally distinct areas of the brain), white matter (the fibrous tracts that connect these areas), and subcortical nuclei. We can take measures such as cortical thickness (how thick the gray matter is in a particular area of the brain), the surface area of the cortex, and measures related to the shape and length of gyri and sulci. We can ask questions about the sizes and shapes of various structures; for example, how does the size and shape of visual cortical regions change as a child learns to read?

It is possible to collect structural MRI scans at all ages – even prenatally. Scans performed on fetuses and infants are often motivated by clinical concerns; however, MRI scans are considered safe for pregnant women and their babies and so provide much research data. However, just as when you take a still photo of a subject in motion, it is impossible to get clear images of the brain if the participant moves. This is particularly problematic for young children, who tend to be quite wiggly. Developmental researchers have gone to great lengths to develop procedures for gathering high-quality MRI data – even from infants and young children (Raschle et al., 2009; Greene et al., 2016).

Analysis of structural MRI data from infants is also challenging, for several reasons (Neil & Smyser, 2018). For example, because the newborn brain has very little myelin, there is low image contrast between gray and white matter – and therefore it is difficult to distinguish anatomical structures. By comparison, as we can see in Figure 2.2B, slightly older children produce higher-contrast brain scans and their brain images are more easily segmented. This figure shows two different types of structural MR pulse sequences. In T1-weighted images, gray matter looks gray and white matter looks white. In T2-weighted images, commonly used in clinical settings, it is easier to detect a brain anomaly.

Note that *in vivo* human brain imaging does not allow us to measure **microscopic** properties of the brain, such as the organization of cells revealed by **histology** – that is, detailed brain tissue analysis of the brain's microstructure. Here, our unit of analysis is the individual **voxel** (a pixel, but in three dimensions rather than two), which – for present-day structural MRI studies – can be as low as 1 cubic mm. A single voxel of this volume in gray matter contains tens of thousands of neurons, mixed in with at least as many glial cells. MRI has poor **spatial resolution** relative to histological analyses in which individual cells are labeled. Ultra-high field strength MRI scanners yield images with higher spatial resolution than the more typical 3 Tesla scanners – for example, 0.5 mm resolution for a 7 Tesla scanner, which makes it possible to visualize cortical layers. However, even these scanners (which are not yet commonly used with pediatric populations) do not compare to what we can glean from postmortem tissue analysis.

As a result, we can only speculate – informed by the converging evidence from histological research – as to the cellular mechanisms that underlie macroscopic structural changes observed with structural MRI. This point will become clear in Chapter 4, when we explore the phenomenon of cortical thinning during childhood. Newer white matter imaging methods are also being validated by histology, thereby giving us a clearer picture of the likely cellular underpinnings of human brain development.

2.3.2   Diffusion-Weighted Imaging (DWI)

DWI refers to a subset of MRI measures that allow us to study the organization and structure of the white matter tracts in the brain. Why might we want to do this? The microstructure of the developing brain is not static: white matter tracts grow and change as a result of experience and

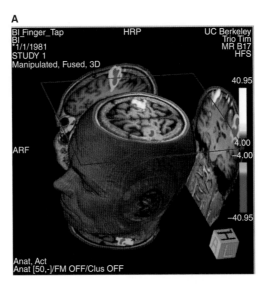

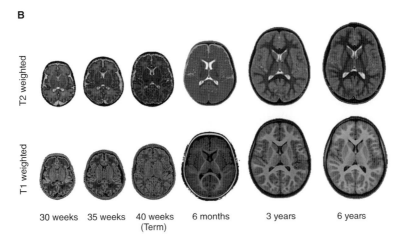

30 weeks   35 weeks   40 weeks   6 months   3 years   6 years
(Term)

Figure 2.2 Structural MRI. A. Three-dimensional reconstruction of a
structural MRI scan, with fMRI activation associated with a finger-
tapping task overlaid on it. Horizontal (H), anterior (A), and lateral
(L) views of the brain are shown in axial, coronal, and sagittal slices,
respectively. (Image courtesy of Ben Inglis at the University of California,
Berkeley Brain Imaging Center) B. Two types of structural MRI
scans, T2-weighted and T1-weighted, are shown at different ages, from
gestational age of 30 weeks to age of 6 years. (Reprinted from Batalle
et al., 2018)

natural maturation processes (and they degrade with aging). Following these changes allows
us to diagnose certain brain disorders, to track the growth of myelin (the sheath of lipids that
insulates and nourishes axons), and to see how experience and learning impact brain connectivity. The most common of these DWI techniques is **diffusion tensor imaging (DTI)** (Box 2.1).

Figure 2.3 The diffusion of water molecules in different types of brain tissue, and the tensors that describe the directionality of diffusion in each case. (Reprinted from Mukherjee et al., 2008)

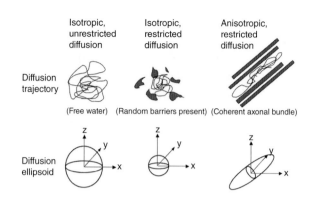

DWI works by tracing the flow of water molecules. Why would measuring the diffusion of H_2O molecules tell us anything about white matter? Well, the water content of the brain is surprisingly high at around 68 percent of the chemical composition of white matter, and around 80 percent of gray matter (Wolthuis et al., 2001). As shown in Figure 2.3, water molecules have a property that is highly relevant for our purposes: they travel randomly if unconstrained, but they tend to travel along the path of least resistance (just as rainwater does). By tracking their movement, we can learn much about the structure and organization of white matter.

Diffusion that occurs equally in all directions is **isotropic**. The dense tissues in the brain restrict the diffusion of water molecules; if these barriers are oriented randomly, the resulting diffusion is still isotropic. Water molecules are less likely to diffuse into or out of a tightly packed axon fiber bundle than they are to travel along its length because that is the path of least resistance. That is, water molecules show highly directional, or **anisotropic**, diffusion in white matter tracts. (To remember these terms, it may help to know that the Greek word stem *an-* means not, *iso-* means equal, and *-tropic* refers to direction).

Now that you have the general idea, let's look at the DTI parameters that are used as indices of white matter microstructure. A **tensor**, shown at the bottom of Figure 2.3, is a shape that describes the mathematical relations between vectors in a multidimensional space. In this context, a vector represents the diffusivity (i.e., the potential for diffusion) of water molecules in a particular direction, and a tensor describes the movement of all the water molecules within a voxel of the brain. A spherical tensor indicates that water molecules in the voxel have the potential to move equally in all directions (isotropic diffusion). By contrast, a cigar-shaped tensor, like the one shown here, indicates greater diffusivity along one dimension than the others – that is, anisotropic diffusion. Coherent white matter tracts are anisotropic: the long axis of the tensor represents the orientation of the fibers. By contrast, gray matter and cerebrospinal fluid are isotropic.

For each voxel in the brain, we can model the tensor and derive various DTI parameters. **Axial diffusivity** (or parallel diffusivity) refers to the degree to which water diffuses along the longest axis of the tensor (vector y, parallel to the axonal bundle, in the rightmost column in Figure 2.3). By contrast, **radial diffusivity**, also called perpendicular diffusivity, reflects water diffusion *perpendicular* to the long axis (vectors x and z in the figure). **Mean diffusivity** refers to the *average* diffusivity in all directions; this value is low in areas of the brain that are tightly packed with structures. (Thus, the tensor in the middle column in Figure 2.3 is depicted as a smaller sphere than the one in the leftmost column.) **Fractional anisotropy** (FA) is a ratio that reflects how much more diffusion there is in a voxel along one axis than the others – that is, how *directional* it is. The value of FA would be 0 for a perfect sphere, and 1 for a needle. As we shall see in Chapter 4, these parameters change over childhood. In particular, a decrease in radial diffusivity – and resulting increase in the value of FA – is thought to reflect, at least in large part, the myelination of long-range axons.

In addition to calculating diffusion parameters for each voxel, it is possible to trace the probable direction of a white matter tract by stitching together the tensors across voxels. This method is referred to as **probabilistic tractography**. The term "probabilistic" reminds us that we can't be confident that individual fiber reconstructions are accurate, as they must be inferred from voxels that are not perfectly anisotropic – and because there are many decision points in the complex process of defining tracts. In fact, current DTI-based tractography both fails to pick up on many axonal projections and yields false positives (Aydogan et al., 2018). However, it does pick up on large, known white matter tracts, and is therefore useful for characterizing the development of these major pathways.

Additional white matter imaging methods, based on a variety of MRI pulse sequences, are being validated by the converging approach of histology (Lazari & Lipp, 2021; Möller et al., 2019). Those interested in delving into this literature more deeply will come across measures of myelin water fraction, iron concentration, macromolecular density, and more. Importantly, studies employing different white matter imaging techniques have drawn somewhat different conclusions regarding the developmental trajectory of different tracts (Lynch et al., 2020). This textbook features data from DTI, both because it is the most extensively validated and widely used white matter imaging method and because fractional anisotropy is moderately correlated with postmortem measures of myelin (Lazari & Lipp, 2021).

2.4 Probing Human Brain Function: Measures of Electrical Activity

The most direct way to measure brain activity is to record the electrical signals produced by neurons, in the form of voltage fluctuations detected either in brain tissue or on the scalp. The suite of techniques that fall into this category are forms of **electrophysiology**. Recording directly from brain tissue, of course, is highly invasive, as it requires intracranial surgery. Intracranial recording is common in systems neuroscience (lab animal) research; however, it is rare in human research – and rarer still in DCN (but see, e.g., Yin et al., 2020) because it is conducted only on patients undergoing brain surgery. Here, we review forms of electrophysiology that are non-invasive and used routinely in pediatric populations.

2.4.1 Electroencephalography (EEG)

EEG is the oldest functional brain imaging technique. It originated with the discovery in the 1920s that brain electrical activity could be recorded from electrodes placed on the scalp (Stone & Hughes, 2013). This technique is still widely used today because of its ability to provide real-time measurement of brain activity. An EEG cap with electrodes embedded in it is shown in Figure 2.4A and B.

As you know, neurons fire with electrical charges – small ones, on the order of 100 microvolts (μV; a back-of-the-envelope calculation indicates that you'd need about one million neurons to power the circuits of your cell phone, and about four million neurons to charge its battery). Because voltage changes in the brain are so small, their detection requires power amplifiers to

A

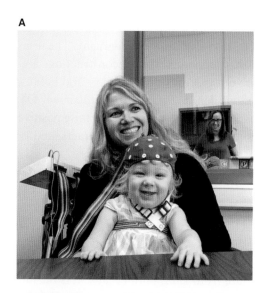

B

Figure 2.4 EEG testing with infants and children. A. An infant wearing an EEG cap. (Photo courtesy of Angie Cimmarrusti and Kimberly Cuevas) B. Older child with experimenter and close-up of cap. (Photos courtesy of Elif Isbell) C. Cross-section of the brain and skull, with an EEG electrode placed on the scalp. Pyramidal neurons are lined up in parallel in the cortex, with the dendrites facing towards the surface of the brain and axons facing downward.

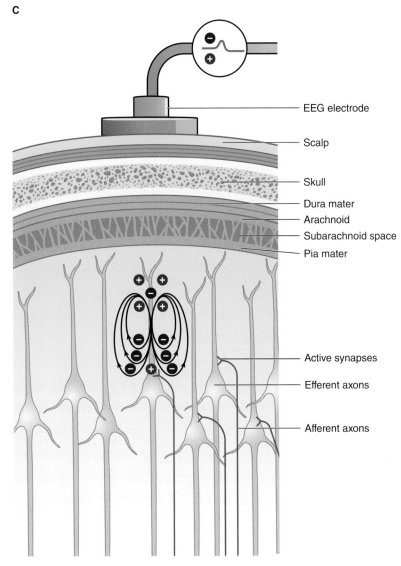

Figure 2.4 (cont.)

boost the signal for analysis purposes; this, in turn, makes EEG sensitive to radiofrequency and other electromagnetic disturbances. For this reason, EEG labs are often built with lead lining in the walls, or contain modified Faraday cages, enclosures that block electromagnetic fields; at the very least, the electronic equipment requires dedicated, filtered electrical circuits. There are many stories about the refrigerator or freezer in some biology lab located near an EEG room rendering data useless.

EEG measures the small **voltage changes** that result from electrical current flowing through the brain and skull in response to neural activity. As you may recall from physics class, voltage is defined as the potential energy, or difference in electrical charge, between two points on a circuit; it is calculated as the product of current and resistance: $V = IR$. Extracellular voltage changes in the brain are generated by the simultaneous excitation of many thousands of cortical neurons known as **pyramidal neurons**, shown in Figure 2.4C. These voltage changes are called **postsynaptic potentials**.

Pyramidal neurons constitute the major class of neurons in the cortex. By virtue of the way the cortex develops (Chapter 4), these characteristically large neurons are lined up perpendicular to the surface of the brain. As a result of this anatomical feature, electrical current flows in the same direction down the length of aligned pyramidal neurons that are activated in tandem. This generates an increase in voltage (depolarization) that is large enough to be detected at the scalp with EEG electrodes and an amplifier (Figure 2.4B). As shown here, the release of an excitatory neurotransmitter at the active synapses leads to the flow of positive ions into the postsynaptic neuron, leaving a negative extracellular voltage. These charged ions then leave the neuron near the cell body, completing the circuit and generating a positive extracellular voltage at the cell body.

The parallel orientation of these pyramidal neurons in the cortical gray matter makes it possible to detect small voltage fluctuations at the scalp. Importantly, however, neurons are not neatly lined up everywhere in the brain. Subcortical brain structures have clusters of neurons oriented in all directions, and so there is little or no net current flow in a particular direction when averaging across them. Compounding this problem, subcortical nuclei are buried deep in the brain, and the ability to detect voltage changes drops off rapidly as a function of distance from the source. Thus, the EEG signal is largely based on activity of the outer cortical mantle of the brain; this is a technical limitation to keep in mind.

Another important limitation is that it is difficult to be sure of the source of the signal in the brain. Imagine you're standing inside a large sphere – a weather balloon perhaps – and shining a penlight at different points on the inside surface. An observer on the outside could see where you're shining the light, but not exactly where you're shining it from. You could be shining it from just near the surface or from the opposite side; this ambiguity is known generally as the Poisson inverse problem, or the inverse problem. Now, you might be thinking, if I'm farther away from the surface the light will be weaker than if I'm close, and that should form a clue as to location. But imagine that the penlight had a brightness button; this is analogous to neurons firing at different rates. Imagine now that inside the balloon there are contours, objects that resemble the folds and creases of the brain: the light could be bouncing off an object and ricocheting around before it reaches the surface.

Various source localization approaches have been developed whose aim is to find the brain areas responsible for EEG signals of interest – that is, solve the inverse problem. However, localizing the source of the signal requires solving the forward problem, meaning calculating the potentials that reach a particular electrode from a given electrical source. Because anatomical differences across individuals affect the forward solution, they also affect the inverse solution, meaning that modeling the forward solution is much more complex than it may at first appear. For decades, simplified spherical head models were used to model sources; more recently, a combination of imaging modalities is helping more accurately describe the geometry of the head model (see Nunez et al., 2019). Despite this, the precision with which we can pinpoint brain activity with EEG, or its **spatial resolution**, is relatively low. But EEG has excellent **temporal resolution**: it faithfully tracks signals with precision on the order of several milliseconds (ms), allowing researchers to dissect the time course of the phenomenon of interest. As we will see below, fMRI has the *opposite* pros and cons: good spatial resolution, as human neuroimaging methods go, but poor temporal resolution! Historically, our understanding has been constrained by a kind of Heisenberg-like uncertainty principle for brain imaging, whereby we could know with great precision when something happened in the brain, or where something happened, but not both. Fortunately, recent advances in bringing multiple imaging modalities together are overcoming this constraint.

As we discuss here and in the next section, there are several ways to use EEG to study the brain. The most basic approach is to plot the **global EEG** signal, shown in Figure 2.5A, to visualize whole-brain rhythms: that is, we can examine coordinated oscillatory activity across the brain associated with different brain states. Plotted as raw voltage changes over time, the global EEG timeseries looks very different depending on whether we are alert, drowsy, or in one of several stages of sleep.

The differences between the awake state and various sleep stages are visible to the naked eye. However, for more fine-grained analysis, these complex waveforms are decomposed into a set of underlying frequencies of brain oscillations using a technique called Fourier analysis. The brain's intrinsic rhythms have been classified into six **frequency bands**: ranges of frequencies of oscillations expressed as Hertz (Hz; cycles/second). From the slowest to the fastest frequencies, these are labeled delta (δ), theta (θ), alpha (α), beta (β), and gamma (γ) – and high-gamma, which is best measured with intracranial recordings. The slowest oscillations (delta waves) are on the order of 0.5–4 Hz, and the fastest ones that can be detected with EEG (gamma waves) may be higher than 70 Hz.

2.4.2 Event-Related Potentials (ERPs) Derived from EEG

In addition to analyzing brain rhythms over time, EEG is used to measure discrete voltage changes in response to a specific event – that is, **event-related potentials (ERPs)**. It is in this domain that EEG's exquisite temporal resolution comes into play. For ERPs, EEG activity is measured in relation to a particular event, such as the presentation of a stimulus; it is then averaged over a series of instances (or trials) of the same event. Averaging over many trials yields a cleaner signal, as various sources of noise (both physiological and non-physiological) are averaged out. This process is illustrated in Figure 2.5A. EEG data are recorded from a set of electrodes in the EEG cap; the resulting waveform from different EEG channels – that is, electrodes – is plotted over time in different colored lines.

In this example, the participant is shown a visual stimulus on a series of trials. The continuous EEG signal is **time-locked** to the onset of these trials (marked by vertical lines) and is averaged across them, yielding a waveform that constitutes the ERP measured at a particular EEG channel. Voltage (in μV) is plotted over time (in milliseconds, or ms). This schematic illustrates the exquisite temporal resolution of EEG: a neural response can be detected within the first 100 ms after the stimulus is presented, reflecting early stimulus processing.

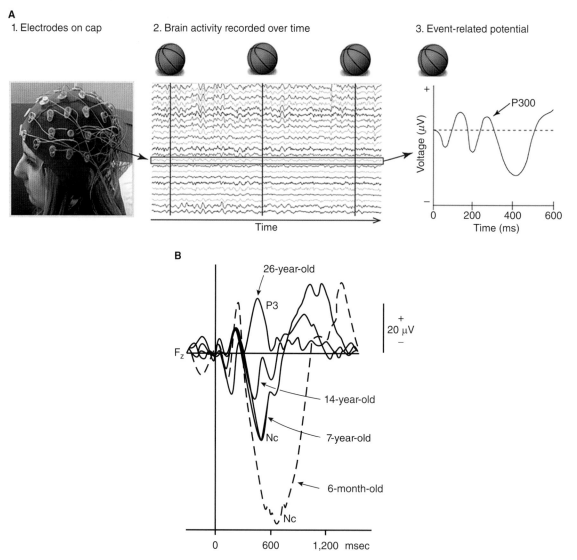

Figure 2.5 ERP basics, focusing on P300/P3. A. Illustration of the derivation of ERP waveforms from continuous EEG data, time-locked to the onset of a specific event that occurs repeatedly over the course of an experiment. The component of interest in this example is the P3 (also known as the P300), which reflects participants deciding whether a basketball appeared or not. (Reprinted from Kam, 2017) B. Event-related potentials change with age. Here, what starts as an Nc potential in infancy in response to infrequently presented novel stimuli becomes the P300/P3 by young adulthood. Notice that even the valence of this particular response changes across the course of development. (Reprinted from Courchesne, 1979)

Importantly, whether a voltage change is positive or negative doesn't map onto activation or silencing of neurons. Both positive and negative deflections reflect neural activity (specifically, postsynaptic potentials in pyramidal neurons); what differs is the spatial orientation of these neurons within the brain. Positive voltage deflections are typically plotted downward, per convention, although this is admittedly counterintuitive; in Figure 2.5 they are plotted upward. Best to simply make a note of the directionality of the axes in any given paper you're reading, a practice that will save you much confusion. The labels given to specific ERPs will serve as a cue too (N for negative going; P for positive going). Indeed, the distinct peaks and troughs in ERP waveforms can be identified reliably under specific task requirements (Luck, 2014), and the well-characterized ERP components have names like the N1 (a negative potential at ~100 ms from onset), P300 (a positive potential at ~300 ms from onset), N400, or the error-related negativity. Each of these components has been linked to specific mental processes; for example, the P300 (or the P3, as it's commonly referred to by researchers) is consistently elicited by stimuli that require decision-making.

As mentioned, the question of where in the brain a specific ERP component originates is unclear, given that electrical current sums and spreads passively across the head in complex ways that depend on an individual's anatomy (e.g., head size and shape and skull thickness) and the location and orientation of the source. Basically, different configuration of sources could lead to the same voltage distribution on the scalp. Between source localization algorithms and multimodal imaging studies, identifying the source of ERP components in the brain is getting more accurate. Nonetheless, localizing ERPs beyond a specific quadrant of the brain remains controversial.

Researchers using ERP measures with children have an additional factor to consider: the maturity of the response. For example, as can be seen in Figure 2.5B, the same waveform changes from infants to children to adolescents to adults. In this case, the Nc gradually lessens in amplitude with age, becoming the P3 in adults. All of these responses were elicited by infrequently presented novel stimuli, and yet there is a striking difference in the ERP waveforms as a function of age. Such age-related changes provide researchers with a means of identifying mechanistic changes associated with development.

2.4.3   Magnetoencephalography (MEG)

Magnetoencephalography (MEG) is similar to EEG in that it is a scalp-based recording technique that detects postsynaptic potentials in pyramidal neurons in the outer layer of cortex. However, while EEG detects voltage fluctuations generated by electrical currents in the brain, MEG detects magnetic field disturbances created by these electrical currents. This signal is very weak (10 fT–1 pT), so detecting it amongst other magnetic field sources requires construction of a magnetically shielded room. As a result, MEG facilities, shown in Figure 2.6, are not as common as EEG setups.

Like EEG, MEG has exquisitely high temporal resolution (less than a millisecond); unlike EEG, MEG also has excellent spatial resolution, down to the level of a few millimeters (Hämäläinen et al., 1993). This is because neural activity creates a localized magnetic field disturbance; it does not spread passively across the brain and scalp the way electrical current does. Thanks to technical advances, MEG can be used from infancy onwards (Kao & Zhang, 2019) – actually, even prenatally by imaging the mother's belly (Anderson & Thomason, 2013). In fetal imaging, the neural source of the signal remains unclear because the pyramidal neurons are still developing (Vasung et al., 2019). Fetal and infant MEG systems are not currently commercially available, and this research is still rare (Kao & Zhang, 2019). More generally, although MEG is a superior imaging technique, at least when it comes to measuring activity at the surface of the brain and localizing it, it is not yet as widely used as the methods discussed here in greater detail.

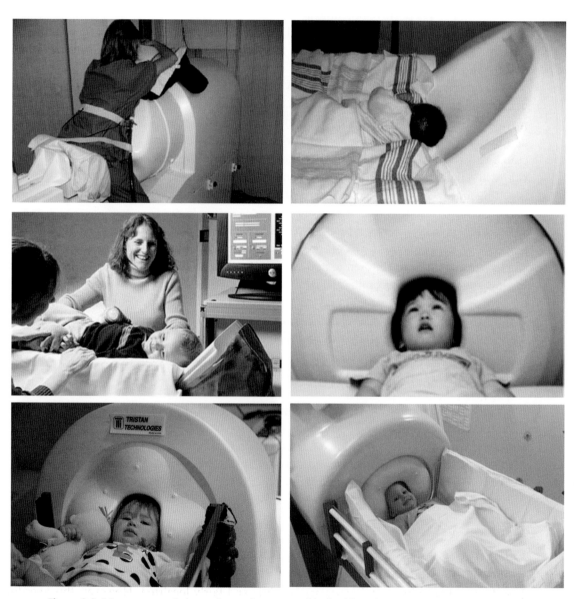

Figure 2.6 Magnetoencephalography equipment used in fetal imaging and with infants and young children. (Reprinted from Chen et al., 2019)

2.5   Probing Human Brain Function: Blood-Based Measures

Whereas the skull, meninges, and cerebrospinal fluid protect against physical damage of the brain, there is a barrier between the brain's blood vessels (capillaries) and tissue. This barrier protects the brain from disease-causing pathogens and toxins that may be present in our blood. A number of imaging techniques now allow for the study of the brain specifically by taking advantage of the dynamic nature of the blood vessels that deliver oxygen to neural tissue.

2.5.1   Cerebral Blood Volume and Flow

The brain is full of blood vessels, as illustrated in the resin cast in Figure 2.7A. These include large vessels like the internal carotid arteries, which carry large volumes of blood to the brain. There are also small blood vessels – a vast network of **capillaries** – that interface with cells. In other words, the cerebral vasculature is a system of highways and small roads that service the whole brain. **Cerebral arteries** (and arterioles, or the small-diameter arteries in the capillaries) deliver oxygenated blood and glucose, as well as other nutrients, that brain cells require to function. This is vital: even a brief interruption of this blood supply, as occurs when an artery is occluded during a stroke, is sufficient to cause cell death. By the same token, **cerebral veins** (and venules in the capillaries) remove deoxygenated blood and waste (products of cell metabolism like carbon dioxide and lactic acid) from the brain.

When neurons have a high firing rate, they require an extra influx of fresh blood to support the heightened metabolic demand. Glial cells known as **astrocytes**, shown in Figure 2.7B, sense the level of neural activity and regulate the amount of blood that flows into the local area by dilating or constricting the arterioles in the capillaries. They accomplish this feat via protrusions called end feet that wrap around both neurons and capillaries, enabling cell signaling between them. The close communication between neurons, astrocytes, and capillaries is referred to as **neurovascular coupling**. We capitalize on the biological phenomenon of neurovascular coupling to study brain function, using several imaging techniques discussed below.

The idea that blood flow increases to active areas of the brain is an old one. An Italian physiologist named Angelo Mosso (1846–1910) studied patients whose brains were exposed due to having undergone intracranial surgery. He observed that the brain pulsated – and that the rate of pulsation seemed to vary according to mental activity, which he attributed to changes in blood circulation. In his landmark book, *Principles of Psychology* (1890), William James recounted an inventive experiment conducted by Mosso: "the subject to be observed lay on a delicately balanced table which could tip downward either at the head or at the foot if the weight of either end were increased. The moment emotional or intellectual activity began in the subject, down went the balance at the head-end, in consequence of the redistribution of blood in his system" (James, 1890, p. 98). Now, it's unclear whether this was a reliable finding; this seems unlikely, as the whole brain is constantly active and a transient increase in blood flow based on a change in mental processes is subtle and fairly localized. However, this anecdote indicates that neurovascular coupling was conceptualized well over 100 years old.

Developmental studies show that cerebral metabolic rate and blood flow velocity and volume are greater in childhood than adulthood (Chugani & Phelps, 1986; Moses et al., 2014). Initial

Figure 2.7 Blood delivery to the brain. A. Resin cast of blood vessels in the brain. (Reprinted from Vendel et al., 2019) B. Schematic showing how astrocytes make contact with both neurons and blood vessels. (© 2019 Nishanth & Schlüter, published by Elsevier Ltd.)

A

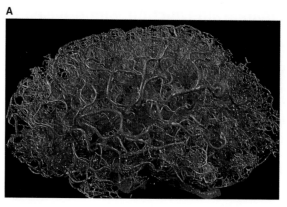

B

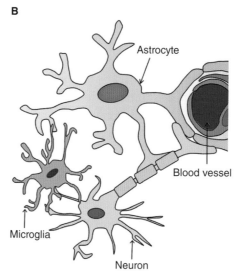

evidence for this comes from positron emission tomography (PET), a technique that involves injection of radioactive isotopes into the bloodstream. Because PET involves radiation exposure, it is rarely used in healthy children; thus, Chugani and Phelps (1986) analyzed PET data collected from pediatric neurological patients, involving a radioactive tracer used to measure glucose metabolism. Another way to estimate cerebral blood flow is through arterial spin labeling, a non-invasive MRI technique that transiently tags water molecules in arterial blood. Studies involving PET and arterial spin labeling show that cerebral blood flow rises from infancy to childhood, peaking sometime between 3 and 8 years at a level that is 40–50 percent higher than in adulthood, and then falls during late childhood and adolescence (Moses et al., 2014).

The conceptual forerunner of PET and MRI was the CT (computed tomography) scan, developed by the radiologist Geoffrey Hounsfield in 1971, who eventually won a Nobel Prize for his work. His insight was that he could take successive slices or angles of X-rays through the body, including the brain, and stitch them together using mathematical techniques to reveal 3D images. CT scans are still used today in clinical applications for diagnosing injury and disease. An invention like this was expensive to create, but Hounsfield was working at EMI Laboratories, whose R&D arm was supported by revenue generated by the Beatles' record company. If your grandparents bought a copy of *Sgt. Pepper's Lonely Hearts Club Band* or *Revolver* you can thank them for supporting science.

In the sections below, we will discuss two brain imaging methods that capitalize on the fact that active neural tissue receives an onslaught of freshly oxygenated blood. The first, **functional magnetic resonance imaging (fMRI)**, is based on electromagnetic forces. The second, **functional near-infrared spectroscopy (fNIRS)**, involves the properties of light absorption. Importantly, both of these are *indirect measures of brain activity*, as they are based on blood vessel dilation in response to neural activity. We have astrocytes to thank for our ability to measure brain function with fMRI and fNIRS!

2.5.2 Overview of fMRI

During fMRI scans, participants lie inside the same type of scanner used to collect structural MRI scans. As we have seen, when there is increased neural activity in a sufficiently large area of brain tissue, nearby capillaries release a surplus of freshly oxygenated blood. This so-called **hemodynamic response** can be measured with fMRI by virtue of the fact that oxygenated and deoxygenated blood have different magnetic properties (see Box 2.1). In brief, this is because hemoglobin, the protein in red blood cells that transports oxygen (and that makes blood red), has iron atoms at its core that are differentially affected by a magnetic field depending on whether they are bound to O_2 molecules. A decrease in the ratio between deoxygenated and oxygenated blood in response to neural activity leads to an increase in MRI signal that is called the **Blood-Oxygen Level Dependent (BOLD)** signal, plotted in several figures below. Because fMRI is based on a sluggish vascular response (known as the hemodynamic lag), it does not provide an instantaneous readout of brain activity: it measures changes on the order of seconds rather than milliseconds – that's three orders of magnitudes lower than EEG! In other words, the **temporal resolution** of fMRI is much lower than that of EEG. On the other hand, unlike EEG, fMRI can measure activity deep in the brain, and the source of activation can be pinpointed much more precisely.

There are two main types of fMRI scans. During **resting-state scans**, discussed in Section 2.6.3, participants aren't given anything to do: they can simply lie there and let their thoughts wander. During **task-based fMRI scans**, by contrast, participants are presented with stimuli, such as images or sounds, and asked to attend to them. Often, they must also respond to them in some way. A common approach is a **subtraction paradigm**, where researchers compare brain activation between conditions that differ only in one way, in an effort to isolate specific cognitive processes (e.g., Posner, 2012). For example, to study how people process grammar, the experimenter might ask the participant to listen to properly formed sentences (*the pizza was too hot to eat*) and compare activation to improperly formed sentences (*the pizza was too hot to sleep*) by subtracting one set of activations from the other.

Some of the regions of the brain that we've named and identified, such as the hippocampus, are defined anatomically – that is, by their shape and location in the brain; others, like the planum temporale or the fusiform face area, are defined *functionally*, meaning that their location in the cortex varies from person to person, and we can only localize them based on fMRI contrasts. (Another way to localize functionally defined regions is via intracortical electrical stimulation; see the classic studies by Wilder Penfield or more recent ones from Josef Parvizi and others.)

In the typical setup for an fMRI experiment (shown in Box 2.1), the participant lies inside the center, or bore, of the scanner with their head positioned within a head coil. The coil fits around the head like a helmet (with extra padding to accommodate small heads). Visual stimuli may be projected onto a mirror placed above the participant's eyes, and the experimenter's instructions and auditory stimuli may be presented via headphones. The participant may hold an MR-compatible device (i.e., one that does not interfere with the magnetic field gradients), such as a button box, made for use in task-based fMRI scans. Typically, the stimuli are visual or auditory and the responses are button presses. However, other types of stimuli (somatosensory, olfactory, or gustatory) and motor responses (e.g., using a track pad to draw, speaking aloud, or even playing an instrument) are also possible with careful experimental control.

To get a general sense of task-based fMRI and the BOLD signal, take a look at Figure 2.8, based on landmark research by Nancy Kanwisher beginning in the mid-1990s. Kanwisher sought to understand whether faces are processed differently in the human visual system from other images. To this end, she conducted studies in which participants viewed series of stimuli, such as faces, scenes, objects, or animals. She then tested for regions showing statistically higher BOLD activation in response to faces than these other classes of visual stimuli. Figure 2.8 shows an axial (horizontal) slice through the brain, slightly above the level of the ears, and a small pink region in ventral temporal cortex. Kanwisher dubbed this the fusiform face area (FFA), because it responded preferentially to faces. Indeed, the fMRI timeseries extracted from this region shows elevated BOLD activation during blocks of face trials relative to other blocks of visual stimuli – including hands, shown here. We will look at fMRI data analysis more closely in Section 2.5.

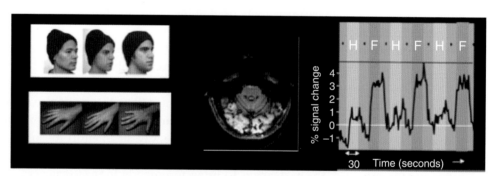

Figure 2.8 fMRI study showing BOLD activation in response to blocks of trials involving faces and hands in ventral temporal cortex. The region outlined in green represents the FFA, defined from a "localizer scan" identifying regions engaged more strongly in response to faces than objects. Average % BOLD signal change within the FFA is plotted across blocks of presentation of hand (H) and face (F) stimuli. (Courtesy of Nancy Kanwisher, based on data from Downing et al., 2006)

The types of behaviors that can be captured while lying in a small tube are rather limited by comparison with the possibilities afforded by EEG and fNIRS. Although fMRI lends itself to studying basic brain processes, it is simply not a naturalistic setting in which to study human behavior in all its complexity. Further, MRI scans (both anatomical and functional) are noisy: the radiofrequency pulses described in Box 2.1 make loud buzzing and clanging sounds. Although participants wear hearing protection, most do not find it a relaxing experience – in fact, studies show that it can induce negative emotions, as well as negatively impact cognitive task performance. Importantly, it is likely that some participants and populations' emotional and cognitive processing are more negatively affected by the scanner environment than others. Collecting additional cognitive (and psychophysiological) data outside the scanner may therefore be helpful.

To make matters worse, it is imperative that participants lie perfectly still during MRI and fMRI data acquisition, as head motion causes artifacts in the BOLD signal (Friston et al., 1996). (Note that it also affects the quality of anatomical scans.) As a result, participants who move their head frequently over the course of a 5- to 10-minute scan – even if only a few millimeters – are typically excluded from the study. A critical confound for DCN studies is that younger participants wiggle in the scanner more than older ones. Moreover, researchers have observed anecdotally that the children who are able to stay still for the full duration of a scan session tend to be those who have a better-developed capacity for self-control – and there is evidence to back this up (Kong et al., 2014). Therefore, young children whose data are included in studies may not be representative of the broader population. However, DCN researchers go to great lengths to minimize head motion in the scanner, and to remove motion artifacts from the data after the fact.

Ironically, researchers are more likely to get high-quality fMRI data from infants than from children: as noted above with regards to structural MRI, infants can be scanned after they fall asleep. But you might be wondering: what kind of fMRI data could one possibly collect on a sleeping infant? Typically, these are data from resting-state scans, as these do not require attention. However, task-based fMRI data have been acquired during sleep for paradigms involving auditory stimuli or flashing lights (Redcay et al., 2007). And, in rare cases, fMRI data have been conducted when infants remain awake (Dehaene-Lambertz et al., 2002).

2.5.3 fNIRS

Although fMRI can be used in infants and young children, the technological hurdles we've reviewed mean that the vast majority of fMRI studies in children focus on children aged 6 years and above. This lack of data from younger children must be addressed if we are to understand the profound cognitive and socioemotional changes that take place during infancy and early childhood. Although infants under 1 year of age can be swaddled and structurally scanned, with some functional imaging mixed in, the developmental period between 1 and 6 years of age is a difficult one for testing children with fMRI. As we have seen, one alternative to fMRI, particularly for children in this age range, is EEG; another is fNIRS. This method is similar to fMRI in that it is based on measurement of regional blood oxygenation changes. It is similar to EEG in that it involves placement of a cap on the head to facilitate non-invasive measurements to be made through the skull. Let's examine how the method works, and then discuss the strengths and weaknesses of this functional brain imaging method relative to the others.

Different wavelengths of light are differentially absorbed by oxygenated (HbO2) vs. deoxygenated hemoglobin (Hb). Thus, changes in how much light is emitted into and detected exiting from the head can be used to reliably estimate changes in concentration of these two states of hemoglobin. Fortunately for DCN researchers, young infants have thinner skin than adults, and their scalp has less hair, allowing the light to be better transmitted through the scalp and skull. As light passes through the skull and brain, it is alternately scattered or absorbed by the tissue through which it travels. Each fNIRS light source emits at least two wavelengths within the near-infrared range: one that is shorter than 770 nm (to detect deoxygenated hemoglobin) and another that is longer than 808 nm, up to 920 nm (to detect oxygenated hemoglobin) (Scholkmann et al., 2014; Bortfeld, 2019). The intensity of light at a given frequency that is passed by an emitter all the way through the brain and is then picked up by a nearby fNIRS detector reflects the oxygenation status of the blood in the area of cortex underlying the emitter and detector at that moment in time. Thus, for example, the less light between 808–920 nm emitted and picked up at the nearby detectors, the more oxygenated the blood is in the underlying patch of cortical tissue.

Practically speaking, using fNIRS involves placing a cap or probe on a participant's head, as shown in Figure 2.9A. The cap is fitted with an array of light emitter and detector pairs, which are spatially located to target the cortical region(s) of interest. Each emitter–detector pair measures optical density changes in the light that travels through the layer of cortex underneath (see Figure 2.9B). The detectors are situated at distances from the emitters to maximally capture light that has traveled through the superficial layer of the brain. Additional detectors can be placed much closer to the emitters to collect information about superficial physiological hemodynamics not related to the brain itself. These short channel detectors provide information about extracerebral signals, such as blood pressure waves, respiration, Mayer waves, and cardiac cycles, which add physiological noise to the signal from the brain itself (Brigadoi & Cooper, 2015). Having a reliable measure of this extracerebral noise allows it to be filtered out, leaving only data from the brain itself. Optical density measures collected at the scalp are then converted into arbitrary units of oxygenated and deoxygenated hemoglobin concentration, which can be analyzed to identify whether and where significant changes in concentration of the two chromophores occurred in the brain during performance of a task. In short, fNIRS allows researchers to measure relative changes in concentration of oxygenated and deoxygenated hemoglobin – an indirect indicator of amount of neural activation – in relation to a task. Hypotheses can then be tested about how brain activity is affected by different behaviors. Although the fNIRS signal is strongly correlated with fMRI (Cui et al., 2011), the measurement is based on optical density units, which are then used to estimate concentration of oxygenated and deoxygenated hemoglobin. Thus, fNIRS data presentation should always include both the oxy- and deoxygenated signals.

The chief advantage of fNIRS is its non-invasiveness, along with its portability and low-cost relative to fMRI. The temporal resolution of fNIRS is better than that of fMRI but worse than EEG/MEG. Its spatial resolution is around 1–2 cm (Scholkmann et al., 2014), worse than

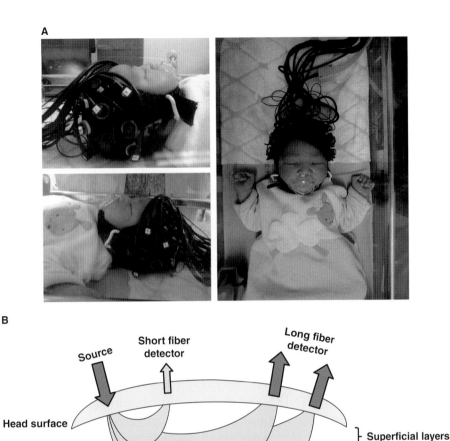

Figure 2.9 Overview of fNIRS. A. Infant with an fNIRS probe in place. (© 2015 Bouchon et al.) B. Schematic of fNIRS light source ("emitter") and three detectors positioned at varying distances from the emitter. (Reprinted from Rupawala et al., 2018)

that of fMRI but better than EEG. Furthermore, unlike fMRI, fNIRS is limited to measuring the hemodynamics of superficial cortical regions. Of relevance to developmental researchers, fNIRS allows infants to be tested while they are awake, along with children of any age who cannot tolerate being placed in a scanner, as is often the case with clinical research. The technique also can be used to test individuals of all ages who have ferromagnetic implantations that prevent them from being anywhere near a scanner's magnet. One such population is deaf individuals who hear artificially via a device called a cochlear implant. In Box 2.2, we discuss research using fNIRS to assess auditory processing in the brains of individuals with cochlear implants.

Box 2.2 The Potential for fNIRS to Guide Cochlear Implant Programming

Cochlear implants (CIs) are small electronic devices that provide the experience of sound to a person with sensorineural hearing loss. Although CIs are now commonly used to support hearing and spoken language learning in deaf and hard-of-hearing children, the sounds conveyed by a cochlear implant are much less precise than those experienced via normal hearing. This is important because while typically developing children are learning language, they extract structure from the signal, which in turn shapes the structure of their developing brains.

What happens to language learning when the speech signal is introduced late, and is not as high fidelity as natural speech? This is exactly the situation in which deaf children find themselves if they learn to hear and speak via a cochlear implant. Although many factors influence the ability of a deaf child hearing through a CI to develop speech and language skills, an important factor is whether the CI is stimulating the auditory cortex adequately. However, obtaining behavioral measurements from young children that adequately reflect this is difficult. Thus, measures of cortical responsivity provide a window into what they are experiencing auditorily.

In response to the need for measurements of cochlear implant-processed speech, researchers have been using fNIRS to analyze cortical activation patterns in cochlear implantees. Because cochlear implantees have a ferromagnetic object implanted in their skulls and thus cannot be anywhere near an MRI scanner, fNIRS is particularly well suited for use with them because it is compatible with implanted devices. Sevy et al. (2010) first compared cortical responses to specific speech stimuli using fNIRS and fMRI in normal-hearing adults, where comparable levels of activation could be verified using the two imaging modalities. These researchers then used fNIRS to examine cortical responsivity to speech in hearing children, deaf children who had been hearing through their implant for four or more months, and deaf children whose cochlear implant had been activated the day of testing. The findings demonstrated speech-evoked cortical activation in all three groups.

In follow-up work (Pollonini et al., 2014; Olds et al., 2016), the researchers sought to determine whether fNIRS is sensitive enough to detect differences in cortical activation patterns evoked by different levels of speech distortion. When postlingually deafened adults were exposed to four distinct listening conditions, the more distorted a listener's experience of speech was as measured by "gold standard" audiological tests, the less distinguishable were the patterns of brain activation observed in response to the different stimulus conditions. Box Figure 2.2E shows a poor CI perceiver's responses, which contrast notably to those from a hearing control (Box Figure 2.2C) and a good CI perceiver (Box Figure 2.2D). In other words, cochlear implantees who were assessed as having poor speech perception through standard audiological tests showed patterns of brain activation that were indistinguishable across all stimulus conditions, including those that contained no detectable speech. In contrast, implantees who performed well on standard perception tests showed activation patterns that approximated those of hearing adults for both normal and channelized speech conditions, as well as to the two non-speech conditions. Keep in mind that the "channelized" speech condition would be doubly distorted for a CI user relative to a hearing control.

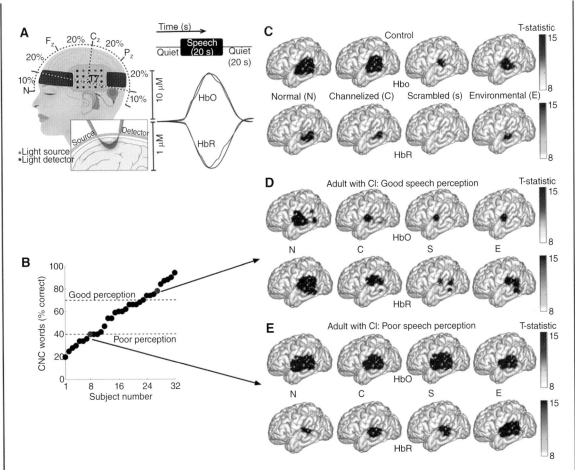

Box Figure 2.2 A. Schematic of the probe location and model of typical hemodynamic response function, with an increase in oxygenated hemoglobin concentration and corresponding decrease in deoxygenated hemoglobin concentration. B. Participants arrayed according to the accuracy of their CNC word performance. On the right, activation maps of the sampled area. C. A normal hearing control participant, and in two cochlear implant users. D. One with good speech perception and E. One with poor perception as assessed via performance on the Consonant-Nucleus-Consonant (CNC) word test. (Reprinted from Olds et al., 2016)

Overall, patterns of cortical activation measured via fNIRS correlated with implant users' audiological test results, thus providing an important demonstration that fNIRS can distinguish good from poor speech perception in cochlear implantees. Ongoing research has the goal of using cortical activation patterns to maximize an implant's signal-to-noise ratio for both adult and pediatric cochlear implantees. Findings from this work will inform our understanding of the neural basis of speech processing via implantation and cortical plasticity for auditory learning in cochlear implant users of all ages.

2.6   fMRI Data Analysis

As we shall see in the following chapters, DCN researchers design tasks to probe the neural basis of such mental functions as attention, language, memory, and more. Importantly, what we refer to as fMRI activation on a task is based on statistical tests comparing the *relative* BOLD signal between task conditions – that is, an fMRI contrast. Participants typically perform numerous trials of each task condition, so as to yield a reliable estimate of brain activation. The ubiquitous images of brain activation we see in papers and the media represent the results of statistical tests between conditions, shown in color and superimposed on anatomical images (colored blobs don't actually show up in the brain, they are used to help us visualize BOLD activation!). There is no such thing as an *absolute* BOLD signal: it is always relative to something else. The BOLD signal is measured in arbitrary units, and it is not comparable from scan to scan. It is often presented as a difference in activation between conditions. In fact, the term *activation* is a misnomer: brain regions are never dormant; they simply vary in terms of level of activity depending on what a person is doing at that moment. It would be more accurate to say that a brain region is *sensitive* to a particular task manipulation. In addition to performing fMRI contrasts, we can examine the coupling of activation over time between brain regions. We will revisit this type of analysis in Section 2.6.3; however, note that such analyses are also conducted to examine coordinated brain activity during task performance.

Another important thing to keep in mind as we move forward is that it is an oversimplification to think that a particular cognitive operation takes place in a particular part or region of the brain. When a brain region is active during a particular behavior, such as listening to speech or planning a motor response, this does not always mean that the region is *necessary* for this behavior. The brain comprises a massively parallel, and massively distributed, set of interrelated neural systems. The brain circuit for a cognitive operation can thus involve parts of the brain that are far removed from one another spatially.

2.6.1   The Basics

fMRI contrasts can be general, identifying all regions engaged during performance of a task, or more specific, identifying regions involved in a specific aspect of a task. A general fMRI contrast compares activation on a task – such as reading sentences – relative to a **baseline** period involving a blank screen (or a screen displaying a fixation cross for participants to look at). However, complex behaviors invoke many mental processes. To read sentences, for example, we must attend to and encode the visual stimuli, recognize individual letters and words, and access their phonology (how they sound) and their meaning. Therefore, such a general contrast yields activation in many brain regions, for many reasons. To identify regions involved in specific mental processes, researchers compare activation across conditions that differ in subtle ways. For example, to identify regions involved in accessing the meaning of words, one might compare BOLD activation when participants read real words vs. nonsense words. To the extent that nonsense words are a good control condition, this more specific fMRI contrast should identify regions involved in extracting meaning from the written word, rather than language processing more generally.

As we saw for structural MRI, the unit of analysis in fMRI is called a voxel. fMRI analyses are based on statistical tests – typically an ANOVA or regression analysis – performed at each voxel. In **whole-brain analyses**, the test is performed on all voxels of the brain (on the order of 100,000 voxels, depending on scan parameters). For those who have learned statistics: rest assured that it is standard practice to statistically correct for this huge number of multiple comparisons so as to reduce the likelihood that the test performed at an individual voxel is significant purely by chance. Another approach is to limit the search space (and therefore the number of comparisons) by testing for activation within a **region of interest** selected based on one's predictions.

When reporting where fMRI activations are located in the brain, we typically use a **standard coordinate system** – essentially, a GPS for the brain. Every point in the brain can be described in terms of its location in space, with standard x, y, and z coordinates. This system serves as a common language: for example, if a paper reports that peak activation for a given fMRI contrast was observed at [−42, 24, 0], we can pinpoint it precisely within the left inferior frontal gyrus. Even better, we can bring to bear everything we know from prior studies about the functions of this region to guide our interpretation of a result.

What we have described here is the standard **univariate fMRI** analytic approach, which has been adopted since the inception of fMRI and is still widely used. More sophisticated, **multivariate fMRI** analyses have gained prominence in cognitive neuroscience research more recently (Kriegeskorte et al., 2008; Dimsdale-Zucker & Ranganath, 2018). In brief, univariate analyses are designed to test for a significant difference between task conditions (null-hypothesis testing). By contrast, multivariate analytic approaches consider the pattern of activation in a more nuanced way, across individual voxels and trials. For example, representational similarity analysis is used to fit a model of the predicted level of brain activation across all individual trials. Thus, this and other multivariate fMRI approaches provide a more nuanced view of brain function than the standard approach. They are not yet very common in DCN, but likely will become so in the near future.

2.6.2 Interpretation of Pediatric fMRI Data

As the field of DCN hinges on our ability to measure how brain activity changes with age, a question of vital importance is whether the BOLD signal is comparable across participants of different ages. As we have just seen, cerebral blood flow (both velocity and volume) is much higher in early childhood than later on; does this affect our ability to draw conclusions about changes in brain function as measured by BOLD? After all, the BOLD response is based on greater delivery of blood to brain tissue during heightened mental activity relative to a *baseline* condition. Therefore, one might imagine that children's higher baseline blood flow would result in a lower BOLD response: that is, there might be a ceiling effect limiting how much more the BOLD signal could increase above and beyond the baseline. However, this concern appears to be unfounded based on studies showing differences between 8-year-olds, 12-year-olds, and adults in cerebral blood flow but not in the BOLD signal (Moses et al., 2014). Indeed, as we will discuss below, the hemodynamic response is quite similar for older children and adults. The stability of this signal from middle childhood into early adulthood likely results from the counteracting effects of various physiological changes (Moses et al., 2014). In short, differences in BOLD signal between children and adults are thought to stem from differences in neurocognitive processes rather than cerebral blood flow itself.

Another important consideration relates to the fact that it is useful to be able to compare, across participants, activation at specific voxels in the brain – and also to report results using a standard coordinate system, as described above. Because individual brains differ in size and shape, however, it is first necessary to resize and warp each participant's data to fit a **standard brain template**, a process referred to as **spatial normalization**. But is it legitimate to normalize brains of different ages to the same standard brain?

An early fMRI study addressed both issues: questions about the comparability of the localization of children's and adults' fMRI activation, and questions about the timing and amplitude of the **hemodynamic response function** (the elemental neurovascular response to a transient stimulus, which is used to model complex BOLD timeseries data). Answering these questions requires the use of simple fMRI tasks, so as to minimize the possibility that age-related differences in location, time course, or magnitude of brain activation are related to differences in task performance and/or strategy use. Kang et al. (2003) undertook this important endeavor, conducting an fMRI experiment in which 7- to 8-year-olds and adults performed a simple visuomotor task. In the study, a visual stimulus appeared on the screen for just over a second, and the participant's job was to press a button at both the onset and offset of the stimulus. Kang and colleagues found a high degree of similarity between children and adults in the overall shape, time course, and magnitude of the BOLD timeseries drawn from visual and motor regions of the brain implicated in the task. This similarity was observed despite the fact that children performed less well than adults (even on this simple task). Thus, we conclude that differential BOLD responses between children and adults are neurocognitively meaningful – and the common approach of normalizing child and adult brains to the same standard template is not necessarily problematic.

However, the picture is quite different for infants and young children: direct comparison to older children and adults is not advised. Due to physiological differences, infants' hemodynamic response function differs from that of older participants in terms of shape, time course, and magnitude. This difference has important implications for data analysis, as BOLD timeseries data are typically modeled with a fixed hemodynamic response function. If infants' data are modeled incorrectly, a BOLD response may go undetected, and one might conclude that they have not yet developed a particular neural/cognitive function. In these cases, using other methods may be advised. For example, a more representative hemodynamic response function may be obtained from infants using fNIRS, for which modeling the response isn't necessary (see Bortfeld et al., 2007). Other constraints involve anatomy, as normalizing infants' or young children's brains to a standard adult template brain is not appropriate. Therefore, both methodological and analytic approaches should be adapted to maximize sensitivity for each age group under investigation, and to facilitate comparison between them (Cusack et al., 2018). When reviewing pediatric fMRI studies – especially those involving infants – it is important to keep these caveats in mind.

2.6.3 Functional Connectivity

fMRI is used not only to localize brain activation, but also to measure so-called **functional connectivity** between brain regions: the strength of their temporal coupling of activation over time (Biswal et al., 1995). Regions whose activation levels fluctuate in tandem are thought to communicate with one another – either directly, via direct anatomical projections between them – or indirectly, via intermediary regions.

In a pioneering study, Bharat Biswal et al. (1995) showed that regions that are known to be anatomically connected and that are co-activated during task performance also show these low-frequency fluctuations at rest. Biswal and colleagues reported, "We have discovered that low-frequency fluctuations in resting brain from regions of the primary sensory motor cortex that are associated with hand movement are strongly correlated both within and across hemispheres … It is concluded that correlation of low frequency fluctuations, which may arise from fluctuations in blood oxygenation or flow, is a manifestation of functional connectivity of the brain" (Biswal et al., 1995, p. 537).

Functional connectivity can be measured during task performance, to get a sense of the degree of coordination between brain regions involved in the task. It can also be measured at rest, in the form of low-frequency fluctuations that cannot be explained by the timing of a specific task. This type of coupling is so-called **intrinsic functional connectivity** (Fox et al., 2005), where "intrinsic" implies that the regions have enduring interactions rather than that they are merely coordinating temporarily to solve a particular task. Patterns of resting-state (rs) functional connectivity are thought to reflect a history of co-activation; indeed, studies examining the neural effects of cognitive or motor training support this conclusion (Guerra-Carrillo et al., 2014).

A set of brain regions that show stronger functional connectivity with one another than with other regions is referred to as a **functional brain network**. A number of distinct networks have been identified via rs-fMRI, as we shall see throughout this book. A landmark study by Michael Fox, Marcus Raichle and colleagues (Fox et al., 2005) identified two anticorrelated large-scale brain networks, shown in Figure 2.10. The researchers conducted whole-brain correlational analyses to identify voxels, shown in warm or cool colors, whose BOLD fluctuations at rest were positively or negatively coupled, respectively, with a region of interest in the posterior cingulate cortex (PCC). To illustrate these results, the timeseries of activation across an rs-fMRI scan is plotted, with the PCC in yellow, medial prefrontal cortex (MPF) in red, and the inferior parietal sulcus (IPS) in blue.

As we shall see later in this book, functional brain networks change markedly in infancy, and continue to be reconfigured through adolescence. When probing the neural basis of cognitive development or individual differences, resting-state functional connectivity is preferred over task-based functional connectivity because it is an independent measure of brain function. That is, it is unrelated to a task for which we want to understand the neural basis of developmental changes or individual differences in cognition. With rs-fMRI, neural differences cannot be explained by how individuals or groups of individuals approach a task (e.g., level of effort or type of strategy). Additionally, rs-fMRI data can be collected in sleeping infants – and even in fetuses (van den Heuvel & Thomason, 2016). However, one important caveat is that functional connectivity estimates are highly sensitive to a variety of factors, including head motion, as well as heart rate and respiration (Grayson & Fair, 2017). Of particular concern to DCN researchers, head movement tends to inflate estimates of short-range functional connectivity (i.e., connections between neighboring regions), and decrease estimates of long-range functional

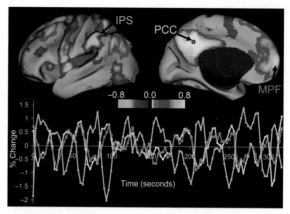

Figure 2.10 Resting-state functional connectivity between a seed region in the posterior cingulate cortex (PCC) and all other voxels in the brain. Voxels showing positive and negative correlations with the PCC are shown in warm and cool colors, respectively. The time course of BOLD fluctuations is plotted below for the PCC and the intraparietal sulcus (IPS). (Reprinted from Fox et al., © 2005 National Academy of Sciences, USA)

connectivity. We will return to this point in Chapter 4. Thus, as noted earlier, it is critical to minimize head movement and to correct for it to the extent possible.

Various statistical approaches are used to characterize brain networks (van den Heuvel & Hulshoff Pol, 2010). One is seeded functional connectivity, shown in Figure 2.10, wherein voxels whose activation correlates with a seed region are identified. It is also common to conduct pairwise connectivity analyses by simply computing the average strength of correlation between voxels in regions of interest. Pairwise connectivity between nodes of a network can be submitted to a graph theoretic analysis, from which various summary metrics of network organization can be computed (e.g., Bassett & Sporns, 2017). Having extracted these network properties, it is possible to examine how they change over development. Damien Fair, featured in our Scientist Spotlight in Box 2.3, Steve Petersen, Bradley Schlaggar, Jonathan Power, and others were pioneers in the application of graph theory to the study of functional brain development (Power et al., 2010). Research along these lines is described further by Ted Satterthwaite in Box 4.3.

Box 2.3 Scientist Spotlight on Damien Fair (University of Minnesota)

Damien Fair (Box Figure 2.3) is a Professor in the Institute of Child Development and Department of Pediatrics and Founding Director of the Masonic Institute for the Developing Brain at the University of Minnesota. His laboratory studies lifespan brain development (from infancy to aging), in different disorders (ADHD, Autism Spectrum Disorder, Parkinson's Disease), and

across different species (humans, non-human primates, and rodents). His team spans the fields of neuroscience, developmental and clinical psychology, psychiatry, biomedical engineering, and computer science.

I was on a winding path to where I'm at, I would say. I was thinking about going to medical school, but then I decided to check whether I really want to do it, so I ended up going to the Yale Physician Associate Program. After graduating, I landed a position as a Physician's Assistant in the Yale New Haven Hospital in the Neurology Department, working with a stroke neurologist who let me do research on large-scale clinical trials. I also had an opportunity to do some side research with a resident named Dave Weisman. We tried to use fMRI, a relatively new technique at the time, to study brain injury. We ran some terrible experiments that were never going to work, but it was my first taste into using non-invasive imaging to look at function inside the brain without actually ever touching it. I knew at that point that this is what I wanted to do, so I applied to graduate programs in Neuroscience. I ended up meeting Brad Schlaggar, a pediatric neurologist who was doing fMRI with perinatal stroke patients, and it was an obvious fit, so I ended up in his and Steve Petersen's lab at Washington University and started doing fMRI research. Around that time the functional connectivity craze was taking off, and I was asked to work with Michael Fox in Mark Raichle's lab to modify code and make it useful for the various work we were doing in the lab. I did that and we applied it to some fMRI studies on task control being led by Nico Dosenbach. It confirmed many of the models of task control we were developing – and poof! Everything changed and my career just went from there.

We do a lot of methods development, because a lot of the measurements we have are very low signal and high noise. So we have put a lot of effort into making them better. I've never wanted to be methods guy, but I always seem to end up there! We also study developmental origins: we think that a lot of the mental health disorders we see in later childhood and adolescence likely start at the time of the making of a brain, during pregnancy and early infancy. So we've been zeroing in on the maternal period and trying to figure out how all the "stuff" that's happening to a mom – from societal influences to stress, to diets, to inflammation – can affect the brain in infancy, and then how that relates to longer-term outcomes. The nice thing about doing MRI at infancy, and specifically the perinatal period, is that you're fairly certain that the majority of

Box 2.3 (cont.)

what you're seeing in terms of environmental exposure is related to the maternal period. We have studies now showing that an increased inflammatory response during pregnancy can affect the starting point, which has long-term implications for fundamental processes like working memory. We also do a lot of work around heterogeneity: there is quite a bit of variation in brain topology and topography – how the brain is organized – and different brain mechanisms might lead to similar phenotypes, so understanding that variability is critical. The fourth leg of the stool is the work we've been doing in animal models and using brain imaging as a bridge to try to better understand the biological phenomena underlying these indirect measures of neurobiology that we get with humans and MRI.

My current job includes building the new Masonic Institute of the Developing Brain at the University of Minnesota. This is an enormous effort led by the UMN Medical School and College of Education and Human Development to bring together basic research, clinical care, applied sciences, work with disabilities, along with policymakers, educators, and importantly *community leaders and organizers* to accelerate discoveries for improving healthy brain development and to streamline the next generation of personalized care.

SUMMARY

- Habituation and dishabituation procedures and preferential looking paradigms have provided important insights about infant cognition
- Child and adolescent cognition are probed with a variety of tasks, questionnaires, and observational measures
- Standardized, psychometrically validated behavioral assessments are essential for drawing valid conclusions about cognitive development
- Cross-sectional research characterizes age-related differences between individuals; longitudinal research characterizes individuals' growth trajectories
- Study participants are rarely representative of the population as a whole
- Structural MRI and diffusion-weighted imaging are used to measure brain structure at a macroscopic level in humans
- EEG and MEG involve scalp recordings of electrical activity in the brain
- EEG data can be used to study brain rhythms or to derive ERPs
- fMRI and fNIRS capitalize on the physical properties of oxygenated and deoxygenated blood
- Univariate fMRI data analysis involves measurement of contrasts between task conditions; multivariate fMRI is a more fine-grained approach
- Functional connectivity analyses of fMRI data are used to study brain networks
- Resting-state fMRI is used to identify intrinsic brain networks
- Every method for studying brain function has distinct benefits and drawbacks with regards to spatial resolution, temporal resolution, ease of use with children, and more

REVIEW QUESTIONS

What is the logic behind habituation/dishabituation procedures and preferential looking paradigms? How do they capitalize on infants' natural tendencies?

Cohort-sequential (or accelerated longitudinal) study designs combine cross-sectional and longitudinal approaches. What does this mean, and why is this useful?

What can, and can't, we measure with structural MRI?

What does diffusion-weighted imaging actually measure? What are the main metrics derived from this method, and how are they interpreted? What is probabilistic tractography?

Why is EEG considered a direct measure of brain activity, and how is it measured? What are ERPs, and what is the utility of identifying well-characterized ERP components?

Why are fMRI and fNIRS considered indirect measures of brain activity? What is similar about what these techniques actually measure, and what is different?

What is meant by an fMRI contrast? How do univariate and multivariate fMRI analyses differ?

What is resting-state fMRI, and how and why is it used?

What is meant by functional connectivity, in the context of fMRI analyses? What is it thought to reflect, and what does it actually measure?

What are some potential concerns regarding the interpretability of age differences in fMRI data, particularly with regards to infants versus older participants?

Which functional brain imaging measure(s) would you use with babies, and/or to study naturalistic behaviors, and why? Which would you use to detect and precisely localize activation anywhere in the brain? Which would you use to tease apart mental processes that take place in rapid succession? Justify your answers.

Further Reading

Aslin, R. N., Shukla, M., & Emberson, L. L. (2015). Hemodynamic correlates of cognition in human infants. *Annual Review of Psychology*, 66(1), 349–379. https://doi.org/10.1146/annurev-psych-010213-115108

Luck, S. J. (2014). *An introduction to the event-related potential technique*, 2nd edition. MIT Press.

Vasung, L., Abaci Turk, E., Ferradal, S. L., Sutin, J., Stout, J. N., Ahtam, B., Lin, P. Y., & Grant, P. E. (2019). Exploring early human brain development with structural and physiological neuroimaging. *NeuroImage*, 187, 226–254. https://doi.org/10.1016/j.neuroimage.2018.07.041

References

Anderson, A. L., & Thomason, M. E. (2013). Functional plasticity before the cradle: A review of neural functional imaging in the human fetus. *Neuroscience and Biobehavioral Reviews*, 37(9 Pt B), 2220–2232. https://doi.org/10.1016/j.neubiorev.2013.03.013

Aslin, R. N. (2007). What's in a look? *Developmental Science*, 10(1), 48–53. https://doi.org/10.111/j.1467-7687.2007.00563.x

Aydogan, D. B., Jacobs, R., Dulawa, S., Thompson, S. L., Francois, M. C., Toga, A. W., Dong, H., Knowles, J. A., & Shi, Y. (2018). When tractography meets tracer injections: A systematic study of trends and variation sources of diffusion-based connectivity. *Brain Structure & Function*, 223(6), 2841–2858. https://doi.org/10.1007/s00429-018-1663-8

Baillargeon, R. (1987). Object permanence in 3½- and 4½-month-old infants. *Developmental Psychology*, 23(5), 655–664. https://doi.org/10.1037/0012-1649.23.5.655

Bassett, D. S., & Sporns, O. (2017). Network neuroscience. *Nature Neuroscience*, 20(3), 353–364. https://doi.org/10.1038/nn.4502

Batalle, D., Edwards, A. D., & O'Muircheartaigh, J. (2018). Annual research review: Not just a small adult brain: Understanding later neurodevelopment through imaging the neonatal brain. *Journal of Child Psychology and Psychiatry*, 59(4), 350–371. https://doi.org/10.1111/jcpp.12838

Biswal, B., Yetkin, F. Z., Haughton, V. M., & Hyde, J. S. (1995). Functional connectivity in the motor cortex of resting human brain using echo-planar MRI. *Magnetic Resonance in Medicine*, 34(4), 537–541. https://doi.org/10.1002/mrm.1910340409

Bortfeld, H. (2019). Functional near-infrared spectroscopy as a tool for assessing speech and spoken language processing in pediatric and adult cochlear implant users. *Developmental Psychobiology*, 61(3), 430–443. https://doi.org/10.1002/dev.21818

Bortfeld, H., Wruck, E., & Boas, D. A. (2007). Assessing infants' cortical response to speech using near-infrared spectroscopy. *NeuroImage*, 34(1), 407–415. https://doi.org/10.1016/j.neuroimage.2006.08.010

Bouchon, C., Nazzi, T., & Gervain, J. (2015). Hemispheric asymmetries in repetition enhancement and suppression effects in the newborn brain. *PloS One*, 10(10), e0140160. https://doi.org/10.1371/journal.pone.0140160

Brigadoi, S., & Cooper, R. J. (2015). How short is short? Optimum source-detector distance for short-separation channels in functional near-infrared spectroscopy. *Neurophotonics*, 2(2), 025005. https://doi.org/10.1117/1.NPh.2.2.025005

Burbacher, T. M., & Grant, K. S. (2012). Measuring infant memory: Utility of the visual paired-comparison test paradigm for studies in developmental neurotoxicology. *Neurotoxicology and Teratology*, 34(5), 473–480. https://doi.org/10.1016/j.ntt.2012.06.003

Chen, Y. H., Saby, J., Kuschner, E., Gaetz, W., Edgar, J. C., & Roberts, T. (2019). Magnetoencephalography and the infant brain. *NeuroImage*, 189, 445–458. https://doi.org/10.1016/j.neuroimage.2019.01.059

Chugani, H. T., & Phelps, M. E. (1986). Maturation changes in cerebral function in infants determined by 18FDG positron emission tomography. *Science*, 231(4740), 840–843. https://doi.org/10.1126/science.3945811

Courchesne, E. (1979). From infancy to adulthood: The neurophysiological correlates of cognition. In J. E. Desmedt (Ed.), *Cognitive components in cerebral event-related potentials and selective attention: Progress in clinical neurophysiology* (Vol. 6, pp. 224–242). Karger.

Cui, X., Bray, S., Bryant, D., Glover, G., & Reiss, A. L. (2011). A quantitative comparison of NIRS and fMRI across multiple cognitive tasks. *NeuroImage*, 54(4), 2808–2821. https://doi.org/10.1016/j.neuroimage.2010.10.069

Cusack, R., McCuaig, O., & Linke, A. C. (2018). Methodological challenges in the comparison of infant fMRI across age groups. *Developmental Cognitive Neuroscience*, 33, 194–205. https://doi.org/10.1016/j.dcn.2017.11.003

Dehaene-Lambertz, G., Dehaene, S., & Hertz-Pannier, L. (2002). Functional neuroimaging of speech perception in infants. *Science*, 298(5600), 2013–2015. https://doi.org/10.1126/science.1077066

Dimsdale-Zucker, H. R., & Ranganath, C. (2018). Representational similarity analyses: A practical guide for functional MRI applications. In D. Manahan-Vaughan (Ed.), *Handbook of Behavioral Neuroscience* (Vol. 28, pp. 509–525). Academic Press. https://doi.org/10.1016/b978-0-12-812028-6.00027-6

Downing, P. E., Chan, A. W., Peelen, M. V., Dodds, C. M., & Kanwisher, N. (2006). Domain specificity in visual cortex. *Cerebral Cortex*, 16(10), 1453–1461. https://doi.org/10.1093/cercor/bhj086

Eimas, P., Siqueland, E., Jusczyk, P., & Vigorito, J. (1971). Speech perception in infants. *Science*, 171, 303–306. https://doi.org/10.1126/science.171.3968.303

Fagan, J. F. (1970). Memory in the infant. *Journal of Experimental Child Psychology*, 9, 217–226. https://doi.org/10.1016/0022-0965(70)90087-1

Fantz, R. L. (1964). Visual experience in infants: Decreased attention to familiar patterns relative to novel ones. *Science*, 146, 668–670. https://doi.org/10.1126/science.146.3644.668

Fox, M. D., Snyder, A. Z., Vincent J. L., Corbetta, M., Van Essen, D. C., & Raichle, M. E. (2005). The human brain is intrinsically organized into dynamic, anticorrelated functional networks. *Proceedings of the National Academy of Sciences of the United States of America*, 102(27), 9673–9678. https://doi.org/10.1073/pnas.0504136102

Friston, K. J., Williams, S., Howard, R., Frackowiak, R. S. J., & Turner, R. (1996). Movement-related effects in fMRI time-series. *Magnetic Resonance in Medicine*, 35(3), 346–355. https://doi.org/10.1002/mrm.1910350312

Grayson, D. S., & Fair, D. A. (2017). Development of large-scale functional networks from birth to adulthood: A guide to the neuroimaging literature. *NeuroImage*, 160(15), 15–31. https://doi.org/10.1016/j.neuroimage.2017.01.079

Greene, D. J., Black, K. J., & Schlaggar, B. L. (2016). Considerations for MRI study design and implementation in pediatric and clinical populations. *Developmental Cognitive Neuroscience*, 18, 101–112. https://doi.org/10.1016/j.dcn.2015.12.005

Guerra-Carrillo, B., Mackey, A. P., & Bunge, S. A. (2014). Resting-state fMRI: A window into human brain plasticity. *The Neuroscientist,* 20(5), 522–533. https://doi.org/10.1177/1073858414524442

Hämäläinen, M., Hari, R., Ilmoniemi, R. J., Knuutila, J., & Lounasmaa, O. V. (1993). Magnetoencephalography: Theory, instrumentation, and applications to noninvasive studies of the working human brain. *Reviews of Modern Physics*, 65(2), 413–497. https://doi.org/10.1103/RevModPhys.65.413

Henrich, J., Heine, S. J., & Norenzayan, A. (2010). The weirdest people in the world? *Behavioral and Brain Sciences*, 33(2–3), 61–83. http://doi.org/10.1017/S0140525X0999152X

Hunter, M. A., & Ames, E. W. (1988). A multifactor model of infant preferences for novel and familiar stimuli. *Advances in Infancy Research*, 5, 69–95.

James, W. (1890). *The principles of psychology*, Vol. 1. Henry Holt and Co. https://doi.org/10.1037/10538-000

Jensen, S. K. G., Kumar, S., Xie, W., Tofail, F., Haque, R., Petri, W. A., & Nelson, C. A. (2019). Neural correlates of early adversity among Bangladeshi infants. *Scientific Reports*, 9, 3507. https://doi.org/10.1038/s41598-019-39242-x

Jusczyk, P. W., & Aslin, R. N. (1995). Infants' detection of the sound patterns of words in fluent speech. *Cognitive Psychology*, 29(1), 1–23. https://doi.org/10.1006/cogp.1995.1010

Kagan, J., & Lewis, M. (1965). Studies of attention in the human infant. *Merrill-Palmer Quarterly,* 11, 95–127.

Kam, J. (2017). The wandering mind: How the brain allows us to mentally wander off to another time and place. *Frontiers of Young Minds*, 5(25). https://doi.org/10.3389/frym.2017.00025

Kang, H. C., Burgund, E. D., Lugar, H. M., Petersen, S. E., & Schlaggar, B. L. (2003). Comparison of functional activation foci in children and adults using a common stereotactic space. *NeuroImage*, 19(1), 16–28. https://doi.org/10.1016/s1053-8119(03)00038-7

Kao, C., & Zhang, Y. (2019). Magnetic source imaging and infant MEG: Current trends and technical advances. *Brain Sciences*, 9(8), 181. http://dx.doi.org/10.3390/brainsci9080181

Kidd, C., Piantadosi, S. T., & Aslin, R. N. (2014). The Goldilocks effect in infant auditory attention. *Child Development*, 85(5), 1795–1804. https://doi.org/10.1111/cdev.12263

Kong, X. Z., Zhen, Z., Li, X., Lu, H. H., Wang, R., Liu, L., He, Y., Zang, Y., & Liu, J. (2014). Individual differences in impulsivity predict head motion during magnetic resonance imaging. *PloS One*, 9(8), e104989. https://doi.org/10.1371/journal.pone.0104989

Kovacs, A. M., Teglas, E., & Endress, A. D. (2010). The social sense: Susceptibility to others' beliefs in human infants and adults. *Science*, 330(6012), 1830–1834. https://doi.org/10.1126/science.1190792

Kriegeskorte, N., Mur, M., & Bandettini, P. (2008). Representational similarity analysis: Connecting the branches of systems neuroscience. *Frontiers in Systems Neuroscience*, 2. https://doi.org/10.3389/neuro.06.004.2008

Lazari, A., & Lipp, I. (2021). Can MRI measure myelin? Systematic review, qualitative assessment, and meta-analysis of studies validating microstructural imaging with myelin histology. *NeuroImage*, 230, 117744. https://doi.org/10.1016/j.neuroimage.2021.117744

Lloyd-Fox, S., Papademetriou, M., Darboe, M., Everdell, N. L., Wegmuller, R., Prentice, A. M., Moore, S. E., & Elwell, C. (2014). Functional near infrared spectroscopy (fNIRS) to assess cognitive function in infants in rural Africa. *Scientific Reports*, 4, 4740. https://doi.org/10.1038/srep04740

Luck, S. J. (2014). *An introduction to the event-related potential technique*, 2nd edition. MIT Press.

Lynch, K. M., Cabeen, R. P., Toga, A. W., & Clark, K. A. (2020). Magnitude and timing of major white matter tract maturation from infancy through adolescence with NODDI. *NeuroImage*, 212, 116672. https://doi.org/10.1016/j.neuroimage.2020.116672

McIntyre, L. C. (2019). *The scientific attitude: Defending science from denial, fraud, and pseudoscience*. MIT Press.

Möller, H. E., Bossoni, L., Connor, J. R., Crichton, R. R., Does, M. D., Ward, R. J., Zecca, L., Zucca, F. A., & Ronen, I. (2019). Iron, myelin, and the brain: Neuroimaging meets neurobiology. *Trends in Neurosciences*, 42(6), 384–401. https://doi.org/10.1016/j.tins.2019.03.009

Moon, C., Lagercrantz, H., & Kuhl, P. K. (2013). Language experienced in utero affects vowel perception after birth: A two-country study. *Acta Paediatrica*, 102(2), 156–160. https://doi.org/10.1111/apa.12098

Moses, P., DiNino, M., Hernandez, L., & Liu, T. T. (2014). Developmental changes in resting and functional cerebral blood flow and their relationship to the BOLD response. *Human Brain Mapping*, 35(7), 3188–3198. https://doi.org/10.1002/hbm.22394

Mukherjee, P., Berman, J. I., Chung, S. W., Hess, C. P., & Henry, R. G. (2008). Diffusion tensor MR imaging and fiber tractography: Theoretic underpinnings. *American Journal of Neuroradiology*, 29(4), 632–641. https://doi.org/10.3174/ajnr.A1051

Neil, J. J., & Smyser, C. D. (2018). Recent advances in the use of MRI to assess early human cortical development. *Journal of Magnetic Resonance*, 293, 56–69. https://doi.org/10.1016/j.jmr.2018.05.013

Nesselroade, J. R., & Baltes, P. B. (Eds.). (1979). *Longitudinal research in the study of behavior and development*. Academic Press.

Nishanth, G., & Schlüter, D. (2019). Blood-brain barrier in cerebral malaria: Pathogenesis and therapeutic intervention. *Trends in Parasitology*, 35(7), 516–528. https://doi.org/10.1016/j.pt.2019.04.010

Nunez, P. L., Nunez, M. D., & Srinivasan, R. (2019). Multi-scale neural sources of EEG: Genuine, equivalent, and representative. A tutorial review. *Brain Topography*, 32, 193–214. https://doi.org/10.1007/s10548-019-00701-3

Olds, C., Pollonini, L., Abaya, H., Larky, J., Loy, M., Bortfeld, H., Beauchamp, M. S., & Oghalai, J. S. (2016). Cortical activation patterns correlate with speech understanding after cochlear implantation. *Ear and Hearing*, 37(3), e160–e172. https://doi.org/10.1097/AUD.0000000000000258

Pollonini, L., Olds, C., Abaya, H., Bortfeld, H., Beauchamp, M., & Oghalai, J. (2014). Auditory cortex activation to natural speech and simulated cochlear implant speech measured with functional near-infrared spectroscopy. *Hearing Research*, 309, 84–93. https://doi.org/10.1016/j.heares.2013.11.007

Posner, M. I. (2012). Imaging attention networks. *NeuroImage*, 61(2), 450–456. https://doi.org/10.1016/j.neuroimage.2011.12.040

Power, J. D., Fair, D. A., Schlaggar, B. L., & Petersen, S. E. (2010). The development of human functional brain networks. *Neuron*, 67(5), 735–748. https://doi.org/10.1016/j.neuron.2010.08.017

Qu, Y., Jorgensen, N. A., & Telzer, E. H. (2021). A call for greater attention to culture in the study of brain and development. *Perspectives on Psychological Science*, 16(2), 275–293. https://doi.org/10.1177/1745691620931461

Raschle, N. M., Lee, M., Buechler, R., Christodoulou, J. A., Chang, M., Vakil, M., Stering, P. L., & Gaab, N. (2009). Making MR imaging child's play: Pediatric neuroimaging protocol, guidelines and procedure. *Journal of Visualized Experiments*, 29. https://doi.org/10.3791/1309

Redcay, E., Kennedy, D. P., & Courchesne, E. (2007). FMRI during natural sleep as a method to study brain function during early childhood. *NeuroImage*, 38(4), 696–707. https://doi.org/10.1016/j.neuroimage.2007.08.005

Rupawala, M., Dehghani, H., Lucas, S., Tino, P., & Cruse, D. (2018). Shining a light on awareness: A review of functional near-infrared spectroscopy for prolonged disorders of consciousness. *Frontiers in Neurology*, 9, 350. https://doi.org/10.3389/fneur.2018.00350

Scholkmann, F., Kleiser, S., Metz, A. J., Zimmermann, R., Mata Pavia, J., Wolf, U., & Wolf, M. (2014). A review on continuous wave functional near-infrared spectroscopy and imaging instrumentation and methodology. *NeuroImage*, 85(1), 6–27. https://doi.org/10.1016/j.neuroimage.2013.05.004

Sevy, A. B., Bortfeld, H., Huppert, T. J., Beauchamp, M. S., Tonini, R. E., & Oghalai, J. S. (2010). Neuroimaging with near-infrared spectroscopy demonstrates speech-evoked activity in the auditory cortex of deaf children following cochlear implantation. *Hearing Research*, 270(1–2), 3947. https://doi.org/10.1016/j.heares.2010.09.010

Sirois, S., & Mareschal, D. (2002). Models of habituation in infancy. *Trends in Cognitive Sciences*, 6(7), 293–298. https://doi.org/10.1016/S1364-6613(02)01926-5

Stone, J. L., & Hughes, J. R. (2013). Early history of electroencephalography and establishment of the American Clinical Neurophysiology Society. *Journal of Clinical Neurophysiology*, 30(1), 28–44. https://doi.org/10.1097/wnp.0b013e31827edb2d

van den Heuvel, M. P., & Hulshoff Pol, H. E. (2010). Exploring the brain network: A review on resting-state fMRI functional connectivity. *European Neuropsychopharmacology*, 20(8), 519–534. https://doi.org/10.1016/j.euroneuro.2010.03.008

van den Heuvel, M. I., & Thomason, M. E. (2016). Functional connectivity of the human brain in utero. *Trends in Cognitive Science*, 20(12), 931–939. https://doi.org/10.1016/j.tics.2016.10.001

Vasung, L., Abaci Turk, E., Ferradal, S. L., Sutin, J., Stout, J. N., Ahtam, B., Lin, P. Y., & Grant, P. E. (2019). Exploring early human brain development with structural and physiological neuroimaging. *NeuroImage*, 187, 226–254. https://doi.org/10.1016/j.neuroimage.2018.07.041

Vendel, E., Rottschäfer, V., & de Lange, E. C. M. (2019). The need for mathematical modelling of spatial drug distribution within the brain. *Fluids and Barriers of the CNS*, 16, 12. https://doi.org/10.1186/s12987-019-0133-x

Wetherford, M. J., & Cohen, L. B. (1973). Developmental changes in infant visual preferences for novelty and familiarity. *Child Development*, 44(3), 416–424. https://doi.org/10.2307/1127994

Wijeakumar, S., Kumar, A., Delgado Reyes, L. M., Tiwari, M., & Spencer, J. P. (2019). Early adversity in rural India impacts the brain networks underlying visual working memory. *Developmental Science*, 22(5), e12822. https://doi.org/10.1111/desc.12822

Wolthuis, R., van Aken, M., Fountas, K., Robinson, J. S., Bruining, H. A., & Puppels, G. J. (2001). Determination of water concentration in brain tissue by Raman spectroscopy. *Analytical Chemistry*, 73(16), 3915–3920. https://doi.org/10.1021/ac0101306

Yin, Q., Johnson, E. L., Tang, L., Auguste, K. I., Knight, R. T., Asano, E., & Ofen, N. (2020). Direct brain recordings reveal occipital cortex involvement in memory development. *Neuropsychologia*, 148. https://doi.org/10.1016/j.neuropsychologia.2020.107625

3   Genes and Epigenetics

LEARNING OBJECTIVES

- Appraise the current state of the "nature vs. nurture" debate
- Explain the concept of heritability, and summarize how the study of heritability began
- Describe how development itself contributes to individual variability
- Describe the two different roles genes play in development
- Identify some of the sources of variation in the human genome

As famed cultural anthropologist Margaret Mead wryly noted, "Always remember that you are absolutely unique. Just like everyone else." Part of what makes us unique is that we have experienced different things in life. Indeed, the astonishing capacity of the human brain to be molded by experience is a major contributor to our individuality – and to our being the most successful and adaptable species on the planet. But any parent can tell you that children arrive with their own personalities, predispositions towards certain behaviors or attitudes, starting in the crib. Even monozygotic (so-called "identical") twins are not exactly the same. To what extent do abilities appear naturally as a result of preprogrammed brain maturation, and to what extent are they learned? This is the age-old **nature versus nurture debate**, with strict **nativists** at one extreme and strict **empiricists** at the other. Nativists have emphasized competencies that seem to be preordained, unfolding naturally according to a genetic blueprint written into our DNA. In contrast, empiricists emphasize the importance of powerful learning mechanisms that are shaped by the environment.

Here, we'll take into consideration two important concepts that are essential for understanding how brains and bodies develop. The first involves what genes are, what they do, how they guide development, and how they contribute to human variation. We will examine the regulatory processes necessary for genes to be expressed, including the influence of epigenetics on this process. The second concept we will tackle is how the mature brain emerges from a dynamic process that starts *in utero* and is influenced by both genetics and epigenetics. As we proceed, we will challenge the view that genes simply code for aspects of who we are, emphasizing instead the interactive influence of genes and the environment (both extrinsic and intrinsic influences on the developing brain, as mentioned above with regard to the interactive specialization framework). Generally speaking, we avoid the use of the word "innate" throughout this book, as the term has come to carry different meanings for different people, and because it wrongly suggests that some behaviors are completely hard-wired. Indeed, the story of developmental cognitive neuroscience is the story of the amazing plasticity of the human brain-gene system, and its extraordinary ability to adapt, adjust, and modify itself based on experience. Therefore, our aim is to fully embrace the dynamic and complex interactions of genetics and environment: how the physical expression of a genotype becomes a person's phenotype, the observable expression of their genes.

3.1   Interactive Specialization

Nativism dominated developmental research for much of the second half of the twentieth century, but its influence waned as researchers documented the powerful influence that environment and experience have on nearly all life outcomes. Meanwhile, neuroscientists found evidence that higher-level cognitive and socioemotional processes are **emergent properties** of the complex interplay between genes, brains, culture, and the environment.

In the field of DCN, Mark Johnson's **interactive specialization perspective** (Johnson, 2001, 2011) provides a framework for understanding how genes and the environment dynamically interact across developmental time to build brains, bodies, and behavior. This perspective explains how the interactions between connected brain regions shape their emerging function. For example, neural firing in one region influences gene expression in another, along with the brain's functional and anatomical structure. Moreover, the intrinsic environment of the brain (i.e., the anatomical connections that influence brain activity and therefore function) interacts with its extrinsic environment (i.e., the external environment and specific experiences of its owner). Two of the central ideas are that development is not unidirectional, and that biology is responsive to the environment from conception onward. In short, researchers in the field of DCN aim to characterize how each individual emerges from a variable blend of inputs.

The interactive specialization framework builds on Jean Piaget's (1952) theoretical contributions to understanding the origins and development of knowledge. It also owes a great deal to theoretical groundwork laid by Gilbert Gottlieb, whose **probabilistic epigenesis** (see Gottlieb, 1976, 1998, 2007) countered earlier views that there was a clear and predetermined path to trait development (Figure 3.1A). Gottlieb argued that the development of any organism is dependent on bidirectional influences – that biological and environmental forces interact to form a larger system with emergent properties that are not reducible to the component processes alone (see Figure 3.1B).

Other indirect sources of influence on the interactive specialization framework are Eleanor Gibson's work on perceptual learning (Gibson & Pick, 2000) and Esther Thelen's work on motor development (Thelen, 2000). In the 1970s, both these researchers began examining

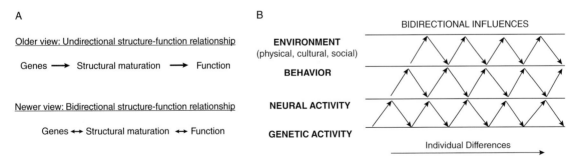

Figure 3.1 Changing views on the influence of genes on development. A. The unidirectional versus bidirectional structure–function relationships. (Adapted from Gottlieb, 1976) B. A more detailed view of the bidirectional relationship. (Adapted from Gottlieb, 1992)

contextual influences on the developing human: Gibson showed that perception is a crucial component of human adaptation; Thelen conceptualized motor development as emergent and exploratory and as integral to cognition. Considered radical in their time, these researchers helped psychology and related fields move away from both strict nativism and strict empiricism.

As often happens, we have had to rediscover what we knew in the past. It is time to lay the nature–nurture debate to rest altogether. Pioneering neuroscientist Donald Hebb, whose ideas we will revisit in Chapter 5, recognized this well ahead of his time:

> The student may find it said … that 80 per cent of intelligence is determined by heredity, 20 per cent by environment. This statement is, on the face of it, nonsense. […] both these variables are of 100 per cent importance: their relation is not additive but multiplicative. To ask how much heredity contributes to intelligence is like asking how much the width of a field contributes to its area. (Hebb, 1958, pp. 128–129)

3.2   Tracking Sources of Individual Variation

The human genome differs critically from the genomes of other species. All humans share 99.9 percent of their genes with other humans. That 0.1 percent difference is a major contributor to what makes each of us unique, even if it's now appreciated that the genome doesn't entirely define a person. Our understanding of genetics, human and otherwise, has surged in recent years, in part due to research programs that seek to understanding genetic factors in disease. Some genetic changes have been associated with an increased risk of having a child with a birth defect or developmental disability, not to mention developing cancer or heart disease. DCN has benefited enormously from these advances, but likewise owes much to the research that preceded its emergence as a field.

Early efforts to understand how the interplay of biology and environment underlies human behavior formed the foundation for the nature vs. nurture debate. The phrase itself was popularized by the polymath Sir Francis Galton well over a century ago (Galton, 1869). Galton was obsessed with measuring human variability, developing an array of behavioral and statistical techniques aimed at making measurement of human traits tractable. He took to heart the dictum of Galileo Galilei that the job of the scientist is to "measure what is measurable, and render measurable that which is not." Galton's fascination with the influence of heredity and environment on social advancement spawned the field of **eugenics**, the study of how to arrange reproduction within a human population to increase the occurrence of heritable characteristics regarded as desirable. Galton (1883) was a strong proponent of using this as a means of improving the human race. Tragically, this line of thinking was most appealing to those who sought to discriminate against others and "weed out" undesirables. This approach served as the basis for the adoption of eugenic policies in both the United Kingdom and United States (Davenport, 1923). For example, in the United States, laws were enacted that legalized forced sterilization of individuals with perceived mental or physical defects. Eugenics was the basis for the passage of the Immigration Act of 1924, which severely limited how many immigrants could enter the country each year; it stayed in effect until the 1960s (Norrgard, 2008). Eugenics also was the basis for the horrors of Nazi Germany.

Putting aside for a moment this dark history of its misuse, Galton's focus on the measurement of variation across an array of human attributes led him to anticipate an important tool in how researchers disentangle genetic from environmental influences in humans: twin and adoption studies (Chapter 2). Critically, Galton recognized the need to understand and measure sources of variability to understand human nature.

3.2.1 Heritability

Variance is the amount of variability observed across a distribution of values. You can plot continuous measurements of any trait – for example, of height – with a histogram to observe its variance, reflected in the shape of the distribution of those values. Generally, if the trait is normally distributed, as height is, more people will be located in the middle section of the inverted U-shaped distribution curve that emerges from the data than on either extreme. A curve that is flatter, with more values away from the middle, reflects a high degree of variability across the population. Variance, then, characterizes the amount of *deviation* across individuals from the mean value for that trait.

Twin and adoption studies allow researchers to estimate how much of the variance of a trait – physical, psychological, or otherwise – is due to genetic differences, how much is due to family environments, and how much remains unexplained even when the first two things are taken into account. In the terminology of twin studies, this is due to **non-shared environment** – a problematic term to which we will return below. Twin and adoption studies have been conducted for a very long time, revealing important information about the degree to which different traits vary across individuals, as accounted for by variance in genes, a child's environment, and unspecified factors (presumably related to variability in the process of development). Across many (many!) studies, the percentage of variance explained by genetic differences has been shown to be at least moderate. Genes matter. Indeed, the concept of **heritability** – the amount of variance in a trait that can be attributed to genetic variation – is relevant to much of this book. That said, understanding what exactly heritability *is* is critical to understanding development itself. There is far more to heritability than genes alone.

Heritability can be estimated via twin and adoption studies, but it also can be estimated by comparing traits across thousands of people in any general population. Because we humans are all at least distantly related – we all have roughly the same genetic material, or **genome** (99.9 percent) – such comparisons can identify even a small increase in similarity between two people relative to the average in the overall population, indicating genetic relatedness. Large-scale population studies, as well as comparisons of SNP-to-trait associations across thousands of individual genomes via **genome-wide association studies (GWAS)**, have confirmed the heritability of many of the psychological traits initially identified as heritable via twin studies. Yet another method, **genome-wide complex trait analysis (GCTA)**, estimates the variance for a complex trait explained by all the SNPs on a chromosome or across an entire genome rather than by testing the association of any particular SNP to that trait. (SNP is discussed in detail in Section 3.5.2.) The GCTA method has also allowed researchers to determine whether the same genes remain associated with a particular trait across the course of development (Krapohl & Plomin, 2016).

Suffice it to say that for any human trait that has been examined, variation across a population is attributable at least in part to genetic differences. Such traits range from how someone processes information, to features of their personality, to the likelihood that they will have a drinking problem or get divorced. A problem with heritability estimates, however, is that they refer to how much variance within a particular population can be accounted for by genetics – not the extent to which an individual's characteristics are determined by their genes. This is the source of a common misunderstanding: if the heritability of a trait is calculated to be about 40 percent, it does not mean that 40 percent of the absolute value of that trait in a specific individual is attributable to genetics; as Hebb pointed out, that would be akin to saying that 40 percent of the area of a rectangle can be explained by its width. Rather, it means that, across the population in question, 40 percent of the variance in a trait is attributable to genetic differences.

Inherent to the above explanation is another source of confusion: heritability is a measure specific to the population under investigation, not to all humans at any point in time. Practically speaking, this means that, depending on the particular time and place in which participants were sampled, a trait may be more or less influenced by genes. Height again provides a useful example for understanding how this works. If malnutrition affects the growth of a large number of individuals in the population, environmental differences – in this case, access to food – will explain more of the variance between individuals than genetics. (This example is, unfortunately, all too relevant; e.g., in 2020 in the United States, at the height of the Covid-19 pandemic, more than 4 in 10 children lived in households struggling to cover basic expenses; Children's Defense Fund, 2021.) With a substantial number of individuals living under dire conditions, genetic effects on height still exist; they are just less influential proportional to the environment for that population at that particular moment in time. By contrast, if everyone in the population is well-nourished, individual differences in genes that influence height will have a bigger influence than environmental variability. This example underscores the danger of generalizing findings on heritability in one population to other populations: measured heritability is not a biological constant.

3.2.2 Developmental Variance

While there are clear genetic and environmentally based differences between people, these are not the only sources of individual variability. Why don't **monozygotic twins** (we'll refrain from using the misnomer identical twins) raised in the same family look and act and think in exactly the same ways? Psychologists and behavioral geneticists account for this as **non-shared environment**. This term implies that the source of variance not accounted for by genes or environment are the sort of idiosyncratic experiences that each of us has. In the context of a twin study, this would be something that happens to one twin but not the other such as getting less oxygen in the womb or slipping on a banana peel and breaking their leg. However, with further delineation of the processes underlying organismal development, including prenatal brain development, there has been a growing appreciation of the degree to which random noise can be introduced through the normal course of development. Even if you take twins with the exact same genome – that is, with identical instructions for brain-building – their brains won't turn out exactly the same. While their brains will be far more similar than those of **dizygotic twins** (for a review, see Jansen et al., 2015), they'll differ in small but meaningful ways from birth onward. How can this be?

While the twin-study notion of non-shared environment may well capture some subset of the non-genetic and non-environmental variance, it doesn't capture it all. There is also what can be thought of as **developmental variance**. Let us explain. Rather than thinking of the developmental process as following a *blueprint*, which implies precise instructions, it's more helpful to think of the process as following a *recipe* (Mitchell, 2018). Most of us have had the experience of diligently following cooking instructions step-by-step, with the result being a similar, but nevertheless slightly (or grotesquely) different version of whatever dish was being made. It's impossible to create exactly the same dish again, even with painstaking effort to follow the same recipe precisely; there are too many sources of variability (humidity, temperature, age and quality of the ingredients, etc.). So it goes with development. Tens of billions of neurons have to be created through cellular duplication, and then migrate, taking up positions in different layers of the developing brain and sending projections out to the rest of the brain to connect with thousands of different cells (see Chapter 4). Each time this process unfolds, it does so somewhat differently. You can start with the same genome, but you won't get exactly the same outcome. Thus, the unexplained variance in twin studies that is referred to as "non-shared environment" is, at least in part, due to random variability in the developmental process, basically **stochastic noise**. To understand this, we have to review what genes are, as well as the role they play in development. Only then can we really appreciate how developmental processes themselves contribute to the individual differences that make us who we are.

3.3   What Genes Are

The original meaning of "**gene**" was grounded in the science of heredity, whereby scientists tried to understand how traits were passed from parents to offspring. However, when we say that genes influence behavior, what we really mean is that genetic differences contribute to differences across people, including in traits that themselves influence behavior (and the brain itself) over time. Because this issue is relevant to the rest of the book, it is worth clarifying the relationship between genes as units of heredity and genes as a stretch of DNA that codes for a specific protein. Understanding the relationship between these two aspects of genetics is foundational to understanding much of the research we will discuss.

3.3.1   Genes as Units of Inheritance

Most of us likely remember learning in school that Gregor Mendel started the science of heredity in the mid-1800s by tracking the manifestation of different traits across generations of pea plants. Mendel noted whether the peas had green or yellow coats, were wrinkled or smooth, were tall or short, and so on. By observing patterns of inheritance, he concluded that there must be something physical being passed down from one generation to the next that controls whether, for example, a plant has peas with wrinkled or smooth shells. Mendel was able to deduce from the patterns he observed that there must be two copies of this *something* for each trait, one contributed by each of the parent pea plants. Thus, the concept of units of heredity was born in reference to whatever these discrete inherited units were, with the understanding that there must be different units for different traits. The word gene was coined later by Danish botanist Wilhelm Johannsen to refer to Mendelian units of heredity (Johannsen, 1909). But the stuff of these units remained a mystery.

In his time Mendel had no inkling how the hereditary transmissions he observed actually happened. Indeed, it was only as microscopes became increasingly powerful in the late 1800s that chromosomes themselves were first observed in cell nuclei. Once scientists were able to visualize these subcellular structures by staining them (hence the name "chromosome," Greek for colored bodies) – they could observe the processes of cellular division, **mitosis** and **meiosis** (Section 3.4). However, the nature and function of the structures themselves was revealed only slowly over time.

Two independent papers published at the outset of the twentieth century formed the basis for the view that specific genetic material is located on particular chromosomes, now referred to as the **chromosomal theory of inheritance** (Crow & Crow, 2002). With that, the behavior of chromosomes during the generation of germ cells via meiosis could be understood to explain why genes are inherited according to Mendel's laws. Soon thereafter, Thomas Hunt Morgan (1910) determined that specific chromosomes specified sex and eye color in fruit flies, providing the critical evidence to support the link between chromosomes and inherited traits. Later, in 1869, Friedrich Miescher identified **deoxyribonucleic acid (DNA)** as the major chemical constituent of chromosomes, and in 1881 Albert Kossel identified the chemical subunits that make up DNA and RNA, called **nucleotides**.

But once DNA was initially characterized, its four nucleotides were deemed too simple to contain the instructions that make all living creatures unique. As a consequence, the hunt for genetic material (the mysterious heritable substance) then focused on proteins, with their multitude of amino acids and complicated shapes. At that point, Frederick Griffith, a bacteriologist looking for a vaccine for pneumonia, transformed a nonvirulent bacterium to a virulent one, and demonstrated that this change was inherited by the next generation of bacteria (Griffith, 1928). Building on this finding, Oswald Avery and his collaborators showed that the source of the critical information was DNA and not proteins (Avery et al., 1944). Although their important finding was largely ignored at the time, subsequent research confirmed that genetic material was indeed made of DNA. Later still, Watson, Crick, Franklin, and Wilkins discovered the structure of DNA using X-ray crystallography.

The very simplicity of DNA, a feature that led to it being dismissed initially, is now recognized as its incredible strength in carrying information: what matters is the unique sequencing of its four nucleotide bases (see Figure 3.2). A nucleotide, or **base**, is the basic structural unit (and building block) for DNA. Each nucleotide is composed of three parts: a five-sided sugar, a phosphate group, and a nitrogenous (containing nitrogen) base (left side of Figure 3.2A). The sugar and phosphate group make up the long sides of the DNA double helix, with a chemical bond between the phosphate group of one nucleotide and the sugar of a neighboring nucleotide holding each backbone together. The nitrogenous bases themselves are located in between the two backbones, or strands, with chemical (hydrogen) bonds linking the bases that are across from one another. Thus, **base pairs** hold the two strands of the double helix together (A always pairs with T, and C always pairs with G) (right side of Figure 3.2A).

In short, the DNA molecule consists of two strands stuck together in a ladder-like shape, with the bonded base pairs – one base from each strand – forming the ladder's rungs.

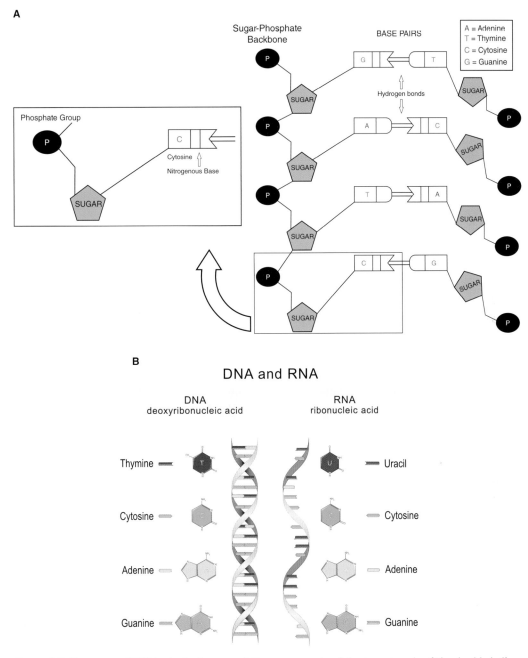

Figure 3.2 Structure of DNA. A. A close-up of the components of the two strands of the double helix, with close-up of the three components of a nucleotide itself. B. A comparison of the helical and base structures of DNA and RNA.

Finally, the ladder is twisted into a helical (i.e., corkscrew) shape; hence the use of the term "double helix" in reference to DNA (left side of Figure 3.2B). This twisting brings the two strands closer while still allowing everything to fit neatly together. Note that the helical structure is not ordinarily visible, as DNA strands are tightly coiled into chromosomes; it has been estimated that if all the chromosomes in a single human cell were uncoiled, the DNA would stretch to a length of around 2 meters! Do that again for all your chromosomes and it would take you to the moon and back – 150 times (National Institute of General Medical Sciences, 2012).

3.3.2   Genes as Protein Encoders

Thus far, we've focused on the role that genes play as units of heredity – but how does that relate to the role of genes in coding for proteins? A gene encodes a protein, but it doesn't *make* the protein. Rather, stretches of DNA called **exons** contain the "code" needed to create a particular protein. For this reason, proteins are the products of genes, and are sometimes referred to as "gene products."

For a protein to be created from a gene, the cell must "read out" the code provided by that gene's stretch of DNA. This is the process of **transcription**, whereby the sequence of bases of a stretch of DNA is transcribed into the reciprocal sequence of bases in a strand of RNA (right side of Figure 3.2B). Thus, the DNA sequence is passed onto a strand of RNA which then carries the information to where proteins are produced, outside of the cell nucleus (DNA stays in the nucleus, as a permanent record that can be called upon again in the future). The RNA molecules that carry out this function are known as **messenger RNA (mRNA)**. Transcription is followed by **translation**, the process by which mRNA molecules are used to create proteins. To achieve this, the specific sequence of nucleotides in the mRNA molecule serves as the code for the corresponding sequence of amino acids needed to produce that gene's protein. In other words, during translation, the sequence of mRNA nucleotides is translated into a corresponding sequence of amino acids (or from RNA "language" into protein "language") to build a protein. **Gene expression** refers to the process by which a protein is synthesized according to "instructions" embedded in a DNA sequence. Transcription and translation are critical components of the process (Figure 3.3). You may have heard about the "production" of proteins; for the sake of clarity, we will use the term "expression" to refer to this process.

A cell only decodes the information in the genome that is relevant to its particular function at a particular time. Because not all of the roughly 18,000 genes in the human genome are transcribed in every cell (not by a long shot) or all the time, transcription is controlled for each gene by the cells themselves, a process guided by large stretches of non-coding DNA – **introns** (as opposed to coding DNA, or exons). Indeed, stretches of non-coding DNA make up well over 95 percent of the genome. Although researchers once thought non-coding DNA was "junk" with no obvious purpose, it is now clear that a good portion of it is integral to the function of cells (Gloss & Dinger, 2018). Non-coding DNA contains many types of regulatory and housekeeping elements (see Plank & Dean, 2014), with sequences determining when, and in which cells, genes are turned on and off. Non-coding DNA also provide sites for specialized proteins – **transcription factors** – to attach or bind to, either activating or repressing the expression of genes as proteins. (If you're wondering how proteins regulate gene expression if gene expression is itself required for protein synthesis, know that this chicken-and-egg problem is an area of research unto itself; for starters, look into self-splicing RNA.) Note that the process of turning gene expression up or down or on or off is called **gene regulation**, the basis for an area of study called

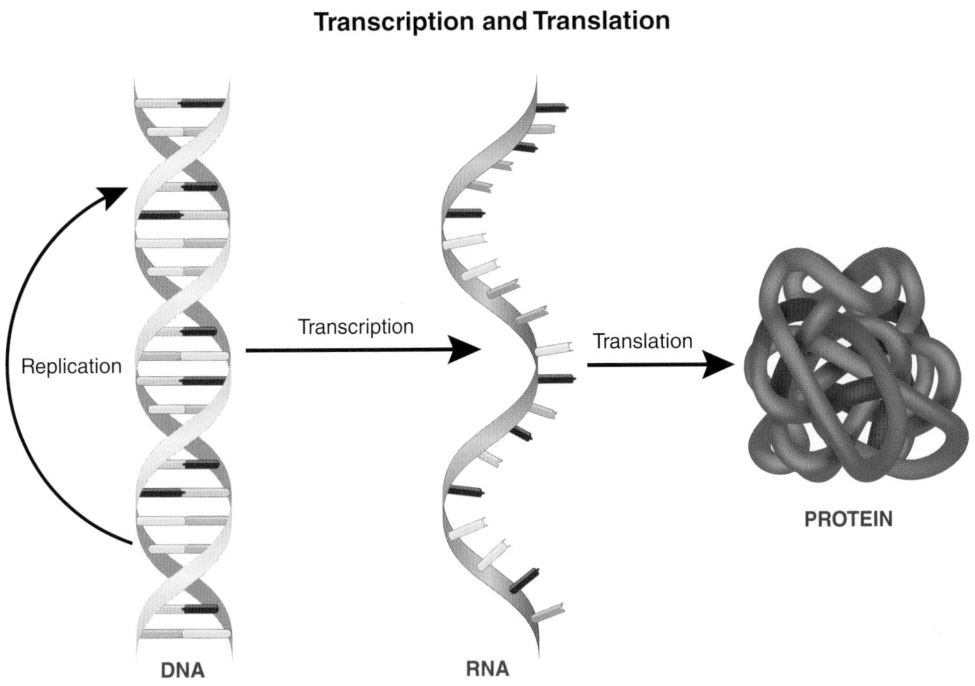

Transcription and Translation

Figure 3.3 In protein synthesis, DNA is transcribed to RNA and RNA is translated into a protein. (Reprinted from Qin et al., 2015, with permission from Elsevier)

epigenetics. The Scientist Spotlight for this chapter focuses on Michael J. Meaney, one of the foremost experts on this issue (Box 3.1). For now, suffice it to say that the regulatory aspect of non-coding DNA introduces additional sources of variability in an organism.

Box 3.1 Scientist Spotlight on Michael J. Meaney (McGill University)

Michael J. Meaney (Box Figure 3.1) is a James McGill Professor of Medicine at Douglas Mental Health University Institute of McGill University, where he is the Director of the Maternal Adversity, Vulnerability and Neurodevelopment Project. Meaney also leads the Integrative Neuroscience Program at the Singapore Institute for Clinical Sciences. He received his PhD from Concordia University, with postdoctoral training at The Rockefeller University. Meaney's studies on stable effects of early maternal care on gene expression and development led to the discovery of novel epigenetic mechanisms for the influence of early experience.

I began my undergraduate work in biology, with a primary interest in developmental biology. We were interested in how the genetic codes play out to create the structure that we call a salamander vs. a bird. But I started to get really interested in individual differences: in other words, what makes one salamander different from another salamander. So my genetics professor told

Box 3.1 (cont.)

me, "you need to take courses in psychology." Those was the days of Harry Harlow, when people were interested in how early experience can shape individual differences in behavior – and right in my hometown of Montreal was the guru of such things: Donald Hebb. He had this brilliant metaphor that has stuck with me. He said that comparing the impact of genes and the environment on an individual is like comparing what contributes more to the area of a rectangle: the length or the width. So for me, nature/nurture was never an issue. When I went off to do graduate studies, I ended up in clinical psychology. As my professor Jane Stewart said, what better way to get to grips with individual variation and development than studying clinical psychology? My thesis work was biological, but as a result of doing the clinical internship and supervision, I was also experienced in dealing with childhood psychopathology.

When it came time to do a postdoc, I went to work with Bruce McEwen, who arguably at the time was the most prominent neuroscientist in the world. At the time, we understood the basic molecular biology: that the environment can create signals inside a cell that ultimately bind to the DNA and turn off genes – but those are all short-term processes. What I was interested in was the long-term enduring effects of early experience … you could call it an imprint. Working in Bruce's lab, we developed a model looking at environmental regulation of stress responses. We had to go through all these processes to understand where in the brain that happens, and which genes are transcribed differentially to influence stress reactivity. This took us to the glucocorticoid receptor – and we weren't alone in that hunt. We found that activation of the glucocorticoid receptor in the hippocampus renders your pituitary-adrenal stress response more modest. And we then showed that maternal licking and grooming could regulate the glucocorticoid receptor in its expression in the hippocampus, and that the offspring whose mothers licked them more frequently were less reactive to stress. So we had an early experience, we had a physiological outcome, and we had a gene that we knew was, at least in part, interlocking those two.

And then the question became: how does maternal licking stably affect the expression of the glucocorticoid receptor in the hippocampus? I did a sabbatical in Edinburgh, where I interacted with people at the Medical Research Council in Genetics, who were interested in the development of cancer. Through these interactions I started to think: what if, for example, maternal licking were actually working through these epigenetic mechanisms? What we knew at the time as being a mechanism for long-term epigenetic marks that could regulate gene expression was DNA methylation. So we came back and started working on DNA methylation, and after around seven or eight years we had the data to convince ourselves that maternal licking was altering the methylation around the glucocorticoid receptor – and that the mark was sustained into adulthood and responsible for the differences in that expression of the gene and the downstream effects of stress response. So, that was proof of principle. Then, we partnered with Gustavo Turecki at McGill, who had postmortem human brain samples from individuals whom we knew did or did not have a history of childhood maltreatment. And we showed that a history of child maltreatment was associated with differences in methylation around the glucocorticoid receptor.

3.3.3 The Big Picture

As should be apparent, taking a molecular biology view of development complicates things considerably, because it embraces the fact that the gene is both a unit of heredity and a repository of information critical for the system to build proteins. These functions are inextricably intertwined. We are each rendered unique through our genetic differences, some big and some small, some inherited and some not. The expression of these genes as proteins at a particular time and in particular cells is guided by the abundant non-coding, regulatory DNA strung in between the genes (i.e., coding DNA) themselves. There's a lot of information in there!

We can simplify matters by zooming out. Living things are different from non-living things because living things are organized (they are called "organisms," after all) and they can adapt to their environments. This organization is not arbitrary: it is very specific, and that specificity is encoded in our genome. The genetic material in each of our cells is the source of that information, arrayed along the 23 pairs of chromosomes, each containing unique chunks of the linear molecule of DNA. (Although differing from species to species, there's nothing particularly special, as far as we know, about how DNA is chunked across chromosomes.) Regardless of species, these chunks include protein coding and non-coding DNA alike. When people use the word "gene," they are referring to the specific bits that provide the information for creating the organized patterns that form our very foundation: the coding DNA. However, those bits wouldn't work without all the non-coding DNA that provides regulatory support for the process of gene expression.

In short, a gene is the unit of heredity, and gene expression generates proteins, a process regulated by the stretches of non-coding DNA between genes, among other things. Proteins are made up of hundreds or thousands of smaller units called amino acids, which are attached to one another in long chains. There are 20 different types of amino acids that can be combined to make a protein. The sequence of amino acids determines each protein's unique three-dimensional structure and its specific function. It is estimated that the human body has the ability to generate 2 million different types of proteins, guided by our 20,000–25,000 protein-coding genes.

The availability of increasingly sophisticated diagnostic tools is revealing a complex human genetic architecture chock-full of different types of genetic mutations, some of which we review below, which themselves vary in frequency across the population, from *de novo* (i.e., immediate changes introduced in us through active processes) to rare to common. Where initial mapping of the human genome promised to paint a clear picture of how genes make us who we are, it is increasingly apparent that our genetic complexity will continue to challenge our ability to find strong genotype–phenotype correlations. Furthermore, individual experiences contribute to an array of gene–environment interactions, underscoring how much the environment also influences genotype-to-phenotype relationships (see Section 3.6 on epigenetics).

3.4   Genetic Variation

Genetic diversity is introduced into a species in a variety of ways, manifesting primarily in the form of different **alleles**, one of two or more versions of a gene. Although the term "allele" was originally used to describe variation among genes themselves, it now also refers to variation among non-coding DNA sequences. An individual inherits two alleles for each gene, one from each parent. If the two alleles are the same, the individual is said to be **homozygous** for that gene; if different, they are **heterozygous**. Sexually reproducing organisms receive unique combinations of alleles from their parents as a direct result of genetic recombination during meiosis and the randomization introduced via the reproductive process itself. The basis for genetic variability – **allelic variation** – is thus a product of the process of reproduction and of the phylogenetic history of humans. Moreover, **mutations** introduce variation into a species' genotype.

Confusingly, geneticists use the term *mutation* to refer to both the process by which a change in DNA sequence is introduced and the resulting change itself. The human genome is an amalgam of millions of mutations accumulated across our ancestral history, some common and some rare, which are then combined with more recent, *de novo* mutations. These sources of variation collectively contribute to making each of us unique.

To identify additional sources of genetic variation, it is helpful to first outline the specific processes of cellular replication: mitosis and meiosis. Here we delineate several sources of variation in the human genome, providing details about the underlying processes and developmental implications of each. While the transcription necessary for protein synthesis involves copying DNA into RNA, the **replication** necessary for cellular division involves copying DNA to make more DNA. Both processes involve the generation of nucleic acids, either DNA or RNA, but the function of each is very different: transcription is involved in gene expression and replication in cellular division. Please note that these terms (transcription and replication) are not synonymous; this is a common source of confusion.

3.4.1   Mitosis

In humans, the nucleus of each cell contains 23 pairs of chromosomes, across which the approximately 3 billion base pairs of DNA are arrayed. During regular cellular division (mitosis), the paired strands pull apart from one another such that each serves as a template for the making of a new, complementary strand. Any cell that is not a gamete (i.e., a sperm or egg cell) is a somatic cell. This category includes cells as diverse as liver cells, blood cells, and skin cells. Mitosis is the process by which such somatic cells divide and make new, identical cells. To achieve this, the DNA unwinds, separating the two strands of the helix. An enzyme – DNA polymerase – binds complementary nucleotides along each strand, thus creating two double-stranded helices that are an exact copy of each other. Thus, as detailed in Figure 3.4, mitosis creates two new daughter cells, each with its own complete genome (i.e., 46 chromosomes packaged across 23 chromosome pairs). Each successive duplicate cell will have the same genetic composition as its parent. Relevant to our purposes, cellular division via mitosis underlies expansion from the embryonic state and growth during development.

3.4.2 Meiosis

Genetic, or sexual, recombination is a complicated process, yet for the vast majority of the time it occurs with remarkable accuracy and precision. Because the number of chromosomes in a species remains the same from one generation to the next, there needs to be a way to reduce the number of chromosomes by half. Meiosis achieves this by producing germ cells (or gametes) that contain half the number of chromosomes found in all other cells in the body. In humans, meiosis occurs in the ovaries of females (to produce eggs) and the testes of males (to produce sperm).

Meiosis is a multi-step process in which a cell makes a copy of each chromosome, and then divides twice (Figure 3.4). Each time it divides, it cuts its DNA content in half. Thus, in humans, a cell goes from having 46 chromosomes to 96 after each is copied. The first division of meiosis cuts that 96 back into 46. The second division cuts that 46 into 23, the number of chromosomes in a sperm or an egg. In this way, meiosis introduces genetic variation into organisms that reproduce sexually. **Genetic recombination** is the overall process of recombining DNA within a chromosome during meiosis so that new combinations emerge that differ from those of either parent.

There are three primary sources of variation introduced during meiosis. In crossing over, two homologous chromosomes – one inherited from each parent – pair along their lengths, gene by gene. Breaks occur along the chromosomes and different parts join up, meaning that chromosomes trade some of their genes in the process. At this point, the chromosomes now have genes in a unique combination relative to when the process started. In **independent assortment**, homologous chromosomes (homologues) – one from each parent – line up in random orientations prior to separating into distinct gametes. Thus, when the homologues separate (or assort), they are distributed across gametes in new ways. Finally, whole chromosomes can be shuffled among the four new gametes in a process called **random segregation**, in which pieces of DNA break and recombine to produce new combinations of genes. Although genes that are very close to one another on a chromosome and are genetically linked stay together, meiosis makes sure that plenty of genetic variability is introduced into each new gamete.

These processes – along with the vagaries of mate selection and the immense randomness involved in the merging of two genomes via fusing gametes at the point of fertilization – contribute enormously to individual variation within any sexually reproducing species. (See Lodish et al., 2016 for a more detailed description of the processes underlying both mitosis and meiosis.)

Figure 3.4 Schematics of DNA replication. Mitotic and meiotic cell divisions.

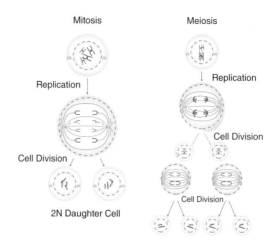

3.5　Mutations

While the normal processes of meiosis and fertilization already introduce substantial variability into the human genome, mutations contribute to genetic variability as well. A mutation is a change that occurs in our DNA sequence, and mutations come in many forms. Mutations can be introduced during mitosis or meiosis, or as the result of environmental factors such as exposure to radiation, cigarette smoke, or toxic chemicals. In fact, many of the now-permanent changes in the genome were introduced via mutations over the course of our ancestral history, and *de novo* **mutations** (i.e., ones that emerge spontaneously rather than are inherited) can be found in any individual as well.

Gene mutations can be classified in two major ways: acquired (also called somatic) and hereditary. Acquired mutations are introduced at some point in an individual's life, and are not passed on to the next generation. Whether acquired mutations are widespread across an individual's cells depends on when they occurred in the developmental process. Those early progenitor cells give rise to cells throughout the body, whereas later ones replicate more locally. Hereditary mutations come from a parent and are present in all of an individual's cells throughout life, beginning prenatally. They are transmitted to the next generation if the mutation is present on the chromosome that is passed down. By contrast, a somatic mutation is a mutation acquired after conception. Somatic mutations can occur in any of the cells of the body except the germ cells (sperm and egg) and therefore are not passed on to children.

3.5.1　Point Mutations

By far the most common type of mutation are **point mutations**, which reflect errors in a single nucleotide of a base pair that is introduced during transcription of a DNA or RNA sequence. Point mutations refer to changes whereby one nucleotide is switched for another, a nucleotide is deleted entirely, or a new single nucleotide is inserted into the existing DNA sequence. All three forms of point mutations introduce a change in the most commonly observed DNA sequence. The consequence of having a point mutation in the genome also varies. A point mutation may have no effect on an organism   that is, it may be "silent" – if it occurs in a region of a gene that does not affect how a protein functions, or in a non-coding region of the DNA that doesn't affect gene expression. In fact, the vast majority of mutations are silent. By contrast, if a mutation changes the amino acid sequence of a protein or alters its expression, there may be phenotypic consequences that then affect the fitness of the organism in its environment – sometimes subtly (e.g., colorblindness), sometimes dramatically, as in the case of cystic fibrosis, a change in a single nucleotide.

Because new mutations arise in each generation and may or may not be transmitted to the next one, it helps to look at the totality of their impact on human variability. A population's genetic variation is increased via the introduction of new alleles, which can result from point mutations or other chromosomal aberrations. Thus, when we talk about allelic variants, we are talking about specific mutations that have become common over the course of human history. In fact, many variations in our genome are the product of ancient point mutations. Whether due to increased fitness incurred by the change or merely to chance, these ancient mutations are the basis for the common allelic variants now recognized in any given population. These mutations were either beneficial or benign (at least they didn't lead to premature death); more serious mutations that impede an individual's ability to have children are culled continuously from the gene pool, although they can still arise as *de novo* mutations.

In this day and age, there's yet another way in which serious genetic mutations can or could disappear from the gene pool: prenatal genetic testing. In Denmark, the incidence of the neurodevelopmental disorder Down syndrome (which is not due to a point mutation but rather to duplication of an entire chromosome, as discussed below) has dropped substantially as a result of universal prenatal screening and family planning (Zhang, 2020). In the not-too-distant future, gene editing in human embryos could further alter the incidence of particular genes in the population. Research on this front is moving forward, given the advent of more precise gene editing tools (Adli, 2018) – in particular, CRISPR-Cas9, for which Jennifer Doudna and Emmanuelle Charpentier received a Nobel Prize in 2020. However, initial studies of this new method show that it can cause chromosomal damage near the stretch of DNA that has been edited (Ledford, 2020). Beyond this issue, which may be resolved with further development of the techniques, there are profound ethical considerations: depending on your point of view, deciding whether or not to have a baby based on an embryo's genetic makeup could sound either utopian or dystopian.

A well-known example of a point mutation that has been somewhat negatively impactful to humans is the mutant allele that causes sickle cell disease. This is an autosomal recessive disorder that affects production of red blood cells. Although it is not a brain disorder per se, individuals with this disease are at elevated risk of strokes. Sickle cell disease is due to a single point mutation – a mutant allele – in the DNA sequence for the HBB gene. If a person receives just one mutant allele on that gene (either from their mother or father), they have what is called the sickle cell trait, meaning they don't have symptoms or problems but can pass the mutant allele on to their children. On the other hand, sickle cell disease results if a person receives the mutant allele for that gene from both the mother and father (i.e., they are homozygous for that allele).

You'd be right to wonder why this mutation is still so prevalent in humans. What has contributed to its maintenance in the human genome? Indeed, although most severely deleterious mutations are eliminated through the process of natural selection, there are some that persist for other reasons. In the case of sickle cell, it can have a positive effect for those heterozygous for it: while still not experiencing full-blown sickle cell disease, they are protected against severe forms of malaria. In other words, not only is sickle cell disease a clear example of a point mutation that is now maintained in the genome and an example of recessive Mendelian inheritance, it also shows the selective advantage of genetic heterozygosity: it gives you more options! In fact, a recent study found that malaria continues to exert strong selective pressure in favor of the mutated sickle cell allele (Elguero et al., 2015).

The sickle cell allele is an example that underscores our broader point about variation in the human genome. This mutant allele is just one example of many potential genetic variants. (Allelic mutants that have become common in the genome are called variants, per Mendel's characterization.) As such, the sickle cell allele serves as a bridge between the concept of a gene as a unit of heredity and that of a gene as a stretch of DNA that encodes a protein. Being homozygous for the mutant sickle cell allele specifically affects the HBB gene's expression of beta-globin, specified by a single chain of 147 amino acids. That change in a single nucleotide in the gene coding for the beta chain of the hemoglobin protein is all it takes to turn a normal hemoglobin allele into a sickle cell allele. And there are literally hundreds of possible mutations of the HBB gene that could result in changes in the expression of beta-globin!

The vast majority of these point mutations cause no noticeable signs or symptoms, but some can and do affect a person's health; they just don't get featured in textbooks because they are far less frequent (and usually messier to explain) than the sickle cell mutant allele example. The point is: the human genome is awash in novel point mutations that will disappear in a few generations, as well as ones that have been with us for millennia as allelic variants. These common variants are also referred to as single nucleotide polymorphisms.

3.5.2 Single Nucleotide Polymorphisms

Over the course of human history, point mutations have introduced substantial variability into the genome. The term **single nucleotide polymorphism** (**SNP**, pronounced "snip") is used to refer to any longstanding allelic difference that was introduced into the genome in this way, via a single point mutation. As a class, SNPs are common across the human genome, with different types of genetic variants more or less common in different populations. When such a mutation spreads throughout a population, it results in two possible versions (i.e., the older one and the newer one) of a particular base at that site in any given genome. Within individuals, SNPs appear on average once every 1,000 nucleotides, and a single person's genome has anywhere from 4 to 5 million SNPs! More than 100 million SNPs have been identified in populations around the world (Auton et al., 2015). Most commonly, these variations are found in non-coding DNA, meaning they occur *between* the protein-coding genes (of course, there is far more non-coding than coding DNA, so this shouldn't be surprising).

Because SNPs within a gene or in a regulatory region near a gene can affect a protein's functionality or level of expression, SNPs are now used as biological markers to help scientists locate genes associated with disease. Indeed, the sickle cell allele discussed above is an example of a SNP, whereby there was a single change in the nucleotide sequence in the HBB gene that has spread to many parts of the globe. That said, most SNPs have no effect on health or development. Nonetheless, SNPs have been identified that can help predict responsivity to certain drugs, susceptibility to environmental factors such as toxins, and risk for particular diseases. SNPs can also be used to track the inheritance of disease genes within families. Researchers in DCN and related fields are working to identify SNPs associated with a range of neurodevelopmental disorders.

3.5.3 Chromosomal Mutations

Although point mutations are the source of most variation in the genome, there are plenty of other forms of mutation. For example, chromosomal abnormalities may emerge far less often than a change to one allele of a base pair, but they tend to be much more impactful. Chromosomal abnormalities are highly variable, but can be sorted into two basic types: structural abnormalities and numerical abnormalities. Structural abnormalities include duplications or deletions of stretches of DNA that occur due to misalignment of the repeated sequences across two chromosomes as they match up during either meiosis or mitosis. For example, Fragile X syndrome – a heritable disorder that involves intellectual disability, often accompanied by autism-like traits and language delays – was *defined* on the basis of a chromosomal mutation: the expansion of a specific triplet of base pairs (CGG) within the Fragile X Messenger Ribonucleoprotein 1 (FMR1) gene. A characteristic of the disorder is that some individuals with Fragile X have a segment of their X chromosome that is broken or fragile (although it is not completely disconnected). Strikingly, the larger the number of repeats of the CGG triplet, the more severe the behavioral symptoms. This is the clearest demonstration in humans of a genetically mediated intellectual disorder. For the vast majority of the disorders of interest to DCN researchers, however, it isn't possible to point to a specific gene as the culprit. Rather, individuals have a genetic risk profile based on the particular set of genetic variants they carry (see Section 3.5).

In numerical abnormalities, mis-segregation of chromosomes during cellular division produces daughter cells that contain the incorrect number of chromosomes (i.e., too many or too few). When such abnormalities happen on the larger chromosomes, the result is generally organismal death due to the larger portion of proteins whose expression is increased or decreased depending on whether there is a chromosomal addition or subtraction. Chromosome pairs are ordered from largest to smallest, with chromosome 23 – the sex chromosomes – anchoring the small end. The size of a chromosome pair corresponds to the number of genes present. Thus, the addition or subtraction of a large chromosome alters gene dosage in a manner generally not compatible with organismal survival. However, in cases in which an addition or subtraction occurs on one of the smaller chromosomes, life may be viable. For example, an extra copy of chromosome 21 – one of the smallest chromosomes – is not lethal, but results in Down syndrome (Trisomy 21). And individuals with Turner syndrome are born with one X chromosome entirely or partially missing.

3.5.4 Environmentally Induced Mutations

A **mutagen** is anything in the environment that can cause a mutation in the DNA. Mutagens include radiation, chemicals, and infectious agents. Our bodies are designed to correct mistakes in cellular replication, but when we are exposed to dangers like these, we increase the risk of experiencing cellular mutations, particularly somatic ones (i.e., not in the germline). Such changes in DNA can have a range of effects, depending on when they are introduced in developmental time and where they occur in the genome. Conveniently, humans are protected from many mutations because they have two active copies of most genes. However, the sex chromosome does not enjoy such redundancy: males have only one copy of genes carried on the X chromosome, and females have an entire copy of this chromosome that is silenced. Thus, mutations of genes on the sex chromosomes can be particularly impactful. And if multiple genes are involved in a process, an entire pathway can be damaged by the mutation of even a single copy of one of those genes.

The role of environmental mutations in the etiology of human development and disease is an active area of research. For example, around 10 percent of the human genome actually comes from viral genetic material that got inserted as a result of infection, known as human endogenous retroviruses (HERVs). These viral genes play a vital role in embryogenesis and other biological processes, contribute to the evolution of the genome, and even allow an organism to adapt to a change in its environment (Padmanabhan Nair et al., 2021). Some HERVs make us more vulnerable to diseases, while others confer resilience. They can be under tight epigenetic control so that they aren't harmful, but environmental triggers like new viral and bacterial infections and UV light can lead them to be expressed. New research involving brain organoids (self-organizing structures grown in the lab from human stem cells; see Box 4.1) suggests that the expression of specific HERVs can negatively impact brain development (Padmanabhan Nair et al., 2021). There is, however, still a lot to be discovered about environmentally induced mutations and their role in neurodevelopmental disorders – and, more broadly, individual differences.

3.6   Epigenetics

As we have seen, our genome provides the instructions to build us, but the resulting phenotype depends on which genes are actually expressed, and when, and how much. It doesn't do us any good to have a recipe if it doesn't get implemented! After all, every cell in the body – in the brain, in the heart, in the bones, and everywhere else – contains the full genome, but any given cell only expresses a subset of genes. Let's explore how this happens.

Epigenetics is the study of heritable changes in gene *expression* that do not involve modifications to the DNA itself, but rather to the regulation of its transcription into RNA. The stem "epi" comes from Greek, meaning "upon" – hence, epigenetics refers to processes that act on genes. Gene expression fluctuates all the time; in some cases, these changes are stable, under tight control by molecules that we refer to as epigenetic markers. Epigenetic markers bind to DNA and indicate to the DNA transcription machinery whether a sequence should be transcribed. Moreover, because these epigenetic markers are replicated during cell division, their instructions are conveyed across developmental time. Relevant to our focus on developmental processes, many differences in gene expression arise during development itself, and the continual process of mitosis retains those differences. Epigenetic modifications are present before you are even born. The difficulty is that these changes are happening all the time, and it has been difficult to isolate them and characterize their effects in humans, although there is a rich animal literature on epigenetics (e.g., see Box 3.1).

3.6.1 Evidence of Epigenetic Effects in Humans

There are, however, examples where nutrition or other aspects of the environment have affected human populations in a way that highlights the impact of epigenetics. Although we can't do the sorts of controlled experiments on human populations that we do with animal models, sometimes nature combined with human-induced events does it for us.

One such example is the Dutch Hunger Winter. In the last year of the Second World War in Europe, German forces imposed a food embargo on the civilian population of the Netherlands. The embargo resulted in a severe famine, which unfortunately coincided with a particularly harsh winter. About 20,000 people died from starvation that winter. Remarkably, and in spite of all the chaos of the time, the Dutch maintained medical care and health records. Thus, years later, scientists have been able to study the effect of famine on human health. Lumey and colleagues (2007) noticed that children who were developing *in utero* at the time of the famine experienced a lifelong increase in their chances of developing various health problems, and many died younger compared to children conceived afterwards (Ekamper et al., 2014).

In a follow-up study (Heijmans et al., 2008), researchers conducted DNA analyses comparing same-sex siblings who had, or had not, been prenatally exposed to famine during the Dutch Hunger Winter *six decades earlier*. Incredibly, in the children who had not been exposed to the adverse effect *in utero*, they found a lower level of an epigenetic marker that downregulates expression of a maternally imprinted gene critical to human growth than in those who had been exposed. In other words, adverse events experienced *in utero* impacted **fetal programming**, whereby the set point of various physiological and metabolic responses for different organ structures and their associated functions are impacted in ways that carry into adulthood.

Numerous other examples of such effects in humans have since been uncovered. For example, Rachel Yehuda and colleagues have documented, among the adult children of Holocaust survivors, a difference in epigenetic markers on at least one gene involved in regulating stress reactivity (e.g., Bierer et al., 2020). This putative epigenetic effect could contribute to the higher vulnerability to stress that has been observed in this population, although there are likely also other mechanisms at play (Dashorst et al., 2019). This work has been at once sensationalized and dismissed in the public sphere (Yehuda et al., 2018), which does not take away from the importance and timeliness of exploring whether or how extreme stressors could have transgenerational effects on behavioral traits, and even susceptibility to disorders like posttraumatic stress disorder. One need not even look to such extreme examples of adversity; for example, research has documented epigenetic effects of adverse childhood events on immune function (Krause et al., 2020).

Coupled with solid evidence from animal research, these observations highlight the fact that developmental plasticity evolved to match an organism to its environment, a bias that can have negative impacts when such adaptive plasticity – adapted to a particular moment in time – is not matched to the subsequent environment. How might this plasticity, and its downstream negative consequences, come about? Early examination of epigenetics has focused on specific molecular mechanisms; two important ones are discussed below. The extent to which environmental effects can provoke a wide range of epigenetic responses is now the focus of intense research, and it is now evident that a host of epigenetic mechanisms allow an organism to respond to the environment through changes in gene expression. Here, we provide a broad overview of the mechanisms underlying the two that are most well understood: DNA methylation and histone modification.

3.6.2 DNA Methylation

It is now well established that one aspect of epigenetics functions through the addition and subtraction of small chemical tags to DNA. You can think of these tags as stop signs that prevent transcription of a particular base. If the RNA molecule can't attach, it won't be able to perform the process of transcription. These chemical tags are **methyl groups** that can modify two of the four bases (cytosine and adenine) that make up our DNA, doing so via enzymes called DNA methyl transferases. In Figure 3.5, you can see that cytosine ("C") has been tagged. When modified in this way, the base is referred to as **methylated** (i.e., 5-methyl cytosine); such methylation blocks a gene from being expressed, while demethylation lifts this obstacle.

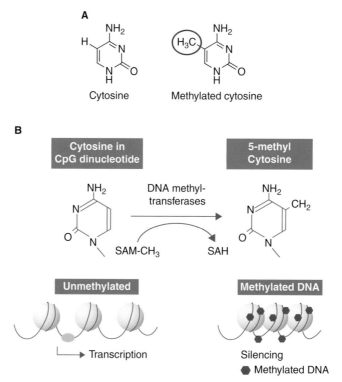

Figure 3.5 DNA methylation and histone modifications are two of the best-defined epigenetic mechanisms of gene expression.
A. An example of chemical change during methylation.
B. Nucleosome spacing in active chromatin is an open structure that allows genes to be expressed; in histone modification, methylation is associated with an inactive, condensed state of the chromosome in which gene expression is blocked.

Thus, DNA methylation is an epigenetic mechanism that can modify the function of genes and affect gene expression, without involving any changes to the underlying DNA sequence. This is the form of epigenetic modification implicated in the offspring of survivors of both the Dutch Hunger Winter and the Holocaust. More broadly, DNA methylation is the primary way in which gene activity is adjusted, especially during early development. Moreover, the changes methylation introduces into gene activity can last for the rest of the cell's life, and even for many generations of cells through cell divisions. Methylation is a means by which environment can influence genes to behave (i.e., be expressed) differently. We should note that, although there is no question that environmentally induced DNA methylation produces epigenetic effects that can be passed to offspring, such effects can also arise stochastically in early development and throughout one's life as well. These effects may or may not be passed on to the next generation, depending on whether they impact germ or somatic cell lines.

3.6.3   Histone Modification

Another epigenetic process involves **histones**, which are proteins that condense and package roughly 2 inches of DNA into a chromosome (National Institute of General Medical Sciences, 2012). A histone is created when strands of DNA wrap around a central core of protein. Basically, histones act as a sort of spool around which DNA can wind, creating structural units called **nucleosomes**. When DNA is tightly wrapped around a histone, its genes cannot be easily accessed for transcription. Some modifications to the histone protein cause nucleosomes to unwind. In this open chromatin conformation, DNA is accessible to binding of transcriptional machinery and subsequent gene activation. In contrast, some modifications strengthen histone–DNA interactions. As can be seen in Figures 3.5B and 3.6, when DNA is wrapped around histones, the genes are prevented from being expressed. Meanwhile, DNA *not* wrapped around histones has genes that can be expressed. Essentially, these histone modifications turn the genes in specific sequences of DNA off or on. If transcriptional machinery cannot access the DNA, the result is gene silencing. Thus, modification of histones can change chromatin architecture and gene activation (Bannister & Kouzarides, 2011). There is a well-populated and growing list of histone modifications, although the role that many of them play in biological processes has not yet been determined. In any case, histone modification is an important process that plays important roles in gene expression.

3.6.4   The Epigenome as a Product of Gene–Environment Interactions

Whereas the genome is the full code for all of the proteins that make up a human being, the **epigenome** can be conceptualized as a system of tags added to the genome that has a major controlling influence on what it does. Without worrying about the mechanistic details, consider the tags as capable of turning a gene on or off, ultimately controlling whether the product of that gene – its protein – can be made. Epigenetic mechanisms help cells become specialized. You wouldn't be you if epigenetics hadn't played a role in controlling which specific genes are active or not across your different cells. Our cells are specialized! Epigenetic mechanisms are a major factor in the processes that lead to this specialization.

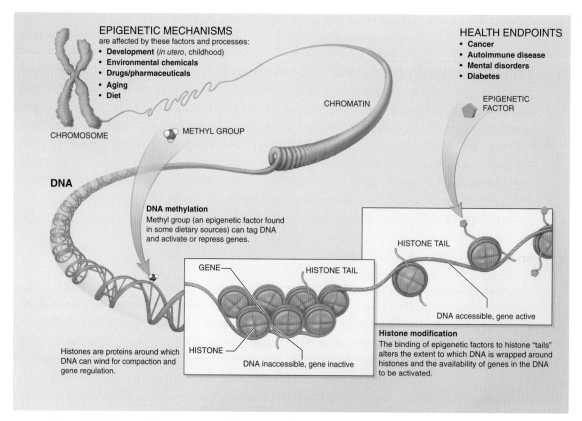

Figure 3.6 Chromatin structure and histone modifications alter gene expression. DNA is wrapped around histones, creating individual nucleosomes. These modifications are associated with increasing/decreasing chromatin accessibility by proteins such as transcription factors, thus leading to an active or repressed chromatin state.

Setting epigenetics aside for the moment, gene–environment interactions that take place through processes like gene expression and brain plasticity have been of interest to developmental researchers for a long time. To understand how the environment interacts with our genome, we have focused in this chapter on describing how different allelic variants populate the genomes of different individuals. Collectively, these variants form an individual's genotype, unique to that person and contributing to differences in that person's phenotype, including a range of psychological traits.

We started this chapter by evaluating how genes contribute to individual variation, and we've worked our way to a seemingly novel means by which genes and environment interact, the focus of epigenetics research. Despite the fact that developmental researchers have been pursuing how the environment influences genes (and vice versa) since the enterprise of understanding developmental processes began, epigenetics has especially captured people's imagination. This is in part because it provides a mechanistic demonstration of environmental impact at a very basic level, right down to our genes. Throughout this book, we will take the view that there is a dynamic interplay of genetic (and epigenetic) and environmental variation in development impacting both behavior and brain.

3.7   "Genetic" Is Not Synonymous with "Heritable"

We have discussed the fact that a gene is a unit of heredity, as well as the source of robust variability in the human genome. Some of this variability was introduced via mutations in our distant past and passed on to us through many generations via the process of inheritance. Some is introduced anew prior to an individual's conception, via the process of meiosis. Additional routes are still being identified. A critical point is embedded here: some variation may be from the genes we get from our parents – that we inherited – while other variation is less tractable, coming from influences of the prenatal environment or from the developmental process itself, including stochastic noise (as described in Section 3.2.2). While such variation may not cause disease, it certainly adds to the uniqueness of who we are. You would be correct to call all of these sources of variability "genetic." Importantly, however, they are not all heritable. Therein lies the source of substantial confusion about genetics and development: when people hear the term "genetic" they think of heredity, but something can be genetic (i.e., in the genes) and not be inherited or heritable. Thus, understanding how genes work in molecular biological terms complements our understanding of genes as sources of inheritance.

3.8   Neurodevelopmental Disorders (NDDs)

The complex interplay of genetics and epigenetics is observed in **neurodevelopmental disorders (NDDs)**, wherein alterations of the tightly coordinated events underlying brain development impact children's cognitive, linguistic, socioemotional, and/or motor development. The hunt for specific genes involved in NDDs has not, by and large, yielded simple answers, with the notable exception being Fragile X syndrome (discussed in Section 3.5.3).

According to the most commonly used system of classification of NDDs (the *Diagnostic and Statistical Manual of Mental Disorders*, Fifth Edition (DSM-5)), these disorders generally fall into one of several camps, organized based on clusters of behavioral symptoms. These include Autism Spectrum Disorder (Chapter 7), Attention Deficit Hyperactivity Disorder (Chapter 10), communication disorders such as Childhood-Onset Fluency Disorder or stuttering, motor coordination disorders such as Tourette syndrome, specific learning disorders that impact academic performance in areas such as reading and writing (Chapters 11 and 12, respectively), and broader learning impairments referred to as intellectual disability/intellectual developmental disorders, such as Down syndrome. Estimates of the incidence of NDDs vary widely, from 3–18 percent of children (Parenti et al., 2020; Leblond et al., 2021).

Additional disorders that stem from atypical brain development include schizophrenia, Obsessive-Compulsive Disorder, Major Depressive Disorder, Bipolar Disorder, and epilepsy, which fall under other categories in the DSM-5. This classification scheme does not account for, say, known overlap in the **etiology** (causes) of Autism Spectrum Disorder and schizophrenia, or between Tourette syndrome and Obsessive-Compulsive Disorder. And so on.

The diagnosis – indeed, the very conceptualization – of NDDs is challenging, for a number of reasons. First, it is almost always difficult to know where to draw a line between typical and atypical development. In other words, although some children are clear outliers, with developmental trajectories that depart drastically from the norm, many children with similar capabilities sit on either side of a diagnostic criterion, such that one will be labeled as having a disorder and the other one will not. This is a good reminder of the fact that individuals fall along a continuum in every behavioral and brain measure; DCN researchers seek to understand the neural underpinnings of this individual variability. Second, there is a fair amount of overlap between disorders: that is, children with behaviors classically associated with one disorder also often have (either concurrently or at another time) symptoms associated with at least one other disorder. That is, there is a high rate of comorbidity between disorders defined by the DSM. This overlap speaks to the fact that when basic neurodevelopmental processes go awry, they can manifest in a variety of ways.

O'Donovan and Owen (2016, p. 1214) summarized the situation well: "As research data have accumulated, it has become clear that the boundaries between diagnostic groups and between illness and wellness are not clear-cut; that there is considerable heterogeneity within diagnostic categories; that patients often have the clinical features of more than one disorder; and that the preponderance of those features in a particular individual can change markedly over time and with development."

Given these challenges, there has been a push in recent years for researchers to move away from investigating individual disorders, instead examining the mechanisms that explain variation along each dimension of behavior, cutting across traditional diagnostic boundaries (see the Research Domain Criteria (RDoC) approach endorsed by the National Institute of Mental Health; Cuthbert & Insel, 2013). Researchers studying NDDs seek to understand the genetic and environmental risk factors that impact brain development writ broadly, as well as the development of specific neural systems.

Nonetheless, advances are being made in the identification of genes associated with NDDs (Vorstman & Ophoff, 2013). In particular, an increasing number of new-but-recurring variants are being identified, for example, in association with disorders such as Autism Spectrum Disorder (ASD) and Attention Deficit Hyperactivity Disorder (ADHD). These variants, as well as the genetic variants identified through a range of other approaches, indicate the involvement of a large number of genes in a given disorder. All in all, on the order of 1,500 gene variants have been implicated in NDDs thus far, and it is estimated that many more are yet to be discovered (Leblond et al., 2021). Each of these gene variants has only a modest effect on behavioral outcomes (Briscoe & Marín, 2020). Many of these gene variants are risk factors for more than one disorder; this speaks to the fact that the lines between disorders in the DSM-5 are blurred (O'Donovan & Owen, 2016; Morris-Rosendahl & Crocq, 2020).

Animal models of NDDs provide crucial insights regarding the role of specific genes in typical and atypical brain development. As but one of many possible examples, let's consider the T*cf*4 gene. Rare, *de novo* mutations of this gene cause a rare neurological disorder called Pitt-Hopkins syndrome, marked by a failure to meet a range of developmental milestones. Common variants of this gene have been associated with an elevated risk of autism, schizophrenia, and Bipolar Disorder (Li et al., 2019). A lot is known about the function of T*cf*4, and where and when in development it is expressed in the brain, far more than we can go into here. Suffice it to say that it is a transcription factor – that is, a regulatory gene that controls the expression of other genes. T*cf*4 expression, which is sensitive to neural activity, supports the initial development of the intricate structure of the cortex. Manipulation of the timing and level of expression of this gene in a specific part of the brain during embryonic development alters the way neurons in that part of the brain migrate and how they synapse, or connect, with each other (Page et al., 2017). Given that this gene helps to specify the way the cortex is wired up, it shouldn't be too surprising that gene variants that affect the functionality of this gene have been implicated in *several* disorders of brain development.

Indeed, genetic variants that confer risk for NDDs have been implicated in several key processes that impact brain development: protein synthesis regulation, transcriptional and epigenetic regulation, and synaptic signaling – in particular, as synapses are initially developing (Parenti et al., 2020). Perturbation of these foundational processes can affect the steps involved in building a brain during prenatal development. (As we will discuss in Chapter 4, these include the birth of neuronal precursor cells, the predictable pattern of migration of these cells to their final position in the brain, and their differentiation into neurons.) Additionally, they can affect the maturation of synapses and circuits in postnatal brain development.

Of course, as we have seen, genes don't function in a vacuum; their expression depends on a whole host of epigenetic factors. This is true even in the case of Down syndrome, for which there is a clear genetic origin: the age of the expectant mother is a known risk factor, as the risk of errors of chromosome division increases with age. It is even more true for the other NDDs discussed above, which emerge as a result of both genetic and environmental vulnerabilities.

The prenatal and early postnatal environment are vitally important with regards to the emergence of NDDs, particularly the first trimester of gestation. Nutrients, hormones, and other chemicals travel into the fetal bloodstream from the placenta, affecting gene expression in the developing embryo. Numerous substances are known **teratogens**: that is, they have been proven to affect embryonic development. These include a variety of drugs, including alcohol and other substances of abuse, as well as medicines. They also include viruses, even some that are relatively benign for healthy younger adults, such as influenza. Other known or potential teratogens include heavy metals like lead, as well as an untold number of chemicals in everyday use (Grova et al., 2019; see Chapter 14). Maternal health factors, including inflammation and extreme psychological stress, along with malnutrition and specific gut microflora (Forssberg, 2019), are all potential risk factors for NDDs. Indeed, elevated risk of Autism Spectrum Disorder and/or schizophrenia have been linked with many, if not all, of these environmental factors.

There is still much to be discovered about the precise mechanisms of action by which external factors influence gene expression, thereby altering molecular and cellular processes and, in turn, brain development. However, although many genes have been implicated in NDDs, they appear to converge on a limited number of neurobiological pathways. Big data approaches are needed to piece together all of these parts (Briscoe & Marín, 2020). In the years to come, viewing NDDs in terms of the neural systems affected and the underlying mechanisms that control their development will hopefully better guide the development of effective treatments and interventions. Possible approaches to intervention informed by this work include the exciting possibility of preventative and preemptive epigenetic medicine (Kubota, 2018). Considering the wide variation among us in genetic variants could lead to greater appreciation for our so-called neurodiversity, and for the strengths that atypically developing individuals bring to the table. At the same time, while appreciation and acceptance of this diversity is warranted, it is also important to combat the societal forces that put some children at greater risk of exposure than others to environmental toxins and maternal health-related risk factors.

SUMMARY

- Development is not unidirectional, and biology is responsive to the environment from conception
- The term "genetic" is not synonymous with the term "heritable"
- Heredity is the passing on of physical or mental characteristics genetically from one generation to another
- By comparing a trait in identical twins versus fraternal twins, researchers can calculate an estimate of its heritability
- Heritability is the amount of phenotypic (observable) variation in a population that is attributable to individual genetic (genotypic) differences
- Developmental noise arises during development from stochasticity (randomness) in cellular and molecular processes, contributing to phenotypic variation
- Point mutations that have become common in the genome are called single nucleotide polymorphisms
- Developmental disorders often underlie children's inability to reach developmental milestones
- Methylation and histone modification are two forms of epigenetic change

REVIEW QUESTIONS

Describe why the nature versus nurture debate is better framed as one about how nature and nurture interact.

What is heritability?

What are the two general roles that genes play in development?

What is the molecular biology perspective on the purpose of genes?

What is stochastic noise in the developmental process and how does it impact the phenotype?

Describe several different forms of genetic mutation.

What are developmental disorders and why are they so difficult to diagnose?

In what way is Down syndrome a genetic disorder? How about sickle cell anemia?

Explain how epigenetics influences individual variability above and beyond that of DNA-based variability.

What do the Dutch Hunger and Holocaust studies suggest about genes and the environment?

Further Reading

Aristizabal, M. J., Anreiter, I., Halldorsdottir, T., Odgers, C. L., McDade, T. W., Goldenberg, A., Mostafavi, S., Kobor, M. S., Binder, E. B., Sokolowski, M. B., & O'Donnell, K. J. (2020). Biological embedding of experience: A primer on epigenetics. *Proceedings of the National Academy of Sciences of the United States of America*, 117(38), 23261–23269. https://doi.org/10.1073/pnas.1820838116

Morange, M. (2001). *The misunderstood gene*. Harvard University Press.

O'Donovan, M. C., & Owen, M. J. (2016). The implications of the shared genetics of psychiatric disorders. *Nature Medicine*, 22(11), 1214–1219. https://doi.org/10.1038/nm.4196

References

Adli, M. (2018). The CRISPR tool kit for genome editing and beyond. *Nature Communications*, 9(1), 1911. https://doi.org/10.1038/s41467-018-04252-2

Auton, A., Brooks, L. D., Durbin, R. M., Garrison, E. P., Kang, H. M., Korbel, J. O., Marchini, J. L., McCarthy, S., McVean, G. A., & Abecasis, G. R. (2015). A global reference for human genetic variation. *Nature*, 526(7571), 68–74. https://doi.org/10.1038/nature15393

Avery, O. T., MacLeod, C. M., & McCarty, M. (1944). Studies on the chemical nature of the substance inducing transformation of pneumococcal types: Induction of transformation by a desoxyribonucleic acid fraction isolated from pneumococcus type III. *The Journal of Experimental Medicine*, 79, 137–158. https://doi.org/10.1084/jem.79.2.137

Bannister, A., & Kouzarides, T. (2011). Regulation of chromatin by histone modifications. *Cell Research*, 21, 381–395. https://doi.org/10.1038/cr.2011.22

Bierer, L. M., Bader, H. N., Daskalakis, N. P., Lehrner, A., Provençal, N., Wiechmann, T., Klengel, T., Makotkine, I., Binder, E. B., & Yehuda, R. (2020). Intergenerational effects of maternal Holocaust exposure on *FKBP5* methylation. *The American Journal of Psychiatry*, 177(8), 744–753. https://doi.org/10.1176/appi.ajp.2019.19060618

Briscoe, J., & Marín, O. (2020). Looking at neurodevelopment through a big data lens. *Science*, 369(6510), eaaz8627. https://doi.org/10.1126/science.aaz8627

Children's Defense Fund. (2021). *The state of America's children*. Center on Budget and Policy Priorities.

Crow, E. W., & Crow, J. F. (2002). 100 years ago: Walter Sutton and the chromosome theory of heredity. *Genetics*, 160(1), 1–4. https://doi.org/10.1093/genetics/160.1.1

Cuthbert, B. N., & Insel, T. R. (2013). Toward the future of psychiatric diagnosis: The seven pillars of RDoC. *BMC Medicine*, 11(126). https://doi.org/10.1186/1741-7015-11-126

Dashorst, P., Mooren, T. M., Kleber, R. J., de Jong, P. J., & Huntjens, R. (2019). Intergenerational consequences of the Holocaust on offspring mental health: A systematic review of associated factors and mechanisms. *European Journal of Psychotraumatology*, 10(1), 1654065. https://doi.org/10.1080/20008198.2019.1654065

Davenport, C. B. (1923). *Eugenics, genetics, and the family*. Williams & Wilkins.

Ekamper, P., van Poppel, F., Stein, A. D., & Lumey, L. H. (2014). Independent and additive association of prenatal famine exposure and intermediary life conditions with adult mortality between age 18–63 years. *Social Science & Medicine*, 119, 232–239. https://doi.org/10.1016/j.socscimed.2013.10.027

Elguero, E., Délicat-Loembet, L. M., Rougeron, V., Arnathau, C., Roche, B., Becquart, P., Gonzalez, J. P., Nkoghe, D., Sica, L., Leroy, E. M., Durand, P., Ayala, F. J., Ollomo, B., Renaud, F., & Prugnolle, F. (2015). Malaria continues to select for sickle cell trait in Central Africa. *Proceedings of the National Academy of Sciences of the United States of America*, 112(22), 7051–7054. https://doi.org/10.1073/pnas.1505665112

Forssberg, H. (2019). Microbiome programming of brain development: Implications for neurodevelopmental disorders. *Developmental Medicine and Child Neurology*, 61(7), 744–749. https://doi.org/10.1111/dmcn.14208

Galton, F. (1869). *Hereditary genius: An inquiry into its laws and consequences*. Macmillan.

Galton, F. (1883). *Inquiries into human faculty and its development*. Macmillan.

Gibson, E. J., & Pick, A. D. (2000). *An ecological approach to perceptual learning and development*. Oxford University Press.

Gloss, B. S., & Dinger, M. E. (2018). Realizing the significance of noncoding functionality in clinical genomics. *Experimental & Molecular Medicine*, 50(97), 1–8. https://doi.org/10.1038/s12276-018-0087-0

Gottlieb, G. (1976). The roles of experience in the development of behavior and the nervous system. In G. Gottlieb (Ed.), *Studies on the development of behavior and the nervous system, vol. 3: Neural and behavioral specificity* (pp. 25–54). Academic Press. https://doi.org/10.1016/B978-0-12-609303-2.50008-X

Gottlieb, G. (1992). *Individual development and evolution: The genesis of novel behavior*. Oxford University Press.

Gottlieb, G. (1998). Normally occurring environmental and behavioral influences on gene activity: From central dogma to probabilistic epigenesis. *Psychological Review*, 105(4), 792–802. https://doi.org/10.1037/0033-295X.105.4.792-802

Gottlieb, G. (2007). Developmental epigenesis. *Developmental Science*, 10(1), 1–11. https://doi.org/10.1111/j.1467-7687.2007.00556.x

Griffith, F. (1928). The significance of pneumococcal types. *The Journal of Hygiene*, 27(2), 113–159. https://doi.org/10.1017/s0022172400031879

Grova, N., Schroeder, H., Olivier, J. L., & Turner, J. D. (2019). Epigenetic and neurological impairments associated with early life exposure to persistent organic pollutants. *International Journal of Genomics*. https://doi.org/10.1155/2019/2085496

Hebb, D. O. (1958). *A textbook of psychology*. W. B. Saunders.

Heijmans, B. T., Tobi, E. W., Stein, A. D., Putter, H., Blauw, G. J., Susser, E. S., Slagboom, P. E., & Lumey, L. H. (2008). Persistent epigenetic differences associated with prenatal exposure to famine in humans. *Proceedings of the National Academy of Sciences of the United States of America*, 105(44), 17046–17049. https://doi.org/10.1073/pnas.0806560105

Jansen, A. G., Mous, S. E., White, T., Posthuma, D., & Polderman, T. J. (2015). What twin studies tell us about the heritability of brain development, morphology, and function: A review. *Neuropsychology Review*, 25(1), 27–46. https://doi.org/10.1007/s11065-015-9278-9

Johannsen, W. (1909). *Elemente der exakten Erblichkeitslehre*. Gustav Fischer.

Johnson, M. H. (2001). Functional brain development in humans. *Nature Reviews Neuroscience*, 2(7), 475–483. https://doi.org/10.1038/35081509

Johnson, M. H. (2011). Interactive specialization: A domain-general framework for human functional brain development? *Developmental Cognitive Neuroscience*, 1(1), 7–21. https://doi.org/10.1016/j.dcn.2010.07.003

Krapohl, E., & Plomin, R. (2016). Genetic link between family socioeconomic status and children's educational achievement estimated from genome-wide SNPs. *Molecular Psychiatry*, 21, 437–443. https://doi.org/10.1038/mp.2015.2

Krause, B. J., Artigas, R., Sciolla, A. F., & Hamilton, J. (2020). Epigenetic mechanisms activated by childhood adversity. *Epigenomics*, 12(14), 1239–1255. https://doi.org/10.2217/epi-2020-0042

Kubota, T. (2018). Preemptive epigenetic medicine based on fetal programming. *Advances in Experimental Medicine and Biology*, 1012, 85–95. https://doi.org/10.1007/978-981-10-5526-3_9

Leblond, C. S., Le, T. L., Malesys, S., Cliquet, F., Tabet, A. C., Delorme, R., Rolland, T., & Bourgeron, T. (2021). Operative list of genes associated with autism and neurodevelopmental disorders based on database review. *Molecular and Cellular Neurosciences*, 113, 103623. https://doi.org/10.1016/j.mcn.2021.103623

Ledford, H. (2020). CRISPR gene editing in human embryos wreaks chromosomal mayhem. *Nature*, 583(7814), 17–18. https://doi.org/10.1038/d41586-020-01906-4

Li, H., Zhu, Y., Morozov, Y. M., Chen, X., Page, S. C., Rannals, M. D., Maher, B. J., & Rakic, P. (2019). Disruption of TCF4 regulatory networks leads to abnormal cortical development and mental disabilities. *Molecular Psychiatry*, 24, 1235–1246. https://doi.org/10.1038/s41380-019-0353-0

Lodish, H., Berk, A., Kaiser, C. A., Krieger, M., Bretscher, A., Ploegh, H., Amon, A., & Martin K. C. (2016). *Molecular cell biology*, 8th edition. W. H. Freeman.

Lumey, L. H., Stein, A. D., Kahn, H. S., van der Pal-de Bruin, K. M., Blauw, G. J., Zybert, P. A., & Susser, E. S. (2007). Cohort profile: The Dutch hunger winter families study. *International Journal of Epidemiology*, 36(6), 1196–1204. https://doi.org/10.1093/ije/dym126

Mitchell, K. J. (2018). *Innate: How the wiring of our brains shapes who we are*. Princeton University Press.

Morgan, T. H. (1910). Sex-limited inheritance in Drosophila. *Science*, 32(812), 120–122. https://doi.org/10.1126/science.32.812.120

Morris-Rosendahl, D. J., & Crocq, M. A. (2020). Neurodevelopmental disorders: The history and future of a diagnostic concept. *Dialogues in Clinical Neuroscience*, 22(1), 65–72. https://doi.org/10.31887/DCNS.2020.22.1/macrocq

National Institute of General Medical Sciences. (2012, June 12). *Genetics by the numbers*. www.nigms.nih.gov/education/Inside-Life-Science/Pages/genetics-by-the-numbers.aspx

Norrgard, K. (2008). Human testing, the eugenics movement, and IRBs. *Nature Education*, 1(1), 170.

O'Donovan, M. C., & Owen, M. J. (2016). The implications of the shared genetics of psychiatric disorders. *Nature Medicine*, 22, 1214–1219. https://doi.org/10.1038/nm.4196

Padmanabhan Nair, V., Liu, H., Ciceri, G., Jungverdorben, J., Frishman, G., Tchieu, J., Cederquist, G. Y., Rothenaigner, I., Schorpp, K., Klepper, L., Walsh, R. M., Kim, T. W., Cornacchia, D., Ruepp, A., Mayer, J., Hadian, K., Frishman, D., Studer, L., & Vincendeau, M. (2021). Activation of HERV-K(HML-2) disrupts cortical patterning and neuronal differentiation by increasing NTRK3. *Cell Stem Cell*. https://doi.org/10.1016/j.stem.2021.04.009

Page, S. C., Hamersky, G. R., Gallo, R. A., Rannals, M. D., Calcaterra, N. E., Campbell, M. N., Mayfield, B., Briley, A., Phan, B. N., Jaffe, A. E., & Maher, B. J. (2017). The schizophrenia- and autism-associated gene, transcription factor 4 regulates the columnar distribution of layer 2/3 prefrontal pyramidal neurons in an activity-dependent manner. *Molecular Psychiatry*, 23, 304–315. https://doi.org/10.1038/mp.2017.37

Parenti, I., Rabaneda, L. G., Schoen, H., & Novarino, G. (2020). Neurodevelopmental disorders: From genetics to functional pathways. *Trends in Neuroscience*, 43(8), 608–621. https://doi.org/10.1016/j.tins.2020.05.004

Piaget, J. (1952). *The origins of intelligence in children*. International University Press.

Plank, J. L., & Dean, A. (2014). Enhancer function: Mechanistic and genome-wide insights come together. *Molecular Cell*, 55(1), 5–14. https://doi.org/10.1016/j.molcel.2014.06.015

Qin, Y., Yalamanchili, H. K., Qin, J., Yan, B., & Wang, J. (2015). The current status and challenges in computational analysis of genomic big data. *Big Data Research*, 2(1), 12–18. https://doi.org/10.1016/j.bdr.2015.02.005

Thelen, E. (2000). Grounded in the world: Developmental origins of the embodied mind. *Infancy*, 1(1), 3–28. https://doi.org/10.1207/S15327078IN0101_02

Vorstman, J. A., & Ophoff, R. A. (2013). Genetic causes of developmental disorders. *Current Opinion in Neurology*, 26(2), 128–136. https://doi.org/10.1097/WCO.0b013e32835f1a30

Yehuda, R., Lehrner, A., & Bierer, L. M. (2018). The public reception of putative epigenetic mechanisms in the transgenerational effects of trauma. *Environmental Epigenetics*, 4(2), dvy018. https://doi.org/10.1093/eep/dvy018

Zhang, S. (2020, December). The last children of Down Syndrome. *The Atlantic*.

4   Brain Development

LEARNING OBJECTIVES

- Outline the basics of brain anatomy
- Describe the difference between a presynaptic and postsynaptic neuron and how they interact
- Demonstrate understanding of Waddington's "epigenetic landscape" as a metaphor for development
- Summarize the process of gastrulation
- Describe how cellular migration proceeds
- Describe the inside-out pattern underlying development of the neocortex
- Delineate the different phases of prenatal brain cell development
- List the stages of postnatal brain development
- Differentiate the overall changes that take place in gray and white matter postnatally

In an infant born at term, the basic brain structure is in place. Any additional neurogenesis – the creation of new neurons – is completed by around the end of an infant's first postnatal year. Yet in infancy and childhood, a vast majority of our energy intake is devoted to brain development. Much more happens beyond neurogenesis! Indeed, while the human brain has high demands for glucose (its source of energy) throughout the lifespan, the glucose requirement rises to adult levels by 2 years of age and doubles through age 9. It returns to adult levels only in the second half of the second decade (Chugani et al., 1987; Goyal & Raichle, 2018).

Both gene expression and environmental input are critical to normal brain development; disruption of either can fundamentally alter neural outcomes. That said, as we emphasized in Chapter 3, neither genes nor input is prescriptive or determinative of outcome. Instead, brain development is best thought of as a complex series of dynamic and adaptive processes that operate throughout the course of development to promote the emergence and differentiation of new neural structures and functions (Stiles, 2008). These processes operate within highly constrained, genetically organized contexts, but they are constantly changing.

Here we begin by introducing key concepts regarding brain anatomy that are necessary to understand how the brain develops. (We will also introduce various brain structures throughout the book; however, we invite readers to review a neuroanatomy or cognitive neuroscience text for a comprehensive overview.) Next, we describe the progression of brain development from first cell to newborn. We will address which nerve cells emerge initially, how and where they are directed to go, and how they connect with one another. We will then summarize the changes that take place postnatally, based on evidence from both histology (brain tissue analysis) and structural MRI.

4.1   Basics of Brain Anatomy

Let's start by getting oriented. The brain, a complex three-dimensional structure, is often visualized in two-dimensional slices called **horizontal (axial)**, **coronal**, or **sagittal** slices or sections. See the color-coded slice orientations and corresponding slices in Figure 4.1, with labels on each section indicating the axes it displays: **dorsal-ventral** (up-down), **rostral/anterior-caudal/posterior** (front-back), and **lateral-medial** (outward-inward). It is worth getting familiar with these different views and axes, as they will come up again and again throughout the book.

A mature human brain has a characteristic pattern of folds; the grooves are called **sulci** and the bumps are called **gyri**. The enfolding of the mature brain is thought to be an adaptation to the dramatic growth in the size of the brain during the course of evolution: it allowed large brains to fit in comparatively small cranial vaults that had to remain small to accommodate the birth process. These folding patterns are far from random, however. They develop in a characteristic pattern, governed in part by physical forces acting on the tissue that cause it to crease, but also in part by specific patterns of gene expression. As a result, the same sulci can be found across individuals (with minor variations that can help explain individual differences in cognition). Some (or perhaps many, or all) sulci constitute functional boundaries between regions; for example, motor and sensory cortices, that support bodily movements and sensations originating in the body, respectively, are subdivided by a large vertical fissure called the central sulcus.

The main subdivisions of the brain are the **cortex**, a set of **subcortical nuclei**, and the **white matter** wedged between them. The cortex, from the Latin term referring to the bark of a tree, is a 2–5 mm thick layer of cells that lies on the surface of the brain. This is apparent from a coronal view of brain tissue (outlined in orange in Figure 4.1), where the cortex is the thin, darker strip that follows the brain surface. The subcortical nuclei consist of numerous clusters of neurons that serve as both relay centers communicating between the cortex and the rest of the body, and as relays among different areas of the cortex. They are located deep in the brain below the cortex (hence the term "subcortical"). Like the cortex, subcortical nuclei are darker in appearance than the white matter. The center of the brain contains a series of interconnected cavities that form the ventricular system, filled with a fluid – cerebrospinal fluid – that is fully recycled several times per day. This fluid serves to cushion and protect the brain, transport hormones within the brain, and remove potentially harmful metabolites, drugs, and other substances away from the brain (Brodal, 2010).

So far, we've reviewed some of the gross anatomy of the brain. Here, "gross" doesn't mean disgusting, but rather the macroscopic level of brain organization: the structural features you can see just by looking at it. When peering under a microscope, the microscopic structures and organization become visible (see Chapter 1 for the hierarchy of brain organization). The two categories of brain cells are **neurons** (or nerve cells) and **glial cells** (glia). There are roughly 86 billion neurons in the human brain and roughly 84 billion glial cells, according to recent estimates. (Estimates were notoriously unreliable until Suzana Herculano-Houzel and colleagues (Azevedo et al., 2009; von Bartheld et al., 2016) developed a pioneering technique that involves turning a brain into what she has called a "brain soup"! (Jabr, 2017).)

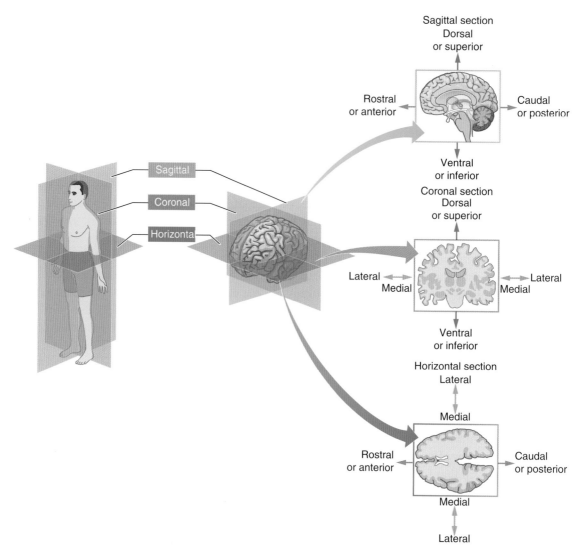

Figure 4.1 The three main slice orientations used to visualize the three-dimensional brain in two dimensions: sagittal (green), coronal (orange), and horizontal or axial (blue). The images at right correspond to the location of the slices through the brain, and the labels indicate the axes along which the images are oriented: dorsal-ventral, rostral/-caudal (or anterior-posterior), and lateral-medial. (*Cognitive Neuroscience*, Banich & Compton. © 2018 Cambridge University Press. Reproduced with permission of the Licensor through PLSclear)

Cortical neurons have two kinds of appendages extending from their **cell bodies**, each of which participates in cell signaling: **dendrites** and **axons** (Figure 4.2A and B). Dendrites are arrays of short fibers that look like the branches of a tree; fittingly, collections of dendrites are often referred to as dendritic arbors. They extend only a short distance away from the cell body and receive chemical signals from other neurons. Axons transmit electrical impulses down the

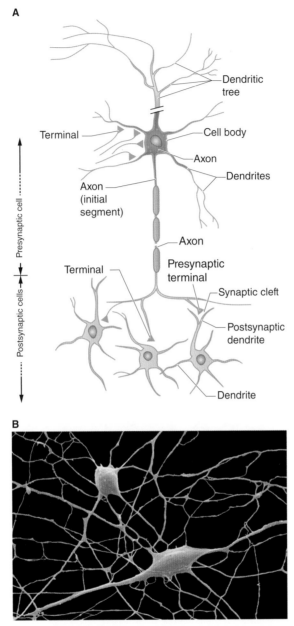

Figure 4.2 Cells in the brain. A. Major components of a pair of neurons and a synapse between them. B. Image of neurons created with electron microscopy. C. Oligodendrocytes wrap their appendages around neurons' axons, creating a myelin sheath. The gaps between myelinated segments of an axon are referred to as the Nodes of Ranvier; the ion channels responsible for transmitting electrical impulses down the length of the axon are clustered here. D. Image of the myelin sheath created with electron microscopy. (*Cognitive Neuroscience*, Banich & Compton. © 2018 Cambridge University Press. Reproduced with permission of the Licensor through PLSclear)

C

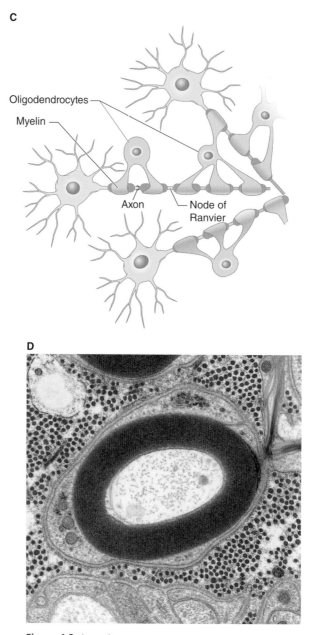

Oligodendrocytes

Myelin

Axon

Node of Ranvier

D

Figure 4.2 (cont.)

length of the neuron at the end of which axon terminals form **synapses** with other neurons. It is at synapses – microscopic gaps between neurons (on the order of one micron, or 10^{-6} meters, in length) – that neurotransmitters are released. For two neurons that are communicating across a synapse, the "sender" of the signal is called the **presynaptic** neuron, and the "receiver" is called the **postsynaptic** neuron. There is a tremendous abundance of types of neurons (and glial cells) in the brain, each with different names and functions. They have different sources of input, different destinations for output, different patterns of dendritic branching, and use different chemical signals, called **neurotransmitters**, to communicate with other neurons.

Neurons transmit signals both locally – to neighboring neurons within the cortex (via **short-range axons**) – and across long distances in the brain (via **long-range axons**, or projections). The cortex has a number of layers (a "laminar" structure) that differ based on their cells' inputs, local connections, and outputs. There are roughly six layers in what is called neocortex, the dominant form of cortex in the human brain, and three or four layers in allocortex.

Bundles of individual axons from many different neurons within one region of the brain form **fiber tracts** that extend to, and make connections with, groups of neurons in distant regions of the brain. Long-range axons are wrapped in a fatty substance called **myelin** that, like insulation on a telephone wire, increases the speed and fidelity of electrical transmission across long distances. This substance is produced by a type of glial cell called **oligo-dendrocytes** (Figure 4.2C and D). In addition to supporting efficient neurotransmission, myelin has at least two other important functions. First, it provides metabolic support to axons, thereby serving a neuroprotective function (Lee et al., 2012). Second, its accrual limits remodeling of neural circuits by inhibiting dendritic and axonal outgrowth; thus, the presence of myelin limits future brain plasticity (see Chapter 5). Myelin has a white appearance because it has a high fat content (phospholipids), which is why fiber pathways are referred to as "white matter," or "white matter pathways."

Broadly speaking, neurons belong to one of three classes: **excitatory**, **inhibitory**, and **modulatory**. As the names suggest, excitatory neurons stimulate other neurons, making them more likely to be electrically active (i.e., to fire action potentials), whereas inhibitory neurons make them less likely to be active. Most excitatory neurons release a **neurotrans-mitter** called **glutamate** onto a synapse, whereas most inhibitory neurons release a neurotransmitter called **GABA**. These neurotransmitters bind to receptors on postsynaptic neurons, eliciting the flow of electrical current that either stimulates or suppresses neural activity in them. Modulatory neurons produce a specific class of neurotransmitters called **neuromodulators** such as dopamine, norepinephrine, and serotonin that are broadly distributed throughout brain tissue and that either amplify or dampen neural signaling. We will mention these various types of neurons and neurotransmitters later in the book. For the most part, however, the book will focus not on individual neurons but rather on higher levels of neural organization – brain regions and networks – and how they emerge and change during development.

4.2 Prenatal Brain Development: An Overview

The potential for variability in the development of any given individual is beautifully captured in Conrad Waddington's (Waddington, 1957) metaphor of an **epigenetic landscape** to describe the different pathways a given cell might take. At various points, the cell (represented by a ball) can take specific permitted trajectories, leading to different outcomes or cell fates. The ball's trajectory will be influenced by the various hills and valleys, representing variations in any given individual's unique genetic makeup, as well as the stochastic (i.e., following random probability distributions) processes inherent to the developmental process (Mitchell, 2007).

If we think of fertilization as being the point at which the ball is at the very top of the hill, and the path it takes its developmental trajectory, we can see that on any given developmental run, it might emerge from the bottom at different locations. In other words, where it emerges represents any number of possible developmental trajectories and outcomes. We should emphasize that Waddington's use of the term "epigenetic" was not in reference to the sort of epigenetics we discussed in Chapter 3 (i.e., mechanisms by which gene expression is regulated). Rather, he was using the term in its Aristotelian sense: the processes of development of an individual cell. In short, the image captures how genetic variation across individuals and random variation combine to affect a given developmental outcome.

This figure – and the conceptualization it represents – has profoundly influenced thinking about development, both in the simple way it captures an individual's development as interacting with their genetic makeup and its self-organizing nature. Moreover, the early entry of the ball into one or another valley highlights what Waddington referred to as **canalization** of the phenotype in the presence of genetic and environmental perturbations. Initially, developmental researchers interpreted this analogy as representing how genetics drives the development of species-typical regularities. Canalization is now also used to represent how genes are part of a hierarchy of influences that contribute to an increasingly fixed developmental trajectory (Gottlieb, 1991).

As should be apparent from our discussion of genetics in Chapter 3, when we say that a gene encodes a protein, we don't mean that the gene *makes* the protein. DNA stores information that can be acted upon – expressed and decoded – by the cell itself to make a protein. By now it should also be apparent that the machinery that does this is itself composed of other proteins. Therein lies evidence of the magnitude of developmental complexity: it's a chicken-and-egg problem, whereby proteins are necessary to make proteins! While this paradox applies to development generally, nowhere is it more apparent than in the process of prenatal brain development. Taking a developmental perspective means that if you want to understand how variation in genes relates to variation in traits, you need to consider the process as it unfolds, and particularly how the process gets started. In other words, the process of development is a prism through which the relationship between genotypes and phenotypes is realized. While the potential relationship is written in the genome, the actual output is determined by how development itself manifests across time in any given instance.

In this section, we will review the stages of early brain development including neural induction and proliferation, cellular migration and differentiation, and exuberant synaptogenesis coupled with programmed cell death and synaptic pruning. Collectively, these processes result in a newborn brain ready for continued postnatal shaping. Keep in mind that much of what we know about brain development – and prenatal brain development, in particular – comes from animal models. By working with any number of non-human species (as well as with human cell-based "blobs" or organoids grown in the lab (see Box 4.1)), we now have a clear picture of how human brains develop, beginning with the differentiation of the neural progenitor cells in the third gestational week. Of course, the term "brain development" can be interpreted as including everything from the molecular events of gene expression to synaptic sculpting due to environmental input.

Box 4.1 Brain Organoids Help Us Understand Brain Development

Box Figure 4.1 Brain organoid with light-sensitive optic vesicles, a simple model of the human eye. (Reprinted from Gabriel et al., 2021)

The discovery of a way to develop cell cultures in three-dimensional structures, as opposed to standard cultures in a dish, has led to the creation of mini, simplified organs that develop some physiological functions that approximate those in a living organ. Scientists use organoids to study the development of a range of different organs including the thyroid, liver, and gut.

In 2008, researchers created the first brain organoids: tiny blobs grown from human stem cells that self-organize into rudimentary brain-like structures, complete with neurons that migrate along radial glial cells to form layers of cortical tissue. Like real brains, these organoids produce patterns of coordinated neural activity, including typical or atypical brain oscillations depending on the source of the stem cells used to create them (Samarasinghe et al., 2021).

The organoid approach has opened up an entirely new way to study how the brain develops. Throughout this book, we refer to animal models of the human brain. The constraint on such models is that they are based on data from animals, not humans. While there are robust commonalities, humans diverged evolutionarily from lab animals eons ago (roughly 96 million years ago in the case of rodents). Because brain organoids are generated from stem cells (Huch & Koo, 2015), they provide a complementary approach to gain insights into human brain development once thought impossible to observe in the laboratory. With stem cells induced from adult somatic cells (cells from the body, such as skin cells), researchers can sidestep the ethical debate around the use of stem cells derived from human embryos (donated after terminated pregnancies).

In just the last decade, researchers have produced a variety of brain organoid protocols and techniques, ranging from the development of region-specific organoids to more complex "whole-brain" organoids that produce patterns of cell interaction and interconnectivity between multiple brain regions. One new organoid model even boasts light-sensitive optic vesicles – precursors to the human eye (Gabriel et al., 2021) (Box Figure 4.1). Researchers adopt either guided or unguided approaches to grow organoids. With the guided approach, they can direct cell fate specification by using patterning factors such as morphogens to reproduce region-specific organoids. However, even the unguided approach, whereby stem cells of different kinds are allowed to self-assemble with minimal influence, has produced blobs with distinct brain regions, including the forebrain, midbrain, and hindbrain (Lancaster et al., 2013), reflecting that early development is to some extent preprogrammed.

Box 4.1 (cont.)

What can these synthetic tissue clusters reveal about brain development? Researchers can manipulate individual genes in the cultured stem cells to gain insights into their precise roles in typical brain development. For example, one study examined the functional significance of a point mutation that occurred over the course of human evolution, providing a glimpse into possible differences in brain structure and function between humans and earlier hominoid species (Trujillo et al., 2021). The organoids generated with gene variants from two extinct human relatives, the Neanderthals and Denisovan, were different in size, shape, and texture from human organoids. Additionally, organoids created from patients with neurodevelopmental disorders can shed light on the genetic contributions to these disorders (Baldassari et al., 2020), which – as we saw in Chapter 3 – have been difficult to ascertain. For example, while there is no satisfactory animal model of microcephaly, a condition resulting in a small brain, an organoid model revealed that premature neuronal differentiation may be a central mechanism (Lancaster et al., 2013). These are but a few examples of how brain organoids can, and will, enhance our understanding beyond what we can learn from other neuroscientific approaches.

Here we consider how these very different levels and kinds of processes interact to support the ongoing series of developmental events (see Morange, 2001) that result in the infants, children, and adolescents whose brains and behaviors we are interested in understanding.

4.3   From First Cell to Newborn

Foundational changes occur during the embryonic period, which in humans begins at conception and extends through the eighth week of gestation. By the end of the embryonic period, the rudimentary structures of the brain and central nervous system are established, and the major compartments of the central and peripheral nervous systems are defined. The early fetal period extends to approximately mid-gestation; it is a period during which critical development of the neocortex continues. Most cortical neurons are generated by the end of that time and many have migrated to their positions in the neocortex, forming essential brain networks. However, the brain continues to grow during the late fetal period, and even postnatally. In fact, the brain increases four times in size in early childhood and reaches approximately 90 percent of adult volume by age six (Lenroot & Giedd, 2006). Nevertheless, structural changes in both gray and white matter continue throughout childhood and adolescence, with parallel changes in functional organization and corresponding behavior. Interestingly, the level of connectivity throughout the developing brain during the early postnatal period far exceeds that of adults (Innocenti & Price, 2005).

4.3.1   Gastrulation and Neural Induction

Embryogenesis is the development of a fully formed organism from a fertilized egg. The initial ball of cells – the blastula – will reorganize into a two- and then a three-layered structure. The process by which the embryo transforms from a one-dimensional layer of epithelial cells (the blastula) into a two- and then a three-layered, multidimensional structure (the gastrula) is called **gastrulation** (Figure 4.3A).

All the tissues of an organism are derived from the gastrula's three initial germ layers. These foundational developmental structures serve as the basis for development of the entire body, including the nervous system. The three germ layers include an outer layer (the **ectoderm**), a middle layer (the **mesoderm**), and an inner layer (the **endoderm**). The ectoderm is the most important layer for our purposes, as cells in this outer layer will become the neural plate, which gives rise to the entire nervous system (the spinal cord, brain, and retina), as well as all our skin cells!

By the end of the fourth week, the embryo begins to assume a more familiar three-dimensional shape, that of the emerging fetus. At this point, the process of **neurulation** is going full throttle (Figure 4.3B). Neurulation is a major event in embryonic transformation, whereby a thickened plate of ectoderm along the dorsal midline of the early vertebrate embryo gives rise to the **neural tube**. The neural tube is the first real neural structure, and it will become the central nervous system (i.e., the brain and spinal cord). For the neural tube to develop, a groove first forms dorsally along the long axis of the neural plate. This groove gradually enfolds, closing it off and giving rise to a tube-like structure. Meanwhile, **somites** develop from the mesoderm and will give rise to body structures, including skeletal muscle, cartilage, tendons, and vertebrae. Finally, the endoderm will give rise to an array of internal organs. The part of the ectoderm that flanks the neural plate will become epidermal skin cells and other external structures.

Once the neural tube is closed at both ends, it is filled with embryonic cerebrospinal fluid. In the meantime, neuroepithelial cells located along the midline of the upper layer of the three-layer disc – now enclosed within the neural tube – receive molecular signals from other cells that induce them to differentiate into neural progenitor cells. As these cells line the inside wall of the neural tube, they establish what will become the zones that will ultimately give rise to neurons and neural support cells (see Saladin, 2011 for a detailed description), thus producing nearly all of the cells that make up the brain.

The neural differentiation of ectodermal cells into one of these cell types, called **neural induction**, is driven by signaling in adjacent tissues, with a remarkable degree of specificity. The **neuroepithelial cells** are the stem cells of the central nervous system. They will go on to generate intermediate **neural progenitor cells** that will themselves differentiate into neurons and glia.

4.3.2 Emergence of Early Structure

This marks the beginning of a protracted process of neural patterning within the central nervous system that begins in the embryonic period; other aspects of brain development continue throughout the prenatal period and postnatally as well (see Figure 4.3C). There are remarkable similarities in this process across animal species, and between animal and human development. Regarding prenatal brain development, the embryos of animals as diverse as frogs, dolphins, and humans can be difficult to distinguish in their early stages, and the cellular differentiation processes even postnatally show some parallels. Fifty years ago, a college student would have been asked to memorize a famous saying by Heckl that "ontogeny recapitulates phylogeny," the idea that ontogenetic development (within a species, such as humans) goes through stages, or recapitulates, the evolutionary stages as we move along the phylogenetic tree from simpler organisms to more complex ones. This view fell out of favor for several decades, but has been

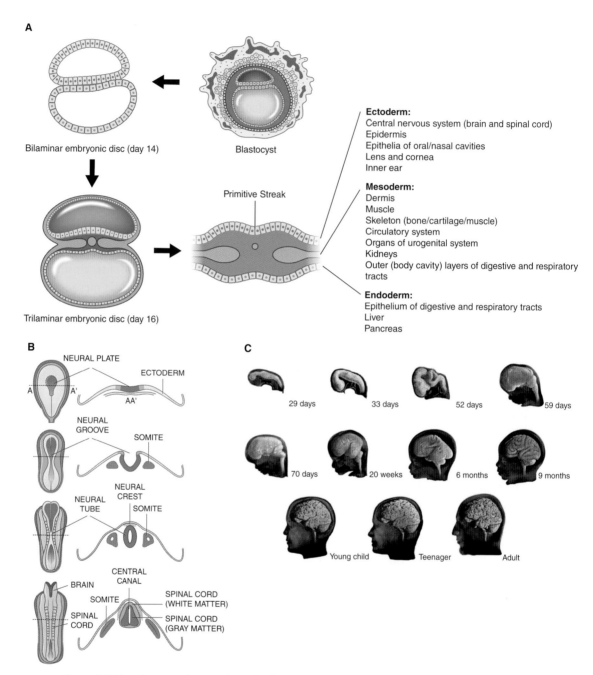

Figure 4.3 Development from embryonic disc to embryo. A. Gastrulation produces three embryonic germ layers, which each will become different primary tissue types. B. The process of neurulation, whereby the neural plate gives rise to the neural tube, which will become the brain and spinal cord. C. Prenatal and postnatal developmental changes of the human brain, including a series of embryonic and fetal stages.

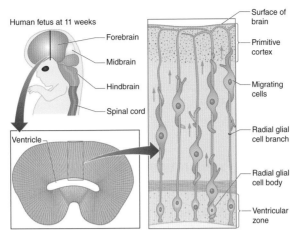

Figure 4.4 Lateral view sketch of human embryo at the 11th week of gestation. The brain and the spinal cord arise in early development from the neural tube, which expands in the front of the embryo to form the main three primary brain divisions: the forebrain, midbrain, and hindbrain. A cross-section through the brain, depicted with a vertical line, reveals the structure of the embryonic brain, with cortical tissue growing outward from the fluid-filled ventricle in the center. A further cross-section within this structure shows the scaffolding created by radial glial cells, along which neural progenitor cells migrate outward, creating the cortex. (*Cognitive Neuroscience*, Banich & Compton. © 2018 Cambridge University Press. Reproduced with permission of the Licensor through PLSclear)

brought back and endorsed by notable biologists, including Neil Shubin, who point out that although the strong version of Heckl's statement – that it applied to all aspects of biological development – is not supported by evidence, ample evidence exists for many of the important and striking similarities between ontogeny and phylogeny.

The transformations in the overall shape of the embryo reflect more specific changes in neural patterning within all regions of the embryonic nervous system. Because the neural tube gives rise to the central nervous system, any mutations at this early stage can lead to fatal deformities or lifelong disabilities (e.g., spina bifida). Structural changes are gradual, following a continuous course of specification and refinement (see Sur & Rubenstein, 2005). The patterning that emerges in the embryonic period thus provides a primitive map of the eventual organization of the nervous system, thereby setting the stage for ever-increasing specificity. At this early juncture the anterior part of the neural tube expands and forms three primary brain vesicles as shown in Figure 4.4. The segments align along the rostral-caudal axis of the embryo, establishing the primary organization of the central nervous system (Stiles, 2008). The structure contains a fluid-filled central chamber that is continuous from the telencephalon to the central canal of the spinal cord, a precursor of the ventricular system.

Both intrinsic and extrinsic molecular signals drive lineage divergence of neural progenitor cells. In particular, **morphogenic signaling** is crucial to the spatial patterning of the brain's structure. A **morphogen** is a signaling molecule that diffuses throughout the developing brain, producing specific cellular responses depending on its local concentration (see Wolpert, 1969, 2007). The different concentration gradients of morphogens thus guide migration of neural progenitor cells to particular locations. Moreover, morphogenic signals trigger expression or suppression of transcription factors within cells, affecting their state and altering the specific types of cells they produce.

4.3.3   Process of Neuronal Proliferation and Migration

Most neural progenitor cells are produced in the **ventricular zone**, inside the neural tube, and migrate radially from that location in the center of the brain out to the developing neocortex (Figure 4.4). Initially, the neurons don't have to travel far and can migrate by extending a long process to just beyond the edge of the ventricular zone and into the outer region of the brain compartment (Nadarajah & Parnavelas, 2002). This basal process attaches to the outer boundary between gray matter and cerebrospinal fluid; at this early stage, this is the outer surface of the developing brain (Miyata et al., 2001). The nucleus of the cell then moves from inside the ventricular zone to where the basal process is on the outer surface. As the nucleus moves, it remains attached to the outer surface, now forming a foundation in the embryonic cortex for additional cells to migrate towards and attach themselves to. This shifting from inside to outside the ventricular zone proceeds until the primary mode of migration has to change because of the need for cells to travel greater distances. At this point, neural progenitor cells require "guides" to support their migration (Rakic, 1972). These **radial glial cells** are now recognized to be progenitor cells themselves. Much like neural progenitor cells that migrate using their own basal process, radial glial cells extend a basal process, attaching it to the outer surface of the brain, while the nucleus of the radial glial cells remains in the ventricular zone. In this way, its basal process forms a kind of scaffold, or climbing rope, along which other neural progenitor cells can migrate outward (shown in Figure 4.4). Each cellular scaffold can support the migration of many neurons.

This orderly vertical pattern of neuron migration creates the laminar, or layered, structure commonly associated with the neocortex, shown in Figure 4.5. Critically, earlier migrating neurons form the deepest layers of cortex and later migrating neurons form successively more superficial layers; thus, the cortex is said to be developed "inside out." Through molecular signaling that is beyond the scope of this chapter, each new wave of migrating neurons bypasses the previous wave of neurons, such that each new wave assumes the most superficial position within the developing cortex. Interestingly, although the initial wave of neurons does not participate in the formation of cortical layers, they are essential for establishing, among other things, the primary sensory inputs to the developing neocortex (Hoerder-Suabedissen & Molnár, 2015).

4.3.4   Neuronal Differentiation and Death

In addition to having a vertical, laminar organization, the cortex is organized into discrete functional areas ultimately distinguished by the types of neurons they contain, the specific pattern of connections they make, and the functions they carry out. During neurogenesis, it

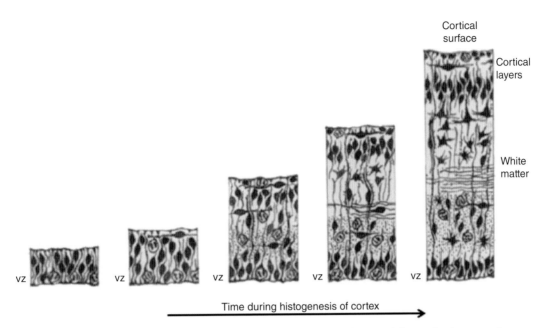

Figure 4.5 Mammalian neocortex neurogenesis. During the establishment of the cerebral cortex, the projection neurons are produced in successive waves and generate six layers organizing one above the other, resulting in an inside-out patterning. Neural progenitor cells divide symmetrically, producing a pool of cortical progenitors, which will transform into ventricular radial glial cells. Radial glial cells divide asymmetrically, generating both a new radial glial cell and an as-yet undeveloped projection neuron. A new neuron migrates radially from the ventricular zone (VZ) along the basal process of a radial glial cell to a region called the cortical plate. As neurogenesis proceeds, diverse subtypes of neurons are generated through successive asymmetric divisions of radial glial cells. (Reprinted from Bystron et al., 2008)

is through complex patterns of molecular signaling within the ventricular zone that the initial "areal fate" of new neurons is determined. Thus, signaling determines whether the cells will migrate anteriorly to brain areas that control motor functions, thus becoming motor neurons, or posteriorly to visual areas to become visual neurons, or laterally to auditory areas to become auditory neurons. This early specification of location sets the stage for subsequent developmental changes that will eventually give rise to functionally distinct cortical regions. However, the process is malleable, and the full commitment of a neuron as being one type or another depends upon many intervening developmental events, including the form of sensory input from the environment (see Sur & Leamey, 2001).

Evolution constructs nervous systems first by overproduction of neural elements, such as neurons, axons, and synapses, and then reduction, through cell death and synaptic pruning. In fact, overproduction of neurons in the prenatal period is so substantial that only about half of the neurons mammalian embryos generate will survive until birth, meaning there is considerable **apoptosis**, or programmed cell death, in the developmental process. Programmed cell death is, as it sounds, a highly regulated sequence of physiological events intrinsic to the system. It involves a cascade of gene expression that ultimately results in the breakdown of chromatin (the DNA, RNA, and protein that constitute chromosomes) and fragmenting of the cell. All neural progenitor cells and neurons (as well as many other types of cells) have this intrinsic "suicide" program. A number of factors can influence the process, with some triggering cell death and others protecting the cell by preventing subsequent steps in the cascade. Apoptosis has been documented within all of the cells in the human brain (Zecevic & Rakic, 2001); rates of cortical apoptosis can go as high as 70 percent (Rabinowicz et al., 1996). A similar process takes place in postnatal brain development, with an over-proliferation of synaptic connections, many of which are subsequently pruned away.

4.4   Postnatal Brain Development

Human gestation takes roughly 265 days, but brain development continues postnatally. Although the processes of production and migration of neurons are largely completed, proliferation and migration of glial progenitors continue for an extended period after birth, and their differentiation and maturation continue at least through childhood. How neurons and glial cells interact across the lifespan remains underspecified, but it is clear that their interactions play an important role in the functional organization of neural circuits throughout postnatal life. Importantly, estimates of the developmental time course of human postnatal processes have largely been based on extrapolation from data acquired in other species and human post-mortem material, meaning that much remains unclear about the temporal pattern of proliferation, migration, differentiation, and regression during the postnatal period in humans, and about the timing of these processes relative to one other.

As we will see throughout this book, brain imaging of infants, children, and adolescents is filling out our understanding of the time course of age-related biological changes in the brain, while also allowing researchers to link these changes to changes in behavior – and also to genes. Many researchers have contributed to this body of knowledge; one of these is Terry Jernigan, whose pioneering work is highlighted in this chapter's Scientist Spotlight (Box 4.2). Most recently, Jernigan and her collaborators have embarked on a large-scale project probing the genetic architecture of the human cerebral cortex and its regional patterning (Grasby et al., 2020). Their results complement other work in showing that the architecture of the cortex is highly polygenic – influenced by more than one gene – suggesting again a complex and dynamic process. Their findings that brain structure plays a role in the causal pathway from genes to variability in general cognitive function underscore the need for us to better understand influences on how the earliest stages of brain development unfold. Consistent with our discussion throughout this chapter, these influences likely reflect both heritable and non-heritable genetic components – including developmental noise and epigenetic effects – meaning there is still much work to do to understand how we become who we are.

4.4.1   Early Cortical Expansion

Total brain volume increases through early childhood and approaches adult levels by middle childhood. Looking a bit more closely, however, there continue to be microstructural changes

Box 4.2 Scientist Spotlight on Terry Jernigan (University of California, San Diego)

Terry Jernigan (Box Figure 4.2) is a Professor of Cognitive Science, Psychiatry and Radiology and Director of the Center for Human Development at the University of California, San Diego. She received her graduate degree in Clinical Psychology from the University of California, Los Angeles. Jernigan is the Coordinating Center Co-director for the Adolescent Brain Cognitive Development (ABCD) Study, the most ambitious study of brain development and child health ever conducted.

For as long as I can remember, I've been interested in differences between people in the way they think and the way they act. So, not surprisingly, I ended up as an undergraduate in psychology. There was a subdiscipline forming that extended into psychology and clinical psychology called neuropsychology or clinical neuropsychology, if you will, but it didn't exist as a formal subfield at that time. So I enrolled in the clinical program at UCLA, and did my internship through a program where there was actually formal training in neuropsychological assessment, and that was at the Stanford-affiliated Palo Alto VA.

But really, my fate was sealed when I discovered that in the basement of that hospital there was a prototype CT scanner. It was extremely exciting to me that there was a machine that would allow you to look inside the human brain. I tried to figure out how to measure things quantitatively from these matrices of images – originally in patients, and then in people of different ages, particularly older people. And the thing that has really hooked me throughout my whole career is being able to produce essentially a statistical parametric map aggregated across groups of individuals, and then show what the systematic distinctions were between them.

From a 30,000 foot view, I'm trying to understand the developmental origins of individual differences in human minds. What makes people individuals – particularly as manifested in their cognitive and other mental phenotypes. On the ground level, what I'm really working on is producing a data resource that can be used by the entire scientific community to model the additive mediating and moderating influences of many plausible factors that we all think are relevant to the generation of behavioral phenotypes in individuals as they develop.

Years ago we completed an imaging genomic project called PING that was designed to look at genetic influences on brain development in 1,500 kids from age 3 to 21. It was the only study of

Box 4.2 (cont.)

its kind, and the dataset has been used by people all over the world. Now, it was cross-sectional, and it turned out that a sample size of 1,500 was way too small for genetic analyses. We were just really beginning to recognize what it would take to actually understand genetic influences on brain development, and brain phenotypes that put people at risk for substance use disorders and so on. [Jernigan co-directs the ongoing ABCD Study, which will be following nearly 12,000 9- to 10-year-olds for at least 10 years using a variety of methods. The original impetus for the study was to identify neural predictors and consequences of substance abuse in adolescence, but its scope has expanded far beyond that.]

When I started in the field, people thought almost all the brain development happens in the first two or three years of life, and then it's all about loading up the software. It was very exciting to be in the right place at the right time to be able to contribute to the now clear evidence coming from *in vivo* brain imaging that biological development of the brain continues over a much more protracted period postnatally. When people ask me at what age the brain is fully mature, I say the correct answer is that the human genome gives rise to the brain's biological processes, and there's a biological lifespan of every brain. When you study large populations, you're looking at this arc of the biology of the brain (the central tendency of it for the most part now, because we're still trying to understand individual differences) and it is really never stable. The more sensitive our methods become, the more obvious this is. But every brain phenotype we come up with in imaging shows a different relationship with age. They accelerate or decelerate in different parts of the age range. We're finally beginning to use the power of multivariate methods and machine learning methods and other ways of modeling the multiple signals that we can measure to get a more integrated picture of the biology as it's unfolding.

even once brain volume reaches a plateau. Figure 4.6 shows data at two timepoints from a study by Catherine Lebel and Christian Beaulieu (Lebel & Beaulieu, 2011). This is an example of an accelerated longitudinal design, discussed in Chapter 2, wherein participants from across a wide age range are sampled more than once, yielding a combination of cross-sectional and longitudinal data. In this study, total brain volume is roughly stable from age 5 to 30; however, this relative stability reflects two counteracting developmental trends: concomitant decreases in gray matter volume and increases in white matter volume over this time period. This study drives home the point that gray and white matter volume are changing in opposite directions over childhood and adolescence. In the sections below, we will delve into the cellular changes that are theorized to underlie these effects.

4.4.2 Large-Scale Changes in Gray and White Matter

Lebel and Beaulieu (Lebel & Beaulieu, 2011) observed that total brain volume appeared to be adult-like by age 5 (Figure 4.7). However, an analysis of longitudinal data from four leading labs shows that it continues to increase slightly through adolescence; after that, it either stabilizes or declines slightly (Mills et al., 2016). As these contrasting findings indicate, estimates of

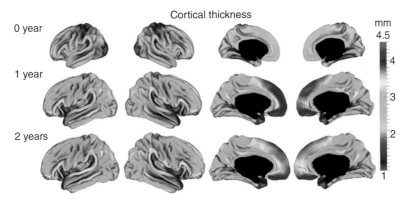

Figure 4.6 Brain changes revealed by an accelerated longitudinal design. (Reprinted from Li et al., 2015)

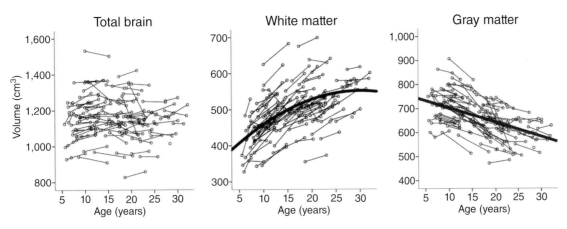

Figure 4.7 Brain volumes, in cubic centimeters. Shown from left to right are total brain volume and gray and white matter volumes. (Reprinted from Lebel & Beaulieu, 2011)

developmental trajectories in brain anatomy differ somewhat across studies (Mills et al., 2016; Walhovd et al., 2017). There are thought to be a variety of reasons for this. First, individual children follow different developmental trajectories, so differences in composition of samples across studies yield different results (LeWinn et al., 2017). Second, the shape of a trendline will differ based on when and how often one draws samples, and which curve fitting methods one adopts (Mills et al., 2016). Third, a variety of other factors, such as type of scanner, scanner pulse sequences, analytic approaches, and even head movement could alter one's estimation of the gray/white matter boundary (which is based on differences in MR signal intensity), and therefore estimates of gray and white matter volumes (Walhovd et al., 2017). Thus, a more accurate picture of developmental change emerges when comparing across large, longitudinal studies with representative samples.

4.4.3   Gray Matter Thinning

We have seen that gray matter decreases during development. What, at a cellular level, could account for this change? We begin here with the research of a pediatric neurologist named Peter Huttenlocher, conducted from the 1970s to the 1990s. Huttenlocher's histological research provided tentative, yet pivotal, insights for subsequent research on brain development, as well as neurological disorders and recovery from brain injury. He took slices of postmortem brain tissue from children of different ages, stained in such a way as to reveal synapses, and counted the number of synapses in each slice of tissue. In Figure 4.8A we see a sample of tissue from dorsolateral prefrontal cortex taken from a 4-year-old. The scale bar indicates 1 μm: less than one thousandth of the dimensions of a voxel in a structural MRI scan. Each arrow indicates the site of a synapse. Huttenlocher did the painstaking work of counting the number of synapses he observed per 100 cubic μm in visual, auditory, and prefrontal cortices. He did so in samples taken at different ages, beginning prenatally at 27 weeks of gestation, and going through adolescence. Figure 4.8B shows the resulting synaptic density measured from a gestational age of 200 to 8,000 days.

These observations led to the inference that rapid synaptic proliferation is followed by gradual synapse elimination ("synaptic pruning") throughout childhood – and, further, that the timing of proliferation and pruning varies across brain regions. Huttenlocher theorized that these different developmental time courses could help explain the development of different cognitive skills at different times, and that it was relevant for the timing of brain plasticity in different neural systems. Of course, these conclusions were tentative as they were based on limited, cross-sectional data, but they have been borne out by subsequent research in laboratory animals.

Huttenlocher's findings have influenced the interpretation of changes in gray matter over childhood observed with structural MRI. In a pioneering longitudinal study (Gogtay et al., 2004), leading researchers in the field (Nitin Gogtay, Jay Giedd, Arthur Toga, Judith Rapoport, and Paul Thompson) collected structural MRI data from 13 children every two years from age 4–21. Although this was a small sample, and a non-representative one at that – the children had an average IQ of 125 – it was a truly unprecedented study. Up to that point, no one had conducted such dense sampling of brain imaging data over child development.

Gogtay and colleagues created color-coded images to illustrate regional differences in gray matter volume changes over development, shown in the now iconic image in Figure 4.9. Rather than finding an increase in gray matter volume from age 4 onwards, as one might expect as brain volume increases, they found a *decrease*. Moreover, they found that the decrease was not uniform across the cortex. In particular, as Huttenlocher had noticed in his tissue sections, association areas involved in higher-level cognition, like prefrontal cortex and parietal cortex, showed more pronounced changes than regions involved in basic sensory processing, like visual and auditory cortex. In fact, Gogtay and colleagues showed that these higher association regions continued to be sculpted into the twenties. This study was a public sensation. In particular, it sparked conversations among legal decision-makers as to when adulthood begins, and among educators as to how long the brain is malleable.

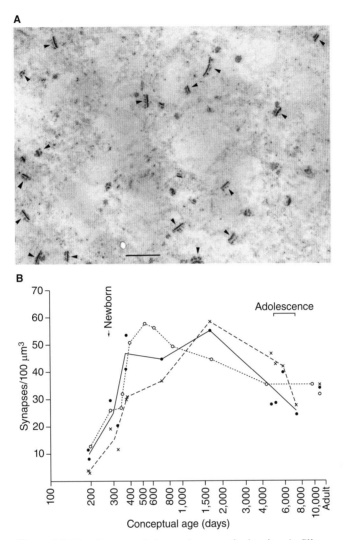

Figure 4.8 Developmental change in synaptic density. A. Slice of tissue taken from prefrontal cortex in a young child and stained for synaptic proteins. B. Synaptic density plotted over time, based on samples of brain tissue taken at different ages. Data are shown for visual cortex (open circles), auditory cortex (filled circles), and prefrontal cortex (crosses). (Reprinted from Huttenlocher & Dabholkar, 1997)

Given Huttenlocher's findings, and the fact that synapses in cortex are localized to the gray matter, it is only natural to wonder – as Gogtay and colleagues did – whether this observed decrease in gray matter can be explained by massive synapse elimination. They also speculated that changes in glia and/or vasculature might also contribute to cortical thinning. However, this is unlikely to be the whole story: in fact, changes in white matter are now hypothesized to play an important role in cortical thinning. As we have seen, long-range fiber tracts become

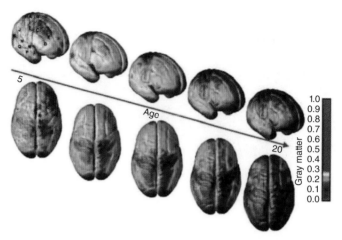

Figure 4.9 Longitudinal changes in local gray matter volume from age 5–20 in a sample of 13 participants. A lateral view of the right hemisphere and a view from the top of the brain are shown over time. Color-coding represents normed units of gray matter. (Reprinted from Gogtay et al., 2004)

increasingly myelinated over childhood and adolescence. As more fibers entering cortex are ensheathed in this fatty substance, that could shift the measured boundary between gray and white matter, on which the measurement of gray matter volume depends. In other words, voxels composed largely of long-range axons that are nearing their terminals in gray matter would be more likely to be classified as gray matter in childhood than adulthood, because of their lower myelin content. As myelin accrues, the apparent gray/white matter boundary would shift, resulting in what looks like a reduction in gray matter thickness over childhood.

There is some support for this idea that myelination contributes to observed cortical thinning, in at least one area of the brain. Adopting a multi-method approach involving structural MRI, diffusion tensor imaging, a technique called quantitative MRI, and consultation of adult postmortem histological maps, Vaidehi Natu, Kalanit Grill-Spector and colleagues (Natu et al., 2019) showed that cortical thinning in ventral temporal cortex in childhood is associated with myelination. The extent to which myelination also contributes to measured cortical thinning in other brain regions is not yet known; however, this type of research is a step in the right direction.

4.4.4 White Matter Microstructural Changes

Thus far, we have discussed developmental changes in white matter volume, as measured by structural MRI. However, this is a crude metric, as white matter is actually made up of fiber tracts running in every direction. As these tracts provide the physical infrastructure for specific brain networks, we want to be able to examine them individually. As we saw in Chapter 2, diffusion-weighted imaging methods such as diffusion tensor imaging (DTI) give us more fine-grained tools for visualizing and quantifying white matter tracts and studying their development.

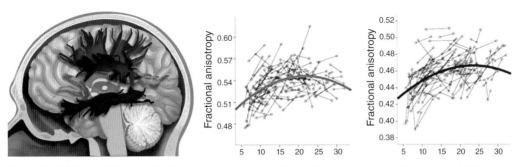

Figure 4.10 Plots of FA as a function of age for two major white matter tracts: the body (middle section) of the corpus callosum (blue) and the inferior longitudinal fasciculus (purple). (Adapted from Lebel & Beaulieu, 2011)

Major white matter pathways in the brain include tracts that connect cortical and subcortical regions (projection fibers), homologous regions in the left and right hemispheres (commissural fibers), and cortical regions within a hemisphere (association fibers). Although the major white matter tracts mature at different rates during prenatal development, they are all in place by the end of the third trimester (see Lebel & Deoni, 2018; Wilson et al., 2021). However, they show a slow developmental trajectory: indeed, diffusion-weighted imaging studies suggest that subtle microstructural changes take place all the way through adolescence. And, as is the case for cortical thinning, white matter development is heterogeneous: individual tracts show different developmental trajectories, as can be seen in Figure 4.10. These data come from the same study as the total white matter volume plotted in Figure 4.7 but provide a more detailed look at the anatomy.

The plots in Figure 4.10 show age-related changes in fractional anisotropy (FA) for two major white matter tracts described below (Lebel & Beaulieu, 2011). As we saw in Chapter 2, FA is an index derived from DTI that describes the directionality of the diffusion of water molecules through tissue. High FA values (on a scale from 0 to 1) are obtained in white matter tracts, as the diffusion of water tends to run parallel to the tracts. An increase in FA values during development is thought to reflect the strengthening of white matter pathways – that is, increased anatomical support for interactions between distant brain regions. We will return to this point below.

Shown in blue on the brain is the corpus callosum, which is the massive bundle of commissural fibers connecting the two hemispheres. Shown in purple is the inferior longitudinal fasciculus: an association fiber tract that connects the occipital and temporal lobes. These fiber tracts were identified via probabilistic tractography (see Chapter 2). As we can see, there is a lot of individual variability, which is of great interest for understanding differences between children! Additionally, the trendlines in the plots show an overall increase in FA over childhood for both tracts – with more protracted changes for the inferior longitudinal fasciculus than the corpus callosum (i.e., for the association fiber tract than the commissural fiber tract, echoing the timing of emergence of these tracts in gestation). For all of the 10 white matter tracts examined in this study, most children showed increased FA through childhood. In fact, for the inferior longitudinal fasciculus and other association fiber tracts, a substantial proportion of individuals continued to show increased FA throughout their twenties.

But what we're measuring here is the directionality of water diffusion. What biological changes might a developmental increase in FA reflect? One plausible explanation is myelination. As axons get wrapped by myelin, they get thicker, reducing the spacing between axons in a fiber tract and restricting the movement of water molecules between them. As explained in Chapter 2, this reduced radial (or perpendicular) diffusivity would lead to an increase in FA. In fact, comparisons between DTI data and postmortem anatomy (Lazari & Lipp, 2021) and newer white matter imaging methods (see Chapter 2) suggest that myelination is a key contributor to the microstructural changes observed with DTI. However, they also suggest that it is not the whole story. Increased FA could additionally result from increasingly dense packing of axons in a fiber tract and/or larger axon diameters, which are also theorized to yield increased efficiency of neural signaling (Feldman et al., 2010). In keeping with this idea, an increase in FA is sometimes referred to as evidence of increased white matter *integrity* or *coherence*, supporting more efficient neural communication. As we shall see below, such changes are thought to contribute to changes in large-scale functional brain networks.

4.4.5   Reorganization of Functional Brain Architecture

If we consider the brain's white matter pathways as roads between regions, we can make the loose analogy that they are transformed during development from bumpy, narrow roads into large, high-speed thoroughfares that make it easier to reach one's destination quickly. If some roads undergo this transformation sooner than others (as is the case for white matter tract development), that is likely to impact the way traffic flows through the system. Likewise, changes in white matter microstructure would be expected to result in changes in the organization of functional brain networks.

As we saw in Chapter 2, one way to investigate interactions between brain regions is via functional connectivity analyses: that is, measurement of the strength of temporal coupling of BOLD activation between brain regions. As discussed previously, the overall pattern of allegiance between regions has led to the characterization of a number of functional brain networks. These networks are evident even in the absence of any specific task demands: so-called resting-state brain networks.

Numerous studies have documented age-related differences in resting-state functional connectivity. Many of these networks can be identified from infancy onward (Gao et al., 2011), and perhaps even prenatally (Thomason et al., 2013). In particular, there is evidence for clearly segregated sensory and motor networks (visual, auditory, and somatomotor) from the get-go. By contrast, higher-order brain networks show protracted changes over childhood and adolescence.

The initial characterization of network development was that networks segregate over childhood, becoming more specialized for their adult roles as they pull apart from one another (Fair et al., 2009). When controlling more rigorously for the confound of head motion, these effects become less pronounced, but are still observed (Satterthwaite et al., 2013; Grayson & Fair, 2017) as discussed in Box 4.3. Increased *within*-network connectivity over childhood and adolescence is observed throughout the brain; this change is thought to result in higher efficiency of neural processing within each of these networks. By contrast, some *between*-network connections get weaker during development while others get stronger, thereby painting a picture of both network segregation and integration (Marek et al., 2016).

To what can we attribute these changes in functional brain architecture? Returning to our road analogy, white matter development would be expected to alter patterns of functional connectivity within and between brain networks. Importantly, however, the converse is not

---

Box 4.3 Developmental Network Neuroscience

One powerful way to study how brain development unfolds in youth is network neuroscience. Broadly, network neuroscience is an interdisciplinary field that applies techniques from the study of networks in other contexts – like social networks, transport networks, and others – to the study of the brain. The rise of network neuroscience responds to abundant evidence that the human brain can be understood as a complex, networked system.

Networks can be studied using measures from **graph theory**; the graphs are constructed of **nodes** and the **edges** that form connections between nodes (Bullmore & Sporns, 2009). Networks can be studied at many scales in the brain, ranging from microscale networks in which the nodes are single neurons in animal models to macroscale networks measured non-invasively in humans, in which the nodes are regions of interest in the brain. Many studies of brain development have used MRI measures to show how brain networks are reshaped in development. Structural networks are typically measured using diffusion imaging, which allows for the measurement of the integrity of white matter tracts, which form the edges that connect different brain regions (nodes). In contrast, functional networks are often constructed by measuring the synchrony of the fMRI signal in different brain regions.

Within macroscale brain networks, a number of network features have been described (Bassett & Sporns, 2017). One of the features that has been particularly informative for understanding the developing brain are network **modules** (also called network communities). Network modules are sets of nodes in the network that are tightly connected to each other and more weakly connected to other brain regions; they can be readily visualized in plots like that shown in Box Figure 4.3. In network neuroscience, these modules reflect well-described brain systems: these modules align with results from animal studies, with lesion studies in clinical patients, and with activation from fMRI studies using cognitive tasks.

In general, these network modules become more defined as children develop through adolescence, in that edges that are *within* a network module – **intra-modular** – get stronger, whereas edges *between* network modules – **inter-modular** – often get weaker. Such development is particularly notable in distributed networks that span association cortex. Notably, a strikingly similar process has also been found to occur in structural brain networks, with network modules becoming more segregated as children grow up. This process has been linked to the development of cognitive abilities, such as executive functioning (see Chapter 10). One current theory suggests that the segregation of network modules may allow for functional specialization of the cognitive sub-systems of the brain. Overall, network neuroscience has provided a new approach to understanding the neural basis of cognitive development.

Box 4.3 (cont.)

Box Figure 4.3
Illustration of the process of segregation of modules in structural networks in youth. Modular segregation results in more defined network modules, which is also associated with better executive function. (Reprinted from Baum et al., 2017)

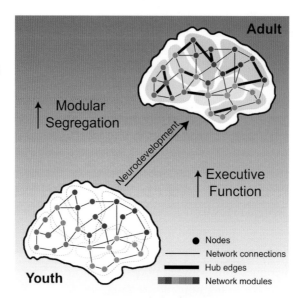

Contributed by Theodore D. Satterthwaite, MD, Associate Professor of Psychiatry, Director, Penn Lifespan Informatics and Neuroimaging Center (PennLINC), University of Pennsylvania Perelman School of Medicine.

true: if – as is often the case – we see an age-related change in functional brain connectivity between two regions, we cannot assume that is due to a change in a white matter pathway that unites them. For one thing, regions that are functionally coupled need not have direct anatomical projections; they may instead both be anatomically connected to a third region. For another, changes in communication between brain regions could stem from any number of other developmental processes: for example, changes in chemical neurotransmission (neurotransmitter release or binding) or synaptic connections within a brain region (e.g., the balance between excitation and inhibition).

Given many brain changes taking place in parallel, it is perhaps not surprising that researchers have tried and largely failed to find strong correspondence between longitudinal changes in white matter microstructure and functional connectivity – at least, using standard brain imaging methods. (There can, however, be interesting dynamic relations between the two: e.g., Wendelken and colleagues (Wendelken et al., 2017) found that white matter FA at one timepoint predicted both cognitive development and future functional connectivity.) The bottom line is that multiple processes likely conspire to produce age-related changes in network strength and organization. As we shall see in the ensuing chapters, such differences have consequences for cognitive development.

SUMMARY

- Embryonic development arises from a well-orchestrated, genetically constrained set of molecular and cellular events
- The neural plate has three layers that form different components of the nervous system, with neural progenitor cells in the ectoderm layer giving rise to the entire nervous system
- Neurulation is the process by which the neural tube forms
- A cell's fate depends on both intrinsic and extrinsic molecular signals
- Overall, both pre- and postnatal brain development is characterized by growth (proliferation of cells and synapses) followed by regression (programmed cell death and synaptic pruning)
- The overall structure of the brain is fully formed by birth, but the brain grows through early childhood and continues to change in subtle ways thereafter
- Synaptic pruning is thought to fine-tune local brain circuits, making them more efficient
- Myelination of long-range fibers enables timely communication between distant brain regions
- Gray matter volume increases over the first few years of life, due to an increased number of neurons and synapses; gray matter volume decreases throughout childhood and adolescence, likely due to both synaptic pruning and myelination
- White matter volume increases through childhood and adolescence, and diffusion-weighted imaging suggests that white matter tract coherence increases
- Changes in the strength of anatomical connections between regions are theorized to contribute to network reconfiguration during development
- Sensory brain networks are refined over early childhood; higher-level cognitive networks mature more slowly

REVIEW QUESTIONS

Where in the brain are the cortex, subcortical nuclei, and white matter, and what are these tissue types composed of? Why are "gray" and "white" matter so named?

What are the three main classes of neurons?

What important functions does myelin have?

Explain Waddington's metaphor of an "epigenetic landscape." What is canalization?

Describe the following developmental processes: neural induction and proliferation, cellular migration and differentiation, synaptogenesis, programmed cell death, and synaptic pruning.

Why is the cortex said to be developed "inside out"? Refer to the neural tube, ventricular zone, and radial glial cells.

What is the advantage of initial overproduction of cells and synapses in early brain development?

Around what age, roughly, does a child's brain volume approximate that of an adult? How do gray and white matter change thereafter?

What cellular processes could contribute to the cortical thinning observed with structural MRI?

What is meant by a functional brain network? How are such networks measured, and how do they change with age?

Further Reading

Karcher, N. R., & Barch, D. M. (2021). The ABCD study: Understanding the development of risk for mental and physical health outcomes. *Neuropsychopharmacology*, 46(1), 131–142. https://doi.org/10.1038/s41386-020-0736-6

Stiles, J. (2008). *The fundamentals of brain development: Integrating nature and nurture*. Harvard University Press.

Sydnor, V. J., Larsen, B., Bassett, D. S., Alexander-Bloch, A., Fair, D. A., Liston, C., Mackey, A. P., Milham, M. P., Pines, A., Roalf, D. R., Seidlitz, J., Xu, T., Raznahan, A., & Satterthwaite, T. D. (2021). Neurodevelopment of the association cortices: Patterns, mechanisms, and implications for psychopathology. *Neuron*, 109(18), 2820–2846. https://doi.org/10.1016/j.neuron.2021.06.016

References

Azevedo, F. A. C., Carvalho, L. R. B., Grinberg, L. T., Farfel, J. M., Ferretti, R. E. L., Leite, R. E. P., Filho, W. J., Lent, R., & Herculano-Houzel, S. (2009). Equal numbers of neuronal and nonneuronal cells make the human brain an isometrically scaled-up primate brain. *Journal of Comparative Neurology*, 513(5), 532–541. https://doi.org/10.1002/cne.21974

Baldassari, S., Musante, I., Iacomino, M., Zara, F., Salpietro, V., & Scudieri, P. (2020). Brain organoids as model systems for genetic neurodevelopmental disorders. *Frontiers in Cell and Developmental Biology*, 8, 590119. https://doi.org/10.3389/fcell.2020.590119

Banich, M., & Compton, R. (2018). *Cognitive neuroscience*, 4th edition. Cambridge University Press. https://doi.org/10.1017/9781316664018

Bassett, D. S., & Sporns, O. (2017). Network neuroscience. *Nature Neuroscience*, 20(3), 353–362. https://doi.org/10.1038/nn.4502

Baum, G. L., Ciric, R., Roalf, D. R., Betzel, R. F., Moore, T. M., Shinohara, R. T., Kahn, A. E., Vandekar, S. N., Rupert, P. E., Quarmley, M., Cook, P. A., Elliott, M. A., Ruparel, K., Gur, R. E., Gur, R. C., Bassett, D. S., & Satterthwaite, T. D. (2017). Modular segregation of structural brain networks supports the development of executive function in youth. *Current Biology*, 27(11), 1561–1572. https://doi.org/10.1016/j.cub.2017.04.051

Brodal, P. (2010). *The central nervous system: Structure and function*. Oxford University Press.

Bullmore, E., & Sporns, O. (2009). Complex brain networks: Graph theoretical analysis of structural and functional systems. *Nature Reviews Neuroscience*, 10(3), 186–198. https://doi.org/10.1038/nrn2575

Bystron, I., Blakemore, C., & Rakic, P. (2008). Development of the human cerebral cortex: Boulder Committee revisited. *Nature Reviews Neuroscience*, 9, 110–122. https://doi.org/10.1038/nrn2252

Chugani, H. T., Phelps, M. E., & Mazziotta, J. C. (1987). Positron emission tomography study of human brain functional development. *Annals of Neurology*, 22(4), 487–497. https://doi.org/10.1002/ana.410220408

Fair, D. A., Cohen, A. L., Power, J. D., Dosenbach, N. U. F., Church, J. A., Miezin, F. M., Schlaggar, B. L., & Petersen, S. E. (2009). Functional brain networks develop from a "local to distributed" organization. *PLOS Computational Biology*, 5(5), e1000381. https://doi.org/10.1371/journal.pcbi.1000381

Feldman, H. M., Yeatman, J. D., Lee, E. S., Barde, L. H., & Gaman-Bean, S. (2010). Diffusion tensor imaging: A review for pediatric researchers and clinicians. *Journal of Developmental and Behavioral Pediatrics*, 31(4), 346–356. https://doi.org/10.1097/DBP.0b013e3181dcaa8b

Gabriel, E., Albanna, W., Pasquini, G., Ramani, A., Josipovic, N., Mariappan, A., Schinzel, F., Karch, C. M., Bao, G., Gottardo, M., Suren, A. A., Hescheler, J., Nagel-Wolfrum, K., Persico, V., Rizzoli, S. O., Altmüller, J., Riparbelli, M. G., Callaini, G., Goureau, O., Papantonis, A., … Gopalakrishnan, J. (2021). Human brain organoids assemble functionally integrated bilateral optic vesicles. *Cell Stem Cell*, 28(10), 1740–1757. https://doi.org/10.1016/j.stem.2021.07.010

Gao, W., Gilmore, J. H., Giovanello, K. S., Smith, J. K., Shen, D., Zhu, H., & Lin, W. (2011). Temporal and spatial evolution of brain network topology during the first two years of life. *PLoS One*, 6(9), e25278. https://doi.org/10.1371/journal.pone.0025278

Gogtay, N., Giedd, J. N., Lusk, L., Hayashi, K. M., Greenstein, D., Vaituzis, A. C., Nugent, T. F., Herman, D. H., Clasen, L. S., Toga, A. W., Rapoport, J. L., & Thompson, P. M. (2004). Dynamic mapping of human cortical development during childhood through early adulthood. *Proceedings of the National Academy of Sciences of the United States of America*, 101(21), 8174–8179. https://doi.org/10.1073/pnas.0402680101

Gottlieb, G. (1991). Experiential canalization of behavioral development: Theory. *Developmental Psychology*, 27(1), 4–13. https://doi.org/10.1037/0012-1649.27.1.4

Goyal, M. S., & Raichle, M. E. (2018). Glucose requirements of the developing human brain. *Journal of Pediatric Gastroenterology and Nutrition*, 66(Suppl 3), S46–S49. https://doi.org/10.1097/MPG.0000000000001875

Grasby, K. L., Jahanshad, N., Painter, J. N., Colodro-Conde, L., Bralten, J., Hibar, D. P., Lind, P. A., Pizzagalli, F., Ching, C. R. K., McMahon, M. A. B., Shatokhina, N., Zsembik, L. C. P., Thomopoulos, S. I., Zhu, A. H., Strike, L. T., Agartz, I., Alhusaini, S., Almeida, M. A. A., Alnæs, D., & Medland, S. E. (2020). The genetic architecture of the human cerebral cortex. *Science*, 367(6484), eaay6690. https://doi.org/10.1126/science.aay6690

Grayson, D. S., & Fair, D. A. (2017). Development of large-scale functional networks from birth to adulthood: A guide to the neuroimaging literature. *Functional Architecture of the Brain*, 160, 15–31. https://doi.org/10.1016/j.neuroimage.2017.01.079

Hoerder-Suabedissen, A., & Molnár, Z. (2015). Development, evolution and pathology of neocortical subplate neurons. *Nature Reviews Neuroscience*, 16(3), 133–146. https://doi.org/10.1038/nrn3915

Huch, M., & Koo, B. K. (2015). Modeling mouse and human development using organoid cultures. *Development*, 142(18), 3113–3125. https://doi.org/10.1242/dev.118570

Huttenlocher, P. R., & Dabholkar, A. S. (1997). Regional differences in synaptogenesis in human cerebral cortex. *Journal of Comparative Neurology*, 387(2), 167–178. https://doi.org/10.1002/(sici)1096-9861(19971020)387:2<167::aid-cne1>3.0.co;2-z

Innocenti, G. M., & Price, D. J. (2005). Exuberance in the development of cortical networks. *Nature Reviews Neuroscience*, 6(12), 955–965. https://doi.org/10.1038/nrn1790

Jabr, F. (2017, December 14). To unlock the brain's mysteries, purée it. *New York Times Magazine*. www.nytimes.com/2017/12/14/magazine/to-unlock-the-brains-mysteries-puree-it.html

Lancaster, M. A., Renner, M., Martin, C. A., Wenzel, D., Bicknell, L. S., Hurles, M. E., Homfray, T., Penninger, J. M., Jackson, A. P., & Knoblich, J. A. (2013). Cerebral organoids model human brain development and microcephaly. *Nature*, 501(7467), 373–379. https://doi.org/10.1038/nature12517

Lazari, A., & Lipp, I. (2021). Can MRI measure myelin? Systematic review, qualitative assessment, and meta-analysis of studies validating microstructural imaging with myelin histology. *NeuroImage*, 230, 117744. https://doi.org/10.1016/j.neuroimage.2021.117744

Lebel, C., & Beaulieu, C. (2011). Longitudinal development of human brain wiring continues from childhood into adulthood. *Journal of Neuroscience*, 31(30), 10937. https://doi.org/10.1523/JNEUROSCI.5302-10.2011

Lebel, C., & Deoni, S. (2018). The development of brain white matter microstructure. *Microstructural Imaging*, 182, 207–218. https://doi.org/10.1016/j.neuroimage.2017.12.097

Lee, Y., Morrison, B. M., Li, Y., Lengacher, S., Farah, M. H., Hoffman, P. N., Liu, Y., Tsingalia, A., Jin, L., Zhang, P.-W., Pellerin, L., Magistretti, P. J., & Rothstein, J. D. (2012). Oligodendroglia metabolically support axons and contribute to neurodegeneration. *Nature*, 487(7408), 443–448. https://doi.org/10.1038/nature11314

Lenroot, R. K., & Giedd, J. N. (2006). Brain development in children and adolescents: Insights from anatomical magnetic resonance imaging. *Neuroscience and Biobehavioral Reviews*, 30(6), 718–729. https://doi.org/10.1016/j.neubiorev.2006.06.001

LeWinn, K. Z., Sheridan, M. A., Keyes, K. M., Hamilton, A., & McLaughlin, K. A. (2017). Sample composition alters associations between age and brain structure. *Nature Communications*, 8(1), 874. https://doi.org/10.1038/s41467-017-00908-7

Li, G., Lin, W., Gilmore, J. H., & Shen, D. (2015). Spatial patterns, longitudinal development, and hemispheric asymmetries of cortical thickness in infants from birth to 2 years of age. *Journal of Neuroscience*, 35(24) 9150–9162. https://doi.org/10.1523/JNEUROSCI.4107-14.2015

Marek, S., Hwang, K., Foran, W., Hallquist, M. N., & Luna, B. (2016). The contribution of network organization and integration to the development of cognitive control. *PLOS Biology*, 13(12), e1002328. https://doi.org/10.1371/journal.pbio.1002328

Mills, K. L., Goddings, A. L., Herting, M. M., Meuwese, R., Blakemore, S. J., Crone, E. A., Dahl, R. E., Güroğlu, B., Raznahan, A., Sowell, E. R., & Tamnes, C. K. (2016). Structural brain development between childhood and adulthood: Convergence across four longitudinal samples. *NeuroImage*, 141, 273–281. https://doi.org/10.1016/j.neuroimage.2016.07.044

Mitchell, K. J. (2007). The genetics of brain wiring: From molecule to mind. *PLOS Biology*, 5(4), e113. https://doi.org/10.1371/journal.pbio.0050113

Miyata, T., Kawaguchi, A., Okano, H., & Ogawa, M. (2001). Asymmetric inheritance of radial glial fibers by cortical neurons. *Neuron*, 31(5), 727–741. https://doi.org/10.1016/S0896-6273(01)00420-2

Morange, M. (2001). *The misunderstood gene*. Harvard University Press.

Nadarajah, B., & Parnavelas, J. G. (2002). Modes of neuronal migration in the developing cerebral cortex. *Nature Reviews Neuroscience*, 3(6), 423–432. https://doi.org/10.1038/nrn845

Natu, V. S., Gomez, J., Barnett, M., Jeska, B., Kirilina, E., Jaeger, C., Zhen, Z., Cox, S., Weiner, K. S., Weiskopf, N., & Grill-Spector, K. (2019). Apparent thinning of human visual cortex during childhood is associated with myelination. *Proceedings of the National Academy of Sciences of the United States of America*, 116(41), 20750–20759. https://doi.org/10.1073/pnas.1904931116

Rabinowicz, T., de Courten-Myers, G., Petetot, J., & de los Reyes, E. (1996). Human cortex development: Estimates of neuronal numbers indicate major loss late during gestation. *Journal of Neuropathology & Experimental Neurology*, 55(3), 320–328. https://doi.org/10.1097/00005072-199603000-00007

Rakic, P. (1972). Mode of cell migration to the superficial layers of fetal monkey neocortex. *Journal of Comparative Neurology*, 145(1), 61–83. https://doi.org/10.1002/cne.901450105

Saladin, K. (2011). *Anatomy & physiology: The unity of form and function*. McGraw-Hill.

Samarasinghe, R. A., Miranda, O. A., Buth, J. E., Mitchell, S., Fernado, I., Watanabe, M., Allison, T. F., Kurdian, A., Fotion, N., Golshani, P., Plath, K., Lowry, W. E., Parent, J. M., Moday, I., & Novitch, B. G. (2021). Identification of neural oscillations and epileptiform changes in human brain organoids. *Nature Neuroscience, 24*, 1488–1500. https://doi.org/10.1038/s41593-021-00906-5

Satterthwaite, T. D., Wolf, D. H., Ruparel, K., Erus, G., Elliott, M. A., Eickhoff, S. B., Gennatas, E. D., Jackson, C., Prabhakaran, K., Smith, A., Hakonarson, H., Verma, R., Davatzikos, C., Gur, R. E., & Gur, R. C. (2013). Heterogeneous impact of motion on fundamental patterns of developmental changes in functional connectivity during youth. *NeuroImage*, 83, 45–57. https://doi.org/10.1016/j.neuroimage.2013.06.045

Stiles, J. (2008). *The fundamentals of brain development: Integrating nature and nurture.* Harvard University Press.

Sur, M., & Leamey, C. A. (2001). Development and plasticity of cortical areas and networks. *Nature Reviews Neuroscience*, 2(4), 251–262. https://doi.org/10.1038/35067562

Sur, M., & Rubenstein, J. L. R. (2005). Patterning and plasticity of the cerebral cortex. *Science*, 310(5749), 805–810. https://doi.org/10.1126/science.1112070

Thomason, M. E., Dassanayake, M. T., Shen, S., Katkuri, Y., Alexis, M., Anderson, A. L., Yeo, L., Mody, S., Hernandez-Andrade, E., Hassan, S. S., Studholme, C., Jeong, J. W., & Romero, R. (2013). Cross-hemispheric functional connectivity in the human fetal brain. *Science Translational Medicine*, 5(173), 173ra24. https://doi.org/10.1126/scitranslmed.3004978

Trujillo, C. A., Rice, E. S., Schaefer, N. K., Chaim, I. A., Wheeler, E. C., Madrigal, A. A., Buchanan, J., Preissl, S., Wang, A., Negraes, P. D., Szeto, R. A., Herai, R. H., Huseynov, A., Ferraz, M., Borges, F. S., Kihara, A. H., Byrne, A., Marin, M., Vollmers, C., … Muotri, A. R. (2021). Reintroduction of the archaic variant of *NOVA1* in cortical organoids alters neurodevelopment. *Science*, 371(6530), eaax2537. https://doi.org/10.1126/science.aax2537

von Bartheld, C. S., Bahney, J., & Herculano-Houzel, S. (2016). The search for true numbers of neurons and glial cells in the human brain: A review of 150 years of cell counting. *Journal of Comparative Neurology*, 524(18), 3865–3895. https://doi.org/10.1002/cne.24040

Waddington, C. (1957). *The strategy of the genes: A discussion of some aspects of theoretical biology.* George Allen & Unwin.

Walhovd, K. B., Fjell, A. M., Giedd, J., Dale, A. M., & Brown, T. T. (2017). Through thick and thin: A need to reconcile contradictory results on trajectories in human cortical development. *Cerebral Cortex*, 27, bhv301. https://doi.org/10.1093/cercor/bhv301

Wendelken, C., Ferrer, E., Ghetti, S., Bailey, S. K., Cutting, L., & Bunge, S. A. (2017). Frontoparietal structural connectivity in childhood predicts development of functional connectivity and reasoning ability: A large-scale longitudinal investigation. *Journal of Neuroscience*, 37(35), 8549–8558. https://doi.org/10.1523/JNEUROSCI.3726-16.2017

Wilson, S., Pietsch, M., Cordero-Grande, L., Price, A. N., Hutter, J., Xiao, J., McCabe, L., Rutherford, M. A., Hughes, E. J., Counsell, S. J., Tournier, J. D., Arichi, T., Hajnal, J. V., Edwards, A. D., Christiaens, D., & O'Muircheartaigh, J. (2021). Development of human white matter pathways in utero over the second and third trimester. *Proceedings of the National Academy of Sciences of the United States of America*, 118(20), e2023598118. https://doi.org/10.1073/pnas.2023598118

Wolpert, L. (1969). Positional information and the spatial pattern of cellular differentiation. *Journal of Theoretical Biology*, 25(1), 1–47. https://doi.org/10.1016/S0022-5193(69)80016-0

Wolpert, L. (2007). *Principles of development*, 3rd edition. Oxford University Press.

Zecevic, N., & Rakic, P. (2001). Development of layer I neurons in the primate cerebral cortex. *Journal of Neuroscience*, 21(15), 5607–5619. https://doi.org/10.1523/JNEUROSCI.21-15-05607.2001

5   Brain Plasticity

LEARNING OBJECTIVES

- Discuss several key ideas and findings that led to the study of brain plasticity
- Outline key cellular mechanisms of brain plasticity
- Provide examples of the three main types of brain plasticity, as distinguished based on their degree of dependence on environmental inputs
- Describe evidence of critical periods of plasticity
- Briefly explain why the opening and closure of critical periods is regulated, and why this is adaptive
- Provide evidence for the expansion-normalization hypothesis of brain plasticity
- Discuss how the potential for plasticity is thought to change over the course of development
- Describe how early life adversity can shape the developing brain

As we grow up, each of us learns skills that differentiate us from one another, like playing the trombone, mastering the Rubik's cube, becoming a champion pole vaulter, or being the sibling who helps to defuse family tensions. Mastering these complex skills takes perseverance – and also alters the brain in the process, tweaking existing neural circuits in response to, and in further support of, novel behaviors. According to the philosopher Will Durant (Durant, 1926, often misattributed to Aristotle), "We are what we repeatedly do. Excellence, then, is not an act, but a habit." Of course, this view of human development ignores genetic differences among people, but it does highlight the ways in which our habits and practices help to shape us over time.

During early development we also master basic competencies that we take for granted, like perceiving the world in three dimensions, or walking, which we tend to think of as abilities that emerge naturally with age. In fact, even these basic competencies are to some extent learned skills. Let's take the case of walking. Nearly every typically developing child across the globe learns to walk within the first 1.5 years of life – with or without extensive coaching from caregivers. In other words, learning to walk seems like an open-and-shut example of nature taking its course. However, learning to walk takes immense effort and a lot of trial-and-error; when they begin, toddlers fall on average 69 times per hour (Adolph et al., 2012). Additionally, cultural practices around the world influence *when* a child learns to walk (Super, 1976; Adolph et al., 2012, 2018). Thus, even for this seemingly most universal of skills, experience – in the form of both practice and external scaffolding – plays a role. So, where does development end and learning begin? We present below some ways of thinking about this question.

5.1 Learning and Development: Broad Categories of Plasticity

Development can be defined broadly as the changes that an individual undergoes over time. If we are changing, we (or our brains) are often learning. This concept of learning can be defined as the acquisition of knowledge or a skill through instruction and/or practice. Can we really tease change and learning apart? Developmental scientists hold different views about this (Galván, 2010). Some think that learning is part and parcel of development; others think these are separate phenomena that can be distinguished along one or more dimensions. Broadly speaking, one relevant dimension to consider is the *magnitude* of plasticity: development has been likened to building a house from the ground up, and learning as small remodeling projects. These differ both in terms of type of construction and scale of the project. A second dimension, related to the first, is the amount of *input* or *effort* required to change a system, with considerably more required for learning once the system is in place. A third dimension is the *timescale* of change: on the order of hours or days in the case of learning, as opposed to weeks, months, or years in the case of development. In this way of thinking, development and learning are on a continuum according to dimensions like magnitude of change, effort involved, and the timescale of change. A related, but more neurally grounded, way of thinking about this development–learning continuum is in terms of the degree to which they involve *different types of brain plasticity*. We will return to this idea below (Section 5.1.4), but first, let us consider three distinct categories of brain plasticity: **experience-independent**, **experience-expectant**, and **experience-dependent**. What are they?

5.1.1 Experience-Independent Brain Development

Experience-independent development is a process of change that unfolds similarly regardless of the individual's environment. Early fetal development is considered largely experience-independent: leaving aside genetic disorders or a gross perturbation such as toxin exposure, development *in utero* follows a tightly regulated sequence of molecular and cellular events with predictable timing and sequence that are determined or at least strongly influenced by genes; this is particularly true of the first trimester. That said, the means by which those genes are decoded to produce relevant proteins is an interactive process, during which individual variability is magnified beyond that attributable to individual genes themselves (Chapter 3). As we saw in Chapter 4, early fetal brain development likewise unfolds in a stereotyped manner across individuals of a species. For example, we each underwent a process of neural tube development and differentiation, and our layered cortex was built by the genetically controlled migration of neuronal precursor cells away from the center of the neural tube. Our brains all have the same major subdivisions, and even the same major gyri and sulci. More than that: it is possible to identify, in each of us, boundaries between cortical regions – say, between primary and secondary visual cortices – on the basis of subtle cytoarchitectonic differences that arise from gradients of gene expression. Although our brains differ in terms of the precise cortical folding patterns and the precise location of each anatomical boundary, they are remarkably similar in broad strokes.

However, development that unfolds similarly regardless of experience is the exception rather than the rule; in fact, we can think of no examples of experience-independent brain development aside from early fetal development. As gestation progresses and the sensory organs mature, experience plays an increasingly important role. For example, the sounds a fetus is exposed to in the third trimester impact auditory processing after birth (Partanen et al., 2013).

5.1.2 Experience-Expectant Brain Development

Bill Greenough and colleagues (Greenough et al., 1987) drew an important distinction between two ways in which environmental inputs can change the brain. They referred to these forms of plasticity as experience-expectant and experience-dependent. Let's review these in turn.

Experience-expectant brain development will unfold *if and only if* the individual is exposed to certain stimuli, within a particular window of development. As with experience-independent development, this form of plasticity is under tight genetic control and follows a precise temporal sequence across individuals of a species. However, like a Rube Goldberg machine, it requires a little push to get the ball rolling – after which it goes down a predictable path. What kind of push is needed to initiate experience-expectant brain plasticity? It is triggered by the sounds, sights, touches, etc. that a typically developing organism is highly likely to experience, given their natural habitat and sensory organs. For example, from the moment our eyes open for the first time, humans and most other mammals are exposed to patterned light – and our visual system does not develop properly unless we are exposed to this detailed visual input as newborns.

How do we know this? An initial insight came from children born with bilateral cataracts, which cause the lens of their eye to be clouded. These children grow up to be heavily visual impaired, or even blind – unless they have cataract removal surgery right away (Maurer & Lewis, 2012). The American Academy of Ophthalmology recommends that cataracts be removed by 2 months of age to achieve the best possible outcome for visual development. This narrow window of time within which the visual system must receive proper input is referred to as a **critical period**. We delve into this research more deeply below (Section 5.3).

5.1.3 Experience-Dependent Brain Development

Finally, experience-dependent brain development is the kind of sculpting of the brain that results from a child's environment: characteristics of their home, neighborhood, and schools, and how they spend their time. This form of plasticity is highly idiosyncratic: it's part of what makes you *you*. Unlike experience-expectant plasticity, it requires a whole lot more than a single environmental trigger. Although our brains register every event we experience, at least briefly, a lasting change generally requires repeated or prolonged exposure to a particular input or practice of a skill. A single event, such as a stressful experience, is unlikely to dramatically alter the course of brain development, but chronic stress exposure can. Likewise, practicing a foreign language sporadically is unlikely to have a significant impact the brain's language system, but the experience of growing up in a bilingual household does (Neville & Bavelier, 1998). Unlike experience-*expectant* brain plasticity, experience-*dependent* plasticity doesn't require

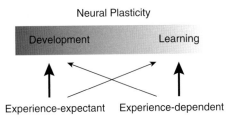

Figure 5.1 The conceptualization of
a continuum between development,
dominated by experience-expectant brain
plasticity, and learning, dominated by
experience-dependent plasticity. (Adapted
from Galván, 2010)

input during a very narrow time frame. For this reason, some researchers refer to the period of maximal potential for experience-dependent brain plasticity as a **sensitive period** rather than a **critical period**. However, it is still the case that timing matters; for example, learning a new language is particularly effortful if we wait too long to get started.

5.1.4 A Continuum from Development to Learning

So, let's get back to the question of the distinction between development and learning. Galván conceptualizes it as a continuum, with development involving predominantly *experience-expectant* brain plasticity and learning involving predominantly *experience-dependent* plasticity, as depicted in Figure 5.1. Note that the gradient in the figure maps roughly onto chronological age: experience-expectant plasticity occurs only during infancy, whereas experience-dependent plasticity takes place from infancy through old age. What do you think? Is it more helpful to think of development and learning as processes that differ along multiple dimensions, or as falling along a continuum? Perhaps some of the neuroscientific research we review will change your mind or reinforce your views.

5.2 Foundations of Research on Brain Plasticity

The notion that the brain can be modified by experience wasn't widely accepted by the public until the 1970s, but research interest in it can be traced back much farther than that (Rosenzweig, 1996; Raz & Lindenberger, 2013). Before getting into modern research on brain plasticity, we shall explore how this idea came to be.

5.2.1 Origins of the Idea

Let's begin in 1779, when an Italian surgeon and anatomist named Michele Vincenzo Giacinto Malacarne was exchanging letters with his friend, a Swiss naturalist named Charles

Bonnet. Malacarne remarked that he had noticed a structural difference in the layers of the cerebellum (the large, intricate structure at the base of the brain) between individuals of differing levels of intellectual capacity. In response, Bonnet speculated that intellectual capacity did not depend on the number of layers, but the number of layers depended on the exercise of intellectual capacity. This provocative claim deserved to be tested empirically, and Malacarne set about to do just that. He took two puppies from the same litter, and put one of them through a training regime. He then sacrificed both animals and analyzed the structure of their cerebella, and noted that the dog who had undergone training had more layers. Alas, this intriguing observation didn't take hold in the intellectual community at that time.

More than a century later, William James used the term *plasticity* in the context of learning: "the phenomena of habit in living beings are due to the plasticity of the organic materials of which their bodies are composed" (James, 1890, p. 105). From there, it was not a big leap to the concept of neural (or brain) plasticity. Meanwhile, in Spain, James' contemporary, Santiago Ramón y Cajal, one of the most important founders of modern neuroscience, was painstakingly examining neuron after neuron in cortical tissue under the microscope. He was using the recently developed Golgi technique for staining a fraction of neurons with silver nitrate, so that he could examine them one by one and draw each one in detail. He and Camillo Golgi later shared a Nobel Prize for their work visualizing neural circuitry. By 1891, Cajal's observations led him to formulate the now-universally accepted **Neuron Doctrine**: the idea that the nervous system is made up of independent cells (neurons) that serve as the fundamental unit of communication and that are densely interconnected.

5.2.2 Dendritic Spines

Cajal looked closely at the dendrites of neurons – the branches that receive inputs from other neurons – and took note of tiny bumps on them that looked like thorns on a rose that he called *spines* (DeFelipe, 2006; Yuste, 2015). Others had also noticed them but assumed they were artifacts of the Golgi staining process, but Cajal showed that they were visible with other stains as well. Observing that their presence increased the surface area available for synapses, he hypothesized that **dendritic spines** played a key role in neuronal communication. Inspired by the experiments and ideas of French neuroscientist Micheline Stefanowska, Cajal promoted the hypothesis that spines grow during neural activity and retract with inactivity, thereby playing a role in learning (DeFelipe, 2015). With modern microscopy techniques for visualizing the surface of the brain in living mice, it is possible to watch spines growing and retracting over minutes and hours (Fischer et al., 1998).

We now know that specific experiences do in fact elicit changes in spines; these changes are observed in parts of the brain that encode the experience. Moreover, research from Linda Wilbrecht and Karel Svoboda using transgenic mice (Wilbrecht et al., 2010) shows that the stabilization of new spines after learning – a lasting anatomical change – depends on the presence of a specific protein that has been implicated in memory formation. This protein is essential for **long-term potentiation (LTP)**.

5.2.3 Long-Term Potentiation and Hebbian Plasticity

LTP is a term for an increase in synaptic strength – increased response of a neuron to presynaptic input – that is induced in brain tissue via trains of strong electrical stimulation. This phenomenon was first discovered by accident (Lømo, 1966; Bliss & Lomo, 1973), and its relevance to actual learning and memory was doubted at first. Over time, however, research on LTP has revealed a lot about the anatomical and neurochemical basis of brain plasticity. For one thing, it has provided evidence for Donald Hebb's famous postulate from 1949 that if a neuron (cell A) repeatedly fires and takes part in causing another neuron (cell B) to fire, "some growth process or metabolic change takes place in one or both cells such that *A*'s efficiency, as one of the cells firing *B*, is increased" (Hebb, 1949, p. 62). This hypothesis is commonly *but inaccurately* summarized as "Cells that fire together wire together." In fact, the cells in this scenario were already wired together, but the synapse gets stronger if the presynaptic neuron (cell A) repeatedly fires right before the postsynaptic one (cell B). Conversely, a synapse gets weaker if the two neurons' activity patterns are decoupled – a phenomenon now known as **long-term depression (LTD)**. (In very learned journals we still see this inaccurate summary; you, dear reader, now know better.)

A lot is now known about these mechanisms of **Hebbian plasticity**; if you're curious to learn more, we recommend taking a course that covers cellular and molecular neuroscience. For our present purposes, suffice it to say that coupled activation of two interacting neurons results in synaptic changes that further strengthen the connection between them (LTP); on the flipside, decoupled activation leads to weakening or elimination of the synapse (LTD). These general principles of Hebbian plasticity will be helpful when we get to the topic of ocular dominance column plasticity later in this chapter. It is also foundational to our understanding of long-term memory, discussed in Chapter 8: LTP and LTD in the hippocampus support memory formation by changing the strength of synaptic connections between neurons that will form a memory trace (engram).

5.3 Characterizing Brain Plasticity

Having looked at how individual synapses are strengthened or weakened as a result of patterns of neural activity, we zoom out and look at the impact of specific types of experiences on the brain (which exert their effects by altering patterns of neural activity). As we shall see, both an animal's living conditions and its exposure to normal sensory input shape its brain development. At the end of this section, we will outline the many ways in which experience can influence the brain's microstructure.

5.3.1 Environmental Enrichment

Donald Hebb, mentioned above for his highly influential theory of synaptic plasticity, humorously likened the question how much of behavior is dependent on heredity and how much on environment to asking "how much of the area of a field is due to its length, how much to its width" (Hebb, 1953, p. 44). Around the early 1960s or thereabouts, he and his children raised pet rats at home and let them roam freely. One day, he decided to take them into the laboratory, where he was conducting experiments testing laboratory rats' ability to memorize routes through a maze. Maze tests have long been used to study how rats develop cognitive maps of space – that is, **spatial learning** (Tolman & Honzik, 1930). Hebb noticed that his pet rats were able to learn the routes more quickly. He hypothesized that this difference in spatial learning stemmed from the fact that his pet rats had grown up in a more stimulating environment. This anecdote inspired a team of Tolman's colleagues at the University of California, Berkeley, David Krech, Edward Bennett, and Mark Rosenzweig, to test this idea formally, raising rats in either an **enriched environment**, involving a large cage with many rats and toys, as shown in Figure 5.2A, or an **impoverished environment**, with only a small cage, one rat, and no toys (Diamond, 1996). These researchers replicated Hebb's initial observation, showing better spatial learning among rats raised in the enriched environment rather than the impoverished one.

Figure 5.2 Research examining the effects of manipulating animals' housing conditions on cortical thickness. A. Rats housed in an enriched environment. (Reprinted from Bennett et al., 1964) B. A coronal section through the rat brain, showing somatosensory cortex. The lines represent the points at which cortical depth was measured. (Reprinted from Diamond et al., 1964)

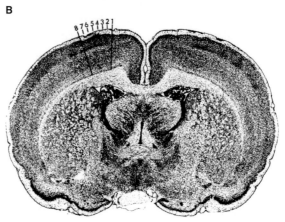

Marian Diamond, a young neuroanatomist at UC Berkeley, was fascinated by these behavioral results, and proposed to test for anatomical differences in the brains of these two groups of rats. They began by comparing the weight of visual and somatosensory cortices, and found that visual cortex was reliably heavier among rats in the enriched condition (Diamond et al., 1964). Seeking to understand the possible causes, they conducted a follow-up study involving postmortem brain tissue analysis (histology), as shown in Figure 5.2B, in which they tested for differences in gray matter – cortical thickness – between the groups. Through careful measurement of tissue slices under a microscope, Diamond and colleagues found a small but consistent effect for visual cortex (the results for somatosensory cortex were small and not reliable): visual cortex was 6 percent thicker in the rats raised in the enriched versus the impoverished environment (Bennett et al., 1964; Diamond et al., 1964).

This discovery ran counter to the prevailing view in the early 1960s that brain structure was entirely determined by genetics. The findings amounted to a bombshell. Diamond later recounted her experience presenting this paper at the American Association of Anatomists:

There were hundreds of people in the room—very few of them women—and this was the first scientific paper I had presented at a big conference. I explained the projects as calmly as I could, people applauded politely, and then—I'll always remember this—a man stood up in the back of the room and said in a loud voice, "Young lady, [the] brain cannot change!" (Diamond, 1996, p. 76)

In subsequent years, Diamond ran a number of additional studies to explore the phenomenon further. She found that, although the enriched environment was associated with thicker visual cortex, there were 7 percent fewer neurons in this tissue. Rather than having more neurons, the existing neurons just took up more space! Indeed, they had bigger cell bodies, more dendrites and dendritic spines, longer dendrites, and larger capillaries (small blood vessels nourishing the cortex). Additionally, there were more glial cells. Additionally, Diamond showed that the degree of change varied by the *amount* of exposure to the environment, as well as the *age* at exposure. Four days of exposure (but not one) was sufficient to see a *small* change in cortical thickness. Diamond recounts in a brief autobiography (Diamond, 1996) that the intervention that led to the most widespread changes across the cortex was 30 days of exposure between postnatal days 60 and 90 – a time frame spanning the late juvenile and early adult periods (Sengupta, 2013). This effect of the home environment can be said to be experience-dependent rather than experience-expectant because it is not – unlike the phenomenon we shall discuss next – an all-or-nothing change that depends on exposure to a specific stimulus during a narrow window in development.

5.3.2 A Critical Period for Plasticity

As we have discussed previously, experience-expectancy refers to the types of inputs that are *compulsory* for the development of specific brain systems – predominantly sensory systems. These inputs are stimuli that an individual of a given species is highly likely to encounter in their environment and, importantly, that its sensory organs are able to detect. We humans detect specific frequencies of light and sound (but are completely oblivious to some that other animals detect, like infrared and ultraviolet light or infrasonic or ultrasound); exposure to these inputs during a particular time window is necessary for the visual and auditory cortices to develop normally.

The concept of a critical period for brain development was born in the 1960s, when future Nobel Laureates David Hubel and Torsten Wiesel were studying the visual system of the cat. They had already conducted landmark neurophysiological research describing the response properties of neurons across visual cortex. In particular, they had discovered that **primary visual cortex (V1)** is composed of **ocular dominance columns**, shown in Figure 5.3A. In this work, the researchers observed that many V1 neurons receiving retinal inputs (those in Layer 4, the input layer of the cortex) responded to stimulation of one eye but not the other, and that neurons responding to light flashed to a given eye were clustered together in alternating cortical columns. (Incidentally, it is because of these alternating columns, which look like stripes when visualized with a technique called autoradiography, that V1 got its alternate name, *striate cortex*.)

We now know that the *initial formation* of ocular dominance columns does not require visual input; rather, this organization emerges from a combination of molecular cues that roughly guide axons to different sites in the cortex, as well as from spontaneous patterns of brain activity that refine and maintain these separate cortical columns (Fair & Schlaggar, 2008). In other words, the basic formation of these columns is experience-independent. However, as we shall see below, Hubel and Wiesel showed that the *maintenance* (i.e., stabilization) of these columns is experience-expectant, in that it requires that both eyes receive visual stimulation in infancy, while the visual system is still developing.

Reflecting back on their initial foray into brain plasticity, Hubel later described a pivotal experiment involving **monocular deprivation** (depriving one eye of visual input):

By about 1962 ... [we] knew enough about the adult animal that we could ask direct questions aimed at learning whether the visual system was malleable. So Torsten Wiesel and I took a kitten a week old, when the eyes were just about to open, and sewed shut the lids of one eye. The procedure sounds harsh, but it was done under anesthesia and the kitten showed no signs of discomfort or distress when it woke up, back with its mother and littermates. After ten weeks we reopened the eye surgically, again under an anesthetic, and recorded from the kitten's cortex to learn whether the eye closure had had any effect on the eye or on the visual path [...] When we opened the lids of the kitten's eye, the eye itself seemed perfectly normal: the pupil even contracted normally when we shined a light into it. Recordings from the cortex, however, were anything but normal. (Hubel, 1988)

What Hubel and Wiesel discovered was that unexpectedly few neurons in the kitten's visual cortex responded to light flashed to the eye that had been deprived of visual input. Indeed, the ocular dominance columns corresponding to that eye were much narrower than those corresponding to the spared eye. The lack of input from the visually deprived eye led to a corresponding expansion of columns receiving information from the spared eye. Notably, the researchers observed a critical period for this effect: columnar contraction occurred only if monocular deprivation took place sometime between eye opening and three months of age, but not if it happened later (Wiesel & Hubel, 1963). They thus showed that ocular dominance columns in the visual cortex develop irreversibly: that is, once they are established, they remain in place. Their findings were important for understanding a type of visual loss called deprivation amblyopia that occurs in humans, and for understanding strabismus.

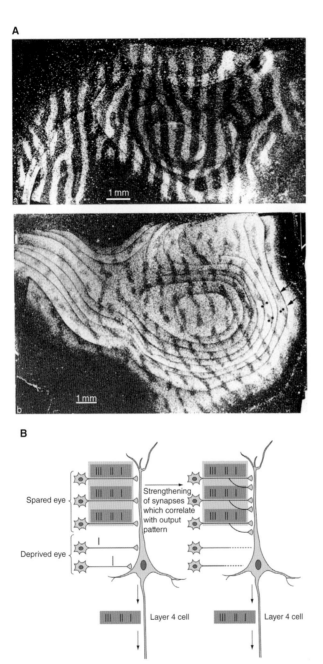

Figure 5.3 Experience-dependent plasticity in visual cortex.
A. Ocular dominance columns in Layer 4 of primary visual cortex (V1), visualized via autoradiography in a typically reared macaque (above) and a macaque who had experienced early monocular deprivation (below). Expansion of the cortical territory associated with the spared eye, shown in white, is visible in the lower image (Reprinted from Hubel & Wiesel, 1977).
B. Diagram depicting how monocular deprivation could lead to ocular dominance plasticity (Reprinted from Purves et al., 1997).

Hubel and Wiesel later showed systematically that healthy competition between inputs from both eyes to their respective visual cortical neurons led to maintenance of ocular dominance columns. In contrast, monocular deprivation resulted in a hostile takeover of sorts of the cortical territory corresponding to the deprived eye by that of the spared eye. As shown in Figure 5.3B, each Layer 4 visual cortical neuron receives input from multiple neurons in the **thalamus**, a deep-brain structure that transmits sensory inputs to the cortex in a spatially precise manner (see Chapter 6 for additional details). Some of these thalamic neurons relay signals from the left eye, and others from the right eye. If one eye is closed, associated thalamic neurons do not fire much, and therefore do not cause the postsynaptic neurons in visual cortex to fire as much as the neurons associated with the spared eye. Because the thalamic neurons from the spared eye drive visual cortical neurons more strongly, this results in strengthening of synapses between them (LTP) and, correspondingly, weakening of the synapses between thalamic neurons from the deprived eye and visual cortex (LTD). If deprivation takes place during the critical period, these changes lead to permanent expansion of columns in V1 associated with the spared eye.

5.3.3   Types of Structural Brain Changes

So far, we have talked mainly about how synapses between neurons are strengthened by neural activity, which in turn depends on external input. However, experiences can sculpt the brain in a variety of other ways as well. As Diamond showed when she documented experience-dependent changes not only in neurons but also in glial cells and vasculature, neurons aren't the only game in town. Figure 5.4 shows *ten classes* of brain changes observed at the cellular level.

Several of these classes of structural change involve neurons. One is **axon sprouting**, resulting in a presynaptic neuron making contact with a larger number of other neurons. A second is increased **dendritic branching** (or **arborization**) in the postsynaptic neuron, and consequently **synaptogenesis** – that is, the formation of new synapses ("genesis" means creation). Notice the larger dendrites, as well as the increased number of spines, which are depicted as red dots in Figure 5.4. If extensive enough, either of these types of changes could be detected as changes in cortical gray matter in a structural MRI scan. A third type is **neurogenesis** – the formation of new neurons – which does not happen on a mass scale after infancy (see Chapter 9 regarding the debate about adult hippocampal neurogenesis in humans). Changes at the neuronal level cannot be directly observed with MRI, but can be observed via other techniques, such as in animal models of plasticity.

Other possible neural changes include **myelination** of previously unmyelinated axons, as well as myelin remodeling – changes in the amount of myelin wrapped around an axon, as mentioned in Chapter 3. If dramatic enough, these changes can be detected as changes in white matter volume as measured via structural MRI, or as changes in white matter microstructure, as measured with diffusion-weighted imaging (a technique described in Chapter 2).

Non-neural forms of experience-dependent plasticity include an increase in the number and/ or size of **glial cells** (or glia). Glial cells are the unsung heroes of brain development and plasticity, as well as brain function (Barres, 2008). Of particular relevance to the current chapter are one type of glial cell called **astrocytes**, which regulate levels of neural activity as well as synapse formation and elimination. Perhaps not surprisingly, then, a disruption in signaling between

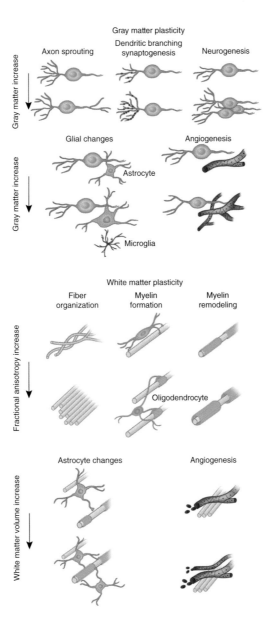

Figure 5.4 Ten classes of cellular changes in brain structure observed at the cellular level. (Adapted from Zatorre, 2012)

glial cells and neurons is thought to play a key role in several neurodevelopmental disorders: Autism Spectrum Disorders, schizophrenia, and epilepsy (Chung et al., 2015). As it turns out, glia are highly plastic, showing changes in structure in the minutes and hours following heightened activity of neighboring neurons (Zhou et al., 2019). Such changes could perhaps account for, or contribute to, gray matter changes observed with structural MRI (see Section 5.5). Astrocytes also promote **angiogenesis**, or the formation of new blood vessels. As neural tissue becomes more active, astrocytes orchestrate the sprouting of small blood vessels to bring extra oxygenated blood to the area. Increased vasculature and associated increases in blood flow could help account for experience-dependent changes in activation observed via fMRI. All in all, experiences can trigger a variety of cellular changes in the brain that might or might not be detected – and whose sources are difficult to tease apart – at the macroscopic level. Thus, animal research on brain plasticity provides insights that we cannot glean from brain imaging in humans.

5.4   Cortical Reorganization under Sensory Deprivation

We have seen in Chapter 4 that ontogeny of the cortex is genetically specified, but that its actual development is the product of a complex series of self-organizing steps that include receipt of input from other parts of the brain. In the case of a sensory region, a substantial portion of the input comes from the body by way of the thalamus. What happens to a sensory region if it no longer receives – or has never received – typical (experience-expectant) thalamic input? One might think that it would simply be dormant, or that it may even atrophy (just as a muscle atrophies if it is no longer stimulated by motor neurons). Instead, it can actually be *co-opted* for other functions.

As we have seen with ocular dominance columns (Figure 5.3), there is robust competition for cortical real estate: if neurons in a particular cortical area are not being stimulated by what would ordinarily have been the dominant inputs to that area, they will form stronger connections with neurons from neighboring regions. Indeed, the cellular structure of the cortex is quite similar from region to region, and can take on different functions depending on its inputs. The cortex has even been called **pluripotent** (in Latin, *pluri* means several, and *potent* = able to). In other words, it can take on a variety of functions, depending on the inputs that have honed it during development (Bedny, 2017). Below, we will discuss cortical reorganization in response to several forms of sensory deprivation.

5.4.1   Somatosensory Deprivation: The Case of the Phantom Limb

A vivid demonstration of cortical takeover can be found in the realm of **somatosensation**, or the sense of touch, through which we can perceive a cut on the ankle or the wind caressing our forearm. The somatosensory cortex takes projections from the skin, tongue, and internal organs and maps them onto its cortical surface, forming a **topographic** map of the body (Penfield & Rasmussen, 1950). Of particular interest here is the **phantom limb** phenomenon, whereby a patient who has had an extremity amputated has the sensation that it is still part of the body – often experiencing pain in a part of the body that is no longer there (Ramachandran & Hirstein, 1998). This occurs because the cortical real estate that was devoted to that limb still exists, and remapping of neuronal projections takes time.

A famous example of phantom limb pain was provided by the British naval commander Admiral Nelson, who was shot in combat in 1797 and had to have part of his arm amputated. For the rest of his life, he experienced pain that felt as though it was emanating from the missing arm, including the distinct feeling of his non-existent nails digging into the palm of his non-existent hand. (Incidentally, he interpreted this sensation, divorced from the body, as evidence of the existence of the soul.)

Roughly two centuries later, Jon Kaas, Michael Merzenich, and other neuroscientists, studying plasticity in somatosensory cortex in rodents and macaques, provided a plausible explanation for phantom limb pain: the takeover of the newly unused cortical tissue by thalamic neurons carrying signals from other parts of the body. Because we rely on the topographic map of our body in somatosensory cortex to localize sensations on the body, the sensation associated with stimulation of thalamic neurons that have encroached on the unused territory could now be misperceived as emanating from the missing limb.

Neurologist V. S. Ramachandran has provided compelling evidence of this account based on his work with patients, such as Patient V.Q.: a 17-year-old who, four weeks previously, had undergone amputation of part of his left arm as a result of a car accident, and who now experienced a phantom hand attached to the stump of his arm (Ramachandran et al., 1992). Ramachandran and his colleagues explored V.Q.'s sensory experience through a clever form of clinical examination. The researchers asked him to close his eyes, and then stroked different parts of his body with a cotton swab and asked him to report what he felt. When they stroked his left cheek, he reported feeling stimulation of that cheek – but also, at the same time, a tingling sensation in his phantom left thumb. When they stroked right below that (i.e., just above the left side of his mouth), he felt a tingling on his left pinky or index finger, respectively. By systematically stroking different parts of his face across two separate visits, the investigators were able to show that V.Q.'s phantom limb was now represented in a stable, topographic manner on his face. There were sharp boundaries between areas representing different parts of the phantom hand. Given the solid base of neuroscientific evidence on topographic maps and neuronal competition, we can infer that this patient's phantom hand must have resulted from cortical expansion of the somatosensory area devoted to his face.

This remarkable example of sensory remapping occurred within days or weeks of amputation. In some cases, phantom limb sensations fade after a few days; in others, like Admiral Nelson's, they persist for decades. Why? There are likely a variety of factors at play, but a large study sample would be needed to explore them further (Ramachandran & Hirstein, 1998), and phantom limb pain is relatively rare, making it difficult to identify participants. It also bears mentioning that this cortical plasticity occurred well beyond the early developmental period during which the somatosensory maps are first formed – giving us even more evidence that brain plasticity can continue throughout the lifespan. But, as we shall see below, cortical reorganization can be even more dramatic if it occurs during a critical period of development.

5.4.2 Visual Deprivation: Congenital Blindness

Visual cortex makes up a large part of the primate brain, so deprivation of visual stimulation can leave a substantial amount of cortex available for other uses. What happens to V1 in an individual who is blind from birth, thereby missing the critical period for experience-expectant plasticity triggered by visual input? Researchers have used fMRI to examine the response properties of V1 in congenitally blind individuals, finding that they engage this region on a range of cognitive tasks, such as those that require language comprehension, working memory, or mental arithmetic (Bedny, 2017). Marina Bedny and colleagues scanned congenitally blind adults and compared them to adults who lost sight later in life and sighted adults while

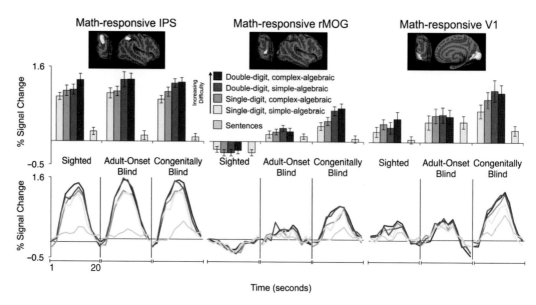

Figure 5.5 Effects of early visual deprivation on the activation of V1 during performance of arithmetic calculations. A cluster of voxels in V1 exhibited stronger activation, across all participants, on the math tasks than the language tasks. The fMRI timeseries shows activation in V1 on the math conditions, separately for three groups of adults: sighted, adult-onset blind, and congenitally blind. Progressively darker lines indicate more and more difficult arithmetic problems. (Reprinted from Kanjlia et al., 2019)

each performed math and language tasks involving auditorily presented stimuli (Kanjlia et al., 2019). In the math task, participants heard two algebraic equations, one after the other (e.g., $5 - 4 = x$; $3 - 2 = x$) and were asked whether the variable x had the same value in the two equations. There were four math conditions, which varied in difficulty in two ways: first, they involved either single-digit or double-digit numbers, and second, they involved either simple algebraic expressions (e.g., $7 - 3 = x$) or more complex ones (e.g., $x - 3 = 7$). In the language task, participants heard two sentences, one presented in the active voice and the other in the passive voice, and were asked if the two meanings were the same.

The brain image in Figure 5.5 shows a large cluster of voxels in V1 that was more active on the math task than the language task across all participants. The investigators looked more closely at the BOLD activation pattern for V1 for each of the three groups of participants. In the right-hand panel, we can see that the congenitally blind participants showed stronger V1 responses for the math tasks than either the sighted or adult-onset blind participants. Upon closer inspection, we also see that the V1 response is more strongly modulated by task difficulty in the congenitally blind participants, a conclusion borne out by statistical tests.

These results demonstrate that, for adults deprived of visual input from birth, activation in V1 increases as a function of cognitive demands in a way that parallels what we see in higher-order cortical areas (i.e., lateral parietal and prefrontal cortices), whose role in working memory is discussed in Chapter 9. In other words, it appears that this cortical tissue has been co-opted as an additional workspace for maintaining and/or manipulating mental representations of number! How is this possible? To understand this, it is important to know that the visual cortex not only receives projections from the visual part of the thalamus, but also receives many projections from higher-order cortical areas. In the absence of visual stimulation during the critical period for visual development via the thalamus, inputs from these higher cognitive areas appear to dominate and shape the emerging function of this region.

5.4.3 Auditory Deprivation: Congenital Deafness and Cochlear Implantation

As with congenital blindness, **congenital deafness** affects a child's development by eliminating another source of sensory information: hearing. The most common reason for congenital deafness is a problem with the conveyance of sound from the inner ear to the brain, either due to damage to the tiny hair cells in the **cochlea** – the coiled structure shown in Figure 5.6 – or to the **auditory nerve**, shown in yellow, which leads from the cochlea to the brain. Auditory nerve damage, or **sensorineural hearing loss**, normally affects both ears. Congenital sensorineural hearing loss can result from premature birth, maternal diabetes, lack of oxygen during birth, a genetic condition, or an infectious disease passed from the mother to child in the womb. The incidence of neonatal hearing loss is 1.1 per 1,000 infants in the United States and has a prevalence of 3.1 percent among children and adolescents (Mehra et al., 2009). This makes hearing loss the fourth most common developmental disorder in the United States.

Some hearing parents opt to learn sign language in order to communicate with their deaf children; others get their deaf children a **cochlear implant (CI)**. A CI is an electronic device that processes incoming sounds and bypasses the inner ear to directly stimulate the auditory nerve, as shown in Figure 5.6. Cochlear implantation has become the most widely used brain–machine interface, and is the most successful intervention for total sensory function loss (Prochazka, 2017). The device has both internal and external components that work together. First, sound energy is picked up by a behind-the-ear microphone/speech processor, which filters, analyzes, and converts the sound energy into a digital code. This signal is sent through the skin via radio frequency to a receiver/stimulator embedded under the scalp, which then distributes that signal along an array of tiny electrodes surgically placed inside the cochlea.

The **basilar membrane** runs along the length of the (coiled up) cochlea and has been likened to a prism: the wide range of frequencies that accompany most sounds – speech, music, environmental noises, and so on – are dispersed along the basilar membrane into different locations. Frequency-selective cells, tuned to specific frequencies, thus represent the range of frequencies from low to high, like a piano keyboard. (This frequency map is called a **tonotopic map** (Chapter 6).) The basilar membrane then passes on precise frequency information to the auditory cortex. In humans, the basilar membrane consists of approximately 3,500 of these frequency selective cells (Oxenham, 2018), and yet most CIs consist of only 12–24 electrodes, CIs don't convey sound with the same degree of richness or resolution as an intact cochlea. If an individual loses their hearing as an adult, they can learn to understand speech and environmental noises, but often only with great effort. The power of youthful neuroplasticity is that when CIs are implanted before the age of 2.5 or so, the chance that recipients will find them beneficial is much higher, but still not perfect. Cochlear implants are not the miracle cure that some YouTube videos make them out to be (Cooper, 2019). They can improve hearing in most cases,

Figure 5.6 Cross-section showing how a cochlear implant transmits sound to the brain. (Reprinted from Kral, 2013)

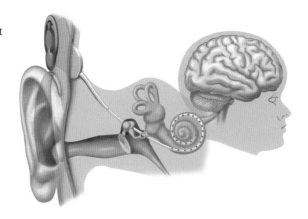

but are often not sufficient to restore full communication with others. Whether CIs alone, sign language alone, or the combination of both yields the best results remains controversial (Geers et al., 2017; Hall et al., 2019).

Continued advances in cochlear implantation technology and surgical techniques have enabled deaf and hard-of-hearing people of all ages to achieve a good level of speech understanding, whether their hearing loss is congenital or acquired. The intervention has been particularly impactful for congenitally deaf infants and young children, as surgery has been approved for younger and younger ages. In 2020, the United States Food and Drug Administration (FDA) approved some forms of implantation in children as young as 9 months based on the results of clinical studies and increasing awareness that significant perceptual tuning in normal-hearing infants takes place across the first year of life (Miyamoto et al., 2018). Early implantation maximizes auditory benefits of the device (Silva et al., 2017). However, language outcomes are highly variable – particularly for children who became deaf before learning language. Systematic research in animal models of deafness (Yusuf et al., 2017) and in humans (Chen & Oghalai, 2016; Benchetrit et al., 2021) has determined that a range of factors contribute to the quality of both hearing and language outcomes, including age of hearing loss – and corresponding effects of prior auditory experience – duration of implant use, whether hearing loss is unilateral or bilateral, facility with perceptual learning, and exposure to a fluent manual (sign) language. Animal models likewise show variable plasticity depending on time of implantation (see Box 5.1).

While many children can and do learn to use the implant's signal to acquire age-appropriate language skills (Fitzpatrick, 2015), better understanding of the mechanisms underlying the variability in language outcomes for human implant users is of significant clinical importance. Using a portable signal processor and consistent stimulation using ambient natural sounds paired with auditory training, congenitally deaf cats show notable cortical responsivity and reorganization following implantation that takes place early in life (see Kral & Lomber, 2015). As can be seen in Figure 5.7, responsivity in an area of primary auditory cortex expanded given consistent stimulation from an early implant. In contrast, later implantation produced far less responsivity.

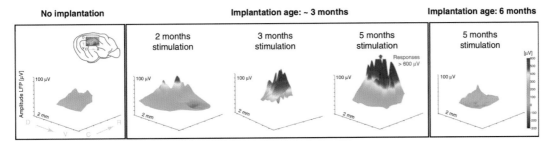

Figure 5.7 Maps of activity in the primary auditory cortex of congenitally deaf cats implanted early and late. The panel on the far left shows the area from which electrophysiological measurements were taken. The middle panel shows responsivity in that area in deaf cats implanted early. The panel on the far right shows comparable measures in animals implanted late. (Reprinted from Kral et al., 2019)

Box 5.1 Cross-Modal Cortical Plasticity Following Congenital Sensory Deprivation

Increasing evidence has demonstrated the impressive ability of the brain to rewire its components as a function of experience. Recognizing the dynamic nature of cortical circuitry is crucial to understanding how the nervous system adapts after sensory deprivation. Many studies have demonstrated that deafness or blindness leads to massive cross-modal recruitment of the cortices deprived of their natural inputs (Bavelier & Neville 2002). Importantly, these neuroplastic changes are believed to be the underlying cause of superior abilities in the remaining modalities of sensory-deprived individuals.

Lomber et al. (2010) found evidence for this hypothesis regarding superior abilities in congenitally deaf cats (Kral & Lomber, 2015), and further demonstrated that specific regions in the deaf auditory cortex are responsible for distinct aspects of enhanced visual performances. The study first showed that congenitally deaf cats performed better than hearing controls in specific visual psychophysical tests. Specifically, deaf cats had superior localization abilities within the peripheral visual field and lower visual movement detection thresholds.

In a second set of experiments aimed at pinpointing the neural mechanisms underlying this phenomenon, different portions of the auditory cortices of both groups of animals were reversibly deactivated using cooling loops (Lomber et al., 2010). These experiments demonstrated that the superior performance in peripheral visual field localization and motion detection were separately and selectively altered in the deaf cats when specific portions of posterior or dorsal auditory cortex, respectively, were transiently deactivated (Box Figure 5.1A). Essentially, a visual double dissociation was identified in what would normally be auditory cortex: while deactivation of posterior auditory field (PAF) altered peripheral localization performance without affecting motion detection thresholds, deactivation of the dorsal zone (DZ) of auditory cortex resulted in the opposite profile. Importantly, none of these manipulations altered visual performance in the hearing cats.

The neural basis for the enhanced visual localization skills of the deaf cats can be ascribed to the PAF. In hearing cats, PAF is involved in the accurate localization of acoustic stimuli. Thus, in deafness, PAF maintains a role in localization – albeit in visual rather than acoustic localization. These intriguing results demonstrate that cross-modal plasticity can substitute one sensory modality for another, while maintaining the functional repertoire of the reorganized region.

Box 5.1 (cont.)

A

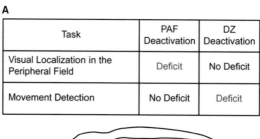

Task	PAF Deactivation	DZ Deactivation
Visual Localization in the Peripheral Field	Deficit	No Deficit
Movement Detection	No Deficit	Deficit

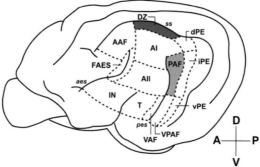

B

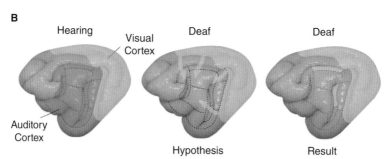

Box Figure 5.1 Example of cross-modal cortical plasticity. A. Summary diagram illustrating the double dissociation of visual functions in auditory cortex of the deaf cat. Bilateral deactivation of PAF, but not DZ, results in the loss of enhanced visual localization in the far periphery. On the other hand, bilateral deactivation of DZ, but not PAF, results in higher movement detection thresholds. (Adapted from Lomber et al., 2010). B. An illustration of the effects of auditory deprivation on visual pathways. In the hearing brain, large regions of the cerebral cortex in hearing subjects are dedicated to processing visual (yellow) or acoustic (orange) information. Dashed lines show individual areas within auditory cortex. In congenitally deaf subjects, visual inputs are theorized to invade (yellow arrows) deaf auditory cortex. (Adapted from Lomber, 2017)

   This study arguably provides one of the most complete and convincing demonstrations that congenital sensory deprivation induces functionally specific cross-modal changes in the cerebral cortex, resulting in superior visual perceptual abilities in the congenitally deaf (Box Figure 5.1B). These cross-modal effects do not occur uniformly across regions of deaf cortex, but principally occur in an adaptive fashion in those regions whose functions are also represented in the replacement modality. Likewise, cross-modal compensatory effects are specific and appear to enhance those functions that the deprived and replacement modalities hold in common. Ultimately, these considerations are important when evaluating the potential for compensatory forms of cross-modal plasticity resulting from any form of sensory loss.

Contributed by Stephen G. Lomber, PhD, Canada Research Chair in Brain Plasticity and Development, Department of Physiology, McGill University.

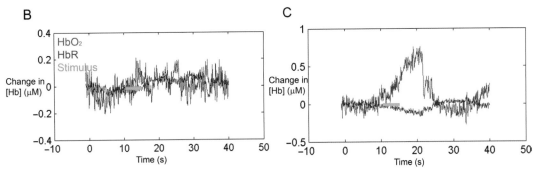

Figure 5.8 fNIRS study examining the effect of cochlear implantation on brain responses to auditory stimulation. A. Example of an early fNIRS array used to measure blood concentration changes in pediatric cochlear implant users on the day of implant activation. B. Prior to activation of a child's implant, auditory stimulation (green bar) produced no change in oxygenated (red trace) or deoxygenated (blue trace) hemoglobin concentrations. C. Following initial activation, auditory stimulation delivered via the implant evoked an increase in oxygenated hemoglobin and a corresponding decrease in deoxygenated hemoglobin. (Reprinted from Bortfeld, 2019).

These findings from laboratory animals guided the search for a similar critical period biomarker in deaf humans. Similar differences were observed in EEG responses collected from congenitally deaf children fitted with cochlear implants across a wide range of ages (i.e., 1–17 years) confirming the importance of early implantation (Ponton & Eggermont, 2001) and making the central auditory evoked potential (CAEP) a primary indicator of the malleability of auditory pathways in deaf children hearing through a cochlear implant. As can be seen in Figure 5.8, fNIRS has since been introduced as a tool for measuring hemodynamic indicators of auditory processing in children following cochlear implantation (Sevy et al., 2010). Up until only recently, people with cochlear implants could not be imaged using fMRI, because of the ferromagnetic components of the implantation. Thus, fNIRS opened up an exciting approach to tracking changes in cortical hemodynamics in both pediatric and adult implant users, and clinical application of fNIRS has increased, with cortical responsivity serving as a guide to device programming in the service of improving speech and language outcomes (e.g., Anderson et al., 2019).

The question of whether or not to receive a cochlear implant has become politicized. Many deaf individuals feel that there is nothing "broken" about them that requires fixing, and they fear the loss of deaf culture. Accordingly, they perceive cochlear implantation as an effort by members of hearing culture to impose their own societal norms on a group of people who are perfectly happy and accepting of who they are. There are complex arguments on both sides of the issue which are not just scientific issues, but cultural and ethical ones about individual autonomy and the role of the state (see, e.g., Cooper, 2019; Maia, 2020).

5.5   Experience-Dependent Plasticity

As we have discussed, experience-dependent brain plasticity refers to the ways in which our unique experiences subtly shape our brains over time. The things we do, or are exposed to, repeatedly over the course of many months or years leave a lasting trace – for better and for worse. Although there is not a specific critical period during which such protracted experiences affect the brain, and each neural system is thought to be maximally plastic at different times in development, we can nevertheless conclude that experience-dependent brain plasticity is more prominent in infancy and early childhood than in adulthood. Below we will discuss two ways in which researchers have examined how the brain changes in response to intensive practice.

5.5.1   Musical Training

Learning to play a musical instrument requires years of practice: it is an immersive experience that involves coordination between auditory, visual, somatosensory, and motor systems, not to mention memory, categorization, and emotional systems (Schlaug, 2015). It is therefore reasonable to wonder whether or how musical training shapes the brain, and whether there is a sensitive period for musical development; after all, most concert musicians began playing their instrument when they were very young. MRI studies comparing musicians with non-musicians have reported a number of structural and functional differences between them, including – but by no means limited to – auditory regions and the part of **primary motor cortex** that controls hand and finger movements (Schlaug, 2015; Wenger et al., 2021). Indeed, differences between groups have been reported throughout the brain; this stands to reason, as many neural systems are involved in playing music.

In interpreting these findings, however, we must keep in mind that musicians – and the adults who enrolled them in music lessons – likely differ from non-musicians in one or more ways: higher musical aptitude, a more musical or nurturing home environment, a more strictly regimented childhood, more access to music lessons, and so on (Wesseldijk et al., 2021). Likewise, individuals who started their musical training earlier in life may differ in other ways from those who started later. Therefore, it is hard to know whether *all* of these neural differences reflect differences in musical training, specifically. A more compelling study design compared pairs of identical twins in which only one of the two siblings actively played a keyboard instrument (piano, organ, keyboard; de Manzano & Ullén, 2018). Although a clever study design, the sample for this study is too small to allow us to draw firm conclusions: it turns out to be difficult to find monozygotic twins in which one learned to play a musical instrument and the other did not.

Even assuming that observed brain differences between groups are related to musical practices, which is not a given, such studies do not address the chicken-and-egg problem: did practicing an instrument lead to brain changes over time, or were there preexisting differences in the brain that predisposed some individuals to become musicians? The answer is likely to be both of these things. Unfortunately, cross-sectional group comparisons (i.e., in which comparisons of the brains of musicians and non-musicians are made at a single timepoint) do not lend themselves to exploring when and how musical experience shapes the brain. This is a fascinating and clinically relevant topic of research (Pantev & Herholz, 2011), but to address it properly we need to examine whether or how the brain changes over time as individuals – in particular children – learn an instrument.

In one study, Elisabeth Wenger, Simone Kühn, Ulman Lindenberger and colleagues tested for changes in cortical gray matter and resting-state functional connectivity across multiple timepoints, comparing aspiring musicians undergoing professional training in one of various instruments to individuals who play music as a hobby (Wenger et al., 2021). The researchers observed a preexisting difference in gray matter volume between the two groups in several of the same brain regions as in prior studies. More importantly, however, they observed differential structural and functional changes in the two groups across three scanning sessions over a 6-month period. Most notably, the aspiring musicians, but not the musical hobbyists, showed a subtle decrease in gray matter volume in the **planum polare**. This is an auditory region adjacent to primary auditory cortex that has been implicated in musical processing in several fMRI studies. You may be surprised that they saw a decrease rather than an increase in gray matter volume; the next section may explain why.

Seeking to test for brain network changes involving the planum polare, Wenger and colleagues used the planum polare as a seed region for resting-state functional connectivity analysis, see Chapter 2 for details on this approach to fMRI research. This approach revealed that the aspiring musicians (but not the hobbyists) showed an increase in connectivity between the planum polare and a number of other brain regions over the course of their training! Hopefully, future researchers will build on these intriguing findings, examining whether they relate to changes in musical proficiency – and adopt the same approach to study the initial phase of musical learning over time in young children.

5.5.2   Dynamics of Plasticity across Skill-Learning

Teaching individuals a novel motor skill in the laboratory is a particularly well-controlled way to study brain plasticity. After all, in this way we can know exactly what, and how much, instruction and practice each individual is getting, and the experience can be standardized across participants. Further, the motor system, unlike, say, conceptual learning, is so clearly delineated and well-characterized that we know where in the brain to look for to find experience-dependent changes. Indeed, there is a rich literature on motor plasticity; however, the vast majority of these studies (and other brain imaging studies of experience-dependent brain plasticity) have two time-points: prior to and immediately following an intervention. One notable exception is a study (Wenger, Kühn et al., 2017) whose results demonstrate that testing for changes at multiple time-points over the course of the intervention can reveal effects that might otherwise go unnoticed.

A common prediction in MRI studies of brain plasticity is an increase in gray matter over the course of training. However, sometimes learning leads to a decrease in gray matter, as we saw above in the study of musical training; sometimes it leads to an increase in white matter tracts. Many times, of course, it leads to no change at all in a given region; thus, it is necessary to examine the trajectory of change *during* learning, rather than simply looking at the end-points (Wenger, Brozzoli et al., 2017). As justification, these researchers cite evidence in the animal literature of initial expansion of cortical maps in response to training, which is then followed by partial renormalization. The **Expansion-Renormalization Model** of plasticity and learning (Reed et al., 2011) is based on findings that learning is associated with overproduction of dendritic spines, some of which are subsequently eliminated. This "overshoot" is theorized to allow for the creation of more efficient connections. On this view, cortical map expansion does not lead to improved behavioral performance in and of itself; rather, it is a mechanism that supports the fine-tuning of neural circuitry that underlies behavior.

The Expansion-Renormalization Model of plasticity has been expanded to the context of human learning and structural MRI measurements (Wenger, Brozzoli et al., 2017). Figure 5.9A illustrates, in theory, how learning could progress over the course of training – rising and ultimately stabilizing – and how associated changes in gray matter volume need not mirror these changes precisely, but rather rise during skill acquisition and fall thereafter. At the microscopic level, these non-linear gray matter volume changes could reflect increased dendritic arborization and axon sprouting, followed by stabilization of efficient neural connections and pruning (elimination) of excess synapses. Additionally, or alternatively, these volumetric changes could reflect proliferation and activation of glial cells, followed by partial renormalization.

Drawing on this framework, Wenger and colleagues sought to test whether intensive motor training in humans would result in an initial increase and subsequent decrease in gray matter volume in motor-related regions. They conducted dense sampling by scanning a group of 15 adult participants up to 18 times each over the course of 7 weeks. During this time, the participants practiced drawing and writing with their non-dominant (left) hand for 30 to 45 minutes per day. As shown in Figure 5.9B, the intervention included exercises that required tracing outlines and writing words on a tablet computer as precisely as possible.

Wenger and colleagues compared gray matter volume changes at pre-training, the training mid-point (Week 4), and post-training to a group of controls who were given no special tasks,

A

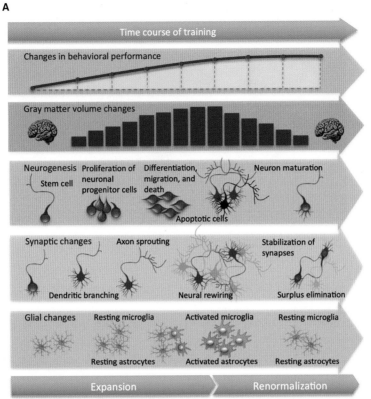

B

Figure 5.9 The Expansion-Renormalization Model of brain plasticity.
A. Schematic of changes at multiple levels, from behavioral improvements
to macroscale changes (gray matter volume) to cellular (neural and glial)
changes. (Adapted from Wenger, Brozzoli et al., 2017) B. Drawing and
[writ]ing exercises undertaken with the non-dominant hand in a motor
[learnin]g study. C. Non-linear changes in gray matter volume observed
[over] weeks of training in right motor cortex. (Adapted from Wenger,
[...] 2017)

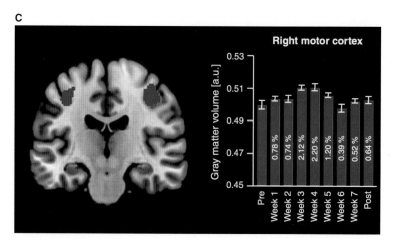

Fig. 5.9 (cont.)

and who were also scanned at the same time intervals. At Week 4, just over halfway through the experiment, participants in the motor training group exhibited larger gray matter volume than controls in left and right primary motor cortices. This difference was not observed prior to training, nor was it observed three weeks later! Looking more closely at changes over time in the experimental group in Figure 5.9C, we see a rise and fall in gray matter in right motor cortex, which controls left hand movements.

Notably, if the investigators had only collected data pre- and post-training, as most others do, they would have concluded that there was *no change* in gray matter as a result of motor training. This leaves us wondering: how many instances of gray matter plasticity have failed to be detected in studies involving the standard pre-/post-intervention design? These results provide initial support for the Expansion-Normalization Model of plasticity in humans, at least at the macroscopic level. This type of dense sampling MRI study has not been conducted in children — either in motor learning or any other domain — so we have yet to discover how the magnitude and trajectory of change compares to what we might see in children as they are first learning to write with their dominant hand. (Maybe you will be the one who conducts this study as you continue your training.)

5.6   Timing of Plasticity

The brain displays functional plasticity at all ages, meaning that there is some degree of age independence. Historically, however, the concept of age-based plasticity implied that adaptive functional responses of the immature brain were greater than those of the mature brain. However, data on age-based functional plasticity are mixed. Early neural connections tend to be somewhat transient, and recruitment of brain regions with transient rather than stable connections seems to provide a mechanism of functional reorganization for parts of the immature brain. On the other hand, factors other than age often distinguish brain injuries in children and adults, complicating comparisons made between child and adult brain injuries. Because plasticity is variably observed in recovery of function following brain insult at least in part as a function of age, the topic merits further exploration.

5.6.1 Recovery from Brain Injury

A disconcerting number of children incur brain damage from traumatic brain injury, neuropsychological procedures, or strokes (nearly 500,000 per year in the United States alone; Frieden et al., 2015). Some patients with **pediatric acquired brain injury** have excellent long-term outcomes, while others have lifelong cognitive and/or behavioral difficulties. The most extraordinary cases of recovery of function after early brain injury are those of a subset of children who have had an entire hemisphere of their brain removed. This most extreme form of treatment, **hemispherectomy**, is undertaken only in the most severe cases of epilepsy that haven't responded to other treatments; indeed, it is becoming obsolete as more benign surgical approaches (including intracranial implants) have been developed. Nevertheless, these are cases from which we can learn much: although children who have undergone full hemispherectomy often have enduring cognitive and motor difficulties, in some cases they are not as dramatic as one would expect, often at least partially attributable to the seizure disorder itself. In fact, the cognitive and motor development of patients with brain injury depends on a complex interplay between factors related to the location, type, severity, and timing of the injury, along with environmental and genetic factors that influence brain plasticity and development.

It is often assumed that patients who incur brain injury early in development are far more likely to recover than those who incur such damage later in life. This idea is often referred to as the **Kennard Principle**, after a series of experiments conducted by Margaret Kennard involving lesions to motor cortex in young primates (Finger, 1999). Lesion studies in rodents also support the idea that earlier damage is better. Reparative changes occur in rats who have undergone perinatal lesions, including synaptogenesis – and even the birth of new neurons – if the damage takes place at the height of neurogenesis (Kolb & Teskey, 2012). In humans, some of the evidence supporting this idea comes from the observation that a patient who suffers a prenatal or perinatal lesion (i.e., a lesion incurred just before or shortly after birth) in left-hemisphere regions associated with language processing can show quite remarkable recovery via functional reorganization of the cortex, with the right hemisphere taking over more of this function. Joan Stiles and colleagues have followed such children over time and found that they can, after a few years, catch up to their peers in terms of language development (Stiles et al., 2005). By contrast, an elderly adult who suffers a stroke in a similar brain region might never fully recover linguistic abilities (Dronkers et al., 2007; Stefaniak et al., 2020).

In adulthood, there are two important challenges that limit brain plasticity. The first is a structural constraint: it is simply harder to modify a system once the foundation is firmly in place. Think of it this way: if you want a sunnier bedroom, it's harder to enlarge the windows than it would have been to make this change when your apartment was first being built. The second challenge is that there are mechanisms in the adult brain that actively prevent plasticity, so-called **molecular brakes** (see Section 5.6.3), driven in part by genetic constraints. In adults, pharmacological interventions and electrical brain stimulation are used to try to remove these brakes and boost plasticity after injury (Kolb & Teskey, 2012).

5.6.2   Earlier Is Not Always Better for Recovery from Brain Injury

Contrary to the Kennard Principle that behavioral outcomes are better following earlier rather than later brain injury, a growing body of evidence suggests that brain injury occurring early in development does not *necessarily* lead to a better outcome than brain injury later in life – and could in some cases lead to a worse outcome. Hebb made this preliminary observation early on with respect to intellectual functioning (Hebb, 1942), and it has since been borne out by larger, more systematic studies. Coming back to hemispherectomy patients, there is some evidence of better intellectual outcomes when the surgery was conducted later in childhood, once the patients had acquired important developmental milestones (e.g., Samargia & Kimberley, 2009; Althausen et al., 2013).

Similarly, in research focused on focal (as opposed to diffuse, i.e., widespread) brain injuries, Anderson et al. (2010) found that brain injury before three years of age produced broad deficits in *higher cognitive functions*, specifically, in working memory and executive functions (discussed in Chapters 9 and 12). These functions depend on a brain network, involving **prefrontal cortex**, that has a very long developmental time course. Damaging the prefrontal cortex early in its development is now thought to be particularly harmful. Quoting Kolb and Teskey (who drew an analogy to explain a specific finding in the rodent literature), "One way to think about the difference in outcome is to think of the effects of damaging a plant just as it emerges from the ground versus somewhat later when it is trimmed. In the former case the plants are likely to die, or at least be stunted in growth" (Kolb & Teskey, 2012, p. 316). Another way to think about it is as a *snowball effect*: higher-level brain regions like prefrontal cortex are essential for learning; therefore, even minor deficits in their functions early on in development could lead to a reduced ability to acquire new skills, thereby leading to more and more severe deficits over time in comparison with peers (Hebb, 1942; Anderson et al., 2005). Thus, when it comes to late-developing higher cognitive functions – albeit not lower-level ones like motor control, or even speech – early brain injury can have a particularly severe impact. Because different brain systems have different developmental trajectories, and are differentially involved in scaffolding the development of other brain systems, it stands to reason that the site of injury would determine the optimal window for plasticity.

5.6.3   Multiple Windows of Plasticity across the Brain

As we have seen, the common assumption that brain plasticity simply declines across development is an oversimplification. The emerging view can be summarized by quoting Ecclesiastes (or The Byrds): "to everything there is a season (turn, turn turn) … a time to be born, and a time to die; a time to plant, and a time to pluck up that which is planted; a time to kill, and a time to heal; a time to break down, and a time to build up." (This song, recorded in 1959, is an oldie but a goodie.)

Put another way, each brain network has a different time window of maximal potential for plasticity – a period of heightened vulnerability *and* opportunity – that depends on its developmental time course. This idea is supported by research in rodents indicating that peak brain plasticity occurs at different times in different cortical areas (Reh et al., 2020). Figure 5.10A

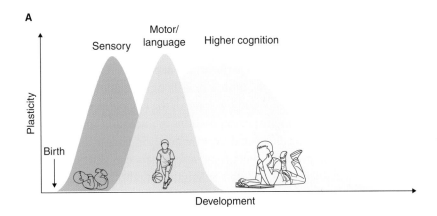

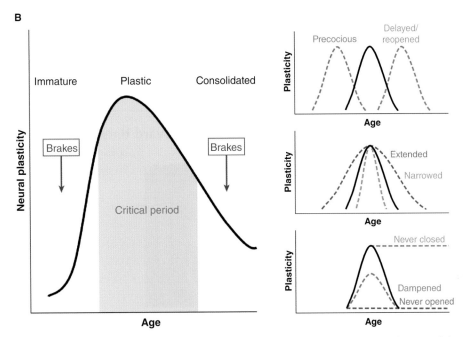

Figure 5.10 Critical periods of brain plasticity. A. Hypothetical illustration of sequential periods of peak brain plasticity across neurocognitive systems. B. Illustrations of the windows of critical period plasticity over development. In typical development, molecular brakes prevent the onset of plasticity, and also shut it off. Various pharmacological and non-pharmacological manipulations can alter this period. (Reprinted from Werker & Hensch, 2015).

plots hypothesized windows of plasticity across different brain regions for child development (although note that this is not exactly the same sequence as has been proposed for mice). Something to ponder is whether this framework helps to make sense of the work on recovery from brain injury at different ages, and the studies examining plasticity after congenital deafness or blindness (Section 5.4).

Importantly, as Takao Hensch (featured in Box 5.2) notes, there isn't some "plasticity factor" that simply decays over time. Rather, the closing of a critical period is an *active* process, involving the molecular brakes we mentioned above, as well as structural factors such as the growth of myelin (McGee et al., 2005) and **perineuronal nets** (Bavelier et al., 2010). Hensch's and others' research in sensory cortices in the mouse reveals tight regulation of the opening, maintenance, and closure of critical periods. We know some of the key molecular and cellular players involved because various pharmacological manipulations in mice (and some non-pharmacological ones), can alter these windows, as illustrated hypothetically in Figure 5.10B. With drugs that affect the production of specific proteins in neurons, researchers can shift the onset of the critical period earlier or later in development, shorten or lengthen it, abolish or dampen it, or even prevent the period from closing (Werker & Hensch, 2015). Such mechanisms are not only at play in rodents: there is evidence – as predicted based on the mouse research – that prenatal exposure to a common class of antidepressants (i.e., selective serotonin reuptake inhibitors) can alter the timing of a critical period for speech discrimination in infants (Weikum et al., 2012)! This is a remarkable set of findings that is worth revisiting after we learn about language development in Chapter 8.

Box 5.2 Scientist Spotlight on Takao Hensch (Harvard University)

Takao Hensch (Box Figure 5.2) is Professor of Molecular Cellular Biology at the Harvard University Center for Brain Science and in Neurology at Harvard Medical School. Hensch's lab studies how early experience shapes brain development, probing the cellular and molecular mechanisms that govern the opening and closure of critical periods of brain plasticity.

Growing up in a multicultural home, I often wondered how my brain differed from all my friends who didn't share this exposure. My motivation to understand the early impacts of experience on the brain thus arose from trying to find out more about myself. At that time, the first wave of interest in AI ("expert systems") was booming, and the prescient possibility that machines might simulate brain function was raised. In my first summer internship at IBM, I plunged into natural language processing – but in college soon realized how little we actually understood the way the brain works. I switched into biology, with the hope of someday returning to AI. The studies of Hubel and Wiesel, Nobel Laureates a few years earlier were deeply inspiring, and I soon became their scientific grandchild.

In those years through the '80s and early '90s, brain research focused on plastic processes at synapses, like long-term potentiation (LTP) and depression (LTD). Elegant studies in the cerebellum, hippocampus, and neocortex left little doubt that excitatory connections are plastic – a major site of rewiring early in life, that we found to include the physical pruning and regrowth of dendritic spines with proteases. But try as we might, manipulating LTP/LTD factors failed to alter *when* the critical periods for plasticity occur, forcing a massive rethink. Two major breakthroughs then propelled the field forward.

One was to shift our attention away from excitatory plasticity towards a role for inhibitory (GABAergic) interneurons. Long regarded as preventing runaway excitation – basically, to prevent epilepsy – their rich morphological diversity and precise connectivity stood in obvious contrast to the more generic excitatory pyramidal cell. Since the time of Cajal, the logic of inhibitory circuits had remained a mystery. We were fortunate to usher in the use of gene-targeted mice to study their role in critical period plasticity. Not only was inhibition necessary to open the window, it was mediated by a specific synaptic GABA receptor and cell type. Decades after Hubel and Wiesel's seminal work, we showed that particular fast-spiking inhibitory basket cells were the first to change in response to early experience.

In other words, these windows were not set in stone by age, but rather reflected the maturational state of inhibitory circuits. This provided a cellular switch, whereby plasticity could be delayed or accelerated – potentially even reopened later in adulthood. For the first time, we could control when a critical period would occur and potentially why they arise in sequence across brain regions. The further discovery that perineuronal nets (PNNs) ultimately enwrap inputs onto basket cells as critical periods fade, confirmed their pivotal role in regulating lifelong plasticity.

Here, then, was the second major breakthrough: the realization that critical period closure is not simply a passive loss of plasticity, but an active process to prevent further rewiring. Several diverse "brakes" on plasticity (like PNNs) have now been identified, which can be lifted in adulthood to rejuvenate the brain. Strikingly, disrupted GABA circuits and plasticity brakes have been linked to cognitive disorders, like autism or schizophrenia, consistent with a developmental etiology. Manipulating critical period timing – once the stuff of science fiction movies – now offers innovative therapies for mental illness, recovery from adult brain injury, and neuroscience-inspired AI, which should be pursued with care. Critical periods, after all, have evolved for a reason, and shape who we are.

At first blush, the idea that there are brakes on the onset and offset of plasticity – particularly the offset – might seem surprising. If adapting to one's environment is a good thing, why should it ever be *actively* inhibited? Well, once the brain reaches the adult state these brakes contribute to stability of the neural architecture that has been fine-tuned over the course of years. Imagine if, every time we were exposed to a new stimulus, it completely rewired our brains. Our memories, and the skills and knowledge we have acquired, would be lost! There are also metabolic consequences: it is energetically expensive to maintain the capacity for plasticity; thus, as long as an individual's environment is fairly stable, it is adaptive to stabilize the brain's architecture (Frankenhuis & Fraley, 2017). However, reopening critical period plasticity could be helpful from a therapeutic standpoint. Indeed, this possibility is an area of active investigation not just for brain plasticity but for the possibility that, like lobsters, we can maintain a cellular plasticity that allows us to replace damaged organs and lost limbs.

5.7   Childhood Adversity

The fact that our brains are fine-tuned by our early experiences means that we are able to adapt to a variety of environments. This is a remarkable feature of the brain – particularly the human brain, as we have an extremely long period of immaturity. However, this malleability is a double-edged sword when it comes to adapting to adverse life experiences. We begin by discussing two perspectives on brain plasticity in response to adversity, then discuss the cumulative risk of various forms of adversity, and finally delve into a few specific examples of ways in which these experiences can, as is often said, "get under the skin" affecting child development.

5.7.1   Brain Plasticity as a Double-Edged Sword

There are different views on the issue of why we should be concerned about early life adversity. One of these is the **mismatch hypothesis**, which holds that being shaped by negative life circumstances is not *intrinsically* problematic: it is a remarkable biological phenomenon that allows individuals to thrive in spite of adversity *in that particular environment*. However, what is problematic, under this view, is when an individual moves into a new environment. Consider a child in an abusive home who learns to disengage from adults to avoid bodily harm. That strategy is an intelligent one in the home environment but can lead to difficulties at school, if the child has an overactive threat detection system that leads them to avoid interacting with teachers.

Therefore, because our society values some cognitive and affective traits over others, individuals who experienced early life adversity can be at a disadvantage when evaluated according to these metrics. However, such individuals may have hidden talents that are simply not appreciated (Frankenhuis et al., 2020). This perspective counters the widespread **deficit model**, wherein children from disadvantaged backgrounds are somehow inferior (on scholastic measures) to those from more privileged ones. This is an important concept, as it promotes understanding and accommodating children from different backgrounds, and combats stereotypes that can further disadvantage children with difficult life circumstances (Ellwood-Lowe et al., 2016). It also allows proponents to make the point that what is considered to be an adverse environment is subjective; for example, adults in different countries may have a very different perspective on what it means to have a fulfilling life and what is the proper way to raise a child.

As valuable as it is, however, the mismatch hypothesis may lead us to ignore valid concerns. While it is certainly true that our perspective on what counts as an adverse environment is subject to our own biases, a child has basic physical, socioemotional, and cognitive needs that must be met in order to thrive. Absence of any of these *expectable inputs* could alter a child's neurodevelopmental trajectory. Further, exposure to stress that is extremely severe and/or chronic can be *physiologically harmful*. This type of exposure is referred to as **toxic stress**: a term coined by the National Scientific Council on the Developing Child (which has reviewed the pivotal work by Bruce McEwen, Megan Gunnar, and others on this important topic). Thus, investigating the effects of early life adversity on the developing brain and behavior has important implications for public health initiatives and policies related to child welfare (Shonkoff et al., 2009; Farah, 2017).

Of course, not all children are equally sensitive to environmental challenges (Boyce, 2019). If you think about it, you likely know – or are – someone who had a very difficult upbringing but got through it relatively unscathed. Why is that? Efforts are underway to better understand sources of resilience, with the ultimate goal of identifying and better supporting those children who are likely to be most susceptible to negative environmental influences. However, the types of interventions that will have the biggest impact on a nation's children are not one-on-one, but rather large-scale economic and policy changes.

5.7.2 Risks Associated with Adverse Childhood Experiences

We have learned a lot about the effects of early life adversity from research on laboratory animals, dating back to early work on monkeys tragically separated from their mothers at birth (Harlow et al., 1965) – but also from children growing up in unusually harsh circumstances. Charles Nelson, Nathan Fox, and Charles Zeanah conducted landmark research on children in Bucharest, Romania who spent their first few years of life in large, warehouse-like institutions (Nelson et al., 2014). The Bucharest Early Intervention Project (BEIP) is the first and only randomized controlled trial using foster care as an alternative to institutional care for orphaned and abandoned children, establishing the degree to which significant neglect in early childhood can profoundly harm early development. The study came about following the 1989 overthrow and death of Romanian dictator Nicolae Ceauşescu. During his decades of authoritarian rule, Ceauşescu imposed a range of nationalist economic policies, including making contraception and abortion illegal. Families that produced fewer than five children were taxed. This had the effect of coercing families into having children they could not afford, and both birth and poverty rates grew correspondingly. Rather than change policies, Ceauşescu expanded a network of institutions where the state vowed to raise abandoned children – implicitly endorsing that abandonment.

At the time of his death, Ceauşescu's orphanages and their thousands of children were revealed to the rest of the world (Nelson et al., 2009). Through longitudinal research spanning well over a decade, the BEIP demonstrated the long-lasting effects of severe neglect and deprivation on the institutionalized children's physical, mental, emotional, and brain development. Encouragingly, the intervention showed that placement in foster care within the first two years of life can mitigate – albeit not entirely prevent – these effects (Vanderwert et al., 2010). As we discuss later (Chapter 14), the findings from the Bucharest project have been considered in the context of the Trump administration's family separation policy in the United States. Fortunately, this level of adversity is the exception rather than the norm; however, challenging life circumstances that are more common can also impact development.

The most vulnerable adult members of our society – those facing poverty, systemic racism, genderism, and/or mental health issues – experience various forms of adversity that can affect both themselves and their children in myriad ways. Effects on children may take many forms, such as emotional or physical neglect or maltreatment, which in turn may stem from or be exacerbated by adult substance abuse, psychiatric conditions, imprisonment, or intolerable stress. Additional factors affecting children may include unstable or unsafe housing, food insecurity, low adult supervision, unpredictable parenting, reduced social interactions and lower conversational engagement, fewer cognitively enriching experiences at home, lack of access to high-quality early education, as well as elevated risk of exposure to toxins and pollutants. Taken together, these many challenges are thought to affect child brain development. Indeed, a number of cross-sectional studies have documented differences in brain structure and function between children from lower and higher socioeconomic family backgrounds (Hackman et al., 2010; Noble et al., 2015; Tooley et al., 2021).

Because multiple risk factors often co-occur – particularly for families facing poverty and/ or racism – it is challenging to assess the impact of any one of them on child development. As a result, one approach has been to consider the cumulative risk of various **adverse childhood experiences (ACEs)**. A highly influential study on ACEs was a large, retrospective survey study of over 17,000 adults in the United States associating their current health conditions with their life experiences (Felitti et al., 1988). The survey asked questions like, "While you were growing up, during your first 18 years of life … Did a parent or other adult in the household often or very often swear at you, insult you, put you down, or humiliate you, or act in a way that made you afraid that you might be physically hurt? [...] Did you often or very often feel that you didn't have enough to eat, had to wear dirty clothes, and had no one protect you, or that your parents were too drunk or high to take you to the doctor if you needed it?" The 10-item questionnaire also asked about emotional neglect, physical and sexual abuse, a family history of substance use, mental illness, imprisonment, and parental separation.

Each "yes" response on the survey received a score of 1, for a total **ACE Score** of up to 10. Researchers found that ACE Score correlated with many negative health outcomes in adulthood, including rate of antidepressant prescriptions and substance use. These risks were progressively higher across participants with ACE Scores of 0, 1, 2, 3, or 4+. Particularly disturbingly, the researchers found that an ACE Score of at least 7 was associated with a 51-fold increase in childhood/adolescent suicide attempts, and a 30-fold increase in adult suicide attempts (Dube et al., 2001).

While the ACES study was pivotal in that it linked childhood experiences to adult health, it is lacking in a number of ways. First, this was a retrospective self-report measure, which limits its reliability. More importantly, it equally weights different types of negative experiences: for example, the experience of having been physically or sexually abused was treated as equally negative as the more commonplace experience of parental divorce. For some children, such events may be experienced as equally aversive; for others, they may not. On the flipside, two people with the same ACE Score could have been impacted very differently by the experiences. Further, the questionnaire was non-specific regarding age or duration of exposure, merely asking about events that occurred prior to age 18. Finally, given very low upward social mobility in the United States, it is fairly likely that many of the individuals with high ACE scores based on their childhood experiences continue to experience serious challenges that could contribute to, or even fully explain, their current health conditions. Despite these limitations, this study has resonated widely with practitioners and policymakers (including the recent Surgeon General in our home state of California, Dr. Nadine Burke-Harris, who identified early life adversity as a top priority and implemented a program to train medical professionals on how to screen their patients for ACEs). On the research front, the ACES study has given way to a large and ever-growing body of research examining how life adversity affects neurodevelopmental trajectories.

5.7.3 Dimensions of Childhood Adversity

There are a number of ways of conceptualizing the mechanisms by which experiences shape child outcomes, including psychopathology (anxiety, depression, etc.) and school performance. The first is the **cumulative risk model** adopted in the ACES study, whereby individual risk factors sum up to influence child outcomes *via a global mechanism* – that is, one that affects the brain (and rest of the body) in the same way. A compelling candidate for a common mechanism linking adverse life experiences with psychopathology is a change in **stress reactivity**: elevation or blunting of activation of the hypothalamo-pituitary-adrenal (HPA) axis of the brain in response to a stressor (Koss & Gunnar, 2018). The HPA axis mounts a well-orchestrated defense against threats of various kinds. This response is adaptive for coping with stressors over the short-term. However, in the face of chronic stressors (Shonkoff et al., 2009; National Scientific Council on the Developing Child, 2010), it leads to chronic inflammation and can wreak havoc on the body and brain (Juster et al., 2010).

While there is lots of evidence that altered stress reactivity and inflammation is a general mechanism by which negative experiences impact our physiology, including our brain function, it doesn't tell the whole story. There is mounting evidence that various environmental factors affect the brain differently. At the limit, one might imagine that each type of adverse experience might affect the brain differently. However, a **dimensional approach** falls partway between the two extremes of a single general mechanism and many fully independent mechanisms. One dimensional framework, proposed by Kate McLaughlin, Margaret Sheridan, and colleagues (2021), outlines three key categories of adversity: deprivation of important cognitive and/or social inputs, exposure to threats and/or harsh caregiving, and an overall unpredictable environment. According to this model, then, each specific form of adversity affects the brain through both general mechanisms, such as stress reactivity, as well as specific mechanisms.

A dimensional approach, such as this one, seems particularly promising as a framework for future research. Already we know a fair amount about the effects of threat exposure on the fear circuitry, including changes in amygdala volumes, activation, and connectivity (Gee et al., 2013; VanTieghem et al., 2021). We also know, for example, that reduced linguistic exposure in early childhood is associated with alterations in brain regions that support language (Merz et al., 2019; Romeo et al., 2018) (Chapter 8). This is a rich and rapidly growing literature that we encourage you to delve into, given the important clinical and societal implications of socioemotional and cognitive development.

SUMMARY

- Development and learning are on a continuum, varying along several dimensions
- Plasticity can be subdivided into three types: experience-independent, experience-expectant, and experience-dependent
- Specific windows during a neural system that can be shaped by environmental inputs are called critical or sensitive periods
- Hebbian plasticity is an important mechanism by which effective synapses are strengthened and ineffective ones are weakened or eliminated

- Rats raised in an enriched environment had thicker visual cortex than those raised in an impoverished one
- Monocular deprivation experiments revealed a critical period for ocular dominance column stabilization
- Environmental influences can trigger neuronal, glial, and vascular changes in the brain
- Sensory deprivation can cause cortical reorganization, which can be rapid, and is particularly dramatic in the case of congenital deprivation
- During learning, gray matter expansion can be followed by contraction; this is consistent with the Expansion-Renormalization Model of plasticity and development
- Animal research indicates that different brain regions have different critical periods, and critical period opening, duration, and closure are tightly regulated at the molecular and cellular levels
- Adverse childhood experiences can have lasting effects on a developing child, and there may be both global and differential effects of distinct kinds of adversity

REVIEW QUESTIONS

Along what dimensions could development and learning be distinguished? Identify at least three.

What are the differences between experience-independent, experience-expectant, and experience-dependent brain development? Do you believe that any one of these forms of maturation is more prominent in child development than the others?

What is Hebbian plasticity, and what are long-term potentiation and long-term depression?

What have we learned about cortical reorganization after visual, auditory, and somatosensory deprivation? Why is the cerebral cortex said to be pluripotent?

Is plasticity always greatest in early childhood? Discuss evidence from studies of sensory deprivation, cochlear implantation, and recovery from brain injury.

Why might it be adaptive for windows of plasticity to close?

Describe the studies examining effects of environmental enrichment in rats.

Name a few forms of structural brain plasticity, including both neuronal and non-neuronal changes.

What is the Expansion-Renormalization Model of cortical plasticity? Provide some evidence for it based on structural MRI. Describe the study and results.

What are some different models regarding the mechanisms by which early life adversity affects child development?

Further Reading

Greenough, W. T., Black, J. E., & Wallace, C. S. (1987). Experience and brain development. *Child Development*, 58(3), 539–559. https://doi.org/10.2307/1130197

Hensch, T. K. (2005). Critical period plasticity in local cortical circuits. *Nature Reviews Neuroscience*, 6(11), 877–888. https://doi.org/10.1038/nrn1787

Lomber, S. G., Meredith, M. A., & Kral, A. (2010). Crossmodal plasticity in specific auditory cortices underlies visual compensations in the deaf. *Nature Neuroscience*, 13(11), 1421–1427. https://doi.org/10.1038/nn.2653

References

Adolph, K. E., Cole, W. G., Komati, M., Garciaguirre, J. S., Badaly, D., Lingeman, J. M., Chan, G. L. Y., & Sotsky, R. B. (2012). How do you learn to walk? Thousands of steps and dozens of falls per day. *Psychological Science*, 23(11), 1387–1394. https://doi.org/10.1177/0956797612446346

Adolph, K. E., Hoch, J. E., & Cole, W. G. (2018). Development (of walking): 15 suggestions. *Trends in Cognitive Sciences*, 22(8), 699–711. https://doi.org/10.1016/j.tics.2018.05.010

Althausen, A., Gleissner, U., Hoppe, C., Sassen, R., Buddewig, S., von Lehe, M., Schramm, J., Elger, C. E., & Helmstaedter, C. (2013). Long-term outcome of hemispheric surgery at different ages in 61 epilepsy patients. *Journal of Neurology, Neurosurgery & Psychiatry*, 84(5), 529–536. https://doi.org/10.1136/jnnp-2012-303811

Anderson, C. A., Wiggins, I. M., Kitterick, P. T., & Hartley, D. (2019). Pre-operative brain imaging using functional near-infrared spectroscopy helps predict cochlear implant outcome in deaf adults. *Journal of the Association for Research in Otolaryngology*, 20(5), 511–528. https://doi.org/10.1007/s10162-019-00729-z

Anderson, V., Catroppa, C., Morse, S., Haritou, F., & Rosenfeld, J. (2005). Functional plasticity or vulnerability after early brain injury? *Pediatrics*, 116(6), 1374–1382. https://doi.org/10.1542/peds.2004-1728

Anderson, V., Spencer-Smith, M., Coleman, L., Anderson, P., Williams, J., Greenham, M., Leventer, R. J., & Jacobs, R. (2010). Children's executive functions: Are they poorer after very early brain insult. *Neuropsychologia*, 48(7), 2041–2050. https://doi.org/10.1016/j.neuropsychologia.2010.03.025

Barres, B. A. (2008). The mystery and magic of glia: A perspective on their roles in health and disease. *Neuron*, 60(3), 430–440. https://doi.org/10.1016/j.neuron.2008.10.013

Bavelier, D., Levi, D. M., Li, R. W., Dan, Y., & Hensch, T. K. (2010). Removing brakes on adult brain plasticity: From molecular to behavioral interventions. *The Journal of Neuroscience*, 30(45), 14964–14971. https://doi.org/10.1523/JNEUROSCI.4812-10.2010

Bavelier, D., & Neville, H. J. (2002). Cross-modal plasticity: Where and how? *Nature Reviews Neuroscience*, 3, 443–452. https://doi.org/10.1038/nrn848

Bedny, M. (2017). Evidence from blindness for a cognitively pluripotent cortex. *Trends in Cognitive Sciences*, 21(9), 637–648. https://doi.org/10.1016/j.tics.2017.06.003

Benchetrit, L., Ronner, E. A., Anne, S., & Cohen, M. S. (2021). Cochlear implantation in children with single-sided deafness: A systematic review and meta-analysis. *JAMA Otolaryngology – Head & Neck Surgery*, 147(1), 58–69. https://doi.org/10.1001/jamaoto.2020.3852

Bennett, E. L., Diamond, M. C., Krech, D., & Rosenzweig, M. R. (1964). Chemical and anatomical plasticity of brain. *Science*, 146(3644), 610–619. https://doi.org/10.1126/science.146.3644.610

Bliss, T. V., & Lomo, T. (1973). Long-lasting potentiation of synaptic transmission in the dentate area of the anaesthetized rabbit following stimulation of the perforant path. *The Journal of Physiology*, 232(2), 331–356. https://doi.org/10.1113/jphysiol.1973.sp010273

Bortfeld, H. (2019). Functional near-infrared spectroscopy as a tool for assessing speech and spoken language processing in pediatric and adult cochlear implant users. *Developmental Psychobiology*, 61(3), 430–443. https://doi.org/10.1002/dev.21818

Boyce, W. T. (2019). *The orchid and the dandelion: Why sensitive children face challenges and how all can thrive*. Allen Lane.

Chen, M. M., & Oghalai, J. S. (2016). Diagnosis and management of congenital sensorineural hearing loss. *Current Treatment Options in Pediatrics*, 2(3), 256–265. https://doi.org/10.1007/s40746-016-0056-6

Chung, W. S., Welsh, C. A., Barres, B. A., & Stevens, B. (2015). Do glia drive synaptic and cognitive impairment in disease? *Nature Neuroscience*, 18(11), 1539–1545. https://doi.org/10.1038/nn.4142

Cooper, A. (2019). Hear me out: Hearing each other for the first time: The implications of cochlear implant activation. *Missouri Medicine*, 116(6), 469–471. www.ncbi.nlm.nih.gov/pmc/articles/PMC6913847/

de Manzano, Ö., & Ullén, F. (2018). Same genes, different brains: Neuroanatomical differences between monozygotic twins discordant for musical training. *Cerebral Cortex*, 28(1), 387–394. https://doi.org/10.1093/cercor/bhx299

DeFelipe, J. (2006). Brain plasticity and mental processes: Cajal again. *Nature Reviews Neuroscience*, 7(10), 811–817. https://doi.org/10.1038/nrn2005

DeFelipe, J. (2015). The dendritic spine story: An intriguing process of discovery. *Frontiers in Neuroanatomy*, 9, 1–13. https://doi.org/10.3389/fnana.2015.00014

Diamond, M. C. (1996). Marian Cleeves Diamond. In L. R. Squire (Ed.), *The history of neuroscience in autobiography, Volume 6* (pp. 62–94). Academic Press. https://academic.oup.com/book/4009/chapter-abstract/145636719?redirectedFrom=fulltext

Diamond, M. C., Krech, D., & Rosenzweig, M. R. (1964). The effects of an enriched environment on the histology of the rat cerebral cortex. *Journal of Comparative Neurology*, 123(1), 111–119. https://doi.org/10.1002/cne.901230110

Dronkers, N. F., Plaisant, O., Iba-Zizen, M. T., & Cabanis, E. A. (2007). Paul Broca's historic cases: High resolution MR imaging of the brains of Leborgne & Lelong. *Brain*, 130(5), 1432–1441. https://doi.org/10.1093/brain/awm042

Dube, S. R., Anda, R. F., Felitti, V. J., Chapman, D. P., Williamson, D. F., & Giles, W. H. (2001). Childhood abuse, household dysfunction, and the risk of attempted suicide throughout the life span: Findings from the adverse childhood experiences study. *Journal of the American Medical Association*, 286(24), 3089–3096. https://doi.org/10.1001/jama.286.24.3089

Durant, W. (1926). *The story of philosophy*. Simon & Schuster.

Ellwood-Lowe, M. E., Sacchet, M. D., & Gotlib, I. H. (2016). The application of neuroimaging to social inequity and language disparity: A cautionary examination. *Developmental Cognitive Neuroscience*, 22, 1–8. https://doi.org/10.1016/j.dcn.2016.10.001

Fair, D., & Schlaggar, B. L. (2008). Brain development. In M. M. Haith & J. B. Benson (Eds.), *Encyclopedia of infant and early childhood development, Volume 1* (pp. 211–225). Elsevier.

Farah, M. J. (2017). The neuroscience of socioeconomic status: Correlates, causes, and consequences. *Neuron*, 96(1), 56–71. https://doi.org/10.1016/j.neuron.2017.08.034

Felitti, V. J., Anda, R. F., Nordenberg, D., Williamson, D. F., Spitz, A. M., Edwards, V., Koss, M. P., & Marks, J. S. (1988). Relationship of childhood abuse and household dysfunction to many of the leading causes of death in adults: The Adverse Childhood Experiences (ACE) Study. *American Journal of Preventative Medicine*, 14(4), 245–258. https://doi.org/10.1016/s0749-3797(98)00017-8

Finger, S. (1999). Margaret Kennard on sparing and recovery of function: A tribute on the 100th anniversary of her birth. *Journal of the History of the Neurosciences*, 8(3), 269–285. https://doi.org/10.1076/jhin.8.3.269.1824

Fischer, M., Kaech, S., Knutti, D., & Matus, A. (1998). Rapid actin-based plasticity in dendritic spines. *Neuron*, 20(5), 847–854. https://doi.org/10.1016/S0896-6273(00)80467-5

Fitzpatrick, E. (2015). Neurocognitive development in congenitally deaf children. In M. J. Aminoff, F. Boller, & D. F. Swaab (Eds.), *Handbook of clinical neurology, Volume 129* (pp. 335–356). Elsevier. https://doi.org/10.1016/B978-0-444-62630-1.00019-6

Frankenhuis, W. E., & Fraley, R. C. (2017). What do evolutionary models teach us about sensitive periods in psychological development? *European Psychologist*, 22(3), 141–150. Elsevier. https://doi.org/10.1027/1016-9040/a000265

Frankenhuis, W. E., Young, E. S., & Ellis, B. J. (2020). The hidden talents approach: Theoretical and methodological challenges. *Trends in Cognitive Sciences*, 24(7), 569–581. https://doi.org/10.1016/j.tics.2020.03.007

Frieden, T. R., Houry, D., & Baldwin, G. (2015). Report to Congress on traumatic brain injury in the United States: Epidemiology and rehabilitation. *Report to the United States Congress*.

Galván, A. (2010). Neural plasticity of development and learning. *Human Brain Mapping*, 31(6), 879–890. https://doi.org/10.1002/hbm.21029

Gee, D. G., Gabard-Durnam, L. J., Flannery, J., Goff, B., Humphreys, K. L., Telzer, E. H., Hare, T. A., Bookheimer, S. Y., & Tottenham, N. (2013). Early developmental emergence of human amygdala-prefrontal connectivity after maternal deprivation. *Proceedings of the National Academy of Sciences of the United States of America*, 110(39), 15638–15643. https://doi.org/10.1073/pnas.1307893110

Geers, A. E., Mitchell, C. M., Warner-Czyz, A., Wang, N. Y., Eisenberg, L. S., & CDaCI Investigative Team. (2017). Early sign language exposure and cochlear implantation benefits. *Pediatrics*, 140(1), e20163489. https://doi.org/10.1542/peds.2016-3489

Greenough, W. T., Black, J. E., & Wallace, C. S. (1987). Experience and brain development. *Child Development*, 58(3), 539–559. https://doi.org/10.1111/j.1467-8624.1987.tb01400.x

Hackman, D. A., Farah, M. J., & Meaney, M. J. (2010). Socioeconomic status and the brain: Mechanistic insights from human and animal research. *Nature Reviews Neuroscience*, 11(9), 651–659. https://doi.org/10.1038/nrn2897

Hall, M. L., Hall, W. C., & Caselli, N. K. (2019). Deaf children need language, not (just) speech. *First Language*, 39(4), 367–395. https://doi.org/10.1177/0142723719834102

Harlow, H. F., Dodsworth, R. O., & Harlow, M. K. (1965). Total social isolation in monkeys. *Proceedings of the National Academy of Sciences of the United States of America*, 54, 90–97. www.ncbi.nlm.nih.gov/pmc/articles/PMC285801/pdf/pnas00159-0105.pdf

Hebb, D. O. (1942). The effect of early and late brain injury upon test scores, and the nature of normal adult intelligence. *Proceedings of the American Philosophical Society*, 85(3), 275–292. www.jstor.org/stable/985007

Hebb, D. O. (1949). *The organization of behavior*. John Wiley & Sons.

Hebb, D. O. (1953). Heredity and environment in mammalian behaviour. *British Journal of Animal Behaviour*, 1, 43–47. https://doi.org/10.1016/S0950-5601(53)80053-5

Hubel, D. H. (1988). *Eye, brain, and vision*. Scientific American Library.

Hubel, D. H., Wiesel, T. N., & LeVay, S. (1977). Plasticity of ocular dominance columns in monkey striate cortex. *Philosophical Transactions of the Royal Society of London. Series B, Biological sciences*, 278(961), 377–409. https://doi.org/10.1098/rstb.1977.0050

James, W. (1890). *The principles of psychology*, Vol. 1. Henry Holt and Co. https://doi.org/10.1037/10538-000

Juster, R. P., McEwen, B. S., & Lupien, S. J. (2010). Allostatic load biomarkers of chronic stress and impact on health and cognition. *Neuroscience and Biobehavioral Reviews*, 35(1), 2–16. https://doi.org/10.1016/j.neubiorev.2009.10.002

Kanjlia, S., Pant, R., & Bedny, M. (2019). Sensitive period for cognitive repurposing of human visual cortex. *Cerebral Cortex*, 29(9), 3993–4005. https://doi.org/10.1093/cercor/bhy280

Kolb, B., & Teskey, G. C. (2012). Age, experience, injury, and the changing brain. *Developmental Psychobiology*, 54(3), 311–325. https://doi.org/10.1002/dev.20515

Koss, K. J., & Gunnar, M. R. (2018). Annual research review: Early adversity, the hypothalamic-pituitary-adrenocortical axis, and child psychopathology. *Journal of Child Psychology and Psychiatry*, 59(4), 327–346. https://doi.org/1doi:10.1111/jcpp.12784

Kral, A. (2013). Auditory critical periods: A review from system's perspective. *Neuroscience*, 247, 117–133. https://doi.org/10.1016/j.neuroscience.2013.05.021

Kral, A., Dorman, M. F., & Wilson, B. S. (2019). Neuronal development of hearing and language: Cochlear implants and critical periods. *Annual Review of Neuroscience*, 42, 47–65. https://doi.org/10.1146/annurev-neuro-080317-061513

Kral, A., & Lomber, S. G. (2015). Deaf white cats. *Current Biology*, 25(9) R351–R353. https://doi.org/10.1016/j.cub.2015.02.040

Lomber, S. G. (2017). What is the function of auditory cortex when it develops in the absence of acoustic input? *Cognitive Development*, 42, 49–61. https://doi.org/10.1016/j.cogdev.2017.02.007

Lomber, S. G., Meredith, M. A., & Kral, A. (2010). Crossmodal plasticity in specific auditory cortices underlies visual compensations in the deaf. *Nature Neuroscience*, 13(11), 1421–1427. https://doi.org/10.1038/nn.2653

Lømo, T. (1966). Frequency potentiation of excitatory synaptic activity in the dentate area of the hippocampal formation. *Acta Physiologica Scandinavica*, 68(Suppl 277), 128.

Maia, T. G. (2020). Cochlear implants in congenitally deaf children: A discussion built on rights-based arguments. *American Annals of the Deaf*, 164(5), 546–559. https://doi.org/10.1353/aad.2020.0002

Maurer, D., & Lewis, T. (2012). Human visual plasticity: Lessons from children treated for congenital cataracts. In J. K. E. Steeves & L. R. Harris (Eds.), *Plasticity in sensory systems* (pp. 75–93). Cambridge University Press. https://doi.org/10.1017/CBO9781139136907.005

McGee, A. W., Yang, Y., Fischer, Q. S., Daw, N. W., & Strittmatter, S. M. (2005). Experience-driven plasticity of visual cortex limited by myelin and Nogo receptor. *Science*, 309(5744), 2222–2226. https://doi.org/10.1126/science.1114362

McLaughlin, K. A., Sheridan, M. A., Humphreys, K. L., Belsky, J., & Ellis, B. J. (2021). The value of dimensional models of early experience: Thinking clearly about concepts and categories. *Perspectives on Psychological Science*, 16(6), 1463–1472. https://doi.org/10.1177/1745691621992346

Mehra, S., Eavey, R. D., & Keamy, D. G. (2009). The epidemiology of hearing impairment in the United States: Newborns, children, and adolescents. *Otolaryngology – Head and Neck Surgery*, 140(4), 461–472. https://doi.org/10.1016/j.otohns.2008.12.022

Merz, E. C., Wiltshire, C. A., & Noble, K. G. (2019). Socioeconomic inequality and the developing brain: Spotlight on language and executive function. *Child Development Perspectives*, 13(1), 15–20. https://doi.org/10.1111/cdep.12305

Miyamoto, R. T., Colson, B., Henning, S., & Pisoni, D. (2018). Cochlear implantation in infants below 12 months of age. *World Journal of Otorhinolaryngology – Head and Neck Surgery*, 3(4), 214–218. https://doi.org/10.1016/j.wjorl.2017.12.001

National Scientific Council on the Developing Child. (2010). *Early experiences can alter gene expression and affect long-term development: Working paper No. 10*. www.developingchild.net

Nelson, C., Fox, N., & Zeanah, C. (2014). *Romania's abandoned children: Deprivation, brain development, and the struggle for recovery*. Harvard University Press.

Nelson, C. A., Furtado, E. A., Fox, N. A., & Zeanah, C. H. (2009). The deprived human brain: Developmental deficits among institutionalized Romanian children – and later improvements – strengthen the case for individualized care. *American Scientist*, 97(3), 222–229. www.jstor.org/stable/27859330

Neville, H. J., & Bavelier, D. (1998). Neural organization and plasticity of language. *Current Opinion in Neurobiology*, 8(2), 254–258. https://doi.org/10.1016/s0959-4388(98)80148-7

Noble, K. G., Houston, S. M., Brito, N. H., Bartsch, H., Kan, E., Kuperman, J. M., Akshoomoff, N., Amaral, D. G., Bloss, C. S., Libiger, O., Schork, N. J., Murray, S. S., Casey, B. J., Chang, L., Ernst, T. M., Frazier, J. A., Gruen, J. R., Kennedy, D. N., Van Zijl, P., Mostofsky, S., ... Sowell, E. R. (2015). Family income, parental education and brain structure in children and adolescents. *Nature Neuroscience*, 18(5), 773–778. https://doi.org/10.1038/nn.3983

Oxenham, A. J. (2018). How we hear: The perception and neural coding of sound. *Annual Review of Psychology*, 69, 27–50. https://doi.org/10.1146/annurev-psych-122216-011635

Pantev, C., & Herholz, S. C. (2011). Plasticity of the human auditory cortex related to musical training. *Neuroscience & Biobehavioral Reviews*, 35(10), 2140–2154. https://doi.org/10.1016/j.neubiorev.2011.06.010

Partanen, E., Kujala, T., Tervaniemi, M., & Huotilainen, M. (2013). Prenatal music exposure induces long-term neural effects. *Public Library of Science One*, 8(10). https://doi.org/10.1371/journal.pone.0078946

Penfield, W., & Rasmussen, T. (1950). The cerebral cortex of man: A clinical study of localization of function. *Journal of the American Medical Association*, 144(16), 1412. https://doi.org/10.1001/jama.1950.02920160086033

Ponton, C. W., & Eggermont, J. J. (2001). Of kittens and kids: Altered cortical maturation following profound deafness and cochlear implant use. *Audiology and Neurotology*, 6(6), 363–380. https://doi.org/10.1159/000046846

Prochazka, A. (2017). Neurophysiology and neural engineering: A review. *Journal of Neurophysiology*, 118(2), 1292–1309. https://doi.org/10.1152/jn.00149.2017

Purves, D., Augustine, G. J., Fitzpatrick, D., Katz, L. C., et al. (Eds.). (1997). Neuroscience. Sinauer Associates.

Ramachandran, V. S., & Hirstein, W. (1998). The perception of phantom limbs. The D. O. Hebb lecture. *Brain*, 121(9), 1603–1630. https://doi.org/10.1093/brain/121.9.1603

Ramachandran, V. S., Rogers-Ramachandran, D., & Stewart, M. (1992). Perceptual correlates of massive cortical reorganization. *Science*, 258(5085), 1159–1160. https://doi.org/10.1126/science.1439826

Raz, N., & Lindenberger, U. (2013). Life-span plasticity of the brain and cognition: From questions to evidence and back. *Neuroscience and Biobehavioral Reviews*, 37(9), 2195–2200. https://doi.org/10.1016/j.neubiorev.2013.10.003

Reed, A., Riley, J., Carraway, R., Carrasco, A., Perez, C., Jakkamsetti, V., & Kilgard, M. P. (2011). Cortical map plasticity improves learning but is not necessary for improved performance. *Neuron*, 70(1), 121–131. https://doi.org/10.1016/j.neuron.2011.02.038

Reh, R. K., Dias, B. G., Nelson III, C. A., Kaufer, D., Werker, J. F., Kolb, B., Levine, J. D., & Hensch, T. K. (2020). Critical period regulation across multiple timescales. *Proceedings of the National Academy of Sciences of the United States of America*, 117(38), 23242–23251. https://doi.org/10.1073/pnas.1820836117

Romeo, R. R., Segaran, J., Leonard, J. A., Robinson, S. T., West, M. R., Mackey, A. P., Yendiki, A., Rowe, M. L., & Gabrieli, J. (2018). Language exposure relates to structural neural connectivity in childhood. *Journal of Neuroscience*, 38(36), 7870–7877. https://doi.org/10.1523/JNEUROSCI.0484-18.2018

Rosenzweig, M. R. (1996). Aspects of the search for neural mechanisms of memory. *Annual Review of Psychology*, 47, 1–32. https://doi.org/10.1146/annurev.psych.47.1.1

Samargia, S. A., & Kimberley, T. J. (2009). Motor and cognitive outcomes in children after functional hemispherectomy. *Pediatric Physical Therapy*, 21(4), 356–361. https://doi.org/10.1097/PEP.0b013e3181bf710d

Schlaug, G. (2015). Musicians and music making as a model for the study of brain plasticity. *Progress in Brain Research*, 217, 37–55. https://doi.org/10.1016/bs.pbr.2014.11.020

Sengupta, P. (2013). The laboratory rat: Relating its age with human's. *International Journal of Preventive Medicine*, 4(6), 624–630.

Sevy, A. B., Bortfeld, H., Huppert, T. J., Beauchamp, M. S., Tonini, R. E., & Oghalai, J. S. (2010). Neuroimaging with near-infrared spectroscopy demonstrates speech-evoked activity in the auditory cortex of deaf children following cochlear implantation. *Hearing Research*, 270, 39–47. https://doi.org/10.1016/j.heares.2010.09.010

Shonkoff, J. P., Boyce, W. T., & McEwen, B. S. (2009). Neuroscience, molecular biology, and the childhood roots of health disparities: Building a new framework for health promotion and disease prevention. *Journal of the American Medical Association*, 301(21), 2252–2259. https://doi.org/10.1001/jama.2009.754

Silva, L. A. F., Couto, M. I. V., Magliaro, F. C. L., Tsuji, R. K., Bento, R. F., De Carvalho, A. C. M., & Matas, C. G. (2017). Cortical maturation in children with cochlear implants: Correlation between electrophysiological and behavioral measurement. *PLoS One*, 12(2), 1–18. https://doi.org/10.1371/journal.pone.0171177

Stefaniak, J. D., Halai, A. D., & Lambon Ralph, M. A. (2020). The neural and neurocomputational bases of recovery from post-stroke aphasia. *Nature Reviews Neurology*, 16, 43–55. https://doi.org/10.1038/s41582-019-0282-1

Stiles, J., Reilly, J., Paul, B., & Moses, P. (2005). Cognitive development following early brain injury: Evidence for neural adaptation. *Trends in Cognitive Sciences*, 9(3), 136–143. https://doi.org/10.1016/j.tics.2005.01.002

Super, C. M. (1976). Environmental effects on motor development: The case of 'African infant precocity.' *Developmental Medicine & Child Neurology*, 18(5), 561–567. https://doi.org/10.1111/j.1469-8749.1976.tb04202.x

Tolman, E. C., & Honzik, C. H. (1930). Introduction and removal of reward, and maze performance in rats. *University of California Publications in Psychology*, 4(17), 257–275.

Tooley, U. A., Bassett, D. S., & Mackey, A. P. (2021). Environmental influences on the pace of brain development. *Nature Reviews Neuroscience*, 22(6), 372–384. https://doi.org/10.1038/s41583-021-00457-5

Vanderwert, R. E., Marshall, P. J., Nelson III, C. A., Zeanah, C. H., & Fox, N. A. (2010). Timing of intervention affects brain electrical activity in children exposed to severe psychosocial neglect. *PloS One*, 5(7), e11415. https://doi.org/10.1371/journal.pone.0011415

VanTieghem, M., Korom, M., Flannery, J., Choy, T., Caldera, C., Humphreys, K. L., Gabard-Durnam, L., Goff, B., Gee, D. G., Telzer, E. H., Shapiro, M., Louie, J. Y., Fareri, D. S., Bolger, N., & Tottenham, N. (2021). Longitudinal changes in amygdala, hippocampus and cortisol development following early caregiving adversity. *Developmental Cognitive Neuroscience*, 48, 100916. https://doi.org/10.1016/j.dcn.2021.100916

Weikum, W. M., Oberlander, T. F., Hensch, T. K., & Werker, J. F. (2012). Prenatal exposure to antidepressants and depressed maternal mood alter trajectory of infant speech perception. *Proceedings of the National Academy of Sciences of the United States of America*, 109(Suppl 2), 17227–17227. https://doi.org/10.1073/pnas.1121263109

Wenger, E., Brozzoli, C., Lindenberger, U., & Lövdén, M. (2017). Expansion and renormalization of human brain structure during skill acquisition. *Trends in Cognitive Sciences*, 21(12), 930–939. https://doi.org/10.1016/j.tics.2017.09.008

Wenger, E., Kühn, S., Verrel, J., Mårtensson, J., Bodammer, N. C., Lindenberger, U., & Lövdén, M. (2017). Repeated structural imaging reveals nonlinear progression of experience-dependent volume changes in human motor cortex. *Cerebral Cortex*, 27(5), 2911–2925. https://doi.org/10.1093/cercor/bhw141

Wenger, E., Papadaki, E., Werner, A., Kühn, S., & Lindenberger, U. (2021). Observing plasticity of the auditory system: Volumetric decreases along with increased functional connectivity in aspiring professional musicians. *Cerebral Cortex Communications*, 2(2), tgab008. https://doi.org/10.1093/texcom/tgab008

Werker, J. F., & Hensch, T. K. (2015). Critical periods in speech perception: New directions. *Annual Review of Psychology*, 66, 173–196. https://doi.org/10.1146/annurev-psych-010814-015104

Wesseldijk, L. W., Mosing, M. A., & Ullén, F. (2021). Why is an early start of training related to musical skills in adulthood? A genetically informative study. *Psychological Science*, 32(1), 3–13. https://doi.org/10.1177/0956797620959014

Wiesel, T. N., & Hubel, D. H. (1963). Single-cell responses in striate cortex of kittens deprived of vision in one eye. *Journal of Neurophysiology*, 26(6), 1003–1017. https://doi.org/10.1152/jn.1963.26.6.1003

Wilbrecht, L., Holtmaat, A., Wright, N., Fox, K., & Svoboda, K. (2010). Structural plasticity underlies experience-dependent functional plasticity of cortical circuits. *Journal of Neuroscience*, 30(14), 4927–4932. https://doi.org/10.1523/JNEUROSCI.6403-09.2010

Yuste, R. (2015). The discovery of dendritic spines by Cajal. *Frontiers in Neuroanatomy*, 9, 1–6. https://doi.org/10.3389/fnana.2015.00018

Yusuf, P. A., Hubka, P., Tillein, J., & Kral, A. (2017). Induced cortical responses require developmental sensory experience. *Brain*, 140(12), 3153–3165. https://doi.org/10.1093/brain/awx286

Zatorre, R. J. (2012). Beyond auditory cortex: Working with musical thoughts. *Annals of the New York Academy of Sciences*, 1252, 222–228. https://doi.org/10.1111/j.1749-6632.2011.06437.x

Zhou, B., Zuo, Y. X., & Jiang, R. T. (2019). Astrocyte morphology: Diversity, plasticity, and role in neurological diseases. *CNS Neuroscience and Therapeutics*, 25(6), 665–673. https://doi.org/10.1111/cns.13123

6   Attention and Perception

LEARNING OBJECTIVES

- Discuss the process of visual control in infants
- Describe the three main types of attention and their developmental trajectories
- Characterize infants' sensory capabilities at birth, and how audition and hearing change during infancy
- Explain the dual-route hypothesis of the development of visual perception
- Distinguish between the dorsal and ventral stream visual pathways, and how they develop
- Describe in what way, and why, the perceptual tuning of the fusiform face area changes with age
- Recount research on multisensory integration in infants

For centuries, it was thought that the womb was little more than a dark, isolated environment and that brain development didn't begin until after birth. We now know this could not be further from the truth. Babies may not be able to see in there (after all, it's not a womb with a view), but they *do* experience visual stimulation, hear sounds, and respond to the world at a much earlier age than was originally believed. There is even compelling evidence that the fetus is responding to external stimuli while *in utero*. Indeed, the transition from pre- to postnatal development is continuous, with early brain development impacted in part by the environmental stimulation that is transmitted through the walls and amniotic fluid of the uterus. Postnatal brain volume continues its prenatal trajectory of growth, increasing enormously from infancy to adulthood, with much of that increase occurring in the first few years of life. Part of this growth is due to the explosion of synaptic connectivity that develops as a response to sensory input from the environment, thus shaping an infant's understanding of the complex and dynamic environment. This rich, multimodal input would seem to be overwhelming, but the infant brain responds by gradually building prior knowledge based on latent statistical patterns in what they experience, all in the service of learning.

In this chapter, we first examine attention, how it develops and how it is measured. We then present current arguments about the nature of early perceptual learning, particularly those that characterize infants as masters of Bayesian inference – statistical learning machines. Such arguments provide a foundation for how infants are able to enter the perceptual world and quickly derive knowledge and generate expectations about its structure. Thus, with perceptual learning serving as an important tool for making sense of the world, we are able to focus on how infants process different forms of sensory information, focusing in particular detail on auditory and visual processing, as those senses are the most well understood. We examine aspects of higher-level vision, including the development of neural substrates that support specific aspects of visual processing, with the example of face processing serving as the basis for an extended discussion of perceptual learning and plasticity. Finally, we acknowledge the critical importance of understanding how different sensory modalities develop together and influence one another. Such multisensory processing is, after all, the way most humans experience patterns in the world. But first, the infant has to attend to those patterns.

6.1   Attention

The way an infant manages its attention is a predictor of the quality of executive function and self-control later in life (Chapters 10 and 13). Thus, developing the ability to direct attention, particularly in the face of distraction, is a vital component of goal-directed behavior. Initially, early attention is driven by **exogenous** (external) cues that alert the infant to things in the world; attention gradually becomes more purposeful, self-guided, and **endogenous**. Posner and Petersen (Posner & Petersen, 1990; Petersen & Posner, 2012) outlined three systems of attention that are available to infants at different times. The first, **attentional arousal (alerting)** appears from birth. The second, **selective attention**, starts to emerge at around 2 months and solidifies by 6 months. One source of confusion in this distinction is that the term "orienting" is often used interchangeably with "alerting," when in fact, orienting (e.g., turning your head towards a sound) is relevant to both types of attention. You can *orient* unconsciously to exogenous cues (such as a sudden loud sound) and you can orient for endogenous reasons of your own choosing – such as watching closely as your mother prepares food for you. We reserve the term "alerting" for the *arousal* sense of attentional allocation. The third form of attention, **executive attention**, emerges later in infancy and continues to develop well into toddlerhood. It constitutes the top-down regulation of attention and, as such, is foundational to the development of executive function (Chapter 10).

The relative separation of these three attention types manifests by around 18 months (de Jong et al., 2016), with executive attention undergoing the greatest developmentally-based change, as projections connecting the thalamus, cingulate cortex, and prefrontal structures consolidate as a differentiated network. Toddlers show a corresponding range of cognitive achievements (Alcauter et al., 2014) and considerable development of executive attention skills continues through the second year.

6.1.1   Underpinnings of Arousal

How does the first form of attention, arousal, develop? The primary actor in this process is the **locus coeruleus**, the main source of the **norepinephrine** transmitted to the rest of the brain (Aston-Jones & Cohen, 2005; Tucker et al., 2015). Norepinephrine is a stress hormone and neurotransmitter, driving arousal of the central nervous system via the brainstem and modulating activation of the cortex. The norepinephrine-containing locus coeruleus goes through phasic and tonic modes of activity. In the phasic mode, the system reacts on a short timescale, associated with behavioral responses to salient stimuli; in the tonic mode, it promotes exploratory alertness (Vazey et al., 2018). In adults, locus coeruleus activity is prominently connected to the anterior cingulate and orbitofrontal cortices, structures involved in task switching, representing action goals and intentions, and that help monitor task-related needs (Chapter 13), and that continue developing well into adolescence. Recent studies suggest that phasic changes in infants' arousal levels influence their individual patterns of sustained attention in the first months of life, with low arousal levels relating to longer looking times (de Barbaro et al., 2017). Thus, it appears that this brainstem-based alerting mechanism serves as a primitive way for infants to modulate their attentional focus: high arousal levels may serve to enhance sensitivity to external stimuli, whereas low arousal may help them focus attention longer by reducing reactivity to potential distractors. In other words, early infant attention is dynamically influenced by autonomic arousal, and individual differences in ability to sustain attention may be traced back to this system. As infants develop, this dynamic form of sustained attention gives way to attention under their own control.

6.1.2 Measuring Attention

Infants' patterns of visual fixation change as they transition from arousal/alerting to endogenously controlled selective attention (Colombo et al., 1991). Beyond looking times, infant attention is studied using indicators of distractibility (Ruff & Capozzoli, 2003), heart rate (Richards, 1997), observer reports (Johansson et al., 2015), and composite variables consisting of several measures (Rose et al., 2005, 2012). More recently, researchers are using ERPs (Reynolds & Romano, 2016) and **pupillometry** (Cheng et al., 2019) as measures of attentional focus. (Pupillometry takes advantage of the fact that pupils dilate in response to increased stimulation; Granholm & Steinhauer, 2004; Eckstein et al., 2017.) Findings from these different approaches converge in support of the basic framework that early externally-guided attention transitions to self-guided attention.

As Posner and Rothbart (2013) proposed, the different forms of attention rely on separate but related brain networks. When the reactive alerting networks that are available early (from birth) give way to infants' own attentional control, attention becomes a critical component of lifelong learning (e.g., Kane & Engle, 2002; Klingberg et al., 2002; Cowan & Morey, 2006; Astle & Scerif, 2011; Amso & Scerif, 2015), consistent with findings on the development of working memory (Chapter 10). Thus, attentional processes underpin the development of abilities described throughout the remainder of this book.

6.2 Continuity from Pre- to Postnatal Perceptual Development

Historically, it was thought that human newborns have minimal awareness of their surroundings. On the contrary, newborns are extremely sensitive to their environment. From birth, they react to all forms of sensory input, indicating that their alerting system – involving the brainstem and other subcortical structures – is intact and highly functional. Having detailed knowledge about how newborns perceive perceptual stimuli in the environment can guide how parents and caregivers tailor these early experiences. The fetus experiences external environmental sensory stimulation – particularly sound – albeit in an altered form, filtered by the uterine walls and amniotic fluid, and thus substantially modified. The same sensory stimulation experienced postnatally, without the uterine filtering, is far more detailed and intense, but the *in utero* experiences provide the developmental foundations for perceptual learning.

At birth, after relying solely on the placenta rather than the lungs for respiratory exchange (Koos & Rajaee, 2014), newborns must adjust to breathing through their nose. They also learn to tolerate light, the full frequency range of ambient noises, and significant temperature fluctuations, as well as to feed. All these experiences will be novel, as will the many routine procedures that are performed on them immediately following their arrival in the world.

6.2.1 Little Statisticians

Just how infants process and learn about these new sensations, including their contingent relationships, is not entirely understood. However, an emerging consensus is that infant brains, like their adult counterparts, are, in some sense, statistical machines. Of course, this is not to say that infants have learned anything about numbers, or counting for that matter (Chapter 12), but they implicitly learn the statistical regularities in the world through repeated exposure (Saffran & Kirkham, 2018). In terms of Marr's levels of analysis (Chapter 1), infants' brain structure is directly and uniquely shaped by input from the environment. This shaping impacts infants' responses to the environment. One account for how infants bridge brain and behavior – how they make sense of the world around them – is that they use **Bayesian inferencing** (Gweon et al., 2010), a process positioned firmly at Marr's algorithmic level (Chapter 1).

Bayesian inferencing is just a fancy name for updating your representation of the world as new information comes in. The Bayesian approach does not specify how babies engage with the world, but it does specify how the ongoing inputs and outputs about the world add up. We engage in Bayesian inferencing all the time: you take your baseline information (the *prior* probabilities you've been exposed to) and update it as new information comes in (producing *posterior* probabilities). That is the essence of Bayes' rule. Indeed, the brain is a big Bayesian machine, trying to evaluate the probability of a particular form given observation about the data relevant to it, and adjusting as needed to reduce error.

There's a vigorous debate among computational neuroscientists about whether the brain is *actually* Bayesian or if it just *appears* to be Bayesian, and about how it is implementing these computations. At the moment, this is all up for grabs. There's also an interesting debate about Bayes inferencing works at higher cognitive levels, or only at lower perception levels. For example, people fall prey to all sorts of misunderstandings when they think about probabilities (Kahneman, 2011), often deviating from the logic of Bayes' rules. It often comes down to the way the information is presented. For example, if people are presented with event frequencies, they tend to perform better in their predictions than if they are presented with probabilities. The tension here is that people may primarily use Bayesian inferencing implicitly, but when they try to solve problems explicitly, they resort to heuristics which can lead to irrational decision making. Babies are still developing the foundation for higher-level cognition, which seems to work to their advantage in making sense of the statistical structure around them.

Thus, if we think of perception as the act of inferring what is causing the sensory stimulation that one experiences at any given moment, the evidence in support of the inherent statistical structure of the world guiding this process is unequivocal. This position was first proposed in 1867 by von Helmholtz in his work on **unconscious inference**, resting on early work by Francis Bacon in the 1600s. It was reintroduced and formalized by Irvin Rock in his magnum opus, *The Logic of Perception* (Rock, 1983). The problem for the sensory system is that the input is often ambiguous, partly degraded, or interrupted (such as a cough that obscures part of a spoken word). Perception, like memory, is a *constructive process* that builds the likeliest mental representation of what is out-there-in-the-world.

As seasoned perceivers, adults have acquired an internal model of the world that incoming sensory information gets compared to. The brain adjusts the model to accommodate that incoming information. In essence, the brain is calculating the error between its model of the world and what the sensory information is saying about the actual world. The only way to reduce the error is to update the model – the essence of Bayes' rule. Of course, if we are very certain of our model, we can misunderstand the incoming signal, as is the case with perceptual illusions. Infants start out with only the sparsest of models (although their modeling gets jump-started by their perceptual experiences *in utero*). Once they're out in the world with all senses working, they've got a lot of catching up to do in updating their model! Fortunately for them, the world tends to be highly structured, and that helps to shape their brains and their models. They don't have to think explicitly about probabilities, they just have to learn to make sense of the world. Cognition comes online as the model fills out probabilistically. This accounts for why infants who are raised in an unstructured or disordered world can have trouble later in life.

6.2.2 Timing Matters in How Environmental Structure Impacts the Developing Brain

Because we now understand that both pre- and postnatal sensory stimulation play important roles in perceptual development, researchers are examining continuities (and discontinuities) in infants' experiences to address a range of issues. Nowhere is this more significant than in the case of prematurely born (preterm) infants, whose intrauterine experiences are truncated and whose experience of the extrauterine environment happens far earlier than evolutionary forces were responding to (Pineda et al., 2014). Increased understanding of these issues has led to evidence-based adaptation of care environments for pre- and full-term newborns alike. For example, very premature infants (born between 25 and 32 gestational weeks), exposed to environments enriched with maternal voice and heartbeat while in the neonatal intensive care unit, showed larger gains in growth of their auditory cortices than a matched group of control infants who received no such enrichment (Webb et al., 2015). Such findings complement behavioral data on early sensitivities, telling us that the sounds fetuses are exposed to prenatally prepare their brains for postnatal hearing and language development (Chapter 11). Such knowledge is a prerequisite for assessing the impact of the physical environment and routine procedures that are performed for newborns' welfare.

The idea that auditory information from the environment influences prenatal brain development is consistent with the theme of environmentally dependent developmental change (Chapter 5). Because the pre- to postnatal period is a time of rapid system-wide change, DCN research is interrogating how various forms of input impact fetal and newborn development – perceptual and otherwise – both behaviorally and neurally. For example, early and continuous environmental enrichment has been shown to selectively enhance endogenous repair of developing white matter following brain injuries induced by perinatal hypoxia, promoting myelination and functional recovery in prematurely born infants (Forbes et al., 2020).

All of our senses are present from birth, although none have reached their "peak" sensitivity. One theory is that senses are hyperconnected at birth (**synesthesia**), and that cortical pruning, combined with early sensory experience, creates the typical differentiation most of us experience as adults (Hubbard et al., 2011; Maurer et al., 2020; about 1 in 2,000 adults fail to differentiate and remain synesthetic). We next review the typical developmental timelines for each sense, as all are important, but we spend considerably more time on audition and vision because of their outsized role in language, social cognition, and learning.

6.3   Touch, Taste, Smell

An infant is born with functioning somatosensory (touch), kinesthetic (movement), proprioceptive (position), vestibular (motion-head), and chemosensory (smell and taste) systems. Each system is structurally in place by around 20 gestational weeks and beginning to be functionally operative. Newborns are sensitive to pressure on their skin and different temperatures. They also experience pain, responding with crying and heightened cardiovascular activity (Balaban & Reisenauer, 2013). Not surprisingly, male newborns who are **circumcised** without anesthesia show increased blood pressure and heart rate, as well as decreased oxygen levels in their blood, and a noticeable surge of stress hormones, leading the American Academy of Pediatrics Task Force on Circumcision (2012) to recommend appropriate analgesia for pain management during this procedure.

The olfactory receptor neurons that will process odors begin to develop very early, around weeks 6 and 7 of prenatal development. Likewise, the nasal cavities form in the first trimester, although it will take some time before they open and connect the mouth to the nostrils. Eventually, the olfactory smell receptors will connect with the olfactory bulb in the brain and together these structures support a fetus's ability to smell by early in the third trimester. In postnatal studies of taste, newborns respond with different facial expressions to sour, bitter, sweet, and salty flavors (with a preference for sweet) suggesting that specific receptor sensitivities are already in place.

Newborns also prefer the smell of their mothers, and they are born with preferences acquired in the womb from the smell and taste of **amniotic fluid**, influenced by the mother's diet. As early as 6 days postnatal, infants turn significantly more towards a breast pad saturated with milk from their own mother than to that of another baby's mother (Macfarlane, 1975; Porter et al., 1992). A well-established finding is that, within hours of birth, an infant prefers the face of its own mother to another unfamiliar woman (Bushneil et al., 1989). Given newborns' poor visual acuity, the basis for this early preference has been argued to have as much to do with smell as with vision (Schaal & Durand, 2012).

6.4   Audition

The mother's heartbeat, the sounds of her digestive system, and even the voice and the voices of other family members are part of a baby's prenatal auditory experience. Once a baby is born, the sounds of the outside world come are loud and clear, but the early exposure to sounds while still *in utero* prepare the infant for processing auditory input postnatally. Sound is relayed to the cortex via deep brain structures, but the primary processes underlying hearing are conductive transmission and cochlear stimulation. With these processes in place, neural transmission of auditory input can begin.

6.4.1   Overview of the Primary Auditory Pathway

We distinguish the peripheral from the central auditory systems. For sound to be perceived, it needs to travel from the peripheral hearing structures to the central auditory system. The **peripheral auditory system** includes the outer, middle, and inner ear, along with the cochlea; the **central auditory system** extends from the cochlear nucleus to the auditory cortex. Sound-induced neural stimulation is carried by the auditory (or cochlear) nerve via the **primary auditory pathway**. This pathway carries messages exclusively from the cochlea, up to the nuclei in the brainstem (cochlear nucleus and superior olive), midbrain (inferior colliculus) and thalamus (medial geniculate nucleus), before reaching the primary auditory cortex (see Figure 6.1). A secondary auditory pathway mediates unconscious sound-based perceptual attention, emotional responsivity, and reflexes. A significant number of nerve fibers cross over to make connections with neurons in the hemisphere opposite from the side of the ear in which they begin (Figure 6.1). This crossing produces robust bilateral representation of sound in support of inter-aural comparisons, an important source of information for sound localization.

Neural representation of sound has a long journey before it arrives at the primary auditory cortex, and it is only at this early cortical level that higher-order processing of the content and meaning of sound can begin. At this point, hearing is conscious, and auditory information can be integrated with information from other sensory stimuli (Romanski & Averbeck, 2009).

6.4.2   Converting Sound to Neural Energy

There are three critical acoustic dimensions to consider when thinking about human audition: a sound's intensity, its frequency, and its duration, along with the modulation (changes) in each over time. All this information needs to be maintained when sound waves are converted into neural representation. Sounds are transmitted with fidelity from the ear to the cortex by a series of hierarchical processing pathways, beginning at the **pinna**, the external part of the ear. Hearing relies on environmentally produced sound waves being transmitted from the outer to the inner ear, during which they are physically amplified by three bones in the middle ear (ossicles). The neural processing of sound starts in the inner ear (see Figure 6.2), which consists of both the **cochlea**, for hearing, and the **semicircular canals**, for balance. Sound waves are transmitted from the air in the outer ear to the liquid in the inner ear/cochlea via the ossicles interfacing with the

Figure 6.1 Overview of the primary auditory pathway. The pathway carries nerve impulses from the cochlea, and each relay nucleus does a specific work of decoding and integration. This pathway is short (only 3–4 relays), fast (with large myelinated fibers), and ends in the primary auditory cortex. (Reprinted from Butler & Lomber, 2013)

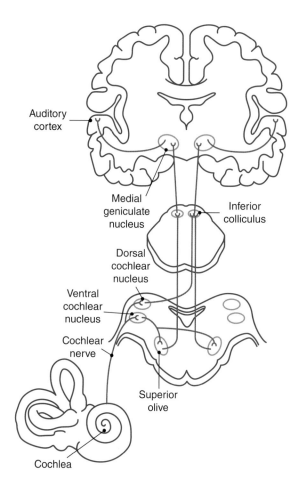

oval window. These sound-induced ripples in the cochlear liquid move the **basilar membrane** – the structure separating the two cochlear compartments – in a wave-like fashion. As the basilar membrane is maximally displaced at different points along its length, it moves sensory receptors, hair-like stereocilia referred to as **hair cells** that are arrayed along the **organ of Corti**. Which hair cells are impacted depends on the specific sound frequency and thus which part of the basilar membrane is maximally displaced. Sound waves dissipate via the round window.

The hair cells are the first point at which sound is converted into the sensation of hearing. It is at this point that **auditory transduction** takes place, whereby sound waves are converted into neural (electrical) signals. The physical nature of the stimulation means that hair cells are mechanoreceptors: their physical bending (if only microscopically so) produces graded neural potentials, helping convey all the different features of complex sound.

Sound frequency is maintained in the transduction process because hair cells are arrayed **tonotopically**, corresponding to where sound waves in the cochlear fluid maximally displace the basilar membrane. High frequencies correspond to points at the membrane's base; low frequencies, at its apex (as shown in Figure 6.3A). Meanwhile, the intensity (volume) of sound is determined by how many hair cells at a particular location are affected by the basilar membrane's

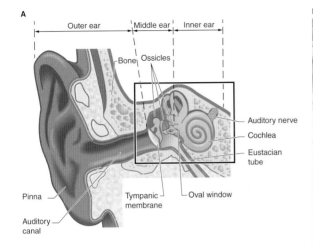

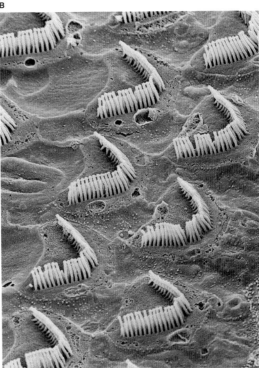

Figure 6.2 How the ear conveys sound to the brain. A. The outer, middle, and inner ear. The inner ear is where sound waves are converted to electrical signals (nerve impulses). B. The spiral shape of the cochlea allows sound wave-induced displacement of the basilar membrane to bend the hair cells on the organ of Corti, depolarizing them, and sending afferent nerve impulses upstream to the brain. (*Cognitive Neuroscience*, Banich & Compton. © 2018 Cambridge University Press. Reproduced with permission of the Licensor through PLSclear)

movement, with bigger waves displacing more hair cells. Hair cells transmit their graded signals to bipolar neurons, the first neurons in the auditory system to fire action potentials. As with the hair cells, bipolar neurons are arranged tonotopically, thus maintaining the **tonotopic organization** of stimulation provided by the hair cells and delivering it further up the auditory processing hierarchy. If you uncoiled the cochlea, frequencies would be laid out in order, like a piano keyboard; this tonotopic map is maintained in primary auditory cortex as well. Figure 6.3A shows the differential exposure to the full range of frequencies pre- and postnatally. The green shaded region highlights those frequencies a fetus is exposed to, while the yellow shaded regions are audible if at high enough intensities. It is only postnatally that the red shaded frequencies are typically experienced, underscoring the importance of protecting prematurely born infants from the full range of auditory stimulation (Lahav & Skoe, 2014).

Hair cells synapse onto spiking neurons whose axons exit the cochlea along its central axis and form the auditory nerve. At each subsequent step, the tonotopic organization that started in the cochlea is maintained, all the way to the auditory cortex itself (see Figure 6.3B), which – along with nearby association areas – collects, deconstructs, and analyzes complex sounds to

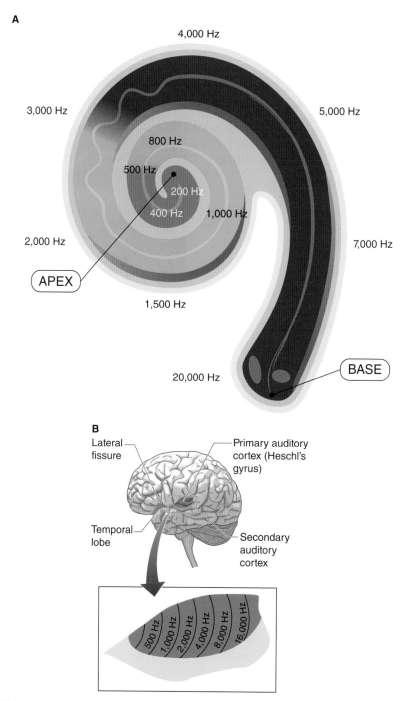

Figure 6.3 Tonotopic organization from cochlea to cortex. A. The cochlea represents the range of frequencies that humans can hear from very high (20,000 Hz) at the base to very low (< 100 Hz) at the apex (Reprinted from Lahav & Skoe, 2014) B. The tonotopic organization of receptors in the cochlea is maintained in the primary auditory cortex (*Cognitive Neuroscience*, Banich & Compton. © 2018 Cambridge University Press. Reproduced with permission of the Licensor through PLSclear)

give rise to auditory perception (Hackett, 2015). In parallel with the ascendant processing of sound information, descending efferent pathways travel from the cortex back to the brainstem, providing an important route for hearing modulation.

6.4.3 Early Hearing Abilities from the Pre- to Postnatal Period

Hearing relies on signals received from the cochlea being transmitted upstream to the auditory cortex, meaning that both peripheral and central auditory systems impact auditory perception. These systems follow different developmental trajectories prenatally, as well as through infancy and childhood. The anatomical components of the peripheral auditory system develop early: the outer, middle, and inner ear form between the gestational ages of 15 and 20 weeks (Graven & Browne, 2008). The components of the central auditory system develop more slowly, emerging around 20 gestational weeks. Although auditory evoked responses have been elicited from a fetus prior to 20 weeks gestational age (Hepper & Shahidullah, 1994), higher-order auditory processing relies on functional connection between the peripheral and central auditory systems, which develops between 25 and 29 weeks (Chapter 8). It is only at this point that the ganglion cells in the cochlea connect to nuclei in the brainstem and can generate a sound-based physiological response. By 25–26 gestational weeks, a loud noise – whether experienced *in utero* or in a neonatal intensive care unit – will produce changes in autonomic function such that heart rate, blood pressure, respiratory pattern, gastrointestinal motility, and oxygenation can all be affected.

Once the peripheral auditory system is in place and connected to the central auditory system, responses to patterned sensory input can begin and will continue postnatally. The entire central auditory system undergoes organization *in utero* in response to stimulation – both endogenous and exogenous. The development of tonotopy in the auditory cortex begins around 30 gestational weeks. Tonotopic representation underlies an infant's ability to receive, recognize, and react to language, music, and other meaningful environmental sounds. Based on their exposure to sounds *in utero*, newborns can discriminate familiar voices, languages, music, and environmental sounds from comparable but novel versions of the same sounds (Chapter 8).

6.4.4 Measurements Specific to Hearing Development

The minimum intensity of a sound that can be detected is the **auditory threshold**, and these thresholds vary by frequency. With brain maturation comes great sensitivity. Overall thresholds improve from about 40–55 dB sound pressure level (SPL) in 1-month-old infants to 10–30 dB SPL in 6- to 12-month-old infants. Behavioral-based threshold estimations for newborns rely on different methods than those used to test older infants (Chapter 2), and are notably higher (70–80 dB SPL). This has led to some questions about their accuracy. Nonetheless, infants' high-frequency auditory thresholds improve between 1 and 6 months of age, with 6-month-olds showing a 4 KHz threshold that is only about 10 dB higher than that of an adult. Low-frequency thresholds mature more slowly, not reaching adult levels until late childhood/pre-adolescence. Longitudinal findings indicate that between 1 and 6 months of age, infants' hearing thresholds improve exponentially (Tharpe & Ashmead, 2001).

EEG is used in various ways to assess hearing. Many countries have introduced so-called universal newborn hearing screening to help ensure that all babies who are born deaf or hard of hearing are identified as soon as possible, with the goal of referring them for early intervention services that will be critical to their early communication and language development. An EEG-based newborn hearing screening tool measures how stimulation from sound moves from the auditory nerve to the brainstem. Crucially, it does not rely on attention from the participant, which is important as newborns generally sleep through the procedure! This measure, alternately referred to as the auditory brainstem response (ABR) or the brainstem auditory evoked potential/response (BAEP/R), involves clicks or tones being played to a newborn through soft earphones while electrodes on the head measure the brainstem's response. ABR analysis focuses on the earliest portion of (0–12 millisecond) of the evoked potential. EEG can be used to test a range of other hearing-based issues as well. For example, repetitive click-sounds of specific frequencies can be presented at different stimulus intensity levels (20 dB, 25 dB, 30 dB, 40 dB, 50 dB, and 70 dB) to determine an individual's hearing SPL at different frequencies. Other analyses – far too many for us to review here – are used to assess, for example, the maturity of the central auditory system.

6.5   Vision

What would it be like to look at the world through the eyes of an infant? And how can we study that? One approach is to see whether an infant looks at and visually follows an object or toy. Another is to check whether an infant blinks in response to a bright light or to check the responsivity of the pupil by shining a small light directly at the eye. Newborns show consistent oculomotor behaviors, interpreted as reflecting visual system organization at birth (Haith, 1980). For example, newborns prefer to look at patterned over non-patterned visual stimuli. Exploiting this bias, Robert Fantz pioneered a technique still widely used in studies with infants and young children (Chapter 2). In its initial form, the technique involved presenting newborns with pairs of pictures or two-dimensional patterns while recording which of a pair most attracted the infant's visual attention, scored as the proportion of fixation times per exposure (Fantz, 1961, 1964). As Fantz observed, infants typically looked longer at a bull's eye versus stripes and checkerboards versus solid forms. Extensive research has revealed a number of additional newborn visual preferences: moving versus static patterns, three- versus two-dimensional forms, and high- versus low-contrast patterns (Slater, 1995), to name just a few.

When newborns emerge from the womb, they aren't able to see much; vision is the slowest of our senses to develop. However, visual perception catches up very quickly with the other senses. Although newborns react to visual stimulation with head and eye movements, their **visual acuity** (detection of fine detail) is relatively poor. At birth, babies see 20/400 (Figure 6.4), but their acuity improves dramatically in the first 3 months, and by 6 months they have 20/20 vision and, assuming they have normal color vision, perceive the full spectrum of colors (some form of color blindness affects 1 in 12 males and 1 in 200 females). Initially, newborns see only black, white, and shades of gray, with red and green emerging between 3 and 4 months (Adams et al., 1994). Their perception of blue and violet lags a bit further in time due to the human

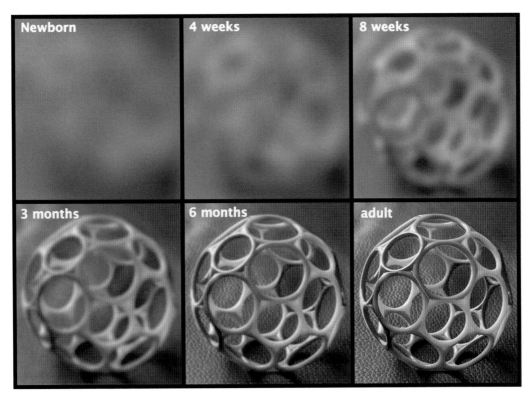

Figure 6.4 Estimation of acuity and color perception changes in infants in the first six months and compared to adults.

retina's comparably fewer receptors specific to the shorter wavelengths of blue light. Infants' perceptual sensitivity to contrast and to motion direction also starts out relatively limited and then improves (Banks & Salapatek, 1983). In addition to reduced visual acuity, newborns' field of view is limited, meaning that they often miss visual targets that are too far away, or too far from their central focal point (in their peripheral vision). Moreover, at birth, infants lack stereopsis, the perception of depth supported by the slight difference in input from each of the two eyes (i.e., binocular disparity). Stereopsis emerges about 8 weeks postnatally (Brown & Miracle, 2003) but only when infants are exposed to a 3D environment.

In short, infants' eyesight improves across the first 6 months of postnatal life with each specific aspect of vision improvement occurring on a distinct timeline, corresponding to development of the neural underpinnings supporting each. Maturation of the eye and the cortical structures, increased synaptic connectivity and myelination, and learning about the visual environment itself all contribute to these developmental advances.

6.5.1 The Neural Basis for Vision

Human vision relies on light reflecting off objects in the world. Light (i.e., electromagnetic radiation) propagates as a wave with a certain amplitude, wavelength (the inverse of frequency), which our visual system has evolved to transduce into neural energy that our brain uses to derive meaningful information. Light waves enter the eye through the cornea, refract, and traverse through the pupil and lens where they are focused onto the retina.

The conversion of light energy into neural activity starts in the retina, which consists of several layers of cells (Figure 6.5). Light-induced neural energy propagates through these layers, first impinging on the **photoreceptors (rods and cones)**. Cones are concentrated in the fovea and process visual detail; rods cover the retinal periphery and process low-level contrast. Although infants are born with the retinal layers and neurons in place, the outer segments of the foveally based cones are underdeveloped, which accounts for their poor acuity in the first months of life (Abramov et al., 1982).

Light information encoded by the photoreceptors is transmitted by downstream retinal neurons in a graded fashion. The **retinal ganglion cells** are the first neurons in the visual processing pathway to fire all-or-none action potentials, and their axons form the optic nerve upon exiting the retina. Optic nerve fibers cross from one hemisphere to the other at the optic chiasm, meaning that visual input to the left visual field of each eye is conveyed to the right hemisphere and vice versa. (This contralateral organization holds for many other processing pathways in the brain as well, for example, audition and sensory-motor.) Thus, damage to left hemisphere visual cortex can result in loss of vision in the right visual field and vice versa, much as damage to left hemisphere motor cortex can result in loss of motor function in the right side of the body.

After leaving the optic chiasm, about 90 percent of the neural activation related to vision is carried to the **lateral geniculate nucleus (LGN)** in the thalamus, and on to the **primary visual cortex** and the rest of the brain. (Primary visual cortex is also referred to as **V1** or **striate cortex**.) This **geniculostriate pathway** underlies our detailed perception of shapes and colors. Connections between the cortex and the thalamus are reciprocal, such that visual cortical neurons provide feedback to the LGN to further support processing and visual attention.

Retinal ganglion cells can be distinguished by their responsivity to distinct flavors of visual information. The two best characterized ones, identified according to their processing-specific characteristics, are known as **magnocellular (M cells)** and **parvocellular (P cells)**. These cells represent parallel processing pathways that convey different forms of visual information. (Another cell type, referred to as koniocellular, appears to be involved in color vision.) M cells contribute to fast/transient processing (i.e., visual motion perception, eye movements) and P cells contribute to recognition (i.e., objects, faces). These two classes of cell are anatomically, physiologically, and functionally distinct: M cells receive input largely from the rods; P cells from the cones. Critically, M cells fire action potentials when a stimulus is introduced, but quickly quiet down if the stimulus does not change. P cells, meanwhile, respond in a sustained manner to stimuli in their receptive fields. The cumulative effect is that M cells conduct neural signals faster and P cells convey constant and detailed information about a stimulus. Collectively, M and P cells provide complete (or nearly complete) coverage of the entire retina.

The inputs from these retinal ganglion cells to the LGN are organized into six distinct layers: the bottom two defined by M cell projections, and the top four by P cell projections. Additional segregation of input to the thalamus by eye of origin maintains information about each eye's left and right visual fields (Figure 6.5). This organizational structure is further maintained in early visual cortex, with M and P cells projecting to different layers of V1. V1 itself is the primary distributor of almost all visual information, with higher-level visual areas receiving almost all input for further analysis either directly or indirectly from V1.

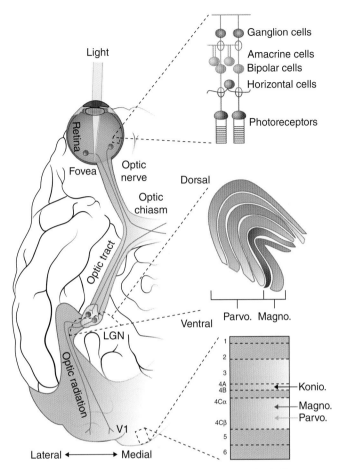

Figure 6.5 Visual pathway from retina to cortex, including a cross-section of the cells in the back of the retina, and the structure of the lateral geniculate nucleus. Optic nerves from each eye meet at the optic chiasm, where nerve fibers associated with the nasal (inner) half of the retina from each eye cross over. Leaving the optic chiasm, nerve fibers from the nasal retina of one eye travel down the optic tract with nerve fibers originating from the temporal retina of the other eye. At the thalamus, the retinal nerve fibers connect with other visual pathway nerves in the LGN. The LGN contains circuits where information is sorted differentially from magno- and parvocellular input. The optic radiation (fibers) then deliver the information to area V1 in the visual cortex. (Reprinted from Jeffries et al., 2014)

6.5.2 Visual Development: From Reflexive Looking to Visual Control

As with other sensory systems, the anatomy of the human visual system develops early. The retina begins to form around 40 days gestational age, and its complete cellular organization is in place by 160 days gestational age. The distinction between retinal cells committed to foveal and extrafoveal visual processing is also present early, although the topology and patterning of receptors and their corresponding neurons will continue to take shape throughout prenatal development and well into the first year of life. Postmortem data show that major subcortical and cortical visual structures (neurons, layers, areas) are in place by the end of the second trimester (e.g., Zilles et al., 1986). The subcortical system (i.e., superior colliculus, brainstem) critical to controlling eye movements – as well as the muscles underlying those movements – also develop prior to birth (Prechtl, 2001).

Given that infants experience visual input only postnatally, how does all this early developing structure get wired up? Although substantial shaping continues postnatally, a basic version of cortical areal patterning is present from the first trimester, including the visual cortex. **Retinotopic mapping** of the visual cortex is further supported *in utero* by spontaneous (intrinsic) neural activity. Starting at the retina and cascading through the visual system, this spontaneous activity contributes to the preservation of the system's sensory structure (Cang et al., 2005), including circuit refinement (Kerschensteiner & Wong, 2008), all before the baby is born! The sudden availability of light to the eyes postnatally corresponds with a surge in synaptogenesis, followed by a more protracted period during which synapses are eliminated in an activity-dependent manner (Chapter 5). Thus, synapses are preserved in active cortical circuits and lost in inactive ones.

A small percentage (~10%) of retinal fibers do not contribute to the geniculostriate pathway to V1, and instead form a **subcortical pathway** providing a low-resolution image of the visual world to guide infants' initial eye movements towards potentially important cues such as object motion and relative size (Johnson, 1990). This subcortical pathway (Figure 6.6) projects from the retina to the **superior colliculus** (in the midbrain) and the pulvinar nucleus (in the thalamus), and includes projections to regions that will contribute to mobilization in response to threats and other salient events (i.e., the amygdala and anterior cingulate cortex) (LeDoux, 1996; Morris et al., 1999). Because the superior colliculus begins functioning in the third trimester, this pathway can be used by infants from birth (Atkinson, 2002), while the geniculostriate pathway matures much more slowly. Ultimately, the subcortical visual pathway will project to area hMT+, thus contributing to the dorsal processing stream of the geniculostriate pathway. At birth, involuntary and exogenously driven visual fixation will dominate infants' looking behavior for the first 2 months of life, at which point they will gradually obtain voluntary control of their eye movements, reaching full control by around 6 months of age (Courage et al., 2006). Note that this timeline is aligned with the description of development of attentional control we outlined earlier; research on infant attention is based largely on visual processes. How well other senses guide attentional allocation in the first months of life is an active topic of research.

6.5.3 Segregation of Vision into Dorsal and Ventral Streams

The visual system is complex, and the primate visual cortex contains over 25 distinct visual cortical areas beyond V1 (Felleman & Van Essen, 1991; Van Essen et al., 1992). Different areas pool input from increasingly large portions of the visual field to support increasingly complex and specific visual functions, including object recognition, motion perception, and the representation of visual space. Given the large number of separate regions, each dedicated to the processing of specific visual cues, the initial view of the neural basis for visual processing was fractionated until Leslie

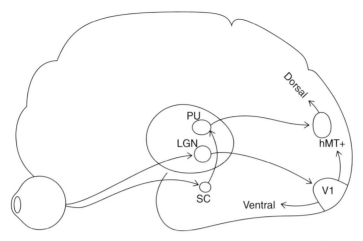

Figure 6.6 A sketch of the subcortical visual pathway. While 90% of optic fibers project to the lateral geniculate nucleus (LGN) and on to primary visual cortex (V1), the remaining 10% project to the superior colliculus (SC) and pulvinar nucleus (PU). A projection also delivers information from the pulvinar to the human middle temporal complex area (hMT+), which contributes to input to the dorsal visual stream, while the ventral stream receives input largely from the LGN via V1. (Reprinted from Strand-Brodd et al., 2011)

Ungerleider and Mortimer Mishkin provided a welcome simplification and a useful framework by proposing two distinct processing streams. These streams, the dorsal and ventral pathways (Ungerleider & Mishkin, 1982), represent an early sorting of visual information into featural and motion dimensions in the LGN (consistent with the P and M cell differentiation of information in the retinae). Indeed, these two major pathways (Figure 6.7A) are distinguished by their processing content. The **ventral visual stream**, or **"what" pathway**, is involved in object recognition and memory; the **dorsal visual stream**, or **"where" pathway**, is involved in perceiving motion.

Beyond V1, the ventral and dorsal pathways emerge as distinct processing trajectories, with the ventral pathway projecting first to extrastriate visual areas V2 and V4, and then ventrally to regions of the inferior temporal lobe that support object recognition. Object perception relies on P cell encoding of many visual processing attributes. As such, different areas in the visual cortex are responsible for processing one or more of the many visual attributes that define edges, surfaces, and objects. The dorsal stream, meanwhile, is largely responsible for processing visual motion coded by M cell inputs. It extends up to visual area MT (also called area V5, or human middle temporal complex (hMT+)) and on to the posterior parietal cortex and other areas implicated in attention, working memory, and motor planning.

The what/where framework has been recast in recent years as reflecting the contribution of each pathway to different functions or output requirements. This reconceptualization posits that the ventral, "what" pathway is responsible for vision-for-perception, while the dorsal pathway – in this context dubbed the **"where/how" pathway** – is responsible for vision-for-action (Goodale & Milner, 1992). Integrating these two views, some researchers refer to the dorsal

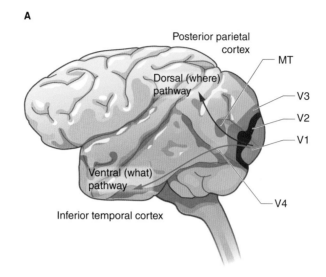

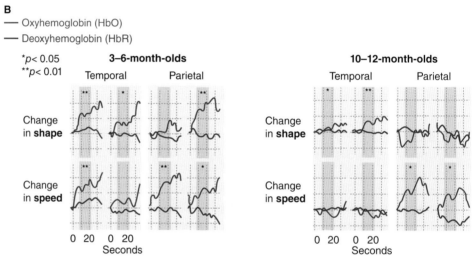

Figure 6.7 Primary visual pathways and how to test for them in infants. A. The dorsal (where/how) and ventral (what) visual pathways. B. Findings from infants of different ages indicate a dissociation of ventral and dorsal stream engagement in the processing of shape and speed changes across the first year of life, as indicated by relative changes in concentration of oxygenated (oxy) in red and deoxygenated (deoxy) hemoglobin in blue. A mature hemodynamic function as measured by fNIRS shows an increase in oxy concentration and a corresponding decrease in deoxy concentration. Significance is measured by comparing concentration of oxygenated hemoglobin during a targeted time window relative to its concentration measured during a pre-stimulus baseline. (Adapted from Wilcox et al., 2014)

stream as the where/how pathway. Indeed, although the general division of labor in the ventral/dorsal streams is supported by decades of research employing a wide range of methods (for a review, see Goodale & Milner, 2018), there is evidence that neither of these frameworks (what/where or what/how) fully captures the array of functional capabilities of each pathway.

For example, the dorsal pathway has been shown to play a role in object perception (Freud et al., 2016), specifically in diverse perceptual functions such as 3D perception, localization of objects, and spatiotemporal integration.

Nonetheless, the overall dorsal/ventral framework holds, helping make the complex array of visuoperceptual and visuospatial functions performed by the human visual system – and how this information contributes to higher-level cognitive processes – easier to understand.

6.5.4 Development of Advanced Visual Processing Capabilities

How do infants come to perceive objects as individual entities in what must first appear to be a cluttered visual world? An early view – the object-first hypothesis (Xu & Carey, 1996) – held that children organize information in their visual field much like adults do, namely, in terms of space, objects, and movement. According to this view, infants experience objects moving through time and space as coherent, cohesive entities. This would mean that infants represent objects using both spatiotemporal and categorical information: that is, information about when, where, and what is presented visually. However, infants' performance in tasks that require them to use featural information haven't always supported this perspective. To address this discrepancy in the literature, Renée Baillargeon and colleagues have suggested that infants integrate featural information using what they have called physical reasoning abilities (Stavans et al., 2019). According to this account, they are able to use featural information to guide understanding of when and where they occur earlier than for distinguishing objects in the environment. Others suggest that a more parsimonious account would focus on infants' physical reasoning abilities alone (Hildebrandt et al., 2020).

While this debate is ongoing, tools from DCN have provided some insight into the developmental time course by which infants show neural evidence of processing different visual features. For example, Teresa Wilcox and colleagues used fNIRS to dissociate infants' neural responses to featural and spatiotemporal information (Wilcox et al., 2005, 2008, 2009). To test infants' sensitivity to different visual features, a gloved hand moved objects back and forth behind a central occluder while infants observed the live event. In this way, researchers were able to introduce featural (i.e., shape) changes or spatiotemporal (i.e., speed) changes to an otherwise uniform visual scene. How infants' process these two visual features becomes neurally dissociable by the end of the first year of life. From 3 months until 7 or 8 months of age, both shape and speed engage dorsal stream processing. (Wilcox et al., 2014); however, between 7 and 12 months, the dorsal stream ceases to be engaged during shape processing (Figure 6.7B). Thus, younger infants appear to rely as much on motion as on shape for early object processing, likely due to their poor visual acuity and to the subcortical processing pathway.

As children develop into early and middle childhood, an array of additional visual processing capabilities – including object tracking, depth perception, and visual focus – continue to develop as well. This means that what children do visually can impact their visual development. In fact, the amount of time young children spend outdoors in natural light reduces the likelihood that they will develop myopia (near sightedness). People with myopia can see close-up objects clearly, but their distance vision is blurry. A growing incidence in children appears to be related to modern changes in their behavior, such that children who spend more time indoors in front of screens rather than outdoors in natural light show the greatest increase

(Wang et al., 2021). Sadly, what had already been a notable increase in myopia diagnoses grew larger still during the Covid-19 pandemic, a time during which children the world over stayed indoors staring at screens rather than attending school in person and engaging in activities outside in natural daylight (Klaver et al., 2021).

6.6   Higher-Level Vision

Visual perception is among the most vigorously researched topics in neuroscience. Low-level visual processing is concerned with issues such as how the retina transduces light and how the visual system extracts features from retinal stimulation. Moving up to mid-level vision, DCN researchers study how these features are used to recognize objects (via statistical inferencing to follow "the logic of perception"). But beyond how surfaces are segmented into separable objects, we want to understand how the visual system recognizes what category each object belongs to – that this one is a "dog," that one a "car," that one a "cup." Imaging data have revealed much about how the human brain is organized into systems specialized for recognizing objects, faces, and scenes, along with many other specific cognitive functions; questions remain relating to how such capabilities arise. Are these networks – and the regions comprising them – already specialized at birth, or do they develop over time with experience? We'll pursue these and other questions in the remaining sections of this chapter, first with a focus on face processing, as it requires sophisticated visual analysis and develops quite slowly.

6.6.1   Face Recognition

The **ventral temporal cortex** has been associated with face processing since Penfield first elicited hallucinations of faces by stimulating his surgical patients' fusiform gyri (Penfield & Perot, 1963). Based on the extensive structural and functional neuroimaging of adult brains that has taken place since, the consensus is that the **face processing network** (Figure 6.8) in most adults contains a highly systematic functional organization whereby the P cell-fueled ventral visual stream emerges at V1, passes this information on to subsequent occipital areas, and delivers it to higher-level visual regions in the occipitotemporal and temporal cortices. This transmission of information doesn't end there, however, and it's worth noting that information is passed bidirectionally; there are at least as many projections back to V1 as there are afferents to it (Pennartz et al., 2019)! Despite this complexity, the processing trajectory and face network are highly structured and reliable across individuals.

Consistent with Penfield's observations, the ventral temporal cortex includes regions that respond to a range of behaviorally significant stimulus categories, including faces, bodies, and scenes. Of note are two regions whose responsivity to particular classes of objects is demonstrated by robust and highly replicated research (Varoquaux et al., 2018): the fusiform gyrus (**fusiform face area, FFA**) in response to faces and the parahippocampal gyrus (**parahippocampal place area, PPA**) in response to visual scenes or places. Accordingly, the FFA is one of the most extensively studied cortical areas, described first by Justine Sergent (Sergent & Signoret, 1992), and then characterized in greater detail by Nancy Kanwisher (Kanwisher et al., 1997; see also

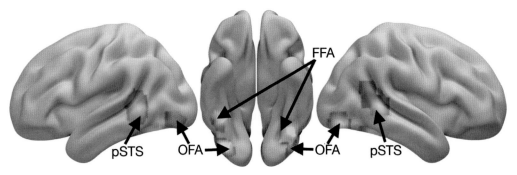

Figure 6.8 The adult face processing network includes the occipital face area (OFA), the fusiform face area (FFA), and the posterior superior sulcus (pSTS). Here bilateral FFA, OFA, and a region in the pSTS responded more to faces than to scrambled faces and objects. (Reprinted from Davies-Thompson et al., 2019)

Kanwisher, 2017). An analogous region in macaque monkeys, the superior temporal sulcus (STS), shows face selectivity in fMRI scans (Tsao et al., 2006). Moreover, single-cell recordings from the same monkeys show face-selective responses in that region. These face-selective cells form "face patches" akin to those observed in humans (Tsao et al., 2008), all of which has led some to conclude that face processing is a strongly modular ability in primates (and has led some to describe this specificity proof of the existence of "grandmother cells" that perceive only Grandma (Gross, 2002)).

Another approach is to functionally define regions in human ventral temporal cortex (Weiner & Grill-Spector, 2013). For example, fMRI multivariate pattern analysis shows that face identities can be distinguished based on their elicited response patterns not only in the FFA, but in the larger face processing network (Figure 6.8), including the occipital face area and the posterior superior temporal sulcus (pSTS) (Davies-Thompson et al., 2019). While the features that drive activation of specific regions within this network are only just being delineated (see Tsantani et al., 2021), the consensus view is that we use a broadly defined perceptual system when we process faces, one that underpins the general face network observed in human adults (Arcaro et al., 2019).

6.6.2   Dedicated Brain Areas Are Further Tuned to Faces through Experience

Although some still consider the FFA (actually, we now know there are two face-selective areas; see Box 6.1) to be hard-wired for face processing across healthy individuals, and already in place for infants to use as they begin processing faces, the picture is more far more nuanced. First, there is the broader face processing network, which includes many co-activated regions (Freiwald et al., 2016). At first blush, that these regions are all responsive to faces may seem to underscore the face-specificity of the network, but the way in which this network develops in the first year of life and progresses developmentally into adulthood reveals that experience with faces is a critical component of the formation of this network.

How does face-specific cortical processing come about? One possibility is that it relies on development of the ventral visual pathway. Another possibility is that there's an early-developing subcortical pathway that focuses infants on faces early on, along with the later-maturing one that enables fine-grained discrimination between faces. This **dual-route hypothesis**, proposed by Mark Johnson and colleagues (Johnson et al., 1991), holds that newborns' sensitivity to faces is initially driven by a primitive bias to be alert to patterns with face-like configurations. Indeed, newborns respond preferentially to face-like stimuli, but only when conditions favor subcortical processing – for example, when the image is moving, or located in their visual periphery rather than centrally (Morton & Johnson, 1991). Even with the neocortex fully engaged, adults continue to use subcortical structures in face processing, including the superior colliculus, amygdala, and hippocampus (Mende-Siedlecki et al., 2013). This means that initial processing of faces doesn't start in the FFA, or anywhere else in the cortex – even if the brain has evolved to process faces there – and that the FFA is not the sole contributor to humans' face processing prowess.

The face-favoring functional organization observed in adults is the product of accrual of experience and improved face discrimination abilities. Developmental changes in the face network reflect this, becoming increasingly specific based on dedicated processing of certain things (i.e., faces) over others (Golarai et al., 2010). For example, face recognition is better in adults than children, with response properties of the neural regions in the face network changing during the transition from childhood to adolescence, and between adolescence and adulthood (Gomez et al., 2017). Neural sensitivity in face-selective regions to face identity improves perceptual discriminability of those faces across development time (Natu et al., 2016). And, although differential activation to faces relative to other stimulus categories has been observed in the ventral fusiform in 4- to 6-month-old infants (Deen et al., 2017), this localization is broad and not specific to the FFA.

Thus, it is clear that newborn visual attention is attracted to low-level perceptual properties of visual stimuli whose effect is to create increasingly complex visual preferences, including for parts of faces, then for faces, and then for specific faces. This shaping, narrowing, or **perceptual tuning**, is a consequence of the species-specific environment in which a child is born (a detailed examination of this perspective applied to faces is presented in Box 6.1). Face tuning has two developmentally based outcomes: stronger neural responses (and correspondingly longer looking times) to faces relative to other visual stimuli (i.e., face identification), and differential responses to different faces (i.e., face discrimination/recognition). The face network also gains a more expansive representation of face-related categories, or classes, with progressive and gradual specialization of the cortical brain areas that ultimately are involved in face processing.

6.6.3   Is It Expertise in Faces, or Configurations?

Our species-specific environment ensures that we see a lot of faces. What if one's experience is uniquely focused on something other than faces? Isabel Gauthier and her colleagues wondered whether *expertise* – accrued through extensive experience discriminating visually similar exemplars of a particular category of objects – drives specialization of face-specific

Box 6.1 High-Level Visual Cortex as a Window into Brain Development

How brain anatomy and function change with childhood experience and underlie our behavior are central questions in DCN. They are explored here using, as a test-bed, regions of high-level visual cortex that respond preferentially to face stimuli (two patches that constitute the fusiform face area; FFA) and scenes (parahippocampal place area; PPA), shown in Box Figure 6.1A. The neural selectivity of these regions appears to emerge from early and prolonged visual experience (e.g., Srihasam et al., 2014; Arcaro et al., 2017). Indeed, there is a rich behavioral literature demonstrating that face recognition skill takes time to develop – likely into one's thirties (Germine et al., 2011).

While the general response pattern across high-level visual cortex seems to be qualitatively present as early as age 5, there is ongoing development and tuning of functional responses – at least for face areas. Face regions increase in size and response magnitude to faces with age; by contrast, the place area shows on average little or no increase in size or selectivity by this point in development (see Box Figure 6.1B and C). This uniquely protracted development of face areas is thought to represent the extensive exposure to, and social pressure to differentiate, faces.

Two characteristics have been shown to change as children get better at recognizing faces: the neural tuning of face regions gets sharper with development, and the way children scan faces changes, with fixations becoming more central by adulthood (Gomez et al., 2018). In fact, it is hypothesized that it is the small and central image a face makes on our retina (compared to the more peripherally extending image of a building or place) that biases face information towards the fusiform gyrus in visual cortex, which has more connectivity to foveal inputs compared to peripheral ones (Box Figure 6.1D). Over development, this consistent foveal versus peripheral input may drive responses differentially to the fusiform gyrus and CoS [collateral sulcus], which respectively have more connectivity to the center (warm colors) and periphery (cool colors) of visual inputs. This **"retinal eccentricity" hypothesis** (Malach et al., 2002) has even been shown to predict the location of new learned visual categories (Gomez et al., 2018). Hence, experience plays a critical role in sculpting the cortical circuitry that underlies our learned perceptual skills.

If face-selective regions mature in size and selectivity, do their underlying tissue structures grow to accommodate these improvements? Prevailing views hypothesized that the gray matter of the brain thins with age, often ascribed to pruning of unnecessary structures for more refined functions in adulthood. Contrary to this hypothesis, using quantitative MRI, a novel MRI scan that taps into cortical tissue properties, it is now believed that there is tissue growth as school-aged children learn to recognize faces and read. This growth is likely linked to dendritic arborization (Gomez et al., 2017) and increased myelination of axons (Natu et al., 2019). In contrast, the place region, which showed no functional development during childhood, displayed no tissue growth.

To fully understand the origins of human socio-cognitive skills, future work on the infant brain is critical (see Deen et al., 2017; Lochy et al., 2019), as is additional research on individuals with prosopagnosia, impairment in face recognition ability that is thought to result from atypically developing face regions (e.g., Song et al., 2015).

Box 6.1 (cont.)

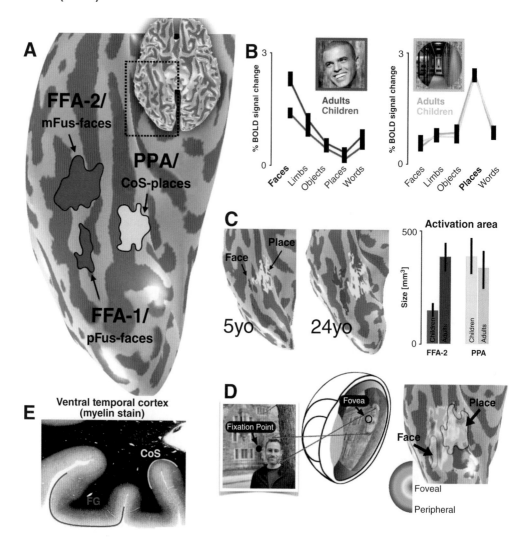

Box Figure 6.1 Brain anatomy and function change with visual experience. A. A sample participant's brain showing the FFA (FFA-1 and FFA-2 combined) in red and the PPA in yellow. B. With development, the BOLD signal differs between 5- to 12-year-olds and 22- to 30-year-olds in the FFA in responses to faces, but not in the PPA in response to scenes. Black bars show the standard error across individuals. C. Face- and place-selective regions in a 5-year-old and 24-year-old, illustrating an increase in the size of FFA with age, as shown in the bars on the right. D. The image produced on the retina by a face embedded in a scene shows that when we fixate on a face within a typical conversational viewing distance (5–6 feet away) the face overlaps the fovea and extends only 5–7 degrees beyond the fovea, while the building in the background extends to the periphery of the retina. The outlined gray regions show where the face and place regions are located within a colormap showing how high-level visual cortex is connected to visual inputs from retinotopic low-level visual cortex.

Contributed by Vaidehi S. Natu, PhD, Research Associate, Stanford Vision and Perception Neuroscience Lab, Department of Psychology, Stanford University, and Jesse Gomez, PhD, Assistant Professor, Princeton Neuroscience Institute, Princeton University

processing regions. In a theoretical challenge to the received wisdom at the time about the primacy of faces to the FFA, Gauthier and her colleagues scanned individuals who had developed extreme visual expertise in categories beyond faces (Gauthier et al., 2000). Results showed FFA responsivity to faces, as well as adjacent activation in response to experts' particular objects of expertise. For example, car experts exhibited greater activity in response to cars than to other objects (i.e., birds), while bird experts exhibited greater activity in response to birds than to cars. This elegant double dissociation was an early demonstration of the critical impact of experience on perceptual tuning of face areas. Moreover, to determine whether unique aspects of car and bird experts were the source of this effect rather than their visual expertise, the research trained naïve participants to recognize novel creature-like objects ("greebles"). Following extensive greeble-training, these newly minted greeble-experts showed greeble-specific activation in the vicinity of FFA, akin to that seen in the car and bird experts (Gauthier et al., 1999). Thus, while humans generally use their FFA for processing faces, it's a region that can be recruited in support of a range of other fine-grained, subordinate level visual processing (Tarr & Gauthier, 2000). (Your authors find this result very agreeble.)

In a study akin to the greeble findings, Jesse Gomez and colleagues identified a sufficient number of adults who had played a particular Pokémon computer game extensively as children (Gomez et al., 2019), contrasting scans of these people with scans from non-experts. Results showed increased cortical activation in the ventral temporal cortex in the Pokémon experts relative to the Pokémon novices. Notably, this activation was not in classically defined face areas

Figure 6.9 The occipitotemporal sulcus (OTS) of adults who played Pokémon extensively as children activated more (right) upon seeing images of Pokémon characters from their childhood videogames compared to adults who did not (left). (Image credit: Jesse Gomez)

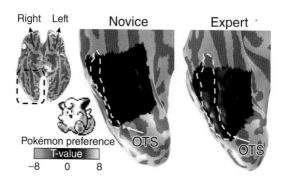

but rather in the occipital temporal sulcus (see Figure 6.9). Because these Pokémon experts had been focused on tiny screen-based animations of the characters on Nintendo Game Boys, the visual information was hitting their retinae differently than when we normally look at faces, meaning it was being delivered to different subregions of the ventral temporal system. This accounts for why the Pokémon-induced activation was observed somewhere other than the traditional face processing regions!

A critique of this "expertise" account of the face processing network is that cars, birds, and greebles all have something like a face, as do Pokémon figures: they are configurally structured like faces (Kanwisher, 2000). Indeed, initial imaging work with individual Pokémon experts (James & James, 2013) found activation specifically in the FFA. This argument turns the expertise account on its head by claiming that the increased involvement of face regions of the brain observed in experts of non-face objects comes about because people use their "face processing module" to individuate those objects. We'll admit that, given the long evolutionary history of humans looking at faces and not at cars or Pokémon, face-specific pressures cannot be discounted. However, face processing is clearly not as modular as originally surmised.

One caveat to this is the existence of **developmental prosopagnosics**, people who from birth are unable to recognize familiar faces, including their own (!), despite intact visual processing and intellectual functioning abilities. Developmental prosopagnosia affects about 1 in 50 individuals (acquired prosopagnosia can occur following brain damage). Prosopagnosia was long thought untreatable, but Ken Nakayama and colleagues have shown that holistic face processing can help remediate it (DeGutis et al., 2014).

The existence of prosopagnosics has been taken as more evidence that the brain evolved the face-specific network (and particularly the FFA) for face-specific processing. For example, some (e.g., Avidan et al., 2014) have interpreted findings that prosopagnosics show normal FFA activation during face recognition but no activation in other regions of the face network (as well as reduced connectivity overall within that network) as supporting a modular view. But as we have seen, it's not just the FFA that matters to face processing; it's how the FFA communicates with other regions to support the exquisite perceptual work we do when we process faces. One can imagine a neurodevelopmentally-based constraint on connectivity that would lead to such a condition, whereby the full network is prevented from wiring up. This interpretation is consistent with findings that different patches of face-specific cortex are tuned to different visual properties of faces and that they all work in concert to support face processing. In short, what looks like an evolutionarily adapted region for faces is more likely a network that takes on the function of discriminating faces by virtue of the fact that, from an early age, it is engaged to process stimuli with those particular visual features (see Grill-Spector & Weiner, 2014).

6.6.4 Effects of Face Deprivation

The results we have reviewed here highlight the inherent plasticity of even the most modular-seeming processing (i.e., faces), as well as the neural structures that support it. Evidence of an interplay between genetic predispositions and environmental influences in the face processing domain comes from behavioral and brain imaging studies in which infant macaque monkeys had no exposure to faces or face-like stimuli during a critical window of development (Sugita, 2008; Arcaro et al., 2017, 2020). Although these studies involved small numbers of monkeys (with good reason) the results are quite thought-provoking. For example, Yoichi Sugita (2008) separated monkeys from their mothers immediately after birth. The researchers wore masks when handling the monkeys, and they positioned the cages in such a way that the face-deprived monkeys couldn't see – but could hear, smell, and interact with – other monkeys in the colony. The human caregivers/researchers did their best to nurture these **face-deprived** monkeys, providing them with a visually rich environment with lots of colorful toys and decorations. Nonetheless, it must be acknowledged that maternal separation negatively impacts socioemotional development (Waddoups et al., 2019).

Critical to the face perception issue, the researchers varied the face-deprivation period for different monkeys, for 6, 12, or 24 months of life. The period of total face deprivation was followed by one month of *selective* face deprivation. Six monkeys were exposed first to human faces, interacting with unmasked humans for around 2 hours per day for 1 month before being reintroduced to their monkey colony. Another group of face-deprived monkeys was exposed first to monkey faces by being housed with another monkey while continuing to interact with masked humans.

Like humans, monkeys are naturally attracted to faces (or, at least, face-like stimuli) from infancy onward (Leopold & Rhodes, 2010). Looking times to different pictures were used to test the monkeys' visual preferences (Figure 6.10A), along with a summary of looking time data (Figure 6.10B). Control monkeys that were raised with other monkeys and exposed to humans preferred to look at monkey faces over human faces. Prior to being exposed to actual faces, the face-deprived infant monkeys preferred to look at pictures of faces relative to objects, looked at human and monkey faces equally, and discriminated equally between them. Thus far, these findings are consistent with arguments for a biologically-based face predisposition. However, after 1 month of being exposed only to humans, the face-deprived monkeys no longer

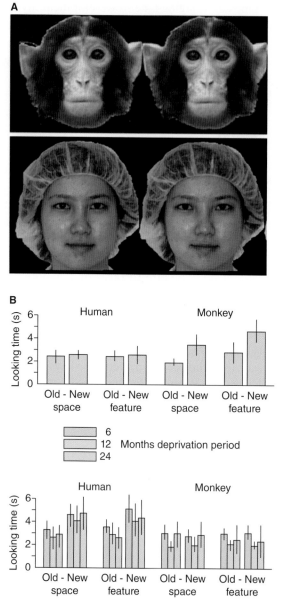

Figure 6.10 Face perception in monkeys. A. Two sample face discrimination trials, one with monkey faces, and another with human faces. Both trials feature subtle differences in the spacing between the two eyes, and between the eyes and mouth. (Adapted from Sugita, 2008.) B. Gray bars show looking time, in seconds, to human faces and monkey faces in typically-reared adult monkeys. The comparison of "old" and "new" bars indicates whether monkeys exhibited a preference for novel faces. Trials involving a manipulation of the spacing between features, or the features themselves, are labeled as "space" and "feature," respectively. Colored bars show looking time after 6, 12, or 24 months of face deprivation followed by 1 month of exposure only to human faces. (Adapted from Sugita, 2008) C. Cortical flat maps showing visual brain areas in individual monkeys, with differential activation for faces vs. objects (in warm colors) and objects vs. faces (in cool colors) in the right and left hemispheres. Data from two control monkeys are featured on the left, and two face-deprived monkeys on the right. Dotted white ovals indicate the STS region of interest. (Reprinted from Arcaro et al., 2017)

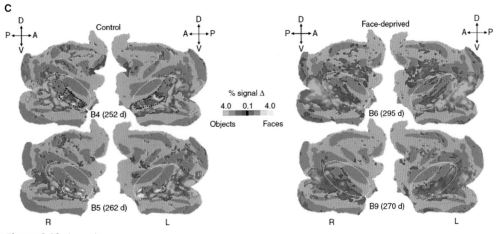

Figure 6.10 (cont.)

looked preferentially at monkey faces relative to objects. Likewise, the monkeys exposed only to monkey faces no longer looked preferentially at human faces relative to objects. Thus, selective visual exposure abolished the monkeys' early global face predisposition. Moreover, eye-tracking data showed that the face-deprived monkeys did not look preferentially at faces of any kind; in fact, they looked longer at people's hands than their faces, likely because they had experience viewing their own hands and those of the humans who interacted with them. Collectively, these findings highlight the importance of visual experience in shaping the biological basis for face processing.

Recall that control monkeys (i.e., monkeys raised viewing both monkeys and humans) look longer at a monkey face than a human face. This preference for a *specific class* of faces is not present early in infancy; rather, this visual preference emerges as infants gain experience with their visual world, presumably dominated by other monkeys with only occasional visits from human researchers. Thus, Sugita's (2008) findings on face-deprived monkeys provide evidence that this preference for conspecific faces depends on environmental input! Strikingly, given one month of selective exposure to humans, face-deprived monkeys developed a preference for human faces over monkey faces. And face-deprived monkeys who were exposed to monkeys for a month before seeing human faces showed a preference for monkey faces. In other words, the preference for conspecific faces is not innate; it is a direct result of visual experience!

How does such deprivation affect the development of face-selective regions in the brain? Using high-resolution anatomical MRI in monkeys reared under typical viewing conditions, Michael Arcaro, Margaret Livingston, and colleagues identified small sulcal "bumps," or buried gyri, within the STS that reliably predict the location of face patches in the same monkeys (Arcaro et al., 2020). The researchers then looked for these anatomical features in face-deprived monkeys. The answer is yes: the structure of this area of the STS looks very similar in face-deprived and control monkeys, suggesting that it is genetically specified. In another study (Arcaro et al., 2017), the researchers tested whether face-deprived monkeys actually develop face patches, as their brains had the anatomical features that would seem to enable development of face patches

(Arcaro et al., 2020). However, the face-deprived monkeys did *not* develop face-selective patches (Arcaro et al., 2017; Figure 6.10C). Thus, the anatomical structure appears to be *necessary but not sufficient* for the species-typical function. Experience is necessary for that to develop! Recall also that the infant's brain is a statistical processing (Bayesian inferencing) machine – or at least functions like one – and it is wired to be efficient. If an infant sees only one person in its first few years with a particular set of facial features, it may overgeneralize and not attend to nuanced differences. This may account for why people in a monocultural environment find it difficult to recognize faces of people from other cultures, even as adults. It appears to be a physiological byproduct of limited experience and constrained early learning.

6.7   Multisensory Perception

To achieve experimental control, researchers traditionally study one sensory modality at a time. However, we don't experience the world that way. An additional scientific complexity is that sensory systems are not fully mature at birth; they continue improving over the course of development, and they mature at different rates. How does the brain integrate information across the senses and between the sensory and motor systems across developmental time even as their maturation rates change?

6.7.1   The Emergence of Experience-Based Integrative Circuitry

As with unisensory perception, the development of multimodal perception in human infants has been studied using variations on the habituation and preferential looking techniques (Chapter 2). From this work, it is clear that multisensory processing, whether manifesting as cross-modal facilitation, cross-modal transfer, or multisensory matching, is present early (Lewkowicz, 2000), with young infants matching input across sensory modalities (Dodd, 1979; Lewkowicz & Turkewitz, 1981). For example, they are sensitive to synchrony between visual and auditory motion (Lewkowicz, 1992), discriminate changes in tempo and rhythm across modalities (Bahrick et al., 2002), and match visual and tactile shapes (Rose & Ruff, 1987). They even make cross-modal matches based on duration (Lewkowicz, 1986). These and other early findings raised tough questions about whether infants are born with their senses integrated or whether true integration comes only with developmental time and experience.

Fortunately, neuroscientists have developed detailed animal models to determine how sensory organs transduce signals, and how the brain segregates and distributes those signals for further processing. This work underscores the critical interaction of neural structure and experience for the development of **multisensory integration**. Barry Stein and his colleagues define multisensory integration as a statistically significant difference between the number of impulses evoked in a single neuron by a cross-modal combination of stimuli and the number evoked by the most effective of those stimuli individually (Meredith & Stein, 1983). The superior colliculus plays an important role, receiving converging unisensory inputs from sensory organs and from an array of cortical regions (Stein et al., 2014). Over time, this structure develops multisensory neurons, thus becoming a critical component of several multisensory processing networks.

Thus, multisensory integration requires anatomical convergence of input on individual neurons or groups of neurons from different sensory systems (Adrian, 1949; Stein & Meredith, 1993). Some indicators of multisensory integration from single neurons are increased magnitude of neural response, shorter response latency, and higher firing rate, all with a corresponding behavioral effect. In addition to subcortical regions, including the superior colliculus and thalamus, many cortical regions engage in multisensory integration, including the parietal, superior temporal cortex, and frontal cortices (Calvert et al., 2004).

When animals are deprived of a single sense (i.e., through dark-rearing or white-noise masking), the neurons in the superior colliculus fail to develop multisensory processing capabilities. However, they don't experience a general problem integrating information from different senses; rather, their inability is specific to the modality that was restricted. The animals integrate non-deprived input just fine (i.e., dark-reared animals integrate auditory-somatosensory stimuli; noise-masked animals integrate visual-somatosensory stimuli). Interestingly, the size of the integrative products for these animals (i.e., the neural responses and behavior) surpass those seen in normally reared animals, demonstrating a form of a cross-modal reorganization as the product of the atypical sensory experience. In short, single-neuron findings from animal models highlight the critical role of experience-dependent plasticity (Chapter 5) in the development of multisensory processing capabilities.

6.7.2   Is It Multisensory Integration, or Convergence?

For multisensory neurons to integrate their inputs, two or more sensory inputs must converge onto a common neuron. But even then, integration is not automatic or even inevitable; it takes developmental time and experience. In other words, convergence precedes integration. This raises questions about whether the precocious behavioral abilities observed in human infants reflect multisensory integration at the neuronal level, or associations (via neural convergence) that are necessary for multisensory integration, but require developmental time and repeated experience (Burr & Gori, 2012; Shaw & Bortfeld, 2015).

Whether the numerous behavioral findings from infants reflect multisensory convergence or true integration remains unknowable, as the available methods for testing human infants are limited. For now, an array of behavioral (e.g., Baart et al., 2015) and neural (e.g., Brandwein et al., 2011) findings point to an extended developmental time frame for nuanced multisensory processing. While the difference between multisensory convergence and integration may seem merely semantic, the debate matters, as there are a number of human conditions in which multisensory processing is disrupted or anomalous. These include Autism Spectrum Disorder, dyslexia, Sensory Processing Disorder, and schizophrenia. In some cases, these disruptions improve with age (Beker et al., 2018); in others, they present lifelong challenges. How such deficits relate to the development of full-blown multisensory integration – at the neuronal level – remains to be determined and thus merits additional research attention.

6.7.3   Novel Approach to Multisensory Research in Infants

Up to this point, we've focused on infants' sensitivity to general coherence across sensory modalities (i.e., the sound and sight of a ball bouncing or of hands clapping). Human speech is also a multisensory domain (Chapter 8). In adults, the sensory experience of seeing a moving mouth affects hearing speech, and young infants can match auditory and visual speech, even for non-native consonants and vowels they've never heard before (Pons et al., 2009). In addition to the auditory and visual components of speech, sensorimotor signals from the vocal tract also guide speech production and perception (Guenther, 2016). Indeed, the emergence of speech capabilities in humans points to an evolutionary (phylogenetic) basis for connectivity between motor and auditory components.

One question is whether this connectivity extends to individual (ontogenetic) development of speech. We know that the neural pathways that support speech processing are in place before birth (Chapter 8), and that the arcuate fasciculus looks relatively mature by 2 months of age (Leroy et al., 2011). Critical to the multisensory processing question, this pathway underpins interaction between auditory and motor speech functions.

Recently, Janet Werker (featured in the Scientist Spotlight in Box 6.2) has investigated whether sensorimotor influence on articulators (vocal organs about the larynx, including the tongue, lips, teeth, and hard palate) impacts infant perception even prior to the onset of babbling. Earlier behavioral findings pointed to multimodal phonetic representation by 2 months of age (Kuhl & Meltzoff, 1982; Patterson & Werker, 2002), and when 2-month-old infants were shown repetitions of a face articulating the same or a different vowel speech sounds, ERPs revealed a mismatch negativity response to a vowel category change (Bristow et al., 2009). These findings suggest multisensory representation of some form. Moreover, when the configuration of infants' lips was manipulated by placing an appropriately shaped object in their mouth, infants' ability to audiovisually match an /i/ or an /u/ vowel was influenced if the manipulation contradicted articulator positioning for the vowel (Yeung & Werker, 2013). Likewise, when an infant's tongue-tip movement was inhibited by a teether, discrimination of the /ɗa/-/ɖa/ contrast – which heavily relies on tongue-tip position – was likewise disrupted (Bruderer et al., 2015).

As in the Bristow et al. (2009) study, Werker and colleagues (Choi et al., 2021) recently used behavioral and ERP measures to test 3-month-old infants' sensitivity to two distinct phonetic contrasts with and without tongue-tip manipulation (Figure 6.11A). When no manipulation was introduced, infants discriminated both contrasts equally well. However, sensorimotor manipulation of the infants' articulators – specifically, inhibition of their tongue-tip movement – influenced their ability to discriminate the auditorily presented speech sounds and impacted their neural processing as well (Figure 6.11B). Blocking infants' tongue-tip inhibited their ability to discriminate /ɗa/-/ɖa/, sounds whose production depends on tongue-tip movement. Moreover, the manipulation actually enhanced infants' discrimination of /ba/-/ɗa/, as /ba/ relies on completely different articulators. These findings suggest that infants' auditory–sensorimotor connectivity is more robust than previously thought. While the results don't address the broader debate over convergence/integration in the development of multisensory processing, they do underscore arguments that speech is a unique domain in which perception and action interact in unique and complex ways.

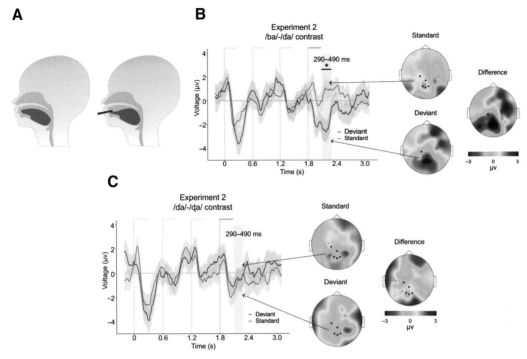

Figure 6.11 Infant articulator manipulation impacts speech discrimination. A. Across two experiments, infants' tongue-tips were left free (left) or were gently inhibited with a teething toy (right). B. ERP results with tongue-tip inhibited during /ba/-/ɖa/ contrast produced a grand averaged ERP time course differentiating the deviant (red line) and the standard (blue line) trials. Mean voltage and standard errors for each condition are plotted for the left-anterior cluster of sensors. Vertical dotted lines mark each syllable onset (1–4), with 1–3 the standard sound, and 4 either standard or deviant. The gray bar indicates the time window of the significant spatiotemporal electrode cluster. The voltage topographies reflect deviant and standard trials (right) and their difference (deviant − standard) averaged across the time window of the cluster (far right). C. The grand averaged ERP time courses to the /ɖa/-/ɖa/ contrast from the same spatiotemporal cluster shown in B, also with tongue-tip inhibited. Here ERP responses indicate no discrimination of the /ɖa/-/ɖa/ contrast. The gray bar indicates the time window of the significant cluster observed in response to the /ba/-/ɖa/ contrast in B. The voltage topographies reflect standard and deviant trials (right), and their difference (deviant − standard) (far right). (Reprinted from Choi et al., 2021)

Box 6.2 Scientist Spotlight on Janet Werker (University of British Columbia)

Janet Werker (Box Figure 6.2) is a Professor in the Department of Psychology at the University of British Columbia, where she directs the Infant Studies Centre. Werker is also the founder of the Early Development Research Group, a consortium focused on the development of language, learning, and social understanding. She studies language acquisition and speech perception in infants and toddlers.

I had always thought that I would be a biologist, because I was really interested in how it is that we fit into and adapt to our particular ecological niche. And then I took a developmental

Box 6.2 (cont.)

Box Figure 6.2 Scientist Spotlight:
Professor Jenet Werker.

psychology course, among other psychology courses, and was hooked. When I was in grad school working with Richard Tees I started thinking about language as our quintessential capability as a species, and where it comes from. While taking a directed reading course on speech perception from John Gilbert, I realized that it was really the nexus of the kinds of things that I was interested in: perception is of course our entry into learning about our worlds, and we have perceptual biases and sensory systems that have evolved to work for our human environments. And perception of course is our entry into our particular cultural environment, and in this case linguistic environment. And so we don't learn "language"; we learn the language or languages that are used in our community.

I came across work by Eimas, Siqueland, Jusczyk, and Vigorito [Eimas et al., 1971] that showed that babies might be showing something like categorical perception for phonemes. And there were a couple of papers by Streeter and by Trehub showing that among the repertoire of speech sounds that babies discriminated were non-native sounds that they hadn't heard before. And yet we also had studies by people like Winifred Strange and Jim Jenkins indicating that adults have difficulty discriminating speech sounds that are not used in their native languages. So, I was interested in understanding when and how this change from broad-based to only native language speech perception might occur. To test it, I needed to look for speech sound contrasts that are not used in English so we could tease apart babies who hadn't had exposure to them from those who had – and when things change. I went to the linguistics department at UBC, where I became aware of the rich consonant repertoires that exist in Hindi and in an Interior Salish First Nations language used in British Columbia, Nlaka'pamux. A linguist took me to the community and introduced me to the elders, and they graciously let me record them. And I was able to go test Hindi speakers from a Hindu temple in Vancouver.

I initially thought that the ability to distinguish non-native sounds would be lost after around age 12, because Lenneberg had said that's when the critical period for language acquisition ends. That was my hypothesis. But we found that they couldn't discriminate the non-native sounds – and neither could 7- to 8-year-olds, so then we tested 3- to 4-year-olds, because there was some work at the time suggesting that 4-year-olds become very rigid about roles – about applying social categories and things that would maybe affect speech perception, but they were lousy as well. And then we started thinking, well, maybe around 18–20 months, when there was supposed to be a word learning explosion. So we started testing kids in that toddler range. But they were lousy, too. Then Pat Kuhl came up to UBC and taught me how to use the conditioned head-turn procedure to test babies, and I started testing every age of baby that could come in. Then there was a day when two moms came into the lab together. They were friends and they had babies close to the same age. The 8-month-old discriminated the non-native speech sounds, and the 10-month-old did not. The conditioned head-turning procedure is not like the continuous data you get with habituation: you can say conclusively whether or not the baby reached criterion on the task. So that's when we started focusing on the infancy period, even though it was not an a priori hypothesized stage. I think it's important to be guided by the data. You have to have a theory and you have to have a hypothesis, since there's no point in just collecting facts that don't relate to each other or make any sense. But on the other hand, you have to be open to what the data are going to tell you.

SUMMARY

- From birth, infants react to all forms of sensory input, indicating that their alerting system is intact and highly functional
- Young infants rely on external stimulation to arouse their attention, though by the age of around 9 months they are able to inhibit certain distractors and focus on a stimulus
- Hearing and vision continue to improve during infancy, due to the development of associated neural pathways
- Infants learn the statistical regularities of the world through repeated exposure
- Vision can be separated into the dorsal and ventral streams, ventral being the "what" pathway, and dorsal being the "where/how pathway"
- There is some evidence from fNIRS that the dorsal stream ("where/how") and ventral stream ("what") pathways become neurally dissociable over the first year of life
- Regions in the fusiform gyrus are preferentially tuned to specific categories of visual stimuli
- The fusiform face area shows increasingly preferential activation to faces over childhood; this tuning is experience-dependent
- Multisensory integration is the product of extended multimodal convergence on a neuron or set of neurons

REVIEW QUESTIONS

What is Bayesian inferencing, and what is the argument that infants engage in it?

Describe the process of auditory perception, all the way from sound waves reaching the ears to tonotopic organization in primary auditory cortex.

List some of the differences in hearing between the pre- and postnatal periods.

How are infants' sensory capabilities measured, and how do hearing and vision change during infancy?

Delineate the geniculostriate pathway, beginning with retinal cells and ending in the cortex. Describe the dorsal and ventral visual streams, and their functions.

How does the dual-route hypothesis potentially explain infants' visual capabilities, and their maturation over time?

Explain the role of the superior colliculus in visual perception in early development and into adulthood.

How does the broader face processing network emerge over development? What is meant by perceptual tuning?

What evidence is there that regions involved in face perception are shaped by experience?

Why is it still unclear whether data from human infants reflect multisensory convergence or integration?

Further Reading

Corrow, S. L., Dalrymple, K. A., & Barton, J. J. (2016). Prosopagnosia: Current perspectives. *Eye and Brain*, 8, 165–175. https://doi.org/10.2147/EB.S92838

Maurer, D., Ghloum, J. K., Gibson, L. C., Watson, M. R., Chen, L. M., Akins, K., Enns, J. T., Hensch, T. K., & Werker, J. F. (2020). Reduced perceptual narrowing in synesthesia. *Proceedings of the National Academy of Sciences of the United States of America*, 117(18), 10089–10096. https://doi.org/10.1073/pnas.1914668117

Saffran, J. R., & Kirkham, N. Z. (2018). Infant statistical learning. *Annual Review of Psychology*, 69, 181–203. https://doi.org/10.1146/annurev-psych-122216-011805

References

Abramov, I., Gordon, J., Hendrickson, A., Hainline, L., Dobson, V., & LaBossiere, E. (1982). The retina of the newborn human infant. *Science*, 217(4556), 265–267. https://doi.org/10.1126/science.6178160

Adams, R. J., Courage, M. L., & Mercer, M. E. (1994). Systematic measurement of human neonatal color vision. *Vision Research*, 34(13), 1691–1701. https://doi.org/10.1016/0042-6989(94)90127-9

Adrian, E. D. (1949). *The Sherrington lectures. I: Sensory integration.* Liverpool University Press.

Alcauter, S., Lin, W., Smith, J. K., Short, S. J., Goldman, B. D., Reznick, J. S., Gilmore, J. H., & Gao, W. (2014). Development of thalamocortical connectivity during infancy and its cognitive correlations. *Journal of Neuroscience*, 34(27), 9067–9075. https://doi.org/10.1523/JNEUROSCI.0796-14.2014

American Academy of Pediatrics Task Force on Circumcision. (2012). Circumcision policy statement. *Pediatrics*, 130(3), 585–586. https://doi.org/10.1542/peds.2012-1989

Amso, D., & Scerif, G. (2015). The attentive brain: Insights from developmental cognitive neuroscience. *Nature Reviews Neuroscience*, 16(10), 606–619. https://doi.org/10.1038/nrn4025

Arcaro, M. J., Mautz, T., Berezovskii, V. K., & Livingstone, M. S. (2020). Anatomical correlates of face patches in macaque inferotemporal cortex. *Proceedings of the National Academy of Sciences of the United States of America*, 117(51), 32667–32678. https://doi.org/10.1073/pnas.2018780117

Arcaro, M. J., Schade, P. F., & Livingstone, M. S. (2019). Universal mechanisms and the development of the face network: What you see is what you get. *Annual Review of Vision Science*, 5, 341–372. https://doi.org/10.1146/annurev-vision-091718-014917

Arcaro, M. J., Schade, P. F., Vincent, J. L., Ponce, C. R., & Livingstone, M. S. (2017). Seeing faces is necessary for face-domain formation. *Nature Neuroscience*, 20(10), 1404–1412. https://doi.org/10.1038/nn.4635

Astle, D. E., & Scerif, G. (2011). Interactions between attention and visual short-term memory (VSTM): What can be learnt from individual and developmental differences? *Neuropsychologia*, 49(6), 1435–1445. https://doi.org/10.1016/j.neuropsychologia.2010.12.001

Aston-Jones, G., & Cohen, J. D. (2005). An integrative theory of locus coeruleus-norepinephrine function: Adaptive gain and optimal performance. *Annual Review of Neuroscience*, 28, 403–450. https://doi.org/10.1146/annurev.neuro.28.061604.135709

Atkinson, J. (2002). *The developing visual brain*. Oxford University Press.

Avidan, G., Tanzer, M., Hadj-Bouziane, F., Liu, N., Ungerleider, L. G., & Behrmann, M. (2014). Selective dissociation between core and extended regions of the face processing network in congenital prosopagnosia. *Cerebral Cortex*, 24(6), 1565–1578. https://doi.org/10.1093/cercor/bht007

Baart, M., Bortfeld, H., & Vroomen, J. (2015). Phonetic matching of auditory and visual speech develops during childhood: Evidence from sine-wave speech. *Journal of Experimental Child Psychology*, 129, 157–164. https://doi.org/10.1016/j.jecp.2014.08.002

Bahrick, L. E., Flom, R., & Lickliter, R. (2002). Intersensory redundancy facilitates discrimination of tempo in 3-month-old infants. *Developmental Psychobiology*, 41(4), 352–363. https://doi.org/10.1002/dev.10049

Balaban, M. T., & Reisenauer, C. D. (2013). Sensory development. In N. J. Salkind (Ed.), *Encyclopedia of human development* (pp. 1144–1147). Sage Publications.

Banich, M., & Compton, R. (2018). *Cognitive neuroscience*, 4th edition. Cambridge University Press. https://doi.org/10.1017/9781316664018

Banks, M. S., & Salapatek, P. (1983). Infant visual perception. In M. M. Haith & J. J. Campos (Eds.), *Handbook of child psychology, Volume 2: Infancy and developmental psychobiology*, 4th edition (pp. 435–571). John Wiley & Sons.

Beker, S., Foxe, J. J., & Molholm, S. (2018). Ripe for solution: Delayed development of multisensory processing in autism and its remediation. *Neuroscience and Biobehavioral Reviews*, 84, 182–192. https://doi.org/10.1016/j.neubiorev.2017.11.008

Brandwein, A. B., Foxe, J. J., Russo, N. N., Altschuler, T. S., Gomes, H., & Molholm, S. (2011). The development of audiovisual multisensory integration across childhood and early adolescence: A high-density electrical mapping study. *Cerebral Cortex*, 21(5), 1042–1055. https://doi.org/10.1093/cercor/bhq170

Bristow, D., Dehaene-Lambertz, G., Mattout, J., Soares, C., Gliga, T., Baillet, S., & Mangin, J. F. (2009). Hearing faces: How the infant brain matches the face it sees with the speech it hears. *Journal of Cognitive Neuroscience*, 21(5), 905–921. https://doi.org/10.1162/jocn.2009.21076

Brown, A. M., & Miracle, J. A. (2003). Early binocular vision in human infants: Limitations on the generality of the Superposition Hypothesis. *Vision Research*, 43(14), 1563–1574. https://doi.org/10.1016/s0042-6989(03)00177-9

Bruderer, A. G., Danielson, D. K., Kandhadai, P., & Werker, J. F. (2015). Sensorimotor influences on speech perception in infancy. *Proceedings of the National Academy of Sciences of the United States of America*, 112(44), 13531–13536. https://doi.org/10.1073/pnas.1508631112

Burr, D., & Gori, M. (2012). Multisensory integration develops late in humans. In M. M. Murray & M. T. Wallace (Eds.), *The neural bases of multisensory processes* (pp. 345–362). CRC Press.

Bushneil, I. W., Sai, F., & Mullin, J. T. (1989). Neonatal recognition of the mother's face. *British Journal of Developmental Psychology*, 7(1), 3–15. https://doi.org/10.1111/j.2044-835X.1989.tb00784.x

Butler, B. E., & Lomber, S. G. (2013). Functional and structural changes throughout the auditory system following congenital and early-onset deafness: Implications for hearing restoration. *Frontiers in Systems Neuroscience*, 7, 92. https://doi.org/10.3389/fnsys.2013.00092

Calvert, G., Spence, C., & Stein, B. E. (Eds.). (2004). *The handbook of multisensory processes*. MIT Press.

Cang, J., Rentería, R. C., Kaneko, M., Liu, X., Copenhagen, D. R., & Stryker, M. P. (2005). Development of precise maps in visual cortex requires patterned spontaneous activity in the retina. *Neuron*, 48(5), 797–809. https://doi.org/10.1016/j.neuron.2005.09.015

Cheng, C., Kaldy, Z., & Blaser, E. (2019). Focused attention predicts visual working memory performance in 13-month-old infants: A pupillometric study. *Developmental Cognitive Neuroscience*, 36, 100616. https://doi.org/10.1016/j.dcn.2019.100616

Choi, D., Dehaene-Lambertz, G., Peña, M., & Werker, J. F. (2021). Neural indicators of articulator-specific sensorimotor influences on infant speech perception. *Proceedings of the National Academy of Sciences of the United States of America*, 118(20), e2025043118. https://doi.org/10.1073/pnas.2025043118

Colombo, J., Mitchell, D. W., Coldren, J. T., & Freeseman, L. J. (1991). Individual differences in infant visual attention: Are short lookers faster processors or feature processors? *Child Development*, 62(6), 1247–1257. https://doi.org/10.2307/1130804

Courage, M. L., Reynolds, G. D., and Richards, J. E. (2006). Infants' attention to patterned stimuli: Developmental change from 3 to 12 months of age. *Child Development*, 77, 680–695. https://doi.org/10.1111/j.1467-8624.2006.00897.x

Cowan, N., & Morey, C. C. (2006). Visual working memory depends on attentional filtering. *Trends in Cognitive Sciences*, 10(4), 139–141. https://doi.org/10.1016/j.tics.2006.02.001

Davies-Thompson, J., Elli, G. V., Rezk, M., Benetti, S., van Ackeren, M., & Collignon, O. (2019). Hierarchical brain network for face and voice integration of emotion expression. *Cerebral Cortex*, 29(9), 3590–3605. https://doi.org/10.1093/cercor/bhy240

de Barbaro, K., Clackson, K., & Wass, S. V. (2017). Infant attention is dynamically modulated with changing arousal levels. *Child Development*, 88(2), 629–639. https://doi.org/10.1111/cdev.12689

Deen, B., Richardson, H., Dilks, D., Takahashi, A., Keil, B., Wald, L. L., Kanwisher, N., & Saxe, R. (2017). Organization of high-level visual cortex in human infants. *Nature Communication*, 8, 13995. https://doi.org/10.1038/ncomms13995

DeGutis, J., Cohan, S., & Nakayama, K. (2014). Holistic face training enhances face processing in developmental prosopagnosia. *Brain*, 137(6), 1781–1798. https://doi.org/10.1093/brain/awu062

de Jong, M., Verhoeven, M., Hooge, I. T., & van Baar, A. L. (2016). Factor structure of attention capacities measured with eye-tracking tasks in 18-month-old toddlers. *Journal of Attention Disorders*, 20(3), 230–239. https://doi.org/10.1177/1087054713516002

Dodd, B. (1979). Lip reading in infants: Attention to speech presented in- and out-of-synchrony. *Cognitive Psychology*, 11(4), 478–484. https://doi.org/10.1016/0010-0285(79)90021-5

Eckstein, M. K., Guerra-Carrillo, B., Miller Singley, A. T., & Bunge, S. A. (2017). Beyond eye gaze: What else can eyetracking reveal about cognition and cognitive development? *Developmental Cognitive Neuroscience*, 25, 69–91. https://doi.org/10.1016/j.dcn.2016.11.001

Eimas, P. D., Siqueland, E. R., Jusczyk, P., & Vigorito, J. (1971). Speech perception in infants. *Science*, 171(3968), 303–306. https://doi.org/10.1126/science.171.3968.303

Fantz, R. L. (1961). The origin of form perception. *Scientific American*, 204, 66e72. https://doi.org/10.1038/scientificamerican0561-66

Fantz, R. L. (1964). Visual experience in infants: Decreased attention to familiar patterns relative to novel ones. *Science*, 146, 668e670. https://doi.org/10.1126/science.146.3644.668

Felleman, D. J., & Van Essen, D. C. (1991). Distributed hierarchical processing in the primate cerebral cortex. *Cerebral Cortex*, 1(1), 1–47. https://doi.org/10.1093/cercor/1.1.1-a

Forbes, T. A., Goldstein, E. Z., Dupree, J. L., Jablonska, B., Scafidi, J., Adams, K. L., Imamura, Y., Hashimoto-Torii, K., & Gallo, V. (2020). Environmental enrichment ameliorates perinatal brain injury and promotes functional white matter recovery. *Nature Communications*, 11(1), 964. https://doi.org/10.1038/s41467-020-14762-7

Freiwald, W., Duchaine, B., & Yovel, G. (2016). Face processing systems: From neurons to real-world social perception. *Annual Review of Neuroscience*, 39, 325–346. https://doi.org/10.1146/annurev-neuro-070815-013934

Freud, E., Plaut, D. C., & Behrmann, M. (2016). "What" is happening in the dorsal visual pathway. *Trends in Cognitive Sciences*, 20, 773–784. https://doi.org/10.1016/j.tics.2016.08.003

Gauthier, I., Skudlarski, P., Gore, J. C., & Anderson, A. W. (2000). Expertise for cars and birds recruits brain areas involved in face recognition. *Nature Neuroscience*, 3(2), 191–197. https://doi.org/10.1038/72140

Gauthier, I., Tarr, M. J., Anderson, A. W., Skudlarski, P., & Gore, J. C. (1999). Activation of the middle fusiform 'face area' increases with expertise in recognizing novel objects. *Nature Neuroscience*, 2(6), 568–573. https://doi.org/10.1038/9224

Germine, L. T., Duchaine, B., & Nakayama, K. (2011). Where cognitive development and aging meet: Face learning ability peaks after age 30. *Cognition*, 118(2), 201–210. https://doi.org/10.1016/j.cognition.2010.11.002

Golarai, G., Liberman, A., Yoon, J. M., & Grill-Spector, K. (2010). Differential development of the ventral visual cortex extends through adolescence. *Frontiers in Human Neuroscience*, 3, 80. https://doi.org/10.3389/neuro.09.080.2009

Gomez, J., Barnett, M., & Grill-Spector, K. (2019). Extensive childhood experience with Pokémon suggests eccentricity drives organization of visual cortex. *Nature Human Behaviour*, 3(6), 611–624. https://doi.org/10.1038/s41562-019-0592-8

Gomez, J., Barnett, M. A., Natu, V., Mezer, A., Palomero-Gallagher, N., Weiner, K. S., Amunts, K., Zilles, K., & Grill-Spector, K. (2017). Microstructural proliferation in human cortex is coupled with the development of face processing. *Science*, 355(6320), 68–71. https://doi.org/10.1126/science.aag0311

Gomez, J., Natu, V., Jeska, B., Barnett, M., & Grill-Spector, K. (2018). Development differentially sculpts receptive fields across early and high-level human visual cortex. *Nature Communications*, 9(1). https://doi.org/10.1038/s41467-018-03166-3

Goodale, M. A., & Milner, A. D. (1992). Separate visual pathways for perception and action. *Trends in Neurosciences*, 15, 20–25. https://doi.org/0166-2236(92)90344-8

Goodale, M. A., & Milner, A. D. (2018). Two visual pathways: Where have they taken us and where will they lead in future? *Cortex*, 98, 283–292. https://doi.org/10.1016/j.cortex.2017.12.002

Granholm, E., & Steinhauer, S. R. (2004). Pupillometric measures of cognitive and emotional processes. *International Journal of Psychophysiology*, 52(1), 1–6. https://doi.org/10.1016/j.ijpsycho.2003.12.001

Graven, S. N., & Browne, J. V. (2008). Auditory development in the fetus and infant. *Newborn and Infant Nursing Reviews*, 8(4), 187–193. https://doi.org/10.1053/j.nainr.2008.10.010

Grill-Spector, K., & Weiner, K. S. (2014). The functional architecture of the ventral temporal cortex and its role in categorization. *Nature Reviews Neuroscience*, 15(8), 536–548. https://doi.org/10.1038/nrn3747

Gross, C. G. (2002). Genealogy of the "grandmother cell." *The Neuroscientist*, 8(5), 512–518. https://doi.org/10.1177/107385802237175

Guenther, F. H. (2016). *Neural control of speech*. MIT Press.

Gweon, H., Tenenbaum, J. B., & Schulz, L. E. (2010). Infants consider both the sample and the sampling process in inductive generalization. *Proceedings of the National Academy of Sciences of the United States of America*, 107(20), 9066–9071. https://doi.org/10.1073/pnas.1003095107

Hackett, T. A. (2015). Anatomic organization of the auditory cortex. In M. J. Aminoff, F. Boller, & D. F. Swaab (Eds.), *Handbook of clinical neurology, Volume 129* (pp. 27–53). Elsevier. https://doi.org/10.1016/B978-0-444-62630-1.00002-0

Haith, M. M. (1980). *Rules that babies look by: The organization of newborn visual activity.* Lawrence Erlbaum Associates.

Hepper, P. G., & Shahidullah, B. S. (1994). Development of fetal hearing. *Archives of Disease in Childhood. Fetal and Neonatal Edition*, 71(2), F81–F87. https://doi.org/10.1136/fn.71.2.f81

Hildebrandt, F., Lonnemann, J., & Glauer, R. (2020). Why not just features? Reconsidering infants' behavior in individuation tasks. *Frontiers in Psychology*, 11, 564807. https://doi.org/10.3389/fpsyg.2020.564807

Hubbard, E. M., Brang, D., & Ramachandran, V. S. (2011). The cross-activation theory at 10. *Journal of Neuropsychology*, 5(2), 152–177. https://doi.org/10.1111/j.1748-6653.2011.02014.x

James, T. W., & James, K. H. (2013). Expert individuation of objects increases activation in the fusiform face area of children. *NeuroImage*, 67, 182–192. https://doi.org/10.1016/j.neuroimage.2012.11.007

Jeffries, A. M., Killian, N. J., & Pezaris, J. S. (2014). Mapping the primate lateral geniculate nucleus: A review of experiments and methods. *Journal of Physiology, Paris*, 108(1), 3–10. https://doi.org/10.1016/j.jphysparis.2013.10.001

Johansson, M., Marciszko, C., Gredebäck, G., Nyström, P., & Bohlin, G. (2015). Sustained attention in infancy as a longitudinal predictor of self-regulatory functions. *Infant Behavior & Development*, 41, 1–11. https://doi.org/10.1016/j.infbeh.2015.07.001

Johnson, M. H. (1990). Cortical maturation and the development of visual attention in early infancy. *Journal of Cognitive Neuroscience*, 2, 81–95. https://doi.org/10.1162/jocn.1990.2.2.81

Johnson, M. H., Dziurawiec, S., Ellis, H., & Morton, J. (1991). Newborns' preferential tracking of face-like stimuli and its subsequent decline. *Cognition*, 40(1–2), 1–19. https://doi.org/10.1016/0010-0277(91)90045-6

Kahneman, D. (2011). *Thinking, fast and slow.* Farrar, Straus & Giroux.

Kane, M. J., & Engle, R. W. (2002). The role of prefrontal cortex in working-memory capacity, executive attention, and general fluid intelligence: An individual-differences perspective. *Psychonomic Bulletin & Review*, 9(4), 637–671. https://doi.org/10.3758/BF03196323

Kanwisher, N. (2000). Domain specificity in face perception. *Nature Neuroscience*, 3(8), 759–763. https://doi.org/10.1038/77664

Kanwisher, N. (2017). The quest for the FFA and where it led. *Journal of Neuroscience*, 37(5), 1056–1061. https://doi.org/10.1523/JNEUROSCI.1706-16.2016

Kanwisher, N., McDermott, J., & Chun, M. M. (1997). The fusiform face area: A module in human extrastriate cortex specialized for face perception. *Journal of Neuroscience*, 17(11), 4302–4311. https://doi.org/10.1523/JNEUROSCI.17-11-04302.1997

Kerschensteiner, D., & Wong, R. O. (2008). A precisely timed asynchronous pattern of ON and OFF retinal ganglion cell activity during propagation of retinal waves. *Neuron*, 58(6), 851–858. https://doi.org/10.1016/j.neuron.2008.04.025

Klaver, C., Polling, J. R., & Enthoven, C. A. (2021). 2020 as the year of quarantine myopia. *JAMA Ophthalmology*, 139(3), 300–301. https://doi.org/10.1001/jamaophthalmol.2020.6231

Klingberg, T., Forssberg, H., & Westerberg, H. (2002). Training of working memory in children with ADHD. *Journal of Clinical and Experimental Neuropsychology*, 24(6), 781–791. https://doi.org/10.1076/jcen.24.6.781.8395

Koos, B. J., & Rajaee, A. (2014). Fetal breathing movements and changes at birth. *Advances in Experimental Medicine and Biology*, 814, 89–101. https://doi.org/10.1007/978-1-4939-1031-1_8

Kuhl, P. K., & Meltzoff, A. N. (1982). The bimodal perception of speech in infancy. *Science*, 218(4577), 1138–1141. https://doi.org/10.1126/science.7146899

Lahav, A., & Skoe, E. (2014). An acoustic gap between the NICU and womb: A potential risk for compromised neuroplasticity of the auditory system in preterm infants. *Frontiers in Neuroscience*, 8, 381. https://doi.org/10.3389/fnins.2014.00381

LeDoux, J. (1996). *The emotional brain: The mysterious underpinnings of emotional life*. Simon & Schuster.

Leopold, D. A., & Rhodes, G. (2010). A comparative view of face perception. *Journal of Comparative Psychology*, 124(3), 233–251. https://doi.org/10.1037/a0019460

Leroy, F., Glasel, H., Dubois, J., Hertz-Pannier, L., Thirion, B., Mangin, J. F., & Dehaene-Lambertz, G. (2011). Early maturation of the linguistic dorsal pathway in human infants. *Journal of Neuroscience*, 31(4), 1500–1506. https://doi.org/10.1523/JNEUROSCI.4141-10.2011

Lewkowicz, D. J. (1986). Developmental changes in infants' bisensory response to synchronous durations. *Infant Behavior and Development*, 9(3), 335–353. https://doi.org/10.1016/0163-6383(86)90008-1

Lewkowicz, D. J. (1992). Infants' responsiveness to the auditory and visual attributes of a sounding/moving stimulus. *Perception & Psychophysics*, 52(5), 519–528. https://doi.org/10.3758/bf03206713

Lewkowicz, D. J. (2000). The development of intersensory temporal perception: An epigenetic systems/limitations view. *Psychological Bulletin*, 126(2), 281–308. https://doi.org/10.1037/0033-2909.126.2.281

Lewkowicz, D. J., & Turkewitz, G. (1981). Intersensory interaction in newborns: Modification of visual preferences following exposure to sound. *Child Development*, 52(3), 827–832. https://doi.org/10.2307/1129083

Lochy, A., de Heering, A., & Rossion, B. (2019). The non-linear development of the right hemispheric specialization for human face perception. *Neuropsychologia*, 126, 10–19. https://doi.org/10.1016/j.neuropsychologia.2017.06.029

Macfarlane, A. (1975). Olfaction in the development of social preferences in the human neonate. *Ciba Foundation Symposium*, 33, 103–117. https://doi.org/10.1002/9780470720158.ch7

Malach, R., Levy, I., & Hasson, U. (2002). The topography of high-order human object areas. *Trends in Cognitive Sciences*, 6(4), 176–184. https://doi.org/10.1016/S1364-6613(02)01870-3

Maurer, D., Ghloum, J. K., Gibson, L. C., Watson, M. R., Chen, L. M., Akins, K., Enns, J. T., Hensch, T. K., & Werker, J. F. (2020). Reduced perceptual narrowing in synesthesia. *Proceedings of the National Academy of Sciences of the United States of America*, 117(18), 10089–10096. https://doi.org/10.1073/pnas.1914668117

Mende-Siedlecki, P., Said, C. P., & Todorov, A. (2013). The social evaluation of faces: A meta-analysis of functional neuroimaging studies. *Social Cognitive and Affective Neuroscience*, 8(3), 285–299. https://doi.org/10.1093/scan/nsr090

Meredith, M. A., and Stein, B. E. (1983). Interactions among converging sensory inputs in the superior colliculus. *Science*, 221(4608), 389–391. https://doi.org/10.1126/science.6867718

Morris, J. S., Ohman, A., & Dolan, R. J. (1999). A subcortical pathway to the right amygdala mediating "unseen" fear. *Proceedings of the National Academy of Sciences of the United States of America*, 96(4), 1680–1685. https://doi.org/10.1073/pnas.96.4.1680

Morton, J., & Johnson, M. H. (1991). CONSPEC and CONLERN: A two-process theory of infant face recognition. *Psychological Review*, 98(2), 164–181. https://doi.org/10.1037/0033-295x.98.2.164

Natu, V. S., Barnett, M. A., Hartley, J., Gomez, J., Stigliani, A., & Grill-Spector, K. (2016). Development of neural sensitivity to face identity correlates with perceptual discriminability. *Journal of Neuroscience*, 36(42), 10893–10907. https://doi.org/10.1523/JNEUROSCI.1886-16.2016

Natu, V. S., Gomez, J., Barnett, M., Jeska, B., Kirilina, E., Jaeger, C., Zhen, Z., Cox, S., Weiner, K. S., Weiskopf, N., & Grill-Spector, K. (2019). Apparent thinning of human visual cortex during childhood is associated with myelination. *Proceedings of the National Academy of Sciences of the United States of America*, 116(41), 20750–20759. https://doi.org/10.1073/pnas.1904931116

Patterson, M. L., & Werker, J. F. (2002). Infants' ability to match dynamic phonetic and gender information in the face and voice. *Journal of Experimental Child Psychology*, 81(1), 93–115. https://doi.org/10.1006/jecp.2001.2644

Penfield, W., & Perot, P. (1963). The brain's record of auditory and visual experience: A final summary and discussion. *Brain*, 86, 595–696. https://doi.org/10.1093/brain/86.4.595

Pennartz, C., Dora, S., Muckli, L., & Lorteije, J. (2019). Towards a unified view on pathways and functions of neural recurrent processing. *Trends in Neurosciences*, 42(9), 589–603. https://doi.org/10.1016/j.tins.2019.07.005

Petersen, S. E., & Posner, M. I. (2012). The attention system of the human brain: 20 years after. *Annual Review of Neuroscience*, 35, 73–89. https://doi.org/10.1146/annurev-neuro-062111-150525

Pineda, R. G., Neil, J., Dierker, D., Smyser, C. D., Wallendorf, M., Kidokoro, H., Reynolds, L. C., Walker, S., Rogers, C., Mathur, A. M., Van Essen, D. C., & Inder, T. (2014). Alterations in brain structure and neurodevelopmental outcome in preterm infants hospitalized in different neonatal intensive care unit environments. *Journal of Pediatrics*, 164(1), 52–60.e2. https://doi.org/10.1016/j.jpeds.2013.08.047

Pons, F., Lewkowicz, D. J., Soto-Faraco, S., & Sebastián-Gallés, N. (2009). Narrowing of intersensory speech perception in infancy. *Proceedings of the National Academy of Sciences of the United States of America*, 106(26), 10598–10602. https://doi.org/10.1073/pnas.0904134106

Porter, R. H., Makin, J. W., Davis, L. B., & Christensen, K. M. (1992). Breast-fed infants respond to olfactory cues from their own mother and unfamiliar lactating females. *Infant Behavior & Development*, 15(1), 85–93. https://doi.org/10.1016/0163-6383(92)90008-T

Posner, M. I., & Petersen, S. E. (1990). The attention system of the human brain. *Annual Review of Neuroscience*, 13, 25–42. https://doi.org/10.1146/annurev.ne.13.030190.000325

Posner, M. I., & Rothbart, M. K. (2013). Development of attention networks. In B. R. Kar (Ed.), *Cognition and brain development: Converging evidence from various methodologies* (pp. 61–83). American Psychological Association. https://doi.org/10.1037/14043-004

Prechtl, H. F. R. (2001). Prenatal and early postnatal development of human motor behavior. In A. F. Kalverboer & A. Gramsbergen (Eds.), *Handbook of brain and behaviour in human development* (pp. 425–427). Kluwer Academic Publishers.

Reynolds, G. D., & Romano, A. C. (2016). The development of attention systems and working memory in infancy. *Frontiers in Systems Neuroscience*, 10, 15. https://doi.org/10.3389/fnsys.2016.00015

Richards, J. E. (1997). Effects of attention on infants' preference for briefly exposed visual stimuli in the paired-comparison recognition-memory paradigm. *Developmental Psychology*, 33(1), 22–31. https://doi.org/10.1037//0012-1649.33.1.22

Rock, I. (1983). *The logic of perception*. MIT Press.

Romanski, L. M., & Averbeck, B. B. (2009). The primate cortical auditory system and neural representation of conspecific vocalizations. *Annual Review of Neuroscience*, 32, 315–346. https://doi.org/10.1146/annurev.neuro.051508.135431

Rose, S. A., Feldman, J. F., & Jankowski, J. J. (2012). Implications of infant cognition for executive functions at age 11. *Psychological Science*, 23(11), 1345–1355. https://doi.org/10.1177/0956797612444902

Rose, S. A., Feldman, J. F., Jankowski, J. J., & Van Rossem, R. (2005). Pathways from prematurity and infant abilities to later cognition. *Child Development*, 76(6), 1172–1184. https://doi.org/10.1111/j.1467-8624.2005.00843.x

Rose, S. A., & Ruff, H. A. (1987). Cross-modal abilities in human infants. In J. D. Osofsky (Ed.), *Handbook of infant development* (pp. 318–362). John Wiley & Sons.

Ruff, H. A., & Capozzoli, M. C. (2003). Development of attention and distractibility in the first 4 years of life. *Developmental Psychology*, 39(5), 877–890. https://doi.org/10.1037/0012-1649.39.5.877

Saffran, J. R., & Kirkham, N. Z. (2018). Infant statistical learning. *Annual Review of Psychology*, 69, 181–203. https://doi.org/10.1146/annurev-psych-122216-011805

Schaal, B., & Durand, K. (2012). The role of olfaction in human multisensory development. In A. Bremner, D. J. Lewkowicz, & C. Spence (Eds.), *Multisensory development* (pp. 29–62). Oxford University Press.

Sergent, J., & Signoret, J. L. (1992). Functional and anatomical decomposition of face processing: Evidence from prosopagnosia and PET study of normal subjects. *Philosophical Transactions of the Royal Society of London. Series B, Biological Sciences*, 335(1273), 55–62. https://doi.org/10.1098/rstb.1992.0007

Shaw, K. E., & Bortfeld, H. (2015). Sources of confusion in infant audiovisual speech perception research. *Frontiers in Psychology*, 6, 1844. https://doi.org/10.3389/fpsyg.2015.01844

Slater, A. (1995). Visual perception and memory at birth. In C. Rovee-Collier & L. P. Lipsitt (Eds.), *Advances in infancy research, Volume 9* (pp. 107–112). Ablex.

Song, S., Garrido, L., Nagy, Z., Mohammadi, S., Steel, A., Driver, J., Dolan, R. J., Duchaine, B., & Furl, N. (2015). Local but not long-range microstructural differences of the ventral temporal cortex in developmental prosopagnosia. *Neuropsychologia*, 78, 195–206. https://doi.org/10.1016/j.neuropsychologia.2015.10.010

Srihasam, K., Vincent, J. L., & Livingstone, M. S. (2014). Novel domain formation reveals proto-architecture in inferotemporal cortex. *Nature Neuroscience*, 17(12), 1776–1783. https://doi.org/10.1038/nn.3855

Stavans, M., Lin, Y., Wu, D., & Baillargeon, R. (2019). Catastrophic individuation failures in infancy: A new model and predictions. *Psychological Review*, 126(2), 196–225. https://doi.org/10.1037/rev0000136

Stein, B. E., & Meredith, M. A. (1993). *The merging of the senses*. MIT Press.

Stein, B. E., Stanford, T. R., & Rowland, B. A. (2014). Development of multisensory integration from the perspective of the individual neuron. *Nature Reviews Neuroscience*, 15(8), 520–535. https://doi.org/10.1038/nrn3742

Strand-Brodd, K., Ewald, U., Grönqvist, H., Holmström, G., Strömberg, B., Grönqvist, E., von Hofsten, C., & Rosander, K. (2011). Development of smooth pursuit eye movements in very preterm infants: 1. General aspects. *Acta Paediatrica*, 100(7), 983–991. https://doi.org/10.1111/j.1651-2227.2011.02218.x

Sugita, Y. (2008). Face perception in monkeys reared with no exposure to faces. *Proceedings of the National Academy of Sciences of the United States of America*, 105(1), 394–398. https://doi.org/10.1073/pnas.0706079105

Tarr, M. J., & Gauthier, I. (2000). FFA: A flexible fusiform area for subordinate-level visual processing automatized by expertise. *Nature Neuroscience*, 3(8), 764–769. https://doi.org/10.1038/77666

Tharpe, A. M., & Ashmead, D. H. (2001). A longitudinal investigation of infant auditory sensitivity. *American Journal of Audiology*, 10(2), 104–112. https://doi.org/10.1044/1059-0889(2001/011)

Tsantani, M., Kriegeskorte, N., Storrs, K., Williams, A. L., McGettigan, C., & Garrido, L. (2021). FFA and OFA encode distinct types of face identity information. *Journal of Neuroscience*, 41(9), 1952–1969. https://doi.org/10.1523/JNEUROSCI.1449-20.2020

Tsao, D. Y., Freiwald, W. A., Tootell, R. B., & Livingstone, M. S. (2006). A cortical region consisting entirely of face-selective cells. *Science*, 311(5761), 670–674. https://doi.org/10.1126/science.1119983

Tsao, D. Y., Moeller, S., & Freiwald, W. A. (2008). Comparing face patch systems in macaques and humans. *Proceedings of the National Academy of Sciences of the United States of America*, 105(49), 19514–19519. https://doi.org/10.1073/pnas.0809662105

Tucker, D. M., Poulsen, C., & Luu, P. (2015). Critical periods for the neurodevelopmental processes of externalizing and internalizing. *Development and Psychopathology*, 27(2), 321–346. https://doi.org/10.1017/S0954579415000024

Ungerleider, L. G., & Mishkin, M. (1982). Two cortical visual systems. In D. J. Ingle, M. A. Goodale, & R. J. W. Mansfield (Eds.), *Analysis of visual behavior* (pp. 549–586). MIT Press.

Van Essen, D. C., Anderson, C. H., & Felleman, D. J. (1992). Information processing in the primate visual system: An integrated systems perspective. *Science*, 255, 419–423. https://doi.org/10.1126/science.1734518

Varoquaux, G., Schwartz, Y., Poldrack, R. A., Gauthier, B., Bzdok, D., Poline, J. B., & Thirion, B. (2018). Atlases of cognition with large-scale human brain mapping. *PLOS Computational Biology*, 14(11), e1006565. https://doi.org/10.1371/journal.pcbi.1006565

Vazey, E. M., Moorman, D. E., & Aston-Jones, G. (2018). Phasic locus coeruleus activity regulates cortical encoding of salience information. *Proceedings of the National Academy of Sciences of the United States of America*, 115(40), E9439–E9448. https://doi.org/10.1073/pnas.1803716115

Waddoups, A. B., Yoshikawa, H., & Strouf, K. (2019). Developmental effects of parent child separation. *Annual Review of Developmental Psychology*, 1, 387–410. https://doi.org/10.1146/annurev-devpsych-121318-085142

Wang, J., Li, Y., Musch, D. C., Wei, N., Qi, X., Ding, G., Li, X., Li, J., Song, L., Zhang, Y., Ning, Y., Zeng, X., Hua, N., Li, S., & Qian, X. (2021). Progression of myopia in school-aged children after COVID-19 home confinement. *JAMA Ophthalmology*, 139(3), 293–300. https://doi.org/10.1001/jamaophthalmol.2020.6239

Webb, A. R., Heller, H. T., Benson, C. B., & Lahav, A. (2015). Mother's voice and heartbeat sounds elicit auditory plasticity in the human brain before full gestation. *Proceedings of the National Academy of Sciences of the United States of America*, 112(10), 3152–3157. https://doi.org/10.1073/pnas.1414924112

Weiner, K. S., & Grill-Spector, K. (2013). Neural representations of faces and limbs neighbor in human high-level visual cortex: Evidence for a new organization principle. *Psychological Research*, 77(1), 74–97. https://doi.org/10.1007/s00426-011-0392-x

Wilcox, T., Bortfeld, H., Woods, R., Wruck, E., Armstrong, J., & Boas, D. (2009). Hemodynamic changes in the infant cortex during the processing of featural and spatiotemporal information. *Neuropsychologia*, 47, 657–662. https://doi.org//10.1016/j.neuropsychologia.2008.11.014

Wilcox, T., Bortfeld, H., Woods, R., Wruck, E., & Boas, D. A. (2005). Using near-infrared spectroscopy to assess neural activation during object processing in infants. *Journal of Biomedical Optics*, 10(1), 11010. https://doi.org/10.1117/1.1852551

Wilcox, T., Bortfeld, H., Woods, R., Wruck, E., & Boas, D. A. (2008). Hemodynamic response to featural changes in the occipital and inferior temporal cortex in infants: A preliminary methodological exploration. *Developmental Science*, 11, 361–370. https://doi.org/doi10.1111/j.1467-7687.2008.00681.x

Wilcox, T., Hawkins, L. B., Hirshkowitz, A., & Boas, D. A. (2014). Cortical activation to object shape and speed of motion during the first year. *NeuroImage*, 99, 129–141. https://doi.org/10.1016/j.neuroimage.2014.04.082

Xu, F., & Carey, S. (1996). Infants' metaphysics: The case of numerical identity. *Cognitive Psychology*, 30(2), 111–153. https://doi.org/10.1006/cogp.1996.0005

Yeung, H. H., & Werker, J. F. (2013). Lip movements affect infants' audiovisual speech perception. *Psychological Science*, 24(5), 603–612. https://doi.org/10.1177/0956797612458802

Zilles, K., Werners, R., Busching, U., & Schleicher, A. (1986). Ontogenesis of the laminar structure in areas 17 and 18 of the human visual cortex: A quantitative study. *Anatomy and Embryology*, 174, 339–353. https://doi.org/10.1007/BF00698784

7 Social Cognition

LEARNING OBJECTIVES

- Consider how imitation might ground subsequent social learning
- Identify different ways in which humans process information about themselves and others
- Differentiate cortical regions that support mental state reasoning
- Recognize that social cognition can be affected by individual and cultural differences
- Identify how social cognition is affected in people with Autism Spectrum Disorder (ASD)
- Differentiate ASD diagnostic and intervention techniques

Humans are social animals. We are not unique in this way, and it is hard to think of any mammal for whom the regulation of social behavior is not important. Even the development of cognitive abilities is dependent on extensive and extended social interaction. From birth, social and cognitive processes influence one another bidirectionally: the skills and abilities that accrue over the course of development are supported by interacting with other people, and interactions with other people contribute to children's future social behavior. This chapter will examine early impacts on social development, including how social interaction influences children's **action understanding and interpersonal attention**.

We start by reviewing the early biases that support social cognition, including the chain of learning that starts with contingency awareness, builds into an understanding of physical and psychological causation, and culminates in the ability to track mental state reasoning in other people. We will then discuss how interest in other people's faces and eyes contributes to infants' sensitivity to biological motion and their ability to distinguish between animate and inanimate objects. Because the lack of basic social competencies is a characteristic of a variety of neurodevelopmental disorders, including Autism Spectrum Disorder (ASD), extensive research focuses on understanding the basis for atypical **social cognition** and whether typical **social cognition can be taught**. Indeed, the huge body of research on ASD alone has contributed to our growing understanding of how social cognition develops; we will give substantial attention to the basis for and the consequences of that disorder.

7.1 Early Social Cognition

Babies have an inborn predisposition to interact with others: they **find it rewarding**. This early interaction grounds social and cognitive development by teaching infants to communicate with others, which helps them learn things. How social cognition emerges provides a window on how infants perceive and interpret the actions of others in relation to themselves. This has enormous implications for the trajectory of their subsequent development and life outcomes.

Infants initially engage in social interactions for seemingly simple reasons, such as maintaining proximity to their caregiver (Gergely, 2010), and engaging mechanisms that attract attention so that they get their needs met. One of these mechanisms is imitation.

7.1.1   The Developmental Onset of Imitation

Watch any new parent with a newborn and sooner or later you'll catch them sticking their tongue out and the baby responding in kind. Thus, Andrew Meltzoff was hardly the first adult to stick his tongue out at a baby, but he *was* the first to study it scientifically. Meltzoff and Moore (1983) found that newborn infants imitated an adult model's facial gesturing, tongue protrusion, and mouth opening. Meltzoff argued that imitation is fundamentally based on infants' ability to represent the analogy between other people and themselves: that is, that others are like me (Marshall & Meltzoff, 2014). Infant copying may reflect a motor schema or action pattern that is available early on as a neurally based motion repertoire. Regardless of the mechanism, it has the effect of getting people's attention.

In a clever extension of this work, baby monkeys born in research facilities also were found to imitate their (human) caretakers' facial gestures (Simpson et al., 2016). This suggests a strong evolutionary basis such that infants will imitate caretakers that aren't even from the same species! Moreover, that imitation served as a scaffold for the infant monkeys to learn another socially relevant behavior: their early imitation ability predicted how well they followed others' gazes at a later date. Follow-up research has further related infant monkeys' imitation abilities to their development of broader social behaviors (Wooddell et al., 2019).

The neonatal-imitation finding has been replicated over the years, but the effect can be persnickety; results depend on the exact age of the infants, and on the gestures being performed for them. Adding to the confusion is that sticking one's tongue out is in some cases an autonomic response to stimulation driven in part by the cerebellum; individuals with cerebellar disorders, or developmental disorders such as Williams syndrome, stick out their tongues not in imitation, but in response to surprising or emotional events, and sometimes without external provocation (Trauner et al., 1989). Thus, because almost any stimulation can lead neonates to stick out their tongues, we shouldn't infer that they are imitating someone when they do so. Moreover, the original study by Meltzoff and Moore (1983) involved a relatively small number of infants, and a small number of gestures, causing some researchers to wonder about the replicability and generalizability of the finding. Getting to the bottom of the imitation issue took a series of increasingly complicated experiments. Indeed, things came to a head with the publication of a large and comprehensive study (Oostenbroek et al., 2016) that concluded that human neonates don't imitate, followed by a counter-response (Meltzoff et al., 2018) arguing that the Oostenbroek study had several methodological flaws. A rebuttal to the rebuttal soon followed (Oostenbroek et al., 2019), and the debate continues (Keven & Akins, 2017).

A more conservative interpretation (Jones, 2017) is that initial gestures by neonates that seem imitative are instead a reflexive behavior produced in response to arousal (Jones, 2017), similar to what happens to infants when they are exposed to blinking lights or to tickling, but that they

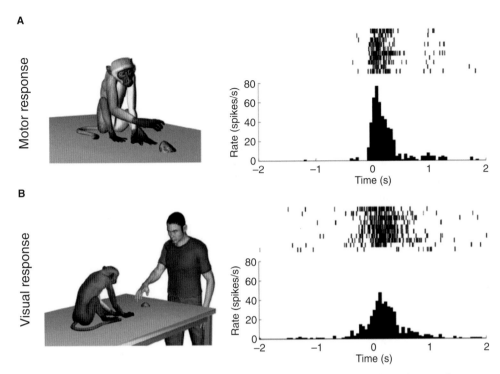

Figure 7.1 Mirror neurons. A. Monkey performing a motor response (top left) and raster plot and spike density histogram (top right) showing that response of a neuron during active goal-directed motor response by the monkey. B. Monkey observing another perform a motor response (bottom left) and raster plot and spike density histogram (bottom right) showing that response of the same neuron when the monkey watches the same goal-direct motor response performed by another. Note: in raster plots, each vertical bar indicates an action potential firing; each distinct line represents a different trial; t = 0 is the moment of contact by monkey or by another with goal object.

underpin true imitative behaviors which develop later. This very Piagetian argument is consistent with the broader view we espouse in this book that development is an emergent process.

7.1.2 Neuronal Mirroring System

Critical support to the self–other analogy hypothesis came from the discovery of **mirror neurons**. Giacamo Rizzolatti and colleagues were studying the neural correlates of simple motor actions, using single cell recordings from electrodes implanted in the cortex of monkeys (the implantation is done under anesthesia, and because the brain itself doesn't have any sensory receptors, the monkeys feel no discomfort from the implants). When a monkey reached for a banana, a distinctive set of neural firings were observed. The researchers replicated this finding across several monkeys. Just by chance, a monkey that was not being tested but whose cell firings were still being recorded saw the first monkey reach for the banana. To everyone's astonishment, the second monkey showed remarkably similar patterns of neural firing, *even though he was not moving* (Figure 7.1; Rizzolatti et al., 2001; Rizzolatti & Craighero, 2004). In short, these monkeys had neurons that "mirrored" others' actions (a kind of proto-"monkey-see monkey do" system).

The concept of mirror neurons exploded among both scientists and the public, with some arguing that they are crucial for many social abilities that humans take for granted.

The relevance of mirror neurons to human behavior has been the subject of intense disagreement and debate ever since (Hickok, 2009). Despite claims that mirror neurons underlie much of what makes humans unique, only one study (Mukamel et al., 2010) has decisively identified these neurons in humans. This is because single cell recording is invasive, and in the case of the Mukamel study, required testing epilepsy patients who had been implanted with intracranial electrodes to identify the foci of seizures for potential surgical treatment. A number of studies have failed to find evidence for mirror neurons (e.g., Lingnau et al., 2009) and the debate remains contentious (Heyes & Catmur, 2021; Turella et al., 2009) – for each study that finds evidence, an equally rigorous study fails to. The object lesson here is that just because there is a reason to think that the brain should be doing something (in this case, because we share a common ancestor with monkeys, many of our brain structures are homologous, and so if monkeys have mirror neurons it stands to reason that humans would), doesn't mean that the brain is doing what we expect it to do. (Much scientific backsliding has been caused by making assumptions rather than appealing to data.)

Nonetheless, there is plenty of indirect evidence for a relationship between the neural basis for processing our own and others' physical actions. Findings from early fMRI studies have shown activation in the inferior frontal and superior parietal lobes both when a person performed an action and when they saw someone else performing the action (Iacoboni et al., 1999). However, the MRI signal is based on averages of vast numbers of neurons, so whether the same neurons are engaged in processing one's own and others' actions remains unclear. Thus, a nuanced understanding of how the so-called **mirror neuron system** works in humans remains out of reach. The current debate focuses on how the system of motoric mirroring develops, with a focus on Hebbian (Keysers & Gazzola, 2014) versus associative learning (Catmur et al., 2016) accounts. (In fact, Hebbian learning seems likely to be the basis for associative learning (Johansen et al., 2014), although that too is a topic of debate (Gallistel & Matzel, 2013).)

Evidence specific to mirror neurons in human infants and young children comes from EEG frequency domain analysis, focusing specifically on mu rhythms (Meltzoff & Marshall, 2018). These are waves that repeat at a frequency between 7.5 and 12.5 Hz and are most prominent when the body is physically at rest; they are suppressed when the motor mirroring system is engaged. Thus, desynchronization of mu rhythms ("mu suppression"; Fox et al., 2016) is hypothesized to reflect representation of activity in one's own body as action is observed in the world. While there are numerous findings on mu suppression from different age groups, the methodology is subject to interference from other waves and by attentional engagement (Hobson & Bishop, 2016). These issues, together with the inherent difficulties of testing very young infants, mean that it remains unclear whether mirror neurons underlie our ability to imitate others early in life.

The current consensus is that mirror neurons alone cannot explain the human capacity for early imitation (leaving aside the issue of neonatal imitation). Despite this, the terms "mirror neuron" and "human mirror neuron system" have been embraced by popular science and are appealed to as explanatory for everything from empathy to Autism Spectrum Disorder. Given the lack of evidence about how these neurons acquire their properties in the first place, and the ongoing debate about neonatal imitation, it seems likely that the co-activation of neurons in response to own and others' movements is the product of either Hebbian or associative learning. On this view, the system is put in place through experience interacting with others.

7.1.3 Contingent Learning Is Social Learning

Parent–child imitation is the basis for social routines that provide a context for infants to learn that they are agents in their interactions: from early on they are treated as participants (Nomikou et al., 2017). In the game peek-a-boo, for example, the caregiver covers their face with the palms of their hands and then uncovers it, revealing wide eyes and surprise (often accompanied by an enthusiastic exclamation of peek-a-boo!). Even newborns enjoy the eye contact inherent to the game, and from early in life, infants find it endlessly amusing. Given the ubiquity of the game across cultures (Fernald & O'Neill, 1993), we might ask: Does this serve a developmental purpose? Peek-a-boo is an example of a **contingent behavior** because the infant's responses are contingent (i.e., dependent) upon what the caregiver does and vice versa. Thus, imitation serves as a foundation for contingency learning.

John S. Watson (1972) showed that 2-month-olds increased their leg kicking when it produced a highly contingent outcome, such as making a mobile rotate, but not when the mobile rotating was similar but not contingent on the infant's behavior. Three-month-olds preferred high – but not perfect – contingency between what their own legs were doing and recordings of their moving legs taken previously (Bahrick et al., 1985). In other words, infants seem driven by a desire to effect causality, to be agents of change. When the correlation of their own movements and the recording was too perfect, infants realized they are not controlling the video.

By their second month, infants smile (display positive affect) during live interactions with their mothers that contain variable contingency. But if they are shown video footage of their mothers from these interactions, in which their mother is doing the same things but non-contingently (i.e., the infant is not able to control the interactions) the infants display *negative* affect (Nadel et al., 1999). This is in spite of these replays having just as much emotion and social stimulation – indeed, the identical content – as the live interaction! Thus, contingency helps establish correspondence between oneself and others and builds an infant's sense of agency in the world – an understanding that their own behavior can control *others'* behavior. Infants' sensitivity to contingency motivates them to attend more closely to their own behaviors, which builds self-awareness. The emerging awareness of their own and others' internal states is critical to developing self-control, an ability that requires self-representation. And awareness of others' mental states helps build a **theory of mind** (Section 7.3.2), the understanding that other people have their own mental states, emotions, and knowledge.

In other words, what might seem to be a simple, silly game provides cues to learning about one*self* and critically supports the larger process of social development.

7.1.4 Mental Representations and Distinguishing between Social and Non-Social Objects

Understanding the basis for imitation in infancy contributes to our understanding of other dimensions of social knowledge. Does early imitative behavior require mental representation of the action being imitated? Infants (human and non-human primates alike) mimic biological beings – or things that at least appear to be biological – and not machines or other inanimate, non-biological objects (Simion et al., 2008; Vanderwert et al., 2015). At a later developmental stage, young children will play imitating inanimate objects like trees and teapots; they find these games engaging and fun, presumably because they are leaving behind the childish habit of only imitating animate objects. It's clear that these children have a mental representation and intentionality behind their imitation – what about infants?

If imitation is reserved for representations that are person- (or biological being-) specific, it points to an evolutionary basis for this ability. While we'll remain agnostic about how the ability comes about initially, if such an ability exists, it provides a basis for infants' drive to interact with others (as opposed to, say, a chair). Indeed, there is both behavioral (Poulin-Dubois, 1999; Träuble et al., 2014; Poulin-Dubois et al., 2015) and neural (Kaduk et al., 2013) evidence that infants distinguish between animate and inanimate objects.

The basis for this ability may be the motion such objects produce. Visual processing is specialized for the extraction of animacy from visual cues of motion, which may partly explain why infants so enjoy mobiles above their cribs. In a classic study, Heider and Simmel (1944) showed that the sense of animacy can arise from dynamic visual cues, even very basic ones. Decades later, researchers realized that lights can be placed on the limbs and joints of a moving human (or animal) to capture their motion in a dark room, and adult observers immediately perceive that motion as being generated by a human. Infants detect and prefer such biological motion early in life (Fox & McDaniel, 1982), a discovery that led to a wave of developmental research on this topic. Recent work shows that both form and speed of motion matter. A recent study found that newborns, despite their notoriously bad visual acuity (Chapter 6) distinguish between things whose speed is constant and those whose speed changes abruptly (Di Giorgio et al., 2021). This indicates an attentional bias towards the types of visual motion cues that underlie animacy. Biological motion from living things can provide cues about their behaviors, goals, and intentions – are they coming towards me or moving away? Are they moving predictably or unpredictably?

7.2   Faces and Eyes Are Social

Faces and eyes convey various forms of information that have social significance, including a person's identity, their emotional state, and what they're reacting to. Not surprisingly, perceiving faces is one of humans' most developed skills. In typically developing children, face recognition is a foundational component of social cognition. A host of findings has converged on the relevant perceptual mechanisms supporting the development of face recognition abilities and helped delineate the neural mechanisms underlying them (Chapter 6). Overall, it is clear that infants enter the world with a bias to orient towards face-like stimuli, which itself drives subsequent face-specific learning. Infants' facial discrimination abilities continue to develop throughout childhood, based on the incorporation of a range of cues, including featural (eyes, nose, mouth) and configural information (the particular pattern of two ovals at the top of the face, an oblong oval in the middle, and a horizontal shape at the bottom – eyes, nose, and mouth). Configural processing is what caused monkeys to mistake a toilet brush for another monkey (an oval shape with hair all around it; Desimone et al., 1984) and infants to recognize even cartoon faces (Tong et al., 2000).

It is not just whose face they are looking at that matters to infants; they also care about the manner and direction in which the different components of that face – particularly the eyes – are moving.

7.2.1 The Importance of Eye Gaze

Early in life, infants orient towards faces with direct gaze, initiating eye contact. Perception of eye contact is supported in early infancy by a subcortical processing route (Senju & Johnson, 2009) that helps infants prioritize processing of the relevant sensory information. Human newborns show a preference for face-like patterns in which darker elements stand out against a lighter background (Farroni et al., 2005), a bias that optimizes detection of an eye's darker iris against its white sclera (Gliga & Csibra, 2007). This high contrast feature detection is supported by the visual cortex in humans, but not in non-human primates (Kobayashi & Kohshima, 2001). The early-emerging predisposition for direct gaze is adaptive, with eyes serving important social and communicative functions in how children learn from other people (Csibra & Gergely, 2009). Thus, children learn the importance of other people's eyes early and demonstrate an implicit awareness that they are cues to a person's knowledge state. Infants who are born blind must learn to use other sensory cues and they do so with equal effectiveness (Bedny et al., 2015), another demonstration of the power of neuroplasticity in developing brains.

In a study on the dynamic relationship between moment-to-moment fluctuations of mutual gaze and underlying neural processing, pairs of children (aged between 9 and 15 months) and adults were simultaneously scanned (**hyperscanned**) with fNIRS while they looked at one another to solve a task (Piazza et al., 2020). Time-locked neural coupling within the dyads was compared to the activation observed during a control condition with no mutual gaze. For both members of the mutual gaze dyads – a social cue available to both individuals simultaneously – the prefrontal cortex (PFC) was significantly coupled to the time course of the mutual gaze. PFC has been shown in a range of studies to contain specialized prediction circuits (e.g., Brodmann area 47, within PFC, tracks and predicts patterns in visual, tactile, and auditory stimuli).

Critically, neural alignment both preceded and anticipated the joint eye contact, with mutual gaze lagging slightly behind the PFC activation itself. Moreover, the adult PFC data tracked infant–adult joint attention to objects, also in a time-locked manner – indicating the adult's anticipation of infant smiles and other positive reactions to the objects. That is, the PFC data appeared to track the adult's motivation to use toys to engage infants in joint attention and thereby elicit positive emotional responses from them. These findings provide neural evidence of the degree to which caregivers monitor the direction of children's eye gaze to follow their attention, results that build on previous fNIRS hyperscanning data that likewise showed heightened PFC activation in infants in response to direct gaze (Urakawa et al., 2015). **Joint attention** emerges as children learn to follow the gaze of others, and that contributes substantially to development in the second year of life.

Seeing is a "mental act" that provides information about what another person is thinking, with eyes providing critical social cues to the mental contents of others. fMRI findings in adults show that eye contact can modulate activity in a range of brain structures (i.e., the "social brain network"), including the fusiform face area (FFA), the superior temporal sulcus (STS), and the amygdala. Whereas gaze following becomes a robust behavior by the middle of the first year, already by the beginning of the second year, infants begin to actively coordinate their visual attention with other people (Bakeman & Adamson, 1984). Indeed, joint attention has been identified as a critical early component of cognitive development, impacting a range of skills, including language development.

But there is growing evidence that even something as seemingly fundamental as our predisposition to focus on and follow eyes is sculpted by our environment. In an elegant example of how quickly experience-dependent processes work, newborns' predisposition to look at others' eyes has been found to adapt quickly to specific cultural norms about eye contact – and thus an infant's relative exposure to communicative eye gaze (Senju et al., 2013). Likewise, infants and children who develop in different cultures show somewhat different patterns of face scanning and are sensitive to different emotion cues conveyed by the face (Geangu et al., 2016; Kelly et al., 2011). Finally, sighted infants of blind parents, who experience qualitatively different eye gaze communication from birth, also show distinct patterns of face scanning and gaze following, and their ERPs in response to gaze shifting are significantly different from those from sighted infants of sighted parents (Senju et al., 2015; Vernetti et al., 2018). Such rapid adaptation to an individual's particular social environment is critical to the formation of distinct cultural groups (Han et al., 2013), in addition to supporting effective social learning and communication.

7.2.2 A Visual Pathway That Supports Social Perception

As discussed in Chapter 6, humans manifest two primary visual pathways: the "what" ventral pathway used to identify objects, and the "where" dorsal pathway used for locating and manipulating objects. Up until recently, the consensus view was that social information was distilled from these two pathways. However, a growing body of empirical evidence suggests there is a third visual pathway dedicated to processing social information (Pitcher & Ungerleider, 2021). Much of the direct (single cell recording) evidence for this third pathway comes from non-human primate studies, but there is substantial indirect (i.e., fMRI) human-based evidence for it as well. Critically, findings from tractography support the notion that there is a pathway leading from the visual cortex to the STS, the region we have described as engaged in a range of socially relevant tasks, including biological motion, dynamic face perception, and theory of mind processing.

According to the proposal, this third pathway is dedicated to processing moving biological objects, including moving faces. Thus, in contrast to the FFA, the "face-selective" region of the third pathway responds much more strongly to moving faces than static ones – distinguishing, for example, live people from photographs or statues. Data from adults show that disrupting the ventral pathway has no effect on the STS in this regard, meaning the two pathways operate largely independently (Bauer, 1984; Gao et al., 2019). These data also show that, in addition to processing moving bodies and faces, the third pathway is engaged in a number of higher-level processes relevant to social cognition. For example, the STS is engaged when people perceive, evaluate, and respond to facial expressions and eye gaze, bodies, and point-light displays (or walkers, a collection of moving dots or light-points that reproduce the visual experience of

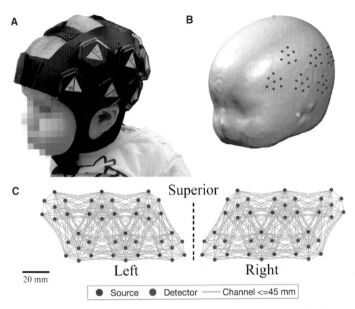

Figure 7.2 High-density fNIRS probes for better spatial resolution.
A. Side view photograph of an infant wearing a cap with tiles visible over the left hemisphere. Note the Velcro strap connections running over the midline of the head (A, B, and C). B. The source positions (red points), detector positions (blue points), and cranial landmarks (green points) shown on the subject-registered 6-month anatomical atlas model. C. 2D representation of the full high-density array, showing channels with source-detector separation of approximately 45 mm or less. (Adapted from Frijia et al., 2021)

seeing a moving body). The STS is also engaged in speech processing and the integration of visual and auditory speech.

A growing body of evidence from DCN is consistent with this proposal. For example, extensive work by Sarah Lloyd-Fox and colleagues using fNIRS with infants demonstrates engagement of superior temporal and other "social pathway" regions during presentation of dynamic social stimuli (Lloyd-Fox et al., 2009, 2011, 2015). These findings include point-light walkers that are presented upright and inverted, which infants respond to differentially, both behaviorally and neurally. However, due to limited spatial resolution, fNIRS data cannot provide clear evidence of a delineation between this processing and ventral visual processing (i.e., FFA). How these regions become integrated over developmental time with frontal regions (i.e., medial prefrontal cortex, or mPFC) likewise remains a question ripe for future research, although there is evidence that the mPFC is engaged in infants in response to social stimuli (Grossman et al., 2008). Future DCN research using high density fNIRS optode arrays (Frijia et al., 2021) will no doubt provide additional insights into when and how this third visual pathway becomes specialized for social perception. Figure 7.2 shows an example of newer high-density fNIRS probes, the likes of which should produce better spatial resolution and localization of cortical activation in infants and young children for whom time in a scanner is unrealistic. Such developments are particularly important if DCN findings are to be applied clinically (i.e., helping identify neurodevelopmental disorders earlier in life). Differences in the processing of social stimuli between typically developing controls and children at risk for ASD, for example, have already been observed (Lloyd-Fox et al., 2013).

7.3   Representation of Self and Other

Infants' awareness of themselves as intentional agents in the world seems largely implicit in the first two years. The first clear evidence of explicit self-awareness emerges at the end of the second year when children are able to pass the mirror mark task (Amsterdam, 1972), in which a noticeable spot of blush or lipstick is placed on a child's nose with the goal of seeing whether, when placed in front of a mirror, the child will notice the spot and touch their own nose. It is quite striking to witness younger children who are unable to pass this test do all sorts of behaviors in response to the child in the mirror, but without any apparent recognition that that child is them. Passing the mirror mark task cannot be taught; a child needs to make the connection between the person in the mirror and themselves, which requires self-awareness. Interestingly, the perfect contingency in behavior between the child and their mirror image is not enough for the child to recognize themselves before a certain age (recall the section above about imperfect contingencies being preferred). Because the child appears to think that the mirror image is another child, not themselves, the representation of *other* seems to precede the representation of self, at least at the perceptual level.

Self-awareness is critical to social development, as children's own intentional and affective states become increasingly and explicitly salient to them. In effect, they reach the point at which they realize "I am a distinct entity … I am hungry … I need to go to the bathroom" and ultimately, they need to recognize that others can be in different states. Just because I am hungry doesn't mean that *you* are. Just because I know where the cookies are hidden doesn't mean that *you* do. This is important: our representation of others' representations underlies how we make predictions about their behaviors. One aspect of perceiving others from birth is watching their actions have consequences.

7.3.1   Goal-Directed Actions and Intentionality

How do we know whether infants expect people to execute actions based on goals? In an innovative application of habituation (Chapter 2), Amanda Woodward (1998) pursued understanding how infants' physical reasoning (Chapter 6) can be extended to reasoning about the action of others. She first habituated 9-month-old infants to either an actor's arm or to a cardboard tube – normally inanimate, but here controlled by an actor hidden out of view – reaching towards one of two toys (Woodward, 1998). Following habituation, the position of the two toys was switched and the arm and the cardboard tube began reaching again towards toys. In one condition, the arm or tube either reached for the same object as before, thus introducing a "new path," or reached for the different toy which introduced a "new goal."

Infants who had seen the *actor* reaching now looked longer at the new goal event than at the new path event; infants who had seen the *cardboard tube* reaching did not show a preference for either the new goal or the new path. Critically, they did dishabituate to both forms of reaching in these new trials, meaning they noticed the change in actions. Similar findings were obtained in a follow-up experiment conducted with 6-month-old infants. Woodward suggested infants were surprised by the actor's change in goal, but not the cardboard tube's, presumably because they understand that inanimate objects (notwithstanding R2-D2 and the like) don't have goals. If this interpretation is correct, it reveals some remarkably sophisticated reasoning about goal-directed actions and intentions.

When younger (3-month-old) infants were habituated to the two different reaching behaviors they dishabituated to both new events, but did not look longer at one or the other (Sommerville & Woodward, 2005). In contrast, another group of 3-month-old infants were habituated to the reaching behaviors only after they had spent time with the two objects. They were first shown the objects and then allowed to interact with them. Now, 3-month-olds normally would not be able to do much with toys given their underdeveloped motor abilities, but with a pair of Velcro covered mittens, they were able to "pick up" the two objects directly, thereby experiencing themselves as goal-directed agents. After they were habituated to the actor or cardboard tube reaching to one of the two objects, in contrast to those who did not "handle" the objects, this group of infants dishabituated to both of the new reaching events, and they looked longest at the new goal event, similar to the 6-month-olds. The researchers argued that the 3-month-olds with "sticky mittens" received physical experience with the toys, thereby becoming sensitive to the "goal directedness" of the reaching and the goal structure of the two different reaching events. This underscores a point we make throughout the book – that experience, interacting with genes and brains, can profoundly affect development.

Most of us understand others' actions by making inferences about their mental states, and observing goal-directed actions may play a role in infants' understanding of intentionality. Much research on whether and how infants interpret goals has been built on Woodward's findings described above (Flack-Ytter et al., 2006; Kanakogi & Itakura, 2011), with corresponding debates over whether infants really understand others' goals. For example, strong arguments have been made that the teleological nature of the events themselves – that is, the purpose they served the actors in the moment – may be the basis for infants' behavior rather than others' intentions (Gergely & Csibra, 2003). This is a subtle but important distinction. Do you need to know what someone else is thinking – the product of their mental activity – to predict what they'll do? Or is it enough to know *what* someone is doing without resorting to a theory about what they might be *intending*? These results can also be framed as a product of event segmentation, by which statistical structure in the world shapes infants' ability to generate action predictions without prior knowledge about the actions themselves (Levine et al., 2018) – essentially, babies are little statistical machines (Chapter 6) and they learn what follows what very effectively (indeed, as we show in Chapter 8, this is how they learn the rules of their native language). In short, while the learning mechanisms that underlie infants' sensitivity to goal-directness and intentionality remain underspecified, the wealth of data indicates that the sensitivity is real. Therein lies a gateway for infants to understand far more complex, mentally based behavior.

7.3.2   False Beliefs and Theory of Mind

Our brains are biological entities that we can see; our minds and the thoughts they contain are conceptual, unobservable, and immaterial entities. A neurosurgeon once told philosopher Daniel Dennett that he had seen hundreds of brains, but he had never seen a single thought. Philosophers have long discussed the means by which we come to know that others have "personhood" as we do. The understanding that others have minds enables us to understand that others' actions depend on the knowledge and beliefs they hold in those immaterial and unobservable minds. We can understand that others' knowledge and beliefs may differ from the ones that we hold in our own heads, meaning people can have false beliefs about the veridical state of the world. You may believe that Seth and Emma broke up and are no longer dating, but I may know for a fact that they are. You have a **false belief**, and I know that you do, and that this will affect decisions you make (such as not inviting both of them to your house for a party).

This is complicated – but critically important – stuff! To have representations of others' representations is to have theories about what is in other people's minds, or *to have a theory of mind*. Where does this theory of mind come from? Interestingly, well before they are able to pass the mirror test and show explicit self-awareness, infants appear to make mentally based interpretations about the goal-directedness of other people's action.

Not long ago, it was thought that a fundamental shift in children's ability to understand the minds of other people was needed in order for them to achieve the kind of attributional thinking inherent to false belief reasoning. It was assumed that children could not perform such reasoning until around 4 years of age, the point at which children are able to respond correctly in a standard elicited-response false belief task, in which children are asked direct questions about how a mistaken person will act in a hypothetical scenario. The original version of such a task involves presenting a child with two dolls, Sally and Anne, and describing the following scenario (Wimmer & Perner, 1983):

One doll (Sally) hides something (a marble) in a basket, then leaves the room. The other, Anne, moves the marble from the basket to a box. Then Sally returns.

The child is then asked where Sally will look for her marble. To pass the task, the child has to understand that Sally will not have the same knowledge about the location of the marble that they do. The child should thus report that Sally will search in the original location (the basket) rather than the true location (the box). Consistent with the notion that such reasoning requires a fundamental shift in mental state reasoning, typically developing children generally do not pass the Sally-Anne task until late preschool, around 4 years of age (Wellman & Liu, 2004). Tasks like the Sally-Anne task often are referred to as false location tasks. Another version, a false contents task, involves showing a child a container, usually of a popular candy, and then showing them that it contains something other than candy, such as pencils (Hogrefe et al., 1986). The child is asked what another person who has just arrived will think is in the container. To pass this task, children must understand that the person just arriving will have a false belief that there is candy in the container, even though they know that is incorrect. As with the false location task, the standard age for passing a false contents task is around 4 years. The ability to pass such tasks was considered evidence that a child had come to understand that the minds of others can hold beliefs that are not necessarily a direct reflection of reality.

Complicating matters considerably, researchers discovered that when false location or false contents tasks are adjusted to not require an explicit response, younger children – even infants – demonstrate false-belief understanding. The basis for these findings was behavioral methods that did not require anything more from infants than that they observe a scene (Chapter 2). For example, in an early study, 15-month-old infants showed sensitivity – by looking longer in a violation-of-expectation task – to an actor behaving contrary to her false belief about where a toy was hidden (Onishi & Baillargeon, 2005). In the past 15 years, many variations of such false belief paradigms have been created for use with very young children (Scott, 2017). Using a cartoon version involving a table, a box, and an occluder, researchers extended findings about false belief understanding to 7-month-olds (Kovács et al., 2010). Not surprisingly, the question of whether infants are capable of making sense of others' behavior based on their unseeable and subjective mental states and processes has generated considerable debate. Some critics argue that mental state attribution is well beyond the ability of preverbal infants, providing alternative accounts of infants' performance that focus on superficial features of the tasks that may be driving infants' looking behavior (Priewasser et al., 2018), or they question the reproducibility of the results from infants based on nuanced methodological details (Phillips et al., 2015; Poulin-Dubois & Yott, 2018). While it is assured that these debates will continue (Heyes, 2014; Phillips et al., 2015; Baillargeon et al., 2018), the methods of DCN are providing insight into possible mechanisms of support for the emerging ability to mentalize.

7.3.3 Understanding Others' Minds

Mentalizing – being able to impute mental states to oneself and to others – is having a theory of mind. A mechanistic question for understanding early mentalizing is whether the implicit and explicit forms of theory-of-mind tasks are based on the same underlying cognitive and neural mechanisms (a single system), or rather reflect qualitatively different kinds of processing (two systems). One argument (Apperly & Butterfill, 2009) is that the behavioral results from infants and children reflect two distinct systems, whereby the first system is present early in life while the second comes online only later (there are other systems that work this way, such as in perception, with absolute versus relative processing, and global versus local processing). The early developing system is fast, efficient, and operates spontaneously/unconsciously; such a system would underlie infants' and young children's impressive performance on modified (implicit) false belief tasks. The second system is explicit, deliberate, and dependent on working memory, but also flexible, thus accounting for older children's ability to overtly (explicitly) reason about mental states. Another argument (Scott, 2017) is that a single system operates automatically in early infancy, and that the tasks that tap into it need to be designed so as not to require the production of overt, explicit responses. A third argument integrates the two systems into one. On this view, with developmental time, the automatic, early system comes to work in conjunction with the overall goal of anticipating people's behavior, which itself manifests in a controlled way, engaging both working memory and executive functions (Carruthers, 2018). On this view, rather than a two-system account, one of the systems encompasses the other, having access to the same conceptual resources. In short, while there are numerous and strong opinions about when and how, developmentally speaking, mentalizing comes about, the disagreements are over the instantiation of the transition from automatic to overt awareness of another's mind. It is precisely these sorts of debates whose resolution is helped enormously by additional evidence from the brain.

7.4   Brain Basis for Mentalizing

As we have seen, the neural systems that support mentalizing appear to be in operation – at least in rudimentary form – in early infancy, allowing for implicit attribution of intentions and belief. Between years 4 and 6, children begin to reason explicitly about the basis for false beliefs. What are the neural substrates that support the differential emergence of these mentalizing abilities? A primary constraint on understanding the nature of early mental state reasoning is young children's inability to explicitly respond to overt questions. For this reason, researchers focused largely on using fMRI to establish which brain regions responded during performance of different mentalizing tasks in adults, although the tasks themselves were often adapted from those used with preschool-aged children (Frith & Frith, 2006). Collectively, findings from this imaging work revealed that adults use a bilateral network of brain regions involved in social cognition, including the medial prefrontal cortex (mPFC), superior temporal sulcus (STS), anterior temporal areas, precuneus, and bilateral temporoparietal junction (TPJ), as detailed in Figure 7.3. That's a lot of brain!

To begin to narrow the focus, it helps to consider the specific functions these different regions support. For example, the mPFC region appears to support decoupling mental state

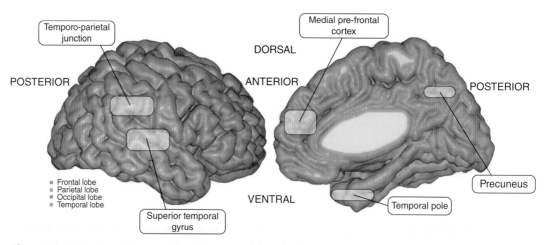

Figure 7.3 Depiction of the neural regions comprising the theory-of-mind network. Although shown here for only one hemisphere (the right), the regions are bilateral, with both hemispheres contributing to theory-of-mind reasoning in adults and children alike.

representations from physical state representations. The STS region is probably the basis for detection of agency, with its sensitivity to direction of eye gaze and other aspects of biological motion. The anterior temporal areas, also referred to as the temporal poles, seem to be involved in access to language- or memory-based social knowledge, while the precuneus is involved in consciousness. Interestingly, the TPJ, particularly in the right hemisphere (rTPJ), has been found to serve two roles: redirecting attention and reasoning about others' mental states. In other words, collectively, these regions represent a wide range of processes relevant to mentalizing. If activation of these different brain regions supports various aspects of mentalizing in adults, does it do the same in children?

7.4.1 Developmental Time Course of Mentalizing

DCN methods have augmented looking times and eye-tracking by adding alternative approaches to tracking the development of mentalizing abilities. Initially, electrophysiological techniques helped characterize the brain-based dynamics of false belief reasoning in young children. In an early experiment, Liu, Wellman, and colleagues asked adults and children between 4 and 6 years of age to reason about the beliefs of characters in animated false belief vignettes in which location switches took place, as well as about reality. ERPs were time-locked to participants' "think" and "reality" judgments (Liu et al., 2009). As can be seen at the top of Figure 7.4, when differentiating others' beliefs from reality, adults showed an event-related component peaking around 800 ms post-stimulus (P8 response) with a left frontal scalp distribution. The researchers interpreted this as a reflection of the decoupling that is necessary for someone to distinguish others' mental states from objective reality. This response was also observed in the children who correctly reasoned about others' false beliefs (middle of Figure 7.4), although the effect occurred quite a bit later. Critically, the effect was not observed in the children who failed to correctly reason about others' false beliefs (bottom of Figure 7.4). In other words, this left-lateralized, late slow wave appears to be the product of representing another person's mental state, as seen in both the adults and the child-passers. In contrast, the child-failers did not show such an ability behaviorally, nor did they show a corresponding neural marker of such representation.

In addition to the late slow wave, when distinguishing false belief from true belief, children showed a late positive wave with a posterior distribution. This component has been interpreted by some as a product of the second of the two systems necessary for robust mental state reasoning. Taken together, these two late waveforms may correspond to the neural systems that guide mental state reasoning. Finally, regardless of whether children were passers or failers, they showed more posterior localization of the late positive wave than adults, whose own late positive wave is generally more centrally distributed (Meinhardt-Injac et al., 2011). This localization change perhaps reflects continued developmental progress into adulthood in conceptualizing mental domains.

Researchers have also used frequency domain analysis of the EEG signal (Chapter 2) to determine whether the neural regions associated with mental state reasoning in older children and adults are also engaged in younger, 4-year-old children (Sabbagh et al., 2009). The measure of interest was the alpha frequency band, because in early childhood alpha becomes the highest amplitude

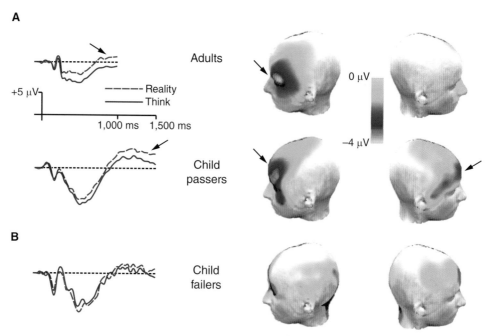

Figure 7.4 Event-related brain potentials (ERPs) show a late slow wave in adults and child-passers relative to child-failers (left), as do maps of their scalp electrical activity (right). A. ERP waveforms extend for 1,000 ms for adults and 1,500 ms for children. The dashed red lines indicate reality judgments, and the solid blue lines indicate think judgments. Arrows point to the late slow wave. B. Maps of scalp electrical activity show mean amplitude difference between conditions (reality subtracted from belief) in the 775- to 850-ms post-stimulus epoch for adults (top) and in the 1,400- to 1,500-ms post-stimulus epoch for child passers (middle) and child failers (bottom). (Reprinted from Liu et al., 2009)

resting EEG rhythm over all regions of the scalp, peaking between 6 and 9 Hz (Marshall et al., 2002). Regional increases in resting/baseline alpha power and coherence reflect more mature functional organization of underlying neural systems (Thatcher, 1994).

Individual differences in resting-state alpha oscillation were observed in areas roughly corresponding to the rTPJ and the mPFC that mapped to individual children's performance on a standard behavioral test of mentalizing ability. These associations held after controlling for children's executive functioning and vocabulary skills. These data were a good start; however, the location of the sources of EEG signals obtained from the scalp can only be approximated (i.e., the Poisson inverse problem; Chapter 2). Because of this, hypotheses about regional localization of EEG signals are heavily guided by findings from, among other things, adult fMRI data.

Subsequent fMRI findings from children have supported the general findings, showing that the higher the rTPJ activation when children reason about mental state content (and not other general social characteristics), the better those children perform on behavioral theory-of-mind tasks (Saxe et al., 2009; Gweon et al., 2012; Bowman et al., 2019). In other words, more advanced theory-of-mind performance corresponds to increasing "selectivity" of the rTPJ for mental state processes. Thus, it appears that frontal contribution to mental state reasoning lags in developmental time relative to the core contribution of the rTPJ, supporting the view that differential maturation of TPJ and mPFC may be linked to children's differential emergence of accurate false belief reasoning.

Recent fNIRS findings are consistent with those obtained from adults, showing activation in an area in the vicinity of rTPJ in 7-month-olds while they tracked the beliefs of another person in an infant-adapted false location task (Hyde et al., 2018). The spatial specificity of fNIRS is more precise than the modeling techniques used to localize EEG sources of activation (Chapter 2), but is nowhere near as precise as fMRI, meaning these results must be interpreted with caution. On the other hand, Hyde et al. (2018) did not observe differential activation of other temporal and prefrontal regions during infants' processing of either true or false belief scenarios, indicating that the rTPJ is engaged for processing belief-relevant events early on, while the frontal regions necessary to support more nuanced mental representations are still not, at 7 months, actively engaged. Interestingly, findings from a recent fNIRS study found significantly stronger fronto-temporoparietal connectivity in 18-month-olds who recognized themselves in a mirror versus those who did not, providing support for the hypothesized relationship between mirror-self recognition and self-awareness in infancy (Bulgarelli et al., 2019).

7.4.2 Interpreting the Data

Why would the rTPJ support theory-of-mind processes at all? There are various views on this. For one thing, it is near superior temporal regions, which support processing biological motion, so perhaps other people's motions (of eyes, hands) contribute to how we reason about their mental state. The rTPJ is also near parietal regions that control attentional orientation. Attention to subtle cues is an important part of deducing somebody's mental state. Thus, the rTPJ has been characterized as an anatomical nexus for different abilities, including not only attention, but memory and language too, all of which are critical to social cognition (Carter & Huettel, 2013). Fortunately, our focus on a specific type of mentalizing – in this case, false belief reasoning – circumscribes the network. Indeed, as highlighted by the results of a meta-analysis (Figure 7.5), the rTPJ is the region that is uniformly active in adults across a wide range of false belief tasks.

7.4.3 Changes in Neural Connectivity Support Mentalizing

Up until now, we have focused exclusively on the specific regions involved in different types of mental state reasoning without characterizing the connections between them. Developmentally focused fMRI studies on mentalizing consistently show primarily TPJ activation in children, while comparable adult data show engagement of a broader, more distributed network of cortical regions. How and when do these other areas engage with the TPJ?

Tractography studies revealed maturation in 3- and 4-year-old children's local white matter structure – quantified as increases in fractional anisotropy of white matter (see

Social animations (n = 14)

Mind in the eyes (n = 10)

False belief vs. photo (n = 15)

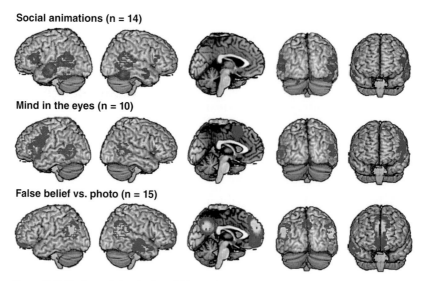

Figure 7.5 Brain activity during different false belief tasks compared to (non-mentalizing) photo viewing, based on a meta-analysis. The social animations task elicits activity in the inferior frontal cortex and temporoparietal junction, as does the mind in the eyes task. The false belief task elicits activity in medial frontal cortex and the temporoparietal junction.) (*Cognitive Neuroscience*, Banich & Compton. © 2018 Cambridge University Press. Reproduced with permission of the Licensor through PLSclear)

Chapter 2) – in areas surrounding many of the same regions associated with better theory-of-mind reasoning (Grosse Wiesmann et al., 2017). Thus, it seems that white matter maturation in this network correlates with the emergence of explicit false belief understanding in these young children.

When controlling for additional measures often confounded in assessments of children's mentalizing performance (i.e., language, executive function performance, children's earlier performance on an implicit false belief task), Grosse Wiesmann and colleagues (2017) observed that increased white matter connectivity between temporoparietal and inferior frontal regions was independent of co-developing cognitive abilities. In short, the researchers' findings demonstrate that the emergence of mental state representation is related to the maturation of specific cortical regions and their emerging connectivity to the prefrontal cortex. These findings highlight the transition from implicit to explicit mental state reasoning during which developmental processes gradually emerge. What about the one- vs. two-system debate? In a more recent study (Grosse Wiesmann et al., 2020), the same researchers found that, although younger children are already capable of implicitly predicting others' behavior based on what they think, this prediction relies on a different brain network than the explicit task, one that matures earlier. By comparing children's responses on a false belief task with structural MRIs from the same children, the researchers found that different brain structures were involved in verbal reasoning about the task and their non-verbal predictions about the task based on eye-tracking (Figure 7.6), again underscoring the distinction between implicit and explicit (or declarative) processes.

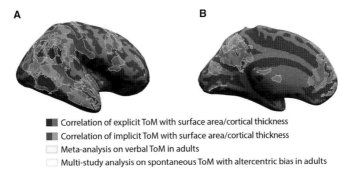

Figure 7.6 Distinct and independent brain regions are associated with success on explicit (blue) and implicit (red, orange) theory-of-mind tasks as shown for A. the surface area and B. cortical thickness. Effects are shown on the inflated surface of the common group template. (Reprinted from Grosse Wiesmann et al., 2020)

7.5 Mentalizing Supports Learning

Premack and Woodruff (1978) were the first to use the term "theory of mind," referring to the behavior of a chimpanzee they were working with who showed evidence of distinguishing the intentions of an agent from the agent's observable behavior. Not surprisingly, as developmental research on mentalizing in human infants and young children ramped up, research with non-human primates continued apace. Initially, a string of findings (Call & Tomasello, 1999; Wyatt Kaminski et al., 2008) showed that great apes were unable to perform at a level comparable to human infants on tasks designed to resemble standard explicit theory-of-mind tasks. However, when the false belief tasks employed were of the type adapted for infants, great apes have been found to behave as coherently as human infants (Krupenye et al., 2016; Buttelmann et al., 2017). Some have interpreted this as additional evidence of a dissociation between the two types of mentalizing tasks, implicit and explicit, thus providing support for two processing levels, or levels of difficulty, account of theory-of-mind reasoning.

Tomasello (2018), however, has proposed an alternative explanation for the transition from implicit to explicit theory-of-mind reasoning that humans make and that apes appear unable to make. Rather than a two-system or nested structure, Tomasello focuses on the critical role played by social and communicative interaction in the development of perspective taking, characterizing the findings from infants and preschoolers as a "U-shaped" pattern of development. Initially, at the left-hand top of the U, infants perform well in infant-specific tasks. Later, at the right-hand top of the U, 4-year-olds perform well on explicit tasks. But between those two time points, things get murky. When presented with explicit theory-of-mind questions, 3-year-olds default to the "reality-based" interpretation – reality from their perspective – not taking the other's perspective and thus answering incorrectly. On this view, what has changed for the 4-year-olds is not that they have shifted to a second, more mature system. Rather, they are better able to deal with what Tomasello refers to as "perspective problems," or problems that are the product of different people having what seem to be incompatible perspectives on objective reality. This seems like a subtle difference in framing, but it does account for the behavioral results we have reviewed from 3-year-olds that don't jibe with a binary, or Piagetian stage-like characterization of mental state reasoning (Király et al., 2018). Rather than adjudicating between these alternative proposals, the two-system account and the perspective-taking account, we will turn our attention to a line of research that, while relevant to the development of mentalizing, likewise acknowledges the relevance of faces – particularly eyes, and the information they carry – to social cognition.

7.5.1   Social Referencing and Emotion Regulation

Another way that gaze provides access to the mental states of others is through **social referencing** (Campos & Stenberg, 1981; Walden & Ogan, 1988), a process whereby children use others' affective displays to regulate their own behavior. Infants literally *look* to the parent for guidance in navigating both emotional and physical landscapes. The classic experimental demonstration of this uses the visual cliff apparatus to observe the influence of mothers' emotional responses on their infants as the infants crawl nearer to the "edge" of an apparent cliff (Sorce et al., 1985). When mothers made a fearful face, the majority of infants stopped crawling. Conversely, when mothers made a happy face, the infants kept on crawling right over the edge. Of course, no infants were harmed in the running of these studies as the children were supported on both sides of the "cliff" (Figure 7.7). Thus, social referencing works in both positive and negative affective directions (Walle et al., 2017). As development proceeds, children learn to interpret increasingly subtle emotions from others' faces, particularly based on others' eyes. In this way, a process that reveals one's own reactions to environmental stimuli has likewise evolved to communicate our deepest emotions to others (Lee & Anderson, 2017).

Learning to encode increasingly subtle cues about others' emotions is a cornerstone of early social development. Rodent models of emotion highlight a sensitive period for amygdala-to-mPFC connections between the periods of weaning and puberty (Yang et al., 2012), and a recent optogenetic study found that amygdala-to-mPFC connections in mice develop prior to the reverse regulatory connections (Arruda-Carvalho et al., 2017). In other words, emotions precede the internally generated ability to control them, something quite relevant to adolescent development. Indeed, functional imaging findings from humans reveal that the neural mechanisms underlying emotion regulation change in qualitative ways from infancy to adolescence, and again from adolescence to adulthood. Parents have a much greater influence in the early years and, as social referencing demonstrates, it is in childhood – a period of profound mPFC immaturity and limited amygdala–mPFC connectivity – that caregivers most influence children's emotional reactions to the world around them. Conveniently, this is in concert with humans' species-specific expectation that the attachment figure will be available throughout early development. Although social referencing provides a means by which caregivers can provide *healthy* support to children as they learn to self-regulate, it also accounts for findings of intergenerational transmission of anxiety and emotion *dysregulation* during the pre-pubertal period (Aktar et al., 2019). Not surprisingly, deficits in

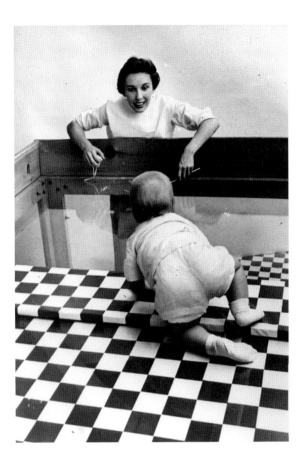

Figure 7.7 The visual cliff apparatus consists of a sheet of Plexiglas covering a cloth with a high-contrast checkerboard pattern. The cloth is placed immediately beneath the Plexiglas on one side of the apparatus, and on the other it drops down about four feet (1.2 m). (Created by psychologists Eleanor J. Gibson and Richard D. Walk at Cornell University)

the domain of social cognition and emotional control are a red flag for a number of neurodevelopmental disorders.

7.5.2 Brain Injury at Different Ages Highlights Developmental Basis for Social Abilities

Acute brain injury in childhood has the potential to lead not only to direct, injury-specific deficits, but can also derail ongoing developmental processes, including social development. Doesn't this contradict what you've learned about neuroplasticity in young brains? In adults, a common approach to studying acute brain injury has been to focus on the location of the lesion as a means of predicting its functional impacts. However, because the developing brain changes dynamically and in interrelated ways we still don't fully understand, brain injury in childhood can affect the whole brain in a generalized or diffuse manner: injury to a specific, local region can lead to both primary and additional, "downstream" impairments. Because principles from adult neuropsychology (i.e., functional localization) do not readily apply to children, a relatively new domain of research has emerged that focuses on the potential for emergent developmental disorders that are a product of early, as compared with later, brain injury. We highlight one approach to research on this topic in Box 7.1.

Box 7.1 Social Cognition in Children with Brain Injury

Emotional and social difficulties are common among children who have suffered acute brain injury. These children often display emotional distress, poor conduct, or problematic peer relationships (Ryan et al., 2015), and symptoms may endure into adulthood with lasting and disturbing consequences. In a recent study, D'Hont and colleagues (2017) examined the electrophysiological correlates of children's processing of emotional facial expressions after early mild traumatic brain injury (mTBI). Eighteen preschool children with mTBI (mean age 53 ± 8 months) and 15 matched healthy controls (mean age 55 ± 11 months) were presented with pictures of faces expressing anger, happiness, or no emotion (neutral) while event-related potentials (ERPs) were recorded (Box Figure 7.1). Stimuli controlled for extrafacial characteristics and low-level physical differences between angry, neutral, and happy faces, such that the groups of pictures only differed on emotional expression. Results revealed that only the healthy controls showed greater P1 amplitudes for happy faces than for angry faces, a well-established finding in typically developing children. Moreover, only controls had a shorter N170 latency for emotional than neutral faces. These findings show differential processing of happy faces by control and brain injured children,

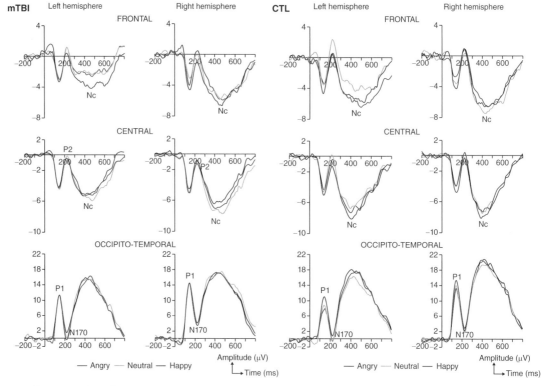

Box Figure 7.1 Grand average ERP waveforms for control (CTL) and mild traumatic brain injury (mTBI) groups. From top to bottom, grand averaged ERPs in the angry, neutral, and happy conditions at the frontal, central, and occipitotemporal ROIs in the left and right hemisphere. The three analyzed ERP components are identified (P1, N170, Nc). (Adapted from D'Hont et al., 2017)

highlighting their salience for healthy preschoolers and suggesting that preschool children who sustain even mild brain injury do not present the early emotional effects that are observed in healthy preschool children for visuospatial processing and visual expertise. Alterations in processing of emotional facial expressions following even mild brain injury early in childhood likely have consequences for the development of socioemotional processing, as it is an ability known to underlie social competence and appropriate social interactions.

The long maturational period of the prefrontal cortex relates to the emergence of increasingly competent social abilities, developmental changes that are the hallmark of prefrontal engagement. However, higher-level abilities are built at least in part on early sensitivity to and rapid processing of cues to others' intentions and desires, as we have seen. Cueing off others' emotions likewise contributes to this developmental cascade. Sensitivity to subtle cues to emotion is present in early infancy; by 3 years of age children show complex and elaborate emotional responsivity that will continue to be enhanced and expanded well past adolescence. Just as abnormal input can negatively influence this developmental trajectory, early brain injury may impair development of these skills as well. The influence of early interruptions is relevant to rehabilitation approaches, development of which has been hampered by the fact that early childhood brain damage may only show overt effects in the social domain at a later stage of development. This temporal disconnect in cause-and-effect has important clinical implications (Tonks et al., 2008). Fortunately, cognitive rehabilitation resources are now available to support children with brain injuries before social deficits emerge. However, much research is needed to understand which approaches work best, and how. For example, emotion regulation strategies that focus on attentional control to different emotional responses show promise (Gross, 2008), and the neural mechanisms by which such interventions have an effect are just beginning to be investigated (Iordan et al., 2019).

7.6 Atypical Social Cognition

Neurodevelopmental disorders are a growing societal challenge (Chapter 3), and the search for the basis of atypical social development in human infants and young children has been prioritized by researchers and funding agencies alike. As diagnostic tools become increasingly sophisticated, they are revealing a complex array of sometimes overlapping features across these different disorders. A widely studied diagnosis is ASD, a pervasive developmental disorder characterized by an array of abnormal or impaired processes.

7.6.1 ASD Phenotype

ASD is complex and heterogeneous, associated with a wide range of life outcomes, from being a "disorder" for about a third of those affected and who develop minimal language and intellectual disability, to "differences" for those who have well-above-average abilities and accomplishments. Developmentally, the symptoms for ASD emerge to various degrees and in various combinations between the end of the first and second years of life. Diagnostic criteria include an array of features, and must be assessed while keeping in mind that their manifestation is quite varied across individuals. Early intervention maximizes the benefits of treatment and improves outcomes for children with ASD, a process that depends on efficacious early screening and identification practices. The persistence of a significant lag between symptom onset and formal diagnosis underscores the urgency of improving methods for early screening (CDC, 2018).

ASD can manifest by 3 years of age, the result of complex gene–environment interactions with clear genetic influences. Symptoms include (1) difficulties with social attention and social communication, (2) the presence of repetitive behavior with objects, (3) atypical body movements and motor development, and (4) an atypical temperamental profile (Zwaigenbaum et al., 2015).

A subset of (1) includes problematic social interaction, in particular, a consistent deficit in theory-of-mind reasoning of the sort we have been discussing. This has moved ASD to the forefront of developmental science research on social cognition. ASD is not caused by deficits in social cognition, but it is very often characterized by socio-cognitive difficulties, particularly weaknesses in these children's ability to mentalize. This unique aspect of ASD spurred Simon Baron-Cohen and colleagues to propose the theory-of-mind hypothesis (a strange name, since the argument is that those with ASD *don't* have a theory of mind) as an explanation of these deficits (Baron-Cohen et al., 1985).

In recent decades, the complexity of ASD has come into full view. The more we learn about its genetics, the more complicated the story becomes, and hundreds of different genes are believed to be associated with it (Sestan & State, 2018) – which has led some to argue that the phenotype is poorly defined, and that ASD possibly encompasses several distinct disorders. Nonetheless, twin studies have revealed that if one twin is diagnosed with ASD, the other has a very high likelihood of also being diagnosed (Sandin et al., 2017). And yet, as with other complex phenotypes, environmental triggers during pregnancy can increase the risk (Thapar & Rutter, 2021). ASD is thus understood to be a complex and heterogeneous set of related developmental disorders in which no single cognitive mechanism or cause can account for the variety of symptoms and range in their expression. While social-communication impairments in ASD cannot be explained exclusively on the basis of theory-of-mind impairments, the impairments in this population have provided important insights about social cognition more generally.

7.6.2   Advances in ASD Diagnosis

The National Institute of Mental Health Research Domain Criteria (RDoC) project (Chapter 3) (Insel & Gogtay, 2014) has as its goal delineating the heterogeneity inherent in different neurodevelopmental profiles to improve understanding of the symptom diversity and variability across various complex neuropsychiatric disorders. The RDoC project emphasizes neurodevelopmental disorders – ASD being one of many – precisely because of the cascading developmental effects of early abnormalities. Early studies focused on older children who had already been diagnosed and whose age ranges were quite broad. To the degree that these studies compared age groups, the work was also largely cross-sectional rather than longitudinal. Not surprisingly, due to the inherent heterogeneity of the disorder, these results were often conflicting.

As the heritability of the disorder has come into focus, along with the risk for reoccurrence within and across generations, researchers introduced the infant-sibling study design (Szatmari et al., 2016), in which younger siblings of an older child with ASD are identified as "high risk" for developing the disorder. These "infant siblings" typically are followed by clinicians and researchers from the first year of postnatal life through to at least 36 months of age, the point at which ASD diagnosis becomes highly reliable and remains stable. The use of this "high-risk design" has already provided major insights into the disorder. What started out as retrospective identification of symptoms after a child was diagnosed (i.e., based on family recollections, family photos, and home videos) has shifted to systematic research involving prospective, longitudinally collected data to identify predictive symptomology. This approach has led to more precise estimation of the sibling risk of diagnosis: 20 percent of younger siblings develop ASD themselves (Ozonoff et al., 2011). A longer-term advantage has been the ability to examine the full range of the disorder's genotype-to-phenotype relationship – for both behavior and brain. There is a large and growing literature on the early behavioral development of ASD (see Jones et al., 2014 for a review of prospective infant sibling findings).

Researchers have begun coupling the high-risk design with longitudinal data collection to establish early developmental dynamics of ASD. As just one example, infants between 2 and 6 months who were later diagnosed with ASD were found to exhibit increased visual fixation on the body of a socially engaging woman and decreased fixation on her eyes relative to low-risk controls (Jones & Klin, 2013). The longitudinal nature of this study allowed the researchers to assess monthly changes in children's fixation levels (rather than absolute levels on any given month), an approach that maximally discriminated between the high- and low-risk groups. Thus, a strong indicator of potential risk – consistent with the social deficits associated with ASD – is the relative perceptual salience of social and non-social stimuli in early infancy.

Further support for this approach comes from ERP data showing early differences between high- and low-risk infant siblings in neural responsivity to faces with dynamic gaze shifts (Elsabbagh et al., 2012). In another study (Orekhova et al., 2014) high-density EEG recordings were obtained from 14-month-olds while they watched videos that had a mix of social (i.e., a woman singing nursery rhymes or playing peek-a-boo) and non-social (i.e., brightly colored toys making sounds and moving by themselves or made to do so by a human hand) content. Analyses showed that heightened activity in the alpha range (7–9 Hz) at 14 months correlated with the emergence of restricted and repetitive behaviors at 3 years in the high-risk group. We have discussed task-independent studies using alpha power as a potential indicator of more mature functional organization of underlying neural systems. Here, the measures were task-dependent (i.e., in response to the social vs. non-social videos). The observation of regionally specific surges in alpha power in response to these videos in a subset of high-risk children who went on to develop ASD-like behaviors (i.e., restricted interests/repetitive behaviors) was interpreted as evidence of exuberant and precocious intercortical communication earlier in life, a finding that was replicated with a much larger group of children (Haartsen et al., 2019). Such approaches demonstrate how the socio-cognitive deficits that correspond to an ASD diagnosis may be tapped into for neural markers that can help speed ASD identification and, thus, intervention.

7.6.3   Structural and Functional Indicators of the ASD Brain

Functional and structural applications of neuroimaging are helping derive brain phenotypes (i.e., neurophysiology; neuroanatomy) with maximum potential to distinguish infants at risk for ASD from typically developing children at a time when behavioral symptomology has yet to emerge. Just as the past several decades of ASD-focused research show that early behavioral symptoms of the disorder are dynamic, so too are the neural markers associated with those symptoms.

It is now clear that a constellation of anatomical features differentiate typically developing infants from those who go on to develop ASD (Courchesne et al., 2020). These include brain overgrowth, altered white matter development, and increased volume of cerebrospinal fluid in the subarachnoid space between the brain and the skull. These structural abnormalities correlate with structural and functional connectivity abnormalities: hyperconnectivity, particularly in the frontal regions, a decrease in long-range connectivity with a corresponding reduction in reciprocal interactions across brain regions, and disconnection among higher-order cortical association areas (Girault & Piven, 2020). Arguments for specific sources of such pathophysiology include abnormal stem cell proliferation and neuronal migration (Casanova & Casanova, 2014), as well as defective synaptogenesis, synaptic pruning and maintenance, and refinement of neural circuitry (Zoghbi & Bear, 2012).

An emerging view is that abnormal anatomical development of the sort seen in ASD prevents species-typical connections from forming, particularly those that underlie the "default mode network" (DMN), an interconnected network of brain structures typically more active during rest than during active task performance. In typically developing individuals, the DMN is engaged during self-reflection and mentalizing (Padmanabhan et al., 2017). Recently, certain types of tasks, particularly higher-order tasks such as attributing mental states to others, have been found to activate a network of areas at least partly overlapping with the DMN (Mars et al., 2012). Indeed, both at the level of the network and that of individual brain areas there is consistent overlap between the DMN and areas that are active during certain types of social cognitive tasks, most notably mentalizing tasks.

Lombardo and colleagues (2019) compared resting-state functional imaging data (rsfMRI) across two subtypes of ASD toddlers (ages 12–48 months) and three other non-ASD control groups. The ASD subtypes were identified using eye-tracking with side by side displays of geometric shapes and social scenes. One ASD group ("GeoPref ASD") showed pronounced early social visual engagement difficulties, fixating geometric shapes far more often than social scenes, while the other did not show such a bias. The researchers hypothesized that whole-brain connectivity analyses would reveal atypical and heterogeneous functional connectivity between higher-level social brain networks – including the default mode network (DMN) – and posteriorly located, lower-level networks that support visual perception and attention, particularly in those ASD children who showed low social visual engagement. As can be seen in Figure 7.8, GeoPref ASD, but not the non-Geo ASD group, showed marked DMN-occipitotemporal cortex hypoconnectivity. This hypoconnectivity was also related to increased severity of social-communication difficulties as measured by the Autism Diagnostic Observation Schedule (ADOS), a gold-standard diagnostic instrument. Early and pronounced social-visual circuit

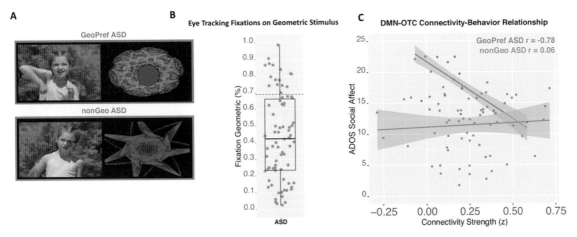

Figure 7.8 Indicators of the ASD brain. A. Distinction between two ASD subtypes. The first ("GeoPref ASD") show pronounced early social visual engagement difficulties, preferring geometric shapes to social images. The second ("non-Geo ASD") do not prefer geometric shapes to social images. B. Scatter-box plot shows eye-tracking data GeoPref ASD, pink; Non-GeoPref, blue). The y-axis represents the percentage of time spent fixating on geometric shapes (middle line in the box represents the median; box boundaries represent the interquartile range). The dashed line represents the threshold by which GeoPref ASD individuals can be identified. C. Increased hypoconnectivity between the default mode network and occipitotemporal cortex (DMN-OTC) is also related to increased severity of social-communication difficulties as measured by the Autism Diagnostic Observation Schedule (ADOS), but only in GeoPref ASD. (Adapted from Lombardo et al., 2019)

hypoconnectivity is a key underlying neurobiological feature in the GeoPref ASD subtype. While DMN dysfunction is a well-established characteristic of older individuals with ASD, these findings are among the first to show DMN abnormalities in toddlers, the age at which initial symptomology for ASD emerges. Precisely at a time when such connections should be rapidly formed, the DMN in children with ASD is functionally disconnected from visual cortices, as well as the dorsal attention network (see Figure 7.7), providing a potential mechanistic account for the social engagement difficulties that characterize early ASD development and that are shared across the majority of ASD toddlers.

7.6.4 Early Intervention

Although the most reliable diagnostic symptoms are still behaviors evident only in the second year, there is widespread hope that identification of early indicators of risk can be coupled with intense intervention to produce "optimal outcomes," a concept introduced by Deb Fein and her colleagues (Fein et al., 2013). The term refers to intervention outcomes in children diagnosed with ASD who, over time and with intensive intervention, stop meeting the diagnostic criteria for the disorder. Demonstrations that early intervention can have such a profound impact on long-term outcomes have made the search for early indicators the holy grail of many ASD research programs.

Problematically, many of the abnormalities that have been identified as emerging in the first year are not specific to ASD and are just as likely to indicate risk for other neurodevelopmental disorders. However, Chawarska and colleagues (Chawarska et al., 2014) found two different combinations of features at 18 months that predicted ASD diagnoses in the same children at 36 months. The first combination (i.e., poor eye contact, limited use of communicative gestures, limited object sharing with others) is associated with greater developmental delays relative to children who exhibit the second combination (i.e., intact eye contact, repetitive behaviors, limited object-based sharing interactions with others). This dissociation indicates that greater cognitive skills can modify the age of onset and severity of ASD symptoms.

Why might this be? For one thing, failing to maintain eye contact or not using communicative gestures has significant downstream repercussions because such "odd" behavior influences how people respond to the child. In other words, a young children with a slight propensity to behave atypically may find themselves dug deeper and deeper into a path of atypicality simply because of the way others respond to them! Because children with ASD are often less interested in people and in social play than other children, these early attentional differences can have major implications for the development of the circuits that support social cognition. Children with little interest in social stimuli, may receive less social input and this in turn will make it increasingly difficult to develop the neural circuits required to support more advanced social skills. The earlier the intervention, the earlier this cascade of effects can be altered.

Sally J. Rogers, featured in this chapter's Scientist Spotlight (see Box 7.2), has been a pioneer in developing early intervention programs for children with ASD, demonstrating the foundational role that parents can play in helping toddlers and preschoolers with ASD connect with others through exercises and routines that target critical developmental skills. Together with Geraldine Dawson, Rogers developed the Early Start Denver Model (ESDM), a structured teaching and relationship-based approach implemented in the child's home that uses play as a learning tool. A randomized, controlled trial over two years found that children aged 18–30 months participating in ESDM significantly improved their IQs, social interaction, and language abilities (Dawson et al., 2010). A partial replication was achieved in a recent follow-up study (Talbott et al., 2019) representing the first randomized, intent-to-treat, multisite evaluation of the efficacy of the ESDM intervention and the first replication of any comprehensive early intervention approach for ASD. Evidence that both younger age and more intervention hours positively affect developmental rates has implications for clinical practice, service delivery, and public policy. Moreover, Rogers has worked to help parents identify ASD early on by teaching them how to observe and look for behavioral signs of the condition. These signs typically involve lack of interaction – not initiating or responding to cuddling, for instance, or not responding to their name or not smiling by 9 months of age.

More recently, Rogers and her team have been pursuing the use of telecommunication for families with early concerns about infant symptoms of ASD who have limited access to experienced professionals for screening and guidance. Telehealth has been used to reduce access disparities in other pediatric populations and has shown promise in parent-implemented interventions for

Box 7.2 Scientist Spotlight on Sally J. Rogers (University of California, Davis)

Sally J. Rogers (Box Figure 7.2) is a Professor Emeritus of Psychiatry and Behavioral Sciences at the Department of Psychiatry, MIND Institute, University of California, Davis, and co-developed the Early Start Denver Model. Rogers obtained Master's and doctoral degrees in Developmental Psychology from the Ohio State University. Rogers has devoted her career to the study of autism and the mitigation of the severe and often lifelong impairments associated with ASD and other neurodevelopmental conditions.

Although my work in early intervention for children with autism is best known, I actually began my professional work in infant intervention at University of Michigan then at Southwest Missouri State University in Springfield, Missouri, where I received my first federal grant through the Regional Center for a project focused on how to get early intervention services to young children with disabilities and their families living in the rural area of southern Missouri. This demonstration project from the US Department of Education allowed me to use the infant-toddler assessment and intervention experience and the tools and procedures developed in Michigan for rural parent coaching and generalist service models. This rural project was a pivotal experience in my career development, in learning how to build a team, train and direct a team in developing interdisciplinary knowledge across the group and supporting each other, in developing parent coaching skills, in building community relationships, and in reaching families who are far away from resources.

The intervention model I've worked from began in the Michigan project and was strongly influenced by the original concepts underlying IDEA and services for children birth to three years: that the appropriate focus for serving very young children should be supporting their learning through everyday activities in their everyday environments by the people who care for them – parents and others. My work in Denver on the Denver Model, and now in Sacramento, on the Early Start Denver Model (esdm.co), developed with my colleagues Geraldine Dawson and Laurie Vismara, focuses on improving intervention approaches for young children with ASD for professionals and for parents. The principles embedded in this early work continue to drive my activities: developing and improving intervention approaches, supporting families and professionals to learn powerful strategies for helping children learn, getting help into the hands of families and interventionists everywhere, working with an interdisciplinary team, applying the tools of developmental and learning science for each individual child.

We are so fortunate in these times to have the technology tools for reaching families and professionals across the country and the world. My colleague Aubyn Stahmer and I have just put a

Box 7.2 (cont.)

set of video modules online for parents working with their young children with autism symptoms at home [https://helpisinyourhands.org] and for the professionals working with them. Parents are so motivated to help their children; we need to demystify what intervention is all about and put it in their hands. Young children with autism and other developmental conditions are far more like any other infant than they are different. We need to see them all as young children constantly engaged in learning. Helping young children with ASD or other neurodevelopmental conditions access the learning opportunities that exist all around them – that is the core of my work, and the core of successful early intervention.

ASD. In a recent study (Talbott et al., 2019), Rogers and her colleagues investigated the feasibility of a novel level-2 telehealth assessment of infants' early social communication and ASD symptoms, the Telehealth Evaluation of Development for Infants (TEDI). Parents of infants aged 6 to 12 months were coached to administer specific semi-structured behavioral probes. Initial feasibility, reliability, and acceptability benchmarks were met, and findings suggest that screening infants via telehealth is a viable approach. The researchers are now pursuing larger-scale efforts to validate this method for longitudinal monitoring of symptomatic infants in community settings.

SUMMARY

- Imitation is a form of contingency learning
- Contingency detection sets infants up for social learning
- Mentalizing, the ability to impute mental states to oneself and to others, underlies having a theory of mind
- Implicit and explicit false belief tasks differentiate early and late childhood mentalizing abilities
- The right temporoparietal junction is active early in life and appears to be engaged early during mental state reasoning tasks
- Children with Autism Spectrum Disorder have difficulty developing the skills associated with theory-of-mind reasoning
- Identifying early neural predictors of ASD are important because early intervention is far more effective than later intervention.

REVIEW QUESTIONS

Describe the basis for the debate about whether human neonates can imitate or not.

What are some of the problems with using the mirror neuron system as an explanation for social behavior?

Are humans born with a theory of mind, or does it develop over time?

What might be the evolutionary basis for theory of mind?

What are the two components of neural processing that support mentalizing?

How does the development time course of implicit and explicit false belief reasoning differ?

Which regions of the brain are engaged during the processing of information about the self?

What is the goal of the National Institute of Mental Health Research Domain Criteria (RDoC) project?

Outline the four domains in which early behavioral markers for ASD have significant empirical support.

Describe why early intervention is so important for children with ASD.

Further Reading

Courchesne, E., Gazestani, V. H., & Lewis, N. E. (2020). Prenatal origins of ASD: The when, what, and how of ASD development. *Trends in Neurosciences*, 43, 326–342. https://doi.org/10.1016/j.tins.2020.03.005

Csibra, G. (2017). Cognitive science: Modelling theory of mind. *Nature Human Behavior*, 1, 0066. https://doi.org/10.1038/s41562-017-0066

Scott, R. M., & Baillargeon, R. (2017). Early false-belief understanding. *Trends in Cognitive Sciences*, 21, 237–249. https://doi.org/10.1016/j.tics.2017.01.012

Stephenson, L., Edwards, S. G., & Bayliss, A. (2020). From gaze perception to social cognition: A neurocognitive model of joint and shared attention. *Perspectives on Psychological Science*, 16(3), 553–576. https://journals.sagepub.com/doi/10.1177/1745691620953773

References

Aktar, E., Qu, J., Lawrence, P. J., Tollenaar, M. S., Elzinga, B. M., & Bögels, S. M. (2019). Fetal and infant outcomes in the offspring of parents with perinatal mental disorders: Earliest influences. *Frontiers in Psychiatry*, 10. https://doi.org/10.3389/fpsyt.2019.00391

Amsterdam, B. (1972). Mirror self-image reactions before age two. *Developmental Psychobiology*, 5(4), 297–305. https://doi.org/10.1002/dev.420050403

Apperly, I. A., & Butterfill, S. A. (2009). Do humans have two systems to track beliefs and belief-like states? *Psychological Review*, 116(4), 953–970. https://doi.org/10.1037/a0016923

Arruda-Carvalho, M., Wu, W. C., Cummings, K. A., & Clem, R. L. (2017). Optogenetic examination of prefrontal-amygdala synaptic development. *Journal of Neuroscience*, 37(11), 2976–2985. https://doi.org/10.1523/JNEUROSCI.3097-16.2017

Bahrick, L. E., Watson, J. S., Areola, M., Huber, N., Kaufman, B., Kennedy, D., Roscelli, N., & Bahrick, E. (1985). Detection of intermodal proprioceptive-visual contingency as a potential basis of self-perception in infancy. *Developmental Psychology*, 21(6), 963–973. https://doi.org/10.1037/0012-1649.21.6.963

Baillargeon, R., Buttelmann, D., & Southgate, V. (2018). Invited commentary: Interpreting failed replications of early false-belief findings: Methodological and theoretical considerations. *Cognitive Development*, 46, 112–124. https://doi.org/10.1016/j.cogdev.2018.06.001

Bakeman, R., & Adamson, L. B. (1984). Coordinating attention to people and objects in mother-infant and peer-infant interaction. *Child Development*, 55(4), 1278–1289. https://doi.org/10.2307/1129997

Baron-Cohen, S., Leslie, A. M., & Frith, U. (1985). Does the autistic child have a "theory of mind?" *Cognition*, 21, 37–46. https://doi.org/10.1016/0010-0277(85)90022-8

Bauer, R. (1984). Autonomic recognition of names and faces in prosopagnosia: A neuropsychological application of the guilty knowledge test. *Neuropsychologia*, 22(4), 457–469. https://doi.org/10.1016/0028-3932(84)90040-X

Bedny, M., Richardson, H., & Saxe, R. (2015). "Visual" Cortex Responds to Spoken Language in Blind Children. The Journal of neuroscience : the official journal of the Society for Neuroscience, 35(33), 11674–11681. https://doi.org/10.1523/JNEUROSCI.0634-15.2015

Bowman, L. C., Dodell-Feder, D., Saxe, R., & Sabbagh, M. A. (2019). Continuity in the neural system supporting children's theory of mind development: Longitudinal links between task-independent EEG and task-dependent fMRI. *Developmental Cognitive Neuroscience*, 40, 100705. https://doi.org/10.1016/j.dcn.2019.100705

Bulgarelli, C., Blasi, A., de Klerk, C. C. J. M., Richards, J. E., Hamilton, A., & Southgate, V. H. (2019). Fronto-temporoparietal connectivity and self-awareness in 18-month-olds: A resting state fNIRS study. *Developmental Cognitive Neuroscience*, 38, 100676. https://doi.org/10.1016/j.dcn.2019.100676

Buttelmann, D., Buttelmann, F., Carpenter, M., Call, J., & Tomasello, M. (2017). Great apes distinguish true from false beliefs in an interactive helping task. *PLoS One*, 12(4). https://doi.org/10.1371/journal.pone.0173793

Call, J., & Tomasello, M. (1999). A nonverbal false belief task: The performance of children and great apes. *Child Development*, 70(2), 381–395. https://doi.org/10.1111/1467-8624.00028

Campos, J. J., & Stenberg, C. R. (1981). Perception, appraisal, and emotion: The onset of social referencing. In M. E. Lamb & L. R. Sherrod (Eds.), *Infant social cognition* (pp. 273–314). Lawrence Erlbaum Associates.

Carruthers, P. (2018). Young children flexibly attribute mental states to others. *Proceedings of the National Academy of Sciences of the United States of America*, 115(45), 11351–11353. https://doi.org/10.1073/pnas.1816255115

Carter, R. M. K., & Huettel, S. A. (2013). A nexus model of the temporal-parietal junction. *Trends in Cognitive Sciences*, 17(7), 328–336. https://doi.org/10.1016/j.tics.2013.05.007

Casanova, E. L., & Casanova, M. F. (2014). Genetics studies indicate that neural induction and early neuronal maturation are disturbed in autism. *Frontiers in Cellular Neuroscience*, 8. https://doi.org/10.3389/fncel.2014.00397

Catmur, C., Press, C., & Heyes, C. (2016). Mirror neurons from associative learning. In R. A. Murphy & R. C. Honey (Eds.), *The Wiley handbook on the cognitive neuroscience of learning* (pp. 515–537). Wiley-Blackwell. https://doi.org/10.1002/9781118650813.ch20

CDC. (2019). Autism spectrum disorder. www.cdc.gov/ncbddd/autism/index.html

Chawarska, K., Shic, F., Macari, S., Campbell, D. J., Brian, J., Landa, R., Hutman, T., Nelson, C. A., Ozonoff, S., Tager-Flusberg, H., & Young, G. S. (2014). 8-month predictors of later outcomes in younger siblings of children with autism spectrum disorder: A baby siblings research consortium study. *Journal of the American Academy of Child & Adolescent Psychiatry*, 53(12), 1317–1327. https://doi.org/10.1016/j.jaac

Courchesne, E., Gazestani, V. H., & Lewis, N. E. (2020). Prenatal origins of ASD: The when, what, and how of ASD development. *Trends in Neurosciences*, 43(5), 326–342. https://doi.org/10.1016/j.tins.2020.03.005

Csibra, G., & Gergely, G. (2009). Natural pedagogy. *Trends in Cognitive Sciences*, 13(4), 148–153. https://doi.org/10.1016/j.tics.2009.01.005

Dawson, G., Rogers, S., Munson, J., Smith, M., Winter, J., Greenson, J., Donaldson, A., & Varley, J. (2010). Randomized, controlled trial of an intervention for toddlers with autism: The early start Denver model. *Pediatrics*, 125(1). https://doi.org/10.1542/peds.2009-0958

Desimone, R., Albright, T. D., Gross, C. G., & Bruce, C. (1984). Stimulus-selective properties of inferior temporal neurons in the macaque. *Journal of Neuroscience*, 4(8), 2051–2062. https://doi.org/10.1523/JNEUROSCI.04-08-02051

D'Hont, F., Lassonde, M., Thebault-Dagher, F., Bernier, A., Gravel, J., Vannasing, P., & Beauchamp, M. H. (2017). Electrophysiological correlates of emotional face processing after mild traumatic brain injury in preschool children. *Cognitive, Affective & Behavioral Neuroscience*, 17(1), 124–142. https://doi.org/10.3758/s13415-016-0467-7

Di Giorgio, E., Lunghi, M., Vallortigara, G., & Simion, F. (2021). Newborns' sensitivity to speed changes as a building block for animacy perception. *Scientific Reports*, 11, 542. https://doi.org/10.1038/s41598-020-79451-3

Elsabbagh, M., Mercure, E., Hudry, K., Chandler, S., Pasco, G., Charman, T., Pickles, A., Baron-Cohen, S., Bolton, P., & Johnson, M. H. (2012). Infant neural sensitivity to dynamic eye gaze is associated with later emerging autism. *Current Biology*, 22(4), 338–342. https://doi.org/10.1016/j.cub.2011.12.056

Farroni, T., Johnson, M. H., Menon, E., Zulian, L., Faraguna, D., & Csibra, G. (2005). Newborns' preference for face-relevant stimuli: Effects of contrast polarity. *Proceedings of the National Academy of Sciences of the United States of America*, 102(47), 17245–17250. https://doi.org/10.1073/pnas.0502205102

Fein, D., Barton, M., Eigsti, I. M., Kelley, E., Naigles, L., Schultz, R. T., Stevens, M., Helt, M., Orinstein, A., Rosenthal, M., Troyb, E., & Tyson, K. (2013). Optimal outcome in individuals with a history of autism. *Journal of Child Psychology and Psychiatry and Allied Disciplines*, 54(2), 195–205. https://doi.org/10.1111/jcpp.12037

Fernald, A., & O'Neill, D. K. (1993). Peekaboo across cultures: How mothers and infants play with voices, faces, and expectations. In K. MacDonald (Ed.), *Parent–child play: Descriptions and implications* (pp. 259–285). State University of New York Press.

Flack-Ytter, T., Gredebäck, G., & von Hofsten, C. (2006). Infants predict other people's action goals. *Nature Neuroscience*, 9, 878–879. https://doi.org/10.1038/nn1729

Fox, N. A., Bakermans-Kranenburg, M. J., Yoo, K. H., Bowman, L. C., Cannon, E. N., Vanderwert, R. E., Ferrari, P. F., & van IJzendoorn, M. H. (2016). Assessing human mirror activity with EEG mu rhythm: A meta-analysis. *Psychological Bulletin*, 142(3), 291–313. https://doi.org/10.1037/bul0000031

Fox, R., & McDaniel, C. (1982). The perception of biological motion by human infants. *Science*, 218(4571), 486–487. https://doi.org/10.1126/science.7123249

Frijia, E. M., Billing, A., Lloyd-Fos, S., Rosas, E. V., Collins-Jones, L., Crespo-Llado, M. M., Amadó, M. P., Austin, T., Edwards, A., Dunne, L., Smith, G., Nixon-Hill, R., Powell, S., Everdell, N. L., & Cooper, R. J. (2021). Functional imaging of the developing brain with wearable high-density diffuse optical tomography: A new benchmark for infant neuroimaging outside the scanner environment. *NeuroImage*, 225, 117490. https://doi.org/10.1016/j.neuroimage.2020.117490

Frith, C. D., & Frith, U. (2006). The neural basis of mentalizing. *Neuron*, 50(4), 531–534. https://doi.org/10.1016/j.neuron.2006.05.001

Gallistel, C. R., & Matzel, L. D. (2013). The neuroscience of learning: Beyond the Hebbian synapse. *Annual Review of Psychology*, 64, 169–200. https://doi.org/10.1146/annurev-psych-113011-143807

Gao, X., Vuong, Q. C., & Rossion, B. (2019). The cortical face network of the prosopagnosic patient PS with fast periodic stimulation in fMRI. *Cortex*, 119, 528–542. https://doi.org/10.1016/j.cortex.2018.11.008

Geangu, E., Ichikawa, H., Lao, J., Kanazawa, S., Yamaguchi, M. K., Caldara, R., & Turati, C. (2016). Culture shapes 7-month-olds' perceptual strategies in discriminating facial expressions of emotion. *Current Biology*, 26(14), R663–R664. https://doi.org/10.1016/j.cub.2016.05.072

Gergely, G. (2010). Kinds of agents: The origins of understanding instrumental and communicative agency. In U. Goswami (Ed.), *The Wiley-Blackwell handbook of childhood cognitive development*, 2nd edition (pp. 76–105). Wiley-Blackwell. https://doi.org/10.1002/9781444325485.ch3

Gergely, G., & Csibra, G. (2003). Teleological reasoning in infancy: The naïve theory of rational action. *Trends in Cognitive Sciences*, 7(7), 287–292. https://doi.org/10.1016/S1364-6613(03)00128-1

Girault, J. B., & Piven, J. (2020). The neurodevelopment of autism from infancy through toddlerhood. *Neuroimaging Clinics of North America*, 30(1), 97–114. https://doi.org/10.1016/j.nic.2019.09.009

Gliga, T., & Csibra, G. (2007). Seeing the face through the eyes: A developmental perspective on face expertise. *Progress in Brain Research*, 164, 323–339. https://doi.org/10.1016/S0079-6123(07)64018-7

Gross, J. (2008). Emotion and emotion regulation: Personality processes and individual differences. In O. P. John, R. W. Robins, & L. A. Pervin (Eds.), *Handbook of personality: Theory and research* (pp. 701–724). Guilford Press

Grosse Wiesmann, C., Friederici, A. D. Singer, T., & Steinbeis, N. (2020). Two systems for thinking about others' thoughts in the developing brain. *Proceedings of the National Academy of Sciences of the United States of America*, 117(12), 6928–6935. https://doi.org/10.1073/pnas.1916725117

Grosse Wiesmann, C., Schreiber, J., Singer, T., Steinbeis, N., & Friederici, A. D. (2017). White matter maturation is associated with the emergence of Theory of Mind in early childhood. *Nature Communications*, 8. https://doi.org/10.1038/ncomms14692

Grossman, T., Johnson, M. H., Lloyd-Fox, S., Blasi, A., Deligianni, F., Elwell, C., & Csibra, G. (2008). Early cortical specialization for face-to-face communication in human infants. *Proceedings of the Royal Society B: Biological Sciences*, 275, 2803–2811. https://doi.org/10.1098/rspb.2008.0986

Gweon, H., Dodell-Feder, D., Bedny, M., & Saxe, R. (2012). Theory of mind performance in children correlates with functional specialization of a brain region for thinking about thoughts. *Child Development*, 83(6), 1853–1868. https://doi.org/10.1111/j.1467-8624.2012.01829.x

Haartsen, R., Jones, E. J. H., Orekhova, E. V., Charman, T., Johnson, M. H., Baron-Cohen, S., Bedford, R., Blasi, A., Bolton, P., Chandler, S., Cheung, C., Davies, K., Elsabbagh, M., Fernandes, J., Gammer, I., Garwood, H., Gliga, T., Guiraud, J., Hudry, K., … Volein, A. (2019). Functional EEG connectivity in infants associates with later restricted and repetitive behaviours in autism: A replication study. *Translational Psychiatry*, 9(1). https://doi.org/10.1038/s41398-019-0380-2

Han, S., Northoff, G., Vogeley, K., Wexler, B. E., Kitayama, S., & Varnum, M. E. W. (2013). A cultural neuroscience approach to the biosocial nature of the human brain. *Annual Review of Psychology*, 64, 335–359. https://doi.org/10.1146/annurev-psych-071112-054629

Heider, F., & Simmel, M. (1944). An experimental study of apparent behavior. *American Journal of Psychology*, 57, 243–249. https://doi.org/10.2307/1416950

Heyes, C. (2014). False belief in infancy: A fresh look. *Developmental Science*, 17(5), 647–659. https://doi.org/10.1111/desc.12148

Heyes, C., & Catmur, C. (2021). What happened to mirror neurons? *Perspectives on Psychological Science*, 17(1). https://doi.org/10.1177/1745691621990638

Hickok, G. (2009). Eight problems for the mirror neuron theory of action understanding in monkeys and humans. *Journal of Cognitive Neuroscience*, 21(7), 1229–1243. https://doi.org/10.1162/jocn.2009.21189

Hobson, H. M., & Bishop, D. V. M. (2016). Mu suppression: A good measure of the human mirror neuron system? *Cortex*, 82, 290–310. https://doi.org/10.1016/j.cortex.2016.03.019

Hogrefe, G. J., Wimmer, H., & Perner, J. (1986). Ignorance versus false belief: A developmental lag in attribution of epistemic states. *Child Development*, 57(3), 567–582. https://doi.org/10.2307/1130337

Hyde, D. C., Simon, C. E., Ting, F., & Nikolaeva, J. I. (2018). Functional organization of the temporal–parietal junction for theory of mind in preverbal infants: A near-infrared spectroscopy study. *Journal of Neuroscience*, 38(18), 4264–4274. https://doi.org/10.1523/JNEUROSCI.0264-17.2018

Iacoboni, M., Woods, R. P., Brass, M., Bekkering, H., Mazziotta, J. C., & Rizzolatti, G. (1999). Cortical mechanisms of human imitation. *Science*, 286(5449), 2526–2528. https://doi.org/10.1126/science.286.5449.2526

Insel, T. R., & Gogtay, N. (2014). National Institute of Mental Health clinical trials: New opportunities, new expectations. *JAMA Psychiatry*, 71(7), 745–746. https://doi.org/10.1001/jamapsychiatry.2014.426

Iordan, A. D., Dolcos, S., & Dolcos, F. (2019). Brain activity and network interactions in the impact of internal emotional distraction. *Cerebral Cortex*, 29(6), 2607–2623. https://doi.org/10.1093/cercor/bhy129

Johansen, J. P., Diaz-Mataix, L., Hamanaka, H., Ozawa, T., Ycu, E., Koivumaa, J., Kumar, A., Hou, M., Deisseroth, K., Boyden, E. S., & LeDoux, J. E. (2014). Hebbian and neuromodulatory mechanisms interact to trigger associative memory formation. *Proceedings of the National Academy of Sciences of the United States of America*, 11(51), E5584–E5592. https://doi.org/10.1073/pnas.1421304111

Jones, E. J. H., Gliga, T., Bedford, R., Charman, T., & Johnson, M. H. (2014). Developmental pathways to autism: A review of prospective studies of infants at risk. *Neuroscience and Biobehavioral Reviews*, 39, 1–33. https://doi.org/10.1016/j.neubiorev.2013.12.001

Jones, S. (2017). Can newborn infants imitate? *Wiley Interdisciplinary Reviews: Cognitive Science*, 8(1–2). https://doi.org/10.1002/wcs.1410

Jones, W., & Klin, A. (2013). Attention to eyes is present but in decline in 2–6-month-old infants later diagnosed with autism. *Nature*, 504(7480), 427–431. https://doi.org/10.1038/nature12715

Kaduk, K., Elsner, B., & Reid, V. M. (2013). Discrimination of animate and inanimate motion in 9-month-old infants: An ERP study. *Developmental Cognitive Neuroscience*, 6, 14–22. https://doi.org/10.1016/j.dcn.2013.05.003

Kanakogi, Y., & Itakura, S. (2011). Developmental correspondence between action prediction and motor ability in early infancy. *Nature Communication*, 2, 341. https://doi.org/10.1038/ncomms1342

Kelly, D. J., Liu, S., Rodger, H., Miellet, S., Ge, L., & Caldara, R. (2011). Developing cultural differences in face processing. *Developmental Science*, 14(5), 1176–1184. https://doi.org/10.1111/j.1467-7687.2011.01067.x

Keven, N., & Akins, K. A. (2017). Neonatal imitation in context: Sensorimotor development in the perinatal period. *Behavioral and Brain Sciences*, 40. https://doi.org/10.1017/S0140525X16000911

Keysers, C., & Gazzola, V. (2014). Hebbian learning and predictive mirror neurons for actions, sensations and emotions. *Philosophical Transactions of the Royal Society of London B: Biological Sciences*, 369(1644), 20130175. https://doi.org/10.1098/rstb.2013.0175

Király, I., Oláh, K., Csibra, G., & Kovács, Á. M. (2018). Retrospective attribution of false beliefs in 3-year-old children. *Proceedings of the National Academy of Sciences of the United States of America*, 115(45), 11477–11482. https://doi.org/10.1073/pnas.1803505115

Kobayashi, H., & Kohshima, S. (2001). Unique morphology of the human eye and its adaptive meaning: Comparative studies on external morphology of the primate eye. *Journal of Human Evolution*, 40(5), 419–435. https://doi.org/10.1006/jhev.2001.0468

Kovács, Á. M., Téglás, E., & Endress, A. D. (2010). The social sense: Susceptibility to others' beliefs in human infants and adults. *Science*, 330(6012), 1830–1834. https://doi.org/10.1126/science.1190792

Krupenye, C., Kano, F., Hirata, S., Call, J., & Tomasello, M. (2016). Great apes anticipate that other individuals will act according to false beliefs. *Science*, 354(6308), 110–114. https://doi.org/10.1126/science.aaf8110

Lee, D. H., & Anderson, A. K. (2017). Reading what the mind thinks from how the eye sees. *Psychological Science*, 28(4), 494–503. https://doi.org/10.1177/0956797616687364

Levine, D., Buchsbaum, D., Hirsh-Pasek, K., & Golinkoff, R. M. (2018). Finding events in a continuous world: A developmental account. *Developmental Psychobiology*, 61(3), 376–389. https://doi.org/10.1002/dev.21804

Lingnau, A., Gesierich, B., & Caramazza, A. (2009). Asymmetric fMRI adaptation reveals no evidence for mirror neurons in humans. *Proceedings of the National Academy of Sciences of the United States of America*, 106(24), 9925–9930. https://doi.org/10.1073/pnas.0902262106

Liu, D., Sabbagh, M. A., Gehring, W. J., & Wellman, H. M. (2009). Neural correlates of children's theory of mind development. *Child Development*, 80(2), 318–326. https://doi.org/10.1111/j.1467-8624.2009.01262.x

Lloyd-Fox, S., Blasi, A., Elwell, C. E., Charman, T., Murphy, D., & Johnson, M. H. (2013). Reduced neural sensitivity to social stimuli in infants at risk for autism. *Proceedings of the Royal Society B: Biological Sciences*, 280, 20123026. https://doi.org/10.1098/rspb.2012.3026

Lloyd-Fox, S., Blasi, A., Everdell, N., Elwell, C. E., & Johnson, M. H. (2011). Selective cortical mapping of biological motion processing in young infants. *Journal of Cognitive Neuroscience*, 23(9), 2521–2532. https://doi.org/10.1162/jocn.2010.21598

Lloyd-Fox, S., Blasi, A., Volein, A., Everdell, N., Elwell, C. E., & Johnson, M. H. (2009). Social perception in infancy: A near infrared spectroscopy study. *Child Development*, 80, 986–999. https://doi.org/10.1111/j.1467-8624.2009.01312.x

Lloyd-Fox, S., Széplaki-Köllőd, B., Yin, J., & Csibra, G. (2015). Are you talking to me? Neural activations in 6-month-old infants in response to being addressed during natural interactions. *Cortex*, 70, 35–48. https://doi.org/10.1016/j.cortex.2015.02.005

Lombardo, M. V., Eyler, L., Moore, A., Datko, M., Carter Barnes, C., Cha, D., Courchesne, E., & Pierce, K. (2019). Default mode-visual network hypoconnectivity in an autism subtype with pronounced social visual engagement difficulties. *eLife*, 8, e47427. https://doi.org/10.7554/eLife.47427

Mars, R., Neubert, F. X., Noonan, M., Sallet, J., Toni, I., & Rushworth, M. (2012). On the relationship between the "default mode network" and the "social brain". *Frontiers in Human Neuroscience*, 6, 189. https://doi.org/10.3389/fnhum.2012.00189

Marshall, P. J., Bar-Haim, Y., & Fox, N. A. (2002). Development of the EEG from 5 months to 4 years of age. *Clinical Neurophysiology*, 113(8), 1199–1208. https://doi.org/10.1016/S1388-2457(02)00163-3

Marshall, P. J., & Meltzoff, A. N. (2014). Neural mirroring mechanisms and imitation in human infants. *Philosophical Transactions of the Royal Society B: Biological Sciences*, 369(1644). https://doi.org/10.1098/rstb.2013.0620

Meinhardt-Injac, B., Persike, M., & Meinhardt, G. (2011). The context effect in face matching: Effects of feedback. *Vision Research*, 51(19), 2121–2131. https://doi.org/10.1016/j.visres.2011.08.004

Meltzoff, A. N., & Marshall, P. J. (2018). Human infant imitation as a social survival circuit. *Current Opinion in Behavioral Sciences*, 24, 130–136. https://doi.org/10.1016/j.cobeha.2018.09.006

Meltzoff, A. N., & Moore, M. K. (1983). Newborn infants imitate adult facial gestures. *Child Development*, 54(3), 702–709. https://doi.org/10.2307/1130058

Meltzoff, A. N., Murray, L., Simpson, E., Heimann, M., Nagy, E., Nadel, J., Pedersen, E. J., Brooks, R., Messinger, D. S., Pascalis, L. D., Subiaul, F., Paukner, A., & Ferrari, P. F. (2018). Re-examination of Oostenbroek et al. (2016): Evidence for neonatal imitation of tongue protrusion. *Developmental Science*, 21(4), e12609. https://doi.org/10.1111/desc.12609

Mukamel, R., Ekstrom, A. D., Kaplan, J., Iacoboni, M., & Fried, I. (2010). Single-neuron responses in humans during execution and observation of actions. *Current Biology*, 20(8), 750–756. https://doi.org/10.1016/j.cub.2010.02.045

Nadel, J., Carchon, I., Kervella, C., Marcelli, D., & Râ Eserbat-Plantey, D. (1999). Expectancies for social contingency in 2-month-olds. *Developmental Science*, 2(2), 164–173. https://doi.org/10.1111/1467-7687.00065

Nomikou, I., Leonardi, G., Radkowska, A., Rączaszek-Leonardi, J., & Rohlfing, K. J. (2017). Taking up an active role: Emerging participation in early mother-infant interaction during peekaboo routines. *Frontiers in Psychology*, 8, 1656. https://doi.org/10.3389/fpsyg.2017.01656

Onishi, K. H., & Baillargeon, R. (2005). Do 15-month-old infants understand false beliefs? *Science*, 308(5719), 255–258. https://doi.org/10.1126/science.1107621

Oostenbroek, J., Redshaw, J., Davis, J., Kennedy-Costantini, S., Nielsen, M., Slaughter, V., & Suddendorf, T. (2019). Re-evaluating the neonatal imitation hypothesis. *Developmental Science*, 22(2), e12720. https://doi.org/10.1111/desc.12720

Oostenbroek, J., Suddendorf, T., Nielsen, M., Redshaw, J., Kennedy-Costantini, S., Davis, J., Clark, S., & Slaughter, V. (2016). Comprehensive longitudinal study challenges the exercises of neonatal imitation in humans. *Current Biology*, 26(10), 1334–1228. https://doi.org/10.1016/j.cub.2016.03.047

Orekhova, E. V., Elsabbagh, M., Jones, E. J., Dawson, G., Charman, T., Baron-Cohen, S., Bedford, R., Bolton, P., Fernandes, J., Ganea, N., Garwood, H., Gliga, T., Hudry, K., Murias, M., Ribeiro, H., Tucker, L., Volein, A., & Webb, S. J. (2014). EEG hyper-connectivity in high-risk infants is associated with later autism. *Journal of Neurodevelopmental Disorders*, 6(1). https://doi.org/10.1186/1866-1955-6-40

Ozonoff, S., Young, G. S., Carter, A., Messinger, D., Yirmiya, N., Zwaigenbaum, L., Bryson, S., Carver, L. J., Constantino, J. N., Dobkins, K., Hutman, T., Iverson, J. M., Landa, R., Rogers, S. J., Sigman, M., & Stone, W. L. (2011). Recurrence risk for autism spectrum disorders: A baby siblings research consortium study. *Pediatrics*, 128(3), e488–e495. https://doi.org/10.1542/peds.2010-2825

Padmanabhan, A., Lynch, C. J., Schaer, M., & Menon, V. (2017). The default mode network in autism. *Biological Psychiatry: Cognitive Neuroscience and Neuroimaging*, 2(6), 476–486. https://doi.org/10.1016/j.bpsc.2017.04.004

Phillips, J., Ong, D. C., Surtees, A. D. R., Xin, Y., Williams, S., Saxe, R., & Frank, M. C. (2015). A second look at automatic theory of mind: Reconsidering Kovács, Téglás, and Endress (2010). *Psychological Science*, 26(9), 1353–1367. https://doi.org/10.1177/0956797614558717

Piazza, E. A., Hasenfratz, L., Hasson, U., & Lew-Williams, C. (2020). Infant and adult brains are coupled to the dynamics of natural communication. *Psychological Science*, 31(1), 6–17. https://doi.org/10.1177/0956797619878698

Pitcher, D., & Ungerleider, L. G. (2021). Evidence for a third visual pathway specialized for social perception. *Trends in Cognitive Sciences*, 25(2), 100–110. https://doi.org/10.1016/j.tics.2020.11.006

Poulin-Dubois, D. (1999). Infants' distinction between animate and inanimate objects: The origins of naive psychology. In P. Rochat (Ed.), *Early social cognition: Understanding others in the first months of life* (pp. 257–280). Lawrence Erlbaum Associates.

Poulin-Dubois, D., Crivello, C., & Wright, K. (2015). Biological motion primes the animate/inanimate distinction in infancy. *PloS One*, 10(2), e0116910. https://doi.org/10.1371/journal.pone.0116910

Poulin-Dubois, D., & Yott, J. (2018). Probing the depth of infants' theory of mind: Disunity in performance across paradigms. *Developmental Science*, 21(4). https://doi.org/10.1111/desc.12600

Premack, D., & Woodruff, G. (1978). Does the chimpanzee have a theory of mind? *Behavioral and Brain Sciences*, 4, 515–526. https://doi.org/10.1017/S0140525X00076512

Priewasser, B., Rafetseder, E., Gargitter, C., & Perner, J. (2018). Helping as an early indicator of a theory of mind: Mentalism or teleology? *Cognitive Development*, 46, 69–78. https://doi.org/10.1016/j.cogdev.2017.08.002

Rizzolatti, G., & Craighero, L. (2004). The mirror-neuron system. *Annual Review of Neuroscience*, 27, 169–192. https://doi.org/10.1146/annurev.neuro.27.070203.144230

Rizzolatti, G., Fogassi, L., & Gallese, V. (2001). Neurophysiological mechanisms underlying the understanding and imitation of action. *Nature Reviews Neuroscience*, 2(9), 661–670. https://doi.org/10.1038/35090060

Ryan, N. P., Catroppa, C., Cooper, J. M., Beare, R., Ditchfield, M., Coleman, L., Silk, T., Crossley, L., Beauchamp, M. H., & Anderson, V. A. (2015). The emergence of age-dependent social cognitive deficits after generalized insult to the developing brain: A longitudinal prospective analysis using susceptibility-weighted imaging. *Human Brain Mapping*, 36(5), 1677–1691. https://doi.org/10.1002/hbm.22729

Sabbagh, M. A., Bowman, L. C., Evraire, L. E., & Ito, J. M. B. (2009). Neurodevelopmental correlates of theory of mind in preschool children. *Child Development*, 80(4), 1147–1162. https://doi.org/10.1111/j.1467-8624.2009.01322.x

Sandin, S., Lichtenstein, P., Kuja-Halkola, R., Hultman, C., Larsson, H., & Reichenberg, A. (2017). The heritability of Autism Spectrum Disorder. *JAMA*, 318(12), 1182–1184. https://doi.org/10.1001/jama.2017.12141

Saxe, R. R., Whitfield-Gabrieli, S., Scholz, J., & Pelphrey, K. A. (2009). Brain regions for perceiving and reasoning about other people in school-aged children. *Child Development*, 80(4), 1197–1209. https://doi.org/10.1111/j.1467-8624.2009.01325.x

Scott, R. M. (2017). The developmental origins of false-belief understanding. *Current Directions in Psychological Science*, 26(1), 68–74. https://doi.org/10.1177/0963721416673174

Senju, A., & Johnson, M. H. (2009). Atypical eye contact in autism: Models, mechanisms and development. *Neuroscience and Biobehavioral Reviews*, 33(8), 1204–1214. https://doi.org/10.1016/j.neubiorev.2009.06.001

Senju, A., Tucker, L., Pasco, G., Hudry, K., Elsabbagh, M., Charman, T., & Johnson, M. H. (2013). The importance of the eyes: Communication skills in infants of blind parents. *Proceedings of the Royal Society B: Biological Sciences*, 280(1760). https://doi.org/10.1098/rspb.2013.0436

Senju, A., Vernetti, A., Ganea, N., Hudry, K., Tucker, L., Charman, T., & Johnson, M. H. (2015). Early social experience affects the development of eye gaze processing. *Current Biology*, 25(23), 3086–3091. https://doi.org/10.1016/j.cub.2015.10.019

Sestan, N., & State, M. W. (2018). Lost in translation: Traversing the complex path from genomics to therapeutics in Autism Spectrum Disorder. *Neuron*, 100(2), 406–423. https://doi.org/10.1016/j.neuron.2018.10.015

Simion, F., Regolin, L., & Bulf, H. (2008). A predisposition for biological motion in the newborn baby. *Proceedings of the National Academy of Sciences of the United States of America*, 5(2), 809–813. https://doi.org/10.1073/pnas.0707021105

Simpson, E. A., Miller, G. M., Ferrari, P. F., Suomi, S. J., & Paukner, A. (2016). Neonatal imitation and early social experience predict gaze following abilities in infant monkeys. *Scientific Reports*, 6, 20233. https://doi.org/10.1038/srep20233

Sommerville, J. A., & Woodward, A. L. (2005). Pulling out the intentional structure of action: The relation between action processing and action production in infancy. *Cognition*, 95(1), 1–30. https://doi.org/10.1016/j.cognition.2003.12.004

Sorce, J. F., Emde, R. N., Campos, J., & Klinnert, M. D. (1985). Maternal emotional signaling: Its effect on the visual cliff behavior of 1-year-olds. *Developmental Psychology*, 21(1), 195–200. https://doi.org/10.1037/0012-1649.21.1.195

Szatmari, P., Chawarska, K., Dawson, G., Georgiades, S., Landa, R., Lord, C., Messinger, D. S., Thurm, A., & Halladay, A. (2016). Prospective longitudinal studies of infant siblings of children with autism: Lessons learned and future directions. *Journal of the American Academy of Child and Adolescent Psychiatry*, 55(3), 179–187. https://doi.org/10.1016/j.jaac.2015.12.014

Talbott, M. R., Dufek, S., Zwaigenbaum, L., Bryson, S., Brian, J., Smith, I. M., & Rogers, S. J. (2019). Preliminary feasibility of the TEDI: A novel parent-administered telehealth assessment for autism spectrum disorder symptoms in the first year of life. *Journal of Autism and Developmental Disorders*, 50(9), 3432–3439. https://doi.org/10.1007/s10803-019-04314-4

Thapar, A., & Rutter, M. (2021). Genetic advances in autism. *Journal of Autism and Developmental Disorders*, 51(12), 4321–4332. https://doi.org/10.1007/s10803-020-04685-z

Thatcher, R. W. (1994). Psychopathology of early frontal lobe damage: Dependence on cycles of development. *Development and Psychopathology*, 6(4), 565–596. https://doi.org/10.1017/S0954579400004697

Tomasello, M. (2018). How children come to understand false beliefs: A shared intentionality account. *Proceedings of the National Academy of Sciences of the United States of America*, 115(34), 8491–8498. https://doi.org/10.1073/pnas.1804761115

Tong, F., Nakayama, K., Moscovitch, M., Weinrib, O., & Kanwisher, N. (2000). Response properties of the human fusiform face area. *Cognitive Neuropsychology*, 17(1–3), 257–280. https://doi.org/10.1080/026432900380607

Tonks, J., Williams, H., Frampton, I., Yates, P., Wall, S., & Slater, A. (2008). Reading emotions after childhood brain injury: Case series evidence of dissociation between cognitive abilities and emotional expression processing skills. *Brain Injury*, 22(4), 325–332. https://doi.org/10.1080/02699050801968303

Träuble, B., Pauen, S., & Poulin-Dubois, D. (2014). Speed and direction changes induce the perception of animacy in 7-month-old infants. *Frontiers in Psychology*, 5, 1141. https://doi.org/10.3389/fpsyg.2014.01141

Trauner, D. A., Bellugi, U., & Chase, C. (1989). Neurologic features of Williams and Down syndromes. *Pediatric Neurology*, 5(3), 166–168. https://doi.org/10.1016/0887-8994(89)90066-0

Turella, L., Pierno, A. C., Tubaldi, F., & Castiello, U. (2009). Mirror neurons in humans: Consisting or confounding evidence? *Brain and Language*, 108(1), 10–21. https://doi.org/10.1016/j.bandl.2007.11.002

Urakawa, S., Takamoto, K., Ishikawa, A., Ono, T., & Nishijo, H. (2015). Selective medial prefrontal cortex responses during live mutual gaze interactions in human infants: An fNIRS study. *Brain Topography*, 28(5), 691–701. https://doi.org/10.1007/s10548-014-0414-2

Vanderwert, R. E., Simpson, E. A., Paukner, A., Suomi, S. J., Fox, N. A., & Ferrari, P. F. (2015). Early social experience affects neural activity to affiliative facial gestures in newborn nonhuman primates. *Developmental Neuroscience*, 37(3), 243–252. https://doi.org/10.1159/000381538

Vernetti, A., Ganea, N., Tucker, L., Charman, T., Johnson, M. H., & Senju, A. (2018). Infant neural sensitivity to eye gaze depends on early experience of gaze communication. *Developmental Cognitive Neuroscience*, 34, 1–6. https://doi.org/10.1016/j.dcn.2018.05.007

Walden, T. A., & Ogan, T. A. (1988). The development of social referencing. *Child Development*, 59(5), 1230–1240. https://doi.org/10.2307/1130486

Walle, E. A., Reschke, P. J., Camras, L. A., & Campos, J. J. (2017). Infant differential behavioral responding to discrete emotions. *Emotion*, 17(7), 1078–1091. https://doi.org/10.1037/emo0000307

Watson, J. B. (1972). *Psychological care of infant and child*. Arno Press.

Wellman, H. M., & Liu, D. (2004). Scaling of theory-of-mind tasks. *Child Development*, 75(2), 523–541. https://doi.org/10.1111/j.1467-8624.2004.00691.x

Wimmer, H., & Perner, J. (1983). Beliefs about beliefs: Representation and constraining function of wrong beliefs in young children's understanding of deception. *Cognition*, 13(1), 103–128. https://doi.org/10.1016/0010-0277(83)90004-5

Wooddell, L. J., Simpson, E. A., Murphy, A. M., Dettmer, A. M., & Paukner, A. (2019). Interindividual differences in neonatal sociality and emotionality predict juvenile social status in rhesus monkeys. *Developmental Science*, 22(2), e12749. https://doi.org/10.1111/desc.12749

Woodward, A. L. (1998). Infants selectively encode the goal object of an actor's reach. *Cognition*, 69(1), 1–34. https://doi.org/10.1016/s0010-0277(98)00058-4

Wyatt Kaminski, J., Valle, L. A., Filene, J. H., & Boyle, C. L. (2008). A meta-analytic review of components associated with parent training program effectiveness. *Journal of Abnormal Child Psychology*, 36(4), 567–589. https://doi.org/10.1007/s10802-007-9201-9

Yang, E. J., Lin, E. W., & Hensch, T. K. (2012). Critical period for acoustic preference in mice. *Proceedings of the National Academy of Sciences of the United States of America*, 109(Suppl 2), 17213–17220. https://doi.org/10.1073/pnas.1200705109

Zoghbi, H. Y., & Bear, M. F. (2012). Synaptic dysfunction in neurodevelopmental disorders associated with autism and intellectual disabilities. *Cold Spring Harbor Perspectives in Biology*, 4(3). https://doi.org/10.1101/cshperspect.a009886

Zwaigenbaum, L., Bauman, M. L., Choueiri, R., Fein, D., Kasari, C., Pierce, K., Stone, W. L., Yirmiya, N., Estes, A., Hansen, R. L., McPartland, J. C., Natowicz, M. R., Buie, T., Carter, A., Davis, P. A., Granpeesheh, D., Mailloux, Z., Newschaffer, C., Robins, D., … Wetherby, A. (2015). Early identification and interventions for autism spectrum disorder: Executive summary months? ASD-autism spectrum disorder DSM-5-Diagnostic and Statistical Manual of Mental Disorders, Fifth Edition M-CHAT-Modified Checklist for Autism in Toddlers. *Pediatrics*, 136(1), S10–S40. https://doi.org/10.1542/peds.2014-3667C

8   Language Learning and Social Interaction

LEARNING OBJECTIVES

- Identify the different components of language
- Describe how language can possess both specific and universal attributes
- Understand how the brain derives meaning from linguistic input
- Identify the brain structures and connections that support language comprehension and production
- Understand the difference between language quantity and quality
- Explain how contingent learning supports language development
- Recognize how experience tunes the brain to specific language input
- Consider the evolutionary origins of language

Humans have a unique ability to communicate complex ideas and express abstract thoughts. This ability gets a huge boost from language. Indeed, it is through language that we have built civilizations, developed the scientific method, and generated mind-expanding literature. Humans do not have to learn everything from personal experience because we are able to use language to learn from the experience of others. The development of language in young children is one of their most anticipated early milestones. How does this process happen in the first place, and how is language learned so consistently across so many different people?

In this chapter, we review the two things that are critical to the emergence of language comprehension and production: linguistic input – lots of it – and receptive neural tissue. We discuss what language is (it's not confined to speech!) and review what is known about the neural underpinnings for language in adults. We then compare the brain-basis of mature language processing to language processing in infants, both physically and relative to an array of behavioral and neural findings. We address the various sources of input and feedback that support early language learning, including initial speech sound discrimination and sound production. Early experience prepares a child to develop more advanced comprehension and production abilities, leading to the mastery of a language (or languages) and, eventually, literacy (Chapter 11). We close with a discussion of why humans, and only humans, have "language," while acknowledging that "communication" is prevalent among non-human animals. The examples we focus on in this chapter are grounded in the basic building blocks of language (including phonetics and phonology). In Chapter 11, we address how words and sentences (morphology and semantics) interface with that foundation and contribute to the development of literacy. And in the intervening chapters (Chapters 9 and 10), we discuss the many dimensions of memory – a core cognitive capacity that is critical to language.

8.1   How the Brain Supports Language and How Language Shapes the Brain

Children who develop without any delays master at least one language — and often more — both rapidly and seemingly effortlessly. The complexity of the language system(s) they acquire, the speed, and the seeming ease with which they do so have inspired many to conclude that language learning is a biologically endowed, special, and uniquely human ability (Chomsky, 1965); others have provided alternative accounts (e.g., Shatz, 1978). From a DCN perspective, language learning highlights the broad neural and behavioral changes that come about over the course of development, not magically, but in response to consistent, complex, and varied environmental input interacting with a developing brain. The universal ability of babies to learn language without explicit instruction highlights the power of gene–environment interactions.

The plasticity theme that runs throughout this book and the theoretical framework on which it is founded are both helpful guides to understanding the wide variety of data specific to language development, from longstanding findings grounded in behavioral measures to the most recent work in structural and functional neuroimaging. Here we integrate these findings in a manner that we hope supports a richer understanding of what language is (and isn't), how it develops (and sometimes doesn't), and why other animals (particularly non-human primates) don't have it.

8.2   What Is Language?

How children learn language requires being clear about the difference between general communication abilities and formal language. The two are linked, but differ in a number of important ways. Language imparts information: what we know, what we believe, what we hope for, what we fear. Language helps in the transmission of thoughts and feelings from one person to another, through arbitrarily produced symbols or sounds that convey meaning. We also communicate thoughts and feelings without language: we laugh, we smile, we scream, we shake our fists, and we raise our eyebrows. These gestures – paralinguistic cues – convey information, but "language" can be both more specific and abstract, allowing us to refer to things that happened in the past and things that have yet to happen.

Language is uniquely human, based on a core combination of features that are not found anywhere else in nature (Chomsky, 1966/2009; but see Jarvis, 2019). The biological basis for language processing and learning is the focus of ongoing investigation (Poeppel et al., 2012; Friederici et al., 2017). Human language is **generative**: there is an infinite number of new sentences to be created. We can string words together to create sentences that have never before been uttered, yet that people still understand. We do this according to rules that most of us can't describe – we just *know* when a sentence is lawful, and we know when it ends ... or when it goes on, and on, and on, and on ... before finally, finally, ending. The ability to generate any number of novel sentences on the spot and without difficulty is a distinguishing feature of how humans communicate. Although birds, dogs, whales, and many other animals engage in vocal communication and body postures to exchange information, these appear to be drawn from a fixed set of possible vocalizations and postures, lacking the generativity of human language.

The neurobiology that underpins human language has been difficult to characterize. For one thing, the relation between meaning and sound is highly complex, and largely arbitrary, yet the highly predictable and structured nature of language helps listeners deal with noisy, disfluent, and ungrammatical input. Even on a noisy train where we are not hearing every syllable with perfect fidelity, we know that the conductor has announced the next stop and we often are able to fill in the missing acoustic details. How the brain does this is non-trivial. It is harder still to track how humans go from knowing nothing about a language to being fluent speakers who can fill in missing information on the fly. Yet the fact that this process can be generalized *across* humans, indicating an evolved process, is evident in the similar patterns of neural activity observed in the brains of speakers of different languages while they produce, process, and act on linguistic input.

8.2.1 Building Blocks of Language Comprehension and Production

Language entails the ability to produce and comprehend either spoken or signed symbols (words or gestures) linked together according to the rules of a particular morphology (how words are formed) and grammar (how sentences are formed). Language shapes our social interaction, engaging almost every area of the brain. Speaking requires specialized neural circuits for controlling the muscles of the larynx, tongue, mouth, jaw, and lips. Understanding speech requires circuits for parsing a dense incoming stream of auditory input and assigning meaning to its component parts. Neural circuits simultaneously identify and interpret facial expressions, body language, and tone of voice in order to distinguish between, for example, sincerity and sarcasm. And all of these processes must be integrated in some way as well. The journey from being a preverbal infant to being a mature speaker/listener seems like it should be a long one.

The different levels at which language can be analyzed are: **phonetics, phonology, morphology, syntax, semantics**, and **pragmatics**. Each is rich in research potential, and they interact with one another in complex ways (Box 8.1). Indeed, most university linguistics departments offer full semester courses on each of these levels, and even subsets of these levels! Here, we focus on how the levels of language engage the brain in different ways and are integrated during language use. We focus on spoken language here, but emphasize that sign languages consist of these component parts as well – they are not merely a system of unstructured gestures, but are themsevles complete, complex, natural languages. In fact, commonalities in the brain structures engaged during processing of both sign and spoken language have changed our understanding of the neurobiological basis of language, demonstrating that it is at least in part amodal. For more information about the neurobiology of sign language, Karen Emmorey (2021) provides a detailed overview of research in this domain.

Box 8.1 The Structural Levels of Language

To be a fluent speaker requires interaction of processing across the following levels:

- *Phonetics* describes the physical production and perception of individual speech sounds, or phonemes; different languages use different sets of phonemes. Phonetics is what distinguishes the /c/ of "cat" from the /r/ of "rat" and makes them different words, to which we assign different meanings.
- *Phonology* describes how the subset of sounds in a particular language fit together. For example, the rules of phonology in English allow us to take two different phonemes, /s/ and /t/ and concatenate them to create the sound /st/ as in /string/. But we are not allowed in English to put together /c/ and /d/ to form /cd/, a combination that does not appear in any English word.
- *Morphology* refers to the rules concerning the meaningful substructures of words, including word roots and stems, suffixes and prefixes. You already know several morphological rules, such as adding –er and –ier to a word to indicate that one thing is than another. We say, "Pat is strong but Chris is stronger" or "That soup is spicy, but this one is spicier."
- *Syntax* characterizes how people put words together into phrases and sentences so that they can communicate meaningfully. All languages have underlying syntactic rules that, when combined with morphological rules, make up a language's grammar. For example, many – but not all – languages distinguish an *actor* from an *agent* by where they appear in a sentence, and in relation to other words. This convention allows us to understand the difference between *The boy bit the dog* and *The dog bit the boy*, while still being able to understand an inverted sentence form such as *The dog was bitten by the boy*.
- *Semantics* focuses on meaning, including the significance of words. Think about the difference between a *ball* and a *block*. At the perceptual level, they are different shapes. At first, respective shapes may be all that a young child thinks of when hearing those labels. With experience, they entail more information, such as the different types of balls and blocks there are and the kind of play associated with each.
- *Pragmatics* characterizes how the social context in which language is used contributes to its meaning. It also incorporates paralinguistic cues: aspects of communication that are woven into structured language. For example, if a classmate in your developmental cognitive neuroscience class turns to you and says "pragmatics is *so* interesting," you interpret it differently if they say it with a straight face, as opposed to if they roll their eyes while saying it.

There are famous stories told among linguists about overconfident colleagues who made assertions in conference talks and were soundly rebuked by attendees. In our favorite, Oxford Professor J. L. Austin noted that in English, a double negative makes a positive ("I didn't *not* go" = "I did go") but that in other languages, such as French, a double negative remains negative "Je n'ai pas faim" (literally, I am not not hungry = I am not hungry). Austin declared that there was no language in the world in which a double positive makes a negative. Columbia Professor Sidney Morgenbesser replied, "Yeah, yeah" with the sing-songy descending minor third that is a cultural universal for "no." This lies at the intersection of syntax and semantics (the issue of the double positive) and invokes pragmatics (in the particular way in which Morgenbesser's response was conveyed).

In a related story, a researcher (who is still active, and out of courtesy we are not disclosing her name) declared that "while there is considerable freedom across languages for how words are formed, and many allow a word to be formed without consonants (*oui* in French; *ai* in English), there are no languages that allow a word to be formed without vowels." An audience member replied "Hmmm" to a burst of laughter. Clearly irritated, the researcher explained that in her phonetic understanding, /m/ is a liquid, and therefore treated like a vowel. To which the same audience member replied "Sshhhh."

8.2.2 Specificity and Universality

There currently are between 5,000 and 7,000 spoken human languages in the world, and many more that are extinct. The differences among spoken languages are noteworthy: some are melodic while others are staccato; some have more vowels than consonants while others have very few vowels. French has 20 different tenses (indicating *when* something happened), English has 12, and some, like Chinese, have none. Even within language families, there are notable differences. For example, various Romance languages (i.e., French, Portuguese, Spanish, and Italian) are quite closely related but not mutually comprehensible by their different speakers. Yet learning one is made easier by knowing another. Despite their differences, separate languages engage largely the same systems for comprehending and speaking. This is evident from the 300 different types of sign languages used throughout the world today. There is no universal sign language and different sign languages are used in different countries and geographical regions; all contain the fundamental levels of language (Box 8.1) and are defined by a distinctive grammar. American Sign Language (ASL) is the primary language of many North Americans who are deaf and hard of hearing and is used by many hearing people as well (LSQ is used in French Canada). British Sign Language (BSL) is a different sign language than ASL, and North Americans who know ASL likely will not understand BSL. The overarching similarities across both spoken and sign languages reveal the engagement of common brain structures, in spite of the fact that one is aural and the other is visual (Hickok et al., 1996).

8.2.3 Localizing Language in the Adult Brain

Long before imaging technologies were available, it was well appreciated that language functions are localized in different parts of the brain. By the mid-1800s, neurologists were treating patients with obvious brain injuries that were accompanied by specific language difficulties. For example, Paul Broca's postmortem examinations of people who had speech production difficulties revealed consistent damage to an area in the left *frontal lobe*, anterior to the central fissure. People with damage to this brain region had intact vocal abilities and were able to comprehend language but were unable to speak fluently; the common lesion site came to be named **Broca's area**.

Carl Wernicke described patients who could produce speech but who had great difficulty comprehending it following damage to the posterior region of the left *temporal lobe*. That area came to be called **Wernicke's area**. We now know that Broca's and Wernicke's areas comprise many subregions, and that the role of each is more complex than simply speech production and comprehension.

Aphasia is the general term for the inability to produce or comprehend language. At one extreme, a person with **Broca's aphasia** can understand but cannot speak, and at the other, a person with **Wernicke's aphasia** can speak but cannot comprehend others. This reveals a **double dissociation** between comprehension and production. Wernicke proposed a model for how the two language regions interact to support production and comprehension, thereby introducing the first hypothesis for how the brain supports language. His model was constrained by all the same problems endemic to lesion studies, but it introduced the notion that *function* could be *mapped* to brain in a systematic way.

Wilder Penfield furthered this pursuit in the 1930s by using brain stimulation on patients undergoing elective surgery for treatment of epilepsy. Penfield identified an extensive network of left lateralized regions involved in the language processing of right-handed people, including Broca's and Wernicke's areas, along with primary auditory cortex, and extending to areas of motor and somatosensory cortices that control facial, tongue, and throat muscles. Wernicke's model, later clarified and illustrated by Lichtheim (1885), subsequently was revived by Geschwind (1965, 1970) and has come to be referred to in various combinations of the originators' names: the "Broca–Wernicke–Lichtheim–Geschwind model" (e.g., Poeppel & Hickok, 2004; Hagoort, 2016) or simply, **the Classic Model** (Tremblay & Dick, 2016).

In this model (Figure 8.1A), the necessary information exchange between brain areas (such as in reading aloud) is accomplished via the arcuate fasciculus, a major fiber bundle connecting the language areas in temporal cortex (Wernicke's area) and frontal cortex (Broca's area). The language areas all border one of the major sulcal fissures in the brain, the lateral sulcus, also called the **Sylvian fissure**. Collectively, this part of the brain is often referred to as **perisylvian cortex**.

The Classic Model posits that listening to and understanding spoken words begins with sound stimulating the primary auditory cortex (**Heschl's gyrus**) via ascending pathways from the cochlea (Chapter 6), through the superior olivary complex and inferior colliculus, and on to the medial geniculate nucleus of the thalamus. From there, information continues to Wernicke's area, where meaning is represented and thus can be extracted from the signal. To produce speech, meaning is conveyed from Wernicke's via the arcuate fasciculus to Broca's area where according to the model, representations for articulating words are held. That is, Broca's contains the instructions for moving the muscles in the vocal cords, mouth, glottis, tongue, lips, and jaw that produce phonemes, and strings those phonemes into words and sentences. These instructions are conveyed to the facial area of the motor cortex, and from there to facial motor neurons in the basal ganglia and brainstem, which relay movement commands to facial muscles and produce speech. It's as easy as that (joking)! (In sign languages, Broca's conveys all this information to the fingers, hands, and arms – and in some instances, feet). The finding that Broca's patients can produce comprehensible speech strongly suggests that internal self-comprehension does not necessarily involve the functioning of Wernicke's area.

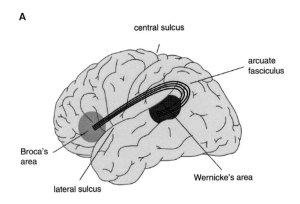

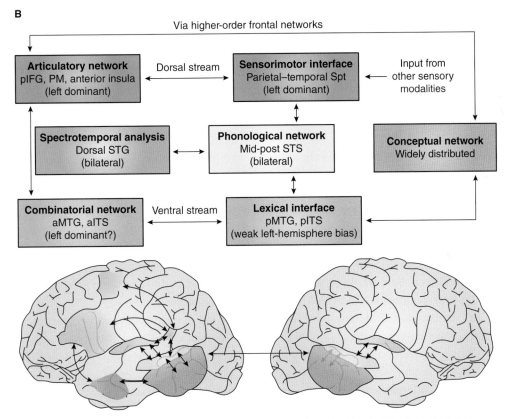

Figure 8.1 Original and recent models of language processing. A. Classic Wernicke–Lichtheim–Geschwind Model of the neurobiology of language. B. Hickok and Poeppel's Dual-Stream Model of language processing. *aITS = anterior Inferior Temporal Sulcus; pITS = posterior Inferior Temporal Sulcus; aMTG = anterior Middle Temporal Gyrus; pIFG = posterior Inferior Frontal Gyrus; PM = Premotor Cortex; STS = Superior Temporal Sulcus; STG = Superior Temporal Gyrus.* (Reprinted from Hickok & Poeppel, 2007)

8.2.4　Complex Processing: Beyond Localization of Language Function

As influential as the Classic Model was, in many ways it was wrong. Imaging methods revealed increasing numbers of regions and white matter tracts involved in language production and processing. The functions assigned to Broca's and Wernicke's areas were overly broad; these brain regions cannot be distinguished solely based on anatomy and must instead be identified based on their functions. And both regions can be parcellated into a number of smaller areas with different **cytoarchitectonic** and **receptoarchitectonic** characteristics (Zilles et al., 2015; Zilles & Amunts, 2018).

An emerging alternative to the Classic Model characterizes language as a functional system built out of (or layered onto) our primate neural architecture. On this view, human language evolved from preexisting structures that initially served different adaptive purposes, with increasing delineation into dorsal-ventral cortical streams that share a range of anatomical characteristics. Although some language-specific mechanisms may well exist, the emerging consensus supports a dual-stream architecture with mutual interactions and phylogenetically common control mechanisms.

A range of dual-stream architectures have been proposed thus far, each based on two functionally distinct neural networks: one interfacing sensory networks with conceptual-semantic systems, and one interfacing sensory networks with motor-articulatory systems. In Hickok and Poeppel's (2007) dual-stream model (Figure 8.1B), two large-scale auditory processing streams are located in the perisylvian cortex, an area encompassing frontal, parietal, and temporal cortices. The *ventral* stream is largely bilateral, mapping phonological information onto semantic representations; it is critical for successful lexical comprehension (e.g., sound to semantics mapping), and includes several white matter tracts (the **uncinate fasciculus**, the **inferior longitudinal fasciculus**, and the **extreme capsule fasciculus**). The *dorsal* stream is largely left lateralized, bridging a region of the temporal-parietal junction and left frontal speech areas; it supports the mapping of auditory sensory representations onto articulatory motor representations, while also providing ad hoc auditory and proprioceptive feedback that is critical for the production of fluent speech. Several major white matter tracts support dorsal stream processing, including the **superior longitudinal fasciculus** and the **arcuate fasciculus**.

The dual-stream model has been further elaborated to include additional white matter tracts within and between cortical regions. Initial versions focused primarily on speech and word processing and not on the complex combinatorial properties of language (à la Chomsky). Some researchers assume that the neural circuitry supporting sentence-level comprehension is fundamentally different from anything seen in non-human primates; others posit human-specific evolutionary-based additions to the dorsal stream that are assumed to have evolved late, phylogenetically speaking, and continue to mature late, in ontogenetic terms. Figure 8.2 represents just one of the more recently proposed dual-stream models. At the top are the main anatomical connections of the perisylvian areas in the left hemisphere, comprising the ventral and the dorsal pathways. The perisylvian cortex, covering frontal, parietal, and temporal cortices, is shaded in light gray. Notice the detailed delineation of subcomponents of the arcuate fasciculus and the additional white matter pathway (e.g., the frontal aslant tract). The primary functions of the dorsal and ventral streams are delineated at the bottom of Figure 8.2. Homologous areas in the right hemisphere (not shown) likely play important roles as well, engaging, for

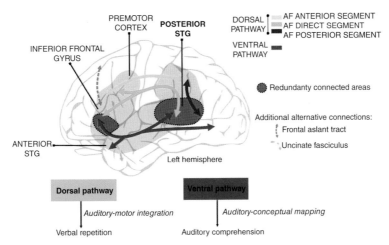

Figure 8.2 Division of labor across the ventral and dorsal language streams. *AF = Arcuate Fasciculus; STG = Superior Temporal Gyrus* (Reprinted from López-Barroso & De Diego-Balaguer, 2017)

example, compensation mechanisms to supplement understanding of speech in noise, interpret the melodic aspects of speech (e.g., prosody), or process the different tones in tonal languages (e.g., Mandarin Chinese). Debates about the details of these architectures will continue for the foreseeable future. Many researchers still think speech is special, but it's becoming harder and harder to defend simplistic characterizations of language; we are well past the view that language is the product of some biologically endowed "black box."

Finally, because speech is a complex form of sound consisting of multiple cues that can be classified largely on the basis of their **spectral and temporal properties**, there has been increasing interest in mapping the processing of the different acoustic properties that characterize speech to specialized neural anatomy (Poeppel, 2014). This mapping commits different computations to the analysis of the temporal versus spectral acoustic features of speech. Temporal features can help differentiate one phoneme from another, as when distinctions in voice onset time as small as 10-50 ms distinguish a /b/ from a /p/. Spectral features, which include the distribution of energy and frequencies within the acoustic signal, distinguish vowels from one another. Distinguishing one person's voice from another when they are saying the same thing is based on myriad temporal-spectral cues, most saliently the timbre (**tam'**-ber), or spectral profile, of the speaker. This is the same process we use to distinguish one musical instrument from another when they are playing the same note.

Processing temporal and spectral cues differentially engages the two hemispheres of the brain. The left hemisphere specializes in analysis of short, fast-changing auditory events with narrow time windows (**temporal cues**), and the right helps integrate frequency rich information over larger time windows (**spectral cues**). This asymmetrical processing of acoustic cue types is a reflection of how the brain divides up processing demands: language is primarily dependent on the left hemisphere, while other aspects of processing related to social cognition, including vocal affect and speaker identity, depend on the right.

8.3   Is the Infant Brain Primed for Language? Evidence from Phonetics and Phonology

Thus far, we have seen that the structural and computational components of language are processed in the adult brain by a number of parallel and hierarchically organized neural circuits. Are neonatal brains preconfigured in this way to learn language? A purely non-nativist view favors bottom-up influences on language development, according to which sensory input shapes a plastic brain; a purely nativist view favors a black-box, modular characterization of how infants can so quickly come to handle the complex, combinatorial features of language (Chomsky's "language acquisition device"). Fortunately, evolving understanding of the neural architectures that support human learning in general has led to a more nuanced view of the neural development that supports language learning in particular. There is increasing evidence that (1) external input in the last trimester interacts with the human-specific genetic–developmental program to produce a fetal brain whose functional organization is primed for processing rhythmically structured stimuli, (2) left/right hemisphere asymmetries emerge early and prominently, and (3) activity across cortical regions, including the frontal lobe, supports the development of the connective pathways underpinning language processing.

8.3.1   Auditory Input Interacts with Developing Brain Structure

When does an individual's experience with language begin, and what impact does this have on the early neural pathways that support further learning?

The tissue and liquid barriers of the womb serve as low-pass filters, absorbing the higher frequency sounds in the speech signal and transmitting only the low frequency sounds (similar to when your ears are below water level in a bathtub). This differential transmission of frequencies means that phoneme-specific information, such as that distinguishing /d/ from /t/, is not experienced by the developing fetus, while prosodic information, such as the acoustic envelope of a spoken utterance, is. Using both behavioral and physiological measures (i.e., fetal movement, heart rate) to extrapolate information about when fetal auditory processing begins and what sorts of auditory distinctions the developing fetus can make, researchers have determined that sound is processed as early as 19 gestational weeks, starting at the lowest frequencies (100 Hz) and increasing up to 3,000 Hz between 30 and 35 gestational weeks (Hepper & Shahidullah, 1994; Lecanuet & Schaal, 1996). Fetal habituation to repeated sounds takes place as early as 32 gestational weeks (Morokuma et al., 2004). Closer to term, infants' sensitivity to more complex sounds improves, allowing them to distinguish variations in music (Kisilevsky et al., 2004) and to differentiate prosodic cues in familiar and novel rhymes (DeCasper et al., 1994). All of this is while the child is still *in utero*! The neural pathways that support language are shaped by this initial, prenatal experience.

Neonates demonstrate what they have learned about sound *in utero* by showing early auditory preferences. In a seminal study, newborns learned to elicit playback of their mother's voice or the voice of an unfamiliar female by sucking on a non-nutritive nipple. They demonstrated a clear preference for their mother's voice over the unfamiliar voice, despite their still limited postnatal experience (DeCasper & Fifer, 1980). Using similar techniques, newborns manifested a preference for a familiar story (Dr. Seuss' *The Cat in the Hat*) over a novel story (DeCasper & Spence, 1986), and for music to which they were exposed repeatedly in the womb over similar music to which they were not exposed (Johansen-Berg, 2001). Newborns also prefer human speech over filtered speech (Spence & DeCasper, 1987), warbled tones (Samples & Franklin, 1978), white noise (Butterfield & Siperstein, 1972; Colombo & Bundy, 1981), and sine-wave analogues of speech (Vouloumanos & Werker, 2007). Moreover, newborns can discriminate speech from non-speech when played forwards, but not backwards (Ramus et al., 2000), they prefer the language of their own environment over another, unfamiliar language (Moon et al., 1993), they can distinguish between stress patterns of different multisyllabic words (Moon et al., 1993), and they can categorically discriminate lexical versus grammatical words (Shi et al., 1999). Newborns can distinguish between two rhythmically dissimilar languages (Mehler et al., 1988), are sensitive to word boundaries (Christophe et al., 1994), and can differentiate between good and poor syllable forms (Bertoncini & Mehler, 1981). While it might initially appear that these early displays of preference show that infants are born with the fundamentals of language, these early perceptual abilities are not due to genetic transmission of the language the caregivers speak. Rather, these preferences are the result of exposure to speech in the womb interacting with our auditory physiology. Infants who were exposed prenatally to two languages do not display differential preference for one or the other when tested as newborns, yet they are still capable of discriminating between the two (Byers-Heinlein et al., 2010). This underscores the impact of early exposure on the developing auditory system.

Such findings are influencing how we treat preterm infants in neonatal intensive care units (NICUs). NICUs are busy places with lots of mechanical noise, alarms, and beeping, all interspersed with long periods of silence. Such atypical auditory experience is potentially disruptive to normal brain development (Matthews et al., 2018), particularly for children born before the 32nd week of pregnancy who are at high risk of developing brain-based disorders. Thus, NICUs are introducing developmental care procedures that include reduction of the noise of alarms and the periods of total silence, and introduction of the sound of a mother's heartbeat, music, and language as they would be heard filtered through amniotic fluid. Indeed, preterm infants exposed to soft music in the NICU show increased coupling between brain networks that previously had been found to be decreased in premature infants (Lordier et al., 2019).

8.3.2 Increasing Sensitivity to Language Sound Specific Structure

A fundamental part of knowing a language is recognizing and producing the language's phonemes and phonology, its sounds and combinations of sounds. Of the hundreds of phonemes that are used across the world's languages, the infant needs to learn *which* of them are used in the ambient language(s). From this, infants develop synaptic connections that support **phonological representations**, critical to recognizing the sound structure of individual words. The neural circuits supporting language are influenced by how acoustic continua produced by the vocal apparatus can be broken up. For example, the voicing continuum (i.e., timing of vibrations of the vocal folds, voice onset time, or VOT) can be divided into small perceptual categories, such as the English minimal pairs /b/ and /p/. Minimal pairs are perceived categorically by adult native speakers and are used contrastively to denote different meanings (e.g., bet vs. pet). Different languages parcellate such continua differently and some distinctions that some languages make (e.g., /u/ and /ou/ in French, or /d/ and /dhi/ in Hindi) are not made in other languages; adult English speakers learning these new contrasts often have difficulty keeping them straight. Because they are not functionally contrastive (i.e., their exchange does not change the meaning of a word), we have lost sensitivity to the fine-grained distinctions between them.

Although many of the acoustic differences for phonetic categories are minute (e.g., a tiny difference in VOT turns /b/ into /p/), young infants are *exquisitely* sensitive to the acoustic distinctions that mark phonetic boundaries. In a groundbreaking study, Peter Eimas and colleagues (Eimas et al., 1971) found that when 1- to 4-month-old English-exposed infants were habituated to one of two synthetic English syllables differing only on VOT, they dishabituated to the other. From this, one might conclude that these language-specific auditory sensitivities are innate to humans. However, the ability to **categorically perceive** such distinctions is not specific to humans, as it is observed in chinchillas (Kuhl & Miller, 1975) and macaques (Kuhl & Padden, 1983) as well. In other words, human phonetic categories evolved from constraints imposed by general characteristics of the mammalian auditory system rather than those unique to human ears and brains (Kuhl, 1986; Smith & Lewicki, 2006).

In another groundbreaking study, Janet Werker and Richard Tees (Werker & Tees, 1984; Werker et al., 1981) demonstrated that 6-month-old infants are able to categorically perceive phonemes in languages they've never before been exposed to (and to which adult English speakers are oblivious). It was subsequently shown that infants undergo a transition from a broad ability to distinguish many/most minimally contrastive phoneme pairs to an increasingly specialized capacity to distinguish primarily the phoneme pairs relevant to their ambient language(s). This **perceptual tuning** takes place in the first year, so that by between 10 and 12 months of age, infants are more adept at discriminating native compared with non-native contrasts. In other words, the ability to discriminate non-native phonetic contrasts declines from ages 6–12 months. Thus, while both monolingual English- and Japanese-exposed infants are able to make the English /r/ and /l/ distinction prior to 6 months of age, by the end of their first year, only the monolingual English-exposed infants will continue to differentiate these sounds (Kuhl et al., 2006). This occurs because the /r/ vs. /l/ distinction is not used in the Japanese language, and perceptual tuning thus renders it increasingly imperceptible to a Japanese-exposed infant. What might be the advantage of *not* being able to recognize every phonetic distinctions in the world? Well, language production and perception are messy. The acoustic signal of different speakers saying the same word is highly variable – not just due to their accents, but to noisy environments, and to *co-articulation effects*. The acoustic signal of, say, the letter /d/, is different when it begins a word (*dog*) than when it is in the middle of a word *(puddle)* or ends the word (*bird*). And the signal is further changed by the phonemes that precede and follow it!

How does perceptual tuning occur? Experience-dependent alteration of functional properties and circuits underlies this form of neuroplasticity (Chapters 4 and 5). Developmental **critical periods** like the one for native language minimal pairs have a constrained timeline, paralleling other examples of the emergence or maintenance of specific abilities. For example, studies with people acquiring a language post-puberty (e.g., second language learners, deaf children raised without robust language input, so-called feral children) show that acquisition of a native language grammar, among other language-specific abilities, is constrained and that lack of stimulation during the early childhood period has lasting effects on the both the brain and behavior. Thus, deprivation during the early developmental time frame leads to lifelong deficits in language – and likely other – abilities. Importance of early exposure to language, whether spoken or signed, to the brain development of congenitally deaf children is a topic of recent research (Hall et al., 2018). An issue for pediatric cochlear implant users is making sure their device is providing appropriate levels of stimulation (Chapter 2). Note that the term *critical periods* applies when a kind of neurally based hard stop exists; for example, few adults are able to acquire native-like pronunciation for languages they learn outside the critical period. *Sensitive periods* are when there is a neurally based bias for learning within a specific period of developmental time, but learning can still occur at other times; many adults are able to acquire native-like vocabulary for languages learned as adults (Chapter 5) – just not native-like accents.

The cellular and molecular mechanisms that control the onset and closure of different critical periods are beginning to come into focus as well. For example, in rat pups, perinatal serotonin reuptake inhibitor (SRI) exposure alters sensory processing and myelin sheath formation, and decreases cortical density in auditory and somatosensory cortex (Simpson et al., 2011). Based on these rat pup data, Weikum and colleagues (Weikum et al., 2012) compared the discrimination abilities of infants of depressed mothers who were treated with SRIs to two other groups of mothers: untreated depressed mothers, and mothers not suffering from depression. They hypothesized that SRIs may alter the timing of the neural development that underlies perceptual tuning for phonetic discrimination in infants. Indeed, fetuses exposed to SRIs showed advanced discrimination abilities *in utero*, perceiving consonant contrasts that were not perceived by fetuses not exposed to SRIs. Moreover, while the infants of non-depressed mothers followed the predicted time course of postnatal phonological development (i.e., at 6 months, they perceived a non-native contrast, and at 10 months, they did not), SRI-exposed infants already failed to discriminate the non-native sounds at 6 months. Thus, it appears that SRIs can open a period of atypical plasticity in a developing infant. On the other hand, the infants of depressed but *untreated* mothers continued to discriminate the non-native sounds at 10 months. The researchers hypothesized that the mechanism behind this delay has to do either with reduced input (a global reduction in speech or of sufficiently engaging speech) or to reduced serotonin levels in the depressed mothers. Together, these findings point to a critical period for perceptual tuning based on the time course of brain development given specific environmental factors.

In sum, we can conclude that infants younger than 6 months can discriminate a wide range of speech sound contrasts, both native and non-native (Saffran et al., 2006). With time and, in many cases, the blurring of perceptual boundaries or non-native contrasts, those precocious discrimination abilities no longer exist. This matters: children's sensitivity to native relative to non-native contrasts at the end of the first year positively predicts their language abilities in the second year, whereas maintenance of sensitivity to non-native contrasts shows a negative relationship with language ability measures in the second year (Kuhl et al., 2005).

8.3.3 Neural Correlates of Language Specific Perceptual Tuning

A strength of the DCN approach is in looking for converging evidence across multiple methodologies. Such an approach can either provide additional support for previous findings, or muddy the waters. ERP data reveal that infants can discriminate both native and non-native consonant contrasts at 7 months, but not 11 months (Rivera-Gaxiola et al., 2005), after which only native contrasts are discriminated. However, when analyses were based on a different parsing of the ERP components, 11-month-old infants' brains appeared to still be sensitive to both types of contrast.

These conflicting results suggest that while infants' sensitivity to native relative to non-native contrasts does increase in the second half of the first year, it is not as systematic as the traditional perceptual tuning account makes it seem. Things get even more complicated from there. For example, Narayan et al. (2010) found that some phoneme contrasts are *not* available to infants prior to perceptual tuning, while other (even non-native) contrasts remain available *after* the tuning period should have ended (i.e., after 8 months). These researchers found that the non-native (Filipino) /na/-/ŋa/ contrast was *not* perceived by English 4- to 12-month-olds, nor was it perceived by Filipino 6- to 8-month-olds. However, older Filipino 10- to 12-month-olds *were* able to make the distinction. These findings are consistent with a report by Anderson et al. 2003, that English-exposed infants showed a loss of sensitivity to a Hindi but not a Salish contrast by the end of their first year. Although this perceptual pattern is unusual – non-native contrasts are typically perceived by pre-tuned infants of any language background (Trehub, 1976; Werker & Tees, 1984; Polka et al., 2001) – these findings indicate that perceptual tuning may be mediated by the relative production difficulty of a contrast pair, or even its **acoustic salience** (Narayan et al., 2010).

Much depends on the specifics of the language being learned and the context in which it is learned. For example, behavioral findings have suggested a somewhat earlier timeline (e.g., 6–8 months) for vowel discrimination compared to consonants (Kuhl et al., 1992; Polka & Werker, 1994), and even 3- to 6-month-old infants have been shown to perceive VOT in a graded, within-category manner given appropriate testing conditions (Miller & Eimas, 1996; McMurray & Aslin, 2005). All this suggests that, although category-like phonetic discrimination may be easily revealed in infants, gradient perception is also possible – think of a rainbow, where the colors blur into one another rather than having sharp boundaries between them. In other words, the devil (or God, or Darwin!) is in the experimental details.

Patricia Kuhl and her colleagues (Kuhl et al., 2014) used MEG to further explore the neural circuits underlying the tuning process. English learning infants between 7 and 11 months were tested on contrasting English and Spanish minimal pairs. The mismatched negativity response (MMN) from younger infants revealed that they could discriminate both languages' contrasts and MEG data showed activation in both auditory (superior temporal gyrus) and motor (inferior frontal gyrus) regions. While the MMN for the older infants showed that they had lost sensitivity to the Spanish (non-native) contrast, the MEG data showed a double dissociation for the acoustic and motor regions, with greater activation in auditory regions for the English (native) speech sounds than for non-native sounds, and greater activation in motor areas for non-native sounds than for native sounds. The researchers replicated their findings with Finnish learning infants using Mandarin contrasts. Adults show the same double dissociation. In other words, different cortical regions take on different tasks over the course of development as a function of what is being learned about the sounds in the environment and when it is learned. By the end of the first year, the speech motor movements are stronger for native than non-native sounds. Correspondingly, they are less efficient/ weaker for non-native speech, thus producing greater cortical activation (indicating greater effort).

Not all phonetic contrasts are perceived the same; how they are perceived depends on who is hearing them and the context in which they are heard. In short, given the behavioral and brain evidence, it is reasonable to conclude that the neural mechanism(s) responsible for perceptual tuning are undergoing concurrent and pronounced development consistent with all the other experience-based perceptual tuning we have reviewed thus far.

8.3.4 Hemispheric Asymmetries

As perceptual tuning data indicate, the infant brain is primed for environmental shaping in the first year. There is growing evidence that a rudimentary version of the left/right architectural arrangement that characterizes adult neural processing is in place in early infancy. Across a series of remarkable studies using multiple methodologies, Ghislaine Dehaene-Lambertz (see the Scientist Spotlight in Box 8.2) and colleagues (e.g., see Dehaene-Lambertz, 2017) have shown that – as in other primates – the neonate auditory cortex is organized into parallel processing streams that filter acoustic information on different timescales. This implies that those aspects of speech processing that require high temporal resolution (e.g., phonetic contrast analysis) are directed relatively early towards the left hemisphere because of its intrinsic, highly-evolved, fine-grained temporal encoding abilities. Recall that the ventral language stream is largely bilateral, while the dorsal stream is predominantly left lateralized. Thus, the components of the two streams in the left hemisphere handle different linguistic processing functions, while sounds whose identification is based in slower spectral cues can be analyzed for message and for context, with a different hemisphere responsible for each.

As Dehaene-Lambertz (2017, p. 52) observed: "Learning your native language and recognizing your parents are both important for human communication." Thus, evolution has routed these two very different acoustic tasks for handling by the two different hemispheres, a solution that has benefited from the hierarchical neural architecture that appears to have been put in place early in the primate brain. An additional benefit is that this neural separation of function allows for a backup system: if injury or disease compromises one system, the other may be spared and made available to step in and compensate for the lost processing abilities.

Box 8.2 Scientist Spotlight on Ghislaine Dehaene-Lambertz (Developmental Neuroimaging Lab, Neurospin, Paris)

Dr. Ghislaine Dehaene-Lambertz (Box Figure 8.1) is CNRS Scientific Director of the Developmental Neuroimaging Lab at Neurospin, a brain-imaging platform dedicated to the human brain in the suburbs of Paris. Originally trained as a pediatrician, she added a PhD in Life and Health Sciences at the Université Paris VI to her MD in order to pursue research on the development of cognitive

Box 8.2 (cont.)

functions in infants and children using brain imaging techniques. These comments are excerpted from a conversation between Dr. Dehaene-Lambertz and the authors.

As a pediatrician trainee, I was working in a neonatal care intensive unit and I wondered: When you resuscitate very premature infants, what is the state of their brains? Do they feel pain? Do they see anything? Are they able to react to the environment? At that time, in the 1980s, there were no responses [to such questions] in the medical field. My colleagues were not at all interested in these kinds of questions that were beyond the scope of immediate medical care. But, I met Jacques Mehler who was also working with babies, but from a very different perspective. He was looking at cognition and how babies perceive language. So, I combined what I was doing in my medical studies and what he was doing – trying to understand how the human brain develops language and speech. I remember that when I was reading articles on baby cognition, I was lost. It was so far from my medical background. But I was captivated, and when we found out with Jacques that newborns were able to recognize their native language, I was hooked and didn't go back to the clinic. My goal at that time was to first understand normal cognitive development and then apply that knowledge to help children with cognitive difficulties.

What I am interested in is how complex cognition can be achieved in a baby's immature brain. Not many of us are trying to understand the neural bases of babies' abilities. When I started, there was this very bottom-up idea of development. First, only the very low-level areas are working, then the associative areas, then higher-level areas and so on. What we have discovered is that this idea is not true: even frontal areas are active in premature infants before term. So my current opinion, though we have not yet done all the necessary studies, is that all networks underlying human cognition are in place early on, before term. You don't develop new circuits as you get older. You do not use more brain areas. What changes is the dynamic within the networks and the relative weight attributed to this or that area at a given age because of its efficiency, which depends on its own stage of maturation but also on the speed of its connectivity with other nodes in the network. Thanks to the combination of EEG and MRI, we can now investigate this aspect.

I don't know if it's controversial, but we still don't fully understand how the human brain is able to do language, [nor] what is the key component or key change between humans and chimps. Many infants' abilities are also present in other animals. But a few years later, there is no doubt that children are better able to perform much more complex cognitive tasks than monkeys. The main difference is not the size of the brain, but its organization. This is why brain imaging in babies is so important: to understand infant cognition.

Studies using fMRI have shown that speech processing by infants engages many of the cortical regions used by adults. Dehaene-Lambertz and colleagues (Dehaene-Lambertz et al., 2002) played a recording of a female voice reading a story in infant-directed speech to 3-month-olds while their brains were scanned. During the scan, the infants heard 20-second excerpts of the speech, played either forwards or backwards. Both the forward and backward speech samples elicited activation in the left temporal lobe, particularly in **Heschl's gyrus**, a region of primary auditory cortex that is typically active during speech processing in adults. There was also significantly greater activity in response to the forward speech than to the backward speech in other left temporal sites, particularly in the **angular gyrus** and the **precuneus**. Based on these findings, the researchers argued that by 3 months, the infant cortex is already parcellated into regions of functional importance for speech-specific processing.

Given the complexity of any language, spoken or signed, it can be hard to know where to begin looking for clues to how the learning process starts. Dehaene-Lambertz has been finding novel ways to address these questions with children at the earliest stages of language learning. For example, in another study (Dehaene-Lambertz, Hertz-Pannier, & Dubois, 2006) she and her colleagues interrogated the hierarchical organization of early auditory processing by using an fMRI slow-event design, an approach that allowed them to focus on the *phase* of the BOLD responses elicited while 3-month-olds heard short sentences in the scanner. Consistent with findings from a similar study with adults (Dehaene-Lambertz, Dehaene, et al., 2006), infants' BOLD responses were evident early in primary auditory areas and then cascaded along the dorsal-ventral and posterior-anterior axis of the superior temporal regions.

Figure 8.3 shows how the hierarchical organization of the perisylvian regions of the brain is evident based on the timing of the response in different regions to a single sentence. The data shown are from both 3-month-old infants and adults. The perisylvian cortex (also referred to as the **perisylvian region**) is so called because it consists of the region around the lateral sulcus (the Sylvian fissure) of the left hemisphere, including both Broca's and Wernicke's areas. The upper row of Figure 8.3 shows the mean BOLD response phase at similar locations on axial slices of an adult standard brain, while the lower row shows the same on axial slices of an infant standard brain and on a right hemisphere sagittal slice. The colors represent the circular mean of the phase of the BOLD response, expressed in seconds relative to sentence onset. These colors reveal a time gradient in both groups along the length of the superior temporal region and extending to Broca's area. The regions highlighted in blue are in counterphase to the stimulation. The slowest responding region, better synchronized with the end than the start of the sentence, is located in the left inferior frontal region. Dehaene-Lambertz and colleagues interpreted these results as a reflection of the temporal window of integration for processing speech, with the signal processed further away from the primary sensory areas (i.e., Heschl's gyrus) as the time window advances, thereby allowing correspondingly larger "chunks" of spoken language input to be handled over time (Overath et al., 2015). In other words, these results suggest a neurally based hierarchical processing organization consistent with behavioral findings showing that even very young infants are sensitive to different aspects of a sentence's component parts, or its structure. Indeed, adult humans and other animals do not simply associate successive items; they are able to abstract hierarchy from the sequential input by engaging different parts of the cortex as the sentence unfolds (Dehaene et al., 2015).

Critically, the cortex also processes sensory input in an associative manner. For example, when an infant sees an object and hears a word, as long as the visual and auditory input occur close together, they can make the association between the object and the word. This is how words are initially learned and has been documented in infants as young as 6 months of age (Bergelson & Swingley, 2012). In other words, what a child learns initially are largely associative dependencies in the input. Initially, even syntactic structure is learned

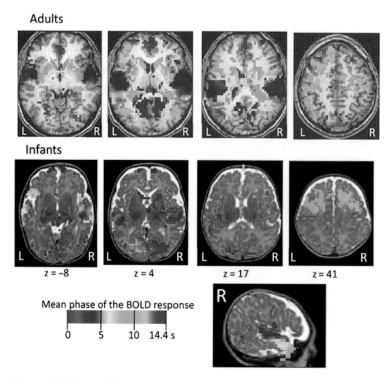

Figure 8.3 Hierarchical organization of language processing in the perisylvian regions in 3-month-old infants and adults as reflected by the mean phase of the BOLD response (reflecting processing time). (Reprinted from Dehaene-Lambertz, 2017)

through association of co-occurring elements. As the infant brain continues to develop and exposure to structured input continues to accrue, the gist of syntactic construction becomes clear, at which point the groundwork has been laid for the comprehension of increasingly complex syntax.

Generally, this model holds across the world's languages: there are rudimentary neural networks in place by the third trimester that are ready for input-based shaping. But relative engagement of different networks depends on which are more or less engaged for processing different languages. For example, we can compare the cortical networks engaged during processing of a case-heavy language (e.g., Russian) to a language with a less synthetic morphology (e.g., English), or to a tonal language (e.g., Chinese). Russian relies on substantial **morphosyntax**, and the brains of Russian speakers have a very dense dorsal fiber tract (Klimovich-Gray et al., 2017). Meanwhile, English is not a strongly **morphosyntactic language**, and it is common to observe a dense ventral fiber tract in English speakers. These languages can be contrasted to Chinese, which as a **tonal language** carries important information via intonation, and is associated with strong connections between the left and the right hemispheres (Ge et al., 2015). In other words, the infant brain begins with what we might think of as a universal language network, agnostic with regard to which language or languages it will be exposed to; its subsequent development is modulated by the language input it receives. Thus, cortical patterns of speech (or sign) processing should be considered in light of the language or languages that shaped them. This also goes a long way towards explaining why learning new languages in adulthood is hard and why some languages are easier to learn than others depending on the structural nuances already made available by the language(s) a person speaks.

8.4 Language Engages the Infant Brain beyond the Language Network

These findings provide insight into how the maturational and functional abilities of the neonate brain interface with the input available from the environment. Moreover, across languages, caregivers exaggerate their speech to infants (Fernald et al., 1989; Fernald & Morikawa, 1993), increasing the pitch of their voice and expanding its range and variability over time while speaking more slowly and using exaggerated prosody called **motherese** (or parentese). Infants quickly come to prefer this over all other acoustic input. Caregivers also repeat themselves. Yes, caregivers repeat themselves. Infants are attracted to this, attend to speech directed at them, and thereby gain experience from the interaction. While the acoustic properties of infant-directed speech appear to underlie its effectiveness in attracting infants' attention, the particular components that drive infants' extended preference are less clear. Infants develop their preference for infant-directed speech postnatally, and are thus not biologically predisposed to exhibit such a preference; our adult propensity to speak motherese appears to be a product of culture, not biology. At birth, infants discriminate between positive and negative emotions (Mastropieri & Turkewitz, 1999) and respond differently to positive and negative emotions as conveyed by tone of voice (Papoušek et al., 1990; Fernald, 1992). Of course, most people are happy when they address infants, so the issues of pitch and affect are tightly intertwined (Kitamura & Burnham, 1998). When affect and pitch are manipulated independently, the (positive) affective properties override the pitch in attracting infants' attention, and they show no preference for infant- over adult-directed speech given a constant (positive) affect (Singh et al., 2002). Since "happy talk" draws infants' attention in a positive way, caregivers (and doting others) are more inclined to manipulate their vocal acoustics to elicit this response. Indeed, and perhaps unsurprisingly, adults rate infants' facial responses to infant-directed speech as more "attractive" than their facial responses to adult-directed speech (Werker & McLeod, 1989). Thus, infants' preference for positive emotion, along with adults' inclination to produce happy talk when speaking to infants, is a critical component of their early preference for infant-directed speech.

In recent years, researchers have linked these behavioral preferences to underlying neural processes. For example, maternally produced infant-directed speech has been shown to increase activity in infants' right frontal cortex, a region important to the development of emotion processing capabilities into adulthood (Naoi et al., 2012), and to improve frontotemporal connectivity more generally (Uchida-Ota et al., 2019). Frontal lobe development is related to positive emotions and positive interactions between mothers and infants (Dawson et al., 1999), and may contribute to the strength of the emotional bond between mother and infant; this in turn may contribute to the strength of bonds between the child and others throughout the lifespan. When cortical activity was assessed while neonates listened to stories read by their mothers in different manners, there was greater frontal lobe activity during the infant-directed than adult-directed portions of the readings (Saito et al., 2007).

In short, the emotional properties of infant-directed speech contribute to positive interactions with caregivers, which in turn provide infants with both emotional and linguistic signals to learn from. With its attention focusing abilities, the maternal voice maximizes neural activity relative to other voices (Purhonen et al., 2004). In an ERP study comparing infants' responses to words produced using infant-directed speech by their mother and by an unfamiliar woman, early auditory components were accelerated in response to the mother's voice and infants were better able to learn those words (Dehaene-Lambertz et al., 2010).

The combination of infants' early exposure to speech and their precocious preference for faces (Chapter 6) – the source of spoken language – helps them to learn the relationship between auditory and visual speech (i.e., the visual information provided by the articulating mouth). Not surprisingly, the language or languages a child is learning in the first year of life influences how they look at a speaker's face. Monolingual English-exposed infants focus their visual attention on an English speaker's eyes at 4 months, her mouth at 8 months, then back to her eyes by 12 months of age (Figure 8.4A). In contrast, when monolingual English-exposed infants view a Spanish speaker, their gaze stays focused predominantly on her mouth at 12 months of age (Lewkowicz & Hansen-Tift, 2012), presumably because they don't recognize the speech and are looking to the mouth for clues to help them parse the input; although you could just as easily imagine they might look at the eyes to understand the emotional intention behind the speech, this is not what they do.

Thus, perceptual tuning for language extends to visual speech. Researchers exposed 4-, 6-, and 8-month-old monolingual English-exposed infants to either English or French faces producing visual speech (i.e., the faces articulating sentences with the sound turned off; Weikum et al., 2007). Results showed that the 4- and 6-month-old, but not 8-month-old, monolingual English-exposed infants detected the difference between English and French from visual cues alone. In other words, the infants were sensitive to these perceptual differences in the first half of the first year of life, much as infants are to non-native speech contrasts. In contrast, English-French-exposed infants *continued* to detect the difference between both the languages at 8 months. Thus, it appears that as the perceptual system becomes more tuned to the native language(s) in the second half of the first year of life, unfamiliar forms become harder to recognize. This loss of sensitivity parallels declines in infants' performance in other perceptual domains, including – as we've discussed – speech sound contrasts, and extends to non-native musical rhythms (Hannon & Trehub, 2005), cross-species individual faces (Pascalis et al., 2005), and cross-species face and voice matching (Lewkowicz & Ghazanfar, 2006). In short, infants selectively retain those perceptual sensitivities that are relevant to their experience and lose sensitivity to those that aren't.

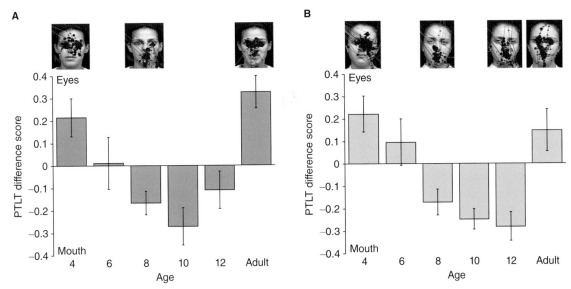

Figure 8.4 Proportion of total looking times (PTLT on x-axis) for different groups of 4- to 12-month-old monolingual English-exposed infants and English-speaking adults when viewing a video of A. an English speaker and B. a Spanish speaker. At 12 months, the infants look longer at the mouth of the Spanish speaker than they do the English speaker. (Reprinted from Lewkowicz & Hansen-Tift, 2012).

The facial motions associated with human speech are impactful. In an influential early study, Kuhl and Meltzoff (1982) observed that when hearing the vowel /a/, 4-month-old infants looked longer at a face articulating /a/ than at a face articulating /i/, demonstrating that they have become sensitive to the particular articulatory gestures required to make different vowel sounds. This finding was later replicated and extended to infants as young as 2 months of age (Patterson & Werker, 1999, 2003). Similarly, 8-month-olds were found to look at a gender-congruent visual display relative to an incongruent one when hearing a gender-specific voice (Patterson & Werker, 2002), demonstrating a sensitivity to pitch and prosody. Five- to 15-month-olds even look longer at a visual speech stream that matches a three syllable non-word with degraded phonetic detail (Baart et al., 2014).

Are infants sensitive to more extended temporal relationships between auditory and visual speech? Lewkowicz and Pons (2013) demonstrated that they are, finding that by between 10 and 12 months of age, infants' representations of speech entail multiple modalities. First, the researchers familiarized infants with either their native (English) or a non-native (Spanish) continuous auditory speech stream. Then the infants were presented with two simultaneous silent videos of a face producing visual speech. In one video, infants saw the face articulating the previously heard string of speech while in the other, they saw a semantically matched version (i.e., a translation) of the same string of speech in the opposite language (the semantic matching makes it more likely that non-linguistic facial expressions would convey the same emotions). Ten- to 12-month-olds looked less at their native visual speech when they were previously familiarized to auditory speech in that language, most likely because they had detected the correspondence between sight and sound and preferred the novel visual speech (i.e., they showed a novelty effect). By the end of the first year, infants appear to have associated the auditory and visual forms of the language they've most been exposed to. A similar study found the same effect in 6-month-olds (Kubicek et al., 2014). Thus, from an early age, infants use multiple sources of information about speech and do so in increasingly complex ways as their experience accrues across the first year of life.

8.4.1 Language Learning Is Contingent Learning

Infants learn language at least in part because they are motivated to interact with others. Kuhl and colleagues (Kuhl et al., 2003) demonstrated this by comparing loss/maintenance of categorical perception in 9-month-old infants learning English. Infants in the experimental group were trained on a Mandarin Chinese contrast that is undetectable by native English speakers. Training took place across 12 sessions, 25 minutes each, over a 4-week period, during which infants interacted with real, live adults; control infants experienced the same play sessions but in English. At the end of the training, the experimental group performed on a discrimination test of that contrast at a level comparable to Mandarin learning infants in Taiwan, while the control group did not. In a second study, the same training sessions took place with a new group of infants, but this time the training was presented by video. As before, half received the training in Mandarin and half in English. Despite showing high engagement with the videos, neither group showed discrimination, highlighting the importance of engaged and **contingent** interaction for language learning to take place.

In other words, language is social, and language learning takes place in responsive social exchanges. If you think this might have implications for the millions of children who are plopped in front of an iPad, you are not alone. Screen time among children has been associated with sleep disorders and in a population study of 718 children, screen time was significantly associated with developmental delay, particularly in the domains of language and communication (Zhu et al., 2020; Varadarajan et al., 2021). Subsequent work has shown that children *can* learn from screens, but only when the interactions are live interactions and thus contingent, as with Zoom, Facetime, and Skype (Roseberry et al., 2014). However, intriguing ERP findings indicate that phonetic learning from a screen can be enhanced when it takes place in the presence of a peer, as opposed to learning alone (Roseberry et al., 2018).

In sum, caregivers elicit speech from their infants and young children by being sensitive to their abilities and responding to their speaking attempts in a supportive and contingent manner. When a child makes a mistake, caregivers either correct it (that's not a *do-o-oo-g*, it's a *ca-a-a-at*) or they indulge the child good naturedly (as when a toddler calls their blanket a *binkie* or their grandma a *gamma* – pretty soon, everyone in the family adopts these words). These kinds of contingencies require actual human interaction on a regular basis. Prime opportunities for language learning occur when adults focus on and talk about things that are relevant to an infant's own attentional focus. Caregivers who provide labels for objects and events when they are the focus of both the caregiver's and the child's attention – **joint attention** – ease the challenge of matching linguistic symbols to their referents and reinforce the social-communicative function of language itself (Tomasello & Farrar, 1986). A child's social-linguistic interaction skills have been shown to influence subsequent development of representational abilities, for example in the language used during play (McCune, 1995; Carpenter et al., 1998; Morales et al., 1998; Delgado et al., 2002; Adamson et al., 2004).

The sensitivity to **contingencies** in the linguistic environment starts early and is important for verbal learning (Chapter 7). In a clever experiment, Michael Goldstein and his colleagues tested the importance of contingency by telling caregivers precisely *when* to respond to infant vocalizations (Goldstein et al., 2003). Half of the infant–caregiver pairs were trained to respond contingently to infants' vocalizations with non-vocal social responses like smiling and touching, while the other half were instructed to respond non-vocally based on the response schedules of the mothers in the contingent group, thus non-contingently. Infants who received social feedback contingent on their vocalizations produced more developmentally advanced vocalizations during the manipulation, as well as after maternal responding was no longer being manipulated, compared to those infants who received feedback independent of when they vocalized. These findings confirm that social interaction is a critical link between early speech perception and subsequent production. Infants who learn the contingency between their own vocalizations and the responses of their caregivers *learn to influence the behavior of social partners*, an important step forward in early communicative development. When caregivers respond contingently to infants' vocalizations with their own speech, infants structure their sounds to match those phonological patterns (e.g., vowel sounds elicit more vowel sounds from infants and words elicit more consonant–vowel combinations) (Goldstein & Schwade, 2008). In more recent work, Goldstein and colleagues (Elmlinger et al., 2019) found that caregivers simplify the statistical and syntactic structure of their speech in response to their infants' babbling: contingent speech contained fewer unique words and contained both shorter utterances and more single-word utterances than non-contingent speech. Infants' immature vocalizations create opportunities for them to learn by eliciting responses from caregivers that contain simplified, more learnable information. Moreover, caregivers who use more linguistically diverse contingent speech with their infants have infants with more advanced vocalizations. Thus, a functional perspective has emerged whereby infant language learning regulates and is regulated by social interactions with adults. This early communication is foundational to the development of complex language going forward.

8.4.2 The Importance of Both Quantity and Quality in Speech Input

Although the social motivation to communicate provides infants with the opportunity for language learning, language exposure is not uniform across all children. In a seminal study, Hart and Risley (1995) demonstrated that the raw number of words children hear varies enormously as a function of a family's **socioeconomic status** (SES), with average income families producing up to double the number of words compared to lower income families. These researchers made the then provocative suggestion that such differences in frequency of exposure might underlie the reliable differences in language outcomes observed as children from these families enter and proceed through formal education. There is now substantial evidence that early differences in both the amount and quality of speech children hear influence their emerging language abilities. The amount of language that children experience before the age of 3 is positively correlated with their language production skills and cognitive development (e.g., Huttenlocher et al., 1991; Bornstein & Haynes, 1998; Huttenlocher, 1998; Shonkoff & Phillips, 2000; Pan et al., 2005; Arterberry et al., 2007). The quality of language exposure, including both linguistic (i.e., vocabulary diversity and sophistication, grammatical complexity, and narrative use (Rowe, 2012)) and interactional features (i.e., contiguous (time-locked), contingent (topically similar), back-and-forth conversation (Hirsh-Pasek et al., 2015)) also matters. Fortunately, caregiver–child conversational turn-taking involves a rich mix of high-quality linguistic, attentional, and social features. Unfortunately, both the quality and quantity of speech input is often mediated by socioeconomic status (Hoff, 2003).

More generally, there is a robust relationship between SES and young children's brain structure and function (for review, see Farah, 2017). But SES covers a great deal – education, access to health care, diet, and parental attention (if both parents are working two jobs, and there are many children in a family, the developing brain may not get as much guided stimulation from adults; Gilkerson et al., 2017). And so, following Galileo Galilei's dictum that we introduced at the beginning of the book, DCN scientists seek to measure this to establish mechanistic knowledge about specific environmental factors associated with specific variation in brain structure. Emerging evidence indicates that children's language environments relate to engagement of prefrontal cortical regions (Sheridan et al., 2012; Garcia-Sierra et al., 2016). Romeo and colleagues (Romeo et al., 2018) demonstrated that greater adult–child conversational experience is related to stronger, more coherent white matter connectivity in the left arcuate and superior longitudinal fasciculi on average, and specifically near the anterior termination at Broca's area in left inferior frontal cortex. Interestingly, these findings were independent of SES and of the sheer quantity of adult speech. Rather, fractional anisotropy measures of tract subregions were found to mediate the relationship between conversational turns and children's language skills, indicating a neuroanatomical mechanism underlying the so-called language gap. In other words, more interaction with adult speakers, rather than simply more words heard, is crucial to children's language abilities.

The left side of Figure 8.5 shows these two left hemisphere white matter tracts. Data plots on the top of the right side of Figure 8.5 show fractional anisotropy in the left arcuate fasciculus and left superior longitudinal fasciculus as a function of the peak number of conversational turns per hour experienced by each participant, while controlling for age, gender, and head motion. The bottom right of Figure 8.5 shows the reconstructed left arcuate fasciculus and left superior longitudinal fasciculus tracts (on the right and the left, respectively) for two participants otherwise matched on age, gender, and SES, but differing in the peak number of conversational turns experienced. Degree of fractional anisotropy is indicated by warmer (higher) to cooler (lower) colors. The individuals are identified by the open black circles imposed on the scatter plots at the top right of Figure 8.5. Whole-brain analyses showed no relationship between language exposure and any other white matter tracts, underscoring the specificity of this relationship. In other words, these results strongly suggest that the development of dorsal language tracts is environmentally influenced and particularly by the quality of early verbal interaction.

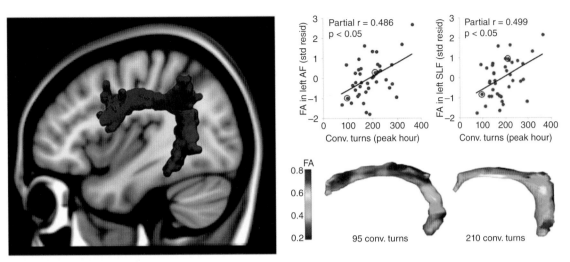

Figure 8.5 Conversational exposure relates to white matter microstructure. The image on the left shows two left hemisphere white matter tracts. The red is the superior longitudinal fasciculus; the blue is the arcuate fasciculus. The scatter plots show fractional anisotropy (FA) in the two tracts (indicated by dot color) as a function of the maximum number of conversational turns per hour experienced by each child in the study (controlling for age/gender/head motion). Below the scatter plots are reconstructions of the two left hemisphere tracts combined for two children matched on age/gender/SES, but differing in number of conversational turns experienced (as indicated by open black circles on scatter plots). Warmer colors represent voxels with higher FA, while cooler colors represent lower FA. (Reprinted from Romeo et al., 2018)

In order to develop normally, starting in infancy, children need to be spoken to and to have such speech evoke reactions based on contingencies. Deprived of this, children don't merely lose language ability – their intellectual, social, and emotional maturation can also be severely stunted. Developmental psychologist Harold Skeels came upon two girls, aged 13 and 17 months, who were housed at the Iowa Soldiers' Orphans' Home in 1934, after being removed from their respective mothers; one mother was an inmate at what was then called an "insane asylum" (what we would now call a psychiatric hospital) and the other mother was a prostitute. In the Orphans' Home they were hardly ever touched, never held, and *only rarely spoken to* (Brookwood, 2021). Skeels put their IQs at 35 and 46, but notes that IQs at that age are unreliable. His qualitative evaluations, and those made by a pediatrician and facility supervisor provided converging evidence of severe mental retardation (Skeels, 1937; Skeels & Dye, 1939). The girls didn't interact with other children or toys in the nursery, showed no interest in standing or walking, and lacked spontaneous vocalization. Skeels arranged for the girls to be transferred to a facility for "feebleminded adults" (what we would now call a facility for adults with special needs) so that they would at least receive minimal care – albeit from women with mental ages of 5–9 years. The women at the facility lavished affection on the girls. Within nine months, Skeels found the two girls transformed, alert and playing like typically developing toddlers. Within 18 months, the girls' IQs had also transformed into the normal range, at 93 and 95. No longer neglected and deprived of contingent language and its social connections, they grew to be adults who got married, had children, and maintained apparently stable, loving households (Wadman, 2021).

Skeels' work captures the big picture of the necessity for early attention and interaction between babies and caregivers for language learning. This is a lesson that we keep learning, as revealed by findings from the Bucharest Early Intervention Project (BEIP) (Chapter 5). As the first and only randomized controlled trial using foster care as an alternative to institutional care for orphaned and abandoned children, the BEIP showed profound cognitive and neural issues in institutionalized children, many of whom go on to develop a range of psychosocial issues in later years (Troller-Renfree et al., 2018). The BEIP screened and selected 136 institutionalized children without preexisting medical conditions, aged between 6 months and 31 months (M = 22 months). Half of the children were then randomly assigned to remain in the institution, and half were assigned to foster care. Across a series of follow-up studies, the negative impact of extended institutionalization on the children – even many years later – was revealed. Negative impacts on the children's language were observed as well, with children placed by the BEIP into foster care by age 2 showing significant advantages in word identification and non-word repetition over those who remained institutionalized (Windsor et al., 2013). As with the Davenport children, those placed by 1.3 years had language skills equivalent to community peers! These findings further highlight the impacts of poor early institutional care on later language development, as well as the critical importance of age of placement into a more optimal environment.

Given how new technologies are transforming the way people interact with each other (often with reduced contingencies), should we be concerned about the influence of digitally based communication on brain and language development? As many have observed first-hand, the average toddler is savvier with digital media than the average septuagenarian. A rising number of toddlers are now put to bed with a tablet instead of a bedtime story. A nationally representative 2013 survey found that children aged 2 years and younger in the United States spent approximately 1 hour per day with screen media, whereas those aged 2–4 years experienced nearly 2 hours per day on average (in the decade since then, screen time has surely increased). If the role of contingent (interactive) language input is crucial to shaping the structural and functional states of the developing brain, what are the consequences for children's acquisition of language and communication? Increased screen-based media use is associated with lower microstructural integrity of the white matter tracts that are critical to language and emergent literacy skills in prekindergarten children (Hutton et al., 2020). Further study is needed, particularly during the rapid early stages of brain development. Traditionally, language learning occurs through face-to-face interaction, accompanied by books or printed or recorded material later during childhood. Digital access to information provides input to infants and children through multiple sensory modalities simultaneously – not just hearing, but vision and touch as well. Is this beneficial, harmful, or neutral with respect to language learning? Are the effects long-lasting or only manifest during early development? What are the long-term consequences of introducing information of a range and on a scale never before experienced by the developing brain? These are just some of the questions researchers entering the field now (perhaps you, dear reader) will grapple with using sophisticated longitudinal designs.

8.4.3   Bilingualism and Multilingualism

If you've tried to learn a second or *n*th language in university, you know how difficult it can be. You need to memorize vocabulary words, learn syntax and different tenses, and learn to understand and pronounce phonemes that may be unfamiliar to you. In all likelihood, even if you continue to study that language for many years, you will speak with an accent. As we've seen, this is a very different way than infants and young children learn, as their brains are literally wiring themselves up to the new sounds, structure, and vocabulary of a language.

For decades, it was thought that learning more than one language would be harmful to the child because they would confuse the languages with one another, or hit a vocabulary limit. After all, if your mental lexicon can only hold a set number of words in total, the argument went, you're dividing it in half (or thirds, or more) and learning fewer words in each language. These capacity limitations are in fact a myth. Much of the early work on this topic was performed by psychologist Wallace Lambert and his colleagues at McGill University in Montreal, a city which is truly bilingual (French and English). Among the first findings was that bilinguals performed significantly better than monolinguals on both verbal and non-verbal intelligence tests (Peal & Lambert, 1962). Several explanations have been suggested as to why bilinguals have this general intellectual advantage. It is argued that they have a language asset, are more agile at concept formation, and have a greater mental flexibility.

In other words, although young children learning two or more languages show smaller vocabulary acquisition in the first couple of years of learning, they gradually catch up to their monolingual peers, and enjoy equal sized vocabularies in the other languages they speak (Genesee, 2009). There is also no evidence that they confuse the languages – their brains create separate lexicons and linguistic stores for the distinct languages. Although many bi- and multilingual speakers engage in "code switching," the linguistic term for inserting words from one language into another, they do so intentionally and deliberately, not by accident (Ramirez & Kuhl, 2017).

In fact, there are no known limits to the number of languages that a person can speak fluently. The *Guinness World Records* lists Ziad Fazah as being able to speak 59 languages. (He himself claims to be fluent in "only" 15 at a time and requires a practice period to get up to speed on the others he knows.) The seventeenth-century poet John Milton could speak English, Latin, French, German, Greek, Hebrew, Italian, Spanish, Aramaic, and Syriac. How's that for neuroplasticity? Or consider the cognitive scientist Douglas Hofstadter, whose hobby is translating poems from one language to another while observing all of the formal and structural constraints of the poetic form. He once took a 500-year-old poem written in Old French and translated it into modern English, Shakespearean English, French, Italian, German, and Russian while preserving the metric features of the original. He even did an English translation in which the first letter of each line spelled out the name of the poem and the poet. Learning languages can be a lifelong pursuit!

8.5   Is Language a "Special" Ability in the Human Toolkit?

The amount of language that most children acquire by age 3 is remarkable. They seem to achieve this through the combined forces of lots of language input, conversational turn-taking (contingencies), and receptive neural tissue. These forces combine with powerful general learning mechanisms and a desire to communicate with others – a desire so strong that many children invent imaginary companions to talk to (Taylor et al., 1993). For phonetic and phonological learning, input is critical. In this chapter, we have seen that infants rely on statistical structure in the signal and distributional properties of the sounds in the language(s) around them to extract relevant phonetic contrasts. The infant brain is sensitive to most phonetic contrasts and continued exposure to them through the language(s) in the environment will maintain and reinforce the ability to make those distinctions while sensitivity to other languages' contrasts declines. Our general auditory abilities have evolved along with our sensitivity to which sounds are easiest to make with our mouth and jaw such that we are able to detect from birth where the boundaries should be placed in most human languages. In other words, perceptual sensitivity to speech categories is part of our evolutionary history, as is loss of these sensitivities if sounds are unused and irrelevant to us.

We have seen how neural data from infants bring new elements to discussions about the origins of language. These studies are still too scarce to add definitive support to current models of adult language processing. Moreover, they are only concerned with spoken languages. Signed languages share many of the same particularities of spoken languages and additional research is needed to understand how hierarchical processing might be relevant to visual language. To discover the principles of the organization of the human brain and how these favor language learning, more and better data on early language processing (whether spoken or signed) are needed, as is the continued use of paradigms that exploit the possibilities that various forms of brain imaging introduce. Finally, examination of the involvement of regions outside the linguistic system, such as the frontal regions, demonstrates that infants' focus on speech as a pertinent stimulus goes well beyond the auditory/linguistic system. Motivation, pleasure, and understanding referential aspects of speech through social cues all have been shown to be important for language learning. In short, language learning is a social process that is best achieved through lots of structured input delivered to a still-plastic brain in an engaged human infant.

8.6   Coda: Why Don't Non-Human Primates Have Language?

One of the main themes of this book is that, although behaviors may seem quite different and discontinuous across species – such as humankind's use of language – brains and genes across species do show a great deal of continuity. Why then do humans have language and other animals, particularly non-human primates, do not?

Although great apes (gorillas, bonobos, orangutans, and chimps) are the living species most closely related to humans, for both ethical and practical reasons, we know much more about the neuroanatomy of other species within the same genus – Old World monkeys – particularly rhesus macaques. Macaques share 93 percent of their DNA with humans, and our common ancestor dates to about 20 million years ago. Their auditory regions are organized in several parallel and hierarchical streams that process different aspects of sounds (Kaas & Hackett, 2000; Tian et al., 2001). The anatomical subdivisions of the brains of humans and macaques are shown side-by-side in Figure 8.6, based on an extensive analysis by Petrides and Pandya (2002). The circled numbers are Brodmann area numbers, which reflect specific regions as identified by the German anatomist Korbinian Brodmann in the early 1900s based on their

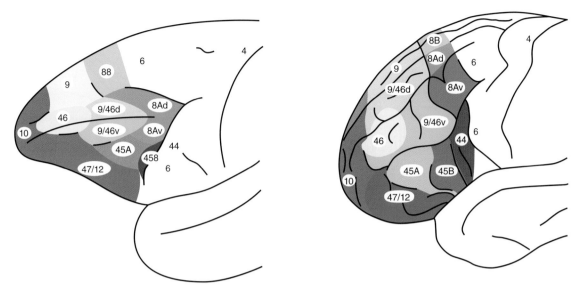

Figure 8.6 View of the frontal portion of the left hemisphere of human (left) and rhesus macaque brains (right).

unique cytoarchitecture (histological structure and cellular organization). The large tongue-shaped structure at the bottom of each brain pictured in Figure 8.6 is the anterior portion of the temporal lobe (the parietal and occipital lobes are not shown). Note the great similarity – each structure found in the human brain is also found in the macaque. The areas of particular interest here are those that subserve three components of what we might call the "linguistic brain": perspective-taking, representation, and rearrangement (for generative grammar). These include the orbital and ventrolateral prefrontal cortex, regions known to be involved in the representation of ideas and the maintenance of them in working memory – those things that you are thinking about at a given moment, whether or not they are in front of you.

Petrides draws attention to the brain region that sits between the representing part of the brain and the orofacial muscle planning part of the brain. In Figure 8.6, this is Area 6, just behind Area 44, part of the premotor cortex, and is involved in moving the lips, jaw, and tongue. Twenty million years is a long time for these brain regions to evolve. It's not too difficult to imagine that a new function would emerge right where these regions meet, gradually enabling the brain to report what it's holding in consciousness – to start talking (or singing, or gesturing) to convey what it is thinking about. Areas 44 and 45 (Broca's area) as well as 47/12 are intimately connected with human speaking and understanding speech, and with playing and understanding music. Why then haven't non-human primates developed speech? Part of the reason is no doubt physiological. Researchers have argued that the higher position of their larynx doesn't give them the fine motor control necessary to produce the variety of speech sounds that give human language its combinatorial power and hence its richness and complexity (Lieberman, 1984; Patel, 2008). Interestingly, in a recent study, Nishimura and colleagues (Nishimura et al., 2022) have provided compelling evidence that the human larynx in fact evolved to have much *simpler* vocal anatomy than that of non-human primates, and that

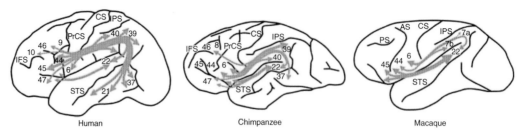

Figure 8.7 The arcuate fasciculus in the human, chimpanzee, and macaque monkey. (Reprinted from Rilling et al., 2008)

it is those simplifications that have provided humans with a stable vocal source. This source, in turn, has served as the foundation for the evolution of human speech (and thus language). By the way, if you're wondering why parrots can make such rich sounds it is because they evolved a completely separate form of vocal organ, the syrinx, that allows them to mimic some of the sounds of human speech (e.g., Larsen & Goller, 2002).

But if the dearth of monkey talk were merely a production limitation, we would expect them at least to learn to recognize speech, or perhaps to communicate with sign language, but researchers have not found this to be the case. There is a *cognitive*, not simply a motor, limitation. Petrides, Pandya, and others have argued that a key difference is not in the gross structure of the brain, but in the fine structure and in its connectivity. The human brain evolved to have more surface area, with far many more folds and convolutions than the macaque brain, making it possible to squeeze millions more neurons into a relatively confined space. Moreover, and partly as a consequence of the greater neural density, human brains have a great deal more connectivity via white matter tracts that carry information bidirectionally. For example, as shown in the schematic left lateral hemisphere views in Figure 8.7, tractographic analyses reveal significant differences in specific white matter tracts across humans, chimpanzees, and macaques, including the arcuate fasciculus, ventral superior longitudinal fasciculus, and medial longitudinal fasciculus. All are more robust and extend farther in humans than in either chimps or macaques. This increase in density and connectivity in the human brain may have added both quantitative and qualitative changes relative to the brains of other, non-human primates. Indeed, higher cognitive operations – such as language and music – may be an emergent property of the complexity of the system. In other words, non-human primates don't have speech because, although the basic architecture is there, the computational power and complexity is not (Levitin, 2008).

More recently, non-primate animal models have gained prominence, particularly those based on songbirds, which have been shown to produce and process complex sound sequences, often in what appears to be a generative fashion. Where non-human primates are not sophisticated vocal learners, songbirds have introduced a non-human model with remarkable vocal complexity and dexterity. Such an approach turns the evolutionary argument on its head, pivoting to evolutionary convergence (i.e., when species have different ancestral origins but have developed similar features) from evolutionary divergence (i.e., when two separate species evolve differently from a common ancestor). Whether or not avian (and other) models will move the non-human animal models of vocal learning beyond word-level processing and into higher-order language, they have diversified the field and broadened the debate (Jarvis, 2019). A recent study found that song learning in the zebra finch is affected by non-vocal, visual feedback from females! Similar to our discussion of infants in Section 8.4.1, young male songbirds given feedback contingent on their immature songs developed higher-quality songs than yoked control birds (Carouso-Peck & Goldstein, 2019). You can count on this line of research to continue.

SUMMARY

- Spoken language consists of several levels of structure: phonetics, phonology, morphology, syntax, semantics, and pragmatics
- Processing spoken and sign languages engage similar brain regions
- The Classic Model of language processing has been replaced by a dual-stream architecture consisting of ventral and dorsal components
- The ventral stream performs acoustic–phonetic analysis and form-to-meaning mapping
- The dorsal stream performs sensorimotor control for sequential analysis
- A complex structural and functional architecture is in place and reacts to the external world from the last trimester of human gestation
- Perceptual tuning to the native language(s) is both maturation- and experience-dependent
- Language is processed in both hemispheres of the brain, with fast temporal cues processed predominantly in the left hemisphere and slower spectral cues processed bilaterally
- Language learning is aided by contingent interaction with caregivers
- Both the quantity and the quality of language input to infants and young children influence their emerging language abilities
- Digital technology is transforming the way people interact with one another and with machines
- The human language processing network has precursors in other animals, particular non-human primates

REVIEW QUESTIONS

How do instances of language deprivation inform the longstanding debate about a child's biological capacities to acquire language?

What is the difference between the Classic Model of language processing and dual-route models?

How do spectral and temporal cues in the speech signal differentially contribute to its structure?

How would you argue that animal communication differs from human language? How is it similar?

What evidence is there to suggest a neurological basis for a critical period?

What evidence is there that infant-directed speech is helpful for language acquisition?

What evidence is there that babies' babbling is influenced by the language they hear?

Explain what it means to have categorical perception.

What evidence do we have that infants have categorical perception? What evidence do we have that non-humans have categorical perception?

Is there evidence that the quantity of language input varies by socioeconomic status (SES)? What about the quality?

Further Reading

Christiansen, M. H., & Chater, N. (2022). *The Language Game: How Improvisation Created Language and Changed the World*. Basic Books.

Dehaene-Lambertz, G., & Spelke, E. (2015). The infancy of the human brain. *Neuron*, 88(1), 93–109. https://doi.org/10.1016/j.neuron.2015.09.026

Friederici, A. D. (2018). The neural basis for human syntax: Broca's area and beyond. *Current Opinion in Behavioral Sciences*, 21, 88–92. https://doi.org/10.1016/j.cobeha.2018.03.004

Rauschecker, J. P. (2018). Where did language come from? Precursor mechanisms in nonhuman primates. *Current Opinion in Behavioral Sciences*, 21, 195–204. https://doi.org/10.1016/j.cobeha.2018.06.003

References

Adamson, L. B., Bakeman, R., & Deckner, D. F. (2004). The development of symbol-infused joint engagement. *Child Development*, 75(4), 1171–1187. https://doi.org/10.1111/j.1467-8624.2004.00732.x

Anderson, J. L., Morgan, J. L., & White, K. S. (2003). A statistical basis for speech sound discrimination. *Language and Speech*, 46(2–3), 155–182. https://doi.org/10.1177/00238309030460020601

Arterberry, M. E., Cain, K. M., & Chopko, S. A. (2007). Collaborative problem solving in five-year-old children: Evidence of social facilitation and social loafing. *Educational Psychology*, 27(5), 577–596. https://doi.org/10.1080/01443410701308755

Baart, M., Stekelenburg, J. J., & Vroomen, J. (2014). Electrophysiological evidence for speech-specific audiovisual integration. *Neuropsychologia*, 53(1), 115–121. https://doi.org/10.1016/j.neuropsychologia.2013.11.011

Bergelson, E., & Swingley, D. (2012). At 6-9 months, human infants know the meanings of many common nouns. Proceedings of the National Academy of Sciences of the United States of America, 109(9), 3253–3258. https://doi.org/10.1073/pnas.1113380109

Bertoncini, J., & Mehler, J. (1981). Syllables as units in infant speech perception. *Infant Behavior and Development*, 4(3), 247–260. https://doi.org/10.1016S0163-6383(81)80027-6

Bornstein, M. H., & Haynes, M. (1998). Vocabulary competence in early childhood: Measurement, latent construct, and predictive validity. *Child Development*, 69(3), 654–671. https://doi.org/10.2307/1132196

Brookwood, M. (2021). *The orphans of Davenport*. Liveright Publishing.

Butterfield, E. C., & Siperstein, G. N. (1972). Influence of contingent auditory stimulation upon non-nutritional suckle. In J. Bosma (Ed.), *Oral Sensation and Perception: The Mouth of the Infant* (pp. 313–334). C. C. Thomas.

Byers-Heinlein, K., Burns, T. C., & Werker, J. F. (2010). The roots of bilingualism in newborns. *Psychological Science*, 21(3), 343–348. https://doi.org/10.1177/0956797609360758

Carouso-Peck, S., & Goldstein, M. H. (2019). Female social feedback reveals non-imitative mechanisms of vocal learning in zebra finches. *Current Biology*, 29(4), R125–R127. https://doi.org/10.1016/j.cub.2018.12.026

Carpenter, M., Akhtar, N., & Tomasello, M. (1998). Fourteen- through 18-month-old infants differentially imitate intentional and accidental actions. *Infant Behavior and Development*, 21(2), 315–330. https://doi.org/10.1016/S0163-6383(98)90009-1

Chomsky, N. (1965). *Aspects of the theory of syntax*. MIT Press.

Chomsky, N. (1966). *Cartesian linguistics: A chapter in the history of rationalist thought*. Harper & Row. Third edition revised and edited with an introduction by J. McGilvray (2009). Cambridge University Press.

Christophe, A., Dupoux, E., Bertoncini, J., & Mehler, J. (1994). Do infants perceive word boundaries? An empirical study of the bootstrapping of lexical acquisition. *Journal of the Acoustical Society of America*, 95(3). https://doi.org/10.1121/1.408544

Colombo, J., & Bundy, R. S. (1981). A method for the measurement of infant auditory selectivity. *Infant Behavior and Development*, 4, 219–223. https://doi.org/10.1016/S0163-6383(81)80025-2

Dawson, G., Frey, K., Panagiotides, H., Yamada, E., Hessl, D., & Osterling, J. (1999). Infants of depressed mothers exhibit atypical frontal electrical brain activity during interactions with mother and with a familiar, nondepressed adult. *Child Development*, 70(5). https://doi.org/10.1111/1467-8624.00078

DeCasper, A. J., & Fifer, W. P. (1980). Of human bonding: Newborns prefer their mothers' voices. *Science*, 208(4448), 1174–1176. https://doi.org/10.1126/science.7375928

DeCasper, A. J., Lecanuet, J., Busnel, M. C., Granier-Deferre, C., & Maugeais, R.(1994). Fetal reactions to recurrent maternal speech. *Infant Behavior and Development*, 17(2), 159–164. https://doi.org/10.1016/0163-6383(94)90051-5

DeCasper, A. J., & Spence, M. J. (1986). Prenatal maternal speech influences newborns' perception of speech sounds. *Infant Behavior and Development*, 9(2), 133–150. https://doi.org/10.1016/0163-6383(86)90025-1

Dehaene, S., Cohen, L., Morais, J., & Kolinsky, R. (2015). Illiterate to literate: Behavioral and cerebral changes induced by reading acquisition. *Nature Reviews Neuroscience*, 16(4), 234–244. https://doi.org/10.1038/nrn3924

Dehaene-Lambertz, G. (2017). The human infant brain: A neural architecture able to learn language. *Psychonomic Bulletin and Review*, 24(1), 48–55. https://doi.org/10.3758/s13423-016-1156-9

Dehaene-Lambertz, G., Dehaene, S., Anton, J. L., Campagne, A., Ciuciu, P., Dehaene, G. P., Denghien, I., Jobert, A., LeBihan, D., Sigman, M., Pallier, C., & Poline, J. B. (2006). Functional segregation of cortical language areas by sentence repetition. *Human Brain Mapping*, 27(5), 360–371. https://doi.org/10.1002/hbm.20250

Dehaene-Lambertz, G., Dehaene, S., & Hertz-Pannier, L. (2002). Functional neuroimaging of speech perception in infants. *Science*, 298(5600), 2013–2015. https://doi.org/10.1126/science.1077066

Dehaene-Lambertz, G., Hertz-Pannier, L., & Dubois, J. (2006). Nature and nurture in language acquisition: Anatomical and functional brain-imaging studies in infants. *Trends in Neurosciences*, 29(7), 367–373. https://doi.org/10.1016/j.tins.2006.05.011

Dehaene-Lambertz, G., Montavont, A., Jobert, A., Allirol, L., Dubois, J., Hertz-Pannier, L., & Dehaene, S. (2010). Language or music, mother or Mozart? Structural and environmental influences on infants' language networks. *Brain and Language*, 114(2), 53–65. https://doi.org/10.1016/j.bandl.2009.09.003

Delgado, C. E. F., Mundy, P., Crowson, M., Markus, J., Yale, M., & Schwartz, H. (2002). Responding to joint attention and language development. *Journal of Speech, Language, and Hearing Research*, 45(4), 715–719. https://doi.org/10.1044/1092-4388(2002/057)

Eimas, P. D., Siqueland, E. R., Jusczyk, P., & Vigorito, J. (1971). Speech perception in infants. *Science*, 171(3968), 303–306. https://doi.org/10.1126/science.171.3968.303

Elmlinger, S. L., Schwade, J. A., & Goldstein, M. H. (2019). The ecology of prelinguistic vocal learning: Parents simplify the structure of their speech in response to babbling. *Journal of Child Language*, 46(5), 998–1011. https://doi.org/10.1017/S0305000919000291

Emmorey, K. (2021). New perspectives on the neurobiology of sign languages. *Frontiers in Communication*, 6, 748430. https://doi.org/10.3389/fcomm.2021.748430

Farah, M. J. (2017). The neuroscience of socioeconomic status: Correlates, causes, and consequences. *Neuron*, 96(1), 56–71. https://doi.org/10.1016/j.neuron.2017.08.034

Fernald, A. (1992). Human maternal vocalizations to infants as biologically relevant signals: An evolutionary perspective. In J. H. Barkow, L. Cosmides, & J. Tooby (Eds.), *The adapted mind: Evolutionary psychology and the generation of culture* (pp. 391–428). Oxford University Press.

Fernald, A., & Morikawa, H. (1993). Common themes and cultural variations in Japanese and American mothers' speech to infants. *Child Development*, 64(3), 637–656. https://doi.org/10.2307/1131208

Fernald, A., Taeschner, T., Dunn, J., Papousek, M., De Boysson-Bardies, B., & Fukui, I. (1989). A cross-language study of prosodic modifications in mothers' and fathers' speech to preverbal infants. *Journal of Child Language*, 16(3), 477–501. https://doi.org/10.1017/S0305000900010679

Friederici, A. D., Chomsky, N., Berwick, R. C., Moro, A., & Bolhuis, J. J. (2017). Language, mind and brain. *Nature Human Behaviour*, 1(10), 713–722. https://doi.org/10.1038/s41562-017-0184-4

Garcia-Sierra, A., Ramírez-Esparza, N., & Kuhl, P. K. (2016). Relationships between quantity of language input and brain responses in bilingual and monolingual infants. *International Journal of Psychophysiology*, 110, 1–17. https://doi.org/10.1016/j.ijpsycho.2016.10.004

Ge, J., Peng, G., Lyu, B., Wang, Y., Zhuo, Y., Niu, Z., Tan, L. H., Leff, A. P., & Gao, J. H. (2015). Cross-language differences in the brain network subserving intelligible speech. *Proceedings of the National Academy of Sciences of the United States of America*, 112(10), 2972–2977. https://doi.org/10.1073/pnas.1416000112

Genesee, F. (2009). Early childhood bilingualism: Perils and possibilities. *Journal of Applied Research on Learning*, 2(2), 1–21.

Geschwind, N. (1965). Disconnexion syndromes in animals and man. I. *Brain*, 88(2), 237–294, https://doi.org/10.1093/brain/88.2.237

Geschwind, N. (1970). The organization of language and the brain. *Science*, 170(3961), 940–944. https://doi.org/10.1126/science.170.3961.940

Gilkerson, J., Richards, J. A., Warren, S. F., Montgomery, J. K., Greenwood, C. R., Oller, D. K., Hansen, J. H. L., & Paul, T. D. (2017). Mapping the early language environment using all-day recordings and automated analysis. *American Journal of Speech-Language Pathology*, 26(2), 248–265. https://doi.org/10.1044/2016_AJSLP-15-0169

Goldstein, M. H., King, A. P., & West, M. J. (2003). Social interaction shapes babbling: Testing parallels between birdsong and speech. *Proceedings of the National Academy of Sciences of the United States of America*, 100(13), 8030–8035. https://doi.org/10.1073/pnas.1332441100

Goldstein, M. H., & Schwade, J. A. (2008). Social feedback to infants' babbling facilitates rapid phonological learning. *Psychological Science*, 19(5), 515–523. https://doi.org/10.1111/j.1467-9280.2008.02117

Hagoort, P. (2016). MUC (memory, unification, control): A model on the neurobiology of language: Beyond single word processing In G. Hickok, & S. Small (Eds.), *Neurobiology of language* (pp. 339–347). Elsevier. https://doi.org/10.1016/B978-0-12-407794-2.00028-6

Hall, W. C., Li, D., & Dye, T. D. V. (2018). Influence of hearing loss on child behavioral and home experiences. *American Journal of Public Health*, 108(8), 1079–1081. https://doi.org/10.2105/AJPH.2018.304498

Hannon, E. E., & Trehub, S. E. (2005). Tuning in to musical rhythms: Infants learn more readily than adults. *Proceedings of the National Academy of Sciences of the United States of America*, 102(35), 12639–12643. https://doi.org/10.1073/pnas.0504254102

Hart, B., & Risley, T. R. (1995). *Meaningful differences in the everyday experience of young American children*. Paul H. Brookes Publishing.

Hepper, P. G., & Shahidullah, S. (1994). Development of fetal hearing. *Archives of Disease in Childhood*, 71(2), F81–F87. https://doi.org/10.1136/fn.71.2.f81

Hickok, G., Bellugi, U., & Klima, E. S. (1996). The neurobiology of sign language and its implications for the neural basis of language. *Nature*, 381(6584), 699–702. https://doi.org/10.1038/381699a0

Hickok, G., & Poeppel, D. (2007). The cortical organization of speech processing. *Nature Reviews Neuroscience*, 8(5), 393–402. https://doi.org/10.1038/nrn2113

Hirsh-Pasek, K., Adamson, L. B., Bakeman, R., Owen, M. T., Golinkoff, R. M., Pace, A., Yust, P. K. S., & Suma, K. (2015). The contribution of early communication quality to low-income children's language success. *Psychological Science*, 26(7), 1071–1083. https://doi.org/10.1177/0956797615581493

Hoff, E. (2003). The specificity of environmental influence: Socioeconomic status affects early vocabulary development via maternal speech. *Child Development*, 74(5), 1368–1378. https://doi.org/10.1111/1467-8624.00612

Huttenlocher, J. (1998). Language input and language growth. *Preventive Medicine*, 27(2), 195–199. https://doi.org/10.1006/pmed.1998.0301

Huttenlocher, J., Haight, W., Bryk, A., Seltzer, M., & Lyons, T. (1991). Early vocabulary growth: Relation to language input and gender. *Developmental Psychology*, 27(2), 236–248. https://doi.org/10.1037/0012-1649.27.2.236

Hutton, J. S., Dudley, J., Horowitz-Kraus, T., Dewitt, T., & Holland, S. K. (2020). Associations between screen-based media use and brain white matter integrity in preschool-aged children. *JAMA Pediatrics*, 174(1). https://doi.org/10.1001/jamapediatrics.2019.3869

Jarvis, E. D. (2019). Evolution of vocal learning and spoken language. *Science*, 363(6461), 50–54. https://doi.org/10.1126/science.aax0287

Johansen-Berg, H, (2001). Music to your baby's ears. *Trends in Cognitive Sciences*, 5(9), 377. https://doi.org/10.1016/S1364-6613(00)01761-7

Kaas, J. H., & Hackett, T. A. (2000). Subdivisions of auditory cortex and processing streams in primates. *Proceedings of the National Academy of Sciences of the United States of America*, 97(22), 11793–11799. https://doi.org/10.1073/pnas.97.22.11793

Kisilevsky, B. S., Hains, S. M. J., Jacquet, A. Y., Granier-Deferre, C., & Lecanuet, J. P. (2004). Maturation of fetal responses to music. *Developmental Science*, 7(5), 550–559. https://doi.org/10.1111/j.1467-7687.2004.00379.x

Kitamura, C., & Burnham, D. (1998). Acoustic and affective qualities of IDS in English. Fifth International Conference on Spoken Language Processing, paper 0909.

Klimovich-Gray, A., Bozic, M., & Marslen-Wilson, W. D. (2017). Domain-specific and domain-general processing in left perisylvian cortex: Evidence from Russian. *Journal of Cognitive Neuroscience*, 29(2), 382–397. https://doi.org/10.1162/jocn_a_01047

Kubicek, C., De Boisferon, A. H., Dupierrix, E., Pascalis, O., Loevenbruck, H., Gervain, J., & Schwarzer, G. (2014). Cross-modal matching of audio-visual German and French fluent speech in infancy. *PLoS One*, 9(2). https://doi.org/10.1371/journal.pone.0089275

Kuhl, P. K. (1986). Theoretical contributions of tests on animals to the special-mechanisms debate in speech. *Experimental Biology*, 45(3), 233–265.

Kuhl, P. K., Conboy, B., Padden, D., Nelson, T., & Pruitt, J. (2005). Early speech perception and later language development: Implications for the "critical period." *Language Learning and Development*, 1(3–4), 237–264. https://doi.org/10.1080/15475441.2005.9671948

Kuhl, P. K., & Meltzoff, A. N. (1982). The bimodal perception of speech in infancy. *Science*, 218(4577), 1138–1141. https://doi.org/10.1126/science.7146899

Kuhl, P. K., & Miller, J. D. (1975). Speech perception by the chinchilla: Voiced-voiceless distinction in alveolar plosive consonants. *Science*, 190(4209), 69–72. https://doi.org/10.1126/science.1166301

Kuhl, P. K., & Padden, D. M. (1983). Enhanced discriminability at the phonetic boundaries for the place feature in macaques. *Journal of the Acoustical Society of America*, 73(3), 1003–1010. https://doi.org/10.1121/1.389148

Kuhl, P. K., Ramírez, R. R., Bosseler, A., Lin, J. F. L., & Imada, T. (2014). Infants' brain responses to speech suggest analysis by synthesis. *Proceedings of the National Academy of Sciences of the United States of America*, 111(31), 11238–11245. https://doi.org/10.1073/pnas.1410963111

Kuhl, P. K., Stevens, E., Hayashi, A., Deguchi, T., Kiritani, S., & Iverson, P. (2006). Infants show a facilitation effect for native language phonetic perception between 6 and 12 months. *Developmental Science*, 9(2), F13–F21. https://doi.org/10.1111/j.1467-7687.2006.00468.x

Kuhl, P. K., Tsao, F. M., & Liu, H. M. (2003). Foreign-language experience in infancy: Effects of short-term exposure and social interaction on phonetic learning. *Proceedings of the National Academy of Sciences of the United States of America*, 100(15), 9096–9101. https://doi.org/10.1073/pnas.1532872100

Kuhl, P. K., Williams, K. A., Lacerda, F., Stevens, K. N., & Lindblom, B. (1992). Linguistic experience alters phonetic perception in infants by 6 months of age. *Science*, 255(5044), 606–608. https://doi.org/10.1126/science.1736364

Larsen, O. N., & Goller, F. (2002). Direct observation of syringeal muscle function in songbirds and a parrot. *Journal of Experimental Biology*, 205(1), 25–35. https://doi.org/10.1242/jeb.205.1.25

Lecanuet, J. P., & Schaal, B. (1996). Fetal sensory competencies. *European Journal of Obstetrics and Gynecology and Reproductive Biology*, 68(1–2), 1–23. https://doi.org/10.1016/0301-2115(96)02509-2

Levitin, D. J. (2008). *The world in six songs: How the musical brain created human nature*. Penguin-Random House.

Lewkowicz, D. J., & Ghazanfar, A. A. (2006). The decline of cross-species intersensory perception in human infants. *Proceedings of the National Academy of Sciences of the United States of America*, 103(17), 6771–6774. https://doi.org/10.1073/pnas.0602027103

Lewkowicz, D. J., & Hansen-Tift, A. M. (2012). Infants deploy selective attention to the mouth of a talking face when learning speech. *Proceedings of the National Academy of Sciences of the United States of America*, 109(5), 1431–1436. https://doi.org/10.1073/pnas.1114783109

Lewkowicz, D. J., & Pons, F. (2013). Recognition of amodal language identity emerges in infancy. *International Journal of Behavioral Development*, 37(2), 90–94. https://doi.org/10.1177/0165025412467582

Lichtheim, L. (1885). On aphasia. *Brain*, 7, 433–485.

Lieberman, P. (1984). *The biology and evolution of language*. Harvard University Press.

López-Barroso, D., & De Diego-Balaguer, R. (2017). Language learning variability within the dorsal and ventral streams as a cue for compensatory mechanisms in aphasia recovery. *Frontiers in Human Neuroscience*, 11. https://doi.org/10.3389/fnhum.2017.00476

Lordier, L., Meskaldji, D. E., Grouiller, F., Pittet, M. P., Vollenweider, A., Vasung, L., Borradori-Tolsa, C., Lazeyras, F., Grandjean, D., De Ville, D. Van, & Hüppi, P. S. (2019). Music in premature infants enhances high-level cognitive brain networks. *Proceedings of the National Academy of Sciences of the United States of America*, 116(24), 12103–12108. https://doi.org/10.1073/pnas.1817536116

Mastropieri, D., & Turkewitz, G. (1999). Prenatal experience and neonatal responsiveness to vocal expressions of emotion. *Developmental Psychobiology*, 35(3), 204–214. https://doi.org/10.1002/(sici)1098-2302(199911)35:3<204::aid-dev5>3.0.co;2-v

Matthews, L. G., Walsh, B. H., Knutsen, C., Neil, J. J., Smyser, C. D., Rogers, C. E., & Inder, T. E. (2018). Brain growth in the NICU: Critical periods of tissue-specific expansion. *Pediatric Research*, 83(5), 976–981. https://doi.org/10.1038/pr.2018.4

McCune, L. (1995). A normative study of representational play at the transition to language. *Developmental Psychology*, 31(2), 198–206. https://doi.org/10.1037/0012-1649.31.2.198

McMurray, B., & Aslin, R. N. (2005). Infants are sensitive to within-category variation in speech perception. *Cognition*, 95(2), B15–B26. https://doi.org/10.1016/j.cognition.2004.07.005

Mehler, J., Jusczyk, P., Lambertz, G., Halsted, N., Bertoncini, J., & Amiel-Tison, C. (1988). A precursor of language acquisition in young infants. *Cognition*, 29(2), 143–178. https://doi.org/10.1016/0010-0277(88)90035-2

Miller, J. L., & Eimas, P. D. (1996). Internal structure of voicing categories in early infancy. *Perception and Psychophysics*, 58(8). 1157–1167. https://doi.org/10.3758/bf03207549

Moon, C., Cooper, R. P., & Fifer, W. P. (1993). Two-day-olds prefer their native language. *Infant Behavior and Development*, 16(4), 495–500. https://doi.org/10.1016/0163-6383(93)80007-U

Morales, M., Mundy, P., & Rojas, J. (1998). Following the direction of gaze and language development in 6-month-olds. *Infant Behavior and Development*, 21(2), 373–377. https://doi.org/10.1016/S0163-6383(98)90014-5

Morokuma, S., Fukushima, K., Kawai, N., Tomonaga, M., Satoh, S., & Nakano, H. (2004). Fetal habit-uation correlates with functional brain development. *Behavioural Brain Research*, 153(2), 459–463. https://doi.org/10.1016/j.bbr.2004.01.002

Naoi, N., Minagawa-Kawai, Y., Kobayashi, A., Takeuchi, K., Nakamura, K., Yamamoto, J. I., & Kojima, S. (2012). Cerebral responses to infant-directed speech and the effect of talker familiarity. *NeuroImage*, 59(2), 1735–1744. https://doi.org/10.1016/j.neuroimage.2011.07.093

Narayan, C. R., Werker, J. F., & Beddor, P. S. (2010). The interaction between acoustic salience and language experience in developmental speech perception: Evidence from nasal place discrimination. *Developmental Science*, 13(3), 407–420. https://doi.org/10.1111/j.1467-7687.2009.00898.x

Nishimura, T., Tokuda, I. T., Miyachi, S., Dunn, J. C., Herbst, C. T., Ishimura, K., Kaneko, A., Kinoshita, Y., Koda, H., Saers, J. P. P., Imai, H., Matsuda, T., Larsen, O. N., Jürgens, U., Hirabayashi, H., Kojima, S., & Fitch, W. T. (2022). Evolutionary loss of complexity in human vocal anatomy as an adaptation for speech. *Science*, 377(6607), 760–763. https://doi.org/10.1126/science.abm1574

Overath, T., McDermott, J. H., Zarate, J. M., & Poeppel, D. (2015). The cortical analysis of speech-specific temporal structure revealed by responses to sound quilts. *Nature Neuroscience*, 18(6), 903–911. https://doi.org/10.1038/nn.4021

Pan, B. A., Rowe, M. L., Singer, J. D., & Snow, C. E. (2005). Maternal correlates of growth in tod-dler vocabulary production in low-income families. *Child Development*, 76(4), 763–782. https://doi.org/10.1111/j.1467-8624.2005.00876.x

Papoušek, M., Bornstein, M. H., Nuzzo, C., Papoušek, H., & Symmes, D. (1990). Infant responses to prototypical melodic contours in parental speech. *Infant Behavior and Development*, 13(4), 539–545. https://doi.org/10.1016/0163-6383(90)90022-Z

Pascalis, O., Scott, L. S., Kelly, D. J., Shannon, R. W., Nicholson, E., Coleman, M., & Nelson, C. A. (2005). Plasticity of face processing in infancy. *Proceedings of the National Academy of Sciences of the United States of America*, 102(14), 5297–5300. https://doi.org/10.1073/pnas.0406627102

Patel, A. D. (2008). Science & music: Talk of the tone. *Nature*, 453(7196), 726–727. https://doi.org/10.1038/453726a

Patterson, M. L., & Werker, J. F. (1999). Matching phonetic information in lips and voice is robust in 4.5-month-old infants. *Infant Behavior and Development*, 22(2), 237–247. https://doi.org/10.1016/S0163-6383(99)00003-X

Patterson, M. L., & Werker, J. F. (2002). Infants' ability to match dynamic phonetic and gender infor-mation in the face and voice. *Journal of Experimental Child Psychology*, 81(1), 93–115. https://doi.org/10.1006/jecp.2001.2644

Patterson, M. L., & Werker, J. F. (2003). Two-month-old infants match phonetic information in lips and voice. *Developmental Science*, 6(2), 191–196. https://doi.org/10.1111/1467-7687.00271

Peal, E., & Lambert, W. E. (1962). The relation of bilingualism to intelligence. *Psychological Monographs: General and Applied*, 76(27), 1–23. https://doi.org/10.1037/h0093840

Petrides, M., & Pandya, D. N. (2002). Comparative cytoarchitectonic analysis of the human and the macaque ventrolateral prefrontal cortex and corticocortical connection patterns in the monkey. *European Journal of Neuroscience*, 16(2), 291–310. https://doi.org/10.1046/j.1460-9568.2001.02090.x

Poeppel, D. (2014). The neuroanatomic and neurophysiological infrastructure for speech and language. *Current Opinion in Neurobiology*, 28, 142–149. https://doi.org/10.1016/j.conb.2014.07.005

Poeppel, D., Emmorey, K., Hickok, G., & Pylkkänen, L. (2012). Towards a new neurobiology of language. *Journal of Neuroscience*, 32(41), 14125–14131. https://doi.org/10.1523/JNEUROSCI.3244-12.2012

Poeppel, D., & Hickok, G. (2004). Towards a new functional anatomy of language. *Cognition*, 92(1–2), 1–12. https://doi.org/10.1016/j.cognition.2003.11.001

Polka, L., Colantonio, C., & Sundara, M. (2001). A cross-language comparison of /d /–/th/ perception: Evidence for a new developmental pattern. *The Journal of the Acoustical Society of America*, 109(5), 2190–2201. https://doi.org/10.1121/1.1362689

Polka, L., & Werker, J. F. (1994). Developmental changes in perception of nonnative vowel contrasts. *Journal of Experimental Psychology: Human Perception and Performance*, 20(2), 421–435. https://doi.org/10.1037/0096-1523.20.2.421

Purhonen, M., Kilpeläinen-Lees, R., Valkonen-Korhonen, M., Karhu, J., & Lehtonen, J. (2004). Cerebral processing of mother's voice compared to unfamiliar voice in 4-month-old infants. *International Journal of Psychophysiology*, 52(3), 257–266. https://doi.org/10.1016/j.ijpsycho.2003.11.003

Ramirez, N. F., & Kuhl, P. (2017). The brain science of bilingualism. *Young Children*, 72(2), 38–44.

Ramus, F., Nespor, M., & Mehler, J. (2000). Correlates of linguistic rhythm in the speech signal. *Cognition*, 75(1), 265–292. https://doi.org/10.1016/s0010-0277(00)00101-3

Rilling, J. K., Glasser, M. F., Preuss, T. M., Ma, X., Zhao, T., Hu, X., & Behrens, T. E. J. (2008). The evolution of the arcuate fasciculus revealed with comparative DTI. *Nature Neuroscience*, 11(4), 426–428. https://doi.org/10.1038/nn2072

Rivera-Gaxiola, M., Silva-Pereyra, J., & Kuhl, P. K. (2005). Brain potentials to native and non-native speech contrasts in 7- and 11-month-old American infants. *Developmental Science*, 8(2), 162–172. https://doi.org/10.1111/j.1467-7687.2005.00403.x

Romeo, R. R., Segaran, J., Leonard, J. A., Robinson, S. T., West, M. R., Mackey, A. P., Yendiki, A., Rowe, M. L., & Gabrieli, J. D. E. (2018). Language exposure relates to structural neural connectivity in childhood. *Journal of Neuroscience*, 38(36), 7870–7877. https://doi.org/10.1523/JNEUROSCI.0484-18.2018

Roseberry, S., Hirsh-Pasek, K., & Golinkoff, R. M. (2014). Skype me! Socially contingent interactions help toddlers learn language. *Child Development*, 85(3), 956–970. https://doi.org/10.1111/cdev.12166

Roseberry Lytle, S., Garcia-Sierra, A., & Kuhl, P. K. (2018). Two are better than one: Infant language learning from video improves in the presence of peers. *Proceedings of the National Academy of Sciences of the United States of America*, 115, 9859–9866. https://doi.org/10.1073/pnas.1611621115

Rowe, M. L. (2012). A longitudinal investigation of the role of quantity and quality of child-directed speech vocabulary development. *Child Development*, 83(5), 1762–1774. https://doi.org/10.1111/j.1467-8624.2012.01805.x

Saffran, J. R., Werker, J. F., & Werner, L. A. (2006). The infant's auditory world: Hearing, speech, and the beginnings of language. In D. Kuhn, R. S. Siegler, W. Damon, & R. M. Lerner (Eds.), *Handbook of child psychology: Cognition, perception, and language* (pp. 58–108). John Wiley & Sons. https://doi.org/10.1002/9780470147658.chpsy0202

Saito, Y., Aoyama, S., Kondo, T., Fukumoto, R., Konishi, N., Nakamura, K., Kobayashi, M., & Toshima, T. (2007). Frontal cerebral blood flow change associated with infant-directed speech. *Archives of Disease in Childhood: Fetal and Neonatal Edition*, 92(2). https://doi.org/10.1136/adc.2006.097949

Samples, J. M., & Franklin, B. (1978). Behavioral responses in 7 to 9 month old infants to speech and non-speech stimuli. *The Journal of Auditory Research*, 18(2), 115–123.

Shatz, M. (1978). On the development of communicative understandings: An early strategy for interpreting and responding to messages. *Cognitive Psychology*, 10(3) 271–301. https://doi.org/10.1016/0010-0285(78)90001-4

Sheridan, M. A., Sarsour, K., Jutte, D., D'Esposito, M., & Boyce, W. T. (2012). The impact of social disparity on prefrontal function in childhood. *PLoS One*, 7(4). https://doi.org/10.1371/journal.pone.0035744

Shi, R., Werker, J. F., & Morgan, J. L. (1999). Newborn infants' sensitivity to perceptual cues to lexical and grammatical words. *Cognition*, 72(2), B11–B21. https://doi.org/10.1016/S0010-0277(99)00047-5

Shonkoff, J. P., & Phillips, D. A. (Eds.). (2000). *From neurons to neighborhoods: The science of early childhood development*. National Academies Press.

Simpson, K. L., Weaver, K. J., De Villers-Sidani, E., Lu, J. Y. F., Cai, Z., Pang, Y., Rodriguez-Porcel, F., Paul, I. A., Merzenich, M., & Lin, R. C. S. (2011). Perinatal antidepressant exposure alters cortical network function in rodents. *Proceedings of the National Academy of Sciences of the United States of America*, 108(45), 18465–18470. https://doi.org/10.1073/pnas.1109353108

Singh, L., Morgan, J. L., & Best, C. T. (2002). Infants' listening preferences: Baby talk or happy talk? *Infancy: The Official Journal of the International Society on Infant Studies*, 3(3), 365–394. https://doi.org/10.1207/S15327078IN0303_5

Skeels, H. M. (1937). A cooperative orphanage research. *The Journal of Educational Research*, 30(6), 437–444. https://doi.org/10.1080/00220671.1937.10880686

Skeels, H. M., & Dye, H. B. (1939). A study of the effects of differential stimulation on mentally retarded children. *Proceedings of the American Association on Mental Deficiency*, 44(1), 114–136.

Smith, E. C., & Lewicki, M. S. (2006). Efficient auditory coding. *Nature*, 439(7079), 978–982. https://doi.org/10.1038/nature04485

Spence, M. J., & DeCasper, A. J. (1987). Prenatal experience with low-frequency maternal-voice sounds influence neonatal perception of maternal voice samples. *Infant Behavior and Development*, 10(2), 133–142. https://doi.org/10.1016/0163-6383(87)90028-2

Taylor, M., Cartwright, B. S., & Carlson, S. M. (1993). A developmental investigation of children's imaginary companions. *Developmental Psychology*, 29(2), 276–285. https://doi.org/10.1037/0012-1649.29.2.276

Tian, B., Reser, D., Durham, A., Kustov, A., & Rauschecker, J. P. (2001). Functional specialization in rhesus monkey auditory cortex. *Science*, 292(5515), 290–293. https://doi.org/10.1126/science.1058911

Tomasello, M., & Farrar, M. J. (1986). Joint attention and early language. *Child Development*, 57(6), 1454–1463. https://doi.org/10.1111/j.1467-8624.1986.tb00470.x

Trehub, S. E. (1976). The discrimination of foreign speech contrasts by infants and adults. *Child Development*, 47(2), 466–472. https://doi.org/10.2307/1128803

Tremblay, P., & Dick, A. S. (2016). Broca and Wernicke are dead, or moving past the classic model of language neurobiology. *Brain and Language*, 162, 60–71. https://doi.org/10.1016/j.bandl.2016.08.004

Troller-Renfree, S., Zeanah, C. H., Nelson, C. A., & Fox, N. A. (2018). Neural and cognitive factors influencing the emergence of psychopathology: Insights from the Bucharest Early Intervention Project. *Child Development Perspectives*, 12(1), 28–33. https://doi.org/10.1111/cdep.12251

Uchida-Ota, M., Arimitsu, T., Tsuzuki, D., Dan, I., Ikeda, K., Takahashi, T., & Minagawa, Y. (2019). Maternal speech shapes the cerebral frontotemporal network in neonates: A hemodynamic functional connectivity study. *Developmental Cognitive Neuroscience*, 39. https://doi.org/10.1016/j.dcn.2019.100701

Varadarajan, S., Govindarajan Venguidesvarane, A., Ramaswamy, K. N., Rajamohan, M., Krupa, M., & Winfred Christadoss, S. B. (2021). Prevalence of excessive screen time and its association with developmental delay in children aged < 5 years: A population-based cross-sectional study in India. *Plos One*, 16(7), e0254102. https://doi.org/10.1371/journal.pone.0254102

Vouloumanos, A., & Werker, J. F. (2007). Listening to language at birth: Evidence for a bias for speech in neonates. *Developmental Science*, 10(2), 159–164. https://doi.org/10.1111/j.1467-7687.2007.00549.x

Wadman, M. (2021). The nature (and nurture) of IQ. *Science*, 373(6554), 498. https://doi.org/10.1126/science.abj6806

Weikum, W. M., Oberlander, T. F., Hensch, T. K., & Werker, J. F. (2012). Prenatal exposure to antidepressants and depressed maternal mood alter trajectory of infant speech perception. *Proceedings of the National Academy of Sciences of the United States of America*, 109(2), 17221–17227. https://doi.org/10.1073/pnas.1121263109

Weikum, W. M., Vouloumanos, A., Navarra, J., Soto-Faraco, S., Sebastián-Gallés, N., & Werker, J. F. (2007). Visual language discrimination in infancy. *Science*, 316(5828), 1159. https://doi.org/10.1126/science.1137686

Werker, J. F, Gilbert, J. H., Humphrey, K., & Tees, R. C. (1981). Developmental aspects of cross-language speech perception. *Child Development*, 52(1), 349–355. https://doi.org/10.2307/1129249

Werker, J. F., & McLeod, P. J. (1989). Infant preference for both male and female infant-directed talk: A developmental study of attentional and affective responsiveness. *Canadian Journal of Psychology*, 43(2), 230–246. https://doi.org/10.1037/h0084224

Werker, J. F., & Tees, R. C. (1984). Cross-language speech perception: Evidence for perceptual reorganization during the first year of life. *Infant Behavior and Development*, 25(1), 121–133. https://doi.org/10.1016/S0163-6383(02)00093-0

Windsor, J., Moraru, A., Nelson, C. A., Fox, N. A., & Zeanah, C. H. (2013). Effect of foster care on language learning at eight years: Findings from the Bucharest Early Intervention Project. *Journal of Child Language*, 40(3), 605–627. https://doi.org/10.1017/S0305000912000177

Zhu, R., Fang, H., Chen, M., Hu, X., Cao, Y., Yang, F., & Xia, K. (2020). Screen time and sleep disorder in preschool children: Identifying the safe threshold in a digital world. *Public Health*, 186, 204–210. https://doi.org/10.1016/j.puhe.2020.07.028

Zilles, K., & Amunts, K. (2018). Cytoarchitectonic and receptorarchitectonic organization in Broca's region and surrounding cortex. *Current Opinion in Behavioral Sciences*, 21, 93–105. https://doi.org/10.1016/j.cobeha.2018.02.011

Zilles, K., Palomero-Gallagher, N., & Amunts, K. (2015). Cytoarchitecture and maps of the human cerebral cortex. *Brain Mapping: An Encyclopedic Reference*, 3, 115–135. https://doi.org/10.1016/B978-0-12-397025-1.00207-4

9 Memory Systems

LEARNING OBJECTIVES

- Classify memory into explicit and implicit memory systems, and provide evidence that they are dissociable
- Within each of these systems, describe different kinds of memory and how they are tested
- Identify the brain systems implicated in different types of memory
- Summarize studies elucidating the types of memory even young infants display
- Describe the overall functions of the hippocampal-dependent memory system
- Provide arguments as to whether or not episodic memory is a uniquely human capacity, and when it emerges in childhood
- Outline what is, and is not, known about infantile amnesia and Highly Superior Autobiographical Memory
- Distinguish between externally and internally guided episodic memory
- Discuss the functions of the hippocampus
- Explain how changing interactions between the medial temporal lobes and other brain systems support episodic memory development

The study of memory development has been stymied by the fact that memory's earliest appearance – in preverbal infants – is near impossible to measure, certainly much more so than it is for older children and adults. In spite of the challenges, intrepid researchers have established a strong foundational understanding of what infants can and cannot remember. Cognitive psychology and neuroscience studies in adult humans and animal models have led to tremendous advances in our understanding of adult memory systems, and this work has served as a scaffold for understanding how these systems emerge in infants and young children. Given the paucity of experiences with which we enter the world, infants must begin life by building knowledge structures; here, genetics provides guidance in building relevant structures and constraints on the emerging neural architecture. As a result, the processes that support early learning are qualitatively different from those that support learning in a mature brain. Nonetheless, these processes are foundational for all subsequent learning. How does memory get started?

In this chapter, we first present a detailed argument for why memory is the foundation for learning. We then outline the different memory systems that have been identified over many years of research, including the neural basis for these distinct systems. We provide a detailed examination of episodic memory, including a review of evidence that it is not unique to humans. Our delineation of the neural basis for the formation of episodic memory serves as an entry point into examining other forms of memory, how they develop, and the role of different neural structures in the developmental process. We follow with an extended discussion of the structural and functional development of the medial temporal lobes and their interaction with other neural structures. Finally, we examine how executive functions and prefrontal cortex play a critical role in memory and its development.

9.1   Memory as the Foundation for Learning

Memory provides the foundation for learning throughout the lifespan. It guides our decisions as we reflect on past experiences and weigh our options: Did this turn out badly for me last time or did it turn out well? Memory is also the basis of our sense of who we are. Without your memory, you don't know what kind of childhood you had; you don't know what subjects in school you're good at and which need extra work; you don't know your favorite flavor of ice cream. That would be a lot of responsibility for any single system! In fact, what we think of as this monolithic cognitive capacity is now understood to be several biologically and cognitively distinct systems, all working together to support mental functioning: systems that may have had independent evolutionary origins as they reacted to different adaptive pressures. The identification of multiple memory systems is arguably the most important discovery in neuroscience in the past century.

Only some of what we experience gets remembered in any practical sense; indeed, one of the evolutionary functions of memory is to abstract out regularities from the world. That is, if we explicitly remembered every sensation, thought, and desire we ever experienced, pulling out a particular memory when we need it would be difficult. It is because we abstract out regularities in the world, a process called **generalization**, that we can treat similar objects as functionally equivalent. If you failed to generalize – as some children with Autism Spectrum Disorder do – you would be taken aback every time you went to a restaurant and were given a fork that doesn't look like the one you have at home.

The dual pressures of needing to remember specific events and also generalize across experiences to establish a knowledge base is one of the core issues in research on memory development. Memory research in adults has provided a strong foundation on which a new century of scientific pursuit can build our understanding of the ontogenetic emergence of memory systems.

It is helpful to remember that, as with other cognitive processes, memory wasn't designed: it evolved as an adaptation to problems in the environment. The different components of memory are not put in place all at once, either phylogenetically or ontogenetically. In fact, their emergence and maturation within individuals develops in a manner that looks somewhat piecemeal. The neuroanatomical substrates of these memory systems are already in place in the womb, as the fetus learns to remember the sound of its mother's heartbeat and the voices and music that it hears through the amniotic fluid – 1-year-olds respond preferentially to those sounds they heard *in utero*, indicating that they remember them. These substrates undergo massive growth and restructuring between infancy and adolescence, as the key brain regions and the pathways that connect them mature. With these neuroanatomical systems in place, experiences can shape the neural connections that form lasting memories.

9.2   Memory Systems

Human memory did not follow a neat evolutionary plan to get where it is. Evolution happened (and continues to happen) in fits and starts, and in response to a range of environmental challenges and pressures. Because different subcomponents of the larger system likely followed separate evolutionary trajectories as they adapted to different problems in the environment, we developed memory subsystems (Gabrieli, 1998).

9.2.1   Memory Classification

Memory systems, depicted in Figure 9.1, differ in multiple ways. They are governed by different principles, store different kinds of information, are influenced by different variables, and are mediated by different neural circuits. Some create richer and more complex memories and are less prevalent across the animal kingdom than others. These forms of memory are typically categorized on the basis of how they are expressed and how long they can persist. Some memory systems can lay down enduring traces – memories that can last for hours, days, years, or even a lifetime (**long-term memory**); others are more contextually dependent and fade quickly, but support goal-directed behavior in the moment – in particular, **short-term** or **working memory**, which we cover in Chapter 10. Even shorter term is **sensory memory** that typically lasts no more than 20 seconds or so, such as the visual "afterimage" that lingers in your brain if there is no subsequent interference. You may have experienced this when looking at a brightly lit object and then closing your eyes: the object appears to be projected on a screen in your mind's eye. Auditory and tactile sensory memory have been documented; due to the nature of the chemical senses – taste and smell – they are less prone to creating sensory memories, although if you've ever had a bad taste in your mouth, or smell in your nose, you may have experienced an "afterimage" in those domains.

Importantly, memory systems do not operate in isolation; several of them may be operating in parallel at any given moment, laying down different kinds of memory traces in response to the same event. Additionally, these systems interact: sometimes they support each other, and sometimes they interfere with one another. That interference is a major cause of forgetting.

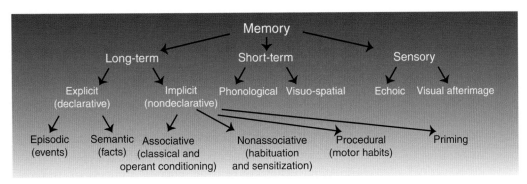

Figure 9.1 Memory can be subdivided into a number of subsystems. This chapter focuses on key forms of long-term memory; Chapter 10 focuses on short-term memory.

Long-term memory systems are commonly distinguished on the basis of whether we have conscious access to them, which determines how they can be tested. **Explicit memory** contains conscious **recollection** of one's own experiences and of facts about the world. This form of memory is often referred to as "**declarative memory**," because tests of explicit memory typically involve verbal recall – in other words, we can declare what we have learned. However, this term confuses the issue with young children who cannot yet speak but who may or may not already have conscious memories; in those cases, we prefer the more general term *explicit memory*. By contrast, **implicit memory** refers to memory that is expressed via changes in behavioral performance. It is also called "**non-declarative memory**" because it is harder to explain, for example, how to walk than it is to just do it.

We study explicit memory using a variety of paradigms. In **recall memory** tasks, we ask you, as a study participant, to tell us explicitly (usually verbally, but sometimes through drawing, singing, or using sign language) what you remember. An example might be to recall the events of your last birthday party, or a set of words the experimenter has presented to you. These types of tasks tap into declarative memory. We can also test **recognition memory** by giving you a list of choices and having you select the one that matches your memory or one that just feels familiar. Which type of memory do you think you are using with short-answer questions, and which type with multiple-choice? Which one taxes your declarative memory more? Short-answer tests use recall memory because you are not given the information explicitly. Multiple-choice tests use recognition memory because you need to recognize the correct answer from among alternatives or distractors. In general, recall memory taxes memory more heavily, because you're starting your memory search from scratch rather than being cued with the answer among several competing choices (the ability to suppress distractors, a form of executive functioning, is covered in Chapter 10).

Two key forms of explicit, or so-called declarative, memory are **semantic memory** and **episodic memory**. Semantic memory refers to the body of general knowledge that we amass over our lifetimes, such as facts about the world or even just the meanings of words. This form of memory is generally impersonal and relatively objective. By contrast, episodic memory consists of your subjective memories for specific events. Such memories are mental simulations that can endure for days or years or even decades; for example, you may remember not only what you did yesterday morning, but also bits of what you did on your tenth birthday. Episodic memory forms the basis for semantic memory, in that we learn new facts or concepts on the basis of singular experiences, but semantic memories are stripped of details about the original experiences that led to the acquisition of this knowledge. Because episodic memory is the most extensively studied form of long-term memory in humans, including children, it will receive disproportionate attention in this chapter.

To make this clearer, knowing that the capital of France in Paris is an example of a semantic memory – it's just something you know, along with the capitals of other countries, and you probably don't remember the particular time and place you learned it. If you remember your first kiss, on the other hand (a salient experience in your life), you are probably remembering the specific time and place where you were (and hopefully, the person you were with). That is an example of an episodic memory: you are remembering that particular episode in your life. One of us was recently explaining the difference between semantic and episodic memory to friends over dinner and their 10-year-old son, Felix, piped in and said, "But I *do* know the time and place I learned it: we learned it today in school!" So, for Felix, it was an episodic memory – and now will probably remain so since we made such a fuss over it. This illustrates an important principle in psychology that has a parallel in quantum physics: that the act of observing or measuring something can actually alter its course. As researchers, we need to be mindful of this.

To study implicit memory, we use tasks that elicit behavioral responses that you yourself might not even be aware of – such as if you've formed an association between an event and an unpleasant outcome. **Conditioning** is an umbrella term for some forms of implicit memory, including simple associations between events, actions, and/or outcomes. These forms of learning are found across many animal species; in humans, they constitute a dominant form of memory during infancy (as we shall see in Section 9.4.1). One well-studied form of conditioning is **classical conditioning**, whereby a stimulus comes to be associated with a specific outcome, which over time results in an involuntary response to that stimulus. The most famous example of classical conditioning is that of Pavlov's dogs, who learned to associate the sound of a bell with food, and thus began to salivate when they heard the bell (the so-called unconditioned stimulus) – even in the absence of food (the so-called conditioned stimulus). (They could also associate food to other inputs, such as the sound of the opening of a dog food container).

A less pleasant form of classical conditioning is the *learned fear response*: for example, a rat will freeze if it hears a specific sound that it had previously heard right before receiving an electric shock. This involuntary response is generally extinguished over time if the events stop co-occurring. However, rodents who experienced adverse early life experiences show slower *extinction* (Callaghan & Richardson, 2012), and fear learning circuitry tends to mature more rapidly in children who experience early trauma (Gee et al., 2013; see Chapter 5).

Operant conditioning or operant learning, which is subtly different from classical conditioning, describes how the prior outcomes of one's behavior shape future behavior. Positive outcomes reinforce the expression of the behavior (a phenomenon also called reinforcement learning) and negative ones diminish it. One vivid example of reinforcement learning is of a rat who learns to press a bar repeatedly to receive a dose of an addictive drug, or even dopamine served up by its own mesolimbic reward system (Olds & Milner, 1954). This type of paradigm has taught us a lot about the brain systems that underlie reinforcement learning, and has become an animal model of addiction.

Another form of implicit memory, **procedural memory**, refers to the largely unconscious knowledge we have about how to *do* things. This includes the learning of motor skills: our memory for the complex set of coordinated muscle movements necessary for walking or writing by hand or swimming. The behavior seems almost automatic, and you aren't entirely aware of what it is you learned to do. In fact, such procedural knowledge is best not thought about at all. When reflected upon, the procedural steps that were linked together as a fluid series of connected motions suddenly stop feeling so fluid! This type of memory, which people often describe as "muscle memory" can persist for a long period; as the old saying goes, "You never forget how to ride a bike" (but you can get rusty if you go without practice for too long).

9.2.2 The Neural Basis of Distinct Memory Systems

For much of the last century, memory was considered a unitary construct. That began to change in the early 1950s, thanks to research on patients with injuries to different parts of the brain (Squire, 2009). A key turning point came when Brenda Milner began studying two of the neurosurgeon Wilder Penfield's patients who had undergone surgeries as a treatment for intractable epilepsy, resulting

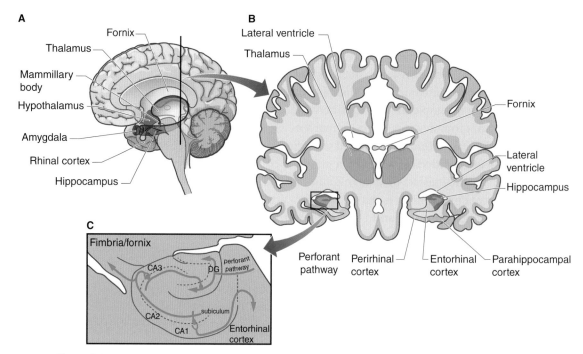

Figure 9.2 Neuroanatomy of the medial temporal lobes. A. A side view of the hippocampus, a structure located deep inside the brain and lateral to the midline. B. A frontal view of the different structures of the medial temporal lobes, based on a cross-section taken at the location of the vertical line in panel A. C. A close-up view of the substructures of the hippocampus and the flow of information therein, as well as the fiber pathways that project into and out of it. (*Cognitive Neuroscience*, Banich & Compton. © 2018 Cambridge University Press. Reproduced with permission of the Licensor through PLSclear)

in removal of one of the **medial temporal lobes**, including the hippocampus, shown in Figure 9.2. Unexpectedly, these patients suffered profound memory loss, becoming densely **amnesic** after the surgeries. Based on this research, Milner had the opportunity to work with another neurosurgeon, William Scoville, who had noticed similar problems with a patient of his. This now-famous patient, H.M. (Henry Molaison, 1926–2008), had had bilateral resection of the medial temporal lobes, and his memory problems were even more severe than those of the other patients. He experienced a loss of memory for events from the years leading up to the surgery, which is called **retrograde amnesia**, as well as an inability to form new explicit memories: a profound **anterograde amnesia**.

We gained tremendous insights into memory systems and their neural underpinnings thanks to extensive neuropsychological research on H.M. (who participated in research for over 50 years, but throughout that period could never remember that he had participated before!) In subsequent research with other patients, the hippocampus and surrounding cortex in the medial temporal lobes came to be understood as critical for the acquisition and recollection of explicit memories (Squire, 1994). Faraneh Vargha-Khadem's research on children who had suffered insults to the medial temporal lobes (as a result of hypoxia–ischemia) reinforces this conclusion (Vargha-Khadem et al., 2003).

Importantly, behaviors that H.M. was not impaired on were ultimately as illuminating as those for which he *was* impaired. Milner taught him a new skill, "mirror-drawing," wherein he had to learn to trace an image that he viewed only through a mirror. Mirror-drawing is of questionable utility, granted, but it was something that he was unlikely to have had any prior experience with. This was important, because he could not report on what he did and didn't already know how to do. After practicing mirror-drawing across ten trials, H.M. got better at it – and three days later, he exhibited good retention of this new skill. Critically, his skill level was far better than it had been at the outset. Yet, stunningly, *H.M. had no conscious recollection of the prior experience of having practiced this skill*, even though a memory trace evidently resided in his motor system! At the time, this striking dissociation between forms of memory was interpreted merely as demonstrating that H.M. was not impaired on a special class of tasks: ones involving motor skills. In subsequent years, however, researchers identified other types of tasks that patients with this form of amnesia are not impaired at, referring to them collectively as forms of non-declarative or implicit memory.

Evolutionarily ancient brain structures have been implicated in implicit memory – that is, classical and operant conditioning and procedural memory. Due to space limitations, we do not go into detail on the neural basis of these forms of memory. In brief, Figure 9.3A shows structures of the **basal ganglia**, which are implicated in both conditioning and procedural memory. Figure 9.3B highlights the **cerebellum**, a distinctive structure involved in rapidly coordinating reflexive responses – that is, behavioral responses associated with conditioning.

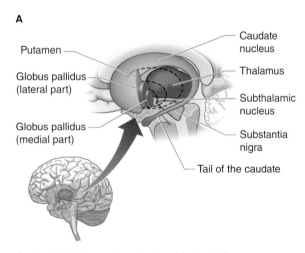

A

Putamen

Globus pallidus (lateral part)

Globus pallidus (medial part)

Caudate nucleus

Thalamus

Subthalamic nucleus

Substantia nigra

Tail of the caudate

Figure 9.3 Brain regions involved in implicit memory. A. The basal ganglia, a group of nuclei deep in the brain that includes the caudate, putamen, and globus pallidus, is critically involved in conditioning and procedural memory. B. The cerebellum, a distinctive structure at the base of the brain, is critical for conditioning. (*Cognitive Neuroscience*, Banich & Compton. © 2018 Cambridge University Press. Reproduced with permission of the Licensor through PLSclear)

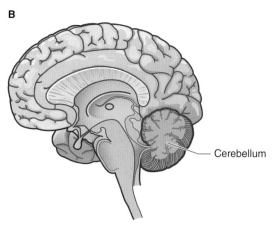

Figure 9.3 (cont.)

Although it is being updated over time, the distinction between explicit and implicit memory revealed by neuropsychological research is still a useful framework. Here, we first probe more deeply into the so-called declarative, or explicit, memory system, focusing on episodic memory and its neural underpinnings. We then return to implicit memory in Section 9.4.1, in the context of infant learning mechanisms.

9.3   Episodic Memory

Episodic memory has captured the imagination of researchers for decades. Endel Tulving (Tulving, 1985) vividly described this ability as "**mental time travel**": a capacity that allows us to reexperience past events, situated in time and space – and also to envision future ones (Suddendorf & Corballis, 1997).

9.3.1   Features of Episodic Memory

As powerful as it is, episodic memory is actually surprisingly fallible: We forget most events – and what we do remember is often inaccurate. This is not always a bad thing, as many memories lose their utility after some time. Imagine if you remembered every place you ever parked your car or bicycle. That could produce a great deal of interference! After all, the only thing you want to know at the end of the day is where you left your car or bike that day. Strikingly, there are a few cases of individuals who exhibit little or no forgetting. One of the most famous cases in the neuropsychological literature is that of a Russian patient known only by his initial S, who saw the physician A. R. Luria (Luria, 1968). Instead of forgetting too much, he remembered too much. His memory capacity was seemingly limitless. This condition, now called **Highly Superior Autobiographical Memory**, is extremely rare: only around 60 cases have been identified in recent years. People with it can recall with exquisite detail everything that happened to them on any date you give them, even if it was a perfectly ordinary day.

You might think that having exceptional memory is a superpower, but it has its drawbacks. One woman with this condition, Rebecca Sharrock, complains that her mind is cluttered; even worse, her vivid recall of negative events from her childhood is emotionally painful, and she suffers from insomnia because her mind races at night. You can hear an interview with her in a podcast called "A Grey Matter" (Queensland Brain Institute, 2021).

We don't yet know much about the neural differences that underlie this fascinating and rare condition (Mazzoni et al., 2019); however, the fact that it can be debilitating suggests that forgetting is adaptive and important for learning (Alberini & Travaglia, 2017). Having said this, most of us have the opposite problem of altogether *too much* forgetting! Well-documented approaches for improving our memory include healthy habits like getting regular exercise and good sleep. Additionally, it is possible to boost one's capacity for memorization by learning mnemonic strategies, such as the "method of loci" developed by the Romans, which is used to great effect by memory champions (Foer, 2012). Practical advice for everyday remembering, offered by memory researchers, is to externalize your memory as much as possible by using calendars and reminders.

Our memories are also fallible in the sense that they are not accurate recordings of our experiences; rather, they often seem like a puzzle with missing pieces that we have to fill in, integrating incoming information with our preexisting knowledge about the world – that is, semantic memory. The renowned developmental psychologist Piaget (Piaget, 1928) noted that new information must be assimilated into existing knowledge frames, and that knowledge has to be updated often in order to adapt to the changing demands of the environment. As critical as it is that we do this filling-in, however, it can lead to mistakes and misrecollection: these additions and distortions often insinuate themselves, becoming part of our "memory." In fact, each time we retrieve a memory, we may pull it up with any additional information we have acquired over the years. Added to the fact that we likely forget some of the initially encoded details, our memories of an event may be radically different from their original form, and the act of remembering itself may pull them farther and farther away from the truth, as we recontextualize (often unconsciously) what happened.

Thus, the **constructive** nature of initial memory formation, and the **reconstructive** nature of memory retrieval, mean that our memories are not as accurate as we'd like to believe. The fact that episodic memory is dynamic (Moscovitch et al., 2016) may make it seem like a fundamentally flawed system, but it is adaptive to keep updating our memories in light of new knowledge we obtain, the cornerstone of Bayesian inferencing (Chapter 6). Daniel Schacter (Addis & Schacter, 2012) refers to these as adaptive constructive processes, arguing that they play a functional role in cognitive processing by allowing past information to be used flexibly in future planning, albeit at the cost of distortions and outright mistakes. A memory process that takes the good with the bad in this way is, at least in part, a product of the multiple systems at work in support of memory.

9.3.2 Is Episodic Memory a Uniquely Human Capacity?

The question of whether humans are the only species that form these richly detailed memories has been heavily debated. After all, "it seems implausible that animals could possess the kind

Figure 9.4 Experiments probing birds' memories related to food caching. A Western scrub jay hiding a delectable treat, wax worms, in one of the wells in a tray. (Reprinted from Clayton et al., 2003)

of autobiographical memory that humans take for granted" (Clayton et al., 2003, p. 685). However, it is difficult to ask a non-human participant – or a preverbal infant, as we shall soon see – what they remember, since they cannot speak. Rather, we need to resort to clever experiments that use indirect measures, such as the improvement in completion times that H.M. exhibited in the mirror-drawing task, in the absence of the ability to say to Brenda Milner, "Hey! I think I'm getting better at this!"

Nicola Clayton designed and carried out a series of clever experiments that take advantage of the way in which Western scrub jays, a species in the crow family (Corvids), hide (or "cache") and recover their food. It is well known that they have excellent memory for the location of their cached foods: the *"where."* Clayton also showed that these birds can also remember the *"what"* and *"when"* of their food storage (Figure 9.4). For example, the birds will locate and dig up their preferred food, wax worms, before digging up peanuts. However, if they are not given access to the food tray for many days, at which point the worms would surely have decayed, the birds go straight for the peanuts. Critically, the birds only switch over to looking for peanuts in this way if they have had the opportunity to learn that wax worms are perishable. In other words, they remember where they hid each type of food, when they hid it, and the fact that their preferred food is perishable!

Consistent with Tulving's description of mental time travel, scrub jays also plan ahead: if another bird watched them cache the food, they will wait until they are alone and re-cache it in a new location, and later retrieve it from the new spot. These behaviors demonstrate what looks a whole lot like episodic memory. Anticipating the inevitable backlash from the human memory community, Clayton referred to the birds' behavior as episodic-*like* memory. Similar paradigms to those used in Corvids have been used in young children, showing that they can recall the what-where-when of episodes at younger ages than would be suggested by standard episodic memory tasks (Jelbert & Clayton, 2017).

9.3.3   The Medial Temporal Lobes

The medial temporal lobes – and, in particular, the **hippocampus** – have been the primary focus of memory research since the early days of neuropsychological research on H.M. and other amnesic patients, and subsequently in laboratory animals. The hippocampus is an intricate structure with a distinctive, seahorse-like shape – so much so that its name is derived from the

Greek word for seahorse. In primates, the portion of the hippocampus near the base of the temporal lobe is broader than the top. Due to the three-dimensional curvature of this structure, two-dimensional sections can be misleading, such that images of the hippocampus may appear as a number of different shapes, depending on the angle and location of the cut. Thus, it is helpful to see it in its three-dimensional form before looking at the component parts shown in Figure 9.2A.

The subdivisions and connections of the hippocampus are highly conserved across the evolution of mammalian species. As a result, animal research has greatly advanced our understanding of the mechanisms by which the hippocampus encodes, consolidates, and retrieves event memories and their details. Many of these findings have yielded important insights that continue to guide research on memory development. For example, electrophysiological research in rats has revealed "neural replay" of events during sleep that supports the consolidation of recent experiences into long-term memories (Chen & Wilson, 2017). As we will discuss in Section 9.4.1, sleep-dependent memory consolidation plays an important role in learning, from infancy through adulthood. Countless other studies have provided insights into hippocampal memory mechanisms, only a few of which we will be able to discuss here.

After years of research and debate, it is now well established that the hippocampus plays a critical role in both encoding and retrieving episodic memories. Likewise, the hippocampus is important for the retrieval of distant memories, as well as ones encoded moments earlier, and is therefore not specific to long-term memory. Finally, while the hippocampus clearly plays a role in explicit memory, it is also involved in conveying the sort of relational knowledge required for implicit memory. For example, we now know that amnesic patients with hippocampal damage can be impaired on implicit tests that tax immediate memory for *relations* between elements of a scene, as their spontaneous eye gaze patterns reveal their failure to register a change in the scene (Hannula et al., 2007). (As we discuss at several points in the book, *where* a participant – even an infant – looks can reveal what they remember.) Thus, Neal Cohen and Howard Eichenbaum have argued that what best characterizes hippocampal-dependent memory is not that it is a form of declarative, or even long-term, memory, but rather that it involves relations among elements of an episode – that is, **relational binding** (Cohen et al., 1997).

At encoding, the hippocampus binds together the different elements of a unique experience – such as the sights and sounds and smells you encountered the first time you explored a marketplace in an unfamiliar country. It does so by coordinating neural activity across all the brain regions that processed the event, laying down a multimodal memory trace via mechanisms of Hebbian plasticity (see Chapter 5.2.3). At retrieval, the hippocampus facilitates the *reactivation* of these associated elements in such a way that we reexperience the diverse elements of the event. This memory can be triggered by a simple cue: if you catch a whiff of a pungent spice, your old memory of the marketplace might come flooding back. A number of leading memory researchers concur that "at encoding the hippocampus obligatorily binds together into a memory trace or **engram** ... those neural elements in the medial temporal lobe and neocortex that give rise to the multimodal, multidomain representations that constitute the content of a conscious experience" (Moscovitch et al., 2016, p. 107).

The term *engram*, introduced by Richard Semon in 1904, has been co-opted in recent years to refer to the cellular connections that underlie memory associations (Josselyn & Tonegawa,

2020). Astonishing methodological advances have enabled researchers to locate engrams within the rodent brain – and not only that, but to reactivate the memories later (Tonegawa et al., 2015)! Incredibly, memory engram technology, described in Box 9.1, has been shown to recover forgotten memories even from as far back as infancy. As we shall see in Section 9.5.2, this line of research is advancing our understanding of memory development by leaps and bounds.

Box 9.1 Labeling and Reactivating Memory Engrams

As we saw in Section 9.5.2, the rapid hippocampal neurogenesis and sprouting of new connections that takes place in infancy seems to contribute to the loss of early memories. Does it destroy these engrams, or are they still in the brain somewhere: intact but inaccessible? In fact, memory engram technology (described below) has yielded evidence that previously lost memories can be recovered. For example, Liu et al. (2012) induced the artificial recall of specific memories in mice in the absence of sensory retrieval cues. This was achieved by directly stimulating the labeled memory engram cells using optogenetics. Specifically, these researchers first subjected mice to contextual fear conditioning, which involves the formation of a contextual engram (primarily in the hippocampus) and its association with a "fear" engram (partly in the amygdala). Mice then normally display conditioned freezing behavior when exposed to the conditioning context. But in this novel experimental paradigm, the engram cells in the dentate gyrus of the hippocampus were labeled with Channelrhodopsin-2 (ChR2), which allows for the activation of these cells with blue light. Stimulating these engram cells in awake and freely moving animals resulted in the specific retrieval of the contextual memories that were associated with fear, resulting in freezing behavior due to artificial memory recall.

Building on this line of research, others have adapted engram labeling technology for experimentation with infant mice. Infant mice can form contextual fear memories, and it is well established they lose these memories as they transition into late infancy. Guskjolen and colleagues tagged engram cells during mouse infancy (postnatal day 17), and then waited for the subjects to develop into adulthood (Guskjolen et al., 2018). Three months later, the investigators optogenetically stimulated the tagged neurons in a different context. Remarkably, this process led to the recovery of the contextual fear memories, such that the mice displayed conditioned fear behavior (they froze)!

How is it possible to label cells that are part of a memory engram? And how can they be stimulated to reactivate a memory? Although this seems like the stuff of science fiction, it's actually achieved through the use of optogenetics, a technique developed in the 2000s that allows researchers to control the function of genetically engineered neurons with light.

Step 1. Using engineered transgenic mouse lines, a subset of neurons in the hippocampus expresses a transgene specifically in neurons that are excited. This is achieved by "hijacking" immediate early genes (IEGs), whose expression is a product of neuronal activity (such as *c-fos*). The neurons that are specifically activated by a learning experience include the memory engram cells. Next, researchers have to tag the allocated neurons at the time of the training event or episode.

Step 2. Tagging neurons in a temporarily specific way involves introducing a co-factor that permits the above transgene to activate a second transgene that can express the ChR2 protein. In some systems, the IEG promoter is used to drive tetracycline transactivator (tTA) protein, which is controlled by the antibiotic doxycycline (DOX) in the animal's diet. In others, the IEG is used to drive inducible Cre recombinase (iCre), which is activated by tamoxifen that is injected into the animal after learning. In either case, the tTA or the iCre then activates or unlocks ChR2 (or whatever destination tag is desired).

Step 3. As shown in (Box Figure 9.1), a subset of neurons in the transgenic mouse's hippocampus (depicted in purple at basal levels of firing) specifically fire when the mouse experiences the training context. These active neurons – the so-called *memory engram cells* – are then labeled by ChR2.

Step 4. Artificial blue light is administered to the hippocampus at defined pulse frequencies via a fiber optic implant. This light stimulation opens the ChR2 ion channels in the tagged neurons, thereby leading to action potentials and the reactivation of the memory engram cells. The original contextual fear memory is thus retrieved, as evidenced by the fact that the mouse displays freezing behavior in a neutral context.

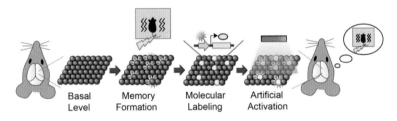

Basal Level   Memory Formation   Molecular Labeling   Artificial Activation

Box Figure 9.1 Memory engram technology. (Reprinted from Tonegawa et al., 2015)

Contributed by Tomás Ryan, PhD, Associate Professor, School of Biochemistry & Immunology & Trinity College Institute of Neuroscience, Trinity College Dublin

Thus far we have treated the hippocampus as a singular structure, but each of its subdivisions processes incoming information in a different way. As a result, although they are tiny, neighboring structures within the hippocampus, they play different roles in memory and learning. In particular, the **dentate gyrus** plays a central role in the formation of new memories.

The dentate gyrus is hypothesized to support **pattern separation** during learning, laying down distinct traces for similar events that allow us to distinguish between them later, as is critical for episodic memory. Consistent with this hypothesis, experimentally boosting neurogenesis in the dentate gyrus boosts discriminability between contexts (e.g., the sights and smells of a cage in which a rodent had previously experienced something aversive), leading to increased separation of memories of experiences that took place in different contexts (Sahay et al., 2011). In contrast, the neighboring **CA3 subfield** is theorized to support **pattern completion**, wherein reactivation of one element of an event enables the retrieval of the full episode via reactivation of neurons involved at encoding. The author Marcel Proust is famous for his extensive memoir that begins with him tasting a French cookie (madeleine), after which his childhood memories come flooding back – presumably thanks in part to pattern completion by the CA3 of his hippocampus!

Are memories actually stored in the hippocampus? The dominant view is that the hippocampus acts like a directory, keeping track of where in the brain (or more accurately, which sets of connections) are implicated for a particular memory. The computer metaphor is apt here: the files on your laptop or tablet are stored in different places on your hard disk or flash memory and your "finder" is a directory telling the operating system where to find the file. If you delete a file, your device typically doesn't delete the file itself, it simply breaks the link between the directory entry and the file location – this is how file recovery programs work, and why, if you sell your device to someone else, it's not enough to delete your personal files without erasing the disk completely: the files are still there. Human memory may operate similarly. Without a distinctive retrieval cue, we can't access the directory. Childhood memories that you didn't know you had can be triggered by a thought or experience that is able to access the (presumably hippocampal) entry point for them.

In rodents, there is evidence of **neurogenesis** – the creation of new neurons – throughout life in the dentate gyrus; the formation of connections involving newly born neurons has been shown to be responsible for encoding new memories in adulthood (Deng et al., 2010). However, the question of whether humans also exhibit lifelong hippocampal neurogenesis is still a matter of debate; if so, it occurs at such low levels that it is often undetectable (Boldrini et al., 2018; Kemperman et al., 2018; Sorrells et al., 2018; Franjic et al., 2022). The degree to which the hippocampus is malleable after early development is important, given – for example – extensive research showing that acute stress suppresses hippocampal neurogenesis in rodents (McEwen, 2000), and, in children, that early life adversity in the form of poverty, early neglect, or physical abuse is associated with smaller hippocampal volumes on average (Hanson et al., 2015). Indeed, a large volume of research shows that the hippocampus, and particularly the dentate gyrus, is exquisitely sensitive to what we experience – and as a result plays a pivotal role in learning and adapting to our environment.

9.3.4 Episodic Memory Networks

Although the structure of the medial temporal lobes is highly conserved across mammalian species, humans have a more complex cortical organization and a richer expression of episodic memory than most or all other animals. (Note that whales – especially orcas – have exquisitely convoluted cortices, but we know next to nothing about their functional brain organization or their memory capabilities.) This richer form of memory is possible thanks to the connections between the hippocampus and other parts of the brain. While the hippocampus is the hub of episodic memory, it is – like all forms of cognition – dependent on a broader brain network, both within and beyond the medial temporal lobes. There are three main fiber tracts that connect the medial temporal lobes with the rest of the brain. The tract that projects to subcortical and midbrain regions – the **fimbria/fornix** – is so essential to memory that a lesion to it causes amnesia. This tract also includes fibers that connect the hippocampus to limbic regions, which explains why we have better memory for events that are affectively salient.

In contrast to the fimbria/fornix, lesions to the other medial temporal lobe tracts (the cingulum bundle and uncinate fasciculus) impact episodic memory in ways that are still being discovered (Wendelken et al., 2015; Bubb et al., 2018). Although we won't delve into the specifics here, we'd like to emphasize that "it's all about connections." The bilateral medial temporal lobes integrate inputs from many sources to create rich memory traces, and in turn influence ongoing cognitive processing and decision-making by recalling relevant prior information (e.g., see Baddeley's model of working memory as detailed in Chapter 10). As we shall see in Section 9.5.5, **prefrontal cortex (PFC)** participates in (among other things) monitoring the veracity and relevance of such retrieved memories.

Depending on the context in which the medial temporal lobes are called upon, different connections come into play. There is an important distinction to be made here between *internally* and *externally guided memory*. When Tulving mused about mental time travel, he was marveling at our capacity to project ourselves into our personal history – autobiographical memory – and various possible futures (autobiographical planning or prospective memory). These types of thoughts take us away from our current surroundings and support our ability to mentally walk through a place we've visited, as well as daydream, mindwander, and brainstorm. During this sort of internally guided memory retrieval, the medial temporal lobes interact closely with the **default mode network** (Buckner & Carroll, 2007; Spreng et al., 2008), which has been broadly implicated in self-generated thought (as discussed in Chapter 10).

Memory retrieval can also be externally guided, helping us to meet challenges in the here-and-now, such as remembering how you know the person who just said hello – or what the professor said last week about the assignment you're working on. This sort of memory supports immediate goal-directed behavior, supported in part by interactions between the hippocampal-dependent memory system and the **frontoparietal network** (Simons & Spiers, 2003), both of which are implicated in working memory and executive functions (see Chapter 10). As it currently stands, we know much more about the neural mechanisms of externally than internally guided episodic memory, for several reasons. First, it is more complicated to carry out well-controlled neuroscientific studies of something as subjective as autobiographical memory than it is to present specific stimuli and test whether they are remembered later.

(However, the practice, in the smart phone era, of continually documenting one's life with photos means that people of your generation, dear reader, may help us advance our scholarship on this important topic.) Secondly, it wasn't until the discovery of the default mode network in the mid-1990s that the distinction between the brain basis of externally and internally guided memory came to light. There has been extremely little fMRI research on the development of autobiographical memory; indeed, we know of only one study involving children to date (Bauer et al., 2017). As such, we focus here on the development of externally guided episodic memory. But first we review the types of memory that are present from birth.

9.4 Development of Memory Systems

Think back to your first memory of an event in your life. What is it? How old were you? How certain are you that you remember it, rather than having been told about it later? Chances are, you can't come up with a memory that took place before you were 3 or 4 years old. As a result of this observation, the prevailing view until the end of the last century was that infants lack the capacity to form conscious memories – a phenomenon referred to as **infantile amnesia**, which we'll revisit in Section 9.4.2. On the other hand, you certainly learned many things during the first few years of life, such as how to walk and talk (and, depending on your family, whether throwing a tantrum got you what you wanted or not), and so it is evident that at least some forms of long-term memory are in place from the beginning.

Guided by evidence of multiple memory systems in adults (Figure 9.1), researchers proposed that young children's profile of performance across different tasks could be explained within the framework of multiple memory systems. Schacter and Moscovitch (1984) were among the first to propose that infants have two memory systems: an **early-developing system** corresponding to *implicit memory*, available from birth, and a **later-developing system** corresponding to *explicit memory*, emerging only in the latter part of an infant's first year and continuing to develop thereafter. Although this model has not been validated (or definitively falsified), it is a useful starting point. The testing of infant memory, and the models based on that testing, have been greatly influenced by adult taxonomies of memory systems. However, ideas about these systems and their development are evolving over time – and, in fact, a developmental perspective on the timing of acquisition of different forms of memory may yet feed back and further refine memory systems models.

9.4.1 Implicit Memory Development

We tend to think of neonates as helpless creatures who exhibit only basic reflexes, like crying when they're hungry or uncomfortable. In fact, however, they're actively forming associations between things they experience, and can, to a limited extent, respond on the basis of these rudimentary memories. How do we know this? It's thanks to clever developmental psychologists who have devised ways to work around infants' underdeveloped sensory and motor systems to infer what is going on in their minds. As noted previously, researchers draw a distinction between children's implicit memories, reflecting the operation of processes acquired unconsciously, and their explicit recollections, involving conscious recall of previous experiences. There is abundant evidence that implicit memory is present from birth and that its function and capacity are relatively consistent (Schneider, 2015).

It is adaptive for infants to adjust their responses to specific demands in the postnatal environment. This adaptation hinges on their ability to learn from experiences. They do so via implicit memory mechanisms introduced in Section 9.2.1. There is evidence that neonates learn from operant conditioning (Tarullo et al., 2011): that is, both approach and avoidance behaviors can be conditioned in awake human newborns through selective reinforcement of their existing reflexes (Lipsitt, 1998). With regards to approach behaviors, neonates readily alter their sucking behavior to obtain good-tasting things, including milk (Papousek, 1961). They also exhibit enhanced sucking behavior to elicit socially relevant auditory stimuli like the sound of their mothers' voice (DeCasper & Fifer, 1980), as we discussed in Chapter 8. An example of an avoidance behavior is eye blinking in response to an anticipated puff of air (Fifer et al., 2010).

Thus, even newborns can modulate their natural behavioral responses based on the prior outcomes of these behaviors – to the extent possible, given their limited repertoire of behaviors. Even more impressively, neonates exhibit classical conditioning, learning to respond to a novel stimulus by virtue of its temporal association with a stimulus that naturally elicits that response. More than that, this learning can be **cross-modal**. For example, as described below, newborns can learn to associate a specific odor or sound with a bodily sensation – and react accordingly when they detect this stimulus again later. This is not a conscious response: these neonates performed the learned response even while asleep. Thus, infants can learn an association between two stimuli across sensory modalities, remember the association over a 24-hour period, and generalize across sleep states!

In fact, infants can even learn *new* associations while they sleep (Gómez & Edgin, 2015). This is a good thing, given that they spend roughly two-thirds of their time in this state. For example, Fifer and colleagues (Fifer et al., 2010) found that sleeping newborns rapidly learned the predictive relationship between a tone and a puff of air to their eye. Specifically, the researchers measured activity of the facial muscles that produce eyeblinks, and showed that infants learned over time to blink in response to the tone, in anticipation of an air puff. They also collected scalp EEG recordings, observing a frontally located positive EEG slow wave emerging towards the latter half of the learning procedure, suggestive of gradual learning over repeated stimulus pairings. Thus, infants can learn from various types of cues while they're sleeping.

Infants also exhibit **recognition memory**, meaning that they have a memory trace for stimuli they've encountered previously – as measured by their production of different behaviors in response to familiar and novel objects. A classic method for assessing recognition memory in infants is the **preferential looking paradigm** described in Chapter 2. Recall that in this paradigm, the infant first becomes well acquainted with one object through a familiarization process. After a delay, both the old object and a new one are shown, and the experimenter measures which one the infant looks at (pays attention to) more. Depending on various factors, including the amount of familiarization provided, infants might look longer at the familiar object or at the novel one. Importantly, either behavior reveals a memory trace for the previously presented object. Recognition memory is evident very early in life; however, as infants mature, they require less extensive familiarization to exhibit memory for an object. They can also retain the memory for longer. For example, Diamond (1990) showed that 4-month-olds can recognize an object after a delay of 10 seconds. By 6 months, they can recognize it after 1 minute, and by 9 months after a delay of 10 minutes. Keep in mind that preferential looking to an object based on memory *doesn't necessarily* reflect a conscious response – although it *could*. Schacter and Moscovitch (1984) theorized that young infants accomplish recognition via the early-developing system, whereas older ones also invoke the later-developing one.

All in all, human infants enter the world with an impressive array of competencies, all of which appear to be adaptive, such as learning to recognize their mother's voice or to orient towards her odor (presumably facilitating nursing). While conditioning mechanisms are relatively age-invariant, recognition memory improves over the course of infancy, potentially transitioning from a reliance on the implicit system alone to involvement of explicit memory as well.

9.4.2   Emergence of Episodic Memory

Although we have no recollection of our first few years of life, even our earliest experiences serve as a scaffold for learning. Yet how can these experiences have lasting effects when they themselves are not remembered? The paradox of infantile amnesia has intrigued developmental researchers for nearly a half-century (Campbell & Spear, 1972; Bauer, 2015). One possibility is that infants are simply unable to form episodic memories; the lack of episodic detail in young children's memories has been attributed to the late development of the hippocampus in human infants (Nadel & Zola-Morgan, 1984), which, as we shall see in Section 9.4.1, undergoes important anatomical development during the earliest stages of life. Another possibility is that infants form episodic memories but that they fade quickly, as we will discuss in Section 9.4.2. In contrast with implicit memory, which is engaged from birth, the precise timing of the development of episodic memory is still unclear. This is no wonder: with implicit memory, it is clear whether the infant has learned the target behavior. With episodic memory, what counts as evidence that an infant explicitly remembers a prior event if they can't tell you about it?

A pioneering researcher, Carolyn Rovee-Collier, set about trying to develop appropriate tests of episodic memory for infants. This endeavor was inspired by her own life. As a graduate student, she needed a way to keep her baby Benjamin busy while working on her dissertation, so she used a ribbon to tie his ankle to a mobile hanging over his crib. That way, when he kicked his leg, the mobile would move. Naturally, Benjamin loved shaking his foot while in the crib. But when Rovee-Collier noticed him shaking his foot even outside the crib, she wondered whether he remembered the experience and wanted to play with the mobile again.

As a researcher, Rovee-Collier capitalized on her curiosity and tested this formally, developing a novel *reinforcement paradigm* called the **mobile task** (Figure 9.5A). In Phase 1 of the experiment (the baseline phase), she tied an infant's foot to the bed to get a baseline measure of the rate of spontaneous kicking. In Phase 2 (the learning phase), she tied the infant's foot to the mobile, providing the opportunity to learn that kicking caused the mobile to move. In Phase 3 (the test phase), she tied the foot to the bed again to measure the rate of kicking. Sure enough, she showed that 6-month-olds exhibited more foot-shaking after learning that it could cause a mobile to move than they had prior to that experience – even though the mobile was no longer attached to their foot. Rovee-Collier argued that 3-month-olds also showed this behavior,

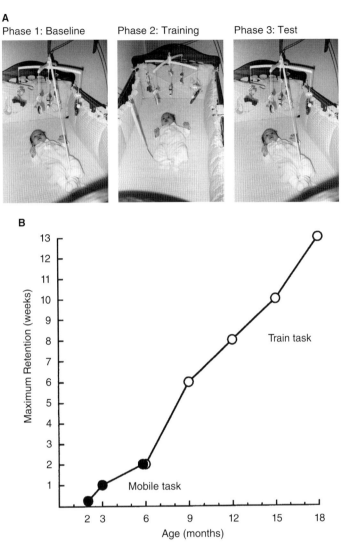

Figure 9.5 Reinforcement paradigms used in infants, and summary of findings. A. Rovee-Collier's mobile task, used in 2- to 6-month-olds. The infant's foot is tied to the bed in Phase 1, to the mobile in Phase 2, and to the bed again in Phase 3. B. Maximum retention of the memory, in weeks, as measured based on elevated kicking rate in Phase 3 relative to Phase 1. Data from mobile task shown in white circles; data from the train task described in the text is shown in black. (Photos from Rovee-Collier, 1999)

although the evidence is not compelling. Her follow-up research showed that 6-month-olds were able to retain this memory for up to two weeks: they showed elevated foot-shaking even if there was a 2-week delay between the experience and the test phase (the white circle at age 6 months plotted in Figure 9.5B).

To study memory in 6- to 18-month-olds, for whom the mobile task was no longer appropriate, Rovee-Collier developed another reinforcement paradigm in which older infants played with a toy train and learned to press a lever to cause it to move. After a delay period of varying lengths, they were given the toy train again. If they were to press the lever more often than they had when they first played with the train, this would be evidence that they remembered their prior experience. Indeed, as shown in Figure 9.5B, Rovee-Collier found that older infants did remember it – and the length of retention increased from 6 to 18 months of age (Rovee-Collier, 1999). These studies made an important contribution, as they provided the first evidence of memory binding capabilities that improve over the first two years of life, and documented factors that influence memory retention at a young age.

But do these experiments provide evidence that infants have episodic memory, or are they simply cases of conditional learning – that is, implicit memory? Rovee-Collier's findings sparked just this debate as to whether the mobile task, and the related train task, are explicit memory tasks (Schacter & Moscovitch, 1984; Tulving, 1985; Clayton et al., 2003). Rovee-Collier proposed that infants have a single memory system, which is present from birth and is strengthened with age. By contrast, Schacter and Moscovitch argued that the implicit memory system is present from birth and the episodic memory system comes online months later. According to the latter view, the marked improvement observed on the train task from 6 to 18 months, not to mention performance in other memory paradigms (Bauer, 2007), could reflect the gradual maturation of episodic memory, working in concert with implicit memory. This latter view seems more plausible, considering behavioral and eye-tracking evidence of rudimentary relational binding – a core feature of episodic memory, as we have seen – within the first 6 months of life (Richmond & Power, 2014; Gómez & Edgin, 2016; Coughlin et al., 2018).

Researchers have further probed the development with the **deferred imitation paradigm**. In deferred imitation tasks, the researcher models an action or action sequence involving an object and, at a later date, hands the object to the infant to test whether they mimic the action(s). This type of paradigm, which probes detailed memory for events, reveals that even 6-month-olds can imitate actions that they witnessed previously (Barr et al., 1996; so can bears: www.youtube.com/watch?v=8qG8bogcd-w). However, 6-month-olds don't seem able to form memories for *singular* events: they must be reexposed to parts of the episode multiple times in order to subsequently imitate it. Patricia Bauer and Jacqueline Leventon showed that laying down a memory trace for an event requires fewer repetitions as infants progress from 13 to 16 months of age (Bauer & Leventon, 2013). By 16 months of age, they could witness an action sequence a single time and then reproduce it one month later.

In summarizing evidence based on her extensive testing of children's memory from birth to 3 years, Harlene Hayne (2007) makes three key points: older infants (1) form new memories more readily, (2) retain memories for longer, and (3) have more flexible memory representations. Collectively, this means they are able to use a wider range of retrieval cues than younger ones. By 2 years of age – a time when infants are able to verbally recount their experiences – they can recount memories of things that occurred days, and sometimes even weeks, earlier (Bauer et al., 2000).

All in all, the prevailing view in the field is that young children leverage implicit memory systems from birth and explicit memory systems that emerge more slowly across the first two years of life. The forms of conditioning observed in infancy are assumed to depend on the basal ganglia, cerebellum, as well as a deep brain structure called the amygdala, and other structures (see Figure 9.3). Recognition memory, observed as early as it is possible to measure it, is thought to depend on medial temporal lobe structures that support object and scene recognition (perirhinal and parahippocampal cortices, respectively). Finally, as we shall see in Section 9.4, the type of rapid, flexible, relational binding that emerges later in infancy is thought to depend on the more protracted maturation of the hippocampus and its connections. Episodic memories can be formed at least by the age of 2; they just can't be retained for very long. Unfortunately, for practical reasons, it has not (yet) been possible to *directly* test the question of when hippocampal-dependent memory first becomes functional. Improvements in infant functional brain imaging will be needed to answer that question (Mullally & Maguire, 2011). However, as we shall see below, we are getting closer to understanding how the medial temporal lobes develop, as well as the cellular mechanisms that may account for the *rapid forgetting* exhibited in early development.

9.4.3 Improvements in Episodic Memory over Childhood

Memory does not suddenly become adult-like after the first two years of life. Ingrid Olson and Nora Newcombe (Olson & Newcombe, 2014) note that children's episodic memories are few and of low quality for several more years. When adults are asked to reflect back on their childhood, the earliest events they report as distinctly *remembering*, rather than simply *knowing*, date back to around age 6. Prior to that age, children can have trouble determining whether what they remember was a real or imagined experience, a waking or a dreaming one: that is, they have difficulty with so-called "source monitoring" of their memories (see Section 9.5.5). Many studies have documented sharp improvements from age 4 to 6 years on tasks that require relational binding. For example, children become less likely to forget where they had seen an object before. Episodic memory continues to improve even after age 6. By middle childhood, children perform quite well on tasks in which they make "old/new" judgments to indicate whether they've encountered a stimulus previously, a process that requires only **recognition memory**. By contrast, tasks that require recall recollection of detailed contextual information, and discrimination between similar test items – that rely more heavily on the episodic memory system – show performance gains well past middle childhood (Ngo et al., 2018).

Attila Keresztes, Nora Newcombe, and colleagues (Keresztes et al., 2018) propose that this pattern of memory development could be explained by a *developmental shift in the balance* between pattern completion and pattern separation (see Section 9.3.3). In other words, very young children are relatively better at generalizing across experiences, supporting semantic memory, than they are at discriminating between similar memories, or between similar test items, whereas the opposite is true for older children and adults. Correspondingly, there is some evidence that children who suffered damage to the hippocampus early in life have relatively spared semantic memory, despite having difficulty remembering individual experiences (Vargha-Khadem et al., 2003). Thus, generalization is possible without individuation of specific memory traces. As we have just seen, performance on tests that require fine-grained discrimination (and therefore pattern separation) improves slowly over childhood and into adolescence.

And, as we shall see below, Keresztes and colleagues argue that this shift depends on the differential development of hippocampal subfields. As this line of research progresses, we will get closer and closer to understanding how children can acquire knowledge without remembering the details of the events surrounding the acquisition of this knowledge.

9.5   Development of the Medial Temporal Lobes

Most of what we know about the early development of the medial temporal lobes comes from research on non-human animals and anatomical MRI studies in humans. However, there has also been some initial fMRI research exploring early hippocampal function.

9.5.1   Structural Development

Animal research reveals that the intricate structures of the medial temporal lobes are built prenatally, through stereotyped patterns of expression of signaling molecules leading to the principled migration of different types of neurons to designated destinations, and to sprouting of specific connections (Khalaf-Nazzal & Francis, 2013). However, development of the medial temporal lobes doesn't end at birth; significant restructuring takes place in infancy. In particular, the dentate gyrus and CA3, discussed earlier in relation to their important functions in pattern separation and pattern completion, mature later than the other subregions. In fact, animal research indicates that most of the neurogenesis (birth of new neurons) in the dentate gyrus takes place *after birth* – and, in fact, continues thereafter. This could explain why pattern separation, which relies on the dentate gyrus, appears to improve more slowly than other forms of memory. The continued restructuring that takes place during infancy could also explain evidence that children who incur damage to the hippocampus tend to have less severe episodic memory deficits if the damage happens prior to 1 year of age (Vargha-Khadem et al., 2003).

Structural MRI studies show that the overall volume of the hippocampus increases dramatically during fetal development and in the first few years of life, but is largely stable thereafter. However, when looking more closely it is apparent that volume subtly changes over the course of childhood, with increases in posterior hippocampus and increases in anterior hippocampus canceling out (Gogtay et al., 2006; Lee et al., 2020). Moreover, several studies have linked volumetric differences in specific parts of the hippocampus to memory performance (e.g., Riggins & Rollins, 2015; Keresztes et al., 2017; Canada et al., 2019; Lee et al., 2020). Several of these studies suggest non-linear changes in hippocampal subfield volumes with age, and changing relationships with behavior over time. However, the overall picture is mixed – likely for a combination of reasons: for example, different age ranges, different ways of subdividing the hippocampus (along the anterior-posterior axis or into subfields, but not both), and potentially because an individual's trajectory of anatomical change is more predictive of cognitive development than volume at a given timepoint (e.g., Shaw et al., 2006).

Overall, while there is evidence that hippocampal development contributes to episodic memory development, it is not the only mechanism at play. As we shall see below, changing connectivity between the hippocampus and cortical regions, and changing functionality of these cortical regions, also play an important role in age-related changes in episodic memory – and this has implications for understanding the precise role of the hippocampus, and where and how memories are stored.

9.5.2 Mechanistic Accounts of Infantile "Amnesia"

In recent years, interest in the neural correlates of infantile amnesia has been reinvigorated due to techniques from development neuroscience that are advancing our understanding of the neurobiology of memory, and of engrams (see Section 9.3.3) in particular. As we have discussed, the hippocampus undergoes tremendous anatomical development during the earliest stages of life. Although neuroscientists have long been interested in the role that neurogenesis plays in memory processes, up until recently, surprisingly little work had examined the impact of ongoing neurogenesis on previously acquired memories. This lack of progress was largely due to technical constraints on the research itself. Now, as new approaches have become available, researchers are interrogating the effect of hippocampal neurogenesis on memory formation. Based on such research, for example, Paul Frankland and his colleagues (Frankland et al., 2013) put forth the seemingly counterintuitive hypothesis that the emergence of new neurons in the hippocampus is the source of early forgetting. Indeed, the researchers predicted that increasing or decreasing neurogenesis after memory formation would respectively shorten or lengthen retention of those memories.

Frankland and colleagues tested this hypothesis by first inducing fear learning (see Section 9.2.1) in adult mice, then artificially boosting neurogenesis, and then testing whether the mice showed infant-like forgetting. Regardless of the manner in which neurogenesis was boosted – via exercise, pharmacological manipulations, or genetic techniques – it led to more pronounced forgetting across a range of hippocampus-dependent memory tasks (Ishikawa et al., 2016; Gao et al., 2018)! In other words, *more* hippocampal neurons led to more forgetting. Even more compellingly, when hippocampal neurogenesis was slowed down in infant mice, they showed improved memory (Akers et al., 2014). These astonishing findings provide the first causal evidence that rapid neurogenesis in infancy contributes to the phenomenon of infantile amnesia. Thus, the infantile amnesia that we observe in children may, at least in part, be a byproduct of the pronounced structural changes that take place in the hippocampus across the course of infancy and early childhood. However, in Box 9.1, we discuss the question of whether the forgotten memory traces have been completely erased or rather still reside in the brain but are rendered inaccessible to conscious awareness.

9.5.3 Hippocampal Function in Early Childhood

Because measuring hippocampal *function* in infancy is much harder than measuring its structure, the question (discussed in Section 9.3.2) of when in infancy the hippocampus and associated regions begin to contribute to memory has not been conclusively answered. Neuroimaging methods such as fNIRS or EEG cannot measure deep structures, so the only option at present to address this question in humans is fMRI. However, this poses an immense challenge. Anatomical MRI scans can be completed while infants are sleeping (albeit not without difficulty) – but how can one possibly get an *awake* infant to lie still and perform a task in an MRI scanner? In fact, Simona Ghetti (see Box 9.2) and her lab pioneered an approach for measuring

Box 9.2 Scientist Spotlight on Simona Ghetti (University of California, Davis)

Simona Ghetti (Box Figure 9.2) is a Professor in the Department of Psychology and the Center for Mind and Brain at the University of California, Davis, where she directs the Memory and Development Laboratory. Ghetti earned her doctoral degree in developmental psychology at UC Davis and moved on to a tenured research professor position at the National Research Council in Bologna, Italy before returning. Ghetti uses behavioral, brain imaging, and eye-tracking methods to study long-term memory development.

I grew up in Italy and did my undergraduate work at the University of Padua. When I started, I did not think in a million years that I would become a Professor of Psychology. I'm the first person in my family to graduate from college. I came to the United States on a fellowship, thanks to the support of several professors, and eventually decided to do my graduate work here.

The first hook into child development and memory for me was eyewitness memory. I began my work as an undergraduate in Italy looking at child abuse cases and testimony in the legal system. I was very interested in how children's needs were considered in the legal system, how their memories were probed and assessed. That's why I came to Davis initially to work with Gail Goodman, who is a world leader in eyewitness memory in children. So, part of my graduate work had to do with looking at long-term memories for victims of child abuse. We studied people who, as young adults, remembered their documented abuse. We were able to compare detailed documents from the courtrooms from 20 years before with what these individuals were saying today about their experiences, and we found that the people who experienced the most severe forms of sexual abuse based on our records were more accurate in their recall, perhaps because it was more memorable or was discussed and validated in court.

While in graduate school, I became interested in memory functioning more generally, and that became the focus of my lab. We spent many years studying hippocampal function in childhood and adolescence, and our finding of protracted hippocampal development beyond early childhood was influential. When we started doing some of this work, the dominant view was that after age 4 or 5, the massive development in memory had to do with children's ability to monitor and control their memories. But I didn't think that could be the whole story, for two reasons. The first is that behaviorally young children's and even older children's memory are still a little more fragmentary, and include less information about space and time than those of adolescents or adults. The second is that it was difficult for me to think that there's a brain structure, like the hippocampus, that doesn't change when it's interacting with cortical regions that are still developing.

But even though the hippocampus is changing in childhood and adolescence, there's a consensus in the field that early hippocampal processes are particularly foundational for getting episodic memory off the ground. Infant brain imaging methods have been a limiting factor, but we have found that you can probe hippocampal function during sleep in very young children [see Section 9.5.3]. We're currently looking at how this relational memory process of putting together pieces of an experience might support learning the association between a word and its referent.

In terms of societal relevance, I am interested in working with children who suffer from chronic disease or otherwise physical, medical conditions that have implications for cognition that have been largely left behind in the literature, including diabetes, heart disease, acute kidney disease, asthma, obesity, and of course traumatic brain injury – conditions that really affect the life of many, many children. These children are typically not recognized as children suffering from a developmental disability, but they still need support in the school setting and beyond.

brain activity while infants sleep (Johnson et al., 2020). This approach builds on the fairly recent discoveries in the adult memory literature demonstrating that memories can be reactivated during sleep via sound presentation, and that memory-related regions are reactivated in response to previously encountered sounds (see Johnson et al., 2020).

In the first study of its kind (Prabhakar et al., 2018), Ghetti and colleagues tested whether sleeping 2-year-olds would activate the hippocampus when hearing a song that they had heard previously in a distinctive context. Over the course of a week, infants played in two different rooms (Rooms A and B), as shown in Figure 9.6A. The rooms had different themes and toys, and different toy characters that they could play with – and, critically, a different song was playing in the background in each room (Songs A and B). After several play sessions, infants were placed in the hallway between the two rooms, where Song A was playing, and were tested on their memory for these experiences, as outlined in Figure 9.6B. They were first asked which room that song had been played in. After that, they were asked which toy character had been in that room: A, B, or a novel character (Character C). Getting these answers right would mean that they remembered specific details of the play episodes: *where* they took place and *what* was there. Remarkably, 62 percent of these toddlers remembered the room, and 40 percent also identified the toy character!

One or two nights after this behavioral test, Prabhakar and colleagues then scanned the toddlers. As the toddlers slept in the MRI scanner, the researchers played Song A, as well as a new song (Song C). Sure enough, as shown in Figure 9.6C, toddlers who had remembered both episodic details exhibited stronger hippocampal activation for the target song than the novel one! In other words, toddlers showed hippocampal activation in response to a memory cue – and this activation was functionally relevant, because it was only observed for toddlers who performed the memory test correctly. This is the first direct evidence in humans that the hippocampus is functional by age 2 (if not sooner).

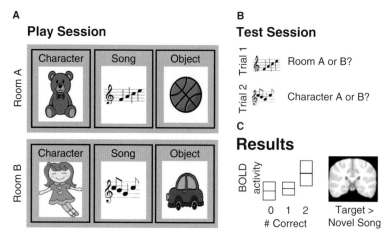

Figure 9.6 Memory task and hippocampal activation during sleep in 2-year-olds. A. Toddlers played in two different rooms, with different toy characters, objects, and songs playing in the background. B. During the test session, they were asked which of two rooms, and which of three characters, a song had been associated with (Trials 1 and 2, respectively). C. Sleeping toddlers exhibited greater hippocampal activation when exposed to a familiar song than a novel one. Level of activation varied across individuals depending on how many of the memory test questions they had got correct. (Adapted from Prabhakar et al., 2018)

9.5.4 Further Development of Hippocampal Function

Although fMRI research on episodic memory in infants is in its infancy (pun intended), there have been a number of studies focused on older children and adolescents (Ofen et al., 2007; Ghetti & Bunge, 2012; Riggins et al., 2020). Some of these studies have examined brain activation during memory formation – encoding – and others during retrieval tasks. Additionally, some have involved tasks that require *recollection* (e.g., selecting which of several objects had been previously paired with a particular scene), whereas others have required only **recognition** of previously seen stimuli (judging an item as old or new). In terms of memory encoding, the emerging picture is that the hippocampus supports *subsequent memory* from at least age 4 onward – the youngest age at which children have performed memory tasks in the scanner (Geng et al., 2019). In short, the hippocampus is more active on trials for which children later remember the item than on those for which they later forget it. The same is true for older children (Ofen et al., 2007). However, a closer look reveals changes in the profile and location of hippocampal activation at both encoding and retrieval during middle childhood (Ghetti et al., 2010; Sastre et al., 2016).

In a study of memory retrieval, Ghetti and colleagues (Sastre et al., 2016) tested three age groups (8- to 9-year-olds, 10- to 11-year-olds, and adults) on a task in which they had to judge whether an object had been encoded previously or not – and, if so, which of three scenes it had been paired with. In 8- to 9-year-olds, as well as low-performing 10- to 11-year-olds, the hippocampus was similarly active when object–scene associations were correctly recalled or when there was a memory failure. In other words, the hippocampus showed increasingly selective activation for episodic memory encoding, suggesting that its role in memory becomes fine-tuned during middle childhood.

9.5.5 Development of Episodic Memory Networks

As we saw in Section 9.3.4, the medial temporal lobes do not operate in isolation; indeed, few brain regions do. Age-related improvements in episodic memory over childhood are also accompanied by changes in other brain regions, as well as in structural and functional connectivity between the hippocampus and these other regions (Ghetti & Bunge, 2012; Riggins et al., 2020). For example, the first study of memory encoding showed increased activation of lateral PFC between 8 and 24 years – and also possibly more mature gray matter in this part of the brain (Ofen et al., 2007). Even in the absence of task demands, the pattern of hippocampal connectivity throughout the rest of the brain changes with age, and also differs as a function of children's memory performance, with some regions showing stronger temporal coupling as a function of age or performance, and others showing weaker coupling (Riggins et al., 2020).

That these functional brain networks change over time stands to reason: after all, the structure of long-range white matter tracts itself changes with age. For example, Catherine Lebel and Christian Beaulieu (Lebel & Beaulieu, 2011) conducted a study using diffusion tensor imaging on participants who ranged in age from 5 to 34 years (see Figure 4.10 in Chapter 4). The results showed increased fractional anisotropy in many tracts, among them the two that connect the medial temporal lobes to various cortical regions (the cingulum bundle and uncinate fasciculus, mentioned in Section 9.3.4). As always when it comes to human brain development, there were also important individual differences across participants. Overall, these changes suggest increased strength of anatomical connections between the hippocampus and various cortical regions, leading to more efficient communication among the disparate brain regions that participate in the same large-scale brain networks (see Chapter 4). Increased anatomical connectivity between hippocampus and many cortical regions also likely supports increased flexibility in the engagement of different brain networks. In other words, the increased possibility of rapid communication along any of a number of white matter pathways likely contributes to increasingly nimble recruitment of the relevant brain regions given the particular task at hand.

Developmental improvements in memory accuracy rely on the emergence of a range of corresponding cognitive skills, including the ability to **monitor** the accuracy and relevance of retrieved memories (this is a form of metacognition, or thinking about our own thoughts). As we have noted previously (Section 9.4.3), children under the age of 6 have difficulty distinguishing between reality and imagination. In fact, improved episodic memory in childhood is likely as much due to improvement in monitoring and other **executive functions** (Chapter 10) that depend on memory representations as it is to inherent memory quality.

Memory monitoring starts early, during the preschool years, but becomes substantially more robust as children progress through middle and late childhood (Ghetti et al., 2010). For example, the neural basis of memory monitoring development was examined with a longitudinal fMRI study involving 8- to 9-year-olds, 10- to 12-year-olds, and young adults tested twice over the span of ~1.5 years (Fandakova et al., 2018). Participants were asked to indicate how certain they were about their selection on an episodic memory task (Figure 9.7A). At encoding, they viewed a series of object–scene pairings, and were asked to decide whether the

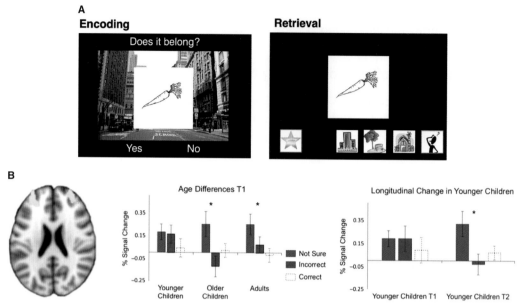

Figure 9.7 Brain changes underlying improvements in memory monitoring during childhood. A. On the encoding task, participants were asked to make a judgment about individual object–scene pairings. On the retrieval task, they were asked to identify the scene it had been paired with at encoding (correct source), or to indicate that they weren't sure. If they were confident that they hadn't seen the object before, they were instructed to indicate that it was new. B. Regions activated at retrieval in anterior PFC, and plots showing activation separately for each age group and type of response. (Adapted from Fandakova et al., 2018)

object belonged in the scene. The purpose of this encoding task was to ensure that children paid attention to the relation between the object and the scene, so that any differences between age groups in performance or in brain activation would not be attributable to differences in a participant's attention to the relevant information. At retrieval, participants were instructed to indicate which of three scenes a previously seen object had been paired with – or to indicate that they remembered the object but couldn't remember the associated scene – the "not sure" response. Alternatively, if they didn't remember the object at all, they were instructed to indicate that.

As expected, episodic memory accuracy increased across the three age groups – and also from 8 to 12 years. When children and adults recognized that they weren't sure of the right answer, as compared to when they selected the right one, they activated several regions, including the anterior insula and anterior cingulate cortex, regions that are broadly implicated in monitoring performance (see Chapter 10), along with anterior PFC (Figure 9.7B). Anterior PFC activation was stronger and more selective for the "not sure" trials as a function of age – and also across the two timepoints for the younger children. Further, the children who engaged anterior PFC most strongly in response to uncertainty at the first timepoint were more likely to have better episodic memory around 1.5 years later! These results show the importance of *knowing what you don't remember*. In other words, being able to monitor the accuracy of one's memories is an important contributor to memory development. More broadly, executive functions help to explain developmental changes and individual differences in episodic memory.

SUMMARY

- There are multiple memory systems that can be broadly classified into explicit and explicit forms of memory
- Remembering is not the same thing as knowing
- The memory systems have different underlying brain systems and developmental trajectories
- The hippocampal-dependent memory system supports episodic memory, and also semantic memory
- The hippocampus is shaped by experiences and supports learning
- Infants display several forms of implicit memory from birth onward
- Although the precise timeline of episodic memory development is debated, it appears to become operational late in infancy, as the hippocampus and its connections mature
- The phenomenon known as infantile amnesia may be a byproduct of early hippocampal maturation
- Hippocampal interactions with various cortical and subcortical regions underpin externally and internally guided episodic memory
- Memory monitoring and other executive functions support episodic memory development

REVIEW QUESTIONS

What key insights have we gleaned from studies of patients regarding different memory systems and their neural bases? Define explicit and implicit memory, and point to key brain structures that support each of these classes of memory.

What are some different forms of conditioning, and how do we know that infants exhibit these types of memory?

What precise function(s) does the hippocampus subserve? Discuss relational binding, pattern completion, and pattern separation, and their functional relevance to episodic and semantic memory.

What are some examples of tasks used to examine memory in infancy?

Why is "declarative memory" a misleading term, particularly in the context of developmental research? Why is explicit memory a more appropriate term?

When in development do explicit and implicit forms of memory emerge?

What is infantile amnesia, and what is one plausible underlying mechanism?

What is the distinction between externally and internally guided memory? Which one do we understand better, developmentally, and why?

Which changes and individual differences in the hippocampal-dependent memory system during childhood (anatomical and/or functional) support improved episodic memory?

Why, based on brain development, are young children thought to have difficulty monitoring their memories? What role(s) do executive functions and prefrontal cortex play in memory and its development?

Further Reading

Olson, I. R., & Newcombe, N. S. (2014). Binding together the elements of episodes: Relational memory and the developmental trajectory of the hippocampus. In P. J. Bauer & R. Fivush (Eds.), *Handbook on the development of children's memory, Volume 1* (pp. 285–308). Wiley-Blackwell.

Prabhakar, J., Johnson, E. G., Nordahl, C. W., & Ghetti, S. (2018). Memory-related hippocampal activation in the sleeping toddler. *Proceedings of the National Academy of Sciences of the United States of America*, 115(25), 6500–6505. https://doi.org/10.1073/pnas.1805572115

Vargha-Khadem, F., Salmond, C. H., Watkins, K. E., Friston, K. J., Gadian, D. G., & Mishkin, M. (2003). Developmental amnesia: Effect of age at injury. *Proceedings of the National Academy of Sciences of the United States of America*, 100(17), 10055–10060. https://doi.org/10.1073/pnas.1233756100

References

Addis, D. R., & Schacter, D. L. (2012). The hippocampus and imagining the future: Where do we stand? *Frontiers in Human Neuroscience*, 5, 173. https://doi.org/10.3389/fnhum.2011.00173

Akers, K. G., Martinez-Canabal, A., Restivo, L., Yiu, A. P., De Cristofaro, A., Hsiang, H.-L., Wheeler, A. L., Guskjolen, A., Niibori, Y., Shoji, H., Ohira, K., Richards, B. A., Miyakawa, T., Josselyn, S. A., & Frankland, P. W. (2014). Hippocampal neurogenesis regulates forgetting during adulthood and infancy. *Science*, 344(6184), 598–602. https://doi.org/10.1126/science.1248903

Alberini, C. M., & Travaglia, A. (2017). Infantile amnesia: A critical period of learning to learn and remember. *Journal of Neuroscience*, 37(24), 5783–5795. https://doi.org/10.1523/JNEUROSCI.0324-17.2017

Barr, R., Dowden, A., & Hayne, H. (1996). Developmental changes in deferred imitation by 6- to 24-month-old infants. *Infant Behavior and Development*, 19(2), 159–170. https://doi.org/10.1016/S0163-6383(96)90015-6

Bauer, P. J. (2007). *Remembering the times of our lives: Memory in infancy and beyond.* Lawrence Erlbaum Associates.

Bauer, P. J. (2015). Development of episodic and autobiographical memory: The importance of remembering forgetting. *Developmental Review*, 38, 146–166. https://doi.org/10.1016/j.dr.2015.07.011

Bauer, P. J., & Leventon, J. S. (2013). Memory for one-time experiences in the second year of life: Implications for the status of episodic memory. *Infancy*, 18(5), 755–781. https://doi.org/10.1111/infa.12005

Bauer, P. J., Pathman, T., Inman, C., Campanella, C., & Hamann, S. (2017). Neural correlates of autobiographical memory retrieval in children and adults. *Memory*, 25(4), 450–466. https://doi.org/10.1080/09658211.2016.1186699

Bauer, P. J., Wenner, J. A., Dropik, P. L., Wewerka, S. S., & Howe, M. L. (2000). Parameters of remembering and forgetting in the transition from infancy to early childhood. *Monographs of the Society for Research in Child Development*, 65(4), 1–213. www.jstor.org/stable/3181580

Boldrini, M., Fulmore, C. A., Tartt, A. N., Simeon, L. R., Pavlova, I., Poposka, V., Rosoklija, G. B., Stankov, A., Arango, V., Dwork, A. J., Hen, R., & Mann, J. J. (2018). Human hippocampal neurogenesis persists throughout aging. *Cell Stem Cell*, 22(4), 589–599.e5. https://doi.org/10.1016/j.stem.2018.03.015

Bubb, E. J., Metzler-Baddeley, C., & Aggleton, J. P. (2018). The cingulum bundle: Anatomy, function, and dysfunction. *Neuroscience & Biobehavioral Reviews*, 92, 104–127. https://doi.org/10.1016/j.neubiorev.2018.05.008

Buckner, R. L., & Carroll, D. C. (2007). Self-projection and the brain. *Trends in Cognitive Sciences*, 11(2), 49–57. https://doi.org/10.1016/j.tics.2006.11.004

Callaghan, B. L., & Richardson, R. (2012). The effect of adverse rearing environments on persistent memories in young rats: Removing the brakes on infant fear memories. *Translational Psychiatry*, 2(7), e138. https://doi.org/10.1038/tp.2012.65

Campbell, B. A., & Spear, N. E. (1972). Ontogeny of memory. *Psychological Review*, 79(3), 215–236. https://doi.org/10.1037/h0032690

Canada, K. L., Ngo, C. T., Newcombe, N. S., Geng, F., & Riggins, T. (2019). It's all in the details: Relations between young children's developing pattern separation abilities and hippocampal subfield volumes. *Cerebral Cortex*, 29(8), 3427–3433. https://doi.org/10.1093/cercor/bhy211

Chen, Z., & Wilson, M. A. (2017). Deciphering neural codes of memory during sleep. *Trends in Neurosciences*, 40(5), 260–275. https://doi.org/10.1016/j.tins.2017.03.005

Clayton, N. S., Bussey, T. J., & Dickinson, A. (2003). Can animals recall the past and plan for the future? *Nature Reviews Neuroscience*, 4(8), 685–691. https://doi.org/10.1038/nrn1180

Cohen, N. J., Poldrack, R. A., & Eichenbaum, H. (1997). Memory for items and memory for relations in the procedural/declarative memory framework. *Memory*, 5(1–2), 131–178. https://doi.org/10.1080/741941149

Coughlin, C., Leckey, S., & Ghetti, S. (2018). Development of episodic memory: Processes and implications. In J. T. Wixted & S. Ghetti (Eds.), *Stevens' handbook of experimental psychology and cognitive neuroscience* (Vol. 4, pp. 133–157). Wiley.

DeCasper, A., & Fifer, W. (1980). Human bonding: Newborns prefer their mothers' voices. *Science*, 208(44448), 1174–1176. https://doi.org/10.1126/science.7375928

Deng, W., Aimone, J. B., & Gage, F. H. (2010). New neurons and new memories: How does adult hippocampal neurogenesis affect learning and memory? *Nature Reviews Neuroscience*, 11(5), 339–350. https://doi.org/10.1038/nrn2822

Diamond, A. (1990). Developmental time course in human infants and infant monkeys, and the neural bases of inhibitory control in reaching. *Annals of the New York Academy of Sciences*, 608(1), 637–676. https://doi.org/10.1111/j.1749-6632.1990.tb48913.x

Fandakova, Y., Bunge, S. A., Wendelken, C., Desautels, P., Hunter, L., Lee, J. K., & Ghetti, S. (2018). The importance of knowing when you don't remember: Neural signaling of retrieval failure predicts memory improvement over time. *Cerebral Cortex*, 28(1), 90–102. https://doi.org/10.1093/cercor/bhw352

Fifer, W. P., Byrd, D. L., Kaku, M., Eigsti, I.-M., Isler, J. R., Grose-Fifer, J., Tarullo, A. R., & Balsam, P. D. (2010). Newborn infants learn during sleep. *Proceedings of the National Academy of Sciences of the United States of America*, 107(22), 10320–10323. https://doi.org/10.1073/pnas.1005061107

Foer, J. (2012). *Moonwalking with Einstein: The art and science of remembering everything*. Penguin Books.

Franjic, D., Skarica, M., Ma, S., Arellano, J. I., Tebbenkamp, A. T. N., Choi, J., Xu, C., Li, Q., Morozov, Y. M., Andrijevic, D., Vrselja, Z., Spajic, A., Santpere, G., Li, M., Zhang, S., Liu, Y., Spurrier, J., Zhang, L., Gudelj, I., Rapan, L., Takahashi, H., Huttner, A., Fan, R., Strittmatter, S. M., Sousa, A. M. M., Rakic, P., & Sestan, N. (2022). Transcriptomic taxonomy and neurogenic trajectories of adult human, macaque, and pig hippocampal and entorhinal cells. *Neuron*, 110(3), 452–469.e14. https://doi.org/10.1016/j.neuron.2021.10.036

Frankland, P. W., Köhler, S., & Josselyn, S. A. (2013). Hippocampal neurogenesis and forgetting. *Trends in Neurosciences*, 36(9), 497–503. https://doi.org/10.1016/j.tins.2013.05.002

Gabrieli, J. D. E. (1998). Cognitive neuroscience of human memory. *Annual Review of Psychology*, 49, 87–115. https://doi.org/10.1146/annurev.psych.49.1.87

Gao, A., Xia, F., Guskjolen, A. J., Ramsaran, A. I., Santoro, A., Josselyn, S. A., & Frankland, P. W. (2018). Elevation of hippocampal neurogenesis induces a temporally graded pattern of forgetting of contextual fear memories. *Journal of Neuroscience*, 38(13), 3190–3198. https://doi.org/10.1523/JNEUROSCI.3126-17.2018

Gee, D. G., Gabard-Durnam, L. J., Flannery, J., Goff, B., Humphreys, K. L., Telzer, E. H., Hare, T. A., Bookheimer, S. Y., & Tottenham, N. (2013). Early developmental emergence of human amygdala–prefrontal connectivity after maternal deprivation. *Proceedings of the National Academy of Sciences of the United States of America*, 110(39), 15638–15643. https://doi.org/10.1073/pnas.1307893110

Geng, F., Redcay, E., & Riggins, T. (2019). The influence of age and performance on hippocampal function and the encoding of contextual information in early childhood. *NeuroImage*, 195, 433–443. https://doi.org/10.1016/j.neuroimage.2019.03.035

Ghetti, S., & Bunge, S. A. (2012). Neural changes underlying the development of episodic memory during middle childhood. *Developmental Cognitive Neuroscience*, 2(4), 381–395. https://doi.org/10.1016/j.dcn.2012.05.002

Ghetti, S., DeMaster, D. M., Yonelinas, A. P., & Bunge, S. A. (2010). Developmental differences in medial temporal lobe function during memory encoding. *Journal of Neuroscience*, 30(28), 9548–9556. https://doi.org/10.1523/JNEUROSCI.3500-09.2010

Gogtay, N., Nugent III, T. F., Herman, D. H., Ordonez, A., Greenstein, D., Hayashi, K. M., Clasen, L., Toga, A. W., Giedd, J. N., Rapoport, J. L., & Thompson, P. M. (2006). Dynamic mapping of normal human hippocampal development. *Hippocampus*, 16(8), 664–672. https://doi.org/10.1002/hipo.20193

Gómez, R. L., & Edgin, J. O. (2015). Sleep as a window into early neural development: Shifts in sleep-dependent learning effects across early childhood. *Child Development Perspectives*, 9(3), 183–189. https://doi.org/10.1111/cdep.12130

Gómez, R. L., & Edgin, J. O. (2016). The extended trajectory of hippocampal development: Implications for early memory development and disorder. *Developmental Cognitive Neuroscience*, 18, 57–69. https://doi.org/10.1016/j.dcn.2015.08.009

Guskjolen, A., Kenney, J. W., de la Parra, J., Yeung, B. A., Josselyn, S. A., & Frankland, P. W. (2018). Recovery of "lost" infant memories in mice. *Current Biology*, 28(14), 2283–2290.e3. https://doi.org/10.1016/j.cub.2018.05.059

Hannula, D. E., Ryan, J. D., Tranel, D., & Cohen, N. J. (2007). Rapid onset relational memory effects are evident in eye movement behavior, but not in hippocampal amnesia. *Journal of Cognitive Neuroscience*, 19(10), 1690–1705. https://doi.org/10.1162/jocn.2007.19.10.1690

Hanson, J. L., Nacewicz, B. M., Sutterer, M. J., Cayo, A. A., Schaefer, S. M., Rudolph, K. D., Shirtcliff, E. A., Pollak, S. D., & Davidson, R. J. (2015). Behavioral problems after early life stress: Contributions of the hippocampus and amygdala. *Biological Psychiatry*, 77(4), 314–323. https://doi.org/10.1016/j.biopsych.2014.04.020

Hayne, H. (2007). Infant memory development: New questions, new answers. In L. Oakes & P. Bauer (Eds.), *Short- and long-term memory in infancy and early childhood: Taking the first steps toward remembering* (pp. 209–239). Oxford University Press.

Ishikawa, R., Fukushima, H., Frankland, P. W., & Kida, S. (2016). Hippocampal neurogenesis enhancers promote forgetting of remote fear memory after hippocampal reactivation by retrieval. *ELife*, 5, e17464. https://doi.org/10.7554/eLife.17464

Jelbert, S. A., & Clayton, N. S. (2017). Comparing the non-linguistic hallmarks of episodic memory systems in corvids and children. *Current Opinion in Behavioral Sciences*, 17, 99–106. https://doi.org/10.1016/j.cobeha.2017.07.011

Johnson, E. G., Prabhakar, J., Mooney, L. N., & Ghetti, S. (2020). Neuroimaging the sleeping brain: Insight on memory functioning in infants and toddlers. *Infant Behavior and Development*, 58, 101427. https://doi.org/10.1016/j.infbeh.2020.101427

Josselyn, S. A., & Tonegawa, S. (2020). Memory engrams: Recalling the past and imagining the future. *Science*, 367(6473), eaaw4325. https://doi.org/10.1126/science.aaw4325

Kempermann, G., Gage, F. H., Aigner, L., Song, H., Curtis, M. A., Thuret, S., Kuhn, H. G., Jessberger, S., Frankland, P. W., Cameron, H. A., Gould, E., Hen, R., Abrous, D. N., Toni, N., Schinder, A. F., Zhao, X., Lucassen, P. J., & Frisén, J. (2018). Human adult neurogenesis: Evidence and remaining questions. *Cell Stem Cell*, 23(1), 25–30. https://doi.org/10.1016/j.stem.2018.04.004

Keresztes, A., Bender, A. R., Bodammer, N. C., Lindenberger, U., Shing, Y. L., & Werkle-Bergner, M. (2017). Hippocampal maturity promotes memory distinctiveness in childhood and adolescence. *Proceedings of the National Academy of Sciences of the United States of America*, 114(34), 9212–9217. https://doi.org/10.1073/pnas.1710654114

Keresztes, A., Ngo, C. T., Lindenberger, U., Werkle-Bergner, M., & Newcombe, N. S. (2018). Hippocampal maturation drives memory from generalization to specificity. *Trends in Cognitive Sciences*, 22(8), 676–686. https://doi.org/10.1016/j.tics.2018.05.004

Khalaf-Nazzal, R., & Francis, F. (2013). Hippocampal development: Old and new findings. *Neuroscience*, 248, 225–242. https://doi.org/10.1016/j.neuroscience.2013.05.061

Lebel, C., & Beaulieu, C. (2011). Longitudinal development of human brain wiring continues from childhood into adulthood. *Journal of Neuroscience*, 31(30), 10937–10947. https://doi.org/10.1523/JNEUROSCI.5302-10.2011

Lee, J. K., Fandakova, Y., Johnson, E. G., Cohen, N. J., Bunge, S. A., & Ghetti, S. (2020). Changes in anterior and posterior hippocampus differentially predict item-space, item-time, and item-item memory improvement. *Developmental Cognitive Neuroscience*, 4. https://doi.org/10.1016/j.dcn.2019.100741

Lipsitt, L. P. (1998). Learning and emotion in infants. *Pediatrics*, 102(Suppl E1), 1262–1267. http://pediatrics.aappublications.org/content/102/Supplement_E1/1262.abstract

Liu, X., Ramirez, S., Pang, P. T., Puryear, C. B., Govindarajan, A., Deisseroth, K., & Tonegawa S. (2012). Optogenetic stimulation of a hippocampal engram activates fear memory recall. *Nature*, 484(7394), 381–385. https://doi.org/10.1038/nature11028

Luria, A. R. (1968). *The mind of a mnemonist: A little book about a vast memory*. Basic Books.

Mazzoni, G., Clark, A., De Bartolo, A., Guerrini, C., Nahouli, Z., Duzzi, D., De Marco, M., McGeown, W., & Venneri, A. (2019). Brain activation in highly superior autobiographical memory: The role of the precuneus in the autobiographical memory retrieval network. *Cortex*, 120, 588–602. https://doi.org/10.1016/j.cortex.2019.02.020

McEwen, B. S. (2000). Effects of adverse experiences for brain structure and function. *Biological Psychiatry*, 48(8), 721–731. https://doi.org/10.1016/S0006-3223(00)00964-1

Moscovitch, M., Cabeza, R., Winocur, G., & Nadel, L. (2016). Episodic memory and beyond: The hippocampus and neocortex in transformation. *Annual Review of Psychology*, 67, 105–134. https://doi.org/10.1146/annurev-psych-113011-143733

Mullally, S. L., & Maguire, E. A. (2011). A new role for the parahippocampal cortex in representing space. *The Journal of Neuroscience*, 31(20), 7441–7449. https://doi.org/10.1523/JNEUROSCI.0267-11.2011

Nadel, L., & Zola-Morgan, S. (1984). Infantile amnesia: A neurobiological perspective. In M. Moscovitch (Ed.), *Infant memory* (pp. 145–172). Plenum Press.

Ngo, C. T., Newcombe, N. S., & Olson, I. R. (2018). The ontogeny of relational memory and pattern separation. *Developmental Science*, 21(2). https://doi.org/10.1111/desc.12556

Ofen, N., Kao, Y.-C., Sokol-Hessner, P., Kim, H., Whitfield-Gabrieli, S., & Gabrieli, J. D. E. (2007). Development of the declarative memory system in the human brain. *Nature Neuroscience*, 10(9), 1198–1205. https://doi.org/10.1038/nn1950

Olds, J., & Milner, P. (1954). Positive reinforcement produced by electrical stimulation of septal area and other regions of rat brain. *Journal of Comparative and Physiological Psychology*, 47(6), 419–427. https://doi.org/10.1037/h0058775

Olson, I. R., & Newcombe, N. S. (2014). Binding together the elements of episodes: Relational memory and the developmental trajectory of the hippocampus. In P. J. Bauer & R. Fivush (Eds.), *The Wiley handbook on the development of children's memory* (pp. 285–308). Wiley-Blackwell.

Papousek, H. (1961). Conditioned head rotation reflexes in infants in the first months of life. *Acta Paediatrica*, 50, 565–576. https://doi.org/10.1111/j.1651-2227.1961.tb08047.x

Piaget, J. (1928). *The child's conception of the world*. Routledge & Kegan Paul.

Prabhakar, J., Johnson, E. G., Nordahl, C. W., & Ghetti, S. (2018). Memory-related hippocampal activation in the sleeping toddler. *Proceedings of the National Academy of Sciences of the United States of America*, 115(25), 6500–6505. https://doi.org/10.1073/pnas.1805572115

Queensland Brain Institute, University of Queensland, Australia. (2021, February 23). Super memory – What it's like to remember being a baby (S1E33), A Grey Matter [Audio podcast]. https://qbi.uq.edu.au/podcast-super-memory-what-its-remember-being-baby

Richmond, J. L., & Power, J. (2014). Age-related differences in memory expression during infancy: Using eye-tracking to measure relational memory in 6- and 12-month-olds. *Developmental Psychobiology*, 56(6), 1341–1351. https://doi.org/10.1002/dev.21213

Riggins, T., Canada, K. L., & Botdorf, M. (2020). Empirical evidence supporting neural contributions to episodic memory development in early childhood: Implications for childhood amnesia. *Child Development Perspectives*, 14(1), 41–48. https://doi.org/10.1111/cdep.12353

Riggins, T., & Rollins, L. (2015). Developmental differences in memory during early childhood: Insights from event-related potentials. *Child Development*, 86(3), 889–902. https://doi.org/10.1111/cdev.12351

Rovee-Collier, C. (1999). The development of infant memory. *Current Directions in Psychological Science*, 8(3), 80–85. https://doi.org/10.1111/1467-8721.00019

Sahay, A., Scobie, K. N., Hill, A. S., O'Carroll, C. M., Kheirbek, M. A., Burghardt, N. S., Fenton, A. A., Dranovsky, A., & Hen, R. (2011). Increasing adult hippocampal neurogenesis is sufficient to improve pattern separation. *Nature*, 472(7344), 466–470. https://doi.org/10.1038/nature09817

Sastre, M., Wendelken, C., Lee, J. K., Bunge, S. A., & Ghetti, S. (2016). Age- and performance-related differences in hippocampal contributions to episodic retrieval. *Developmental Cognitive Neuroscience*, 19, 42–50. https://doi.org/10.1016/j.dcn.2016.01.003

Schacter, D. L., & Moscovitch, M. (1984). Infants, amnesics, and dissociable memory systems. In M. Moscovitch (Ed.), *Infant memory* (pp. 173–216). Plenum Press. https://doi.org/10.1007/978-1-4615-9364-5_8

Schneider, W. (2015). *Memory development from early childhood to emerging adulthood*. Springer.

Shaw, P., Greenstein, D., Lerch, J., Clasen, L., Lenroot, R., Gogtay, N., Evans, A., Rapoport, J., & Giedd, J. (2006). Intellectual ability and cortical development in children and adolescents. *Nature*, 440(7084), 676–679. https://doi:10.1038/nature04513

Simons, J. S., & Spiers, H. J. (2003). Prefrontal and medial temporal lobe interactions in long-term memory. *Nature Reviews Neuroscience*, 4(8), 637–648. https://doi.org/10.1038/nrn1178

Sorrells, S., Paredes, M., Cebrian-Silla, A., Sandoval, K., Qi, D., Kelley, K. W., James, D., … Alvarez-Buylla A. (2018). Human hippocampal neurogenesis drops sharply in children to undetectable levels in adults. *Nature*, 555, 377–381 (2018). https://doi.org/10.1038/nature25975

Spreng, R. N., Mar, R. A., & Kim, A. S. N. (2008). The common neural basis of autobiographical memory, prospection, navigation, theory of mind, and the default mode: A quantitative meta-analysis. *Journal of Cognitive Neuroscience*, 21(3), 489–510. https://doi.org/10.1162/jocn.2008.21029

Squire, L. R. (1994). Declarative and nondeclarative memory: Multiple brain systems supporting learning and memory. In D. L. Schacter & E. Tulving (Eds.), *Memory systems* (pp. 203–231). MIT Press.

Squire, L. R. (2009). The legacy of patient H.M. for neuroscience. *Neuron*, 61(1), 6–9. https://doi.org/10.1016/j.neuron.2008.12.023

Suddendorf, T., & Corballis, M. C. (1997). Mental time travel and the evolution of the human mind. *Genetic, Social, and General Psychology Monographs*, 123(2), 133–167.

Tarullo, A. R., Balsam, P. D., & Fifer, W. P. (2011). Sleep and infant learning. *Infant and Child Development*, 20(1), 35–46. https://doi.org/10.1002/icd.685

Tonegawa, S., Liu, X., Ramirez, S., & Redondo, R. (2015). Memory engram cells have come of age. *Neuron*, 87(5), 918–931. https://doi.org/10.1016/j.neuron.2015.08.002

Tulving, E. (1985). Memory and consciousness. *Canadian Psychology/Psychologie Canadienne*, 26(1), 1–12. https://doi.org/10.1037/h0080017

Vargha-Khadem, F., Salmond, C. H., Watkins, K. E., Friston, K. J., Gadian, D. G., & Mishkin, M. (2003). Developmental amnesia: Effect of age at injury. *Proceedings of the National Academy of Sciences of the United States of America*, 100(17), 10055–10060. https://doi.org/10.1073/pnas.1233756100

Wendelken, C., Lee, J. K., Pospisil, J., Sastre III, M., Ross, J. M., Bunge, S. A., & Ghetti, S. (2015). White matter tracts connected to the medial temporal lobe support the development of mnemonic control. *Cerebral Cortex*, 24(9), 2574–2583. https://doi.org/10.1093/cercor/bhu059

10 Working Memory and Executive Functions

LEARNING OBJECTIVES

- Define working memory and executive functions
- Sketch out the hypothesized subcomponents of working memory
- Describe the types of tasks that are used to measure different aspects of working memory
- Identify key brain regions and networks involved in working memory and executive functions
- Explain key hypotheses regarding the neural mechanisms that support working memory and top-down control
- Describe how different facets of working memory change over childhood and adolescence
- Identify key brain changes that support working memory development
- Explain the neural basis of improvements in the ability to monitor the environment for challenges that require top-down control

When you were in high school, your teachers and parents probably told you explicitly what you needed to do, such as "Review Chapter 2 and write down three things you've learned – and then quietly complete your math worksheet if you finish early." As a college student you are typically given more latitude regarding which goals you complete in your work and personal lives and how you go about them; this requires that you keep more information in mind and balance a larger number of competing demands: that is, you have to be more self-directed. In both cases, successful **goal-directed behavior** requires us to keep in mind and organize all information that is relevant to the tasks at hand, a cognitive ability known as **working memory (WM)**. WM is rooted in attentional processes that emerge in infancy (Cowan, 2016; see Chapter 6); keeping relevant information in mind requires sustained, selective attention. The number of items we can hold in mind at once (and the precision with which we can remember them) is limited, yet it increases throughout childhood and is further honed over the course of adolescence.

Goal-directed behavior also requires control processes to ensure that our behavior is compatible with our goals and appropriate to the circumstances, and to flexibly adjust our behavior as needed. After all, what is an appropriate way to act in one context is not necessarily appropriate in another. Children may be encouraged to freely join in a discussion while sitting around the dinner table, but in the classroom they might have to inhibit that impulse and instead raise their hand and wait to be called on. Collectively, the control processes that allow us to behave appropriately and complete tasks are referred to as **executive functions (EFs)** or **cognitive control**.

Developmental psychologists consider WM one of the core EFs, whereas systems and cognitive neuroscientists studying WM tend not to. Here, we draw a distinction between the active representation of a limited amount of relevant information – WM maintenance, or short-term memory – and EF processes that *operate on* – that is, **manipulate** – these active representations, or *use* them to guide behavior.

WM and EFs are effortful, attention-demanding, and prone to failure – and yet they are essential for goal-directed behavior, impacting academic success and a variety of life outcomes over the lifespan. Children with low WM capacity tend to have difficulty following task instructions and keeping relevant information in mind, and as a result may fall behind in school (Gathercole et al., 2008). School is particularly challenging for children with poor EFs, including those diagnosed with Attention Deficit Hyperactivity Disorder (ADHD; Box 10.1). Children with ADHD can have trouble staying in their seats and focusing on the task at hand – and, on top of falling behind with their coursework, they may be reprimanded for disrupting the class. WM and EFs set the stage for learning by enabling children to stay on task; they are also central to the types of cognitive operations needed to understand complex ideas.

Given that WM and EFs are such important factors for school success, there is great interest in this line of research to improve academic performance. Two different instructional approaches have been proposed: either minimizing WM and EF demands in classroom activities so as to remove these barriers to achievement, or finding ways to hone these foundational cognitive abilities. Much research is aimed at determining whether and how WM and EFs can be improved (Box 10.2). To address these important questions effectively, we must first understand the mechanisms underlying these fundamental cognitive abilities, their developmental trajectories, the sources of individual differences, and the ways in which they support learning.

A distinction is made between **"cool"** and **"hot"** EFs (Zelazo & Carlson, 2012). So-called "cool" EFs control behavior in an emotionally neutral context – for example, when completing a difficult task that is not, in and of itself, personally meaningful, risky, or rewarding. By contrast, so-called "hot" EFs help us to self-regulate when the stakes are high: that is, when the potential for success or failure is salient and highly motivating. In this chapter we focus on "cool" EFs that support the ability to operate on the contents of WM in a neutral context. In Chapter 13, we cover "cool" and "hot" EFs that underpin self-control. Below, we begin by outlining an influential model of WM that includes an EF component, and describing its cognitive development. We then provide an overview of findings from research in adults and non-human primates, which sets the stage for reviewing neuroimaging research on WM and EF development. Finally, we move beyond EFs that support WM by discussing how EFs are – or could be – conceptualized.

Box 10.1 Attention Deficit Hyperactivity Disorder (ADHD)

Symptoms: ADHD is a neurodevelopmental condition that impacts WM and EFs. The core behavioral dimensions are inattention/disorganized (so-called "internalizing" symptoms) and hyperactive/impulsive ("externalizing" symptoms). Individuals with ADHD lie on a spectrum across both dimensions – indeed, we all do! Many individuals diagnosed with ADHD exhibit only internalizing symptoms: they have difficulty exerting top-down control over their thought processes, and as a result tend to be easily distracted and have difficulty getting organized and

Box 10.1 (cont.)

managing their time. By contrast, those who additionally or instead exhibit externalizing symptoms struggle to control their overt behavior, often failing to inhibit inappropriate responses or regulate their emotions. As ADHD is considered a disorder that emerges during development, current diagnostic guidelines specify that symptoms need to be evident by age 12; however, this is an arbitrary cutoff age, and the onset and progression of ADHD vary. Symptoms may already be noticed in the preschool years, and often persist through adulthood.

Diagnosis: The legitimacy of this condition has been questioned, with skeptics noting that it is overdiagnosed and overmedicated – and even that it is a societally constructed disorder. These arguments are not entirely wrong. It is true, after all, that people are all on a continuum with regard to these behaviors, and that WM and EFs develop more slowly in some children than others – and the fact that the prevalence of ADHD diagnosis and medication has increased over time is related in part to increased awareness of the condition, as well as policy changes. It is also true that modern society places demands on us that our ancestors didn't have to contend with: for example, our brains did not evolve to sit still and focus for hours at a time, and yet those of us who are incapable of doing so suffer the consequences. However, for children with a legitimate diagnosis these behaviors are sufficiently severe as to negatively impact their academic performance and interpersonal interactions. For some, the condition can be downright debilitating, as they are at much greater risk of accidents, and of dropping out of high school or delaying graduation. In other words, it is a serious disorder worthy of attention (Hinshaw, 2018).

Etiology: Some individuals are at much higher risk of developing ADHD than others, by virtue of their genetic makeup. Relative to many other neurodevelopmental disorders, the heritability of this condition is considered high. Nonetheless, environmental factors play an important role in determining whether genetic susceptibility manifests as ADHD, such as low birthweight, prenatal exposure to chemical substances that affect brain development *in utero*, and exposure to lead and other toxins in childhood.

WM performance: Of particular relevance for this chapter, a large longitudinal study (Karalunas et al., 2017) measured fluctuations in ADHD symptom severity and cognitive task performance over three years in 7- to 13-year-olds with and without ADHD. The children completed three cognitive measures: the spatial span test described in Section 10.2, the stop-signal task (a measure of response inhibition; see Chapter 13), and a delay discounting task (a measure of delay of gratification; see Chapter 13). They found that children who showed bigger improvements in WM (but not the other measures) across timepoints showed greater symptom remission.

Neural underpinnings: ADHD is associated with altered dopaminergic and noradrenergic activity; medications used to alleviate the symptoms are non-specific stimulants that boost the activity of these neuromodulators. As discussed in Section 10.4.3, dopamine helps to adjust neural "gain" in PFC; the same is true of norepinephrine; thus, it has been proposed that the symptoms of ADHD stem from impaired adjustment of neural gain (Arnsten & Pliszka, 2011; Hauser et al., 2016). In addition to these differences in neurochemistry, numerous neuroimaging studies have documented structural and functional brain differences between children with and without ADHD. The frontostriatal pathway has been implicated, although it is not that simple: multiple brain regions and pathways have been implicated. Longitudinal research suggests that children with ADHD exhibit a delayed or altered trajectory of cortical maturation, as measured by cortical thickness (Shaw et al., 2007). Fully characterizing the structural and functional brain profiles of patients who remit as they mature, as compared with those with persistent symptoms, could provide important insights for treatment approaches and early intervention (Sudre et al., 2018).

Treatments: Behavioral therapies have proven to be as effective in managing symptoms as pharmacological treatment. In some cases, a combination of behavioral and pharmacological approaches is the most beneficial strategy (Hinshaw, 2018). Lifestyle changes, including increased sleep and exercise, are also promising approaches. Finally, cognitive training may hold some promise (see Box 10.2).

10.1 Early Theoretical Framework

If you've ever asked someone for directions, you've had to encode their response (e.g., "Turn right on Elm Street and an immediate left on Spruce Street; go past the first intersection and you will see a store with a red awning on the right-hand side"). You could try to rehearse the gist of what they said, and/or construct a mental map of space that allows you to envision the route you must follow. As you've surely noticed, though, you can only keep a small amount of information in mind at one time: that is, we have a **limited capacity store** for keeping mental representations actively in mind.

In the 1960s, when researchers were beginning to liken the mind to a computer, they drew a distinction between **short-term** and **long-term memory** (STM and LTM) (Atkinson & Shiffrin, 1968). Short-term memory refers to the ability to remember information over a brief period of time, on the order of seconds – as compared with long-term memory, which can persist for hours, days, months, or years. Unlike long-term memory, comprising a vast network of stored knowledge and experiences that lies dormant unless it is retrieved, short-term memory is what allows us to keep in mind a few pieces of information in the service of our immediate goals – for example, dialing a phone number that we've just been given.

The concept of WM encompasses both the short-term **maintenance** and **manipulation** of mental representations (Baddeley, 2003). The key characteristic of WM is that it is active and goal-directed, critical to the sorts of mental processes involved when a limited amount of information must be "worked with" for a brief period before being put to some use. Several component processes support WM, and it is through their coordinated activity that people have the capacity both for temporary storage and reorganization or transformation of that information. We often manipulate information in WM by reordering stored representations on the fly and/or chunking them into smaller, and ideally meaningful, groupings. As a mundane example, we can go to the grocery store with a small list of items in mind (milk, cereal, bananas, granola bars, oranges), and reorder it based on where in the store things are co-located (bananas and oranges; milk; cereal and granola bars).

Figure 10.1 Baddeley's updated model of the components of WM, building on his 1974 model with Hitch. (Reprinted from Baddeley, 2003)

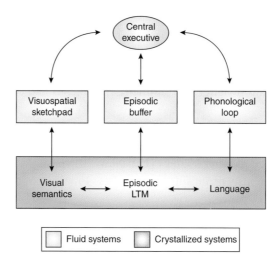

Alan Baddeley and Graham Hitch were the first to propose characterizations of these component parts, suggesting a three-part system: the **phonological loop**, the **visuospatial sketchpad**, and the **central executive**. This theoretical framework was first proposed in 1974, and later amended to include an **episodic buffer**, to better account for interactions between WM and LTM (Baddeley, 2003). Figure 10.1 shows all four of these components; it also illustrates how WM stores interact with long-term memory systems (referred to here as crystallized systems). According to this framework, the central executive coordinates the activity of three systems that keep relevant information in mind, each of which in turn draws on activated representations in long-term memory (see Chapter 9). The visuospatial sketchpad draws on "visual semantics" – that is, our knowledge about the visual world, such as our ability to recognize familiar objects on sight. The phonological loop draws on our language system. Finally, the episodic buffer brings into the realm of conscious awareness our memories for past events (see Chapter 9).

The original three-component theoretical framework was highly influential in guiding neuroscientific (including DCN) research on WM, and conceptualizations of WM have continued to be refined. In particular, developmental psychologist Nelson Cowan's embedded process model (Cowan, 2016) provides a compelling account of the emergence of WM from early-developing attentional processes. Cowan also articulates a number of developmental changes that could contribute to improvements in WM over childhood.

10.1.1 Phonological WM

Alan Baddeley's 2003 model includes two **modality-specific stores** that mediate the temporary storage of different kinds of information. One of these is the above-mentioned phonological loop, which supports active rehearsal of verbally encoded material, such as a phone number you've just heard or seen, via "subvocal articulation," or inner speech. There is robust behavioral evidence that this system, most commonly called **verbal** or **phonological WM**, is indeed mediated by inner speech. For example, one highly replicable phenomenon that informed the development of the WM model is the *word length effect*, wherein the number of words we can recall decreases as a function of the number of syllables in the words. For example, Baddeley and colleagues showed that one is more likely to remember the words "Mumps, School, Maths, Zinc" than "Tuberculosis, University, Physiology, Aluminium" (Baddeley et al., 1975). Additionally, patients with a condition called dyspraxia, who have difficulty orchestrating the complex set of movements needed for speaking, have reduced phonological WM spans. Finally, the brain regions implicated in this ability include regions that are known to be important for language processing.

10.1.2 Visuospatial WM

The other modality-specific store in the model is the visuospatial sketchpad, poetically described as the "blackboard of the mind" by the late neuroscientist Patricia Goldman-Rakic. This system, commonly referred to as visuospatial WM, temporarily stores visual images, representing their colors, shapes, and spatial layouts. Visuospatial representations can be quite complex: if asked to do so, you could probably describe roughly how you get from the front entrance of your home to your bedroom, and what you see along the way. Just as information can be manipulated in phonological WM, so too can it be manipulated in visuospatial WM. For example, we can in theory (if we aren't using GPS) mentally rotate a geographic map to align it with the direction we're headed in. Researchers have examined how many, and how, distinct representations can be retained in visuospatial WM; the tasks they use typically involve simple visual stimuli, such as an array of colored squares on a screen. In addition to testing **WM span**, cognitive psychologists study **WM precision**, or the fidelity with which various attributes of visual stimuli (e.g., their color, orientation, and spatial location) are remembered.

Visuospatial WM is often conceptualized as a singular capacity, commonly referred to as visuospatial working memory; however, an object's visual features and location in space are represented by distinct cortical pathways: the ventral and dorsal streams described in Chapter 6. Thus, some researchers have subdivided the visuospatial sketchpad into separate spatial ("visual") and non-spatial ("object") WM systems, emphasizing the segregation of different visual attributes in WM (Smith & Jonides, 1999). However, distinct visual features of an object are both represented separately and bound together into a single percept, thanks to interactions between the pathways, and so other researchers consider that it is these bound representations that are maintained in WM. In fact, there is evidence for both segregation and integration of visual representations in the brain. Brady and colleagues (Brady et al., 2011) have described the structure of visual WM as a hierarchy wherein we represent individual features, individual objects, and sets of objects. DCN research has predominantly focused on spatial WM, as discussed below.

10.1.3 The "Central Executive" (EFs)

This part of Baddeley and Hitch's model was originally conceptualized as a domain-general pool of processing capacity that controls attention and carries out whatever additional processing is needed, including retrieval of information from long-term memory. In this sense, it was a "catch-all" that was meant to capture all the cognitive capabilities that could not be accounted for by the two domain-specific memory stores (the phonological loop and visuospatial sketchpad). In subsequent years, the term "central executive" has been replaced in the literature by *EFs*, in recognition of the idea that there are multiple distinct (yet interactive) control processes. Although the most elusive component of the Baddeley model, there has been extensive research on development and the neural basis of each component of WM.

10.2 Measuring WM Capacity

Various tasks are used to probe different aspects of WM (Figure 10.2A). Phonological and spatial WM maintenance are typically measured via simple **span** tests that index the number of items an individual can encode and recall. For example, in the **Digit span** test of phonological WM, a participant may be asked to recall sequences of spoken numbers, words, or non-words. In the visual spatial span test, participants are cued to attend to objects at different locations on a board or digital screen and point to each one in turn. On some trials, participants are instructed to recall the items (be they verbal or spatial) in the same order in which they were encoded (**forward span**); on others, they must recall them in the *reverse* order (**backward span**). The number of items in the list grows until participants can no longer remember all the items in the correct order. Your WM span is defined as the highest number of items you are able to recall accurately.

Forward span tasks are sometimes referred to as measures of short-term memory, as opposed to working memory, because they don't technically require "working with" the mental representations. Backward span tasks, by contrast, are universally described as measures of working memory because participants are required to maintain (manipulate) items in WM by rehearsing them. It is worth noting, however, that even on tasks that do not *require* maintenance manipulation, participants – particularly adults – may spontaneously chunk a long list of items into subgroups, thereby invoking EFs to help them keep more items in mind. Chunking is a strategy for creating easily remembered strings of items, rather than trying to memorize individual items. In fact, telephone numbers are subdivided into groups of three or four digits for ease of memorization, precisely because chunking is known to be an effective way to lighten our WM load.

Whereas simple span tests tax memory for a single set of stimuli, **complex span tasks** measure the ability to toggle back and forth between encoding items into WM and completing another task. For example, the **Listening span** task entails processing a series of sentences (e.g., "Giraffes grow on trees"; "Dogs have four legs"; …), indicating, in turn, whether each one is true or false (T; F; …), while encoding the final word of each sentence into WM. At the end of the trial, they would be asked to recall all the final words (trees, legs, …). As for the simple span tests, the number of items to be remembered grows across the trials, and an individual's span on this type of measure is based on the longest number of words they could remember – in this case, while concurrently performing another task. The listening span task and other complex span tasks were designed in such a way as to invoke EFs by requiring participants to switch attention between two tasks.

A number of studies have involved administration of cognitive task batteries to adult participants on verbal and spatial working memory span tasks, with results showing again and again that the best account of the data is a model consisting of two domain-specific stores – verbal and visuospatial – and a domain-general processing component along the lines of Baddeley's Central Executive (Kane et al., 2004). As discussed below, a model with these three components is also the best fit for behavioral data from children (Alloway et al., 2006), and is consistent with findings from neuropsychological and neuroimaging research (Jonides et al., 2005).

Another WM task designed to invoke EFs is the **n-back task**, which is most commonly used in fMRI studies. A series of stimuli is presented one at a time in this task (Figure 10.6A). Participants must continually *update* the set of items in WM; the number of preceding items they must keep online differs across conditions. To understand this, picture a sliding window in which only the last "n" items are currently relevant. On 0-back trials, the task is to press a button when the current stimulus is identical to the immediately preceding one (i.e., it appears twice in a row). On 1-back trials, participants must press a button when the current stimulus matches the one that was presented two stimuli ago (i.e., when there is one intervening stimulus). Similarly, on 2-back trials, participants must press when the stimulus matches the one that was presented three stimuli ago (i.e., two intervening stimuli). As you can see, the width of the sliding window of WM increases from 0-back to 1-back to 2-back, and on and on. This paradigm has been used in working memory training studies (Box 10.2); with practice, children can get up to 5-back or higher!

Box 10.2 Can WM and EFs Be Honed with Intensive Training?

The question of whether general cognitive functions can be strengthened through practice dates back at least as far as Plato, and has been studied and debated since the turn of the twentieth century. The critical question – one that sparked a multi-billion dollar "brain training" industry but which is hotly debated – is whether training on one (or many) specific computerized tasks can *transfer* to improved performance on other types of tasks that require the same cognitive skills and, most importantly, to real-world challenges such as those encountered at school. In the area of WM, specifically, a number of researchers have drawn on the principles of brain plasticity to hypothesize that intensive training on WM tasks should strengthen the underlying neural circuitry (Constantinidis & Klingberg, 2016).

However, evidence of the effectiveness of the WM training approach is mixed. On the one hand are studies showing extensive practice on computerized WM tasks led to improved performance on these and related WM tasks in both neurotypical adults and children, as well as in children with ADHD (e.g., Jaeggi et al., 2008; Klingberg, 2010). That is, these studies showed *near transfer* to related tasks. More importantly, a large meta-analysis showed that WM training led to reduced inattention in daily life, among children both with and without ADHD (Spencer-Smith & Klingberg, 2015). That is, it showed *far transfer* to the types of real-world behavioral difficulties we seek to ameliorate.

On the other hand, other meta-analyses have shown weak and short-lasting effects of WM training (e.g., Hulme & Melby-Lervåg, 2012). A recent meta-analysis of studies involving over 2,000 typically developing children showed small to moderate effects of WM training on near-transfer tasks of WM, but negligible effects on far-transfer tests of intelligence or academic achievement in carefully controlled studies (Sala & Gobet, 2020).

Box 10.2 (cont.)

How can we reconcile these contradictory findings? Researchers who have found evidence in favor of WM training have pointed out that training is not *universally* effective (e.g., Jaeggi et al., 2011) – that is, some participants stand to gain more than others. They have also cautioned that although training gains can persist for months, it is likely that regular or periodic practice is necessary. Perhaps the question, "Does cognitive training work?" is akin to the question "Does medicine cure disease?" (Katz et al., 2018). The answer is: it depends.

The field needs to establish the boundary conditions, identifying *what* works *when*, for *whom*, and *why*. With regards to the "what" question, cognitive scientists would do well to partner with education researchers who are well-versed in evidence-based pedagogical practices. Regarding "when," one cannot assume that the same intervention would work equally well across pre-schoolers, children, teens, and adults. The question of "who" stands to benefit from such training is ill-posed; interventions should be designed with the target population in mind.

Much (although not all) of the controversy has been based on the issue of whether high-functioning individuals – often college students – can improve their cognitive skills. Conclusions from this work do not necessarily extend to children with specific neurodevelopmental disorders, or even to neurotypical children whose home environment has not prepared them adequately for school. Finally, to address the "why" question, the field must better understand the core cognitive processes that support numerous tasks, the learning mechanisms that support transfer, and the factors that lead to individual differences in learning trajectories. There is one additional question that we must ask ourselves with regards to any intervention: Is it worth the time, or does it take away from other potentially enriching activities like exercise or stimulating hobbies or time with friends? Given how much time children spend on digital devices these days, this is a legitimate question – and one that will have to be answered on a case-by-case basis.

10.3   WM Development

Working memory plays an important role in child development, and many cognitive theories take increases in working memory capacity as a starting point for cognitive change. For example, components of WM can be distinguished by the roles they play in knowledge and skill acquisition.

10.3.1 How WM Supports Learning

In pursuing the ways in which WM development impacts learning, Susan Gathercole and colleagues have examined how phonological WM supports literacy and numeracy development, as well as the ability to follow task instructions (Alloway et al., 2006). Other researchers have focused on how spatial WM is correlated with achievement in STEM (Science, Technology, Engineering and Mathematics) fields. Indeed, the ability to visualize and manipulate mental representations in space is thought to help students comprehend (or design) complex systems

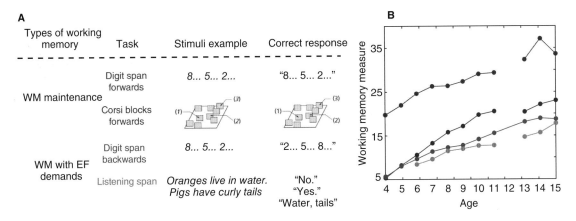

Figure 10.2 Age-related improvements in performance on tests of WM. A. Behavioral tasks commonly used to measure WM in children. B. Age-related improvements from 4 to 15 years on four tests of WM administered to 4- to 15-year-olds. (See Gathercole et al., 2004)

(Cohen & Hegarty, 2014). (As you may have noticed, imagining the structures of the brain in 3D is helpful for learning neuroanatomy.) Finally, the executive component of WM has been broadly associated with learning and achievement.

In one particularly compelling longitudinal study, researchers administered three EF measures to a sample of nearly 9,000 kindergarten children and showed that each of these measures predicted academic achievement in the second grade (Morgan et al., 2019). One of these measures was the Digit span Backward task. Merely being able to reverse a set of numbers in WM predicted reading, math, and science achievement two years later! This result held even when controlling for the children's initial academic performance, sociodemographic variables, and other EF measures. This study also showed that WM manipulation was most strongly predictive of future academic achievement for children with the lowest socioeconomic status. That is, it seems that having strong WM skills made young children less susceptible to negative environmental influences on scholastic performance.

10.3.2 Age-Related Increases in WM Span

Having shown that WM is important, we will now examine how and why it improves over childhood and adolescence. Numerous cross-sectional studies have provided evidence that WM capacity improves from infancy through adolescence (Cowan, 2016). In what may be the largest and most comprehensive dataset to date, Gathercole and colleagues collected data on up to nine tests of WM for over 700 children between ages 4 and 15 (Gathercole et al., 2004). They saw clear developmental improvements on all nine tasks. Figure 10.2B shows the results for four of these tests. Plotted here are two simple span tasks – Digit span Forward and Corsi blocks – that measure phonological and spatial WM maintenance, respectively. Also shown here are two phonological WM tasks designed to tax EFs: Digit span Backward and the complex span task called Listening span. The y-axis shows the list length for each of these tests – that is, the largest number of items that could be remembered accurately, on average, at each age.

Gathercole and colleagues further performed factor analyses to determine whether the tests could be grouped together as measures of the same construct, based on patterns of covariation in performance across participants. For each of the age ranges tested (6–7, 8–9, 10–11, and 13–15), they showed that a confirmatory three-factor model of phonological loop, visuospatial sketchpad, and central executive (EFs) fit the data better than two-factor models, supporting a distinction between these components in Baddeley's models (Figure 10.1).

10.3.3 Age-Related Increases in Spatial WM Precision

So far, we've covered how developmental WM studies test for growth in span, or the number of items that can be recalled. The bulk of the literature to date has focused on span, but some studies have instead focused on WM precision. Fidelity of WM for spatial locations can be measured with eye-tracking. In the **memory-guided saccade task** (shown in Figure 10.3), participants (be they humans or monkeys) view a stimulus that flashes at a specific location on the computer screen. After this stimulus disappears, there is a delay period during which participants must wait for a

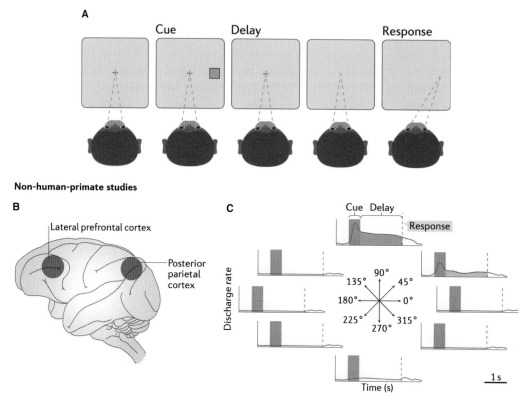

Figure 10.3 Summary of classic electrophysiological studies of spatial working memory. A. Memory-guided saccade task. B. Schematic showing regions implicated in visuospatial working memory in the monkey brain. C. Schematic illustrating activity of a single prefrontal neuron recorded while the monkey performs the spatial WM task. (Reproduced from Constantinidis & Klingberg, 2016)

few seconds, keeping the spatial location in mind. Then, when cued to respond, they must move their eyes – that is, make a saccade – to the location in space where they had previously seen the stimulus. The measure of WM precision is then calculated as the physical distance between the to-be-remembered location and the point on the screen where the participant looked. This task has been widely used in neurophysiological studies of WM in monkeys. In humans, Beatriz Luna and colleagues showed that spatial WM precision increases over adolescence (Luna et al., 2004).

Similarly, other studies have shown developmental improvements in memory precision for visual features; participants are asked to use a dial or slider to change the color of a shape or the orientation of a line to match what they remember. For example, Burnett Heyes and colleagues (Burnett Heyes et al., 2016) conducted a longitudinal study with children 7–14 years of age tested at two timepoints, two years apart. Participants used a dial to change the orientation of a line to match their memory of a cued stimulus, and the investigators calculated the difference in angle between their response and the stimulus. They found that precision increased with age, both cross-sectionally and longitudinally over the two timepoints (see Chapter 2 for the distinction between these two types of analyses). Improvements in WM precision have been theorized to be due to decreased variability or noisiness of stored feature representations, which in turn may depend on developmental differences in encoding precision and/or memory decay over the delay period.

10.4 Neural Basis of WM

Early investigations on the neural substrates of WM implicated **lateral prefrontal cortex (PFC)** in WM maintenance. By the early 1930s, observations of patients with brain injury as well as controlled lesion studies in non-human primates led to the conclusion that PFC was important for "higher intellectual functions," although it was clear that it was not doing this alone – and, in particular, that lateral parietal cortex also played a role (Jacobsen, 1931). Subsequent lesion studies in non-human primates (typically macaques) showed that PFC was essential for performing tasks requiring them to encode a stimulus and remember it over a delay period prior to responding (Fuster, 2001). Based on this research, lateral PFC was identified as playing a key role in what came to be known as WM. In the 1960s, Russian neuropsychologist Alexander Luria systematically studied the cognitive deficits of patients who had sustained damage to lateral PFC. He described the most common characteristic as an inability to consciously represent and execute plans and action sequences (Fuster, 2001), thereby emphasizing the role of lateral PFC in preparing for an upcoming behavioral response.

10.4.1 Early Discoveries

This neuropsychological research in humans and monkeys inspired additional studies, initiated by Patricia Goldman-Rakic, Joaquín Fuster, Michael Petrides, Richard Passingham, and other influential investigators. These studies confirmed that temporarily inactivating, or lesioning, dorsolateral PFC (**DLPFC**) led to impaired WM. Building on this, Fuster and Goldman-Rakic conducted pioneering electrophysiological research characterizing the response properties of

DLPFC neurons. One commonly used task in this research is the **memory-guided saccade task** (Section 10.3.2). The monkey sits in front of a computer screen and maintains gaze fixation on a central crosshair (Figure 10.3A). A stimulus is presented briefly and, after a delay of several seconds, the monkey must make a saccade to the cued location.

Using this paradigm, Fuster, Goldman-Rakic and others showed that neurons in DLPFC and lateral parietal cortex (also called posterior parietal cortex or PPC in the WM literature) represent the to-be-remembered spatial location across the delay period (Figure 10.3B). A schematic of this classic finding is shown in Figure 10.3C, which illustrates activity of a single prefrontal neuron recorded while the monkey performs the spatial WM task. The y-axis shows the average firing rate ("Discharge rate") over the course of a trial ("Time (s)"). The gray bar represents the duration of the cue stimulus; the dashed red line indicates the moment in time when the monkey responds by making an eye movement. In this example, the neuron's preferred spatial location is at 90° relative to the horizon; it also responds, to a lesser extent, to a stimulus presented at 45°. This neuron fires in response to a cue presented at the preferred location ("Cue") and continues to discharge during the delay period ("Delay"). The delay-period activity is spatially selective: that is, PFC neurons with other preferred locations do not fire as strongly during this period. In this example, the neuron shows *persistent delay-period activity*.

These studies revealed that different PFC neurons are preferentially tuned to different stimuli or spatial locations, and that individual PFC neurons coding the to-be-remembered information show heightened neural firing across a delay period, consistent with a role in maintaining the contents of WM (Fuster, 1973; Goldman-Rakic, 1995). As these classic studies reported, some PFC neurons show persistent spiking activity across the entire delay period; however, newer studies have emphasized that the majority of PFC neurons spike at different times across the delay period. As a result, researchers have proposed models wherein persistent delay-period activity emerges from a dynamic (as opposed to stationary) population code involving interactions between many neurons (Mongillo et al., 2008; Meyers, 2018). In other words, large neuronal ensembles exhibit delay-period activity that reflects specific information about the items to be held in WM (in this case, their spatial location; other cases may include perceptual features such as color, size, or temporal order).

The flipside of keeping relevant information in WM is keeping *irrelevant* information *out* of WM. Intriguingly, one early study showed that PFC-lesioned monkeys could perform a simple delayed response task as long as the lights were turned out during the delay period – in other words, when visual interference from the environment was eliminated (Malmo, 1942). We return below, in the section on EFs, to the importance of PFC for **interference suppression** – that is, minimizing the impact of distractors on behavioral performance – and the fact that this capacity improves across development. A model of WM proposed by Earl Miller and Jonathan Cohen (Miller & Cohen, 2001), based on a prior model of visual attention (Desimone & Duncan, 1995), has influenced how we think about the role of PFC in damping down irrelevant activity. Miller and Cohen's **biased competition model** posits that PFC does not actively inhibit interference, but rather biases competing streams of information in sensory and other association cortices to emphasize task-relevant information. This process, referred to as **top-down modulation**, is probably mediated not by PFC alone, but rather by a broader **lateral frontoparietal network (LFPN)**. This framework underscores a point we make throughout this book: that regions do not operate in isolation.

10.4.2 Neuroimaging Studies in Adults

Shortly after fMRI methods became available to the neuroscience community, investigators confirmed that lateral PFC was active during performance of WM tasks in humans (Petrides et al., 1993; Smith & Jonides, 1999). Unlike electrophysiological studies, which offered exquisite temporal resolution, these early functional neuroimaging experiments were unable to tease apart the time course of a trial. Subsequent study designs enabled researchers to isolate the neural correlates of the different processes over time for performance on distinct phases of a task: stimulus encoding, the delay period, and the response period. These studies confirmed that lateral PFC was active at all phases, including the delay period, consistent with the claim that it is involved in stimulus maintenance.

These studies confirmed a partial dissociation between brain regions involved in phonological WM, visuospatial WM, and EFs, in line with Baddeley and Hitch's model (Figure 10.1). In particular, phonological WM tasks implicate left ventrolateral PFC (**VLPFC**; inferior frontal gyrus), a region centrally implicated in language (see Chapter 7). This region is also, to a lesser degree, active in tasks that do not involve verbal material, thereby supporting a broader role in maintenance. By contrast, spatial WM tasks implicate DLPFC – specifically, the superior frontal sulcus, near a region involved in planning eye movements to attended locations in space. Spatial WM tasks also consistently engage parietal cortex – in particular the intraparietal sulcus, a region implicated in spatial attention and planning movements to specific locations in space.

By contrast with these domain-sensitive regions, DLPFC is implicated in a variety of WM tasks that require EFs – and less so in tasks involving maintenance alone (Smith & Jonides, 1999; Petrides, 2000). First, it is implicated in tasks requiring interference suppression (Bunge et al., 2001; Sakai et al., 2002). Of note, Katsuyuki Sakai, Richard Passingham, and colleagues showed that the addition of distraction trials to the memory delay period of a spatial working memory task increased the magnitude of DLPFC activity on correct trials over and above that on trials in which participants made errors. These findings suggest that DLPFC helps to create a distractor-resistant memory trace, harkening back to early work by Malmo (Malmo, 1942) and Miller and Cohen's biased-competition model, described in the previous section. Second, DLPFC is invoked in **task management** when it is necessary to perform two tasks at once (D'Esposito et al., 1995), as in the complex span task described above (Bunge et al., 2001). Third, it is implicated in WM manipulation, as in tasks that require mentally reordering a list of items (Sakai & Passingham, 2003; Crone et al., 2006). Additionally, it is involved during tasks that require flexibly **updating** the contents of WM (Salmon et al., 1996).

While PFC often receives recognition as the "most valuable player" in WM, there are other key regions. A large body of research implicates lateral parietal cortex in both WM maintenance and manipulation. The coordinated activity of lateral PFC, lateral parietal cortex, and associated regions comprises the **lateral frontoparietal network (LFPN)**, which is broadly implicated in WM and EFs. (This network is also called the "executive control network" or the "central executive network." However, ascribing cognitive functions to any brain network is unwise, as our understanding of its functions will likely continue to evolve with further study.) Second, the **frontostriatal pathway** and its **dopaminergic** inputs are also critical for WM. Other essential contributors to WM are the *targets of top-down modulation*, such as visual association areas in occipital cortex in the context of visual WM (see Section 10.4.4). Third, the engagement of the LFPN is thought to be directed by the **cingulo-opercular network** (also known as the "salience network"; Section 10.6). Both WM and EFs emerge from the interactions of large-scale brain networks rather than stemming from a single brain region.

10.4.3 Neuromodulatory Influences on WM

Keeping relevant information in mind and irrelevant information out of mind depends crucially on the action of several neurochemicals, including **dopamine**, as well as norepinephrine and acetylcholine, on the activity of glutamatergic and GABAergic neurons in PFC (Arnsten, 2011). Dopamine and norepinephrine (both in the family of catecholamines) are referred to as neuromodulators because – rather than directly stimulating or inhibiting other neurons – they modulate the strength of a synapse. That is, the amount of dopamine or norepinephrine present in the space between two neurons affects how strongly signaling by one neuron impacts the activity of the other. We focus here on dopamine, which has been more closely linked to WM (see Box 10.1 for more discussion of norepinephrine).

Dopamine is produced in deep nuclei in the brain and is released in the striatum and throughout broad swaths of the cortex, influencing the strength of synaptic transmission in PFC and elsewhere. Through its interactions with GABAergic neurons, dopamine increases the **signal-to-noise ratio**, or **"gain"** of neural activity. That is, it tunes neurons in such a way that they respond preferentially to task-relevant stimuli and task demands by quieting the background activity – as though tuning a radio to a specific station (Cohen & Servan-Schreiber, 1992). Thus, either too much or too little dopamine affects the gain of PFC neurons, abolishing selective delay-period neural activity (Vijayraghavan et al., 2007) – a phenomenon described in the literature as the "inverted-U effect" of dopamine on performance. In fact, dopamine is so essential to PFC function that blocking dopaminergic transmission in the PFC can lead to WM impairments in monkeys nearly as severe as surgical removal of the entire area (Brozoski et al., 1979)!

Behavioral research in adult humans also supports the role of dopamine in WM (Cools & D'Esposito, 2011). WM is often impaired in patients with Parkinson's disease, which is caused by the selective destruction of dopamine-producing cells in the basal ganglia and cerebellum. Second, genetic polymorphisms (gene variants) that influence dopamine activity help to explain individual differences in WM performance. Further, there is evidence that dopamine modulates PFC activity and functional connectivity (Roffman et al., 2016; Bäckman et al., 2017; Salami et al., 2019).

One caveat: nearly every study you read about in the newspaper says that dopamine is doing something important, but it can't be doing all these things alone. We have already mentioned norepinephrine; other important neuromodulators include serotonin, histamine, opioids, and more. There are, in fact, numerous neurochemicals present in low levels in the brain, including ones whose influences on behavior (in particular, human behavior) have not yet been well characterized (Niyonambaza et al., 2019). In the coming years, methods for measuring these chemicals non-invasively will surely refine our thinking about the neurochemistry of the brain.

10.4.4 Mechanisms of WM

Our understanding of the mechanisms underlying WM has advanced substantially over the past two decades. One advance has been an improved understanding of the role of dopamine in WM (Braver et al., 1999; Frank et al., 2001; Cools et al., 2009). This neuromodulator is thought to serve as a **gating signal** that determines whether recent information should be maintained in WM, or whether the contents of WM should be updated. The theory is that dopaminergic input to the PFC promotes stability of WM representations by keeping the "gate" closed, rendering the neurons resistant to distractors by increasing neural gain, as we have discussed previously. By contrast, the theory goes, dopaminergic modulation of the striatum promotes cognitive flexibility by opening the gate and allowing new information to impact neural firing.

This gating model highlights the importance of maintaining a fine balance between stability and flexibility: if the WM system were always open to new inputs, we would be so distracted that we would be unable to maintain focus on a single thought. By contrast, if it were impervious to new inputs, we would be overly rigid in our thinking (D'Esposito & Postle, 2015). Several patient populations are thought to have difficulties with WM gating. Individuals with **Attention Deficit Hyperactivity Disorder (ADHD)** Inattentive Type are – by definition – overly distracted, which could stem from insufficient closure of the gate (Barkley, 1998; see Box 10.1). By contrast, individuals with **Autism Spectrum Disorders (ASD)** tend to be cognitively inflexible, which could stem from insufficient opening of the gate (Dajani & Uddin, 2015; Kriete & Noelle, 2015). Finally, it has been hypothesized that individuals with schizophrenia have a malfunctioning gating mechanism, as they have difficulty with both WM maintenance and updating (Braver et al., 1999).

Another advance relates to the type of information lateral PFC neurons represent. They fire in relation to stimulus-specific information to be retained, and to planned motor responses; they also code for a variety of dimensions of a task, including task rules and feature conjunctions (Fusi et al., 2016; Rigotti et al., 2013). For example, a particular neuron in PFC may respond to several different parameters of either the sensory stimuli themselves or task rules, or to some combination thereof (Mansouri et al., 2006) – and can even take on totally new response properties on a different task (Asaad et al., 2000). These "high-dimensional" prefrontal neurons may be the means by which different combinations of task-relevant features can be coded in categorical ways to guide an appropriate behavioral response.

A third advance has been the formulation of the **sensory recruitment hypothesis**, also called the sensorimotor hypothesis. There is evidence that WM representations are actively maintained in the brain regions that encoded them in the first place (Harrison & Tong, 2009). As a result, PFC and parietal neurons have been reconceptualized as serving as "pointers" to these representations, reactivating task-relevant ones via top-down modulation (Nee & D'Esposito, 2016). One exciting study in humans that combined multivariate fMRI, machine learning, EEG, and transcranial magnetic stimulation (Rose et al., 2016) shows that a recently encoded stimulus attribute that is not currently in mind can be reactivated in WM via electrical stimulation of a category-selective area that encodes this attribute – perhaps mimicking the effect of top-down modulation on visual association cortex. This result shows that information can be maintained in a latent form that does not require persistent activation, and reinforces the sensory recruitment hypothesis, wherein memories reside in the cortical regions that processed them in the first place.

Despite this substantial progress, important questions remain. For example, although theorists converge on the point that lateral PFC prioritizes task-relevant information, it is unclear how it "knows" which mental representations to prioritize via top-down modulation, or when to open or close the WM gate. In other words, who controls the controller? Computational modelers have proposed that the answer to this fascinating problem lies in an *adaptive* gating mechanism involving PFC, the striatum, and dopaminergic inputs to the system that learns from experience when the contents of WM should be protected or updated (Kriete & Noelle, 2015). However, more research is needed to tackle this philosophically important problem.

10.5   Neural Changes That Support the Development of WM

Lateral PFC has, from the very beginning, been front and center in the study of the neural basis of WM development. This line of research was launched by Adele Diamond, who worked with Goldman-Rakic (Diamond & Goldman-Rakic, 1989) on a study comparing the behavior of infants to monkeys with bilateral lesions in DLPFC. Diamond administered the famed developmental psychologist Jean Piaget's AB task (referred to as "A-not-B") to both groups of participants. In this classic task (Piaget, 1952), the participant watches as the experimenter hides a toy (often repeatedly) under one of two boxes positioned next to each other (Box "A"). Then, the experimenter hides the toy at the other location (Box "B") and the infant is allowed to reach out to whichever box is of interest. Piaget showed that 8- to 12-month-olds were more likely to reach to Box A, thereby making a *perseverative error*. While Piaget developed this task to study the emergence of object permanence, the A-not-B task is now considered a test of WM and EF because it requires updating the contents of WM and overriding an inappropriate response. Diamond and Goldman-Rakic found that lesions to DLPFC led monkeys to make many perseverative errors, just like infants. Their pivotal study helped set the stage for DCN to emerge as a domain of research.

10.5.1 Changes in WM Maintenance over Middle Childhood and Adolescence

The majority of functional brain imaging studies of WM development have focused on spatial WM. A number of fMRI studies have shown stronger delay-period activation in adults than children in the regions that have been most strongly implicated in spatial WM: the superior frontal sulcus in lateral PFC and the intraparietal sulcus in lateral parietal cortex (Klingberg et al., 2002; Bunge & Wright, 2007). In addition, a unique longitudinal neurophysiological study in a small group of macaques showed improvements during the transition from puberty to adulthood on the memory-guided saccade test. These behavioral changes were accompanied by increased delay-period neural activity in lateral PFC related to to-be-remembered information, as well as decreased activity in response to distracting stimuli (Zhou et al., 2016). This work supports the hypothesis that robust, distractor-resistant delay-period PFC activity emerges during development, thereby contributing to improved WM capacity.

Several neuroimaging studies in children have combined structural and functional brain measures to study WM development. Of note, Torkel Klingberg and colleagues conducted a structural and functional MRI study of spatial WM capacity of people ranging from 6 to 25 years of age, using an accelerated longitudinal design (as described in Chapter 2). In one study based on this dataset (Darki & Klingberg, 2014), they sought to uncover the anatomical and functional correlates of WM performance at one timepoint (a cross-sectional analysis), as well as the predictors of future performance (a longitudinal analysis). These two types of analyses yielded different insights. Cross-sectionally, higher WM capacity was associated with stronger BOLD activation, thicker gray matter, and more coherent white matter microstructure within a frontostriatal-parietal network. Longitudinally, white matter microstructure in the frontoparietal and frontostriatal tracts at one timepoint predicted individuals' WM capacity two years later, consistent with the cross-sectional results. By contrast, the cortical measures of activation and anatomy from frontoparietal regions were *not* predictive of growth over time. Instead, the caudate nucleus in the basal ganglia now emerged as an important predictor. Darki and Klingberg's results support three key points: (1) long-range frontoparietal and frontostriatal pathways are associated with WM performance at one timepoint as well as improvements in performance during development, (2) the striatum plays an important role in WM development, and (3) more broadly, cross-sectional and longitudinal data can yield complementary results by explaining differences between individuals and changes within individuals, respectively.

While many studies, including those detailed above, have documented increased recruitment of lateral PFC and parietal cortex with age on WM tasks, others have shown the opposite: stronger activation in children than in adults. In a cross-sectional/longitudinal study involving 8- to 30-year-olds scanned at several timepoints, Beatriz Luna (see Scientist Spotlight in Box 10.3) and colleagues observed *decreased* activation in DLPFC and parietal cortex on the memory-guided saccade task (Simmonds et al., 2017). These researchers also observed decreased activation in other regions that support WM and EFs: the anterior insula and anterior cingulate cortex (part of the cingulo-opercular network discussed in Section 10.6), and portions of the basal ganglia involved in motor control (the globus pallidus and putamen). Thus, they found that control-related brain regions are active throughout childhood and adolescence, but that they become more efficient as WM precision increases. Notably, the most pronounced change observed, extending from middle childhood through late adolescence, was an *increase* in activation of visual cortical regions. This finding is consistent with the sensory recruitment hypothesis described earlier (D'Esposito & Postle, 2015), wherein visual stimuli are actively maintained in visual cortical regions. These results suggest that, as WM maintenance in visual cortex becomes more reliable, there is less need for top-down modulation from prefrontal and parietal cortices (Simmonds et al., 2017).

Box 10.3 Scientist Spotlight on Beatriz Luna (Center for Neural Basis of Cognition, University of Pittsburgh)

Beatriz Luna (Box Figure 10.1) is the Staunton Professor of Psychiatry and Pediatrics as well as Professor of Psychology and faculty of the Center for Neural Basis of Cognition at the University of Pittsburgh, where she directs the Laboratory of Neurocognitive Development. As of 2013, Luna is the Founding President of Flux: The International Congress for Integrative Developmental Cognitive Neuroscience. She is also currently Editor-in-Chief of the Developmental Cognitive Neuroscience *journal. In the quest to understand adolescent neurocognitive development, her laboratory uses multimodal neuroimaging methods, including task and rest fMRI, diffusion-weighted imaging (DTI), magnetoencephalography (MEG), magnetic resonance spectroscopic imaging, and positron emission tomography (PET).*

After I received a Bachelor of Arts in Psychology, with a minor in Philosophy, I obtained a Master's degree in Clinical Psychology and Existential Phenomenology. I like to think that the core aspects of phenomenology still guide my scientific thinking. I then took a year off before pursuing a PhD in Developmental Psychology. My dissertation found that the location or extent of brain injury in premature infants due to hypoxic events did not predict behavioral outcome, suggesting that early plasticity impacts brain functional integrity beyond structure. So, I pursued a postdoc with John Sweeney to gain expertise in fMRI, which was first emerging in the field as well as neuroscience and psychiatry. John's lab was using neuroimaging to understand the neural basis of schizophrenia and autism, and he understood that characterizing development was key, particularly during the adolescent period. While I was encouraged to pursue a psychiatric disorder, I knew that we first needed to define normative development through adolescence before we could understand impaired trajectories. This was considered a risky approach, but I knew that this is what I was passionate about and so I persisted. I was motivated to understand the brain basis of adolescent development and why it can deviate at this time to result in psychopathology but also to understand the uniqueness of normative adolescent risk-taking, as I had been a risk-taking adolescent and was aware of its unique place in development. This is still the main aim of our studies probing clinical populations, including: ADHD, autism, schizophrenia, and substance use disorders. Recently, as neuroimaging advances, I have also returned to early development from birth to childhood.

To characterize the neural basis of cognition, I have focused on the core cognitive components of inhibitory control and working memory using eye movement tasks that have been well characterized in non-human primates, where its neurophysiology, neuroanatomy, and neurochemistry are well understood. This approach has led to my programmatic research using multimodal imaging and tasks such as the antisaccade task [see Chapter 13.4.2] and the memory-guided saccade tasks to understand neurocognitive development. These tasks are particularly revealing because, unlike traditional neuropsychological task that can appear mature by childhood due to strategies, eye movement tasks probe the basic circuitry supporting cognition and reliably show maturation into the twenties. Our studies have revealed that, contrary to popular belief, what is unique to adolescence is in fact the access to adult level prefrontal systems. This new, not-yet-mastered, ability is driven by heightened reward processing, informing what we know about sophisticated planning in sensation seeking behaviors at this time. This led to our Driven Dual Systems Model. We have gathered novel evidence showing adult level prefrontal function and increased reward system function in adolescence supported by decreases in frontostriatal connectivity and dopamine function. Some of our latest findings suggest that the amount of dopamine increases through development, stabilizing in adolescence, while receptor densities decrease into young adulthood through specialization. Taken together, our studies suggest that by adolescence all neurocognitive elements are available and development shifts into a process of specialization including decreases in fronto-subcortical connectivity and variability. Our broader model of adolescent development proposes that earlier in development neural and genetic predisposition interact with environmental demands to optimize adaptation. By adolescence, critical period plasticity mechanisms in association cortices establish adult trajectories through closing mechanisms such as myelination.

So, why is better WM performance associated with stronger activation of the LFPN in one study (Darki & Klingberg, 2014), and weaker activation in another (Simmonds et al., 2017)? These studies differ in a number of ways; here we will entertain the possibility that it boils down to differences in task demands. As children mature, they may become better able to *calibrate* their WM network to the task at hand. A task with a higher WM load, such as the forward span task used by Klingberg's lab, may benefit from strong engagement of fronto-parietal regions. By contrast, a task with a lower load but that requires more precise spatial memory, such as the memory-guided saccade task used by Luna's lab, may benefit more from sustained visual cortical representations. Evidence that is compatible with the hypothesis that adults' control system is better calibrated to task demands comes from studies showing that frontoparietal activation ramps up more steeply across WM task difficulty levels in children than in adults (Vogan et al., 2016).

Across studies, there is agreement in the literature that improvements in working memory stem from changes in long-range pathways involving lateral PFC, parietal cortex, the striatum, and domain-specific cortical regions. These findings are consistent with resting-state fMRI data that highlight changes in functional connectivity from childhood to adulthood, including an overall age-related weakening of local networks (i.e., those within the same lobe) and a corresponding strengthening of long-range connections (Fair et al., 2008; Grayson & Fair, 2017). Moreover, the coherence of regional activation – as indicated by the strength of functional connectivity at rest – is strongly associated with WM capacity (Stevens et al., 2011). Available evidence points to the idea that changes in neurochemistry, including but not limited to dopaminergic transmission, sculpt neural firing patterns in such a way that they contribute to increased WM capacity and greater precision (Söderqvist et al., 2012; Luna et al., 2015). Improved calibration of top-down control is likely to be the product of several developmental mechanisms, including increased effectiveness of dopaminergic modulation of the frontostriatal pathway (see Section 10.4.3) and increased influence of the cingulo-opercular network on the LFPN (see Section 10.6).

10.5.2 Neural Basis of Early WM Development

The work outlined above focuses on the period of middle childhood and adolescence. However, performance in this age range is already rather advanced. To capture the period of most dramatic growth, it is necessary to study behavioral and brain function in younger children. EEG and fNIRS (see Chapter 2) have provided the means to do so. For example, Perlman and colleagues (Perlman et al., 2015) used fNIRS to measure lateral PFC activation across a fairly large sample of 3- to 7-year-olds on a spatial WM task with either a short or long delay: 2 or 6 seconds. Figure 10.4A shows the oxyhemoglobin contrast of the long working memory block minus rest. (Note that all activity is located within lateral PFC, because all the sensors were placed there.) Colors represent the T-statistics for the comparison of the two conditions in the general linear model. This figure shows that delay-period activity in lateral PFC was greater during task performance than rest, consistent with prior fNIRS and EEG studies in younger children (Bell & Wolfe, 2007; Buss et al., 2014; Genovesio et al., 2014). Further, this activation was of higher amplitude for the long delay than short delay trials. The researchers divided the sample into two age groups via a median split, with all children below median age, in months, in one group and all those above it in the other. Figure 10.4B shows how average oxyhemoglobin and deoxyhemoglobin concentrations changed over the course of a trial. From these data we can see that both younger and older children engaged PFC more strongly on the long delay blocks. However, examining age as a continuous variable rather than comparing age groups, Perlman and colleagues showed an increase from age 3 to 7 in the PFC oxyhemoglobin response for the long delay blocks. In other words, PFC engagement during WM maintenance increases during early childhood.

10.5.3 Neurodevelopmental Improvements in WM with EF Demands

Several WM tasks that tax EFs have been adapted for use in children, including tasks requiring interference suppression, manipulation, or updating of items in WM. In a study examining interference suppression (Olesen et al., 2006), participants had to encode the spatial location of an array of stimuli. Participants then saw a second array of stimuli that they were supposed to

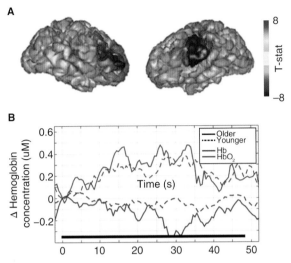

Figure 10.4 Results of fNIRS study of early WM development. (Reproduced from Perlman et al., 2016) A. Reconstructed images of brain activity on the long WM delay blocks, measured by the oxyhemoglobin response. B. Group-averaged time course of the evoked oxy- (red) and deoxyhemoglobin (blue) responses in the right hemisphere for 3- to 7-year-olds above or below the median age (younger and older children). (Reproduced from Perlman et al., 2016)

ignore – that is, distractors. Children exhibited greater superior frontal sulcus activation than adults during this period of distraction, which – given that this region is involved in visuospatial WM – suggests that they were less effective at ignoring the irrelevant visuospatial stimuli. They also showed weaker activation than adults in DLPFC and bilateral parietal cortex, suggesting that they failed to engage these regions sufficiently to create a distractor-resistant memory trace.

In an early study examining WM manipulation, Eveline Crone (see Scientist Spotlight in Chapter 13) and colleagues (Crone et al., 2006) acquired fMRI data while children aged 8–12 years, adolescents aged 13–17 years, and young adults performed simple span tasks involving only three items (Figure 10.5A). Forward span trials required only maintenance: participants had to remember the items in the order in which they had been presented. Backward span trials additionally required manipulation, as participants had to reverse the order of the items in addition to remembering them. The researchers found minimal age differences in performance on Forward span trials; they also found minimal differences in the activation of left VLPFC (Figure 10.5B). As noted previously, this region has been implicated in WM – in particular, phonological WM. By contrast, they found marked behavioral and neural differences on the Backward trials. While adults and, to a lesser extent, adolescents exhibited robust DLPFC activation that was sustained over a 6-second delay, 8- to 12-year-olds did not (Figure 10.5C). Lateral parietal cortex showed

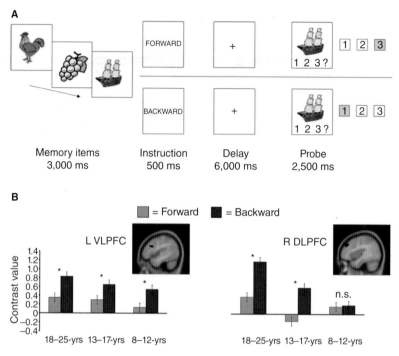

Figure 10.5 Results of fMRI study of working memory maintenance and manipulation in children, adolescents, and adults. A. Task design. The correct answers are shaded in blue for illustrative purposes. B. Average contrast values for delay-period activation in left VLPFC and right DLPFC. (Reproduced from Crone et al., 2006)

a similar pattern. This study suggests that increased delay-period recruitment of DLPFC and lateral parietal cortex supports age-related improvements in the ability to manipulate information in WM.

Another set of studies has used the n-back paradigm (Section 10.2) to examine the process by which we can continuously update contents of WM. In the 0-back task, participants had to respond every time they saw a specific fractal stimulus (Figure 10.6A). In the 1-back task, they had to respond when a stimulus was identical to the one on the previous trial. In the 2-back task, they had to respond when a stimulus was identical to the stimulus that had been presented two trials earlier. Ted Satterthwaite, Raquel Gur, and colleagues employed this task in an fMRI study with nearly 1,000 participants between ages 8 and 22 years (Satterthwaite et al., 2013). They found improvements in performance across the age range, although – as is always the case – they also observed marked individual differences at all ages. They first examined WM activation across the full group of participants. When comparing the challenging 2-back task with the 0-back task, widespread activation was observed compared with the 0-back task. In other words, these regions showed a *load-dependent increase* in activation from the 0-back to the 2-back task.

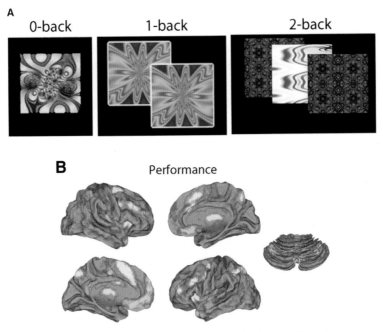

Figure 10.6 fMRI study of WM development. A. An n-back task with three levels of difficulty. B. Regions showing a positive or negative correlation between WM performance and load-dependent increases in activation (warm and cool colors, respectively). (Reproduced from Satterthwaite et al., 2013)

Satterthwaite and colleagues sought to determine whether this WM load effect (i.e., the degree to which activation increased with load) varied as a function of age and/or performance. They found this to be the case, on both counts – and performance was a better predictor of this brain pattern than was age. The warm colors in Figure 10.6B indicate regions that show this brain–behavior correlation: that is, areas for which better performers showed a bigger load-dependent increase in activation. These areas include regions in LFPN, as well as regions in the cingulo-opercular network (dorsal anterior cingulate cortex, anterior insula, and thalamus) – and in the cerebellum, which supports WM and other cognitive functions (Sokolov et al., 2017). These results are in line with the idea that stronger engagement of top-down control is beneficial for performance of challenging WM tasks, as we saw in Section 10.5.1.

However, this is not all that Satterthwaite and colleagues (Satterthwaite et al., 2013) found: they also showed that better WM was associated with a bigger load-dependent *decrease* in activation in a different brain network, known as the **default mode network (DMN)** or the task-negative network (cool colors in Figure 10.6B). This network is so named because the regions in it are *less* active during performance of a task than when participants are engaged in internally directed thought processes such as self-reflection (Raichle et al., 2001). Therefore, it stands to reason that we are better able to focus on tasks when our inner thoughts are suppressed. In fact, the pattern of activation and deactivation of these two networks mediated the positive correlation between age and WM performance, explaining nearly 40 percent of the variance in the relation between age and performance. These findings, based on task activation, go hand in hand with those of resting-state functional connectivity studies (see Chapter 2). Thus, better WM updating is associated both with greater engagement of the network implicated in top-down control and less engagement of the network implicated in introspection. These findings echo a point made earlier: good WM involves both keeping goal-relevant information *in* mind and irrelevant information *out* of mind.

The LFPN and DMN show low between-network functional connectivity in neurotypical adults at rest – not surprisingly, given how the networks are defined: pairs of regions that exhibit weak temporal coupling are assigned to different networks (see Chapter 2). However, a big surprise has been the discovery that the networks don't start out decoupled: Xiaoquian Chai, Susan Whitfield-Gabrieli, and colleagues discovered the LFPN and DMN are often more in sync in children than adults (Chai et al., 2013). We don't yet understand why this is, although a plausible hypothesis is that the decoupling that occurs as the brain matures may stem from changes in the functioning of the cingulo-opercular network, which is thought to control the engagement of the LFPN and DMN (Section 10.6). What we do know is that both adults and children whose LFPN and DMN are more dissociated typically outperform their peers on WM tasks (Hampson et al., 2010; Keller et al., 2015) and other cognitive tasks.

Taking this a step further, a longitudinal study showed that weaker LFPN–DMN connectivity at age 7 was associated with *improvements* in attentional problems over the next four years (Whitfield-Gabrieli et al., 2020). Although we don't have a crystal ball, this neural measure helped to *predict* who would "grow out of" their symptoms over time, and who might benefit from early intervention! This finding is relevant to the treatment of ADHD (see Box 10.1) – and, more broadly, illustrates the potential societal impact of "neuroprediction" (Gabrieli et al., 2015).

In summary, WM and EF development have been linked to functional and structural changes in frontoparietal and frontostriatal regions and pathways, as well as in connections with domain-specific cortical regions involved in stimulus encoding. Thus, the overall pattern of results across task-based fMRI studies supports developmentally based improvements – and substantial individual differences – in the ability to titrate the level of top-down control needed to meet a particular challenge, quieting internally directed thought.

10.6 Developmental Changes in the Recruitment of Top-Down Control

As we have seen, the LFPN has been broadly implicated in the development of WM and EFs. Some studies show increased frontoparietal activation during task performance across childhood and adolescence, and others show decreases (Crone & Steinbeis, 2017). This pattern of results may reflect improvements in neural calibration, whereby top-down control is engaged to the extent required to meet the challenge at hand. Refinement in the allocation of control could perhaps be explained by increased use of deliberate strategies. Additionally, this refinement likely stems from improved communication between the cingulo-opercular network, involved in monitoring task demands and performance, and the LFPN, involved in top-down control.

The dorsal anterior cingulate cortex (dACC) has long been implicated in monitoring one's own performance. This region is thought to sound an alarm when an error has been made (Carter et al., 1998), alerting the LFPN to the need to engage in greater top-down control on subsequent trials. More broadly, this region has been consistently associated with conflict monitoring – not only in detecting conflict between the chosen response and the correct one, but also detecting when there is a need to adjudicate between competing signals in order to select an appropriate response (Botvinick et al., 1999). An influential computational model of EF (cited nearly 1,700 times at the time of writing) distinguished between the alerting function of the dACC and the top-down control function of lateral PFC (Botvinick et al., 2001; for an update, Botvinick & Cohen, 2014). While there have been longstanding debates over the details of this model, the general idea has withstood the test of time.

More recently, researchers have ascribed this alerting function more broadly to the cingulo-opercular network, which is often dubbed the "salience" network, as it is thought to monitor the environment for salient cues and mobilize top-down control to respond effectively to them (Seeley et al., 2007; Uddin, 2017). Devarajan Sridharan and colleagues (Sridharan et al., 2008) proposed that this network serves as a "switch" that leads the brain to toggle between activation of the DMN, involved in internally guided thought, and the LFPN, involved in goal-directed behavior in response to external stimuli (Figure 10.7). Further, Lucina Uddin and colleagues (Uddin et al., 2011) observed stronger resting-state functional connectivity between cingulo-opercular and LFPN network nodes in young adults than in 7- to 9-year-old children – consistent, on the face of it, with the idea that we become better able to engage EFs in response to changes in the environment. As we have discussed at several points in this book, there is now widespread evidence of changing patterns of coupling within and between these and other brain networks from infancy through adolescence. Through diffusion tensor imaging and probabilistic tractography (see Chapter 2), this study also revealed stronger white matter between key nodes in these two networks, as well as within the cingulo-opercular network; thus, the age-related differences in functional coupling appear to be rooted in changing structural connections.

In closing, goal-directed behavior improves over childhood and adolescence for several reasons. First, we become better able to keep goal-relevant information in mind and manipulate it as needed, while filtering out distractors. This capacity for WM depends on the LFPN and frontostriatal pathways. Second, we become better able to monitor our environment and detect situations that require the implementation of top-down control. This capacity to identify challenges and mobilize resources to meet their demands i.e., to exert the necessary level of control relies on the interplay between the LFPN, the cingulo-opercular network, and the DMN. Third, as discussed further in Chapter 13, we become better able to inhibit impulses that are counter-productive to our goals; this capacity, too, relies on PFC. These abilities support academic achievement and performance at work, and also help us to tackle the complexities of day-to-day life.

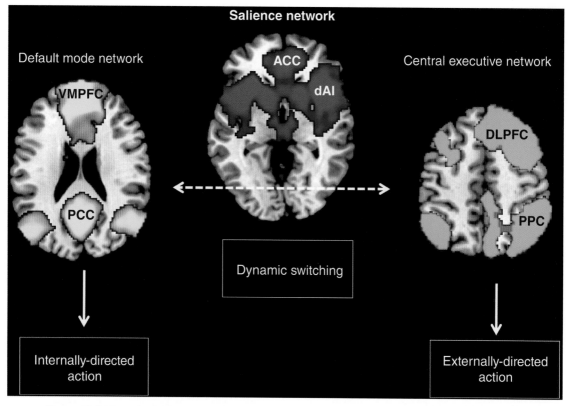

Figure 10.7 Hypothesized interactions between the DMN, cingulo-opercular network, and LFPN. The cingulo-opercular network is hypothesized to switch the brain's dominant mode of activity between the DMN and LFPN. (Figure provided by Lucina Uddin)

SUMMARY

- We have limited-capacity, short-term memory stores for the active maintenance of phonological and visuospatial mental representations
- We can maintain and manipulate these actively maintained representations to achieve immediate goals; this is the defining characteristic of WM
- WM capacity and precision improve over childhood, and to a lesser extent in adolescence
- EFs are slowly developing control processes that support goal-directed thought and behavior; putative EFs include interference suppression, WM manipulation, updating, monitoring, and more
- Lateral PFC, and more generally the LFPN, represent goals and task rules and engage in top-down modulation of the activity of the brain regions that encode information into WM
- Lateral PFC and associated regions are active from an early age, but show more sustained activation across early childhood and may become better calibrated to task demands over middle childhood and adolescence

- Dopamine, acting through the frontostriatal pathway, is thought to play a gating function that influences the balance between stability and flexibility of WM representations
- The dopaminergic system changes through adolescence, and is implicated in several neurodevelopmental disorders
- Subdivisions of PFC make dissociable contributions to WM and EFs, and develop differentially
- The cingulo-opercular, or "salience" network, is thought to alert the LFPN to the need to exert top-down control, leading to reduced activation of the DMN
- Structural and functional changes in the LFPN and cingulo-opercular networks help to explain developmental change and individual differences in WM and EFs

REVIEW QUESTIONS

Draw Baddeley and Hitch's 2003 model of WM. Describe the components, and identify key brain regions associated with each one.

Discuss what we have learned from neurophysiological and lesion studies about the role of the PFC in WM.

Explain the "inverted-U" effect of dopamine on WM.

Explain the biased competition model, and ponder whether it could serve as a unifying principle of PFC function.

Explain the sensory recruitment hypothesis, and how it differs from the classic view that items are maintained in PFC.

Describe how the brain network that supports spatial WM changes over childhood and adolescence, both structurally and functionally.

Discuss a possible reason as to why some studies find that adults engage PFC and parietal cortex more strongly on WM tasks than children, whereas others find the opposite. How might these findings support the idea that the LFPN becomes better calibrated to task demands over development?

Define key nodes in the LFPN, cingulo-opercular network, and the DMN. Explain what roles these networks are thought to play in cognition, and how their engagement and interactions change over development.

Further Reading

Cowan, N. (2016). Working memory maturation: Can we get at the essence of cognitive growth? *Perspectives on Psychological Science*, 11(2), 239–264. https://doi.org/10.1177/1745691615621279

Crone, E. A., & Steinbeis, N. (2017). Neural perspectives on cognitive control development during childhood and adolescence. *Trends in Cognitive Sciences*, 21(3), 205–215. https://doi.org/10.1016/j.tics.2017.01.003

Satterthwaite, T. D., Wolf, D. H., Erus, G., Ruparel, K., Elliott, M. A., Gennatas, E. D., Hopson, R., Jackson, C., Prabhakaran, K., Bilker, W. B., Calkins, M. E., Loughead, J., Smith, A., Roalf, D. R., Hakonarson, H., Verma, R., Davatzikos, C., Gur, R. C., & Gur, R. E. (2013). Functional maturation of the executive system during adolescence. *The Journal of Neuroscience*, 33(41), 16249–16261. https://doi.org/10.1523/JNEUROSCI.2345-13.2013

References

Alloway, T. P., Gathercole, S. E., & Pickering, S. J. (2006). Verbal and visuospatial short-term and working memory in children: Are they separable? *Child Development*, 77(6), 1698–1716. https://doi.org/10.1111/j.1467-8624.2006.00968.x

Arnsten, A. F. (2011). Catecholamine influences on dorsolateral prefrontal cortical networks. *Biological Psychiatry*, 69(12), e89–e99. https://doi.org/10.1016/j.biopsych.2011.01.027

Arnsten, A. F., & Pliszka, S. R. (2011). Catecholamine influences on prefrontal cortical function: Relevance to treatment of attention deficit/hyperactivity disorder and related disorders. *Pharmacology, Biochemistry, and Behavior*, 99(2), 211–216. https://doi.org/10.1016/j.pbb.2011.01.020

Asaad, W. F., Rainer, G., & Miller, E. K. (2000). Task-specific neural activity in the primate prefrontal cortex. *Journal of Neurophysiology*, 84(1), 451–459. https://doi.org/10.1152/jn.2000.84.1.451

Atkinson, R. C., & Shiffrin, R. M. (1968). Human memory: A proposed system and its control processes. In K. W. Spence & J. T. Spence (Eds.), *The psychology of learning and motivation: Advances in research and theory, Volume 2* (pp. 89–195). Academic Press. http://dx.doi.org/10.1016/s0079-7421(08)60422-3

Bäckman, L., Waris, O., Johansson, J., Andersson, M., Rinne, J. O., Alakurtti, K., Soveri, A., Laine, M., & Nyberg, L. (2017). Increased dopamine release after working-memory updating training: Neurochemical correlates of transfer. *Scientific Reports*, 7(1), 7160. https://doi.org/10.1038/s41598-017-07577-y

Baddeley, A. (2003). Working memory: Looking back and looking forward. *Nature Reviews Neuroscience*, 4, 829–839. https//doi.org/10.1038/nrn1201

Baddeley, A. D., Thomson, N., & Buchanan, M. (1975). Word length and the structure of short-term memory. *Journal of Verbal Learning & Verbal Behavior*, 14(6), 575–589. https://doi.org/10.1016/S0022-5371(75)80045-4

Barkley, R. A. (1998). Attention-deficit hyperactivity disorder. *Scientific American*, 279(3), 66–71. https//doi.org/10.1038/scientificamerican0998-66

Bell, M. A., & Wolfe, C. D. (2007). Changes in brain functioning from infancy to early childhood: Evidence from EEG power and coherence during working memory tasks. *Developmental Neuropsychology*, 31, 21–38. https//doi.org/10.1207/s15326942dn3101_2

Botvinick, M. M., Braver, T. S., Barch, D. M., Carter, C. S., & Cohen, J. D. (2001). Conflict monitoring and cognitive control. *Psychological Review*, 108(3), 624–652. https://doi.org/10.1037/0033-295x.108.3.624

Botvinick, M. M., & Cohen, J. D. (2014). The computational and neural basis of cognitive control: Charted territory and new frontiers. *Cognitive Science*, 38(6), 1249–1285. https://doi.org/10.1111/cogs.12126

Botvinick, M., Nystrom, L. E., Fissell, K., Carter, C. S., & Cohen, J. D. (1999). Conflict monitoring versus selection-for-action in anterior cingulate cortex. *Nature*, 402(6758), 179–181. https://doi.org/10.1038/46035

Brady, T. F., Konkle, T., & Alvarez, G. A. (2011). A review of visual memory capacity: Beyond individual items and toward structured representations. *Journal of Vision*, 11(5), 4. https://doi.org/10.1167/11.5.4

Braver, T. S., Barch, D. M., & Cohen, J. D. (1999). Cognition and control in schizophrenia: A computational model of dopamine and prefrontal function. *Biological Psychiatry*, 46(3), 312–328. https://doi.org/10.1016/S0006-3223(99)00116-X

Brozoski, T. J., Brown, R. M., Ptak, J., & Patricia, S. (1979). Dopamine in prefrontal cortex of rhesus monkeys: Evidence for a role in cognitive function. *Catecholamines: Basic and Clinical Frontiers.*

Proceedings of the Fourth International Catecholamine Symposium, Pacific Grove, California, September 17–22, 1681–1683. https://doi.org/10.1016/B978-1-4832-8363-0.50516-4

Bunge, S. A., Ochsner, K. N., Desmond, J. E., Glover, G. H., & Gabrieli, J. D. E. (2001). Prefrontal regions involved in keeping information in and out of mind. *Brain*, 124(10), 2074–2086. https://doi.org/10.1093/brain/124.10.2074

Bunge, S. A., & Wright, S. B. (2007). Neurodevelopmental changes in working memory and cognitive control. *Current Opinion in Neurobiology*, 17(2), 243–250. https://doi.org/10.1016/j.conb.2007.02.005

Burnett Heyes, S., Zokaei, N., & Husain, M. (2016). Longitudinal development of visual working memory precision in childhood and early adolescence. *Cognitive Development*, 39, 36–44. https://doi.org/10.1016/j.cogdev.2016.03.004

Buss, A. T., Fox, N., Boas, D. A., & Spencer, J. P. (2014). Probing the early development of visual working memory capacity with functional near-infrared spectroscopy. *NeuroImage*, 85, 314–325. https://doi.org/10.1016/j.neuroimage.2013.05.034

Carter, C. S., Braver, T. S., Barch, D. M., Botvinick, M. M., Noll, D., & Cohen, J. D. (1998). Anterior cingulate cortex, error detection, and the online monitoring of performance. *Science*, 280(5364), 747–749. https://doi.org/10.1126/science.280.5364.747

Chai, X. J., Ofen, N., Gabrieli, J. D. E., & Whitfield-Gabrieli, S. (2013). Selective development of anticorrelated networks in the intrinsic functional organization of the human brain. *Journal of Cognitive Neuroscience*, 26(3), 501–513. https://doi.org/10.1162/jocn_a_00517

Cohen, C. A., & Hegarty, M. (2014). Visualizing cross sections: Training spatial thinking using interactive animations and virtual objects. *Learning and Individual Differences*, 33, 63–71. https://doi.org/10.1016/j.lindif.2014.04.002

Cohen, J. D., & Servan-Schreiber, D. (1992). Context, cortex, and dopamine: A connectionist approach to behavior and biology in schizophrenia. *Psychological Review*, 99(1), 45–77. https://doi.org/10.1037/0033-295x.99.1.45

Constantinidis, C., & Klingberg, T. (2016). The neuroscience of working memory capacity and training. *Nature Reviews Neuroscience*, 17, 438–449. https//doi.org/10.1038/nrn.2016.43

Cools, R., & D'Esposito, M. (2011). Inverted U-shaped dopamine actions on human working memory and cognitive control. *Biological Psychiatry*, 69(12), e113–e125. https://doi.org/10.1016/j.biopsych.2011.03.028

Cools, R., Frank, M. J., Gibbs, S. E., Miyakawa, A., Jagust, W., & D'Esposito, M. (2009). Striatal dopamine predicts outcome-specific reversal learning and its sensitivity to dopaminergic drug administration. *The Journal of Neuroscience*, 29(5), 1538–1543. https://doi.org/10.1523/JNEUROSCI.4467-08.2009

Cowan, N. (2016). Working memory maturation: Can we get at the essence of cognitive growth? *Perspectives on Psychological Science*, 11(2), 239–264. https://doi.org/10.1177/1745691615621279

Crone, E. A., & Steinbeis, N. (2017). Neural perspectives on cognitive control development during childhood and adolescence. *Trends in Cognitive Sciences*, 21(3), 205–215. https://doi.org/10.1016/j.tics.2017.01.003

Crone, E. A., Wendelken, C., Donohue, S., van Leijenhorst, L., & Bunge, S. A. (2006). Neurocognitive development of the ability to manipulate information in working memory. *Proceedings of the National Academy of Sciences of the United States of America*, 103(24), 9315–9320. https://doi.org/10.1073/pnas.0510088103

Dajani, D. R., & Uddin, L. Q. (2015). Demystifying cognitive flexibility: Implications for clinical and developmental neuroscience. *Trends in Neurosciences*, 38(9), 571–578. https://doi.org/10.1016/j.tins.2015.07.003

Darki, F., & Klingberg, T. (2014). The role of fronto-parietal and fronto-striatal networks in the development of working memory: A longitudinal study. *Cerebral Cortex*, 25(6), 1587–1595. https://doi.org/10.1093/cercor/bht352

Desimone, R., & Duncan, J. (1995). Neural mechanisms of selective visual attention. *American Psychological Association*, 18, 193–222. https://doi.org/10.1146/annurev.ne.18.030195.001205

D'Esposito, M., Detre, J. A., Alsop, D. C., Shin, R. K., Atlas, S., & Grossman, M. (1995). The neural basis of the central executive system of working memory. *Nature*, 378(6554), 279–281. https://doi.org/10.1038/378279a0

D'Esposito, M., & Postle, B. R. (2015). The cognitive neuroscience of working memory. *Annual Review of Psychology*, 66, 115–142. https://doi.org/10.1146/annurev-psych-010814-015031

Diamond, A., & Goldman-Rakic, P. S. (1989). Comparison of human infants and rhesus monkeys on Piaget's AB task: Evidence for dependence on dorsolateral prefrontal cortex. *Experimental Brain Research*, 74(1), 24–40. https://doi.org/10.1007/BF00248277

Fair, D. A., Cohen, A. L., Dosenbach, N. U. F., Church, J. A., Miezin, F. M., Barch, D. M., Raichle, M. E., Petersen, S. E., & Schlaggar, B. L. (2008). The maturing architecture of the brain's default network. *Proceedings of the National Academy of Sciences of the United States of America*, 105(10), 4028–4032. https://doi.org/10.1073/pnas.0800376105

Frank, M. J., Loughry, B., & O'Reilly, R. C. (2001). Interactions between frontal cortex and basal ganglia in working memory: A computational model. *Cognitive, Affective, & Behavioral Neuroscience*, 1(2), 137–160. https://doi.org/10.3758/CABN.1.2.137

Fusi, S., Miller, E. K., & Rigotti, M. (2016). Why neurons mix: High dimensionality for higher cognition. *Current Opinion in Neurobiology*, 37, 66–74. https://doi.org/10.1016/j.conb.2016.01.010

Fuster, J. M. (1973). Unit activity in prefrontal cortex during delayed-response performance: Neuronal correlates of transient memory. *Journal of Neurophysiology*, 36(1), 61–78. https://doi.org/10.1152/jn.1973.36.1.61

Fuster, J. M. (2001). The prefrontal cortex – An update: Time is of the essence. *Neuron*, 30(2), 319–333. https://doi.org/10.1016/S0896-6273(01)00285-9

Gabrieli, J. D. E., Ghosh, S. S., & Whitfield-Gabrieli, S. (2015). Prediction as a humanitarian and pragmatic contribution from human cognitive neuroscience. *Neuron*, 85(1), 11–26. https://doi.org/10.1016/j.neuron.2014.10.047

Gathercole, S. E., Durling, E., Evans, M., Jeffcock, S., & Stone, S. (2008). Working memory abilities and children's performance in laboratory analogues of classroom activities. *Applied Cognitive Psychology*, 22(8), 1019–1037. https://doi.org/10.1002/acp.1407

Gathercole, S. E., Pickering, S. J., Ambridge, B., & Wearing, H. (2004). The structure of working memory from 4 to 15 years of age. *Developmental Psychology*, 40(2), 177–190. https://doi.org/10.1037/0012-1649.40.2.177

Genovesio, A., Tsujimoto, S., Navarra, G., Falcone, R., & Wise, S. P. (2014). Autonomous encoding of irrelevant goals and outcomes by prefrontal cortex neurons. *The Journal of Neuroscience*, 34(5), 1970–1978. https://doi.org/10.1523/JNEUROSCI.3228-13.2014

Goldman-Rakic, P. S. (1995). Cellular basis of working memory. *Neuron*, 14(3), 477–485. https://doi.org/10.1016/0896-6273(95)90304-6

Grayson, D. S., & Fair, D. A. (2017). Development of large-scale functional networks from birth to adulthood: A guide to the neuroimaging literature. *NeuroImage*, 160, 15–31. https://doi.org/10.1016/j.neuroimage.2017.01.079

Hampson, M., Driesen, N., Roth, J. K., Gore, J. C., & Constable, R. T. (2010). Functional connectivity between task-positive and task-negative brain areas and its relation to working memory performance. *Magnetic Resonance Imaging*, 28(8), 1051–1057. https://doi.org/10.1016/j.mri.2010.03.021

Harrison, S. A., & Tong, F. (2009). Decoding reveals the contents of visual working memory in early visual areas. *Nature*, 458(7238), 632–635. https://doi.org/10.1038/nature07832

Hauser, T. U., Fiore, V. G., Moutoussis, M., & Dolan, R. J. (2016). Computational psychiatry of ADHD: Neural gain impairments across Marrian levels of analysis. *Trends in Neurosciences*, 39(2), 63–73. https://doi.org/10.1016/j.tins.2015.12.009

Hinshaw, S. P. (2018). Attention deficit hyperactivity disorder (ADHD): Controversy, developmental mechanisms, and multiple levels of analysis. *Annual Review of Clinical Psychology*, 14, 291–316. https://doi.org/10.1146/annurev-clinpsy-050817-084917

Hulme, C., & Melby-Lervåg, M. (2012). Current evidence does not support the claims made for CogMed working memory training. *Journal of Applied Research in Memory and Cognition*, 1(3), 197–200. https://doi.org/10.1016/j.jarmac.2012.06.006

Jacobsen, C. F. (1931). A study of cerebral function in learning: The frontal lobes. *Journal of Competitive Neurology*, 52(2), 271–340. https://doi.org/10.1002/cne.900520205

Jaeggi, S. M., Buschkuehl, M., Jonides, J., & Perrig, W. J. (2008). Improving fluid intelligence with training on working memory. *Proceedings of the National Academy of Sciences of the United States of America*, 105(19), 6829–6833. https://doi.org/10.1073/pnas.0801268105

Jaeggi, S. M., Buschkuehl, M., Jonides, J., & Shah, P. (2011). Short- and long-term benefits of cognitive training. *Proceedings of the National Academy of Sciences of the United States of America*, 108(25), 10081–10086. https://doi.org/10.1073/pnas.1103228108

Jonides, J., Lacey, S. C., & Nee, D. E. (2005). Processes of working memory in mind and brain. *Current Directions in Psychological Science*, 14(1), 2–5. https://doi.org/10.111/j.0963-7214.2005.00323.x

Kane, M. J., Hambrick, D. Z., Tuholski, S. W., Wilhelm, O., Payne, T. W., & Engle, R. W. (2004). The generality of working memory capacity: A latent-variable approach to verbal and visuospatial memory span and reasoning. *Journal of Experimental Psychology: General*, 133(2), 189–217. https://doi.org/10.1037/0096-3445.133.2.189

Karalunas, S. L., Gustafsson, H. C., Dieckmann, N. F., Tipsord, J., Mitchell, S. H., & Nigg, J. T. (2017). Heterogeneity in development of aspects of working memory predicts longitudinal attention deficit hyperactivity disorder symptom change. *Journal of Abnormal Psychology*, 126(6), 774–792. https://doi.org/10.1037/abn0000292

Katz, B., Shah, P., & Meyer, D. E. (2018). How to play 20 questions with nature and lose: Reflections on 100 years of brain-training research. *Proceedings of the National Academy of Sciences of the United States of America*, 115(40), 9897–9904. https://doi.org/10.1073/pnas.1617102114

Keller, J. B., Hedden, T., Thompson, T. W., Anteraper, S. A., Gabrieli, J. D. E., & Whitfield-Gabrieli, S. (2015). Resting-state anticorrelations between medial and lateral prefrontal cortex: Association with working memory, aging, and individual differences. *Cortex*, 64, 271–280. https://doi.org/10.1016/j.cortex.2014.12.001

Klingberg, T. (2010). Training and plasticity of working memory. *Trends in Cognitive Sciences*, 14(7), 317–324. https://doi.org/10.1016/j.tics.2010.05.002

Klingberg, T., Forssberg, H., & Westerberg, H. (2002). Increased brain activity in frontal and parietal cortex underlies the development of visuospatial working memory capacity during childhood. *Journal of Cognitive Neuroscience*, 14(1), 1–10. https://doi.org/10.1162/089892902317205276

Kriete, T., & Noelle, D. C. (2015). Dopamine and the development of executive dysfunction in autism spectrum disorders. *PloS One*, 10(3). https://doi.org/10.1371/journal.pone.0121605

Luna, B., Garver, K. E., Urban, T. A., Lazar, N. A., & Sweeney, J. A. (2004). Maturation of cognitive processes from late childhood to adulthood. *Child Development*, 75(5), 1357–1372. https://doi.org/10.1111/j.1467-8624.2004.00745.x

Luna, B., Marek, S., Larsen, B., Tervo-Clemmens, B., & Chahal, R. (2015). An integrative model of the maturation of cognitive control. *Annual Review of Neuroscience*, 38, 151–170. https://doi.org/10.1146/annurev-neuro-071714-034054

Malmo, R. B. (1942). Interference factors in delayed response in monkeys after removal of frontal lobes. *Journal of Neurophysiology*, 5, 295–308. https://doi.org/10.1152/jn.1942.5.4.295

Mansouri, F. A., Matsumoto, K., & Tanaka, K. (2006). Prefrontal cell activities related to monkeys' success and failure in adapting to rule changes in a Wisconsin card sorting test analog. *The Journal of Neuroscience*, 26(10), 2745–2756. https://doi.org/10.1523/JNEUROSCI.5238-05.2006

Meyers, E. M. (2018). Dynamic population coding and its relationship to working memory. *Journal of Neurophysiology*, 120(5), 2260–2268. https://doi.org/10.1152/jn.00225.2018

Miller, E. K., & Cohen, J. D. (2001). An integrative theory of prefrontal cortex function. *Annual Review of Neuroscience*, 24, 167–202. https://doi.org/10.1146/annurev.neuro.24.1.167

Mongillo, G., Barak, O., & Tsodyks, M. (2008). Synaptic theory of working memory. *Science*, 319(5869), 1543–1546. https://doi.org/10.1126/science.1150769

Morgan, P. L., Farkas, G., Hillemeier, M. M., Pun, W. H., & Maczuga, S. (2019). Kindergarten children's executive functions predict their second-grade academic achievement and behavior. *Child Development*, 90(5), 1802–1816. https://doi.org/10.1111/cdev.13095

Nee, D. E., & D'Esposito, M. (2016). The representational basis of working memory. In R. E. Clark & S. Martin (Eds.), *Behavioral neuroscience of learning and memory* (pp. 213–230). Springer.

Niyonambaza, S. D., Kumar, P., Xing, P., Mathault, J., De Koninck, P., Boisselier, E., Boukadoum, M., & Miled, A. (2019). A review of neurotransmitters sensing methods for neuro-engineering research. *Applied Sciences*, 9(21), 4719. https://doi.org/10.3390/app9214719

Olesen, P. J., Macoveanu, J., Tegnér, J., & Klingberg, T. (2006). Brain activity related to working memory and distraction in children and adults. *Cerebral Cortex*, 17(5), 1047–1054. https://doi.org/10.1093/cercor/bhl014

Perlman, S. B., Huppert, T. J., & Luna, B. (2015). Functional near-infrared spectroscopy evidence for development of prefrontal engagement in working memory in early through middle childhood. *Cerebral Cortex*, 26(6), 2790–2799. https://doi.org/10.1093/cercor/bhv139

Petrides, M. (2000). Dissociable roles of mid-dorsolateral prefrontal and anterior inferotemporal cortex in visual working memory. *The Journal of Neuroscience*, 20(19), 7496–7503. https://doi.org/10.1523/JNEUROSCI.20-19-07496.2000

Petrides, M., Alivisatos, B., Meyer, E., & Evans, A. C. (1993). Functional activation of the human frontal cortex during the performance of verbal working memory tasks. *Proceedings of the National Academy of Sciences of the United States of America*, 90(3), 878–882. https://doi.org/10.1073/pnas.90.3.878

Piaget, J. (1952). *The origins of intelligence in children*. International University Press.

Raichle, M. E., MacLeod, A. M., Snyder, A. Z., Powers, W. J., Gusnard, D. A., & Shulman, G. L. (2001). A default mode of brain function. *Proceedings of the National Academy of Sciences of the United States of America*, 98(2), 676–682. https://doi.org/10.1073/pnas.98.2.676

Rigotti, M., Barak, O., Warden, M. R., Wang, X.-J., Daw, N. D., Miller, E. K., & Fusi, S. (2013). The importance of mixed selectivity in complex cognitive tasks. *Nature*, 497(7451), 585–590. https://doi.org/10.1038/nature12160

Roffman, J. L., Tanner, A. S., Eryilmaz, H., Rodriguez-Thompson, A., Silverstein, N. J., Ho, N. F., Nitenson, A. Z., Chonde, D. B., Greve, D. N., Abi-Dargham, A., Buckner, R. L., Manoach, D. S., Rosen, B. R., Hooker, J. M., & Catana, C. (2016). Dopamine D1 signaling organizes network dynamics underlying working memory. *Science Advances*, 2(6), e1501672. https://doi.org/10.1126/sciadv.1501672

Rose, N. S., LaRocque, J. J., Riggall, A. C., Gosseries, O., Starrett, M. J., Meyering, E. E., & Postle, B. R. (2016). Reactivation of latent working memories with transcranial magnetic stimulation. *Science*, 354(6316), 1136–1139. https://doi.org/10.1126/science.aah7011

Sakai, K., & Passingham, R. E. (2003). Prefrontal interactions reflect future task operations. *Nature Neuroscience*, 6(1), 75–81. https://doi.org/10.1038/nn987

Sakai, K., Rowe, J. B., & Passingham, R. E. (2002). Active maintenance in prefrontal area 46 creates distractor-resistant memory. *Nature Neuroscience*, 5(5), 479–484. https://doi.org/10.1038/nn846

Sala, G., & Gobet, F. (2020). Cognitive and academic benefits of music training with children: A multilevel meta-analysis. *Memory & Cognition*, 48(8), 1429–1441. https://doi.org/10.3758/s13421-020-01060-2

Salami, A., Garrett, D. D., Wåhlin, A., Rieckmann, A., Papenberg, G., Karalija, N., Jonasson, L., Andersson, M., Axelsson, J., Johansson, J., Riklund, K., Lövdén, M., Lindenberger, U., Bäckman, L., & Nyberg, L. (2019). Dopamine D2/3 binding potential modulates neural signatures of working memory in a load-dependent fashion. *The Journal of Neuroscience*, 39(3), 537–547. https://doi.org/10.1523/JNEUROSCI.1493-18.2018

Salmon, E., Van der Linden, M., Collette, F., Delfiore, G., Maquet, P., Degueldre, C., Luxen, A., & Franck, G. (1996). Regional brain activity during working memory tasks. *Brain*, 119(5), 1617–1625. https://doi.org/10.1093/brain/119.5.1617

Satterthwaite, T. D., Wolf, D. H., Erus, G., Ruparel, K., Elliott, M. A., Gennatas, E. D., Hopson, R., Jackson, C., Prabhakaran, K., Bilker, W. B., Calkins, M. E., Loughead, J., Smith, A., Roalf, D. R., Hakonarson, H., Verma, R., Davatzikos, C., Gur, R. C., & Gur, R. E. (2013). Functional maturation of the executive system during adolescence. *The Journal of Neuroscience*, 33(41), 16249–16261. https://doi.org/10.1523/JNEUROSCI.2345-13.2013

Seeley, W. W., Menon, V., Schatzberg, A. F., Keller, J., Glover, G. H., Kenna, H., Reiss, A. L., & Greicius, M. D. (2007). Dissociable intrinsic connectivity networks for salience processing and executive control. *The Journal of Neuroscience*, 27(9), 2349–2356. https://doi.org/10.1523/JNEUROSCI.5587-06.2007

Shaw, P., Eckstrand, K., Sharp, W., Blumenthal, J., Lerch, J. P., Greenstein, D., Clasen, L., Evans, A., Giedd, J., & Rapoport, J. L. (2007). Attention-deficit/hyperactivity disorder is characterized by a delay in cortical maturation. *Proceedings of the National Academy of Sciences of the United States of America*, 104(49), 19649–19654. https://doi.org/10.1073/pnas.0707741104

Simmonds, D. J., Hallquist, M. N., & Luna, B. (2017). Protracted development of executive and mnemonic brain systems underlying working memory in adolescence: A longitudinal fMRI study. *NeuroImage*, 157, 695–704. https://doi.org/10.1016/j.neuroimage.2017.01.016

Smith, E. E., & Jonides, J. (1999). Storage and executive processes in the frontal lobes. *Science*, 283(5408), 1657–1661. https://doi.org/10.1126/science.283.5408.1657

Söderqvist, S., Nutley, S. B., Ottersen, J., Grill, K. M., & Klingberg, T. (2012). Computerized training of non-verbal reasoning and working memory in children with intellectual disability. *Frontiers in Human Neuroscience*, 6, 271. https://doi.org/10.3389/fnhum.2012.00271

Sokolov, A. A., Miall, R. C., & Ivry, R. B. (2017). The cerebellum: Adaptive prediction for movement and cognition. *Trends in Cognitive Sciences*, 21(5), 313–332. https://doi.org/10.1016/j.tics.2017.02.005

Spencer-Smith, M., & Klingberg, T. (2015). Benefits of a working memory training program for inattention in daily life: A systematic review and meta-analysis. *PloS One*, 10(3), e0119522. https://doi.org/10.1371/journal.pone.0119522

Sridharan, D., Levitin, D. J., & Menon, V. (2008). A critical role for the right fronto-insular cortex in switching between central-executive and default-mode networks. *Proceedings of the National Academy of Sciences of the United States of America*, 105(34), 12569–12574. https://doi.org/10.1073/pnas.0800005105

Stevens, W. D., Kahn, I., Wig, G. S., & Schacter, D. L. (2011). Hemispheric asymmetry of visual scene processing in the human brain: Evidence from repetition priming and intrinsic activity. *Cerebral Cortex*, 22(8), 1935–1949. https://doi.org/10.1093/cercor/bhr273

Sudre, G., Mangalmurti, A., & Shaw, P. (2018). Growing out of attention deficit hyperactivity disorder: Insights from the 'remitted' brain. *Neuroscience and Biobehavioral Reviews*, 94, 198–209. https://doi.org/10.1016/j.neubiorev.2018.08.010

Uddin, L. Q. (2017). *Salience network of the human brain*. Academic Press.

Uddin, L. Q., Supekar, K. S., Ryali, S., & Menon, V. (2011). Dynamic reconfiguration of structural and functional connectivity across core neurocognitive brain networks with development. *Journal of Neuroscience,* 31(50), 18578–18589. https://doi.org10.1523/JNEUROSCI.4465-11.2011

Vijayraghavan, S., Wang, M., Birnbaum, S. G., Williams, G. V, & Arnsten, A. F. T. (2007). Inverted-U dopamine D1 receptor actions on prefrontal neurons engaged in working memory. *Nature Neuroscience,* 10(3), 376–384. https://doi.org/10.1038/nn1846

Vogan, V. M., Morgan, B. R., Powell, T. L., Smith, M. L., & Taylor, M. J. (2016). The neurodevelopmental differences of increasing verbal working memory demand in children and adults. *Developmental Cognitive Neuroscience,* 17, 19–27. https://doi.org/10.1016/j.dcn.2015.10.008

Whitfield-Gabrieli, S., Wendelken, C., Nieto-Castañón, A., Bailey, S. K., Anteraper, S. A., Lee, Y. J., Chai, X. Q., Hirshfeld-Becker, D. R., Biederman, J., Cutting, L. E., & Bunge, S. A. (2020). Association of intrinsic brain architecture with changes in attentional and mood symptoms during development. *JAMA Psychiatry,* 77(4), 378–386. https://doi.org/10.1001/jamapsychiatry.2019.4208

Zelazo, P. D., & Carlson, S. M. (2012). Hot and cool executive function in childhood and adolescence: Development and plasticity. *Child Development Perspectives,* 6(4), 354–360. https://doi.org/10.111/j.1750-8606.2012.00246.x

Zhou, X., Zhu, D., Qi, X.-L., Li, S., King, S. G., Salinas, E., Stanford, T. R., & Constantinidis, C. (2016). Neural correlates of working memory development in adolescent primates. *Nature Communications,* 7(1), 13423. https://doi.org/10.1038/ncomms13423

11   Language and Literacy

LEARNING OBJECTIVES

- Describe the "reading paradox"
- Outline the neuronal recycling hypothesis and its relation to the evolution of reading and writing
- Describe the visual word form area and how it develops
- Explain the cerebral mechanisms engaged during proficient reading
- Delineate the component abilities that underlie reading
- Detail why both quantity and quality of early language input are important to reading
- Describe developmental dyslexia and differentiate it from acquired dyslexia

By the time they enter into formal education, typically developing children have a basic pre-reading toolkit: spoken language, some familiarity with the alphabet (although many children believe that the letter between *k* and *p* is *ellemeno*), and the beginnings of phonological awareness. These skills all serve as a foundation for the development of reading. In particular, early language abilities support children as they learn to decode and comprehend written words, and early measures of discourse-level language skills are strong predictors of reading success. Literacy is built on these basic skills. All else being equal (although that's rarely the case), and assuming no reading-specific disorders, the stronger the early language abilities, the easier the reading development.

At this point it is important to draw a distinction between reading and the many abilities we describe in *Fundamentals of Developmental Cognitive Neuroscience* that have a clear evolutionary basis, such as visual perception, reaching, grasping, and orienting. Language is a product of culture that scaffolds on existing visual perception and language decoding mechanisms in the brain, but the brain did not evolve for reading. We know this because reading is a relatively recent development in human history (about 4,000 years ago) and because of evolutionary lag – the fact that it takes far longer than that for complex abilities to emerge through natural selection.

Reading thus depends on both domain-general and domain-specific abilities: children's early language skills are domain-general, while the finely tuned visual recognition necessary for fluent reading is domain-specific. In the early school years, the focus on mapping written symbols to their phonological form relies on children having representations of the (aural) phonetic components of their language. At a general level, children who score poorly on reading comprehension tests often have difficulty decoding words, as well as understanding spoken language. In this chapter, we discuss the neurobiological basis for both typical and atypical reading development, and we consider a language-specific disorder, dyslexia, that ultimately impacts reading.

11.1   Reading Paradox

Reading is made possible, at least in part, through the development of neuronal tissue that is dedicated to decoding visual symbols. Decoding takes the cues on a written page and derives meaning from them. The most basic component of decoding is applying knowledge of letter–sound relationships, including knowledge of patterns formed by strings of letters, to correctly pronounce written words. This is followed by the ability to decode whole words rather than decoding letter-by-letter, and relies on the sort of statistical inferencing we saw in Chapter 4.

Whereas human beings have been talking, signing, and singing for anywhere between 50,000 and 100,000 years, we've been writing for only about 4,000 years. This means that the brain structures that are dedicated to reading were not selected for that purpose. Rather, they were accommodated to it. Thus, if we want to understand why our brains are the way they are, we need to look to the environment that shaped them and, specifically, to a culture that valued reading and writing. Then, we need to understand how neurons repurpose (or recycle) themselves to allow for new, culturally invented skills.

11.1.1 Writing as a Cultural Invention That Has Enabled Reading

Writing and decoding writing (i.e., reading) are both recently invented social practices that have created reading-specific systems in the brain. Writing is a tool designed by us for us to use, meaning it is unique to human bodies and capacities, as well as to our needs, interests, and circumstances. In inventing writing, humans discovered that the visual cortex can function as a text comprehension system. Thus, reading isn't enabled by our brain any more than swiping a cell phone is to see the next picture; it is something our brains have enabled us to do. The beauty of this perspective is that it allows us to see how the brain constrains our cultural practices even as our cultural practices shape the brain itself.

What we are able to do depends not only on how we are built but also on the cultural and technological environments we find ourselves in. In the case of reading, this relies first and foremost on there being writing in the environment. Next, reading and writing require a specific mapping between the scrawls and scribbles we write down (or chisel) and the way we want them interpreted – a decoding key that linguists call a **script** (not to be confused with what actors read from, or the word used to distinguish handwriting from printed letters).

Reading is fundamentally an application of our ability to see, and depends on everything that seeing depends on, including specific neural systems. When we read, we make use of brain areas dedicated to seeing by recycling the visual system.

11.1.2 Co-invention of Writing and Reading

We have described reading as a cultural invention, but reading requires writing. Writing was the first cultural invention – a technological invention, really – to make the spoken word permanent. In so doing, writing changed the human brain, and changed the human condition along with it. Although reading and writing are distinct processes, the invention of a system of

Figure 11.1 Egyptian hieroglyphs from 13th century BC tomb of Seti I. (Wikipedia)

written symbols necessarily preceded the invention of reading. The term **writing system** refers to the relationship between the symbols of an orthography and the particular type of linguistic units they represent: entire words versus syllables versus single sounds (**phonemes**). In contrast, **orthography** describes the set of symbols used in a writing system, as well as the conventions governing their use when members of a language community communicate via writing.

Suffice it to say that hundreds of different writing systems have come and gone over the past few thousand years. Writing is estimated to have started in a minimal form about 6,000 years ago. Egyptian hieroglyphs were developed around 3200 BC, combining logographs (written symbols that represent an entire word or morpheme), syllabic, and alphabetic elements (Figure 11.1), but it was only around 2000 BC that Phoenicians developed the first alphabet, one consisting entirely of consonants. A thousand years later, the Greeks added vowels (Daniels, 1996). Punctuation marks began appearing as early as the second century BC. It wasn't until 900 AD that spaces were introduced between words! As you can imagine, spacing between words radically facilitated reading by easing the process of text decoding (Houston, 2013).

To this day, writing systems come in all shapes and sizes. The Latin alphabet – the most commonly used writing system in the world – provides specific symbols for each phoneme, including for both the vowel and consonant sounds. Other alphabetic languages don't convey vowel sounds in their writing at all (e.g., standard Hebrew), or use diacritical marks to indicate them (e.g., Arabic). Logographic systems (e.g., Chinese) represent the meaning (i.e., semantic) components of words rather than the phonemes themselves. Both Chinese hanzi and Japanese kanji are logographic writing systems, meaning one symbol can represent a complete word or morpheme (you'll recall from Chapter 8 that a morpheme is the smallest unit of meaning in a language). Japanese hiragan and katakana are both syllabic alphabets, meaning each symbol represents a syllable. You read that right: in Japanese, you can write the same thing using one of three different writing systems!

Some writing systems are very common, others less so. For example, the Arabic script, which is used in Modern Standard Arabic, has also been adapted for Persian. In the past, it was used to write Hausa and Malay. Another common script is Devanagari, which is used by over 120 languages, including Hindi, Nepali, Sanskrit, and Marathi. The Urdu script is derived from Arabic – like the Perso-Arabic script we've mentioned – but it is used for writing Urdu. Clearly, even now, there are a lot of ways to write!

When we learn to read in other languages, we often have to learn to remap a familiar alphabetic symbol to a new sound, such as the *o* in French; sometimes markings help remind us, as in the ñ in Spanish. Learning an entire new alphabet from scratch can be difficult for adults, but a typically developing child can learn any written system humans use.

11.1.3 Shallow (Transparent) and Deep (Opaque) Orthographies Impact Reading Acquisition

In general, orthographies that use an alphabet have a higher degree of correspondence between the written symbol and the sound it represents than do either syllabic or logographic writing systems. Nonetheless, alphabetic languages vary in how directly a letter maps to a sound. For example, English orthography is notorious for its highly variable letter-to-sound mappings, while Spanish orthography is highly systematic.

The different sounds associated with a single letter in English are due to the rapid changes in English pronunciation that have taken place despite a relatively stable orthography. (This is the source of the joke that *fish* can legitimately be spelled *ghoti*, by using the /gh/ sound from *enough*, the /o/ sound from *women* and the /ti/ sound from *action*.) In contrast, Spanish letter-to-sound mappings are highly regular, making Spanish writing relatively easy to decode. This variability in letter-to-sound mappings across different orthographies is characterized as running along a continuum, from deep to shallow (sometimes also described as running from opaque to transparent). How shallow/deep an orthography is impacts how easy it is for early readers of that language to develop phonemic awareness. As an English reader, you will not be surprised to learn that deep orthographies like English present substantial difficulties for early readers of the language, a topic to which we will return.

11.2 Neuronal Specialization and the Creation of Reading-Specific Areas on the Brain

Writing is a human innovation that has led to repurposing of neuronal resources in support of reading. Stanislas Dehaene and his colleagues proposed the **neuronal recycling hypothesis** to account for how a cultural invention can reorganize the brain. Their argument is that reading recycles existing cerebral structure that serves a functionally similar purpose (Dehaene & Cohen, 2007). In the case of reading, the functional ability is detailed visual object recognition. It is hardly radical to recognize that reading makes use of brain areas dedicated to seeing, but the details of how this comes to pass are pretty remarkable.

Becoming a literate human exemplifies the merging of our phylogenetic and ontogenetic histories, whereby culture imposes practices that selectively alter neuronal systems adapted initially to quite different functions. The neuronal recycling hypothesis builds on the idea that there is a "fringe of variability" (Dehaene, 2011) that tolerates an already-evolved system being used differently than the use for which it was originally adapted (Steven Pinker argued as much when he described music as an artifact or byproduct of speech, rather than an evolutionary adaption, a view which has generated much debate). In the case of reading, the brain's visual object recognition system (Chapter 6) provides the necessary degrees of freedom for novel cultural practices to take advantage of those preexisting neural resources. The visual system is highly constrained but also highly plastic, and culture is able to sculpt it within those constraints, transforming specific components of the visual cortex into a text comprehension system.

11.2.1 Visual Object Categories and the Visual Word Form Area (VWFA)

We have argued that reading is complex and multidimensional, yet we've also argued that our reading and writing systems are constrained by the brain networks we recycle in the service of acquiring the ability to read. But networks recycled from what? A critical contribution to understanding literacy comes from watching what happens in the brain when people read, a process that reveals the degree to which reading requires specialized visual object recognition (Cohen et al., 2002). The process starts with recognizing individual letters, but with the development of literacy, readers come to recognize entire words. From there, the rest of the language system can be fully engaged via the visual system alone.

Being an expert reader requires being an expert letter (and word) recognizer. Recall from our discussion of face recognition (Chapter 6) that the fusiform gyrus contains patches of cortex that respond differentially to specific classes of visual stimuli. In the case of face recognition, the ability localizes to a component of the right fusiform gyrus, the fusiform face area (FFA). The parahippocampal place area (PPA) is dedicated to processing places. FFA and PPA specialization helps us navigate our social and physical worlds. There are other regions within the ventral visual cortex dedicated to processing other important visual categories (e.g., tools, body parts).

As one becomes an expert recognizer of the component parts of writing, a similar degree of functional localization takes place for letters and words. A singular advance in our understanding of how the brain enables reading has been the observation that when skilled readers recognize written words, they engage a small region of left fusiform gyrus within the ventral occipitotemporal cortex. This area is now widely referred to as the **visual word form area (VWFA)**. The label VWFA was first introduced to describe PET findings contrasting responsivity to words and non-words (Petersen et al., 1990).

All three regions (FFA, PPA, VWFA) provide exquisite visual recognition about their respective objects of expertise. Face and place recognition have served humans far longer than reading, while the historically recent invention of written symbols makes it unlikely that the VWFA evolved for reading, meaning that experience-driven selectivity for letters and words emerges through the process of learning to read itself. Evidence for this argument comes from various sources. For example, preferential responses to letters and words are found only in literate adults (Dehaene et al., 2010), with the VWFA emerging in the ventral visual processing stream as the process of learning to read results in extraction of linguistic information from visual symbols.

11.2.2 Language-Specific Tuning of the VWFA

We have seen that there are very many different writing systems in use around the globe. Given these various writing systems, you might wonder how the human brain – fundamentally the same regardless of the language spoken by its owner – handles that variability. Do readers of a logographic writing system decode written language in the same way that readers of a syllabic or an alphabetic system do? Indeed, an indisputable consequence of learning to read any written language is the emergence of the VWFA, with this area serving as a functional hub of orthographic processing that links written language to its corresponding sounds (as well as to meaning, but more on that later). In short, the written form of any language engages the VWFA.

Studies comparing brain activation in readers of languages as diverse as English and Chinese have confirmed that the VWFA is engaged by both during reading (Booth et al., 2006; Nakamura et al., 2012). However, while skilled readers of English produce a strongly left-lateralized VWFA response to English letters and words, readers of Chinese produce bilateral activation, most dominantly in the left fusiform gyrus – corresponding to the English readers' VWFA – but also in the right (Nelson et al., 2009). Such variability in the functional localization of the VWFA across languages should not be entirely surprising, considering the specifics of the two orthographies, which represent writing systems with very different levels of representation. English maps from orthography to phonology to semantics; in contrast, Chinese contains far more information about semantics than phonology, and much of semantic understanding is right lateralized, something we learned first from the split-brain experiments of Sperry and Gazzaniga in the 1960s (see Gazzaniga, 2005 for a review).

Although the VWFA is considerably smaller, as well as more variable in precise location across individuals relative to the FFA, it serves a similar visual recognition purpose, one exclusively in the service of reading. Exposure to familiar orthography in literate individuals activates the VWFA more than does any other category of visual stimuli, including faces, objects, houses, and numerical digits. Young children who are learning to read need to focus deliberately on the act of reading. With maturation, reading becomes automatic to the point that we can't turn it off – if there is text in front of us, we read it, even if we are instructed not to, a phenomenon known as the **Stroop effect**. Of course, the extensive practice with a particular written language that leads to fluent reading impacts not just the VWFA, but other levels of the visual system too. For example, expert readers of French and Chinese were found to engage the VWFA while reading their respective languages, but the two groups differed in which parts of lower-level visual cortex were engaged (Szwed et al., 2014). These differences in early visual processing likely stem from the different physical forms in French and Chinese orthography: lines vs. figures. Such findings highlight that reading is complex, and the VWFA is just one part of a larger, distributed neuronal system that it engages. In an expert reader, processing starts at the lowest level of the visual system, as soon as a reader puts eyes to page (or screen), and it's not surprising that the many structural differences across writing systems may impact the precise processing route. Regardless, the processing of all writing systems engages the VWFA along the way.

How do the specifics of one's writing system shape the brain? The extent to which a reader's VWFA is engaged in response to different bigrams (i.e., pairs of letters) depends on the statistics of letter co-occurrences. Figure 11.2 shows the mean percentage change in the fMRI BOLD response from literate English speakers to different meaningless bigrams. With increasing bigram frequency, responsivity in the VWFA increases. The VWFA reflects language-specific orthographic knowledge, and provides us with yet another example of how the statistics of the environment shape our perception.

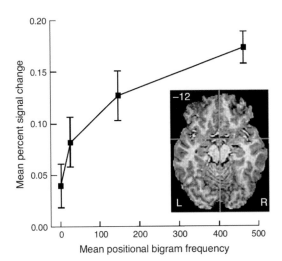

Figure 11.2 VWFA tuning in response to bigram frequency in literate speakers of a written alphabetic language, English. (Adapted from Binder et al., 2006)

11.2.3 Learning to Read "Creates" the VWFA

The emergence of literacy changes a child's brain (Cantlon et al., 2011; Dehaene-Lambertz et al., 2018). Just as specific configurations – individual letters – increasingly engage the VWFA, strings of letters likewise do so. In a test of the neuronal recycling hypothesis, Ghislaine Dehaene-Lambertz and Stanislas Dehaene (Dehaene-Lambertz et al., 2018) tracked how the visual cortex of individual French-speaking children changed during the first months of their reading acquisition. To do so, the researchers used fMRI to scan a group of 6-year-old children longitudinally, up to seven times in total, both prior to and during their first year of school. While in the scanner, children were asked to perform an unrelated target-detection task, during which they saw various pictures, including words, numbers, tools, houses, faces, and bodies. As shown in Figure 11.3, children's reading was also assessed behaviorally, with these measures revealing increases in both their grapheme–to–phoneme mapping abilities and reading speed in the first trimester of school.

These behavioral improvements correspond to changes in how the brain responds to the written word. Figure 11.3A shows the effect of children's reading speed on word-evoked activations relative to rest (their age was entered as a covariable). Moreover, as shown in Figure 11.3B, voxels specific to written words emerged at the VWFA location. Note that digits also begin separating out into their own functional subregion, as the first year of school involves extensive digit-specific experience. Meanwhile, children's brain responses to other categories remained stable, although the face-related activity already in the right FFA increased further and in proportion to the increases in children's reading scores. This increased lateralization of face processing to the right indicates a "release" of the right fusiform gyrus for further specialization in face processing as the VWFA region in the left fusiform becomes increasingly tuned to letters. Connectivity analyses from other studies are consistent with this interpretation (Behrmann & Plaut, 2013). Thus, the emergence of VWFA is left lateralized, and its engagement is in response to letters and words and not to numbers or faces. In short, as a reader gains

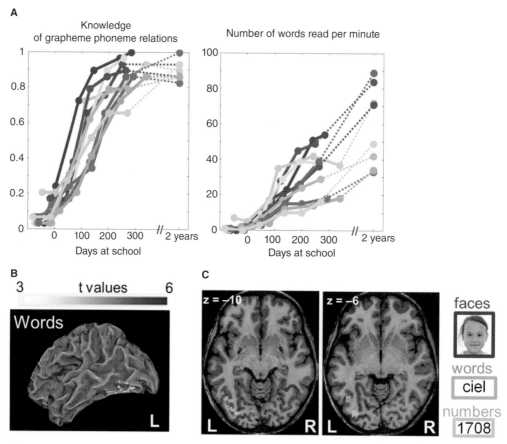

Figure 11.3 Longitudinal tracking of behavior and brain in children learning to read. A. Behavioral indicators of the impact of formal education on reading ability. The different colors each represent one child's performance and the x-axis on both graphs represents children's performance (higher number = better/faster performance). B. In a study of developing readers, reading speed related to the amount of activation evoked by words compared to rest in the VWFA (with age entered as a covariable). C. Activation evoked by faces (in red), words (in green), and numbers (in blue). Activation in the left occipitotemporal pathway in response to words and numbers increased with reading speed, and reading proficiency was associated with increased responses to faces in the right fusiform gyrus. (All figures reprinted from Dehaene-Lambertz et al., 2018)

proficiency with processing the written word, the VWFA shifts from being most responsive to letters relative to any other visual stimulus to being maximally responsive to words. Without engagement with letters and words, what we are calling the VWFA would be used for other visual processes – thus, it really is something that reading creates.

11.2.4 Alternative Perspectives on the VWFA

A challenge to this account of the VWFA comes from the finding that blind individuals engage that region while reading Braille. Braille depends on the use of touch to decode patterns of raised dots, and the Braille characters represent the letters of the alphabet, punctuation marks, numbers, and everything else you can write in print. Not surprisingly, expert Braille readers show more overall neural activation when reading Braille than when touching meaningless dot patterns (Sadato et al., 1996). What is surprising, however, is that blind Braille readers show peak neural responsivity to meaningful dot patterns in the canonical location of sighted readers' VWFA (Reich et al., 2011). You don't need visual experience with print to develop reading selectivity in the ventral occipital cortex! How can this be? One interpretation is that the ventral occipitotemporal cortex is committed to processing shapes for meaning – even 3D shapes created by raised dots – independent of modality (Hannagan et al., 2015). Another possibility is that, in the absence of visual input, the ventral occipitotemporal cortex of blind individuals becomes involved in language processing by virtue of (genetically coded) white matter pathways that provide linguistic feedback to the VWFA, rather than by visual language itself (Kim et al., 2017). According to this view, unlike responses to writing in sighted individuals, VWFA responsivity to Braille reflects feedback to the area from the processing of linguistic information (i.e., syntax, semantics) in the absence of visually mediated letter and word forms. However, only those who are congenitally blind show language-specific specialization in the visual cortex, indicating that the kind of repurposing seen in Braille readers only happens when alternative forms of language input are experienced during a sensitive period in development (Pant et al., 2020).

Reading researchers have begun focusing on the attentional component of VWFA based on a small, but influential subset of findings that highlight the VWFA's intrinsic connectivity to frontoparietal regions involved in attention processing (Price & Devlin, 2003; Vogel et al., 2012). According to this view, the findings from blind Braille readers suggest that there are multiple routes to and from the VWFA, including both language and attentional systems. Indeed, the visual cortices of blind people do not remain inactive, and blindness experienced at any age leads to synchronization during rest between the visual cortices and frontoparietal attention networks. Support for this perspective has grown in recent years in light of findings from larger datasets and more sophisticated imaging techniques. For example, based on the large imaging dataset available via the Human Connectome Project (N = 313), Menon and colleagues (Chen et al., 2019) recently suggested that the VWFA is a "gateway" linking language and attentional systems. This is worth keeping in mind when considering routes by which the VWFA is engaged in language-specific processing.

11.3 Brain Interconnectivity and Literacy

Skilled reading requires the integration of several forms of specialized knowledge, including orthographic awareness (knowing the composition of the written form of language), phonemic and phonological awareness (knowing about the individual sounds of one's language and how they can be combined), and syntactic and semantic awareness (knowing the grammatical structure of sentences and the meanings of words). In a typical population of skilled adult readers, the convergence of these forms of knowledge supports efficient reading.

Studying the development of reading in children helps delineate the mechanisms that stitch the component parts of reading together. Because different aspects of reading emerge at different developmental timepoints, it is only through research targeting different stages of the acquisition process that we have come to understand the neural foundations of literacy.

11.3.1 Interfacing the VWFA with the Rest of the Language System

Beyond emergence of the left-lateralized VWFA, learning to read puts into place a processing network that forms an interface between the visual representation of language – writing – and the larger spoken language system (Dehaene, 2009). As you may remember from your own experiences with reading acquisition, this process takes time and effort.

Learning to read changes the brain – and the better the reader, the more marked the change. Figure 11.4 shows a schematic view of how the VWFA becomes both functionally and anatomically tuned to letters and words, while also being integrated with the frontotemporal language network (Dehaene & Dehaene-Lambertz, 2016).

Tractography analyses (Wandell et al., 2012) highlight three white matter tracts critical to reading: the **superior longitudinal fasciculus**, the **arcuate fasciculus**, both important to speech

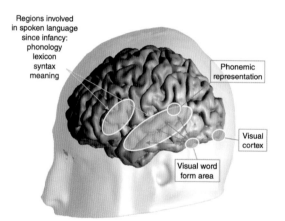

Figure 11.4 Left hemisphere ventral visual areas (in green) increase their activation and specialization during the acquisition of literacy. Additional connections emerge linking ventral visual areas to the broader language network (in yellow), particularly an area in the superior temporal gyrus involved in phonemic (sound) representation. Learning to read gradually establishes a brain network in which visual representation of language is linked to the larger spoken language system. (Reproduced from Dehaene & Dehaene-Lambertz, 2016)

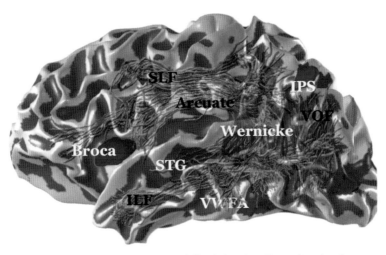

Figure 11.5 Reading generates specialized circuitry. Posterior visual signals are transmitted to the language system (red overlay, white text). Subdivisions of cortical regions that are consistently identified as active during reading: the visual word form area (VWFA); regions within the intraparietal sulcus (IPS), which appear to be a source of top-down modulation; regions near the primary auditory cortex in the superior temporal gyrus (STG); and Wernicke's and Broca's areas, implicated in the comprehension and production of language. Four large tracts (black text) terminate near the functionally defined regions: the VOF, ILF, superior longitudinal fasciculus (SLF), and the arcuate fasciculus. (Reprinted from Wandell & Le, 2017)

and language (see Chapter 8), and the **inferior longitudinal fasciculus**, which connects the VWFA to the anterior and medial temporal lobe (Figure 11.5). A fourth tract, the **vertical occipital fasciculus**, facilitates communication between ventral visual stream regions involved in form perception and dorsal stream regions involved in eye movements and attention. Thus, as reading ability develops, the VWFA becomes increasingly linked to left-lateralized language areas, far more than corresponding regions in the right hemisphere (i.e., FFA, PPA). The process by which such connectivity emerges can be interpreted in interactive specialization terms (Johnson, 2011): the form-sensitive VWFA – focused on letters – becomes increasingly specialized for words as it becomes integrated with the larger language network (Hannagan et al., 2015). This is supported by findings from a longitudinal training study in which changes in the VWFA were tracked over time in kindergarten-aged children using both fMRI and ERP (Brem et al., 2010). Results showed early activation of the VWFA in response to print, with additional changes corresponding to the emergence of letter–speech sound associations.

The neuronal recycling model (Section 11.2) predicts that cortex evolutionarily dedicated to other functions is gradually co-opted for novel uses, such that its original functional responsivity reduces gradually while the new responsivity increases. However, the original functional responsivity is never entirely erased. Thus, reading acquisition displaces other evolutionarily-based functions in the site of the VWFA, yet signs of that function remain. Interestingly, in the fMRI study comparing illiterate to literate adults (Dehaene et al., 2010), Dehaene and colleagues found activation patterns consistent with the view that reading co-opts neural tissue that would otherwise process other visual stimuli. These same researchers found that right-hemisphere responsivity to faces was significantly greater in literate compared to illiterate adults and, with increases in literacy, cortical responsivity to faces decreased in the left fusiform region of former illiterates while responsivity to faces sharply increased in their right as their reading ability improved.

The practice of children learning to read early in life has become widespread only in the past few hundred years: not nearly long enough for us to have evolved a genetically predefined neural system devoted to reading. That literacy has an impact on the brain shouldn't be surprising, however: reading affects all spheres of mental functioning. For one thing, it reinforces and modifies a range of core cognitive abilities, including verbal and visual memory, phonological and phonemic awareness, and visuospatial skills. Reading allows us to offload memory to the external world – if we can look something up, such as a phone number or set of instructions for a recipe, we don't have to memorize it. It allows us to share our thoughts with someone who is not in front of us right now, and may read it months, years, or even centuries later.

As with so many other brain–behavior relationships, studying focal brain lesions in skilled readers formed the basis for understanding the role the brain plays in literacy (Déjerine, 1891). Such studies included descriptions of patients with focal brain injury in the left posterior part of the brain who had acquired difficulties with what had been skilled reading. Moreover, it was recognized that different outcomes were the result of different lesion locations. We now know that ventral lesions and dorsal lesions both have catastrophic effects on a patient's reading ability, but in distinct ways. For example, Figure 11.6A shows lesion data from patients with injuries in and around the left fusiform gyrus, all of which resulted in pure alexia – a selective disorder in which letter and word recognition are completely knocked out (Starrfelt et al., 2009). By contrast, the impact of dorsal lesions, although more variable, is often on phonological processes such as reading aloud (see Figure 11.6B for ventral and dorsal white matter tracts associated with reading components of the brain). Importantly, double dissociations have been found, whereby people who couldn't read could still write (alexia without agraphia) and people who couldn't write could still read (agraphia without alexia). Such double dissociations have even been observed in music reading and writing.

These contrasting effects of area-specific lesions led to early hypotheses about the existence of a direct reading route, between the printed word and its semantic meaning, and an indirect route, between letters and words, spoken language, and semantic meaning (see Warrington & Shallice, 1969 for a review; Harm & Seidenberg, 2004 for a model). The indirect route corresponds to dorsally located brain regions, including the posterior superior temporal gyrus, angular gyrus, and supramarginal gyrus, all associated in some way with phonemic and phonological awareness (Dickens et al., 2019). The past several decades of research have provided a foundation for understanding how the brain enables reading, helping delineate the component processes and underlying neuroanatomy engaged during reading. Convergent findings across a range of technologies and methodologies have confirmed that both ventral (orthographic to semantic) and dorsal (orthographic to phonological to semantic) visual processing routes are critical components of the development of skilled reading.

11.3.2 Anatomy of Visual Reading Circuitry: Dorsal and Ventral Pathways

The brain regions involved in reading are located primarily (but not entirely) in the left hemisphere. As we've discussed, these regions can be grouped into two processing pathways: a dorsal and a ventral route. Figure 11.7 shows the primary components and processes at work in these two routes. The dorsal route supports conversion of orthographical symbols to sound and is involved in phonological processing more generally; the ventral route supports visual analysis of orthography, including words, and linking words to meaning. The dorsal route is particularly involved in integrating sounds (phonemes/phonology)

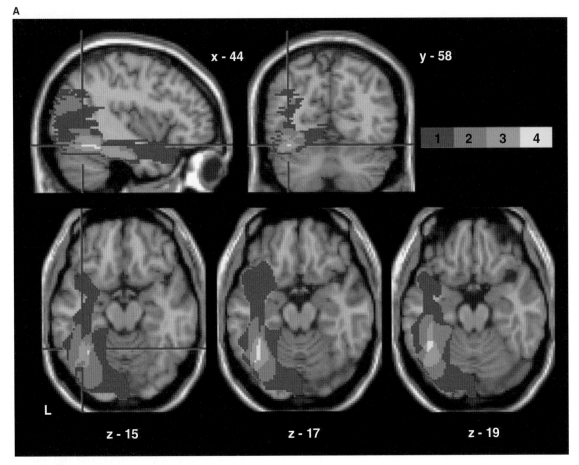

Figure 11.6 Reading and the brain. A. Lesion maps from four pure alexic patients overlaid on a canonical single-subject MRI brain scan in Montreal Neurological Institute (MNI) space. Scale colors refer to the number of voxels common across the patients, with yellow voxels being common to all four. (Reprinted from Starrfelt et al., 2009) B. Ventral and dorsal reading routes. Ventral route includes temporo-occipital (including VWFA) to medial temporal gyrus (MTG); dorsal route includes inferior parietal lobe (IPL), which encompasses both supramarginal gyrus and angular gyrus, and superior temporal gyrus (STG), feeding forward to the inferior frontal gyrus (IFG). (Reprinted from Yablonski et al., 2019)

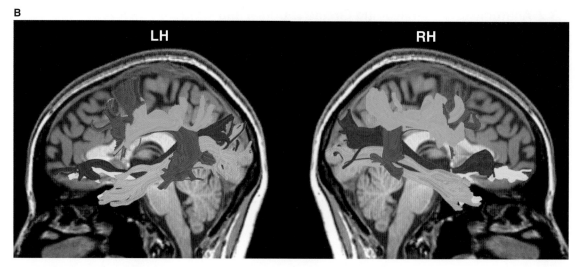

Figure 11.6 (cont.)

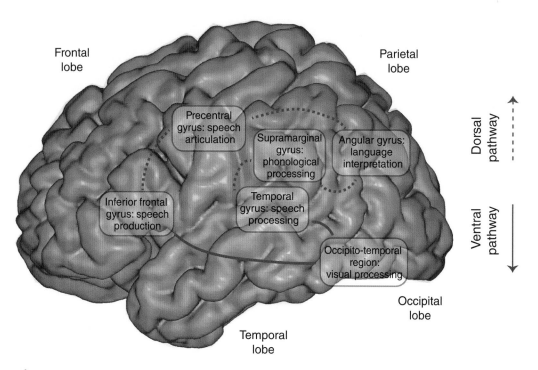

Figure 11.7 Overview of the functions supported by the dorsal and ventral reading pathways.

with their corresponding symbols (orthography) and with attentional control. The dorsal route includes temporoparietal areas (i.e., superior temporal gyrus, supramarginal gyrus, inferior parietal lobe) and the inferior frontal gyrus. The ventral route includes occipitotemporal areas (i.e., VWFA, middle and inferior temporal gyrus) and is related to visual word and semantic recognition (Pugh et al., 2001; Jobard et al., 2003; Cattinelli et al., 2013). Thus, conceptualizing reading as an engagement of these two processing routes provides a "big picture" of the processes at play during skilled reading.

You'll remember that we discussed the dorsal and ventral visual streams in Chapter 6. While the dorsal and ventral reading routes incorporate visual processing, these are well-defined networks specific to reading, related to but distinct from the dorsal and ventral visual processing pathways. Substantial evidence links specific activation of dorsal and ventral reading routes to different reading skills in both children and adults (Booth et al., 2003; Finn et al., 2014; Stites & Laszlo, 2017). Various hypotheses have been put forward about the role the two routes play in reading acquisition, and each is relied on more or less depending on the type of words being read. For example, the dorsal route is more likely to be involved when reading pseudowords – pronounceable but not real words, like *glaph* – whereas the ventral route is more likely to be involved when reading highly familiar words (Taylor et al., 2017).

11.3.3 Improved Reading Proficiency Involves a Dorsal-to-Ventral Shift

Just as the dorsal and ventral streams are used differently for different types of reading, these streams are believed to be used differently during different stages of reading development. For example, an influential early proposal postulated that successful reading acquisition involves transition away from reliance on the dorsal route to increasing reliance on the ventral route (Pugh et al., 2001). Indeed, correlations are seen between reading skill and ventral route activation, as words become increasingly familiar, while correlations between reading ability and dorsal route activation, quite robust during early reading acquisition, lessen as the child achieves reading proficiency. Moreover, this hypothesized **dorsal-to-ventral shift** aligns with behavioral evidence for a shift in the way children read words as they gain proficiency. When young children are first learning to read, they sound words out, relying on their understanding of orthography-to-phoneme mappings to extract linguistic information from the orthographic symbols. The route is engaged even when adults are asked to learn new vocabulary and/or phonology (Hofstetter et al., 2017). The more familiar the correspondence between certain letter combinations and linguistic information becomes, the greater the role of visual word recognition in reading, replacing letter-to-phoneme conversion as the default process (Ziegler & Goswami, 2005). Indeed, neuroimaging evidence has suggested that the ventral stream emerges in response to word forms only as children begin to associate meaning directly with print, without intervening verbalization (Maurer et al., 2005, 2006).

11.4 Language Influences Reading; Reading Influences Language

Reading is a skill learned through extensive exposure to both spoken language and the written word, and early childhood is foundational both for language development and for future reading abilities. Humans are largely ensured success with oral language given "typical" genetic endowment and "normal" environmental input. In contrast, meeting the requirements to successfully acquire the ability to decode and comprehend written language – that is, to achieve literacy – is not at all guaranteed. The skills required to be a proficient reader are far less intuitive than those involved in talking. Becoming literate depends on a complex mapping between visual symbols and the sounds and meanings we've already encountered in learning to speak – reshaping and linking networks supporting vision and oral language to enable an individual to extract meaning from an abstract array of visual symbols (i.e., letters; Dehaene & Cohen, 2011). Not surprisingly, given what we know about brain plasticity, the earlier this reshaping and linking starts, the better. An underappreciated but critical factor in this process is a child's initial oral/aural language abilities, including the level of verbal stimulation a child receives.

We have referred to **phonemic awareness** at various points in this chapter: children who are phonemically aware can treat spoken words as built out of phonemes, breaking words into their component sounds. But phonemic awareness isn't just about sound; it's also about spelling. Learning how orthography relates to the phonology of a language is a major hurdle in learning to read in an alphabetic writing system. As we mentioned in Section 11.2.1, spelling is less daunting in languages with shallow orthographies (e.g., Spanish), but for readers learning a language like English, it can be very frustrating because the correspondences between letters and phonemes in English are so inconsistent. Words as simple as "bat," "cat," and "car" illustrate this. Mapping the /a/ sound from "bat" to "cat" is easy enough, but it's not so straightforward to go from "cat" to "car." It doesn't sound like cat, but it has two of the same letters! Early readers have to learn a lot about individual sounds, but also about how they work together in different words: they have to learn the **phonology** of the language. Thus, phonemic awareness (i.e., awareness of individual sounds within words) stems from **phonological awareness** (i.e., awareness of the sound structure of words). Phonological awareness requires exposure to substantial amounts of oral, as well as written, language. Oral language skills, such as speech sound accuracy and vocabulary, contribute to phonological awareness in children (McDowell et al., 2007).

11.4.1 The Importance of Both Quantity and Quality of Oral Language Exposure

Recall from Chapter 8 that there are dorsally and ventrally located white matter fiber tracts connecting the language-relevant regions of the frontal and temporal cortices. The dorsal language pathway supports speech perception and production by connecting subcomponents of the temporal cortex to the inferior frontal gyrus and precentral gyrus/premotor cortex, while the ventral language pathway supports the mapping of specific combinations of sounds to meaning by linking other subcomponents of the temporal cortex to the ventral inferior frontal gyrus. Although both of these routes are typically referred to as unitary pathways, it is increasingly clear that each consists of more than one major fiber tract, and researchers continue to delineate the precise nature of these pathways (as shown in Figure 11.5). For example, there is now substantial structural evidence at least in humans that the dorsal pathway consists of more than one white matter bundle (e.g., Gierhan, 2013; Friederici, 2015). Regardless of these details, it is safe to say that dorsal connectivity in the left hemisphere undergirds perception and production of spoken language, and its development in early childhood has implications for the later development of reading abilities. Also in Chapter 8, we described a cross-sectional study (Romeo et al., 2018) in which turn-taking (i.e., contingent verbal interaction between a child and caregiver) proved important for development of brain structures that support early language development. In particular, the findings obtained in that study using fractional anisotropy, a metric of white matter coherence (Chapter 2), indicated that the number of conversational turns in parent–child interactions impacted the development of the dorsal pathway for language. These researchers found that more adult–child conversational turn-taking, independent of SES and overall amount of adult speech, is related to stronger, more coherent white matter connectivity in the left arcuate and superior longitudinal fasciculi on average, and particularly in the region near their anterior termination in left inferior frontal cortex (i.e., at Broca's area). Consistent with these findings, fractional anisotropy in the same two white matter tracts has also been associated with individual differences in phonological awareness (Vandermosten et al., 2012) and in overall reading ability (Vandermosten et al., 2015).

Because a common feature of phonological processing skills is phonological *awareness*, the relation between those skills and reading depends upon the development of underlying phonological *representations* (Fowler, 1991; Goswami, 2000). Thus, while phonological awareness and reading abilities are strongly interrelated, the Romeo et al. (2018) findings support the notion that oral language is critical to building these representations. Thus, while early spoken language experience certainly contributes to the development of phonological awareness, it also appears to have a direct effect on emerging white matter microstructure, thus providing a neuroanatomical scaffold for later reading development. All of this underscores the importance of understanding the role of early spoken language to the development of anatomical connections within children's brains. Even before the onset of learning to read, factors in a child's early language environment shape the white matter tracts that will provide critical support for reading acquisition, and whose integrity is correlated with reading proficiency. Because Romeo et al. (2018) reported no other associations between white matter and conversational turn-taking, the relationship was specific to the left arcuate fasciculus and the superior longitudinal fasciculi, critical components of phonological development. And, while this effect held even after controlling for SES and overall amount of speech input to which the children were exposed, it is well documented that SES impacts reading development in other ways, including via other dimensions of the early spoken language environment.

While these findings highlight the complex interplay between different aspects of language input and specific dimensions of language development, individual differences in the white matter pathways underlying oral language and reading are likely influenced by a combination of genetic factors, such as a family history of language or reading impairments, and environmental factors, such as SES and the quality of the early language and literacy environment. Understanding the precise role that the early language environment plays in the development of different brain systems and how these impact subsequent reading abilities may ultimately help to explain why children follow different developmental trajectories in reading. Ideally, researchers will be able to identify various "biomarkers" (i.e., aspects of early brain structure) that indicate the need for specific interventions in early childhood.

11.4.2 Emergent Skills That Are Critical to the Acquisition of Reading

Regardless of background, socioeconomic status, or environmental opportunities, learning to read and write is foundational to children's success in school and to optimizing their overall life trajectory. Although reading continues to develop over the course of one's life, we hope we've made it clear that, from the earliest timepoints in infancy and early childhood, a child can be acquiring abilities that will support the development of reading. Most notably, this process involves the acquisition of language itself. Although reading instruction generally takes place in the first few years of formal schooling, it starts well before that and it will continue to improve over the course of adolescence and adulthood. Understanding the trajectory of reading development was initially a challenge for researchers given that, at its outset, learning to read involves engaging multiple overlapping skills, which themselves are all developing at once. Despite these challenges, what a "normal" reading development trajectory looks like is now well established, and there are a handful of skills that predict the route that this trajectory is likely to follow for any particular child. In particular, oral language, phonological awareness, alphabet knowledge, and print awareness are all strong predictors of how quickly and how well children will read once they are exposed to formal reading instruction in school. We'll briefly review each of these components of reading and review how they become integrated over time with appropriate training and support.

First, as we've discussed, one of the strongest predictors of reading ability is overall exposure to spoken (or oral) language and specific aspects of language exposure that contribute to the development of phonological awareness. The early experiences children have with language have considerable impact on their future reading development. Oral language skills develop in the context of responsive environments, contingent conversation, and consistent language interactions between children and their caregivers. The quantity of parental talk is highly associated with vocabulary size in the early years. Disparities in vocabulary can be seen as early as 18 months of age and the disparities between children from homes where opportunities for language exposure abounds (often wealthier homes) and their peers from homes where language exposure is more limited only widens as children grow older (Gilkerson et al., 2018; Hart & Risley, 2005).

It is widely accepted that children's own spoken language skills, including speech sound production accuracy and overall vocabulary knowledge (both in visual and spoken word form), contribute to the development of phonological awareness. But what about the matter of phonological decoding (translating letters into spoken language)? Although achieving fluent reading in English is commonly assumed to be a byproduct of mastering phonological decoding, because decoding is a skill that is clearly related to phonological processing (Torgesen et al., 1994; Snowling, 1998), there is growing evidence that learning letter–sound correspondences does not by itself lead to improved reading fluency (Torgesen, 2005). This is particularly so in languages with shallow orthographies, for which low reading fluency is confounded with low reading accuracy in both typically developing early readers and children with reading disability (Rakhlin et al., 2019). Thus, to better understand reading development and the nature of the difficulties different children have in acquiring it, regardless of the orthographic depth of their own language(s), researchers continue to examine factors that contribute to decoding accuracy, in addition to phonological awareness. Both contribute to skilled reading.

Decoding accuracy and phonological awareness are skills that depend on the development of strong links between auditory and visual processing, part of which requires simultaneously seeing and hearing letters. On the visual side, we've seen that development of the VWFA requires exposure – and lots of it – to letters themselves and the written words they create. This means children need to be exposed to print! But the sound side of things means that they also need someone to read that print aloud. This is an activity that is passed along culturally: if your grandparents read to your parents while your parents looked at the page, your parents probably read to you in the same way.

Over the course of what needs to be considerable exposure, experience-dependent tuning can take hold, and increasingly focal and left-lateralized patterns of brain engagement emerge in response to print and the sounds it represents. Sensitivity to letters, and to visual word forms more generally, continues to be refined throughout adolescence and into adulthood, resulting in increasingly efficient reading. In this way, fluent word recognition – and all that comes with it – can build on the refinement of early language and perceptual processes, making the critical link between phonological and orthographic components of reading. How and how often a person engages in reading activities will influence this developmental trajectory even further.

11.5 Subtypes and Sources of Poor Reading

Much of the world lacks even basic literacy. In the United States up to 17 percent of the population are not fluent readers, defined as individuals with reading skill at or below the fourth grade level (Stanovich, 1986). This **functional illiteracy** characterizes up to 44 percent of those living in poverty (Baer et al., 2009). This only underscores our repeated point that it is extraordinarily unlikely that the capacity to read is intrinsic to the human brain or that natural selection had an opportunity to specialize brain regions for reading. The amount and kind of overt teaching and practice needed to achieve fluent reading further highlights the lack of intrinsic reading capacity built into the human brain (Schlaggar & McCandliss, 2007). Nonetheless, reading is critical in the modern world. Understanding the different types of poor reading and how they manifest in the brain is a major area of research in DCN.

Around the start of second grade, children begin the transition from learning-how-to-read to reading-in-order-to-learn (and several years later, children learn how to write so that others can read what they've written and understand it – a skill that requires considerable theory of mind and perspective taking). A child failing to make this transition is considered to have a reading difficulty. Reading difficulties can result from a biological deficit, most often in the phonological and/or orthographic components of reading (i.e., dyslexia) or other cognitive components required for reading, such as executive function. Commonly, reading difficulty stems from an environmental cause, such as an under-stimulating home environment, often associated with low socioeconomic status and second language households (i.e., environmental illiteracy; Kozol, 1985). As we have seen here, promising *biomarkers* have been identified to help diagnose the source of a reading deficit. However, it is extremely difficult for educators themselves to differentiate children with a biological cause for reading difficulty (i.e., dyslexia) from children who suffer from reading difficulties due to inadequate environmental exposure to literacy (i.e., environmental illiteracy). Accurate diagnosis is the first step in determining what intervention to pursue. Whereas interventions for children with dyslexia involve rehabilitating impaired emergent literacy abilities, such as letter-to-sound mapping, children with environmentally induced illiteracy require a more comprehensive intervention, one centered on increasing their exposure to oral and written language in the service of developing reading skills (Ardila et al., 2010).

11.5.1 Correlates with Socioeconomic Status

Socioeconomic status (SES) is a common conceptualization of the social and economic status of an individual or group that is typically measured by some combination of parental educational attainment, income, and occupation. Higher SES is associated with better reading outcomes (Peterson & Pennington, 2015), as variations in SES are associated with different environmental factors, including the language environment of the home (Hoff et al., 2002) and the quality of school instruction (Lee & Burkam, 2002). An "achievement gap" refers to the disparity in academic performance and/or educational attainment between students from disparate backgrounds (Reardon, 2011), and one of the most consistent findings in the educational literature in the last half century is that reading achievement differs between lower- and higher-SES children (Reardon, 2011). Interestingly, while the racial achievement gap has shrunk considerably over the course of the last half century, the income-related achievement gap has more than doubled (OECD, 2016).

Lower SES has been associated with lower performance in all the language skills we've reviewed that underpin reading ability, including phonological awareness, single word decoding, and vocabulary size, as well as abilities we haven't highlighted, including reading comprehension and overall grammatical complexity (Noble & McCandliss, 2005). On average, children from lower-SES families are more likely to read below grade level than children from higher-SES backgrounds, as well as to meet the criteria for reading disability (Peterson & Pennington, 2015). Consistent with our discussion of the importance of a range of early experiences to reading development, SES-related gaps in reading begin well before children enter school (Reardon & Portilla, 2016). Not surprisingly, the deficits increase as the children progress through school (Feinstein, 2003). This gap has been getting even wider in recent decades (Reardon & Portilla, 2016). To remediate (and ideally to prevent) the cascading effects of SES on educational achievement, it is imperative that we clearly identify the early impacts of SES on reading development, including on the underlying neurobiology.

Reducing the number of children who enter school with inadequate early literacy experiences is an important step towards preventing reading difficulties and enabling long-term school success. Due to many factors, including inadequate home literacy environment and lack of access to books, as well as lack of early learning opportunities, children in low-resource settings and from high poverty homes tend to lag behind on these emergent literacy skills compared to their peers from higher-resource homes. This puts these children on a path towards early and enduring difficulties with reading. Children who begin school with less prior knowledge and early language skills – notably, these include general verbal abilities, basic phonological awareness, and letter knowledge – are more likely to have difficulty learning to read in a formal educational setting. In addition to performance differences related to SES, there are neural indicators as well. For example, a structural MRI examination of a group of 13- to 15-year-olds from diverse backgrounds revealed that cortical gray matter thickness in temporal and occipital lobes was associated with both SES and performance on standardized tests. Critically, the cortical differences accounted for almost half of the income achievement difference (Mackey et al., 2015)! Another study of children between the ages of 4 and 22 years found that differences in the cortical volume of frontal and temporal gray matter explained as much as 20 percent of test score gaps (Hair et al., 2015). Other studies have confirmed similar relationships between SES, neuroanatomy, and a variety of cognitive domains and/or academic achievement (for review, see Farah, 2017).

As far as neural mechanisms underlying SES disparities in reading skills are concerned, relationships have been observed between SES and brain activation related to phonological awareness in left perisylvian regions in pre-reading 5-year-olds (Raizada et al., 2008). The same relationship has been observed in children aged 8–13 years (Demir-Lira et al., 2016). Another study found that SES modulated the relationship between phonological awareness skills and brain activity in the left fusiform and perisylvian regions during active reading in a group of 6- to 9-year-olds (Noble, Wolmetz, et al., 2006). Interestingly, lower-SES children exhibit a stronger brain–behavior relationship than their peers with higher SES, suggesting that low SES multiplies the effect of low phonological awareness, resulting in weaker decoding skills (Noble, Farah, & McCandliss, 2006). In contrast, it appears that children from higher-SES backgrounds are buffered from the effects of low phonological skill, resulting in increased fusiform recruitment and better reading outcomes. Collectively, findings such as these raise questions about how SES differences in children's language skills arise in the first several years of life, and which aspects of higher and lower SES environments influence either (or both) language and neural development. Of course, SES is a multifaceted construct that includes both economic resources and sociocultural backgrounds, so there are likely many aspects of both higher- and lower-SES environments that contribute to these differences.

11.5.2 Developmental Dyslexia

Reading disability (RD) refers to a significant reading difficulty that cannot be accounted for by deficits in general intelligence or education. The term dyslexia refers to difficulty in reading and is a type of specific learning disability; it too is sometimes called a reading disability or disorder. This is, indeed, confusing. To keep things as simple as possible, we will focus here on dyslexia, with the understanding that there are other forms of reading disability.

Dyslexia is complex, and varied definitions exist across educational, medical, and governmental organizations. Nonetheless, most definitions include one key feature: difficulty recognizing words. Students with dyslexia will encounter difficulty identifying or pronouncing familiar and unfamiliar words accurately and fluently (Hancock et al., 2016; Hulme &

Snowling, 2017). There are two general classes of dyslexia: acquired (through injury) and developmental. The sorts of lesions we described in Section 11.3 are often the source of acquired dyslexia, which itself is highly variable. Here we'll limit our focus to developmental dyslexia, a deficit selectively affecting the visual processing of words, but leaving oral and non-verbal reasoning skills intact.

The primary difference between developing readers with dyslexia and their peers with typical reading skills is that those with dyslexia show less activation in reading-relevant brain regions, including temporoparietal and occipitotemporal regions, while reading and performing reading-related tasks, such as rhyming (Martin et al., 2015). Some studies indicate that readers with dyslexia have less gray matter in temporoparietal regions specifically relevant to decoding, and in occipitotemporal regions involved in word reading (Richlan et al., 2013). These findings of lower activation and smaller amount of gray matter in reading-relevant brain areas align with the fact that students with reading difficulty have weaker decoding skills and more difficulty recognizing words by sight than do their peers with typical reading skills. Recently, researchers have proposed the "neural noise hypothesis" of dyslexia (Hancock et al., 2016), which suggests that the reading disorder is a consequence of deficits in neurotransmission. Glutamate, the main excitatory neurotransmitter in the human brain, appears to be elevated in dyslexic individuals, which may contribute to impaired reading through excessive excitatory activity (hyperexcitability) resulting in heightened noise and instability in information processing. Heightened noise is hypothesized to affect encoding of sensory information and produce impairments in multisensory integration and phonological awareness, key components of reading development. One of the proponents of this hypothesis, Fumiko Hoeft, is featured in the Scientist Spotlight in Box 11.1. An alternative perspective has been proposed by Jason Yeatman and colleagues, who argue that the focus on a "core deficit" approach to dyslexia is misguided. They instead propose a model where by reading skill is explained as a collection of several distinct, additive predictors, or risk factors, of reading (dis) ability (O'Brien & Yeatman, 2020). These are just two of the many (many!) theories about the cognitive and neural underpinnings of developmental dyslexia. Needless to say, given the abundance of competing theories about the basis for dyslexia, various of which posit that this form of reading disability arises from impaired sensory, phonological, or statistical learning mechanisms, among other things, it is clear that research on reading, particularly impaired reading, will continue unabated for years to come.

Dyslexia is best characterized as a developmental disorder. Essayist Malcolm Gladwell created a stir in 2014 when, in his book *David and Goliath*, he listed a number of highly successful individuals who were dyslexic, and from that, concluded that perhaps their dyslexia was an advantage, something that did not need remediation or "fixing." DCN researcher Mark Seidenberg (2018), along with many others, reacted strongly by pointing out that this was neither a scientific deduction, nor logical. As cognitive neuroscientist Stephen Kosslyn explains, this is not a true experiment; we don't know how much more successful these individuals would have been if they could read more easily. Scientific reasoning requires that we consider causal and mechanistic explanations, and that we resist the temptation to jump to conclusions that are thought-provoking and novel, but have no basis in empirical observation.

Box 11.1 Scientist Spotlight on Fumiko Hoeft (Brain Imaging Research Center, University of Connecticut)

Fumiko Hoeft (Box Figure 11.1) is a Professor in Psychological Sciences, Mathematics, Neuroscience and Psychiatry, and Director of the Brain Imaging Research Center at the University of Connecticut. She is also an Adjunct Professor in the Department of Psychiatry at the University of California, San Francisco. Hoeft was trained clinically at Keio University School of Medicine (Tokyo, Japan), and in research at several universities before completing her MD/PhD and postdoctoral fellowship at Stanford University. Hoeft studies the neural basis of dyslexia and individual differences in learning to read.

I always wanted to be a clinician. While I was in medical school in Japan, I got fascinated by the brain, so I chose to be a psychiatrist. That got me interested in brain research, and I packed up, and moved to the United States to get a glimpse of how research was done. I thought it would be temporary, but I haven't gone back to being a clinician or to Japan since. At first, I was doing more basic research that is relevant for medical disorders, but then I started seeing cognitive neuroscientists looking at brain functions for the sake of understanding the brain, and that really fascinated me. I did basic research for several years – and then I found reading and dyslexia, and the work Professor John Gabrieli was doing at Stanford University. I was excited that I could integrate my knowledge in clinical medicine, and basic and cognitive neurosciences, and apply them to a topic that could have a real-world impact.

Reading is exciting to me because it's still thought of (though hotly debated) as something that only humans can do. Dyslexia is a neurobiological disorder where you have difficulties specifically in word reading, and you see this in 5–10 percent of all children, regardless of the language they speak, writing system they use, and how rich/poor they are. People can have it for many reasons, but a large portion seems to stem from problems understanding the sound components of the words. But we now know that just like many other disorders, it is multifactorial, in that it's the amount and balance between risk and protective factors that can lead to dyslexia. And depending on these factors, some can have tremendous challenges, and some will end up barely having symptoms and be resilient, even when they are at high risk like having parents with dyslexia. We are starting to call this the Cumulative Risk and Protection (CRAP) Model (!).

This is what my lab is studying; risk and protective factors, whether neurobiological, cognitive, or socioemotional, because early identification and prevention is so important. So a lot of our work right now is looking at high-risk children, and how parents' genes and environment impact

Box 11.1 (cont.)

their children's language and literacy (and math) skills. We also look at how dyslexic children learn to compensate and become better at reading. It turns out that they are often using the prefrontal cognitive control and memory networks, and/or articulatory networks. Additionally, we develop new theories of dyslexia that link risk genes, neurophysiology, structural and functional brain circuits to behavior, and test them; like the Neural Noise hypothesis we proposed three years ago.

In this multilingual society, we also think it's important to look at how bilingual and multilingual children's brains develop, and how the brain circuits important for reading and dyslexia are different from language to language (note: turns out that it's much more similar and universal than we used to think). A fun project on brain development is to use AI to develop "brain network growth charts" just like the growth charts for height and weight that you may have seen in a pediatrician's office. And finally, we have some projects that translate our discoveries to the society by developing and/or validating apps to screen and prevent dyslexia. Even though we've been doing this for over 10 years, I feel like we're still just scratching the surface.

SUMMARY

- The reading paradox describes the temporal disconnect in humans' use of spoken/signed language and writing/reading, which indicates that the neural structures that support reading did not evolve for that purpose
- The neuronal recycling hypothesis postulates that a cultural invention, such as reading, can recycle existing cerebral structure that serves a functionally similar purpose, thus reorganizing the brain
- The visual word form area (VWFA) is a small region in the left fusiform gyrus that is engaged in skilled readers as they recognize written words, and that emerges as a consequence of learning to read
- The VWFA reflects language-specific orthographic knowledge, and its specific location and degree of laterality varies somewhat by language
- Reading generates specialized networks that reach beyond the VWFA to interface with the rest of the language system
- Brain regions involved in reading are located primarily (but not entirely) in the left hemisphere in most people and can be grouped into two processing pathways that include a dorsal and a ventral route
- The dorsal route supports conversion of orthographical symbols to sound and is involved in phonological processing more generally
- The ventral route supports visual analysis of orthography, including words, and links words to meaning
- During reading acquisition, readers transition from reliance on the dorsal route to reliance on the ventral route, a shift that corresponds to the shift from attention to the orthography-to-phoneme mapping to a more general focus on visual word recognition
- The bidirectional influence between phonemic and phonological awareness and reading demonstrates that language influences reading and reading influences language

- Socioeconomic status is associated with performance in all the language skills that underpin reading ability, including phonological awareness, single word decoding, and vocabulary size, as well as reading comprehension and overall grammatical complexity
- Developmental dyslexia describes significant reading difficulty that is not accounted for by deficits in general intelligence or education

REVIEW QUESTIONS

What is the reading paradox?

What does it mean to describe reading and writing as cultural inventions?

Outline the role of the visual word form area in reading.

What are the factors critical to developing a visual word form area?

What are phonemic and phonological awareness?

What are the two reading routes in the brain and which aspects of reading does each support?

How does exposure to oral and written language, respectively, contribute to the development of reading skills?

What is the difference between acquired and developmental dyslexia?

Why is dyslexia now considered a multifactorial disorder?

Further Reading

Dehaene, S., Cohen, L., Morais, J., & Kolinksy, R. (2015). Illiterate to literate: Behavioral and cerebral changes induced by reading acquisition. *Nature Reviews Neuroscience*, 16(4), 234–244. https://doi.org/10.1038/nrn3924

Seidenberg, M. (2018). *Language at the speed of sight*. Basic Books.

Wandell, B. A., Rauschecker, A. M., & Yeatman, J. D. (2012). Learning to see words. *Annual Review of Psychology*, 63, 31–53. https://doi.org/10.1146/annurev-psych-120710-100434

References

Ardila, A., Bertolucci, P. H., Braga, L. W., Castro-Caldas, A., Judd, T., Kosmidis, M. H., Matute, E., Nitrini, R., Ostrosky-Solis, F., & Rosselli, M. (2010). Illiteracy: The neuropsychology of cognition without reading. *Archives of Clinical Neuropsychology*, 25(8), 689–712. https://doi.org/10.1093/arclin/acq079

Baer, J., Kutner, M., Sabatini, J., & White, S. (2009). *Basic reading skills and the literacy of America's least literate adults. Results from the 2003 National Assessment of Adult Literacy (NAAL) supplemental studies*. Washington, DC: US Department of Education (Report No. NCES 2009-481).

Behrmann, M., & Plaut, D. C. (2013). Distributed circuits, not circumscribed centers, mediate visual recognition. *Trends in Cognitive Sciences*, 17(5), 210–219. https://doi.org/10.1016/j.tics.2013.03.007

Binder, J. R., Medler, D. A., Westbury, C. F., Liebenthal, E., & Buchanan, L. (2006). Tuning of the human left fusiform gyrus to sublexical orthographic structure. *NeuroImage*, 33(2), 739–748. https://doi.org/10.1016/j.neuroimage.2006.06.053

Booth, J. R., Burman, D. D., Meyer, J. R., Lei, Z., Choy, J., Gitelman, D. R., Parrish, T. B., & Mesulam, M. M. (2003). Modality-specific and -independent developmental differences in the neural substrate for lexical processing. *Journal of Neurolinguistics*, 16(4–5), 383–405. https://doi.org/10.1016/S0911-6044(03)00019-8

Booth, J. R., Lu, D., Burman, D. D., Chou, T. L., Jin, Z., Peng, D. L., Zhang, L., Ding, G. S., Deng, Y., & Liu, L. (2006). Specialization of phonological and semantic processing in Chinese word reading. *Brain Research*, 1071(1), 197–207. https://doi.org/10.1016/j.brainres.2005.11.097

Brem, S., Bach, S., Kucian, K., Guttorm, T. K., Martin, E., Lyytinen, H., Brandeis, D., & Richardson, U. (2010). Brain sensitivity to print emerges when children learn letter-speech sound correspondences. *Proceedings of the National Academy of Sciences of the United States of America*, 107(17), 7939–7944. https://doi.org/10.1073/pnas.0904402107

Cantlon, J. F., Pinel, P., Dehaene, S., & Pelphrey, K. A. (2011). Cortical representations of symbols, objects, and faces are pruned back during early childhood. *Cerebral Cortex*, 21(1), 191–199. https://doi.org/10.1093/cercor/bhq078

Cattinelli, I., Borghese, N. A., Gallucci, M., & Paulesu, E. (2013). Reading the reading brain: A new meta-analysis of functional imaging data on reading. *Journal of Neurolinguistics*, 26(1), 214–238. https://doi.org/10.1016/j.jneuroling.2012.08.001

Chen, L., Wassermann, D., Abrams, D. A., Kochalka, J., Gallardo-Diez, G., & Menon, V. (2019). The visual word form area (VWFA) is part of both language and attention circuitry. *Nature Communications*, 10, 5601. https://doi.org/10.1038/s41467-019-13634-z

Cohen, L., Lehéricy, S., Chochon, F., Lemer, C., Rivaud, S., & Dehaene, S. (2002). Language-specific tuning of visual cortex? Functional properties of the visual word form area. *Brain*, 125(5), 1054–1069. https://doi.org/10.1093/brain/awf094

Daniels, P. T. (1996). The study of writing systems. In P. T. Daniels & W. Bright (Eds.), *The world's writing systems* (pp. 3–17). Oxford University Press.

Dehaene, S. (2009). *Reading in the brain*. Penguin Books.

Dehaene, S. (2011). *The number sense: How the mind creates mathematics*. Oxford University Press.

Dehaene, S., & Cohen, L. (2007). Cultural recycling of cortical maps. *Neuron*, 56(2), 384–398. https://doi.org/10.1016/j.neuron.2007.10.004

Dehaene, S., & Cohen, L. (2011). The unique role of the visual word form area in reading. *Trends in Cognitive Sciences*, 15(6), 254–262. https://doi.org/10.1016/j.tics.2011.04.003

Dehaene, S., & Dehaene-Lambertz, G. (2016). Is the brain prewired for letters? *Nature Neuroscience*, 19(9), 1192–1193. https://doi.org/10.1038/nn.4369

Dehaene, S., Pegado, F., Braga, L. W., Ventura, P., Nunes Filho, G., Jobert, A., Dehaene-Lambertz, G., Kolinsky, R., Morais, J., & Cohen, L. (2010). How learning to read changes the cortical networks for vision and language. *Science*, 330(6009), 1359–1364. https://doi.org/10.1126/science.1194140

Dehaene-Lambertz, G., Monzalvo, K., & Dehaene, S. (2018). The emergence of the visual word form: Longitudinal evolution of category-specific ventral visual areas during reading acquisition. *PLOS Biology*, 16(3), e2004103. https://doi.org/10.1371/journal.pbio.2004103

Déjerine, J. (1891). Sur un cas de cécité verbale avec agraphie, suivi d'autopsie. *Mémoires Société Biologique*, 3, 197–201.

Demir-Lira, Ö. E., Prado, J., & Booth, J. R. (2016). Neural correlates of math gains vary depending on parental socioeconomic status (SES). *Frontiers in Psychology*, 7. https://doi.org/10.3389/fpsyg.2016.00892

Dickens, J. V., Fama, M. E., DeMarco, A. T., Lacey, E. H., Friedman, R. B., & Turkeltaub, P. E. (2019). Localization of phonological and semantic contributions to reading. *Journal of Neuroscience*, 39(27), 5361–5368. https://doi.org/10.1523/JNEUROSCI.2707-18.2019

Farah, M. J. (2017). The neuroscience of socioeconomic status: Correlates, causes, and consequences. *Neuron*, 96(1), 56–71. https://doi.org/10.1016/j.neuron.2017.08.034

Feinstein, L. (2003). Inequality in the early cognitive development of British children in the 1970 cohort. *Economica*, 70(277), 73–97. https://doi.org/10.1111/1468-0335.t01-1-00272

Finn, E. S., Shen, X., Holahan, J. M., Scheinost, D., Lacadie, C., Papademetris, X., Shaywitz, S. E., Shaywitz, B. A., & Constable, R. T. (2014). Disruption of functional networks in dyslexia: A whole-brain, data-driven analysis of connectivity. *Biological Psychiatry*, 76(5), 397–404. https://doi.org/10.1016/j.biopsych.2013.08.031

Fowler, R. (1991). *Language in the news: Discourse and ideology in the press*. Routledge.

Friederici, A. D. (2015). White-matter pathways for speech and language processing. In M. J. Aminoff, F. Boller, & D. F. Swaab (Eds.), *Handbook of clinical neurology, Volume 129* (pp. 177–186). Elsevier. https://doi.org/10.1016/B978-0-444-62630-1.00010-X

Gazzaniga, M. S. (2005). Forty-five years of split-brain research and still going strong. *Nature Reviews Neuroscience*, 6(8), 653–659. https://doi/org/10.1038/nrn1723

Gierhan, S. M. E. (2013). Connections for auditory language in the human brain. *Brain and Language*, 127(2), 205–221. https://doi.org/10.1016/j.bandl.2012.11.002

Gilkerson, J., Richards, J. A., Warren, S. F., Oller, D. K., Russo, R., & Vohr, B. (2018). Language experience in the second year of life and language outcomes in late childhood. Pediatrics, 142(4), e20174276. https://doi.org/10.1542/peds.2017-4276

Gladwell, M. (2014). *David and Goliath*. Penguin Books.

Goswami, U. (2000). Phonological representations, reading development and dyslexia: Towards a cross-linguistic theoretical framework. *Dyslexia*, 6(2), 133–151. https://doi.org/10.1002/(SICI)1099-0909(200004/06)6:2<133::AID-DYS160>3.0.CO;2-A

Hair, N. L., Hanson, J. L., Wolfe, B. L., & Pollak, S. D. (2015). Association of child poverty, brain development, and academic achievement. *JAMA Pediatrics*, 169(9), 822–829. https://doi.org/10.1001/jamapediatrics.2015.1475

Hancock, R., Gabrieli, J. D. E., & Hoeft, F. (2016). Shared temporoparietal dysfunction in dyslexia and typical readers with discrepantly high IQ. *Trends in Neuroscience and Education*, 5(4), 173–177. https://doi.org/10.1016/j.tine.2016.10.001

Hannagan, T., Amedi, A., Cohen, L., Dehaene-Lambertz, G., & Dehaene, S. (2015). Origins of the specialization for letters and numbers in ventral occipitotemporal cortex. *Trends in Cognitive Sciences*, 19(7), 374–382. https://doi.org/10.1016/j.tics.2015.05.006

Harm, M. W., & Seidenberg, M. S. (2004). Computing the meanings of words in reading: Cooperative division of labor between visual and phonological processes. *Psychological Review*, 111(3), 662–720. https://doi.org/10.1037/0033-295X.111.3.662

Hart, B., & Risley, T. R. (1995). Meaningful differences in the everyday experience of young American children. P.H. Brookes.

Hoff, E., Laursen, B., & Tardif, T. (2002). Socioeconomic status and parenting. In M. Bornstein (Ed.), *Handbook of parenting, Volume 2*, 2nd edition (pp. 231–252). Lawrence Erlbaum Associates.

Hofstetter, S., Friedmann, N., & Assaf, Y. (2017). Rapid language-related plasticity: Microstructural changes in the cortex after a short session of new word learning. *Brain Structure and Function*, 222(3), 1231–1241. https://doi.org/10.1007/s00429-016-1273-2

Houston, K. (2013). *Shady characters: The secret life of punctuation, symbols, and other typographical marks*. W. W. Norton.

Hulme, C., & Snowling, M. J. (2017). Reading disorders and dyslexia. *Current Opinion in Pediatrics*, 28(6), 731–735. https://doi.org/10.1097/MOP.0000000000000411

Jobard, G., Crivello, F., & Tzourio-Mazoyer, N. (2003). Evaluation of the dual route theory of reading: A metanalysis of 35 neuroimaging studies. *NeuroImage*, 20(2), 693–712. https://doi.org/10.1016/S1053-8119(03)00343-4

Johnson, M. H. (2011). Interactive specialization: A domain-general framework for human functional brain development? *Developmental Cognitive Neuroscience*, 1(1), 7–21. https://doi.org/10.1016/j.dcn.2010.07.003

Kim, J. S., Kanjlia, S., Merabet, L. B., & Bedny, M. (2017). Development of the visual word form area requires visual experience: Evidence from blind braille readers. *Journal of Neuroscience*, 37(47), 11495–11504. https://doi.org/10.1523/JNEUROSCI.0997-17.2017

Kozol, J. (1985). *Illiterate America*. Anchor Press.

Lee, V., & Burkam, D. (2002). *Inequality at the starting gate: Social background differences in achievement as children begin school*. Economic Policy Institute.

Mackey, A. P., Finn, A. S., Leonard, J. A., Jacoby-Senghor, D. S., West, M. R., Gabrieli, C. F. O., & Gabrieli, J. D. E. (2015). Neuroanatomical correlates of the income-achievement gap. *Psychological Science*, 26(6), 925–933. https://doi.org/10.1177/0956797615572233

Martin, A., Schurz, M., Kronbichler, M., & Richlan, F. (2015). Reading in the brain of children and adults: A meta-analysis of 40 functional magnetic resonance imaging studies. *Human Brain Mapping*, 36(5), 1963–1981. https://doi.org/10.1002/hbm.22749

Maurer, U., Brem, S., Bucher, K., & Brandeis, D. (2005). Emerging neurophysiological specialization for letter strings. *Journal of Cognitive Neuroscience*, 17(10), 1532–1552. https://doi.org/10.1162/089892905774597218

Maurer, U., Brem, S., Kranz, F., Bucher, K., Benz, R., Halder, P., Steinhausen, H. C., & Brandeis, D. (2006). Coarse neural tuning for print peaks when children learn to read. *NeuroImage*, 33(2), 749–758. https://doi.org/10.1016/j.neuroimage.2006.06.025

McDowell, K. D., Lonigan, C. J., & Goldstein, H. (2007). Relations among socioeconomic status, age, and predictors of phonological awareness. *Journal of Speech, Language, and Hearing Research*, 50(4), 1079–1092. https://doi.org/10.1044/1092-4388(2007/075)

Nakamura, K., Kuo, W. J., Pegado, F., Cohen, L., Tzeng, O. J. L., & Dehaene, S. (2012). Universal brain systems for recognizing word shapes and handwriting gestures during reading. *Proceedings of the National Academy of Sciences of the United States of America*, 109(50), 20762–20767. https://doi.org/10.1073/pnas.1217749109

Nelson, J. R., Liu, Y., Fiez, J., & Perfetti, C. A. (2009). Assimilation and accommodation patterns in ventral occipitotemporal cortex in learning a second writing system. *Human Brain Mapping*, 30(3), 20762–20767. https://doi.org/10.1002/hbm.20551

Noble, K. G., Farah, M. J., & McCandliss, B. D. (2006). Socioeconomic background modulates cognition-achievement relationships in reading. *Cognitive Development*, 21(3), 349–368. https://doi.org/10.1016/j.cogdev.2006.01.007

Noble, K. G., & McCandliss, B. D. (2005). Reading development and impairment: Behavioral, social, and neurobiological factors. *Journal of Developmental and Behavioral Pediatrics*, 26(5), 370–378. https://doi.org/10.1097/00004703-200510000-00006

Noble, K. G., Wolmetz, M. E., Ochs, L. G., Farah, M. J., & McCandliss, B. D. (2006). Brain–behavior relationships in reading acquisition are modulated by socioeconomic factors. *Developmental Science*, 9(6), 642–654. https://doi.org/10.1111/j.1467-7687.2006.00542.x

OECD (Organization for Economic Cooperation and Development). (2016). *PISA 2015 results: excellence and equity in education, Volume I*. OECD Publishing.

O'Brien, G., & Yeatman, J. D. (2020). Bridging sensory and language theories of dyslexia: Toward a multifactorial model. *Developmental Science*, 24(3), e13039. https://doi.org/10.1111/desc.13039

Pant, R., Kanjlia, S., & Bedny, M. (2020). A sensitive period in the neural phenotype of language in blind individuals. *Developmental Cognitive Neuroscience*, 41, 100744. https://doi.org/10.1016/j.dcn.2019.100744

Petersen, S. E., Fox, P. T., Snyder, A. Z., & Raichle, M. E. (1990). Activation of extrastriate and frontal cortical areas by visual words and word-like stimuli. *Science*, 249(4972), 1041–1044. https://doi.org/10.1126/science.2396097

Peterson, R. L., & Pennington, B. F. (2015). Developmental dyslexia. *Annual Review of Clinical Psychology*, 11, 283–307. https://doi.org/10.1146/annurev-clinpsy-032814-112842

Price, C. J., & Devlin, J. T. (2003). The myth of the visual word form area. *NeuroImage*, 19(3), 473–481. https://doi.org/10.1016/S1053-8119(03)00084-3

Pugh, K. R., Mencl, W. E., Jenner, A. R., Katz, L., Frost, S. J., Lee, J. R., Shaywitz, S. E., & Shaywitz, B. A. (2001). Neurobiological studies of reading and reading disability. *Journal of Communication Disorders*, 34(6), 479–492. https://doi.org/10.1016/S0021-9924(01)00060-0

Raizada, R. D. S., Richards, T. L., Meltzoff, A., & Kuhl, P. K. (2008). Socioeconomic status predicts hemispheric specialisation of the left inferior frontal gyrus in young children. *NeuroImage*, 40(3), 1392–1401. https://doi.org/10.1016/j.neuroimage.2008.01.021

Rakhlin, N. V., Mourgues, C., Cardoso-Martins, C., Kornev, A. N., & Grigorenko, E. L. (2019). Orthographic processing is a key predictor of reading fluency in good and poor readers in a transparent orthography. *Contemporary Educational Psychology*, 56, 250–261. https://doi.org/10.1016/j.cedpsych.2018.12.002

Reardon, S. F. (2011). The widening academic achievement gap between the rich and the poor: New evidence and possible explanations. In G. J. Duncan & R. J. Murnane (Eds.), *Whither opportunity? Rising inequality, schools, and children's life chances* (pp. 91–116). Russell Sage Foundation.

Reardon, S. F., & Portilla, X. A. (2016). Recent trends in income, racial, and ethnic school readiness gaps at kindergarten entry. *AERA Open*, 2(3). https://doi.org/10.1177/2332858416657343

Reich, L., Szwed, M., Cohen, L., & Amedi, A. (2011). A ventral visual stream reading center independent of visual experience. *Current Biology*, 21(5), 363–368. https://doi.org/10.1016/j.cub.2011.01.040

Richlan, F., Kronbichler, M., & Wimmer, H. (2013). Structural abnormalities in the dyslexic brain: A meta-analysis of voxel-based morphometry studies. *Human Brain Mapping*, 34(11), 3055–3065. https://doi.org/10.1002/hbm.22127

Romeo, R. R., Segaran, J., Leonard, J. A., Robinson, S. T., West, M. R., Mackey, A. P., Yendiki, A., Rowe, M. L., & Gabrieli, J. D. E. (2018). Language exposure relates to structural neural connectivity in childhood. *Journal of Neuroscience*, 38(36), 7870–7877. https://doi.org/10.1523/JNEUROSCI.0484-18.2018

Sadato, N., Pascual-Leone, A., Grafman, J., Ibañez, V., Deiber, M. P., Dold, G., & Hallett, M. (1996). Activation of the primary visual cortex by Braille reading in blind subjects. *Nature*, 380(6574), 526–528. https://doi.org/10.1038/380526a0

Schlaggar, B. L., & McCandliss, B. D. (2007). Development of neural systems for reading. *Annual Review of Neuroscience*, 30, 475–503. https://doi.org/10.1146/annurev.neuro.28.061604.135645

Seidenberg, M. (2018). *Language at the speed of sight*. Basic Books.

Snowling, M. (1998). Dyslexia as a phonological deficit: Evidence and implications. *Child Psychology and Psychiatry Review*, 3(1), 4–11. https://doi.org/10.1017/S1360641797001366

Stanovich, K. E. (1986). Matthew effects in reading: Some consequences of individual differences in the acquisition of literacy. *Reading Research Quarterly*, 21(4), 360–407. https://doi.org/10.1598/rrq.21.4.1

Starrfelt, R., Habekost, T., & Leff, A. P. (2009). Too little, too late: Reduced visual span and speed characterize pure alexia. *Cerebral Cortex*, 19(12), 2880–2890. https://doi.org/10.1093/cercor/bhp059

Stites, M. C., & Laszlo, S. (2017). Time will tell: A longitudinal investigation of brain–behavior relationships during reading development. *Psychophysiology*, 54(6), 798–808. https://doi.org/10.1111/psyp.12844

Szwed, M., Qiao, E., Jobert, A., Dehaene, S., & Cohen, L. (2014). Effects of literacy in early visual and occipitotemporal areas of Chinese and French readers. *Journal of Cognitive Neuroscience*, 26(3), 459–475. https://doi.org/10.1162/jocn_a_00499

Taylor, J. S. H., Davis, M. H., & Rastle, K. (2017). Comparing and validating methods of reading instruction using behavioural and neural findings in an artificial orthography. *Journal of Experimental Psychology: General*, 146(6), 826–858. https://doi.org/10.1037/xge0000301

Torgesen, J. K. (2005). Recent discoveries on remedial interventions for children with dyslexia. In M. J. Snowling & C. Hulme (Eds.), *The science of reading: A handbook* (pp. 521–537). Blackwell Publishing. https://doi.org/10.1002/9780470757642.ch27

Torgesen, J. K., Wagner, R. K., & Rashotte, C. A. (1994). Longitudinal studies of phonological processing and reading. *Journal of Learning Disabilities*, 27(5), 276–286. https://doi.org/10.1177/002221949402700503

Vandermosten, M., Boets, B., Wouters, J., & Ghesquière, P. (2012). A qualitative and quantitative review of diffusion tensor imaging studies in reading and dyslexia. *Neuroscience and Biobehavioral Reviews*, 36(6), 1532–1552. https://doi.org/10.1016/j.neubiorev.2012.04.002

Vandermosten, M., Vanderauwera, J., Theys, C., De Vos, A., Vanvooren, S., Sunaert, S., Wouters, J., & Ghesquière, P. (2015). A DTI tractography study in pre-readers at risk for dyslexia. *Developmental Cognitive Neuroscience*, 14, 8–15. https://doi.org/10.1016/j.dcn.2015.05.006

Vogel, A. C., Miezin, F. M., Petersen, S. E., & Schlaggar, B. L. (2012). The putative visual word form area is functionally connected to the dorsal attention network. *Cerebral Cortex*, 22(3), 537–549. https://doi.org/10.1093/cercor/bhr100

Wandell, B. A., & Le, R. K. (2017). Diagnosing the neural circuitry of reading. *Neuron*, 96(2), 298–311. https://doi.org/10.1016/j.neuron.2017.08.007

Wandell, B. A., Rauschecker, A. M., & Yeatman, J. D. (2012). Learning to see words. *Annual Review of Psychology*, 63, 31–53. https://doi.org/10.1146/annurev-psych-120710-100434

Warrington, E. K., & Shallice, T. (1969). The selective impairment of auditory verbal short-term memory. *Brain*, 92(4), 885–896. https://doi.org/10.1093/brain/92.4.885

Yablonski, M., Rastle, K., Taylor, J. S. H., & Ben-Shachar, M. (2019). Structural properties of the ventral reading pathways are associated with morphological processing in adult English readers. *Cortex*, 116, 268–285. https://doi.org/10.1016/j.cortex.2018.06.011

Ziegler, J. C., & Goswami, U. (2005). Reading acquisition, developmental dyslexia, and skilled reading across languages: A psycholinguistic grain size theory. *Psychological Bulletin*, 131(1), 3–29. https://doi.org/10.1037/0033-2909.131.1.3

12 Numeracy

LEARNING OBJECTIVES

- Describe what the "number sense" is, what it entails, and when it emerges
- Describe the evolutionarily-based system that supports magnitude estimation
- Explain how the approximate number representation follows the Weber-Fechner law
- Compare non-symbolic and symbolic number estimation
- Discuss the evidence for whether numbers are innate or a cultural construction
- Understand what it means to be numerate and the role that learning to count plays in that process
- Characterize how the brain changes to support numeracy in young children
- Delineate how the arithmetic network changes from childhood to adulthood
- Describe what is known about the brain basis for developmental dyscalculia
- Develop recommendations for public policy vis-à-vis math education, based on research evidence

Numbers are an integral part of our daily lives: we rely on at least basic numerical skills in most occupations, and also in our daily activities – when we tell time, cut a recipe in half, calculate a tip, or decide which of two products is a better deal. Thus, a certain level of **numeracy** is essential for making good decisions. Beyond that, an understanding of statistics, geometry, algebra, calculus, and other areas of math are essential for STEM fields. After all, they have helped propel our species through four industrial revolutions (so far).

Although mathematical competencies may not seem relevant to the neurodevelopment of infants and young children, the numerical abilities underlying these competencies begin accruing early in life. Indeed, they are a focal topic in DCN research. Children think about numbers long before they start school, and there is substantial growth in numeracy skills prior to the onset of formal education. Children can be encouraged to develop their number understanding across various play situations, with parents taking an important role in developing their children's numeracy skills – at home, in the playground, in stores, in nature.

In this chapter, we review evidence that very young children are sensitive to numerical magnitudes, a type of informal knowledge often referred to as having a **number sense**. Toddlers demonstrate number sense across a range of everyday problem-solving situations, for example, by reasoning about who has more or less ice cream or grape juice, or devising strategies for creating equal shares of countable objects or amounts. These early non-symbolic number skills accrue informally through children's everyday interactions with caregivers and other children, serving as the basis for subsequent development of symbolic number. We will examine the relationship – perceptually, conceptually, and neurally – between non-symbolic and symbolic number. We will review how the brain regions that support number sense are impacted by acquisition of symbolic number, and how variable experience can lead to more or less well-tuned representations of number (both non-symbolic and symbolic). Because mathematical competence is built on these representations, we outline different outcomes in children – and review the brain basis for individual differences. Finally, we present evidence from math intervention studies of their impact on the development of the brain regions underlying numeracy.

12.1   Number Systems

The numerical operations we perform as adults rely on skills honed through years of school- or experience-based mathematics, but the foundation for this learning is present long before formal education begins. A central question for us here is: How do natural number concepts arise? To begin to answer this question, we need to characterize those preverbal cognitive capacities that are in place before schooling begins. In part, this means identifying evolutionary constructs that existed (in animals) long before formal mathematics, and determining the degree to which natural number concepts (in humans) emerged from these foundations.

Numerical cognition can be divided into two broad categories: **non-symbolic** and **symbolic**. Non-symbolic number doesn't refer to number at all. Rather, it is approximate in nature; for instance, you can quickly estimate which of two sections of a parking lot has more cars in it when choosing where to park. Such non-symbolic number sensitivity is ubiquitous, and guides behavior – in human and non-human animals alike – from moment to moment. In contrast, symbolic numbers are *exact quantities* and their corresponding symbols are typically written or spoken.

In symbolic number, symbols are used to represent *natural numbers*: the set of all whole, non-negative numbers that are fundamental to symbolic mathematical thought. Natural numbers are used for counting ("there are *three* apples in the refrigerator") and ordering ("this is the *third* largest country in the world"). The natural numbers are subdivided into **cardinal numbers**, the words used colloquially for counting ("three"), and **ordinal numbers**, the words used to denote relative position in a sequence ("third").

There are many different numerical systems for expressing number in the world, and different ways of using digits and other symbols to represent quantities. How did these different systems develop? Who uses them? Before young children learn the symbols for natural numbers, they already have an intuitive sense of number.

12.1.1   Number Sense

Although they may not be able to solve differential equations, there is abundant evidence that animals across a range of species have a number sense (Dehaene, 1997), a mental system that allows assessment of numerical magnitudes. The classic demonstration of this early capacity in humans involves presenting someone with two sets of objects (e.g., dots), and asking them to determine which set contains more (Buckley & Gillman, 1974; Figure 12.1). For the display shown in Figure 12.1A (5 vs. 10 dots), adults can correctly assess which set has more without counting the individual dots in the set. Number estimation like this is observed across human cultures, even in those with no number words beyond five (Gordon, 2004; Pica et al.,

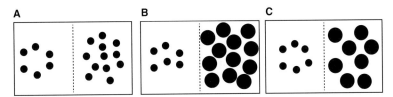

Figure 12.1 Example of dot displays used in different discrimination tasks. Each panel has five dots on the left and ten dots on the right. A. Do number and physical size are congruent. B. The physical dimension of the dot display is not controlled. C. Both dot number and size are incongruent. (Adapted from Leibovich & Ansari, 2016)

2004; some languages represent numbers as, e.g., 1, 2, 3, 4, 5 and *many*). As shown in Figure 12.1B and C, researchers manipulate other dimensions of such displays in an effort to control for alternative visual features and participants' inhibitory control capacities (see Leibovich & Ansari, 2016). How much these properties contribute to people's numerical discrimination abilities, over and above the abstract numerical quantity information, has been the topic of substantial debate. It is now clear that humans of all ages are sensitive to differences in abstract numerical magnitude (Starr et al., 2017). Remarkably, even human infants demonstrate sensitivity to quantity changes, distinguishing between array sizes in both the visual (Xu & Spelke, 2000) and auditory (Lipton & Spelke, 2003) modalities. The "acuity" (i.e., sharpness or resolution) of this ability continues to improve with age and with increases in mathematical ability (Halberda et al., 2012).

12.1.2 Cultural Construction of Symbolic Mathematics

Our non-symbolic representation of number contrasts with symbolic number, which relies on the use of symbols and words to refer to specific numerical quantities (e.g., "three," "3," III, and "third"). It is only over the course of our evolution that we have gained elementary representations of different aspects of the external world: things like time, space, and number. Although these internalized representations may be shared to varying degrees across a range of animal species, they have provided humans, in particular, with the foundation for mathematics and its capacity to integrate these different senses. It is noteworthy that while *Homo sapiens* emerged 200,000 to 300,000 years ago, the first historical records of symbolic numbers date back only to 4,000 BC. Symbolic number systems are a relatively recent addition to our cognitive toolkit. Thus, symbolic number as we know it is culturally derived knowledge (as with written language, there hasn't been enough time for it to be genetically encoded), and the cultural construction of mathematics can be thought of as a human search for coherence across representations, with symbolic number playing a critical role. You probably didn't notice it as a child, but once you began using symbols to represent magnitude, your sense of number itself changed (Leibovich et al., 2017). This process of mapping numerical magnitudes onto symbols has been made part of the human experience and has been the focus of extensive research in DCN. A growing body of evidence is revealing how number symbols acquire meaning in individual minds.

12.1.3 Numerical Systems

The numbers you are familiar with, officially referred to as Hindu-Arabic numerals (henceforth "numerals" or "digits"), consist of a set of 10 symbols – 1, 2, 3, 4, 5, 6, 7, 8, 9, 10 – that represent quantities in the decimal number system. Our decimal system, also called the *base-10 number system*, is the most commonly used system in the world, derived from the number of fingers you have on your two hands (you may remember that as a small child you counted on your fingers, an operation that has probably been moved entirely into your frontal lobes by now). However, there are many other number systems. The simplest of these is the unary numeral system, in which every natural number is represented by a numerically corresponding set of icons. If you were to choose a hash mark ("/") as your icon, then the number seven would be represented as *///////*. Such a system might make you think of tally marks in which each set of four marks is crossed with a fifth, as seen in cartoons to denote the passing of days. That "grouping" of icons into clusters of five is itself a demonstration of the way we can adapt the unary system to handle larger numbers (and is probably related to the fact that you have four fingers and a thumb on each hand). Despite that being a system best reserved for small numbers, ancient recording devices called *tally sticks* were used to document quantities, sometimes growing quite large. Historical reference is made by Pliny the Elder (AD 23–79) about the best wood to use for tallies, and Marco Polo (1254–1324) mentions the use of the tally in China.

You use base-10 all the time but probably don't realize (or remember) that this is a system that you had to learn, often with great difficulty. If you were asked to add 8 and 4 and you answered 12, you are thinking in base-10, even if it doesn't feel like you've done much thinking at all! But when you were learning to use base-10, you had to think about how those symbols are ordered. Base-10 works like this: First, you go through all the digits in the number set: 0, 1, 2 … Once you hit 9, you have no more digits to represent the next number. So, you change it back to 0, and add 1 to the tens digit, giving you 10. The process repeats over and over, and eventually you get to 99, where you can't make any larger numbers with two digits, so you add another, giving you 100, and so on.

Although this all may seem elementary, we shouldn't underestimate the complexity of what is going on. We have only discussed a tiny fraction of the number systems available, but it should already be clear that the systems we have discussed allow humans to do remarkable things (never mind what the base-2 system has enabled computer programmers to do). We all take this for granted but trying to decode other number system bases illustrates the cognitive complexity of what is going on. In base-5, we would run out of digits after the number 5 with the number set: 0, 1, 2, 3, 4 … now we have no more digits (we've used five symbols already, including the 0) and so the number 5 is represented by changing the 4 back to 0 and adding a 1 to the position immediately left of it (the 5s column) and you write it "10." Indeed, although the symbols "10" seem to you like they could not mean anything other than "ten," that constitutes powerful evidence of the interaction between learning, brain development, and culture: we have been *taught* that this set of symbols corresponds to the number ten, just as we have been taught that the symbol "t" is pronounced a certain way. In base-5, we would have been taught that the symbol "10" represents the number "five." In base-2 (binary, the way your digital music and photos are stored) the symbol "10" means the number "two." Confusing? We learn our numeric symbol system so completely that it is impossible to turn the system off – just as it is impossible to turn off our reading system, as demonstrated by the Stroop effect, and indeed, a Stroop effect for numbers has been observed, even in children (Vaid & Corina, 1989).

The goal of this chapter is to understand how children use their early numerical sensitivities to develop symbolic number abilities. What are children's first number-based intuitions – their number sense – and what role, if any, do these intuitions play in their ability to learn the base-10 system and the various forms of mathematics it enables? To answer these questions, we need to distinguish between symbolic and non-symbolic number.

12.2 Non-Symbolic Number

Non-symbolic number refers to representation of numerical magnitude without numerical symbols. Here, we use the term *non-symbolic number* to refer to non-symbolic forms of numerical magnitude (i.e., dot displays), and *symbolic number* for symbolic forms (i.e., numerals). We will use the term *numerosity* to refer to quantity more generally, regardless of its form. Non-symbolic number is conveyed through sensory magnitudes, such as the density of a visual array of dots or the temporal stringing together of auditory beeps. When you wake up to a bright light, it is the *magnitude* of the light that is bothering you. Likewise, loud sounds, salty food, a stubbed toe, all index a larger magnitude of a sensory stimulus than you might consider optimal. The converse is also true – if you can't read in a dark room, hear in a crowded party, or feel the touch of a mosquito on your forearm, the magnitude of the stimulus is too small.

12.2.1 Mechanisms Underlying Non-Symbolic Number Representation

A large body of research has established that humans (and other animal species) are born equipped with mechanisms that render them sensitive to changes in numerical magnitude. Two basic preverbal mechanisms of non-symbolic number have been identified. The first is a domain-general mechanism that tracks the spatiotemporal characteristics of a limited number of visually presented items (up to approximately 3 or 4). This system is referred to as the object tracking system (Klahr & Wallace, 1973), an allusion to the fact that the stimuli are often visual. The second system, the approximate number system, flexibly represents numbers well beyond 4 along a metaphorical number line (Restle, 1970) with increasingly poor resolution as the numbers increase.

Where the object tracking system is argued to account for our ability to **subitize**, or rapidly and accurately determine the number of items in small sets without counting, the approximate number system is invoked to account for how we represent any number, large or small. The crucial signature of the object tracking system, so called because it mimics the limited number of items that can be held in visual short-term memory (Piazza et al., 2011), is its limited storage capacity (i.e., 3–4 elements) and its precision. The approximate number system, on the other hand, is argued to account for our and many other species' ability to discriminate between magnitudes. As it turns out, this ability is based on a coarse code for visually encoded numerical quantity, the brain basis of which we'll examine in Section 12.4. Moreover, recent evidence indicates that it is plausible for number tracking to be supported by a single system that is perceptually precise for smaller quantities and increasingly approximate as quantities increase and processing is limited (Cheyette & Piantadosi, 2020). Here we will refer to a single system based on the conceptual aspects of the approximate number system and its behavioral indicators.

12.2.2 Evidence for Object Tracking

Some researchers have argued that an object tracking system accounts for findings on infants' numerical cognition. As you'll recall from Chapter 2, testing methods investigating discrimination abilities in non-verbal participants, including infants, often employ the habituation-dishabituation paradigm (Fantz, 1964; Oakes et al., 2011). A pioneering study on early number representation by Prentice Starkey and Robert Cooper (1980) repeatedly presented 22-week-old infants with different arrays of 2 dots until they habituated to that specific number. Following habituation to 2 dots, infants saw new arrays with either 2 dots or with 3 dots. Infants' looking times were longer immediately following the presentation of 3-dot arrays, but not before, suggesting that they perceived a change between the familiar and novel arrays. Was it a change in number or a change in shape? In fact, the researchers had manipulated the physical characteristics of the arrays to prevent infants from discriminating based on some non-numerical feature in them. Moreover, the order of number presentation was reversed to verify that infants actually dishabituated to it, rather than to the complexity of the arrays themselves. Infants reliably discriminated 3 vs. 2 dots (along with 2 vs. 3), but they failed to dishabituate when comparing 4 vs. 6 dots (and 6 vs. 4). The same pattern of results was replicated in newborn infants (Antell & Keating, 1983) and in 10- to 12-month-old infants (Strauss & Curtis, 1981), who dishabituated to a comparison of 2 vs. 3 items but not to 4 vs. 5. Infants notice changes in number sets even when the type of item itself (e.g., dots, dashes, dogs), its position, or its size are varied across trials. Finally, 5-month-olds have been found to dishabituate to moving stimuli (van Loosbroek & Smitsman, 1990), thereby supporting the view that children can focus on number without relying on the visual patterns themselves (see also Wynn et al., 2002).

12.2.3 Evidence for Approximate Number

In addition to discriminating small numbers of objects, infants can reliably discriminate between numerical quantities that well exceed the object tracking capacity limit. For numbers greater than 4, infants' discrimination abilities are limited by the ratio of numerical change between sets. For example, Xu and Spelke (2000) habituated 6-month-old infants to arrays of 8 dots whose physical characteristics (e.g., perimeter, density) varied from one array to the next. Following habituation, an array with 16 or 12 dots was presented. Infants looked longer for a change to 16 but not 12 dots. The same pattern of results was observed when infants were initially presented with 16 dots at habituation and 8 dots at dishabituation. In other words, infants only dishabituated to the novel number of dots when the ratio between the smaller amount and the larger amount was 0.5 (e.g., 8 dots vs. 16), but not 0.66 (e.g., 8 dots vs. 12).

A common finding with both adults and infants is that performance in relative numerosity judgments decreases as the numerical ratio between the smaller and the larger group increases (e.g., Xu & Spelke, 2000; Agrillo et al., 2012), although performance improves with age. Such ratio-dependent discrimination was described long ago by Ernst Heinrich Weber (1795–1878), not with regard to numerical magnitude, but for weight. Weber observed that you do not perceive the absolute weight difference between two weights, but their ratio. *Weber's law*, the mathematical function he worked out to characterize his observations, demonstrates that the degree to which two stimuli need to differ for someone to detect a difference between them (i.e., their "just noticeable difference") is a constant ratio of the original stimuli. The resulting *Weber fraction* indicates the smallest variation to a number that can be readily perceived. It seems then that approximate number perception follows Weber's law, something Weber would not have known; DCN seeks to find such generalizable laws of cognition, just as physics seeks to find generalized laws that govern motion.

This ratio-based dependency has become the hallmark for arguments made in support of the *approximate number system*, an hypothesized mechanism that supports estimation of numerical magnitudes without relying on language or symbols. The approximate number system plays a critical role in the development of other numerical abilities, such as the concept of exact number and simple arithmetic. The Weber fraction can be used as an index of an individual's approximate number acuity. Because the approximate number system is ratio dependent, its accuracy varies in predictable ways. For example, the *distance effect* describes how the larger the numerical distance is between two quantities, the easier it is to discriminate them (i.e., shorter response times and lower error rates). Correspondingly, difficulty discriminating any two quantities is dependent on their relative rather than absolute difference. For the distance effect, for example, the specific ratio needed varies across development (Halberda & Feigenson, 2008; Halberda et al., 2008). Newborns are only able to discriminate a 0.3 ratio (1:3, or 4 vs. 12) but not 0.5 (1:2, or 4 vs. 8) (Izard et al., 2009). By ten months, infants' discrimination abilities have already improved to 0.6 (2:3, but not 4:5) (Xu & Arriaga, 2007). This improvement continues throughout childhood and into adulthood, the source of which may be brain maturation, the learning that takes place during formal education, or both. Whichever it is has important implications for understanding the development of more complex numerical skills. Finally, another hallmark of the approximate number system is the *size effect*, whereby it is easier to discriminate smaller numerical magnitudes compared to larger ones at the same distance (2 vs. 4 is easier than 22 vs. 24). It turns out that all animals, humans and non-humans alike, show both these effects.

12.2.4 Origins of the Approximate Number System

Importantly, humans are not the only species who show sensitivity to the ratio between different numerical sets. Rhesus macaque monkeys show a pattern of behavior similar to humans (Merten & Nieder, 2009), one that extends to other non-symbolic tasks as well, including simultaneous non-symbolic comparison (Brannon & Terrace, 2002), non-symbolic ordering (Cantlon & Brannon, 2006), and even non-symbolic arithmetic (Cantlon & Brannon, 2007). The effect holds for animals other than primates too, including dolphins, wolves, parrots, bees, and beetles (see Lyons, 2015 for references). Why might this be? A good example for understanding this is honeybees. They are only very remotely related to humans: they don't have a backbone, so they are not even vertebrates. The last common ancestor between bees and humans likely lived about 600 million years ago. Since that time, these two groups – one leading to bees and the other to vertebrates (including birds, fish, and mammals) – evolved completely independently. Indeed, bees have a very different brain organization than humans with relatively few, although very complex, neurons. Despite these differences, honeybees can discriminate between sets of different sizes (Chittka & Geiger, 1995). This has been shown with dot displays and – more relevant for bees – the number of landmarks they use during navigation. Such findings point to an ancient evolutionary basis for non-symbolic number, one that is based in magnitude representation. The approximate number system has great evolutionary continuity as well (Gebuis et al., 2016). Numerical competence has adaptive value, a core idea of evolutionary theory. For example, when finding food, more food items means more nutrition. In predation situations, animals avoid becoming prey by hiding among large groups of conspecifics. Fish do this all the time. Conversely, many predators have to team up into groups to overpower their prey. Wolves, for example, have different optimal pack sizes depending on the dangerousness of specific prey: six for elk, eight for moose, and more than ten for bison (MacNulty et al., 2014). The approximate number system helps with survival.

12.3 Symbolic Number

In contrast to non-symbolic number, symbolic number allows you to appreciate that the absolute difference between 18 and 19 is exactly the same as the difference between 134 and 135 (although it is not the same relative or ratio difference; 19 is about 5.5 percent larger than 18, 135 is about 0.7 percent larger than 134). It takes humans substantial developmental time to get to the point of understanding absolute difference equivalencies. Between the ages of 2 and 5, children develop an understanding that when they count, they are individuating items in a set. From there, they quickly go beyond having verbal symbolic representation of numbers to having other ways of symbolically representing numbers. Such number symbols are particularly powerful because they allow people to communicate about number quickly, and even without speaking the same language. Symbolic numbers allow representation of large, multi-digit numbers; for example, using the place-value system inherent to the base-10 system (Section 12.1.3) they allow numerical manipulation with arithmetic and much more. But first, children have to learn to count.

12.3.1 A Brief Digression into Language Acquisition and Attentional Focus

As we saw in Chapter 8, language acquisition is a vast topic, and many universities offer one or several courses on just that; we cannot hope to do the topic complete justice in this textbook, but will provide the conceptual outlines of a remarkable interaction between genes, brains, and environment – and how they promote one of the highest and most sophisticated cognitive attributes of any species: true linguistic communication. Learning language has important implications for learning numbers too.

As toddlers are learning to speak, and their caregivers are teaching them words, how does the toddler know which attribute of an object the parent is referring to? A fire engine could be driving down the street and the parent might say any one of these things: *that's a fire engine*, *that's red*, *that's fast*, *that's a truck*, *that's loud*. Children's brains appear to be hard-wired to assume that linguistic labels refer to different attributes according to a complicated hierarchy that depends on the specific stimulus, any comparison stimuli present, and their developmental stage and prior linguistic knowledge. That is, genes create brain structures that are predisposed to focus on general noun object names first and proper names and adjectives later.

When a parent points to the family dog and says "that's Fluffy," young children assume that "Fluffy" is not a proper name, but a general noun name, and may then overgeneralize and refer to *all* dogs as "Fluffy" or even refer to any quadruped they see (if the salient thing to the child is that the animal walks on four legs instead of two). Attending to adjectives (such as colors) tends to come later, although context plays a role: *that apple is green* and *that apple is red* trigger adjectival focus. In general, a focus on prepositions (*the apple is on the plate* or *the plate is under the apple*) emerges after that. Older children thus use context to determine the salient attribute; if you didn't yet know the words "elated" or "despondent," for example, you'd be predisposed to notice that attribute which has changed (and we'd deduce that *I'm elated* or *I am despondent* refer to emotional states).

This remarkable ability is necessary for vocabulary acquisition, for without it, any word could refer to anything. And yet, most of the time, we understand that they don't. So it is with number. When a display varies in number, children automatically ("innately") know that the words refer to number. There may well be a universal order of emergence of linguistic categories, with nouns always learned before adjectives, which are always learned before adverbs, for example; this is an area of active research, as is pinning down the precise ages and phases at which new words are assumed to map onto particular attributes.

12.3.2 Individuation and Counting

At the heart of basic number development lies the ability to enumerate sets – count – based on individuation of the objects in the set. Children initially learn to count sequences through memorization, just as they learn the alphabet. This early counting often takes a song-like form (counting songs are found in almost every culture) that can be meaningless to children, who simply follow the sing-song sequence. That is, they learn the sequence of count words, and often happily recite it, but they don't yet connect the words in that sequence to meaning. Natural numbers are precise and discrete. Although most children recite the count list (i.e. "one," "two," "three"...) around age 2, children only gradually, over the next two years or so, learn the precise and discrete meanings of each of these words.

According to the counting principles theory (Gelman & Gallistel, 1978), children possess "innate" counting principles that guide them in recognizing counting as an activity to determine the quantity in a given set. The acquisition of counting skills represents the first connection between preverbal numerical mechanisms and a culturally determined symbolic system. Around 2 years of age, toddlers begin to implement counting routines to enumerate sets of objects around them (Wynn, 1992). The repeated connection between physical elements in the environment and their corresponding number words contributes to a robust mapping between non-symbolic and symbolic representations of numerical quantities. Without getting into mechanistic details, this procedure is similar to any other mapping between a word and its specific meaning during vocabulary growth. Nevertheless, number words represent a unique case because they refer to the property of a set rather than to a characteristic of a specific object (Wynn, 1992). To accomplish counting, children must respect three basic principles. They have to:

(i)   recite the number word sequence in the established order (stable order principle);
(ii) match each object in a set to one, and only one, number word (one-to-one correspondence principle);
(iii) identify that the last number word represents the number of items in the set (cardinality principle).

There are two additional principles:

(iv) the *abstraction principle* states that any collection of objects can be counted (e.g., oranges, thoughts, clouds, etc.);
(v)   and the *order-irrelevance principle* states that the order in which the items are counted is irrelevant.

Learning the counting principles is a long and error-prone process that takes children in industrialized countries anywhere between the age of 2 and – in extreme cases – the end of second grade at age 8 (National Research Council, 2015). The counting principle theory strongly advocates for the initial role of the principles in shaping the acquisition of counting skills (the *principle first* view), although other theories hold that, initially, counting is a routine that itself enables children to acquire the counting principles (the *principle after* view). According to this view, counting is first an imitation activity (e.g., the sing-song recitation we mentioned) that is shaped by parents, teachers, and peers (Briars & Siegler, 1984; Fuson, 1988). Only later do children learn that counting refers specifically to the determination of the number of items in a given set. Some argue that number words assume different meanings for children depending on the specific context (Fuson, 1988). For example, in the sequence context, children can recite number words aloud in the correct order because they have memorized the unique sequence of sounds without any specific numerical meaning. In the counting context, children segment the numerical sequence and assign a number word to only one counted object (one-to-one correspondence), but nevertheless still lack the understanding that the last number word uttered represents the total number of items in the counted set (cardinal context). In short, learning to count is hard work.

12.3.3 Counting Helps Focus Children on Number Rather than Other Attributes

Another challenge is how children progressively acquire the cardinality principle and how they extend it to the counting list. According to the *knower level theory* (Wynn, 1990, 1992; Carey, 2001), children's acquisition of the cardinal meaning of number words follows predictable developmental stages. Initially, children are considered pre-numerical knowers because they lack any numerical meaning of the number words. When requested to provide a certain number of objects (as in the give-a-number task; Wynn, 1990), children usually collect a handful of items without implementing any counting strategy. Subsequently, children learn the cardinal meaning of the number word "one"; thereafter, they can correctly provide one item when it is requested. However, *one-knowers* still fail with larger quantities. Interestingly, however, they don't respond with one item when larger quantities are requested because they know the cardinal meaning of the number word "one." Similarly, *two-*, *three-*, and *four*-knowers correctly provide 2, 3, and 4 items respectively, but they still fail with larger quantities. These children are usually defined as *subset-knowers* because their understanding of the cardinal meanings of number words is limited to a subset of the counting list (i.e., from 1 to 4; Le Corre et al., 2006).

Progressively, children realize that the next number word in the counting list corresponds to one additional element in the counted set, and that every natural number has a successor (i.e., *successor function*, Gelman & Gallistel, 1978). It is only after the "four-knower" stage that children can extend the cardinality principle to the whole counting list and are on their way to becoming *cardinal-principle knowers*. With the full acquisition of the cardinality principle, children understand that the last recited number word identifies the quantity in the counted set. Susan Carey has suggested that learning to count resembles a conceptual bootstrapping process (Carey, 2009). Initially, by respecting the counting rules (e.g., fixed order of number words, one-to-one correspondence), children create a structure in which number words are simply placeholders with specific relations between each other (e.g., "two" comes after "one"), but the words still lack true numerical meaning. Only later, through conceptual bootstrapping, do children gradually fill the placeholders with numerical meaning. What's interesting is that the same stereotyped order of knower-level emergence has been observed across different languages and cultures (Sarnecka et al., 2007), albeit later in places where children are educated later. For example, the developmental progression from one-knowers to cardinal principle-knowers follows a slower trajectory in an indigenous, farming-forager Amazonian tribe whose children have little formal schooling, but it still goes through the same phases in the same order (Piantadosi et al., 2014). In other words, generalizing the count sequence relies on cognitive abilities that unfold in early childhood, but likewise are heavily influenced by societal factors. Counting is a cognitive universal, despite differences in language and culture.

In summary, children use counting to create a reliable association between objective quantities and symbolic representations of numerical quantities. The initial counting routine progressively leads children to understand that the last pronounced number word corresponds to the cardinality of the set. The acquisition of the cardinality principle, in particular, is a critical milestone in numerical development because it sets a child up for the process of assigning numerical meaning to otherwise arbitrary symbols (i.e., digits).

12.4 Relationship between Non-Symbolic and Symbolic Number

As we have seen, where non-symbolic number allows for ready assessment of approximate magnitude, symbolic number is precise. Some have argued that the entryway to symbolic representation of number, including cardinal and ordinal number words (e.g., "three," "third") and written numerals ("3"), is through their non-symbolic counterparts (Dehaene et al., 2008).

According to this view, the non-symbolic number abilities engendered by the approximate number system are foundational to numerical development in general, and mathematical development in particular (Halberda & Feigenson, 2008).

But thus far, we have been distinguishing between non-symbolic and symbolic number representation. Does this mean that symbolic representation is grounded in an evolutionarily ancient form of non-symbolic magnitude representation? Two factors consistent with this possibility are the cross-species generality of the approximate number system, and brain-based links between numerical and physical magnitude. We will address each of these points and conclude that, while the non-symbolic and symbolic number are clearly related, the relationship between them is not at all unidirectional. Findings from studies on the neural representation of quantity – in humans and non-humans alike – provide important insights into how the brain has evolved a system for representing abstract information about number, one that has been foundational to humans' development of precise symbolic number representations.

12.4.1 The Brain Basis for Number

Investigation of the brain basis for number started with patient studies early in the twentieth century. The Swedish neurologist Salomon Henschen (Henschen & Schaller, 1925) described several patients who had lost the ability to process numbers or perform calculations following brain damage. Although awareness of brain-related calculation deficits had been around for nearly a century, it was Henschen who coined the term *acalculia* to describe these deficits. With no brain imaging capabilities – this was in the early 1900s – many of the patients' brains were never studied, or if they were, were examined postmortem. Thus, it remained unclear what the location-to-function relationship was for number. Over the years, there was some argument among researchers about whether language provides the basis for processing numbers (e.g., Spelke & Tsivkin, 2001), an intuition guided by the fact that numerical ability manifests following the development of counting. Nevertheless, it is now undisputed that numerical representation is independent from language, and relies on its own brain network. For example, patients who have lesions in certain areas of the parietal lobe sometimes develop a deficit in dealing with numbers or calculating while their language function is totally spared. Of course, the clarity of this double dissociation depends on the lesion size and location, but repeated observations along these lines point to an independent number system, at least in the adult brain. How language and number interact in the developing brain is another matter, and has itself become the focus of research (e.g., Spelke & Tsivkin, 2001).

With the advent of functional imaging methods in the 1990s, it became feasible to map neural representation of number in humans. Consistent with lesion studies, the early results pointed to posterior parietal cortex, as well as parts of the prefrontal cortex, as critical to number representation and manipulation. About 10 years later, at the turn of the millennium, single cell recordings in non-human primates began to reveal that single neurons represent specific numerical information, implicating two regions in particular – the intraparietal sulcus (IPS) and the prefrontal cortex (PFC) – in numerical processing. Indeed, because the IPS showed the highest proportion of quantity-specific neurons, researchers focused on that region, often to the exclusion of other brain regions (see Fias et al., 2013; Menon, 2015; for critical analyses).

Although we now recognize that arithmetic skills engage multiple brain regions and are characterized by distributed processing, understanding the role that IPS plays in numerical cognition has been critical to mapping the *arithmetic network*. As we discuss in Section 12.6, this network supports a range of number-related abilities, including counting, retrieval of math facts, and yes, arithmetic. To understand how this network emerged in humans, it helps to understand what the single-cell data reveal about number representation in non-human primates.

12.4.2 The Neuronal Code for Number

In a seminal behavioral study, Elizabeth Brannon and Herbert Terrace (1998) showed that rhesus macaque monkeys could order visual displays of non-symbolic number from smallest to largest quantity, demonstrating an ability to understand the concept of numerical quantity. Because a number of labs had established techniques at that time for recording neural activity from macaque monkeys during behavioral protocols, the finding sparked a rush of research on the neural underpinnings that support such ability. Brannon and others recorded from monkeys while they performed a range of tasks measuring their ability to discriminate different numerosities – the number of elements in a set. This involved recording the activity of individual neurons while the animals held quantities of dots in memory for short periods of time (Figure 12.2). Of course, monkeys first have to be trained to work with different quantities of items, and one of the standard tasks for this purpose is a delayed match-to-numerosity task (Figure 12.2A), a variation of the delayed match-to-sample task used with human participants – including children – that you've read about elsewhere in this book. Using this task, Andreas Nieder and Earl Miller presented monkeys with a specific number of items in a visual array (Nieder et al., 2002; Nieder & Miller, 2004). The monkeys had first been trained to hold the quantity of items – the numerosity – in memory for a short period of time in order to obtain a reward. Following a brief delay, a second array appeared. On half of the trials, the same number of dots was shown in the second as in the first array. For those cases, the animals were trained to respond by releasing a lever, after which they received their reward. On the other half of the trials, the second array contained a smaller or larger number of dots than the first (i.e., a different numerosity). In those cases, the animals were trained to continue holding the lever until they received their reward. Using this behavioral protocol together with single-cell recording (Figure 12.2B and C), the researchers were able to establish that the animals discriminated among different quantities (based on the accuracy of their performance), while simultaneously obtaining information about what the monkeys' neurons were doing. These neural data were obtained from monkeys' PFC, demonstrating how the region engages in both encoding and maintaining a numerical quantity in working memory in the service of a task. Similar data for encoding of numerosity have been obtained from IPS.

The accumulation of neuronal data of this kind has provided a clearer view of the neural foundation of the approximate number system: different magnitudes are encoded by bell-shaped tuning functions with the peak at the preferred quantity, just as auditory neurons are tuned to specific frequencies, or visual neurons are tuned to specific line orientations. Thus, number neurons responses are characterized by neuronal *tuning curves* around the target number. As you probably recall, this is a function we've observed in other perceptual domains; in the case of number, individual neurons are tuned to a specific, preferred abstract numerosity.

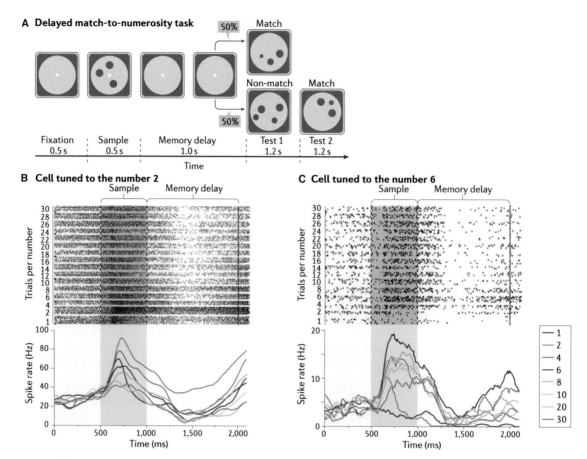

Figure 12.2 Number sensitive neurons in monkeys. A. The delayed match-to-numerosity task used by Nieder and colleagues to test number representation in rhesus macaque monkeys. B. The time course of neuronal firing during trials for different numerosities. At the top of the panel is a dot-raster histogram – each dot represents an action potential – recorded from the PFC in response to all even numbers (and "1") up to "30" across multiple repetitions of each stimulus. Notice that the target numerosity ("2") produces neural engagement in both the presentation phase of the sample ("sample") and in the subsequent delay phase ("memory delay") during which working memory maintains the representation. C. Similar data in response to the numerosity "6." (Reprinted from Nieder, 2016)

For example, a neuron might fire maximally when three dots are displayed, irrespective of how the dots are arranged and even whether they are shown all together, or one at a time: that neuron encodes "three." The same neuron responds less to adjacent quantities, in this case, two and four, and it doesn't respond at all to one and five. This reveals a key characteristic of number neurons: their response is approximate and relatively imprecise. Not only does the preferred quantity elicit responses, but so do adjacent ones, if to a lesser degree. Of course, there are neurons tuned not only to number three, but to two and one and five and six and so on. Based on their specific tunings, all of these neurons together are able represent the entire numerical space, thus informing the animal about which numerosity is being shown.

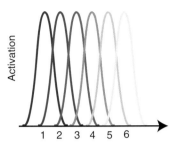

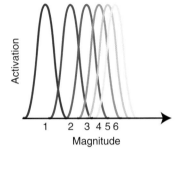

Figure 12.3 Linear versus logarithmic scaling of magnitude.

Data from both monkeys (Nieder & Merten, 2007) and humans (Merten & Nieder, 2009) show that numerical quantity and tuning curve width are positively correlated. As the preferred numerosity for a neuron increases, the width of its response curve – indicating relative imprecision – also increases. This effect is consistent with the numerical ratio effects described by Weber's law. Neuroimaging data also show this ratio-dependent tuning for numerosity in the human parietal cortex (Piazza et al., 2004). However, one point of clarification is needed. In Section 12.2, we said that the approximate number system provides increasingly coarse representation with increasing numerical magnitudes. Weber's law handily accounts for the distance effect. But characterizing the increasing representational coarseness with increasing magnitude can only be characterized with an additional tweaking of that law. In fact, it was Weber's student, Gustav Fechner (Fechner, 1860), who determined that logarithmic, rather than linear, scaling was needed to accommodate findings that our subjective experience of a stimulus is proportional to the logarithm of its objective intensity. This logarithmic scaling also shows up in other domains, such as musical pitch. Figure 12.3 demonstrates this contrast. Indeed, the Weber-Fechner law, as it's now known, helped account for a puzzling feature of the monkeys' bell-shaped neural tuning curves: they were not symmetrical when plotted on a linear number scale (Nieder & Miller, 2003). Rather, the monkeys' tuning curves were systematically distorted such that curves for smaller magnitudes had steeper slopes while those for larger magnitudes had shallower slopes. But when Nieder and colleagues plotted the same data logarithmically – on a compressed number line – the curves became symmetric. Thus, the monkey data reveal what the Weber-Fechner law predicts: that regardless of magnitude, the more numerosity representations overlap, the more difficult it is to discriminate them, and the larger the numerical magnitude the more the representational overlap. Thus, another hallmark of the approximate number system, the size effect, can be accounted for at the neural level.

To summarize, abstract quantity is encoded by specific neurons in the primate brain. The role of the IPS in number judgments has been supported by brain imaging data from adults (Piazza et al., 2002) and children (Cantlon et al., 2009). In fact, modulation of activity in the IPS based on changes in non-symbolic number has been observed in children as young as 4 years of age (Cantlon et al., 2006). The brain's encoding of numerosity is such that values that are closer together have more representational overlap (i.e., distance effects), and that overlap increases as the size of the numbers increases (i.e., size effects). Consistent with the Weber-Fechner law, the approximate number system supports analog representations of numerosity that are subject to the same logarithmic compression observed in perception of physical stimuli varying along a physical continuum (i.e., intensity). Abstract numerical representations share fundamental principles with sensory magnitudes and, correspondingly, the number line for non-symbolic numerical magnitude is logarithmically compressed.

12.4.3 Number Representations and Brain Networks

Thus far, we have focused on the IPS and the PFC in our discussions of the neural basis for number representation. Indeed, lesion, single-cell, and imaging data all seem to point to neurons in these regions. Why might this be? First, the PFC is involved with number because it is at the top of our cortical processing hierarchy, receiving highly refined information from the posterior parietal cortex (PPC) and the anterior temporal cortex. The data featured in Figure 12.2 are from monkeys doing a task that required them to hold a numerical quantity in memory. That this task engaged their PFC is consistent with that region's involvement in a wide range of cognitive processes, including working memory. But what about the PPC? First, recall that the parietal cortex is the endpoint for the dorsal visual stream, or the "where" pathway (Chapter 6). This is just one of several sensory sources that converge in the PPC. The PPC even receives premotor information that can represent a range of different features of movement, including their enumeration. Think about how children start learning to count by using their fingers. Indeed, this region of the parietal cortex is engaged when they do that (Rusconi et al., 2005)! Buried within the PPC is the IPS, a multimodal association area (Duhamel et al., 1998; Schlack et al., 2005) that receives input from all primary sensory systems, including visual, auditory, and somatosensory. The IPS is now appreciated as the site where abstract magnitude – magnitude across space, time, and number – is represented (see target article and commentaries in Walsh, 2003).

You might be wondering whether the other visual stream, the ventrally located "what" pathway, has a job in processing number? Indeed, the endpoint of the ventral visual stream is the ventral temporal occipital cortex (VTOC). You'll recall from Chapter 6 that this pathway encodes high-level object identity. Because digits and number words are visual objects, they are processed via this pathway. Processing of these visual symbols – both the digits and the letters that comprise the number words – develops in the left fusiform gyrus (FG), an area whose handling of specific forms is homologous to the right IFG's handling of face processing (as discussed in Chapters 11 and 6, respectively). Figure 12.4 shows intracranial EEG recordings taken from adults in response to visual number form in the FG, highlighting the specificity of one region's responsivity to digits as opposed to any other form. These findings are further

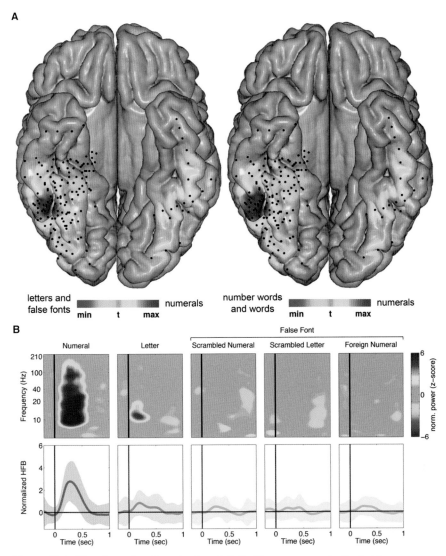

Figure 12.4 Visual number form in the adult fusiform gyrus as indicated by intracranial recordings. A and B. Anatomical coordinates of preferential responses to numbers were estimated based on degree of preferential response to numbers for each electrode (black dots) across seven participants as contrasted with morphologically similar stimuli (false font and letters) and from semantically and phonetically similar stimuli (number words and non-number words). Focal activity for numbers is in the inferior temporal gyrus. C. Activity in the ITG during Experiment 1 in an individual subject (Subject 2). Time-frequency analysis during presentation of five different visual stimuli is shown at top; the y-axis represents the log scale of frequencies from 1 to 210 Hz. Red and blue represent significant increase and decrease of normalized power, respectively. Mean normalized high frequency broadband (HFB) power traces across time during presentation of each of the five different visual stimuli (stimulus onset is at 0). A greater HFB is observed during processing of numerals relative to other conditions. (Reprinted from Shum et al., 2013)

supported by brain imaging data showing involvement of FG in visually mediated numerical judgments in both adults (Holloway et al., 2013) and children (Cantlon et al., 2009). Thus, visual representations of symbolic number appear to be processed via the ventral stream and mapped onto appropriate quantity representations (Shum et al., 2013). Cross-modal phonological information – relevant here to the representation of symbolic number words – likewise includes this pathway. This is because skilled readers develop rich representations for speech that allow them to map printed language onto existing phonological representations (Wagner & Torgesen, 1987; Elbro, 1996). Interaction of the IPS and FG with multiple other regions, including different subcomponents of the PFC, allows for active manipulation (Chapter 10) of numerical magnitude representations, network-level processing that supports increasingly complex numerical problem solving.

12.4.4 How Numerical Symbols Acquire Their Meaning

With the acquisition of counting skills, children begin the process of mapping a specific non-symbolic quantity onto a corresponding symbol. For example, they learn that the last number named when counting a set of objects represents the quantity of objects in that group (i.e., the cardinality principle), and that each subsequent number is generated by adding one to the previous number (i.e., the successor function, or n + 1). However, even mastery of these principles does not guarantee that children can correctly individuate larger numbers (Le Corre & Carey, 2007). To understand magnitude relations between digits, children need to correctly estimate where quantities are located on a number line (Le Corre, 2014). To systematically assess children's number comparison skills, a child might be shown two numbers (of either one or two digits) on the left and right side of a computer screen, and instructed to choose the larger (or smaller) digit by pressing a corresponding key. With expertise, this becomes a relatively simple task and the vast majority of children – except those with severe difficulties, something we discuss in Section 12.6 – perform near perfectly. Because of how easy this task becomes, it is more meaningful to focus on response times. Between 6 and 8 years of age, children become increasingly efficient (i.e., fast) at performing these symbolic number comparisons (Holloway & Ansari, 2009). Critically, their efficiency improves as a function of the numerical distance between the two digits being presented, much as we saw with non-symbolic number. Likewise, as the numerical distance between the two digits decreases, children slow down. By now, you should recognize this as the symbolic version of the distance effect we described in the context of non-symbolic number. In the same vein, if the distance between two symbolic numbers is held constant, children are slower to compare large numbers to smaller numbers. This is the symbolic version of the size effect. Such effects arise due to the lack of precision of the neural representations for different magnitudes. As with non-symbolic number, such imprecision makes it more difficult to distinguish between quantities, although with extensive training, we gradually narrow our representations of symbolic number to the precise quantity represented by a particular digit.

It may seem counterintuitive that symbolic number – the means by which we represent number precisely – would nevertheless produce distance and size effects. After all, these were described in Section 12.2 as being due to the imprecise approximate number system. In fact, the existence of such effects for symbolic number supports the argument that the same noisy non-symbolic representations supported by the approximate number system form the foundation for symbolic number. In its nascent state our understanding of symbolic number is as imprecise as our sensitivity to magnitude differences. With mastery of cultural symbols (i.e., digits and number words), our symbolic representations gain precision, narrowing in on specific quantities as the mapping between symbolic and non-symbolic number strengthens. It is not only children's conceptual representation of numerical symbols that "tunes" with this training; the neural representation of number in the IPS tunes as well. Thus, increasing the mapping strength between non-symbolic and symbolic number increases the representational precision of both.

Not surprisingly, as children become increasingly exposed to digits with formal education, the way in which they map symbolic numbers on a number line becomes less logarithmic (i.e., approximate) and more linear (i.e., precise). A compelling demonstration of this is shown in Figure 12.5, in which increased time in formal education corresponds to children's transition from representing symbolic number on a logarithmic to a linear number line. Critically, this logarithmic-to-linear effect emerges *only* with substantial symbolic number training. This is strong evidence that the precise quantity representation indicated by symbolic number is not something we are born with. If left untrained, for example by living in a culture where number symbols have not been invented and no one is teaching us to count, this logarithmic number line prevails. In Box 12.1, we examine data from cultures in which number representation is nearer to this nascent state. Spoiler alert: as with literacy (Chapter 11), these data likewise demonstrate that symbolic number is not at all guaranteed. Because symbolic number representation feels automatic to us as adults, we tend to forget that we had to be taught about digits. In fact, mastering symbolic number – whereby our culture imposes a linear number scale on our intuitive logarithmic one – is a painful learning process. Our training in precise numerical representations puts a linear framework on our otherwise logarithmic numerical intuitions, thus intertwining the two number systems for the remainder of our lives.

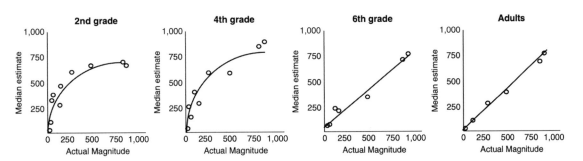

Figure 12.5 Progression from logarithmic to linear pattern of median estimates among individuals of different ages when asked to estimate by marking with a pencil the location they thought different numbers should fall on a line between 0 and 1,000. (Reprinted from Iuculano & Menon, 2018; adapted from Siegler & Opfer, 2003)

Box 12.1 Influence of Culture on Number Representation

Our understanding of the origins of number has been greatly advanced by research conducted with indigenous groups who do not use number symbols, and have not been taught anything about the base-10 system. Such a culture reveals much about human numerical competence with far less cultural learning imposed (no number symbols and no one teaching us to count). For example, Peter Gordon worked with the Pirahã tribe, in the Brazilian state of Amazonas. These people only have number words for one, two, and many. When tested by anthropologists, they discriminated one from two, but for three, they made errors and these errors were more pronounced for higher numbers. But their performance was not random. Rather, and consistent with Weber's law, the distribution of their responses broadened with increasing target numbers (Frank et al., 2008). Similar results have been obtained from another indigenous group, the Munduruku in the Amazonian rainforest of Brazil, by Pierre Pica.

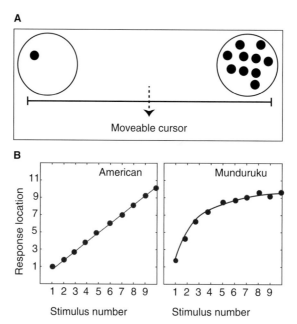

Box Figure 12.1 Method and findings for testing number representation in Munduruku and American adults. A. Participants were asked to indicate where sets of dots ranging from 1 to 10 should be located on a line relative to one another (either in drawing or on a computer screen). B. Western and Amazonian indigene cultures differ in how they map number. Munduruku adults mapped out the numbers 1 through 10 logarithmically, while American adults mapped the same numbers out linearly.

In a particularly clever study, Pica and colleagues (Pica et al., 2004) tested the Munduruku's spatial understanding of number with an unmarked line connecting two sets of dots on each end. On the left side was 1 dot and on the right were 10 dots. Volunteers were asked to point to the location where a third set of dots with a numerical value anywhere between 1 and 10 should be located. The answer was recorded and this was repeated many times with the full range of possible numbers. The question was how the Munduruku spaced the numbers 1 through 10, with the comparison group being an analogous task performed by a group of American adults (Box Figure 12.1A).

The results were clear: Americans placed the numbers at equally spaced intervals along the line (Box Figure 12.1A), a finding that was not surprising, since we do this all the time with rulers and graphs. A linear scale is one with distributed numbers. However, Munduruku showed quite a different pattern, placing groups of five or more dots further to the right end of the line (i.e., where six should be). Overall, they had larger intervals between smaller numbers and smaller intervals between larger numbers: they produced a logarithmic scale (Box Figure 12.1B). This is just as Fechner would have predicted!

The data clearly demonstrate that we naturally present numerical quantities on a logarithmic number line, or scale. We can speculate that this is how the brain represents numerical quantities without the systematic influence of symbolic number (i.e., without cultural influence), but it may be that the logarithmic representation is unique to the Munduruku. However, recall that data based on a similar task performed by American kindergarten children (average age 5.8 years), first graders (6.9 years), and second graders (7.8 years) demonstrate how expertise in counting shapes our number representations (Figure 12.5). The youngest children look like the Munduruku: they map their numbers logarithmically. Even in the first year of school, the curve is logarithmic, but the influence of all that symbolic number training is beginning to show: the estimates are getting a bit more precise. By second grade, the kids are firmly in the linear world: their estimates are evenly laid out. Our linear representation of number is the product of culture, contradicting our logarithmic intuition.

12.4.5 Stepping Stones to Mathematical Competency

We've reviewed how basic numerical abilities – sensitivity to magnitude differences, counting, and symbol mapping – develop to support number processing. An important practical aspect of such knowledge in children is that they have the numerical tools for more advanced mathematical engagement, starting with arithmetic.

As with much DCN research, children who get tested on number representation in developmental labs are from so-called "WEIRD" (i.e., Western, Educated, Industrialized, Rich, and Democratic) samples, likely already having received far more exposure to numerically rich environmental input than the average child on the planet. Thus, conclusions drawn from correlational data acquired from such samples, for example, that the acuity of one's approximate number system is a predictor of the development of mathematical ability (Halberda et al., 2008), are premature. Although the two are clearly linked, it is telling that a large internet-based

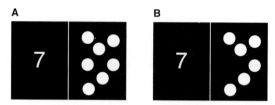

Figure 12.6 Stimuli used to test children's mapping between symbolic and non-symbolic magnitudes. A. Congruent display. B. Incongruent display. (Adapted from Matejko & Ansari, 2019)

study found that children's non-symbolic number acuity improves steadily throughout childhood and well into adulthood (Halberda et al., 2012). If anything, such a trajectory points to the influence of symbolic number on non-symbolic representation. In other words, children who get lots of input about symbolic number are having their magnitude representations tuned in such a way that the acuity of their non-symbolic number improves as well.

Regardless, there is evidence that the strength of children's quantity-to-symbol number mappings predicts their mathematical achievements (Mundy & Gilmore, 2009; Defever et al., 2013). One way to test this is to present children with displays containing both a symbolic and a non-symbolic number, some of which are congruent with one another and some incongruent. Children are asked to determine if they match (Figure 12.6), while response time and accuracy are measured. Using this approach, Brankaer et al. (2014) found that performance in both first and third graders explained a good part of the variance in these children's mathematical abilities, over and above their independently assessed symbolic and non-symbolic skills and whether the math assessment was timed or not. Consistent with this, a clear relationship has been found between the precision of children's symbolic number representations and their math achievement (Lyons et al., 2014). Indeed, in a recent meta-analysis, the association between symbolic number comparison and math abilities was significantly larger than between non-symbolic number and math (Schneider et al., 2017). In short, the direction of causality in the development of non-symbolic and symbolic number is far from clear, while the importance of strong mapping between the two is now apparent. Such findings have led to a shift in focus from what was originally hypothesized to be a one-way developmental influence (i.e., from non-symbolic to symbolic number) to one that is bidirectional at best (Goffin & Ansari, 2019). This reconceptualization is influencing how developmental researchers approach the issue of numerical cognition and has far-reaching practical implications for math education as well.

12.5 Arithmetic

You often hear the terms arithmetic and mathematics used interchangeably. In truth, arithmetic is a particular branch of mathematics, one dealing with addition, subtraction, multiplication, and division, where mathematics is broader, including arithmetic, algebra, geometry, and beyond. Arithmetic describes the use of numbers in calculations. It is to mathematics as spelling is to writing: it is foundational. Knowledge of numerical magnitude and the ability to easily manipulate and move between non-symbolic and symbolic number are critical skills to have to support development of more sophisticated mathematical knowledge.

Well before the start of formal education, children use counting to solve simple sums. Progressively, children begin to count without external aids (i.e., they shift from using their fingers to using a verbal strategy). The efficiency of these strategies increases rapidly, with children going from counting all sets in their entirety to *counting-on*, whereby when adding two numbers they begin counting from the first number and add the second to it. They then shift to adding the smaller to the larger number (*counting-on-larger*) (Geary et al., 1992). Repeated use of increasingly sophisticated counting routines allows children to develop associations between problems and their answers – *arithmetic facts* – which become stored in long-term memory. Because counting is cognitively demanding and error-prone, the acquisition of these arithmetic facts serves as a stand-in for counting, a strategy that is far more efficient and consumes less working memory (e.g., Campbell & Xue, 2001).

Arithmetic facts also enable children to decompose problems into smaller problems. Initially, children use decomposition strategies for problems with larger numbers (i.e., greater than 10) and in multi-digit calculations. Decomposition is used a lot for addition, a bit less for subtraction (Barrouillet et al., 2008), and much less for multiplication. With the onset of multiplication learning – starting around second grade – children begin to rely on fact retrieval as their most dominant strategy (Imbo & Vandierendonck, 2007), accounted for at least in part by the extensive rote memorization that takes place in the service of mastering multiplication tables. Moreover, because multiplication (along with addition) is a commutative operation (e.g., $6 \times 4 = 4 \times 6$), unlike division and subtraction, the formation of problem–answer associations can be better encoded in long-term memory. Although the development of division is not well characterized, the strategies involved are likely different from other forms of arithmetic (Robinson et al., 2006).

12.5.1 The Arithmetic Network in Typically Developing Children

In an effort to characterize the typical neurodevelopmental profile that supports development of basic arithmetic, Kawashima et al. (2004) conducted the first brain imaging study comparing children and adults while they performed addition, subtraction, and multiplication. Results showed that children recruited surprisingly similar neural networks relative to adults, including prefrontal, intraparietal, and occipitotemporal areas, and that engagement was largely comparable across the three arithmetic operations. Although influential, the study was limited by the small number of participants in each age group. That, together with the broad age range made it difficult to detect specific age-based developmental differences. Around the same time, Vinod Menon and his colleagues began investigating the neural correlates of arithmetic skill development. Their examination of 8- to 19-year-olds performing basic addition and subtraction problems revealed that activation varied as a function of years in school (Rivera et al., 2005). In particular, they observed age-related increases in left-parietal cortex and inferior temporal cortex, and decreases in PFC activity.

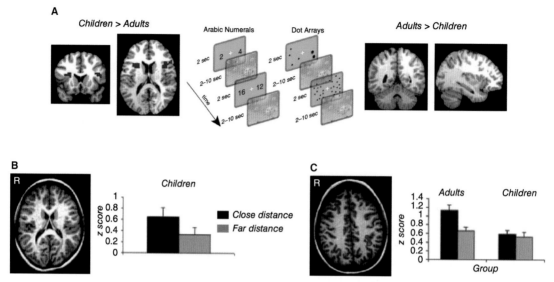

Figure 12.7 Age-related changes in IPS involvement during magnitude representation for both non-symbolic and symbolic number. A. While performing symbolic and non-symbolic number comparison tasks, children show greater activation of prefrontal cortex compared to adults while adults show greater IPS activation compared to children. B. In a non-symbolic distance comparison task, 9-year-old children show activation in the dorsolateral prefrontal cortex as a function of non-symbolic distance. C. Adults show a significant distance effect in left interparietal sulcus; 9-year-olds do not. (Reprinted from Iuculano & Menon, 2018)

Subsequent imaging studies confirmed this: numerical problem solving was found to engage a core parietal-frontal network, with age-related shifts in relative engagement of different neural regions as children shifted to more sophisticated behavioral strategies. During both symbolic and non-symbolic number comparison tasks, 6-year-olds show greater PFC activation than adults, while adults show more IPS activation relative to children (Cantlon et al., 2009; Figure 12.7A). Meanwhile, the ratio-dependent distance effect is shown to involve substantial dorsolateral PFC activation in 9-year-olds (Figure 12.7B), while the same effect in adults corresponds to heightened IPS activation (Ansari & Dhital, 2006; Figure 12.7C). In short, the kinds of problem-solving strategies used early in development and that engage the PFC give way to automatized number representations and long-term memory for arithmetic facts, which rely on regions in and around the PPC.

Although these studies helped identify the neural systems that support the development of arithmetic skills, they generally did not include systematic manipulations of task-specific and other experimental parameters to help discern how different regions are recruited, an approach used in adult arithmetic research (e.g., Tschentscher & Hauk, 2014). In an example of early work addressing this (e.g., De Smedt et al., 2011), problem size (small vs. large) and operation (addition vs. subtraction) were systematically manipulated in a group of children from a relatively narrow age range (10- to 12-year-olds). As had been observed in adults, findings showed that large number problems (i.e., involving numbers greater than 10) and subtraction produced increases in the frontoparietal network, including IPS and PFC (see also Evans et al., 2016), while smaller numbers and addition – both related to fact retrieval – produced greater activation in the medial temporal lobe, specifically the left hippocampus (HC). This was in contrast to the angular gyrus (AG) activation observed in adults when they carried out retrieval-based calculations. Thus, this engagement of the HC is likely related to children's still-ongoing formation of long-term memory for arithmetic facts (see Menon, 2016), whereby differences between children and adults reflect the developmentally specific role of the HC in long-term semantic memory formation. As we saw in Chapter 10, the HC plays a critical role in consolidation of facts acquired early in life. Only later in adulthood does arithmetic fact recall become so automatized that the posterior parietal regions, including the AG, become more engaged during arithmetic calculations.

Findings from other developmental studies likewise reflect the role that HC plays in early arithmetic fact retrieval. Menon and colleagues (Cho et al., 2011) used multivariate pattern analysis (an approach to analyzing brain imaging data that we introduced in Chapter 2) to compare regional activation in 7- to 9-year-old "counters" (procedural strategy users) and "retrievers" (arithmetic fact users). Remember that multivariate pattern analysis allows comparison of finer-grained spatial patterns of brain activity across groups rather than the overall mean activity comparisons allowed by univariate fMRI analyses. Indeed, distinct patterns of brain activity emerged for the two groups of children in the bilateral HC. In short, children who use more fact retrieval, as determined by verbal reports, show increased activity in the bilateral HC (along with several other regions). Menon and his team then replicated these findings with a larger sample of children from a comparable age range (Cho et al., 2012), as well as observing that higher frequencies of retrieval use correlated with increased activation of the HC bilaterally based on a correlation between retrieval fluency, number of facts retrieved, and brain activity during addition.

Finally, in a longitudinal study (Qin et al., 2014) in which 7- to 9-year old children, adolescents, and adults were followed for one year, children were found to rely increasingly on retrieval strategies and showed a corresponding increase in activity in bilateral HC, as well as reductions in activity in areas implicated in more effortful counting strategies (i.e., PFC, left superior parietal cortex, right posterior parietal-occipital cortex). With age, this pattern shifted, whereby HC activity was significantly reduced in adolescents. Activity in adolescents was not significantly different from that seen in adults. Functional connectivity of the hippocampus to cortical areas changed too, such that retrieval use was associated with the strength of hippocampal-cortical functional connectivity rather than with changes in hippocampal activity. Moreover, multivariate pattern recognition revealed greater representational stability across different arithmetic problems in the adolescents and adults than in the children, indicating that engagement of the HC increases in primary school, decreases in adolescence, and stabilizes in adulthood. In sum, these findings confirm the early role that the HC plays in development of the arithmetic network, whereby decreases in parietal-frontal engagement follow the corresponding behavioral shift from procedural to memory-based retrieval strategies.

12.5.2 Difficulties with Number

While dynamic changes generally take place over the course of development in the recruitment of the frontoparietal brain circuits subserving arithmetic, with a "neural shift" from general processing regions in the PFC to more specialized regions in the PPC, additional variability comes in the form of individual differences in numerical competence. An early window onto the degree to which such differences exist, even among adults, is provided by Daniel Ansari and colleagues (Grabner et al., 2007), who found that individuals with higher mathematical competence had greater engagement of the left angular gyrus while solving both single- and multi-digit multiplication problems relative to those with lower mathematical competence. Ansari is featured in this chapter's Scientist Spotlight (Box 12.2). This finding suggests a stronger reliance by more competent individuals on automatic, language-mediated processes during arithmetic problem solving, reflected in greater recruitment of the left angular gyrus. Children likewise fall along a continuum of math performance, and below a certain level, they are given the label "dyscalculic."

Box 12.2 Scientist Spotlight on Daniel Ansari (University of Western Ontario)

Daniel Ansari (Box Figure 12.2) is a Professor and Canada Research Chair in Developmental Cognitive Neuroscience and Learning in the Department of Psychology, the Faculty of Education, and the Brain & Mind Institute at the University of Western Ontario in London, Ontario, where he directs the Numerical Cognition Laboratory. Daniel Ansari received his PhD from University College London in 2003. He studies the development of numerical cognition in typically and atypically developing children.

How I got into studying numerical cognition was accidental, I would say. As an undergraduate student at Sussex University, I quickly discovered that I was really interested in developmental psychology. I took a course on infant development and cognition that was taught by the late George Butterworth. I also took a course on social human development taught by Nicola Yuill and those were kind of my favorite classes. So, then I decided that I really wanted to do something in developmental psychology. One day I saw a post for a PhD scholarship posted by

Annette Karmiloff Smith in the British Psychological Society. I was accepted for this position, which focused on why children with Williams syndrome, a rare genetic developmental disorder, struggle so much with basic number and math.

I discovered that, although on the face of it studying numbers in numerical cognition looks like a very niche and narrow field, it is actually a tremendous springboard for exploring all sorts of issues in psychology and neuroscience: issues related to education, but also issues related to fundamental questions such as how do humanly invented symbols become represented in the brain and what are the sort of learning and developmental trajectories that lead children to sort of combine or merge biological predispositions with things that get transmitted through cultural history. And then you can study typical and atypical development of numerical cognition. I always wanted to branch out a little bit more, but then I found other questions related to number broadly defined that we could pursue as a research group and that's why I continued to study numerical cognition – not necessarily because I'm a math nerd myself but I see number and math as a really neat way of studying human development and human cognition, more generally.

The field has been very focused on foundational competencies, and I think that is because the debate as to whether number is innate or not has driven the research on infants and toddlers. As a function of that, we are not really studying all things that are math – but I think as we get more confident about the foundational systems, people will try to understand how you scale up from them to get to these very complex ways of thinking. I used to be a very strong believer that the approximate number system is the foundation of math – that you're born with these intuitions around number, and those allow you then to transfer to doing things symbolically and doing them exactly. But the more we looked at that we found that the picture may be more complex than that, and symbolic number knowledge may develop largely independently of the approximate number system and may go on to influence the approximate number system as well: that when you start to have these abstract symbolic non-iconic representations of number, you can use them to describe and differentiate between sets of things in your environment.

Dyscalculia is an example of a field of study that was very heavily influenced by adult neuropsychology: you have patients who've got parietal damage, and kids who under-activate their parietal cortex, therefore the two must be somehow the same thing. But my experience working with kids who have math difficulties is that you rarely find kids who have an isolated math difficulty – and those who do are not representative of all the children who need help.

12.5.3 Developmental Dyscalculia

Strong evidence of the importance of the approximate number system to subsequent symbolic number abilities comes from developmental dyscalculia, a disorder in which individuals have severe and lifelong difficulties with arithmetic (American Psychiatric Association, 2003). In its most recent edition, the *Diagnostic and Statistical Manual of Mental Disorders* (DSM), produced by the American Psychiatric Association, uses the term "specific learning disorder" to describe impairments in reading, written expressions, and mathematics. Diagnostic criteria specific to mathematics focus on all the skills we have been discussing: mastering number sense, facts about numbers, and calculation. Such difficulties may be reflected by poor understanding of numbers, their magnitude, and their relationships to one another. The individual may count on fingers rather than using math facts. The individual may get lost in arithmetic computations and will often switch procedures midstream. Dyscalculia is diagnosed through the use of standardized arithmetic tests, with notable underachievement relative to the level expected based on age, education, and overall intelligence (Butterworth & Kovas, 2013). Critically, this disorder is far more prevalent than many realize: somewhere between 5 and 7 percent of the population. Despite popular memes questioning the utility of school-based math education, dyscalculic people earn less and are more likely to be in financial trouble (Butterworth et al., 2011).

Developmental dyscalculia is differentiated from number processing difficulties resulting from, for example, brain injury. However, poor teaching and environmental deprivation have also been implicated in its etiology. Because both hemispheres of the brain are engaged during performance of normal arithmetic functions, dyscalculia can result from dysfunction of either hemisphere, although the left parietotemporal area is of particular significance. The prevalence is as common in girls as in boys. Dyscalculia can occur as a consequence of prematurity and low birthweight and is frequently encountered in a variety of neurologic disorders, such as ADHD, Developmental Language Disorder, epilepsy, and Fragile X syndrome. Developmental dyscalculia has proven to be a persistent learning disability, at least for the short term. Educational interventions for dyscalculia range from rote learning of arithmetic facts to developing strategies for solving arithmetic exercises. The long-term prognosis and the role of remediation in outcomes are yet to be determined.

To help people with dyscalculia, we first have to understand its developmental origins. Poor numerical magnitude processing – based in the approximate number system – appears to be the basis for this disability (e.g., De Smedt et al., 2009), whereby the mapping between non-symbolic and symbolic numerical magnitudes is disrupted (Price et al., 2012; Nosworthy et al., 2013). Because the approximate number system serves as a scaffolding for symbolic number processing, deficits at this basic level cascade into problems with symbolic math as development proceeds (e.g., De Smedt et al., 2013). As we've seen, among typically developing young children, symbolic number processing abilities correlate with mathematical competence, more so than approximate number abilities do. Clearly, the robustness of the mapping between quantities and symbols impacts the development of numerical competence, including arithmetic. The fact that children with dyscalculia often show weak quantity-to-symbol mapping adds further support to this argument, indicating that dyscalculia may arise not from a "core deficit" in the ability to compare quantities, but instead from an "access deficit" – a problem with how the brain links quantities to number symbols (i.e., Arabic numerals), or in how it maps numbers onto verbal or spatial processes.

However, pure dyscalculia is the exception rather than the rule, and needn't always stem from difficulties with the approximate number system. There are several points along the processing stream – well beyond basic magnitude processing – where numerical cognition could be disrupted. These problems can emerge either because of a learning disability or simply due to poor instruction. Regardless, once this happens, children then end up with poor math skills, often along with other cognitive difficulties.

12.5.4 Individual Differences in the Arithmetic Network

You don't have to be dyscalculic to have troubles with math, and there are pronounced individual differences among typically developing, non-dyscalculic children and adults alike. James Booth and his colleagues (Berteletti et al., 2014) examined the influence of such differences, observing that children with low arithmetic ability showed higher activity in the right IPS while working on small number problems than those with higher fluency, indicating their increased effort. The researchers also observed a negative association between number line estimation ability and activity in the IPS during subtraction. Similarly, Daniel Ansari and colleagues found that low mathematical competence in adolescents was associated with increased activity in the right IPS during performance of both addition and subtraction calculations (Price et al., 2013). Thus, overall, individuals with lower mathematical competence seem to engage numerical magnitude processing-related areas of the arithmetic network more than those with higher competence, although both groups show the neural shift from greater PFC to PPC engagement. Perhaps this increase in IPS activity reflects a protracted reliance on immature arithmetic procedures, such as counting, which involve more specific thinking about numerical magnitude. Alternatively, poorer representations of numerical magnitude may prevent individuals with low arithmetic competence from developing more advanced mathematical skills.

12.6 Math Education

Although it is clear that the arithmetic network undergoes considerable change over the course of development, identification of a generalizable developmental profile has been stymied for a number of reasons. For one thing, researchers have only recently acknowledged the inherent variability in instructional approaches and the impact this has on the emergence and ultimate form the arithmetic network takes in any one child's brain. Indeed, children's strategy use is dependent on how arithmetic is taught in their particular classroom. The strategies we described in Section 12.5 are the ones most often modeled in arithmetic instruction in the United States, where rote learning of the multiplication tables has traditionally been encouraged more than counting or decomposing a problem, and where doing subtraction with counting or decomposition is more often encouraged than through memorization. Of course, there is variability in these approaches both within and across US regions. Variability in instruction is even greater from country to country, with some instructors, for example, encouraging counting and others discouraging it. In particular, whether or not the multiplication tables need to be memorized is the stuff of intense national and international disagreement! These are all sources of variability that impact how the emerging mathematical brain is organized. Add to that specific individual differences that are more or less impactful on numerical performance, and you can see why this field is gaining a growing presence in the DCN field. Exciting extensions of numerical cognition research focus on cross-regional/cross-cultural comparisons of both behavioral and neuroimaging data, a trend that should yield important observations in the future. An issue that merits more immediate attention is that the quality of math instruction varies widely within countries as a function of SES.

What we in WEIRD societies consider education in math, in support of industrialized jobs in science, technology, and engineering, typically involves an ability to solve story problems and other abstract problems that may seem very far removed from everyday life. Contrast that with the way that number is used in other societies, or even within WEIRD societies among those who feel disenfranchised from school and who have what we colloquially might call "street smarts."

One of the most powerful examples of this disconnection between symbolic, abstract number concepts and practical number concepts was a study conducted with unschooled children in Brazil who worked as street vendors (a common occupation in developing countries), selling candy, tangerines, or puffed wheat. Children between the ages of 10 and 12 were given money (Brazilian *cruzeiros*) and asked to add or subtract the bills. For example, they might be given 17 bills of different denominations and had to calculate how much money they had. Or they might be told the price of buying candy in the store and were asked to calculate how much change they should receive if they paid with a large bill. As long as the children were counting cruzeiros, or boxes of candy – quantifiable objects – they performed very well. If asked to do exactly the same problems in a school context, for example, adding and subtracting numbers rather than objects, the children did very poorly, often generating completely nonsensical answers (Saxe, 1988). Their practical mathematical knowledge was utterly divorced from their symbolic, "book" mathematical knowledge.

12.6.1 Math Intervention

Regardless of the cause of a particular child's math deficiencies, there is enough evidence that environment often plays a role that focus has turned to whether early interventions, particularly those informed by neuroscience, can improve the outcomes for poor achievers. In particular, the fact that children from disadvantaged backgrounds fall behind their peers in math skill growth starting from an early age (National Center for Education Statistics, 2011) is cause for concern. Identifying early predictors of math skill growth in children from varying backgrounds might aid identification and amelioration of the reasons behind individual differences in math skill growth. Increased understanding of the mechanisms behind these individual differences in turn might have implications for decreasing the achievement gap.

12.6.2 Effects of Math Intervention on the Developing Brain

Of the many ways to conceptualize teaching and learning, a crystal clear one is that they drive biological changes in the brain. By combining innovative approaches to teaching with DCN measurement techniques, we can expand our understanding of what is effective at promoting learning and why. The first step in identifying impactful interventions is to conduct training studies, and nowhere is this more needed than in math education. Examples of such studies are relatively few, but are increasing in number as the field has expanded.

Initial work focused on adaptive software programs instantiated as computer games that were meant to target improvements in the approximate number system. All of these games were some variation of improving precision in discriminating non-symbolic number, for example, by comparing sets of dots. As with so many other brain-training games, the intervention does improve number comparison abilities, but the effect does not appear to generalize even to counting, much less to arithmetic. A more ambitious approach involves one-on-one tutoring, an approach implemented in a study designed to facilitate rapid retrieval of math facts (Supekar et al., 2013). The researchers found that hippocampal–PFC functional circuits predicted performance improvement over an 8-week period, with the children who showed higher intrinsic functional connectivity in those circuits prior to starting the training showing the most performance improvements on numerical problem solving. This points to the importance of circuit reorganization in the shift that children make from effortful counting to more efficient, memory-based forms of problem solving.

Another question that training studies can address is why some children learn better than others. Understanding how children learn to transfer learning from old to new problems is particularly relevant to math interventions. In a recent study, Menon and colleagues (Chang et al., 2019) investigated individual differences in the neurocognitive mechanisms that support math learning and "near" transfer to novel, but structurally related, problems. The researchers found that with just five days of a math tutoring protocol, children between the ages of 8 and 10 years showed significant learning of arithmetic facts, characterized by clear differentiation in both behavioral and brain responses between trained and novel problems. Behaviorally, individual differences in learning rate as measured during the five-day training period predicted near transfer of learning, with faster learners showing greater performance gains on novel, but similarly structured, problems. Neurally, faster learners showed greater overlap in neural representations within medial temporal lobe regions implicated in memory formation, as well as greater segregation of large-scale brain circuits between trained and novel problems. These changes point to the emergence of more distinct specialized functional circuitry with increased learning. These findings demonstrate that speed of learning and near transfer are interrelated. Moreover, they help identify the neural mechanisms by which faster learners transfer their knowledge better.

These are just two examples of how effective behavioral intervention can alter distributed brain systems. These findings raise questions about whether successful behavioral interventions can effectively normalize activity in systems that show atypical functional responses, for example, in children with math-specific learning difficulties, or whether these children recruit neural resources atypically to achieve the same level of performance as typically developing children (see Iuculano et al., 2015). The functional brain changes that follow effective intervention will need to be quantitatively characterized to address these questions, as well as to delineate the mechanisms by which different levels of math problem-solving performance can be improved. In turn, such work will help researchers and educators alike identify the neural factors that mediate individual differences in intervention responsivity. Fortunately, these worthy goals are ones that researchers are actively pursuing.

SUMMARY

- The number sense is an evolutionarily ancient sensitivity that humans share with other animals, including fish
- Symbolic mathematics is a cultural construction
- The approximate number system (ANS) supports representation of relative magnitudes
- The responsivity of number neurons in rhesus macaques is tuned to a target number
- Symbolic number requires moving from a logarithmic to a linear representation of magnitude

- Children use counting to link objective quantities and symbolic representations of numerical quantities
- The intraparietal sulcus (IPS) and prefrontal cortex (PFC) are key brain regions engaged during number processing
- The strength of children's quantity-to-symbol number mappings predicts their mathematical achievements
- Developmental dyscalculia is a disorder in which individuals have severe and lifelong difficulties with arithmetic

REVIEW QUESTIONS

What is the relationship between representations of large, approximate numbers and representations of small numbers?

How do researchers determine that judgments about number are not simply derived from judgments about mass and size?

How does the acuity of the approximate number system (ANS) increase over the course of development?

What is the relationship between the ANS and mathematical achievement?

Is ANS acuity as measured early in life a reliable predictor of later mathematical achievement?

How does becoming numerate change people's representation of magnitude?

What are the behavioral and brain bases for refinement of the ANS over the lifespan?

How do the brains of children and adults differ when engaging in arithmetic problem solving?

What does the finding about engagement of the angular gyrus in mathematically competent individuals indicate?

Describe how people with developmental dyscalculia can be distinguished from people who have had poor numerical training.

Make recommendations about math/arithmetic education.

Further Reading

Cheyette, S. J., & Piantadosi, S. T. (2020). A unified account of numerosity perception. *Nature Human Behavior*, 4, 1265–1272. https://doi.org/10.1038/s41562-020-00946-0

Nieder, A. (2019). *A brain for numbers: The biology of the number instinct*. MIT Press.

Siegler, R. S., & Braithwaite, D. W. (2017). Numerical development. *Annual Review of Psychology*, 68, 187–213. https://doi.org/10.1146/annurev-psych-010416-044101

References

Agrillo, C., Piffer, L., Bisazza, A., & Butterworth, B. (2012). Evidence for two numerical systems that are similar in humans and guppies. *PloS One*, 7(2), e31923. https://doi.org/10.1371/journal.pone.0031923

American Psychiatric Association. (2003). *Diagnostic and statistical manual of mental disorders*, 5th edition. American Psychiatric Association.

Ansari, D., & Dhital, B. (2006). Age-related changes in the activation of the intraparietal sulcus during nonsymbolic magnitude processing: An event-related functional magnetic resonance imaging study. *Journal of Cognitive Neuroscience*, 18(11), 1820–1828. https://doi.org/10.1162/jocn.2006.18.11.1820

Antell, S. E., & Keating, D. P. (1983). Perception of numerical invariance in neonates. *Child Development*, 54(3), 695–701. https://doi.org/10.1111/j.1467-8624.1983.tb00495.x

Barrouillet, P., Mignon, M., & Thevenot, C. (2008). Strategies in subtraction problem solving in children. *Journal of Experimental Child Psychology*, 99(4), 233–251. https://doi.org/10.1016/j.jecp.2007.12.001

Berteletti, I., Prado, J. Ô., & Booth, J. R. (2014). Children with mathematical learning disability fail in recruiting verbal and numerical brain regions when solving simple multiplication problems. *Cortex*, 57, 143–155. https://doi.org/10.1016/j.cortex.2014.04.001

Brankaer, C., Ghesquière, P., & De Smedt, B. (2014). Children's mapping between non-symbolic and symbolic numerical magnitudes and its association with timed and untimed tests of mathematics achievement. *PLoS ONE*, 9(4). https://doi.org/10.1371/journal.pone.0093565

Brannon, E. M., & Terrace, H. (1998). Ordering of the numerosities 1 to 9 by monkeys. *Science*, 282(5389), 746–749. https://doi.org/10.1126/science.282.5389.746

Brannon, E. M., & Terrace, H. (2002). The evolution and ontogeny of ordinal numerical ability. In M. Bekoff, C. Allen, & G. M. Burghardt (Eds.), *The cognitive animal* (pp. 197–204). MIT Press. https://doi.org/10.7551/mitpress/1885.003.0030

Briars, D., & Siegler, R. S. (1984). A featural analysis of preschoolers' counting knowledge. *Developmental Psychology*, 20(4), 607–618. https://doi.org/10.1037/0012-1649.20.4.607

Buckley, P. B., & Gillman, C. B. (1974). Comparisons of digits and dot patterns. *Journal of Experimental Psychology*, 103(6), 1131–1136. https://doi.org/10.1037/h0037361

Butterworth, B., & Kovas, Y. (2013). Understanding neurocognitive developmental disorders can improve education for all. *Science*, 340(6130), 300–305. https://doi.org/10.1126/science.1231022

Butterworth, B., Varma, S., & Laurillard, D. (2011). Dyscalculia: From brain to education. *Science*, 340(6130), 1049–1053. https://doi.org/10.1126/science.1201536

Campbell, J. I. D., & Xue, Q. (2001). Cognitive arithmetic across cultures. *Journal of Experimental Psychology: General*, 130(2), 299–315. https://doi.org/10.1037//0096-3445.130.2.299

Cantlon, J. F., & Brannon, E. M. (2006). Shared system for ordering small and large numbers in monkeys and humans. *Psychological Science*, 17(5), 401–406. https://doi.org/10.1111/j.1467-9280.2006.01719.x

Cantlon, J. F., & Brannon, E. M. (2007). Basic math in monkeys and college students. *PLOS Biology*, 5(12), e328. https://doi.org/10.1371/journal.pbio.0050328

Cantlon, J. F., Brannon, E. M., Carter, E. J., & Pelphrey, K. A. (2006). Functional imaging of numerical processing in adults and 4-year-old children. *PLOS Biology*, 4(5), e125. https://doi.org/10.1371/journal.pbio.0040125

Cantlon, J. F., Libertus, M. E., Pinel, P., Dehaene, S., Brannon, E. M., & Pelphrey, K. A. (2009). The neural development of an abstract concept of number. *Journal of Cognitive Neuroscience*, 21(11), 2217–2229. https://doi.org/10.1162/jocn.2008.21159

Carey, S. (2001). Cognitive foundations of arithmetic: Evolution and ontogenesis. *Mind and Language*, 16(1), 37–55. https://doi.org/10.1111/1468-0017.00155

Carey, S. (2009). *The origin of concepts*. Oxford Scholarship Online. https://doi.org/10.1093/acprof:oso/9780195367638.001.0001

Chang, H., Rosenberg-Lee, M., Qin, S., & Menon, V. (2019). Faster learners transfer their knowledge better: Behavioral, mnemonic, and neural mechanisms of individual differences in children's learning. *Developmental Cognitive Neuroscience*, 40, 100719. https://doi.org/10.1016/j.dcn.2019.100719

Cheyette, S. J., & Piantadosi, S. T. (2020). A unified account of numerosity perception. *Nature Human Behavior*, 4, 1265–1272. https://doi.org/10.1038/s41562-020-00946-0

Chittka, L., & Geiger, K. (1995). Can honey bees count landmarks? *Animal Behavior*, 49(1), 159–164. https://doi.org/10.1016/0003-3472(95)80163-4

Cho, S., Metcalfe, A. W. S., Young, C. B., Ryali, S., Geary, D. C., & Menon, V. (2012). Hippocampal-prefrontal engagement and dynamic causal interactions in the maturation of children's fact retrieval. *Journal of Cognitive Neuroscience*, 24(9), 1849–1866. https://doi.org/10.1162/jocn_a_00246

Cho, S., Ryali, S., Geary, D. C., & Menon, V. (2011). How does a child solve 7+8? Decoding brain activity patterns associated with counting and retrieval strategies. *Developmental Science*, 14(5), 989–1001. https://doi.org/10.1111/j.1467-7687.2011.01055.x

De Smedt, B., Holloway, I. D., & Ansari, D. (2011). Effects of problem size and arithmetic operation on brain activation during calculation in children with varying levels of arithmetical fluency. *NeuroImage*, 57(3), 771–781. https://doi.org/10.1016/j.neuroimage.2010.12.037

De Smedt, B., Noël, M. P., Gilmore, C., & Ansari, D. (2013). How do symbolic and non-symbolic numerical magnitude processing skills relate to individual differences in children's mathematical skills? A review of evidence from brain and behavior. *Trends in Neuroscience and Education*, 2(2), 48–55. https://doi.org/10.1016/j.tine.2013.06.001

De Smedt, B., Swillen, A., Verschaffel, L., & Ghesquière, P. (2009). Mathematical learning disabilities in children with 22q11.2 deletion syndrome: A review. *Developmental Disabilities Research Reviews*, 15(1), 4–10. https://doi.org/10.1002/ddrr.44

Defever, E., De Smedt, B., & Reynvoet, B. (2013). Numerical matching judgments in children with mathematical learning disabilities. *Research in Developmental Disabilities*, 34(10), 3182–3189. https://doi.org/10.1016/j.ridd.2013.06.018

Dehaene, S. (1997). *The number sense*. Oxford University Press.

Dehaene, S., Izard, V., Spelke, E., & Pica, P. (2008). Log or linear? Distinct intuitions of the number scale in western and Amazonian indigene cultures. *Science*, 320(5880), 1217–1220. https://doi.org/10.1126/science.1156540

Duhamel, J. R., Colby, C. L., & Goldberg, M. E. (1998). Ventral intraparietal area of the macaque: Congruent visual and somatic response properties. *Journal of Neurophysiology*, 79(1), 126–136. https://doi.org/10.1152/jn.1998.79.1.126

Elbro, C. (1996). Early linguistic abilities and reading development: A review and a hypothesis. *Reading and Writing*, 8(6), 453–485. https://doi.org/10.1007/BF00577023

Evans, T. M., Flowers, D. L., Luetje, M. M., Napoliello, E., & Eden, G. F. (2016). Functional neuroanatomy of arithmetic and word reading and its relationship to age. *NeuroImage*, 143, 304–315. https://doi.org/10.1016/j.neuroimage.2016.08.048

Fantz, R. L. (1964). Visual experience in infants: Decreased attention to familiar patterns relative to novel ones. *Science*, 146(3644), 668–670. https://doi.org/10.1126/science.146.3644.668

Fechner, G. (1860). *Elements of psychophysics*. Holt, Rinehart, & Winston.

Fias, W., Menon, V., & Szucs, D. (2013). Multiple components of developmental dyscalculia. *Trends in Neuroscience and Education*, 2(2), 43–47. https://doi.org/10.1016/j.tine.2013.06.006

Frank, M. C., Everett, D. L., Fedorenko, E., & Gibson, E. (2008). Number as a cognitive technology: Evidence from Pirahã language and cognition. *Cognition*, 108(3), 819–824. https://doi.org/10.1016/j.cognition.2008.04.007

Fuson, K. C. (1988). *Children's counting and concepts of number*. Springer.

Geary, D. C., Bow-Thomas, C. C., & Yao, Y. (1992). Counting knowledge and skill in cognitive addition: A comparison of normal and mathematically disabled children. *Journal of Experimental Child Psychology*, 54(3), 372–391. https://doi.org/10.1016/0022-0965(92)90026-3

Gebuis, T., Cohen Kadosh, R., & Gevers, W. (2016). Sensory-integration system rather than approximate number system underlies numerosity processing: A critical review. *Acta Psychologica*, 171, 17–35. https://doi.org/10.1016/j.actpsy.2016.09.003

Gelman, R., & Gallistel, C. R. (1978). *The child's understanding of number*. Harvard University Press.

Goffin, C., & Ansari, D. (2019). How are symbols and nonsymbolic numerical magnitudes related? Exploring bidirectional relationships in early numeracy. *Mind, Brain, and Education*, 13(3), 143–156. https://doi.org/10.1111/mbe.12206

Gordon, P. (2004). Numerical cognition without words: Evidence from Amazonia. *Science*, 306(5695), 496–499. https://doi.org/10.1126/science.1094492

Grabner, R. H., Ansari, D., Reishofer, G., Stern, E., Ebner, F., & Neuper, C. (2007). Individual differences in mathematical competence predict parietal brain activation during mental calculation. *NeuroImage*, 38(2), 346–356. https://doi.org/10.1016/j.neuroimage.2007.07.041

Halberda, J., & Feigenson, L. (2008). Developmental change in the acuity of the "number sense": The approximate number system in 3-, 4-, 5-, and 6-year-olds and adults. *Developmental Psychology*, 44(5), 1457–1465. https://doi.org/10.1037/a0012682

Halberda, J., Ly, R., Wilmer, J. B., Naiman, D. Q., & Germine, L. (2012). Number sense across the lifespan as revealed by a massive Internet-based sample. *Proceedings of the National Academy of Sciences of the United States of America*, 109(28), 11116–11120. https://doi.org/10.1073/pnas.1200196109

Halberda, J., Mazzocco, M. M. M., & Feigenson, L. (2008). Individual differences in non-verbal number acuity correlate with maths achievement. *Nature*, 455(7213), 665–668. https://doi.org/10.1038/nature07246

Henschen, S. E., & Schaller, W. (1925). Clinical and anatomical contributions on brain pathology. *Archives of Neurology & Psychiatry*, 13(2), 226–249. https://doi.org/10.1001/atchneurpsyc.1925.02200080073006

Holloway, I. D., & Ansari, D. (2009). Mapping numerical magnitudes onto symbols: The numerical distance effect and individual differences in children's mathematics achievement. *Journal of Experimental Child Psychology*, 103(1), 17–29. https://doi.org/10.1016/j.jecp.2008.04.001

Holloway, I. D., Battista, C., Vogel, S. E., & Ansari, D. (2013). Semantic and perceptual processing of number symbols: Evidence from a cross-linguistic fMRI adaptation study. *Journal of Cognitive Neuroscience*, 25(3), 388–400. https://doi.org/10.1162/jocn_a_00323

Imbo, I., & Vandierendonck, A. (2007). The development of strategy use in elementary school children: Working memory and individual differences. *Journal of Experimental Child Psychology*, 96(4), 284–309. https://doi.org/10.1016/j.jecp.2006.09.001

Iuculano, T., & Menon, V. (2018). Development of mathematical reasoning. In J. T. Wixted & S. Ghetti (Eds.), *Stevens' handbook of experimental psychology and cognitive neuroscience* (Vol. 4, pp. 183–222). Wiley. https://doi.org/10.1002/9781119170174.epcn406

Iuculano, T., Rosenberg-Lee, M., Richardson, J., Tenison, C., Fuchs, L., Supekar, K., & Menon, V. (2015). Cognitive tutoring induces widespread neuroplasticity and remediates brain function in children with mathematical learning disabilities. *Nature Communications*, 6, 8453. https://doi.org/10.1038/ncomms9453

Izard, V., Sann, C., Spelke, E. S., & Streri, A. (2009). Newborn infants perceive abstract numbers. *Proceedings of the National Academy of Sciences of the United States of America*, 106(25), 10382–10385. https://doi.org/10.1073/pnas.0812142106

Kawashima, R., Taira, M., Okita, K., Inoue, K., Tajima, N., Yoshida, H., Sasaki, T., Sugiura, M., Watanabe, J., & Fukuda, H. (2004). A functional MRI study of simple arithmetic: A comparison between children and adults. *Cognitive Brain Research*, 18(3), 227–233. https://doi.org/10.1016/j.cogbrainres.2003.10.009

Klahr, D., & Wallace, J. G. (1973). The role of quantification operators in the development of conservation of quantity. *Cognitive Psychology*, 4(3), 301–327. https://doi.org/10.1016/0010-0285(73)90016-9

Le Corre, M. (2014). Children acquire the later-greater principle after the cardinal principle. *British Journal of Developmental Psychology*, 32(2), 163–177. https://doi.org/10.1111/bjdp.12029

Le Corre, M., & Carey, S. (2007). One, two, three, four, nothing more: An investigation of the conceptual sources of the verbal counting principles. *Cognition*, 105(2), 395–438. https://doi.org/10.1016/j.cognition.2006.10.005

Le Corre, M., Van de Walle, G., Brannon, E. M., & Carey, S. (2006). Re-visiting the competence/performance debate in the acquisition of the counting principles. *Cognitive Psychology*, 52(2), 130–169. https://doi.org/10.1016/j.cogpsych.2005.07.002

Leibovich, T., & Ansari, D. (2016). The symbol-grounding problem in numerical cognition: A review of theory, evidence, and outstanding questions. *Canadian Journal of Experimental Psychology*, 70(1), 12–23. https://doi.org/10.1037/cep0000070

Leibovich, T., Katzin, N., Harel, M., & Henik, A. (2017). From "sense of number" to "sense of magnitude": The role of continuous magnitudes in numerical cognition. *Behavioral and Brain Sciences*, 40, e164. https://doi.org/10.1017/S0140525X16000960

Lipton, J. S., & Spelke, E. S. (2003). Origins of number sense: Large-number discrimination in human infants. *Psychological Science*, 14(5), 396–401. https://doi.org/10.1111/1467-9280.01453

Lyons, I. M. (2015). Numbers and number sense. In J. D. Wright (Ed.), *International encyclopedia of the social & behavioral sciences*, 2nd edition (pp. 46–56). Elsevier. https://doi.org/10.1016/B978-0-08-097086-8.57031-7

Lyons, I. M., Price, G. R., Vaessen, A., Blomert, L., & Ansari, D. (2014). Numerical predictors of arithmetic success in grades 1–6. *Developmental Science*, 17(5), 714–726. https://doi.org/10.1111/desc.12152

MacNulty, D. R., Tallian, A., Stahler, D. R., & Smith, D. W. (2014). Influence of group size on the success of wolves hunting bison. *PLoS One*, 9(11), e112884. https://doi.org/10.1371/journal.pone.0112884

Matejko, A. A., & Ansari, D. (2019). The neural association between arithmetic and basic numerical processing depends on arithmetic problem size and not chronological age. *Developmental Cognitive Neuroscience*, 37, 100653. https://doi.org/10.1016/j.dcn.2019.100653

Menon, V. (2015). Arithmetic in the child and adult brain. In R. C. Kadosh & A. Dowker (Eds.), *The Oxford handbook of numerical cognition* (pp. 502–530). Oxford University Press. https://doi.org/10.1093/oxfordhb/9780199642342.013.041

Menon, V. (2016). Memory and cognitive control circuits in mathematical cognition and learning. *Progress in Brain Research*, 227, 159–186. https://doi.org/10.1016/bs.pbr.2016.04.026

Merten, K., & Nieder, A. (2009). Compressed scaling of abstract numerosity representations in adult humans and monkeys. *Journal of Cognitive Neuroscience*, 21(2), 333–346. https://doi.org/10.1162/jocn.2008.21032

Mundy, E., & Gilmore, C. K. (2009). Children's mapping between symbolic and nonsymbolic representations of number. *Journal of Experimental Child Psychology*, 103(4), 490–502. https://doi.org/10.1016/j.jecp.2009.02.003

National Center for Education Statistics. (2011). *The Nation's Report Card: Mathematics 2011* (NCES 2012–458). National Center for Education Statistics, Institute of Education Sciences, US Department of Education, Washington, DC.

National Research Council. (2015). *Transforming the workforce for children birth through age 8: A unifying foundation*. National Academies Press. https://doi.org/10.17226/19401

Nieder, A. (2016). The neuronal code for number. *Nature Reviews Neuroscience*, 17(6), 366–382. https://doi.org/10.1038/nrn.2016.40

Nieder, A., Freedman, D. J., & Miller, E. K. (2002). Representation of the quantity of visual items in the primate prefrontal cortex. *Science*, 297(5587), 1708–1711. https://doi.org/10.1126/science.1072493

Nieder, A., & Merten, K. (2007). A labeled-line code for small and large numerosities in the monkey prefrontal cortex. *Journal of Neuroscience*, 27(22), 5986–5993. https://doi.org/10.1523/JNEUROSCI.1056-07.2007

Nieder, A., & Miller, E. K. (2003). Coding of cognitive magnitude: Compressed scaling of numerical information in the primate prefrontal cortex. *Neuron*, 37(1), 149–157. https://doi.org/10.1016/S0896-6273(02)01144-3

Nieder, A., & Miller, E. K. (2004). Analog numerical representations in rhesus monkeys: Evidence for parallel processing. *Journal of Cognitive Neuroscience*, 16(5), 889–901. https://doi.org/10.1162/089892904970807

Nosworthy, N., Bugden, S., Archibald, L., Evans, B., & Ansari, D. (2013). A two-minute paper-and-pencil test of symbolic and nonsymbolic numerical magnitude processing explains variability in primary school children's arithmetic competence. *PLoS ONE*, 8(7), e67918. https://doi.org/10.1371/journal.pone.0067918

Oakes, L. M., Hurley, K. B., Ross-Sheehy, S., & Luck, S. J. (2011). Developmental changes in infants' visual short-term memory for location. *Cognition*, 118(3), 293–305. https://doi.org/10.1016/j.cognition.2010.11.007

Piantadosi, S. T., Jara-Ettinger, J., & Gibson, E. (2014). Children's learning of number words in an indigenous farming-foraging group. *Developmental Science*, 17(4), 553–563. https://doi.org/10.1111/desc.12078

Piazza, M., Fumarola, A., Chinello, A., & Melcher, D. (2011). Subitizing reflects visuo-spatial object individuation capacity. *Cognition*, 121(1), 147–153. https://doi.org/10.1016/j.cognition.2011.05.007

Piazza, M., Izard, V., Pinel, P., Le Bihan, D., & Dehaene, S. (2004). Tuning curves for approximate numerosity in the human intraparietal sulcus. *Neuron*, 44(3), 547–555. https://doi.org/10.1016/j.neuron.2004.10.014

Piazza, M., Mechelli, A., Butterworth, B., & Price, C. J. (2002). Are subitizing and counting implemented as separate or functionally overlapping processes? *NeuroImage*, 15(2), 435–446. https://doi.org/10.1006/nimg.2001.0980

Pica, P., Lemer, C., Izard, V., & Dehaene, S. (2004). Exact and approximate arithmetic in an Amazonian indigene group. *Science*, 306(5695), 499–503. https://doi.org/10.1126/science.1102085

Price, G. R., Mazzocco, M. M. M., & Ansari, D. (2013). Why mental arithmetic counts: Brain activation during single digit arithmetic predicts high school math scores. *Journal of Neuroscience*, 33(1), 156–163. https://doi.org/10.1523/JNEUROSCI.2936-12.2013

Price, G. R., Palmer, D., Battista, C., & Ansari, D. (2012). Nonsymbolic numerical magnitude comparison: Reliability and validity of different task variants and outcome measures, and their relationship to arithmetic achievement in adults. *Acta Psychologica*, 140(1), 50–57. https://doi.org/10.1016/j.actpsy.2012.02.008

Qin, S., Cho, S., Chen, T., Rosenberg-Lee, M., Geary, D. C., & Menon, V. (2014). Hippocampal-neocortical functional reorganization underlies children's cognitive development. *Nature Neuroscience*, 17(9), 1263–1269. https://doi.org/10.1038/nn.3788

Restle, F. (1970). Theory of serial pattern learning: Structural trees. *Psychological Review*, 77(6), 481–495. https://doi.org/10.1037/h0029964

Rivera, S. M., Reiss, A. L., Eckert, M. A., & Menon, V. (2005). Developmental changes in mental arithmetic: Evidence for increased functional specialization in the left inferior parietal cortex. *Cerebral Cortex*, 15(11), 1779–1790. https://doi.org/10.1093/cercor/bhi055

Robinson, K. M., Arbuthnott, K. D., Rose, D., McCarron, M. C., Globa, C. A., & Phonexay, S. D. (2006). Stability and change in children's division strategies. *Journal of Experimental Child Psychology*, 93(3), 224–238. https://doi.org/10.1016/j.jecp.2005.09.002

Rusconi, E., Walsh, V., & Butterworth, B. (2005). Dexterity with numbers: rTMS over left angular gyrus disrupts finger gnosis and number processing. *Neuropsychologia*, 43(11), 1609–1624. https://doi.org/10.1016/j.neuropsychologia.2005.01.009

Sarnecka, B. W., Kamenskaya, V. G., Yamana, Y., Ogura, T., & Yudovina, Y. B. (2007). From grammatical number to exact numbers: Early meanings of "one," "two," and "three" in English, Russian, and Japanese. *Cognitive Psychology*, 55(2), 136–168. https://doi.org/10.1016/j.cogpsych.2006.09.001

Saxe, G. B. (1988). The mathematics of child street vendors. *Child Development*, 59(5), 1415–1425. https://doi.org/10.2307/1130503

Schlack, A., Sterbing-D'Angelo, S. J., Hartung, K., Hoffmann, K. P., & Bremmer, F. (2005). Multisensory space representations in the macaque ventral intraparietal area. *Journal of Neuroscience*, 25(18), 4616–4625. https://doi.org/10.1523/JNEUROSCI.0455-05.2005

Schneider, M., Beeres, K., Coban, L., Merz, S., Schmidt, S. S., Stricker, J., & De Smedt, B. (2017). Associations of non-symbolic and symbolic numerical magnitude processing with mathematical competence: A meta-analysis. *Developmental Science*, 20(3). https://doi.org/10.1111/desc.12372

Shum, J., Hermes, D., Foster, B. L., Dastjerdi, M., Rangarajan, V., Winawer, J., Miller, K. J., & Parvizi, J. (2013). A brain area for visual numerals. *Journal of Neuroscience*, 33(16), 6709–6715. https://doi.org/10.1523/JNEUROSCI.4558-12.2013

Siegler, R. S., & Opfer, J. E. (2003). The development of numerical estimation: Evidence for multiple representations of numerical quantity. *Psychological Science*, 14(3), 237–250. https://doi.org/10.1111/1467-9280.02438

Spelke, E. S., & Tsivkin, S. (2001). Language and number: A bilingual training study. *Cognition*, 78(1), 45–88. https://doi.org/10.1016/S0010-0277(00)00108-6

Starkey, P., & Cooper, R. G. (1980). Perception of numbers by human infants. *Science*, 210(4473), 1033–1035. https://doi.org/10.1126/science.7434014

Starr, A., DeWind, N. K., & Brannon, E. M. (2017). The contributions of numerical acuity and non-numerical stimulus features to the development of the number sense and symbolic math achievement. *Cognition*, 168, 222–233. https://doi.org/10.1016/j.cognition.2017.07.004

Strauss, M. S., & Curtis, L. E. (1981). Infant perception of numerosity. *Child Development*, 52(4), 1146–1152. https://doi.org/10.1111/j.1467-8624.1981.tb03160.x

Supekar, K., Swigart, A. G., Tenison, C., Jolles, D. D., Rosenberg-Lee, M., Fuchs, L., & Menon, V. (2013). Neural predictors of individual differences in response to math tutoring in primary-grade school children. *Proceedings of the National Academy of Sciences of the United States of America*, 110(20), 8230–8235. https://doi.org/10.1073/pnas.1222154110

Tschentscher, N., & Hauk, O. (2014). How are things adding up? Neural differences between arithmetic operations are due to general problem solving strategies. *NeuroImage*, 92, 369–380. https://doi.org/10.1016/j.neuroimage.2014.01.061

Vaid, J., & Corina, D. (1989). Visual field asymmetries in numerical size comparisons of digits, words, and signs. *Brain and Language*, 36(1), 117–126. https://doi.org/10.1016/0093-934X(89)90055-2

van Loosbroek, E., & Smitsman, A. W. (1990). Visual perception of numerosity in infancy. *Developmental Psychology*, 26(6), 916–922. https://doi.org/10.1037/0012-1649.26.6.911.b

Wagner, R. K., & Torgesen, J. K. (1987). The nature of phonological processing and its causal role in the acquisition of reading skills. *Psychological Bulletin*, 101(2), 192–212. https://doi.org/10.1037/0033-2909.101.2.192

Walsh, V. (2003). A theory of magnitude: Common cortical metrics of time, space and quantity. *Trends in Cognitive Sciences*, 7(11), 483–488. https://doi.org/10.1016/j.tics.2003.09.002

Wynn, K. (1990). Children's understanding of counting. *Cognition*, 36(2), 155–193. https://doi.org/10.1016/0010-0277(90)90003-3

Wynn, K. (1992). Children's acquisition of the number words and the counting system. *Cognitive Psychology*, 24(2), 220–251. https://doi.org/10.1016/0010-0285(92)90008-P

Wynn, K., Bloom, P., & Chiang, W. C. (2002). Enumeration of collective entities by 5-month-old infants. *Cognition*, 83(3), B55–B66. https://doi.org/10.1016/S0010-0277(02)00008-2

Xu, F., & Arriaga, R. I. (2007). Number discrimination in 10-month-old infants. *British Journal of Developmental Psychology*, 25(1), 103–108. https://doi.org/10.1348/026151005X90704

Xu, F., & Spelke, E. S. (2000). Large number discrimination in 6-month-old infants. *Cognition*, 74(1), B1–B11. https://doi.org/10.1016/S0010-0277(99)00066-9

13   Motivated Behavior and Self-Control

LEARNING OBJECTIVES

- Explain the importance of approach and avoidance behaviors and self-control
- Describe the hallmark characteristics of patients with damage to orbitofrontal cortex
- Discuss the outcomes of patients who underwent frontal leucotomies
- Explain how slow brain maturation could be advantageous for humans
- Characterize different approaches to measuring self-control, and provide examples
- Discuss whether self-control in early childhood predicts future behavior, and if so, how
- Identify key brain regions involved in self-control and reward-related processing, and describe how they change over development or vary across individuals
- Describe how adolescents' brains respond to risky decision-making and peer influence
- Articulate ways in which the standard account of adolescent risk-taking is oversimplified
- Explain the neural and contextual changes in adolescence that can lead to positive or negative growth trajectories

Self-control describes an individual's ability to control immediate desires to achieve longer-term goals. The earliest and most general demand on children by parents and society is the ability to control impulses and modulate emotional expression. Moreover, successful completion of many life goals depends on children's mastery of self-control. In short, self-control has a profound and lasting effect, from the earliest years of life well into adulthood.

In this chapter, we introduce how approach and avoidance drive children's behavior well beyond their capacity for self-control. We outline the history behind our understanding of how frontal regions contribute to behavioral and emotional control, including a range of lesion studies, and review more recent evidence that children show differential engagement of subregions of the prefrontal cortex given neutral or motivationally salient environments. As children age into adolescence, the cortical circuitry underlying their decision-making is changing quickly. We review evidence for differential reward sensitivity in adolescence and how this impacts how decisions are made. Finally, we review how the many changes taking place in adolescence, including pubertal development, continued brain maturation, increases in freedom and responsibility, and new social settings, all can lead to either positive or negative growth trajectories as adolescents transition into adulthood.

13.1   Drivers of Behavior

What motivates us to behave as we do? How do our motivations and behaviors change across the early lifespan, and why are there such big differences between people? Can we explain why some people are more likely than others to engage in unhealthy or unsafe behaviors? These important questions get at the heart of who we are as people, and they have important implications for public health and public policy. To address them, we must study the interplay among neural systems that have differential influences on behavior.

13.1.1 Approach, Avoidance, and Self-Control

On the whole, it is evolutionarily adaptive to engage in behaviors that result in positive outcomes and avoid behaviors and situations that may result in negative ones; these behavioral tendencies are referred to as **approach and avoidance behaviors**. Some of these behaviors are instinctual. For example, infants orient towards the sound of their mother, but away from a sound that sounds like an aversive stimulus. Likewise, a young child instinctively avoids bitter or sour flavors, which could indicate a poisonous substance, but gravitates towards sweet foods, which – in the natural world – are fruits that are safe to eat and a good source of energy.

In addition to these deeply engrained behaviors, we have at our disposal from a very early age powerful learning mechanisms that shape our behavior based on the outcomes of our prior actions: *positive and negative reinforcement learning*. We have previously discussed early-developing forms of implicit memory known as classical and operant conditioning, which guide behavior towards appetitive cues and away from aversive ones (Chapter 9). These forms of memory are based on positive and negative reinforcement learning. A complicating factor is that positive outcomes sometimes require behaviors that are not immediately rewarding (e.g., reading a textbook when you might rather be swimming), and negative outcomes sometimes follow positive behaviors (e.g., getting food poisoning after eating your favorite food).

Overall, approach and avoidance behaviors have helped to ensure the survival of species across the animal kingdom. However, seeking out potential rewards and avoiding potential threats is not always in an individual's best interests. As our society changes, so too do the particular behaviors that guarantee positive outcomes. Moreover, our behaviors change our society itself over time. For example, our natural predilection for sweets has fueled a massive refined sugar industry. Distilled down to its pure form, sugar is powerfully addictive in a way that fruit is not; it hijacks the **reward circuitry** of our brain. Given the ubiquity of refined sugar in our current food supply, it is no wonder that we are seeing unprecedented levels of obesity and diabetes around the globe. Similarly, substances with psychoactive properties that have been distilled from plants, like nicotine, alcohol, and opiates, are highly addictive in their purest form. They, too, hijack our brain's reward circuitry, thereby reinforcing drug-seeking behaviors that are maladaptive, and have led to a range of substance dependencies on a massive scale.

Thus, reward-seeking is vitally important, but can be maladaptive if taken to an extreme (Box 13.1). So, too, can be the avoidance of uncertain, potentially negative outcomes that may yield possibly large rewards. If we are too afraid or insufficiently motivated to take risks, we miss out on opportunities. As former US President Jimmy Carter advised, "Go out on a limb. That's where the fruit is." In other words, surviving and thriving require the *right* level of reward-seeking and threat avoidance: not too much, not too little. Tellingly, atypical motivational circuitry of one form or another has been documented in a variety of clinical conditions: anxiety disorders,

Box 13.1 Public Health Relevance

Adolescent vulnerability. Adolescence is an important but precarious phase of life. Susceptibility to psychiatric disorders is greatest in mid-adolescence, particularly in females (Fairchild et al., 2011). Additionally, accidents stemming from risky behaviors and violence are the leading causes of disease and death among youth across the globe – particularly in males, and particularly in industrialized nations (World Health Organization, 2014). As a result, a number of countries have pointed to adolescent risk-taking – including substance use, unprotected sex, cigarette smoking, binge drinking, and fighting – as a major public health issue.

   Individuals exhibiting problematic behaviors. Importantly, the most problematic behaviors are predominantly observed in a small proportion of teens, perhaps 10–15 percent, who are argued to be atypically developing (Bjork & Pardini, 2015). This subset of individuals tend to have a history of behavioral disinhibition (i.e., lower self-control), with patterns of behavior that would meet criteria for conduct disorder, oppositional-defiant disorder, or ADHD. Because they are at far greater risk than most teens of poor life outcomes and criminal behavior, more DCN research on this population is warranted.

   Substance abuse. Adolescence is a time of heightened vulnerability to substance abuse. Indeed, teens who start to use substances like alcohol and marijuana at an earlier age are more likely to succumb to addiction. These and other drugs are thought to impact the developing dopamine system, thereby enhancing their reinforcing properties – and doing so at a time in life when pre-frontal control circuitry is not fully mature, potentially thereby compounding the risk for substance abuse (Casey, 2015). Substance use in adolescence may also trigger or exacerbate mental health problems; for example, early cannabis use is thought to trigger the onset and increase the severity of schizophrenic symptoms like psychosis (Thorpe et al., 2020). Instead, or additionally, it is possible that individuals with budding mental health problems turn to substances of abuse in an attempt to cope with them, making it difficult to tease apart cause and effect. Likewise, studies showing differences in brain structure and function between teens with and without substance use disorder can be subject to this chicken-and-egg problem, because it is unclear whether the brain anomalies increase susceptibility to, and/or are caused by, substance abuse. The National Institute on Drug Abuse in the United States has co-funded a very large longitudinal study known as the Adolescent Brain Cognitive Development (ABCD) study to tackle this thorny problem.

   Criminality. Just as risk-taking peaks in adolescence, criminal behavior in most parts of the world rises through adolescence and peaks in the early twenties before subsiding: this is referred to as the "age-crime curve" (Bjork & Pardini, 2015). Developmental researchers have argued successfully to the United States Supreme Court that sentences for adolescents should be more lenient than those for adults, based on diminished responsibility as a result of their immaturity (Steinberg, 2009). For example, the 2005 case *Roper v. Simmons* ruled the death penalty unconstitutional for crimes committed under the age of 18, citing three general differences between juveniles and adults: their "susceptibility to immature and irresponsible behavior," their "vulnerability and comparative lack of control over their immediate surroundings," and "the reality that juveniles still struggle to define their identity." Although this case did not explicitly cite

Box 13.1 (cont.)

neuroscientific evidence, subsequent Supreme Court rulings have done so, leading to the abolition of life without the possibility of parole sentencing for both homicide and non-homicide crimes. From the standpoint of public safety, incarcerating juveniles leads to increased recidivism (rate of reoffending) relative to parole sentencing for a whole host of reasons, including reduced opportunity to develop social skills and regulate their behavior (Dmitrieva et al., 2012).

The importance of investing in adolescence. Adolescence is a time of great change during which individuals can get on positive or negative trajectories. Leading developmental researchers argue that policies that take this fact into account could promote positive growth trajectories in the realms of health, education, and social and economic success (Dahl et al., 2018). They propose a number of intervention strategies, including creating opportunities for positive risk-taking, discovery and exploration, development of autonomy, and increased understanding of social experiences, as well as introduction to positive role models and mentors.

depression, bipolar disorder, and even schizophrenia (Whitton et al., 2015). Approach and exploration are linked and form a continuum of risk-seeking behaviors; avoidance and complacency or fear are similarly linked, forming a continuum of risk-avoidant behaviors.

For some species, approach and avoidance behaviors can be sufficient for survival. This is true of species that are highly adapted to a specific environmental niche – living in a specific habitat, in which they eat a limited range of foods and encounter a limited range of predators. However, the more specialized the environment, the more susceptible a species is to loss of habitat or changes in climate. We humans have managed to populate a wider variety of habitats and meet more challenges than any other species other than viruses. After all, *Homo sapiens* managed to survive the last Ice Age. (Hopefully we will find ways to adapt to the current climate crisis!)

What accounts for our species' versatility? We can't rely purely on instinct or by repeating previously rewarded behaviors and avoiding learned threats, because we live in more specialized and complex physical and social environments (Chapter 7). Rather than relying on the genetic transmission of behaviors (such as spiders' knowledge of how to make a web), we evolved to engage in cultural transmission of knowledge and to learn from others' mistakes. Second, we must establish goals, formulate plans to surmount novel challenges, carefully monitor our progress towards our goals, and occasionally curb our natural tendencies — abilities supported by the working memory and executive functions reviewed in Chapter 10. So-called **"hot" executive functions** support decision-making in situations involving high risk with a high potential payoff, and in emotional or personally meaningful contexts. To illustrate the importance of this form of **self-control**, we begin here by reviewing how behavior looks when such executive functions are not fully intact, in patients who have suffered brain injury.

13.1.2 Insights from Patients

You may already have learned about the striking case of Phineas Gage, although it bears repeating as it led to a breakthrough in our understanding of PFC function and behavioral regulation. Gage was a 25-year-old railroad construction supervisor tasked with laying down

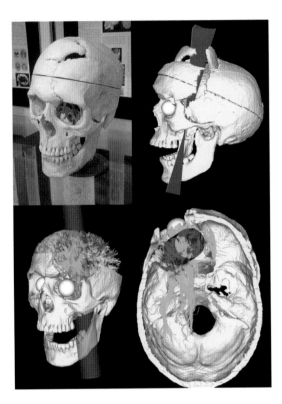

Figure 13.1 3D reconstruction of the path of destruction of the iron rod in Phineas Gage's brain, and the white matter tracts that were likely impacted. (Reprinted from Van Horn et al., 2012)

tracks for a new railroad in Vermont in 1848. One fateful day, an explosion caused a 13-pound iron rod (called a tamping iron) to tear through his skull (Figure 13.1), destroying a large portion of his left **prefrontal cortex (PFC)** in the process. Remarkably, he survived the impact; even more remarkably, he didn't lose consciousness. In fact, he resumed work just a few minutes later, and when his doctor, John Martyn Harlow, arrived, Gage assured the man that nothing was wrong (O'Driscoll & Leach, 1998). As one might imagine, given the cavernous hole in his head, Gage contracted a near-fatal infection. Thanks to his doctor's care, he ultimately survived. However, Harlow noticed profound changes in his patient's behavior, describing him as "exceedingly capricious and childish, but with a will as indomitable as ever." One the other hand, the doctor noted that his patient's memory was intact: "Remembers passing and past events correctly, as well before as since the injury."

Harlow's observations were confirmed by Phineas Gage's employers. While they had previously considered him a highly effective foreman, they found him so changed that they did not allow him to return to work. This is hardly surprising, given what we know from Harlow's description: "He is fitful, irreverent, indulging at times in the grossest profanity (which was not previously his custom), manifesting but little deference for his fellows, impatient of restraint or advice when it conflicts with his desires … A child in his intellectual capacity and manifestations, he has the animal passions of a strong man … His mind was radically changed, so decidedly that his friends and acquaintances said he was 'no longer Gage'."

(An alternative view comes from the Irish comedian Dara Ó Briain (2019). "Doctors noted that after the accident he was noticeably more hostile, and they said that the reason for this is because he damaged the frontal lobes of his brain and maybe this was the region of his brain that served to damp down violent mood swings. Ah, maybe. Or maybe it's because a ?*#&! spike just got shot up the back of his face...")

This clinical observation led to a dramatic reconceptualization of the frontal lobes, whose function had been previously underappreciated. But Harlow's observations of Gage demonstrated that the frontal lobes were behaviorally relevant, and spurred a line of inquiry into frontal lobe function that persists unabated today (see also Chapter 10). Gage's accident destroyed the most ventral portions of PFC, including **orbitofrontal cortex (OFC)** – so-named because it sits right above the orbit, or eye socket. Focal lesion studies in non-human primates confirm that damage to OFC and surrounding tissue can cause emotional lability – exaggerated changes in mood – and other notable behavioral changes (Fuster, 2001). This work also showed that the precise location of the lesions matters, as the PFC has a number of functionally distinct subregions.

As it turns out, Gage's injury extended beyond these regions. Over 150 years later, John Darrell Van Horn, Arthur Toga, and colleagues were allowed to remove Gage's skull and the iron rod from their display case at the Harvard Medical School and perform a 3D reconstruction of the path of destruction (Van Horn et al., 2012). Based on white matter tractography in healthy young adult males (Figure 13.1), they concluded that there would have been widespread damage to white matter tracts connecting left PFC to left hemisphere temporal lobe and limbic regions, as well as to right PFC. Thus, this horrible accident led to widespread damage to bilateral PFC pathways whose regulation of behavior is now much better understood.

Additional evidence regarding the functions of PFC comes from the surgical procedures known as the **frontal leucotomy**, popularly known as a **frontal lobotomy**, whereby PFC was disconnected from the rest of the brain. These surgeries were undertaken beginning in the 1930s in an effort to cure serious mental health conditions, such as schizophrenia and mood disorders. The logic was that these disorders were the result of aberrant activity in the frontal lobes, and that eliminating the activity through surgery would calm patients who were tormented by their own thoughts. The procedure was, in fact, effective for a subset of patients, and the neurologist credited with developing it (António Egas Moniz) was awarded the Nobel Prize for it in 1949. Unfortunately, the procedure sometimes did more harm than good; in fact, Moniz was subsequently shot by a former patient seeking retribution.

Given its apparent success, a psychiatrist who was not licensed to perform this surgery (Walter Freeman) developed a 10-minute outpatient procedure that he could complete in the comfort of his office, whereby an icepick inserted into the eye socket was driven into the brain by a rubber mallet, and then rotated in such a way as to sever white matter fibers. This new procedure, advertised as being "easier than curing a toothache," was prescribed freely. As popular as these so-called psychosurgeries were, they sometimes caused debilitating symptoms – as in the case of Rosemary Kennedy, who became severely mentally and physically incapacitated – or even death. The effects varied wildly across patients, likely in part because of variability in the location and skill of the surgeon (these were a far cry from the precise MRI-guided brain surgeries conducted today). Frontal leucotomies were banned in the United States in 1970, but not soon enough for the tens of thousands of patients who underwent the procedure.

Subject A   Subject B

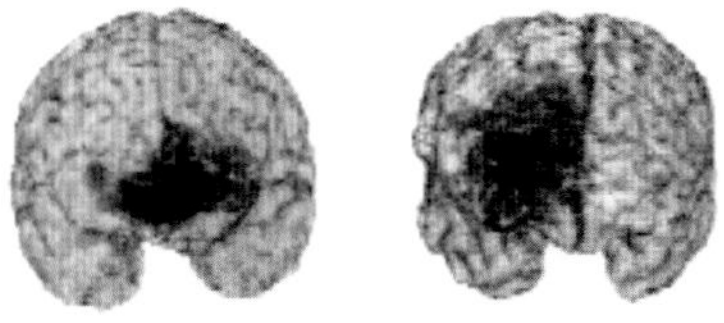

Figure 13.2 3D reconstruction of anatomical MRI scan of patients who had incurred damage to OFC early in childhood. These images show the front of the brains. (Reprinted from Anderson et al., 1999)

13.1.3 PFC Injuries Incurred during Development

Thus far, we've described PFC damage in adults. What happens when PFC is compromised while it is still maturing? Given that the brain undergoes major changes in the first few years and is more plastic then, one might imagine that the brain can reorganize in such a way as to compensate for the injury. On the other hand, one might imagine that an early injury could have a snowball effect, drastically altering a child's developmental trajectory by disrupting foundational mental abilities that must be in place to scaffold the development of more complex ones. (See the discussion of the Kennard principle in Chapter 5.) There doesn't seem to be a hard-and-fast rule – yet. However, PFC injuries during development often have lasting effects.

Steven Anderson, Antoine Bechara, and colleagues (Anderson et al., 1999) reported two cases of young adults who incurred damage to OFC within the first few years of life. One was a 20-year-old woman who had been hit by a car at 15 months; the other was a 23-year-old man who had had a frontal lobe tumor removed at 3 months of age. Figure 13.2 shows the 3D reconstructions of the two individuals' brains. The brain on the left is the woman's and the brain on the right is the man's; both show pronounced orbitofrontal (OFC) lesions.

Both individuals seemed to recover normally from the OFC lesions they had sustained early in life, meeting standard developmental milestones through early childhood. As the two individuals grew older, however, behavioral problems became evident: in all likelihood, their behavior appeared more and more abnormal as their peers' frontal lobes developed and theirs did not. The girl was described as being unresponsive to punishment at age 3. As a child, she was deemed intelligent and academically capable, but she had difficulty completing tasks. Her moods changed at the drop of a hat: that is, she was emotionally labile – like Phineas Gage. She showed no empathy and had no friends. At school and at home, she exhibited disruptive behavior, and lied frequently. She was physically and verbally abusive, and showed no remorse for her misbehavior. She was arrested multiple times for theft, and engaged in early and risky sexual behavior. At age 14, she was placed in a treatment facility. At age 20, she was described as a neglectful mother who had no job and no plans for the future. The boy with OFC damage had an eerily similar behavioral profile (Anderson et al., 1999).

A case that parallels theirs is that of Howard Dully, who, at age 12, became the youngest patient to undergo the outpatient frontal leucotomy, now a 72-year-old former bus driver in San Jose, California. In 1960, his stepmother, who disliked him and found him defiant, marched him into Walter Freeman's office for an ice-pick lobotomy. Dully's early adult life was characterized by alcoholism, homelessness, and incarceration. He argues in his memoir, *My Lobotomy: A Memoir* (Dully & Fleming, 2008), that this surgery profoundly altered his life course.

But how do we know that these individuals' behavioral profiles stemmed from their early frontal lobe injuries? After all, we don't know what they would have been like if they hadn't had them. This highlights the importance of converging methodologies in theory building. These different stories collectively paint a picture that is consistent with carefully controlled lesion studies in monkeys: interactions between OFC and lateral PFC regions are critical for regulating behavior in the face of temptation or in an emotionally charged situation. By contrast, lesions to lateral PFC that leave OFC intact lead to deficits regulating behavior in neutral situations (see Chapter 10). PFC has multiple subregions with different functions, but they work together to support goal-directed behavior by allowing us to represent our goals, articulate plans for achieving them, consider the possible consequences of our actions, inhibit inappropriate behavioral and emotional responses, and more.

Importantly, PFC not only helps us to curb our temptations when giving in to them would interfere with our goals, but also helps us to decide to seek out rewards and take calculated risks in the process. The development of goal-directed behavior involves the interplay between evolving motivational and self-regulatory processes.

13.2 Self-Control

If you have ever stopped yourself from saying or doing something inappropriate or resisted the temptation of dessert, you have engaged in self-control. As you have likely noticed, exerting self-control is taxing; it is also highly fallible. Rewards and punishments are powerful drivers of behavior, and at times our impulses, desires, and emotional responses are simply too strong to override. This is all the more true in development: in particular, infants utterly lack self-control. They wet themselves (and worse), and they cry at even the slightest discomfort. It wouldn't be hyperbole to say that learning to inhibit our natural impulses is one of the most important skills we learn through childhood and adolescence. A rudimentary capacity for self-control emerges in early childhood but is not fully operational for another two decades. Having emphasized early cognitive development in the initial chapters of this book, this final chapter emphasizes middle childhood and adolescence – a time when the neural systems underlying self-control are already in place but are being refined.

13.2.1 The Protracted Neurodevelopment of Self-Control

Some years ago, a car insurance company (Allstate) printed the following advertisement:

Why do most 16-year-olds drive like they're missing a part of their brain? BECAUSE THEY ARE. Even bright, mature teenagers sometimes do things that are "stupid." But it's not really their fault. It's because their brain hasn't finished developing. The missing part is called the dorsal lateral prefrontal cortex, and it plays a critical role in teens' decision-making and understanding of future consequences. Problem is, it doesn't fully develop until their 20s. This is one of the reasons why 16-year-old drivers have crash rates three times higher than 17-year-olds and five times higher than 18-year-olds.

The text was accompanied by a cartoon of a 16-year-old's brain with a car-shaped hole in the frontal lobes. This advertisement has a grain of truth to it, but it got one vital piece wrong: the dorsal lateral PFC (DLPFC), discussed in Chapter 10 as being centrally involved in top-down control over behavior, is not missing in adolescents! Nor is it dysfunctional. (As you already know, dear reader, you can't believe everything advertisers say.) In fact, lateral PFC is active as early in life as we can measure it: in preterm infants at 30-week gestational age (Mahmoudzadeh et al., 2013); see also Chapter 10. Lateral PFC helps us to attend to, and learn from, the world around us. As we shall see, what changes with age is *when and how* it is engaged, and how strongly it influences neural activity elsewhere in the brain.

The human brain develops more slowly than that of any other species, and the neural system that supports self-control develops more slowly than any other of our brain systems. At a population level, this relative delay may be perfectly adaptive for an omnivorous species with no natural predators. With caregivers who can provide for us and protect us from harm, humans have the luxury of being born utterly helpless and developing slowly before we have to make our own way in the world. During this period of extended plasticity, our brains become fine-tuned to our surroundings as we learn to navigate the opportunities and constraints that it affords (see Chapter 5). This feature of the human brain surely contributes to our ability to survive in a wide range of environments: slow and steady wins the race. In fact, the fine-tuning of other brain systems may be best accomplished if they are not under tight top-down control by PFC from the outset. As these other systems mature, so too do the fiber tracts from PFC that modulate brain-wide neural activity in the service of goal-directed behavior.

Although the slow development of self-control may have been beneficial for humankind, it does not always work out for the best for individuals. Even typically developing children and adolescents – and even neurologically healthy adults – vary widely in their capacity for self-control. At the lower end of the distribution, we find children with a wide variety of neurodevelopmental disorders whose symptoms include deficits in executive functioning. Thus, it behooves us to understand how self-control changes over the course of development and varies across individuals.

13.2.2 Measuring Self-Control

How might we measure self-control experimentally? There are two complementary approaches, each of which is valuable in its own way. The naturalistic approach is to place the participant – typically a young child – in a situation that mirrors the kinds of challenges they may face in real life and observe how they behave (Zhou et al., 2012). These ingenious tasks measure, for example, how well children tolerate frustration while trying to build a wooden puzzle without looking at it, how well they manage to avoid being tempted by a delectable treat, like a marshmallow, placed right in front of them – a **delay of gratification task** – or how well they are able to conceal their disappointment when they unwrap an underwhelming present. These types of tasks approximate the types of behaviors we ultimately want to understand, and lend themselves to studies of young children and are said to have ecological validity.

A different approach is to measure performance on abstract tasks designed to drill down to the essence of self-control, stripped away from other potentially confounding variables. One example of such a task is known as the **Day/Night Stroop**, in which a child must say the opposite of what is displayed on a card (e.g., say "day" when they see a picture of the moon, and "night" when they see a picture of the sun (Gerstadt et al., 1994). One large study involving children from 3.5 to 7 years of age revealed that children below the age of 5 struggled with this task, even though they were able to respond "day" to one learned abstract stimulus and "night" to another. In other words, 5-year-olds didn't have any trouble learning associations between words and pictures, but rather found it difficult to suppress their previously learned tendency to say "day" when they saw a sun and "night" when they saw a moon.

13.2.3 Delay of Gratification

The most famous test of self-control in young children is Walter Mischel's delay of gratification task, commonly referred to as the **marshmallow task** (Mischel et al., 1989). (Informal versions of this task have made it into the mainstream: online videos of children undertaking the so-called "candy challenge" total many millions of views!) In this paradigm, a young child is seated alone at a table with something appealing, such as a marshmallow, and is asked whether they would like to have it right away or wait for a larger treat later, such as two marshmallows. More often than not, the young child will say that they would rather wait for the larger treat. The experimenter leaves the child alone in the room with the treat right in front of them, and in some cases with a bell they can ring if they change their mind and would like to have the single treat right away. Unbeknownst to the child, they're being recorded with a video camera so that their behavior can be coded later. The **wait time** refers to the amount of time a child is willing to wait before they give up and request the smaller reward, if in fact they do not wait until the experimenter returns (15 minutes later in the original paradigm). **Hot focus** refers to the proportion of the wait time they spend staring at the treat or the bell, as opposed looking at something else.

This is a difficult task for preschoolers; as they get older, and their impulse control improves, their wait time increases and the amount of time they engage in hot focus decreases. However, it is possible to improve younger children's performance. For example, if preschoolers can't see the treats during the delay, or if the experimenter draws their attention to other thoughts, they can resist temptation for longer. Self-reports suggest that slightly older children spontaneously adopt the strategy of distracting themselves, and even older children instruct themselves on how to behave (Mischel et al., 1989). Layered on top of developmental increases in delay of gratification are individual differences in performance. As we shall see, these individual differences likely reflect both differences in a particular brain and contextual factors – and these differences appear to be linked to a variety of life outcomes (although there are caveats to consider).

13.2.4 Predicting Life Outcomes

Preschoolers who completed the marshmallow task in the late 1960s have been followed for decades, and studies show that the number of seconds a child waits for the larger reward at test is correlated with their later academic achievement, quality of emotional coping, physical health, and drug use in adulthood (Casey et al., 2011). Thus, it would seem that early self-control ability, at least as indexed by the marshmallow task, is a predictor of an individual's ability to regulate multiple aspects of behavior over the entire course of life. However, this conclusion has been called into question (Watts et al., 2018; Michaelson & Munakata, 2020) because performance on the marshmallow test is affected by sociocultural and interpersonal factors, by social norms and social interactions (Mischel et al., 1989; Michaelson & Munakata, 2016). Additionally, children's expectations matter: they wait longer when the experimenter has previously delivered on a promise to the child than when she has failed to do so (Kidd et al., 2013). Based on this finding, Celeste Kidd and colleagues proposed that socioeconomically disadvantaged children tend to live in more unpredictable environments and have less of a reason to trust that the experimenter will ultimately give them two treats. If this is the case, the logical decision for these young children is to take one treat right away. Thus, the marshmallow task isn't a "pure" measure of self-control; nor is it perfectly predictive of life outcomes, as many other factors come into play.

There is, however, a remarkable longitudinal study involving a large sample size and multiple measures of self-control that supports the idea that self-control in childhood predicts later life outcomes. Terrie Moffitt, Avshalom Caspi, and colleagues (Moffitt et al., 2011) followed a cohort of over 1,000 children in New Zealand from birth through middle age, administering a variety of measures along the way, creating a reliable composite measure of self-control based on measures at five timepoints between ages 3 and 11; these included observational measures and parental, teacher, and self-reports of four indices: emotional lability, impulsivity, inattention, and lack of goal persistence.

The composite measure revealed that poor childhood self-control predicted worse life outcomes at age 35, including higher rates of substance dependence, financial struggles, and even likelihood of having had an adult criminal conviction when controlling for socioeconomic status and IQ (race and ethnicity are not discussed) (Figure 13.3). Moffitt, Caspi, and colleagues found that this relationship was partially explained by the fact that children with low self-control were more likely to engage in problematic behaviors in adolescence that put them on a harmful trajectory, including dropping out of school, becoming teenaged parents, and taking up smoking by age 15. However, these *adolescent snares*, as the researchers referred to these problematic behaviors, didn't fully explain the relationship. Thus, these results appear to support the societal relevance of self-control early in childhood.

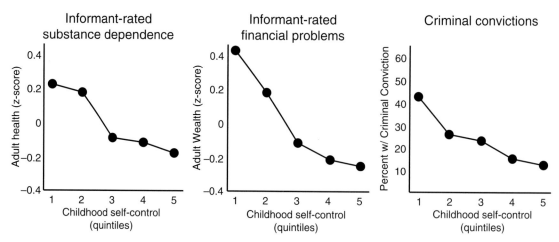

Figure 13.3 Associations between childhood self-control, binned into quintiles, and three life outcomes measured at age 35. (Adapted from Moffitt et al., 2011)

13.3   Neural Basis of Self-Control and Its Development

A fundamental question regarding the development of goal-directed behavior is the extent to which it depends on changes in self-regulation, and/or on basic drivers of behavior such as reward-seeking. In other words, do children get better over development at resisting temptation because they improve at self-control, or because the rewards themselves become less tempting? The neural systems underlying self-control and reward processing interact closely, and both change over development, making this question a tough nut to crack. However, neuroimaging studies have helped us to examine neurodevelopmental changes in each system somewhat independently. In particular, the neural basis of self-control and its development is often probed with fairly abstract, boring, unrewarding tasks – in a so-called *neutral context* – thereby allowing us to home in on the control component while minimizing the complex interplay with motivational circuitry.

13.3.1 Self-Control in a Neutral Context: Inhibiting Motor Responses

Abstract tests of self-control that are commonly used from late childhood onward are typically computerized tasks in which participants must inhibit a motoric response to a stimulus. Despite being very far removed from the real-world behaviors we're ultimately interested in understanding, these types of tasks also have several advantages for researchers. For one thing, they afford more precise measurement of self-control, and they lend themselves to use during brain imaging protocols. By comparing across carefully designed task conditions, it is possible to isolate and measure specific self-control components of both brain and behavioral responses. For another thing, these tasks make it possible to examine the development of self-control across a broad age range. Although abstract computerized tests don't paint a full picture of the complexities of human behavior, as we shall see below, they have provided insights regarding the neural basis of certain aspects of self-control.

Self-control is often measured by tests of **response inhibition** (also known as **inhibitory control**). In these tasks, participants must inhibit or suppress response tendencies. They are typically not rewarded, and so the tasks are considered fairly pure measures of self-control. The two most common tests of response inhibition are **Go/No-Go** and **Stop-Signal paradigms**, both of which require participants to inhibit a response. On a typical Go/No-Go task, participants see a series of images, one after another: say, a large number of dog photos (designated as "Go" stimuli) with a few cat photos mixed in (designated "No-Go" stimuli). They are instructed to respond quickly with a button press every time they see a Go stimulus, but to stop themselves from pressing the button to a No-Go stimulus. If lots of Go stimuli are presented in a row, people develop a tendency to press repeatedly, which makes it hard to inhibit responding to the occasional No-Go stimulus. Performance on this task is chiefly measured by accuracy on the No-Go trials. Stop-Signal paradigms are similar, except that participants see the same stimulus over and over, while only occasionally receiving a cue – and at the last possible moment – instructing them to interrupt their motor plan. This means the stopping cue should stop them in their tracks. Performance on the Stop-Signal task is measured by how much advance warning a person needs in order to successfully withhold their response, effectively establishing how efficient their inhibitory control system is.

The region most closely linked to response inhibition on these sorts of tasks is the **right inferior frontal gyrus (IFG)**, shown in blue in Figure 13.4 (Aron et al., 2014; Cai et al., 2014). This is one of the brain regions that best distinguishes individuals with high and low self-control on the delay of gratification task (Berman et al., 2013). A plausible account of what happens during response inhibition is that the **anterior insula** (Chapter 10) sends a signal to the adjacent IFG, alerting it to a change in the environment. (In the Go/No-Go task, this would be the No-Go stimulus; in Stop-Signal, it would be the stopping cue.) The right IFG in turn sends a signal via the so-called **hyperdirect pathway** to the **subthalamic nucleus** in the basal ganglia, a small nucleus that rapidly inhibits planned motor responses via projections to motor cortical areas (Aron & Poldrack, 2006). In this way, the right IFG signals the need to stop or change a habitual motor response when something changes in the environment (Chatham et al., 2012).

13.3.2 Neurodevelopment of Response Inhibition

DCN research has produced a robust literature on response inhibition that examines how we inhibit manual motor responses, as well as corresponding eye movements, so-called *prepotent responses*. Studies in this domain typically rely on the Go/No-Go and Stop-Signal tasks described above, as well as an eye movement control paradigm that we describe below. The ability to withhold prepotent responses that are not task-appropriate improves significantly throughout childhood, slows down in adolescence, and varies a lot between individuals (Williams et al., 1999; Constantinidis & Luna, 2019). What accounts for this developmentally related change and variability across individuals?

As we have seen, the neural pathway involved in inhibiting manual responses includes right anterior insula and right IFG, projecting via the hyperdirect pathway to the subthalamic nucleus of the basal ganglia to inhibit motor responding. Weidong Cai and Vinod Menon (Cai et al., 2019) found that, in general, 9- to 12-year-olds engage the same brain regions as adults when

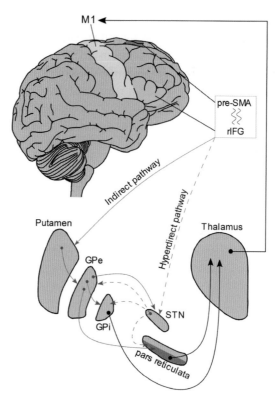

Figure 13.4 Pathways in the basal ganglia involved in response inhibition. The indirect pathway passes through the striatum, which comprises the caudate (not shown here) and the putamen. Projections from the striatum travel to the external segment of the global pallidus (GPe), which projects directly to the output nuclei (the substantia nigra, pars recticulata, and the internal segment of the global pallidus (GPi)) or via the subthalamic nucleus (STN). The hyperdirect pathway projects directly to the STN. The output nuclei send projections to the thalamus, which transmits signals to the primary motor cortex (M1) for the inhibition of motor responses. The wavy lines between the pre-supplementary motor area (pre-SMA) and right inferior frontal gyrus (rIFG) denote functional connections between them. (Reprinted from Obeso et al., 2008)

performing the Stop-Signal task, and they do so to the same extent (Figure 13.5A). Further, these researchers found that children who were faster at inhibiting motor responses (lower Stop-Signal reaction time) tended to activate the subthalamic nucleus more strongly, and to show stronger temporal coupling of fMRI activation (*functional connectivity*; see Chapter 2) between this inhibitory motor nucleus and the anterior insula. This relationship, shown in Figure 13.5B, reinforces the importance of the hyperdirect pathway for inhibitory control.

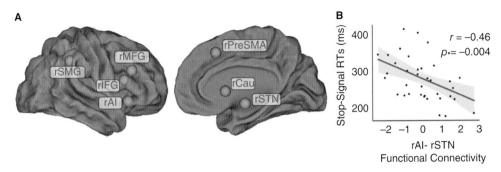

Figure 13.5 Evidence supporting the role of the hyperdirect pathway in inhibitory control. A. Regions engaged on the Stop-Signal task, including the right anterior insula (rAI). B. Children with better Stop-Signal task performance (lower SSRT) showed stronger functional connectivity between rAI and the right subthalamic nucleus (rSTN). (Reprinted from Cai et al., 2019)

Another behavioral paradigm that has been used to study response inhibition is the **antisaccade task**, in which participants are asked to move their eyes to the opposite side of the screen from the location of a briefly presented stimulus (Luna et al., 2015). We naturally orient our eyes towards a visual stimulus that appears suddenly in the periphery of our visual field, so moving our eyes to the *opposite* side of that stimulus is very unnatural. As such, the antisaccade task forces participants to engage in voluntary, top-down control over their eye movements. Needless to say, children make many errors on this task. Adolescents are quite good at it on the whole, but their performance isn't as consistent as that of adults: they perform the task correctly on some trials but not on others. This *trial-to-trial variability* in accuracy on the antisaccade task decreases over adolescence. What accounts for these developmental changes – and for pronounced individual differences – at the level of the brain?

Critically, we know a lot about the neural system that underlies voluntary control over eye movements (Sweeney et al., 1996). The *oculomotor system* drives eye movements; it also includes DLPFC, which is thought to send top-down signals to the oculomotor system when needed. Armed with this knowledge, researchers had a strong idea of where to begin looking for changes that could support the development of voluntary eye movements.

In a longitudinal fMRI study involving 123 participants between 9 and 26 years of age, Luna and colleagues (Ordaz et al., 2013) found that children as young as 9 engaged the same set of brain regions as adults on the antisaccade task, indicating that the system underlying inhibition of eye movements is in place at least by middle childhood. However, the researchers also found a slight *decrease* in activation of DLPFC over childhood on correctly performed antisaccade trials, reductions that reached adult-like activation levels by adolescence. In other words, the top-down control system becomes more efficient during the teenage years. Interestingly, when participants in the antisaccade task are rewarded for accurate performance, adolescents can perform near adult levels. This reveals two things: first, on the whole, adolescents have the capacity to exert strong self-control; second, motivation can enhance response inhibition, as is the case when that behavior is rewarded (Constantinidis & Luna, 2019). We have talked about how temptation can undermine goal-directed behavior, but here we see that reward can actually enhance self-control!

Critically, the biggest age effect Luna and colleagues found was when participants made an error and immediately corrected it, moving their eyes towards the location of the stimulus and then moving them to the opposite side of the display. From ages 9 to 26 years, participants got increasingly fast at correcting their errors; the fMRI scans also showed a pronounced increase in **error-related activation** in the **dorsal anterior cingulate cortex (dACC)**. As discussed in Chapter 10, there is evidence that the dACC (together with the anterior insula, mentioned earlier), alerts DLPFC to the need to exert greater top-down control on subsequent trials. This finding suggests that more robust error signaling, as indexed by dACC activation, supports improvements in response inhibition.

All in all, the neural pathways that underlie self-control are present in childhood but become more effective with age. Adolescents are relatively good at self-control on the whole, and can perform near adult levels if motivated to do so. Research that focuses on typically developing participants serves as a foundation for understanding children and teens who struggle with impulse control, such as a subset of those with ADHD (Box 10.1; Pievsky & McGrath, 2017). Indeed, the tasks we have reviewed here have been used extensively to try to understand how self-control networks, among others, are affected in ADHD (e.g., Samea et al., 2019).

13.4 Neural Basis of Self-Control in a Motivationally Salient Context: Resisting Temptation

Having shown that self-control improves with age in the absence of external rewards or punishments, we are now ready to examine how it interacts with basic drivers of behavior during development. It would be nice to know what's going on inside a child's brain while they're trying to resist temptation or to not get upset. These types of real-world behaviors – and even the laboratory tasks designed to mirror them (e.g., the marshmallow, puzzle box, and disappointing gift tasks described in Section 13.2.2) – are difficult to study with brain imaging. fMRI would, in some ways, be preferable to use here over measures such as EEG or fNIRS (Chapter 2), because fMRI is capable of measuring activity in the subcortical limbic structures that drive approach and avoidance behaviors. However, it is difficult to behave naturally while lying in a scanner, so researchers have looked for other ways to study the neural basis of hot self-control.

13.4.1 Approaches to Studying Hot Self-Control

One approach to studying self-control in a motivationally salient ("hot") context is to collect data about *real-world behaviors* and then relate those to patterns of brain activation obtained during performance of cognitive tasks in the scanner. Another, much less common approach is to try to capture limited real-world behaviors during brain imaging. A third approach, adopted by a majority of studies, is to measure brain activation while participants perform tasks that require decision-making in the face of possible rewards (Section 13.5.3).

B. J. Casey, Marc Berman, and colleagues adopted the first of these approaches in a pair of fMRI studies in which they related real-life behavior to brain activation observed during a scanner-based self-control task. The study was a decades-long follow-up to Mischel's classic longitudinal study on delay of gratification, described earlier. A subset of participants from the original study underwent fMRI scans when they were in their forties. They were preselected based on their classification as having either high or low self-control that was stable across several decades. This classification was based on their marshmallow task performance in pre-school and self-reported executive functioning throughout their twenties and thirties. These two stable groups showed differences in brain activation when they performed tasks requiring inhibitory control of one form or another. Adults with stable high self-control showed stronger activation of the right IFG when inhibiting responses on the Go/No-Go task (Casey et al., 2011). These findings are consistent with data discussed in Section 13.3.1 showing the right IFG heavily implicated in response inhibition in a neutral context. The two groups also showed different patterns of brain activation on a task used in the second fMRI study that required inhibiting memories (Berman et al., 2013).

Brain activation was different enough across the two groups of participants that a machine learning algorithm trained on these patterns of brain activation could predict with 72 percent accuracy whether the brain data of a given child in the sample was from the high or low self-control group. One of the regions whose patterns of activation best discriminated these groups was the IFG (but in contrast to our earlier discussion, this was only in the left hemisphere, likely because the task involved suppressing memories rather than motor responses). Thus, individual differences in self-control are related to differences in underlying prefrontal control circuitry. These findings shouldn't be misinterpreted to mean that children who performed poorly on the marshmallow task as preschoolers *necessarily* became adults with lower self-control. Remember that individuals were selected for this study on the basis of the stability of their behavioral profiles across three decades and across two different assessments of self-control.

13.4.2 Neural Basis of Delay of Gratification

As interesting as these studies are, they don't show us what happens *while* children resist temptation. Insights into how we delay gratification come from a small fMRI study (Luerssen et al., 2015) using a task akin to the marshmallow task. A group of 7- to 9-year-old children were simply asked to lie quietly in the scanner for as long as they could, as the researchers collected resting-state fMRI data to measure patterns of functional connectivity during this waiting period. The mirror inside the scanner that typically projects task stimuli to participants instead projected an image of a pile of cookies that lay on a paper napkin on the children's chests! In other words, the only thing the children could see while lying for an undetermined period were cookies. The children were told that they could stop the scan at any time and get out and have these cookies. Although most of the participants completed the scan – the 8 to 10 minutes was a relatively short time period for children of this age to wait – the brain data are revealing.

Activation patterns obtained during the wait period showed interesting correlations with children's hot focus (Section 13.2.3), as measured on a previous day using Mischel's classic delay of gratification task. Children with lower hot focus outside the scanner exhibited stronger connectivity between multiple PFC regions and the **ventral striatum** – specifically, the **nucleus**

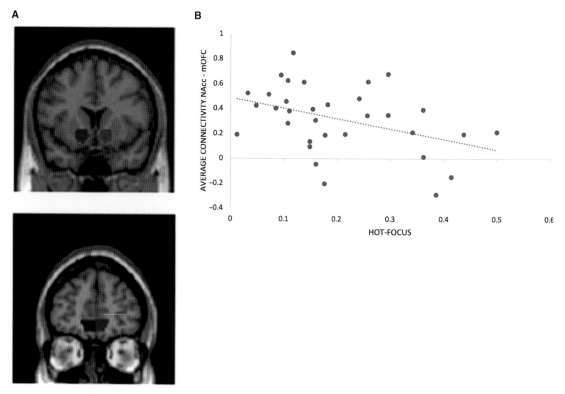

Figure 13.6 Results of resting-state fMRI study of delay of gratification. A. Regions of interest in or near the NAc and medial OFC, shown in coronal slices. B. Stronger functional connectivity between these regions of interest is associated with lower hot focus (better self-control).

accumbens (NAc), a small nucleus deep in the brain whose function is closely tied to reward anticipation and reward processing, driven by dopamine signaling. Figure 13.6A shows regions of interest in the approximate location of the NAc.

Figure 13.6 also shows the left and right **medial OFC**. The relationship between NAc-prefrontal (or, more broadly, **frontostriatal**) coupling and self-control was stronger for medial OFC than for any of the other PFC regions. As we saw with Phineas Gage and other patients, damage to this region is associated with dysregulated emotions and behavior. This study suggests that, even among typically developing children, self-control is associated with stronger communication between medial OFC and other PFC regions and reward-related regions. This conclusion is in line with a large longitudinal study involving 8- to 27-year-olds that showed stronger resting-state functional connectivity between medial OFC and the amygdala, another limbic region, to be associated with lower alcohol use two years later (Peters et al., 2017).

On the whole, though, most of what we know about the neural basis of delay of gratification comes from the *delay discounting paradigm*, in which participants (typically adolescents or adults) are asked to make a series of choices between receiving a small reward soon and a larger reward later. For example, participants are asked: "Would you prefer $5 today, or $10 in one week?" To motivate them to take this task seriously, the experimenter explained that, after the study was finished, they would receive the appropriate reward based on one of their decisions. For example, they would receive $10 one week later if that was the choice they had made on the trial selected at random. Over the course of the experiment, participants perform numerous trials with different combinations of reward values and wait times, allowing experimenters to assess just how much an individual values immediate gratification. In one study, Wouter van den Bos, Sam McClure, and colleagues showed that increased patience from ages 8 to 25 years was associated with increased structural coherence of white matter connecting DLPFC and the striatum (van den Bos et al., 2015). This study, along with the delay of gratification study outlined above (Luerssen et al., 2015) and many others, reveal that deferral of rewards depends on strong frontostriatal connections.

13.4.3 Reward-Based Decision-Making

The delay of gratification and delay discounting tasks are relatively straightforward, in that it's quite clear to participants which behaviors will lead to which outcomes. However, life doesn't often work like that. Much of the time, we have to make decisions under uncertainty, guessing which option will yield the greatest reward. In laboratory studies, such **reward-based decision-making** is often probed using **gambling tasks** on which participants decide whether to take risks, on the off-chance that they will yield a higher reward than the safe bet. Researchers use choice behavior on these tasks as a simplified measure of propensity towards risk-taking. They find, on the whole, that adolescents take a larger number of risky bets on gambling tasks than do either children or adults (Casey, 2015). This developmental pattern roughly mirrors what is observed in real life: we are more likely to take risks in adolescence than at any other time in our lives. As we discuss in Section 13.5, taking risks in moderation is a natural part of growing up. However, it can be highly problematic when taken to an extreme. As a result, researchers have invested substantial effort into trying to understand adolescent decision-making.

A set of related hypotheses is that teens engage in more reward-seeking behavior than other age groups because their brains respond more strongly in the face of potential rewards (Ernst et al., 2006; Steinberg et al., 2008; Casey, 2015). The ventral striatum – which, as we saw above, includes the nucleus accumbens – is a natural region to focus on as a test of this hypothesis, since there is lots of evidence from both animal models and humans that it is involved in anticipating and processing rewards. Thanks to strong input from **dopaminergic neurons** in the substantia nigra, the nucleus accumbens plays a key role in learning the *value* of an item or of a behavioral response. In this way, activation in this area signals motivationally salient events. In fMRI studies, participants engage the ventral striatum more strongly when they expect a larger reward than a smaller one. The ventral striatum is thought to transmit the value of a given option to OFC and other brain regions, biasing decision-making in favor of choices that could yield the most favorable outcomes. Indeed, neuroimaging research in adults indicates that the stronger the ventral striatum activation on a gambling task, the more likely a participant is to select the high-risk/high-payoff option (Kuhnen & Knutson, 2005).

13.4.4 Reward Sensitivity in Adolescence

As with adults, the ventral striatum is involved in reward anticipation in children and adolescents as well; however, adolescents sometimes show *stronger* activation in anticipation of a large reward (relative to a smaller one) than either children or adults (Galvan et al., 2006), suggesting that they are more attuned to reward value. However, this isn't always the case. Sometimes teens actually show *less* reward-related activation than adults (Galvan, 2010). The activation differences likely depend on how motivated teens are to seek out rewards on a particular task (Galvan, 2010; Bjork & Pardini, 2015), and, as we mentioned earlier, how much they trust that the reward will be forthcoming. After all, it stands to reason that if we don't care about a particular outcome, we are not likely to strongly engage reward circuitry when we anticipate it or experience it.

In general, however, studies show that when teens are motivated, they show greater sensitivity to rewards on average than either children or adults. Several neurobiological hypotheses have been proposed to explain this phenomenon. One is that PFC regions and pathways involved in self-control are on a slower developmental trajectory than limbic regions involved in reward processing, and that they therefore have less influence on behavior (Steinberg et al., 2008; Casey, 2015). Another is that *dopamine* activity in the ventral striatum is higher during adolescence, as a way to encourage seeking of new experiences at an age when, evolutionarily, young humans were about to set out on their own, thereby amplifying reward responsivity (Luna & Wright, 2016).

Not surprisingly, researchers have posited that higher reward sensitivity in the ventral striatum helps to explain why teens take more risks than other age groups. However, the brain–behavior relationship is not so simple; recent findings and meta-analytic based summaries suggest that there is rarely a strong relationship between ventral striatum activation and real-world risk-taking behaviors in adolescence (Sherman et al., 2018; Demidenko et al., 2020; Tervo-Clemmens et al., 2020). Indeed, this literature is quite mixed – and for a variety of reasons (Herman et al., 2018). To get the full picture, we will likely need more holistic analyses of the brain that consider the structure, function, and connectivity of multiple brain structures – and, more broadly, consideration of social and demographic factors. We may also need to distinguish between various kinds of risk-taking based on type of activity: say, legal and socially accepted activities like skydiving (which is societally condoned) as opposed to taking illegal street drugs. Thus, we need to distinguish the impact of individuals' risk-taking on other people, for example, whether it is antisocial or prosocial (Section 13.5.2). Perhaps most importantly, the field of DCN will benefit from the use of tasks that more closely relate to real-world behaviors.

There are several other important caveats to the characterization of adolescents as being more likely than children and adults to give in to temptation and engage in imprudent behaviors, as a result of high reward sensitivity and weak top-down control circuitry. First, adolescents vary widely in terms of their propensity towards risk-taking. Second, control regions and reward-related regions don't always work in opposition; they can also work together. For example, reward processing can enhance self-control and learning (Davidow et al., 2018; Constantinidis & Luna, 2019). Third, high reward sensitivity is not always a bad thing, having also been associated with the positive attribute of prosociality (Blankenstein et al., 2020). Fourth, calculated risks are often carefully considered and can ultimately be wise decisions. We will discuss this point below.

13.5 Adolescent Decision-Making

There's no doubt about it: teens have a bad reputation. Parents often brace themselves for their children's teenage years. Right around the time puberty hits, many parents lament that their previously sweet and obedient children are now talking back to them and slamming doors. Later in adolescence, parents might worry about their teens sneaking out of the house and engaging in unsafe behaviors. Here, we consider the broader context of adolescence, with a view to promoting greater empathy for teens.

13.5.1 The Transition to Adulthood

Adolescence is a period of transition between childhood and adulthood, involving both biological changes, including the effects of sex hormones on the body and brain, and social changes, including reduced reliance on caregivers (Dahl et al., 2018). This is a time for exploring the world, garnering the knowledge and skills needed for independence, as well as testing boundaries (Casey, 2015). During this period, seeking out novel experiences is important: as teens plan to leave home and establish new lives and identities, they need to develop a sense of the realm of possibilities for them. Teens have a greater tolerance for ambiguity, meaning a greater willingness to take risks when the outcome is uncertain (Tymula et al., 2012). Indeed, a study conducted in 11 countries around the world shows that, in most of these countries, risk-taking (as measured both by real-world behaviors and two laboratory tasks) follows an inverted-U function: it starts out low in childhood and then rises, peaking in late adolescence before dropping again (Duell et al., 2018).

Adolescence is also a time when one's *self-concept* is under construction (Sebastian et al., 2008). Teens are figuring out who they are, who they want to become, and with whom they want to affiliate. This growing self-concept is an extension of theory of mind and sensitivity to others' thoughts (Chapter 7). Distancing from parents or caregivers and orienting more towards peers is a natural part of this process. As we shall see below, the specific social context teens find themselves in influences decision-making and underlying brain activation as well. This period of elevated risk-taking is a positive development, on the whole; as the old proverb goes, "nothing ventured, nothing gained." For 10–15 percent of adolescents, however, risk-taking does, indeed, lead to problematic behaviors (Box 13.1).

13.5.2 Social Influences on Adolescent Decision-Making

As car insurance companies know very well, adolescents are far more likely to be involved in accidents than adults, particularly if there are adolescents in the car. This is no laughing matter: when controlling for the number of miles driven, drivers between ages 16 and 19 years are nearly *three times* more likely than drivers aged 20 years or older to be in a fatal car accident (Centers for Disease Control and Prevention), and the risk is even higher when the teen driver is male, or when the other passengers are teenagers. This is a sobering example of how the desire for approval from one's peers can lead to questionable behavior. Of course, peer influence is often positive, and is important for shaping teens' emerging adult identities, but it can also promote risky behaviors like unsafe driving, illegal drug use, unsafe sex, and more.

Several fMRI studies have been based on a driving simulation game call the Stoplight task (Figure 13.7A; Chein et al., 2011; Kahn et al., 2015; Sherman et al., 2019). In this game, players drive down a racetrack; the sooner they reach the end, the bigger the reward. However, there are stoplights along the way. When a stoplight turns from green to yellow, the driver has a choice between slowing to a halt, thus slowing down their overall performance, and speeding up to get through the intersection before the light changes. If participants go through the yellow light, there's a chance that it will turn red. If it does turn red, there's a chance they will crash the car, resulting in an even longer delay for them to finish the course than if they had simply waited for the light to change. Players can't predict how long the light will stay yellow, because it varies from trial to trial. Practically speaking, it's unclear whether running a yellow light will pay off in terms of the size of the reward they will receive once they reach the finish line.

In the initial fMRI study involving this paradigm, Jason Chein, Larry Steinberg, and colleagues (Chein et al., 2011) compared behavior and brain activation in 40 participants in three age groups: adolescents (14–18 years), young adults (19–22 years), and adults (24–29 years). Critically, there is another twist to the study: to probe peer influence on risky decision-making, the researchers asked each participant to bring two same-aged friends with them to the MRI scanner. Participants performed the task twice: once alone, and once with their friends watching their driving performance from the MRI control room and talking with them over the intercom. Chein and colleagues found that, on average, adolescents didn't take more risks than older participants when they played alone. However, when participants in the youngest group were watched by their friends rather than playing alone, they ran more yellow lights and crashed more often. This was true even though their friends didn't encourage them to take risks, but rather simply said they were watching and had made predictions about how well the player would perform.

To explore the neural underpinnings of these effects, Chein and colleagues studied brain activation corresponding to the *decision points* in the task: the moments when the stoplight turned from green to yellow and the driver had to decide whether to stop or go. Adults engaged left lateral PFC clusters more strongly than adolescents (Figure 13.7B), indicating greater activation of impulse control circuits. These clusters were identified in a whole-brain analysis as showing a significant main effect of Age in an ANOVA involving Age crossed with Social Context. This finding (illustrated more clearly in the region-of-interest analysis for lateral PFC, labeled as LPFC, in Figure 13.7D) suggests that, on the whole, 24- to 29-year-olds engaged more top-down control than 14- to 18-year-olds while performing the task. The 19- to 22-year-olds showed highly variable activation, intermediate to the other groups but not significantly different from either one. This finding fits with other evidence that our brains are still not fully

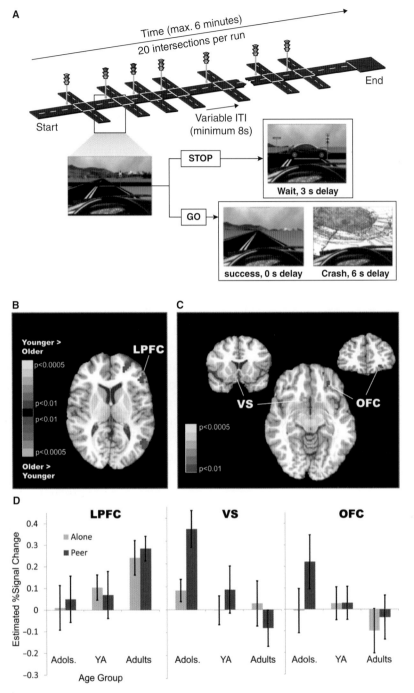

Figure 13.7 Results of fMRI study involving the Stoplight task. A. Sample trial showing the task design. B. Lateral PFC, shown in blue, shows a main effect of Age: it is more strongly engaged by adults than adolescents. C. The ventral striatum (VS) and OFC show an Age × Social Context interaction: these regions show greater sensitivity to social context in adolescents than in adults. D. A closer look at the patterns of activation in lateral PFC, the ventral striatum (VS), and OFC across the age groups and social contexts. (Reprinted from Chein et al., 2011)

adult-like by our early twenties, as initially suggested by Nitin Gogtay, Jay Giedd, and colleagues (Gogtay et al., 2004).

Additionally, Figure 13.7C shows that social context differentially affected activation of two key regions involved in reward-based decision-making – the ventral striatum and OFC – across the age groups. Voxels in these regions showed a significant Age × Social Context interaction in the whole-brain ANOVA. As can be seen in the region-of-interest analyses for the ventral striatum (labeled as VS) and OFC in Figure 13.7D, adolescents showed stronger activation for these regions than did the older age groups – but only when they were in the presence of their peers. In other words, teens engaged brain regions associated with motivation and reward during decision-making when their peers were watching more strongly than when they were alone. Critically, results showed that the teens predominantly engaged the ventral striatum just prior to making a decision to go through the yellow light, suggesting that they either anticipated a positive outcome or potentially found it rewarding to take a risk. In fact, risk-taking on the Stoplight task is correlated with self-reported **sensation seeking**, as measured by questions like, "I like to have new and exciting experiences and sensations even if they are a little frightening," and "I'll try anything once" (Steinberg et al., 2008; Chein et al., 2011).

A follow-up study from Lauren Kahn, Jennifer Pfeifer, and colleagues showed that right IFG is more active just before teens decide to stop at the yellow light than to go through it (Kahn et al., 2015). This result extends findings from the previously described studies showing that right IFG is involved in inhibitory control in neutral contexts (see Section 13.3.1), revealing that it is also involved in self-control in motivationally salient situations. What's more, teens with higher self-reported sensation-seeking and sensitivity to reward and punishment activated the right IFG less strongly, even when they decided to stop at the yellow light.

The Stoplight paradigm (see also Sherman et al., 2019) warrants further use, as it is closer to real-world risk-taking than many of the other studies that aim to characterize risk-taking and sensation-seeking. For example, with a larger participant pool, researchers could more closely examine age-related changes, test for sex differences and relationships with sex hormone levels, and probe relationships with real-life risk-taking. This paradigm could also be a good target for *neuroprediction*: testing whether activation patterns on this task predict future problem behaviors (e.g., Bjork & Pardini, 2015). Another important extension would be to look more closely at the qualities of specific relationships that explain when and why the presence of peers in the MRI scanner suite influences decision-making – whether for better or for worse. For example, Eva Telzer and Adriana Galván showed that strong social support buffers risk-taking behavior and associated brain activation (Telzer et al., 2015). In other words, we must consider the social context in which individuals are making decisions (van Hoorn et al., 2019).

13.5.3 Positive and Negative Growth Trajectories

All in all, many changes take place in adolescence, including pubertal development and continued brain maturation, increasing freedom and responsibility, and new social

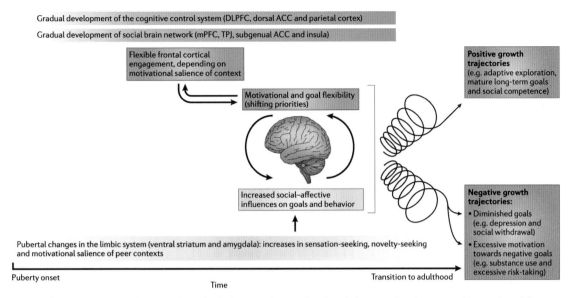

Figure 13.8 Model of the biological changes that underpin adolescent development. (Reproduced from Crone & Dahl, 2012)

settings. These changes can lead to either positive or negative growth trajectories, as illustrated in Figure 13.8. According to Eveline Crone (featured in the Scientist Spotlight, Box 13.2) and Ron Dahl's model (Crone & Dahl, 2012), a rapid rise in sex hormone levels at the onset of puberty sets in motion changes in social and affective processing – probably via changes in the ventral striatum and amygdala, key structures underlying motivated behavior. These changes promote increased novelty-seeking, sensation-seeking, and peer orientation, social and affective changes that occur in concert with changes in brain systems underlying cognitive control (including the anterior cingulate cortex (ACC), dorsolateral PFC (DLPFC), and parietal cortex) and social cognition (including medial PFC (mPFC), the temporoparietal junction (TPJ), subgenual ACC, and the anterior insula). Interactions within and across these systems contribute to flexible engagement of prefrontal control that depends on motivational salience, changes that can produce increased social motivation, exploration, and risk-taking – especially when taking risks may lead to the peers' admiration.

Over time, these tendencies can result in healthy exploration and risk-taking that support adult social competence: a positive, upward spiral. However, these tendencies can also lead to several negative spirals. One is that risk-taking can manifest as problematic behaviors, such as substance abuse or unsafe behaviors. Another is that heightened sensitivity to *social evaluation* can magnify the effects of peer rejection and social distancing, as seen in depression. In general, these changes in social-affective processing and flexible PFC recruitment are developmentally appropriate. However, in combination with risk factors, they can have negative consequences as well.

Box 13.2 Scientist Spotlight on Eveline Crone (Erasmus University, Rotterdam)

Eveline Crone (Box Figure 13.1) is a Professor of Developmental Neuroscience in Society at the Erasmus University in Rotterdam, and a Professor in Neurocognitive Developmental Psychology at Leiden University. She has also served as Vice President of the European Research Council. She received her doctoral degree in Psychology at the University of Amsterdam, and then completed a postdoctoral fellowship at the University of California at Davis before returning to the Netherlands. She studies adolescent brain development, and is interested in this period of life as a window of social opportunity.

When I started as a PhD student, I was mostly interested in adult behavior – how people behave in daily life and the reason for their actions. But then I realized that if you want to understand the different components of behavior, you have to really understand how people get there. My PhD was mostly behavioral and psychophysiological measures such as EEG and heart rate. When I went to the United States for my postdoc I had strong training in experimental psychology, but not yet in neuroimaging, so that was a life-changing experience.

I was interested in changes in cognitive processes from birth to adulthood, but when I started my own lab I got specialized more in adolescence. I could never really figure out why there was so much more variance in these teenage years relative to childhood and adulthood, and that is when I started to combine the motivation perspective with the cognitive development. We started to understand that the combination of subcortical systems and cortical systems, and how they develop relatively to each other, was really the interesting part about adolescent development. After we realized that this reward-cognitive control balance was an important thing to study in this period in life, we also wanted to use it to understand trajectories of development, so we tried to use this information about risk-taking in adolescence to predict bad behavior such as alcohol use, breaking rules. But even though most of those adolescents have this relatively reward-seeking behavior, only very few of them get into trouble – maybe only 10–15 percent. So then I started to wonder: What does this reward-seeking behavior mean if it only predicts a relatively small proportion of problem behavior in adolescence? Most teenagers want to contribute. They want to have impact, respect: autonomy is what they're seeking. So, my interest shifted towards wanting to understand how to create opportunities for learning and adaptation and growth and social development.

We introduced peer influence and peer support into our paradigms to find out how trajectories of motivation and cognition get influenced by multiple factors in the social context – and to better understand where the variation is coming from: which processes are very sensitive to context, and which are relatively stable over time. I am interested in looking more at the subtypes within the population. For example, there are adolescents who show a lot of cognitive control and reward activity; those may be the ones that are most interesting in terms of their potential to have impact in society. So, we're looking more into whether we can define these subtypes within our data and then follow those individuals and see if that tells us something about where they will end up later on. I'm interested in knowing whether we can find ways to predict the potential of young people to really make changes in society. And I want to use more of a citizen science approach – not only because of the moral reason that we have to get people involved, but because it could make our research better. For example, if I'm in my lab studying how young people take risks and teachers are concerned about getting them motivated to go to school, maybe I'm testing completely the wrong questions. I also think it's important that we connect more with sociology. We may find certain behavior against the norms of an individual, but it might be completely in line with the norms of a certain group or neighborhoods. I think that is what we have been ignoring too much in our work: we still focus too much on the individual and not the neighborhood.

In summary, our behavior is guided by the impetus to seek out rewards and avoid threats, and is regulated by top-down control mechanisms when simple approach and avoidance behaviors are insufficient to reach our goals. These regulatory mechanisms mature during childhood and adolescence, with adolescence marked by heightened reward-seeking and peer influence, as well as inconsistent engagement of self-control. On the whole, individual differences in both self-control and sensation-seeking in adolescence can be linked to real-world decision-making differences throughout life.

SUMMARY

- From a young age, we exhibit approach and avoidance behaviors; by contrast, our capacity for self-control matures slowly
- Patient data from individuals with damage to the frontal regions demonstrate a corresponding decrement in behavioral and emotional control
- Injury to the prefrontal regions during childhood limits development of networks of regions that together support goal-directed behavior
- Specific regions in prefrontal cortex have been implicated in self-control in neutral and/or motivationally salient contexts

- Delay-of-gratification tasks approximate the types of behaviors we want to understand and thus have ecological validity and are useful in studies of young children
- Interactions between prefrontal regions and the ventral striatum predict self-control in the face of temptation
- Early self-control ability, as indexed by the marshmallow task, was demonstrated to be a predictor of an individual's ability to regulate multiple aspects of behavior over the entire course of life
- More recent research demonstrates that children's specific experiences and expectations play a role in the nature of the relationship between self-control ability and long-term behavior regulation
- Adolescence is the time in life when sensation-seeking and risk-taking are highest; however, individuals vary widely in these attributes
- Adolescents generally show heightened activation of reward-related regions during risky decision-making

REVIEW QUESTIONS

What are the key drivers of behavior?

What have we learned from patient research about the neural underpinnings of self-control?

How is self-control studied in naturalistic settings, and how is it studied in the laboratory?

What evidence is there that self-control early in childhood predicts future life outcomes? Is there more to the story than that?

When (if ever) does self-control fully mature?

How could it be advantageous for the neural system that underlies self-control to develop slowly?

Are the same brain regions involved in self-control in a neutral context and a motivationally salient one? What types of tasks are used to study each, and what have they shown in terms of developmental change?

Why is risk-taking during adolescence thought to be evolutionarily advantageous, on the whole? What can happen when it goes awry?

What is the traditional account of the neural basis of adolescent risk-taking? What evidence supports it, and in what ways is it incomplete?

What are the changes in adolescence that could lead to either positive or negative life trajectories? What role do peers play?

Further Reading

Casey, B. J. (2015). Beyond simple models of self-control to circuit-based accounts of adolescent behavior. *Annual Review of Psychology*, 66, 295–319. https://doi.org/10.1146/annurev-psych-010814-015156

Chein, J., Albert, D., O'Brien, L., Uckert, K., & Steinberg, L. (2011). Peers increase adolescent risk taking by enhancing activity in the brain's reward circuitry. *Developmental Science*, 14(2), F1–F10. https://doi.org/10.1111/j.1467-7687.2010.01035.x

Mischel, W., Shoda, Y., & Rodriguez, M. I. (1989). Delay of gratification in children. *Science*, 24(4907), 933–938. https://doi.org/10.1126/science.2658056

References

Anderson, S. W., Bechara, A., Damasio, H., Tranel, D., & Damasio, A. R. (1999). Impairment of social and moral behavior related to early damage in human prefrontal cortex. *Nature Neuroscience*, 2(11), 1032–1037. https://doi.org/10.1038/14833

Aron, A. R., & Poldrack, R. A. (2006). Cortical and subcortical contributions to stop signal response inhibition: Role of the subthalamic nucleus. *The Journal of Neuroscience*, 26(9), 2424–2433. https://doi.org/10.1523/JNEUROSCI.4682-05.2006

Aron, A. R., Robbins, T. W., & Poldrack, R. A. (2014). Inhibition and the right inferior frontal cortex: One decade on. *Trends in Cognitive Sciences*, 18(4), 177–185. https://doi.org/10.1016/j.tics.2013.12.003

Berman, M. G., Yourganov, G., Askren, M. K., Ayduk, O., Casey, B. J., Gotlib, I. H., Kross, E., McIntosh, A. R., Strother, S., Wilson, N. L., Zayas, V., Mischel, W., Shoda, Y., & Jonides, J. (2013). Dimensionality of brain networks linked to life-long individual differences in self-control. *Nature Communications*, 4(1), 1373. https://doi.org/10.1038/ncomms2374

Bjork, J. M., & Pardini, D. A. (2015). Who are those "risk-taking adolescents"? Individual differences in developmental neuroimaging research. *Developmental Cognitive Neuroscience*, 11, 56–64. https://doi.org/10.1016/j.dcn.2014.07.008

Blankenstein, N. E., Telzer, E. H., Do, K. T., van Duijvenvoorde, A. C. K., & Crone, E. A. (2020). Behavioral and neural pathways supporting the development of prosocial and risk-taking behavior across adolescence. *Child Development*, 91(3), e665–e681. https://doi.org/10.1111/cdev.13292

Cai, W., Duberg, K., Padmanabhan, A., Rehert, R., Bradley, T., Carrion, V., & Menon, V. (2019). Hyperdirect insula-basal-ganglia pathway and adult-like maturity of global brain responses predict inhibitory control in children. *Nature Communications*, 10(1), 1–13. https://doi.org/10.1038/s41467-019-12756-8

Cai, W., Ryali, S., Chen, T., Li, C. S. R., & Menon, V. (2014). Dissociable roles of right inferior frontal cortex and anterior insula in inhibitory control: Evidence from intrinsic and task-related functional parcellation, connectivity, and response profile analyses across multiple datasets. *The Journal of Neuroscience*, 34(44), 14652–14667. https://doi.org/10.1523/JNEUROSCI.3048-14.2014

Casey, B. J. (2015). Beyond simple models of self-control to circuit-based accounts of adolescent behavior. *Annual Review of Psychology*, 66, 295–319. https://doi.org/10.1146/annurev-psych-010814-015156

Casey, B. J., Somerville, L. H., Gotlib, I. H., Ayduk, O., Franklin, N. T., Askren, M. K., Jonides, J., Berman, M. G., Wilson, N. L., Teslovich, T., Glover, G., Zayas, V., Mischel, W., & Shoda, Y. (2011). Behavioral and neural correlates of delay of gratification 40 years later. *Proceedings of the National Academy of Sciences of the United States of America*, 108(36), 14998–15003. https://doi.org/10.1073/pnas.1108561108

Chatham, C. H., Claus, E. D., Kim, A., Curran, T., Banich, M. T., & Munakata, Y. (2012). Cognitive control reflects context monitoring, not motoric stopping, in response inhibition. *PloS One*, 7(2), e31546. https://doi.org/10.1371/journal.pone.0031546

Chein, J., Albert, D., O'Brien, L., Uckert, K., & Steinberg, L. (2011). Peers increase adolescent risk taking by enhancing activity in the brain's reward circuitry. *Developmental Science*, 14(2), F1–F10. https://doi.org/10.1111/j.1467-7687.2010.01035

Constantinidis, C., & Luna, B. (2019). Neural substrates of inhibitory control maturation in adolescence. *Trends in Neurosciences*, 42(9), 604–616. https://doi.org/10.1016/j.tins.2019.07.004

Crone, E. A., & Dahl, R. E. (2012). Understanding adolescence as a period of social–affective engagement and goal flexibility. *Nature Reviews Neuroscience*, 13(9), 636–650. https://doi.org/10.1038/nrn3313

Dahl, R. E., Allen, N. B., Wilbrecht, L., & Suleiman, A. B. (2018). Importance of investing in adolescence from a developmental science perspective. *Nature*, 554(7693), 441–450. https://doi.org/10.1038/nature25770

Davidow, J. Y., Insel, C., & Somerville, L. H. (2018). Adolescent development of value-guided goal pursuit. *Trends in Cognitive Sciences*, 22(8), 725–736. https://doi.org/10.1016/j.tics.2018.05.003

Demidenko, M. I., Huntley, E. D., Jahn, A., Thomason, M. E., Monk, C. S., & Keating, D. P. (2020). Cortical and subcortical response to the anticipation of reward in high and average/low risk-taking adolescents. *Developmental Cognitive Neuroscience*, 44, 100798. https://doi.org/10.1016/j.dcn.2020.100798

Dmitrieva, J., Monahan, K. C., Cauffman, E., & Steinberg, L. (2012). Arrested development: The effects of incarceration on the development of psychosocial maturity. *Development and Psychopathology*, 24(3), 1073–1090. https://doi.org/10.1017/s0954579412000545

Duell, N., Steinberg, L., Icenogle, G., Chein, J., Chaudhary, N., Di Giunta, L., Dodge, K. A., Fanti, K. A., Lansford, J. E., Oburu, P., Pastorelli, C., Skinner, A. T., Sorbring, E., Tapanya, S., Uribe Tirado, L. M., Alampay, L. P., Al-Hassan, S. M., Takash, H. M. S., Bacchini, D., & Chang, L. (2018). Age patterns in risk taking across the world. *Journal of Youth and Adolescence*, 47(5), 1052–1072. https://doi.org/10.1007/s10964-017-0752-y

Dully, H., & Fleming, C. (2008). *My lobotomy: A memoir*. Crown.

Ernst, M., Pine, D. S., & Hardin, M. (2006). Triadic model of the neurobiology of motivated behavior in adolescence. *Psychological Medicine*, 36(3), 299–312. https://doi.org/10.1017/S0033291705005891

Fairchild, G., Passamonti, L., Hurford, G., Hagan, C. C., von dem Hagen, E. A., van Goozen, S. H., Goodyer, I. M., & Calder, A. J. (2011). Brain structure abnormalities in early-onset and adolescent-onset conduct disorder. *The American Journal of Psychiatry*, 168(6), 624–633. https://doi.org/10.1176/appi.ajp.2010.10081184

Fuster, J. M. (2001). The prefrontal cortex – An update: Time is of the essence. *Neuron*, 30(2), 319–333. https://doi.org/10.1016/S0896-6273(01)00285-9

Galvan, A. (2010). Adolescent development of the reward system. *Frontiers in Human Neuroscience*, 4(6). https://doi.org/10.3389/neuro.09.006.2010

Galvan, A., Hare, T. A., Parra, C. E., Penn, J., Voss, H., Glover, G., & Casey, B. J. (2006). Earlier development of the accumbens relative to orbitofrontal cortex might underlie risk-taking behavior in adolescents. *The Journal of Neuroscience*, 26(25), 6885–6892. https://doi.org/10.1523/JNEUROSCI.1062-06.2006

Gerstadt, C. L., Hong, Y. J., & Diamond, A. (1994). The relationship between cognition and action: Performance of children 3½–7 years old on a Stroop-like day-night test. *Cognition*, 53(2), 129–153. https://doi.org/10.1016/0010-0277(94)90068-X

Gogtay, N., Giedd, J., Lusk, L., Hayashi, K., Greenstein, D., Vaituzis, A., Nugent, T., Herman, D., Clasen, L., Toga, A., Rapoport, J., & Thompson, P. (2004). Dynamic mapping of human cortical development during childhood through early adulthood. *Proceedings of the National Academy of Sciences of the United States of America*, 101, 8174–8179. https://doi.org/10.1073/pnas.0402680101

Herman, A. M., Critchley, H. D., & Duka, T. (2018). Risk-taking and impulsivity: The role of mood states and interoception. *Frontiers in Psychology*, 9. https://doi.org/10.3389/fpsyg.2018.01625

Kahn, L. E., Peake, S. J., Dishion, T. J., Stormshak, E. A., & Pfeifer, J. H. (2015). Learning to play it safe (or not): Stable and evolving neural responses during adolescent risky decision-making. *Journal of Cognitive Neuroscience*, 27(1), 13–25. https://doi.org/10.1162/jocn_a_00694

Kidd, C., Palmeri, H., & Aslin, R. N. (2013). Rational snacking: Young children's decision-making on the marshmallow task is moderated by beliefs about environmental reliability. *Cognition*, 126(1), 109–114. https://doi.org/10.1016/j.cognition.2012.08.004

Kuhnen, C. M., & Knutson, B. (2005). The neural basis of financial risk taking. *Neuron*, 47(5), 763–770. https://doi.org/10.1016/j.neuron.2005.08.008

Luerssen, A., Gyurak, A., Ayduk, O., Wendelken, C., & Bunge, S. A. (2015). Delay of gratification in childhood linked to cortical interactions with the nucleus accumbens. *Social Cognitive and Affective Neuroscience*, 10(12), 1769–1776. https://doi.org/10.1093/scan/nsv068

Luna, B., Marek, S., Larsen, B., Tervo-Clemmens, B., & Chahal, R. (2015). An integrative model of the maturation of cognitive control. *Annual Review of Neuroscience*, 38, 151–170. https://doi.org/10.1146/annurev-neuro-071714-034054

Luna, B., & Wright, C. (2016). Adolescent brain development: Implications for the juvenile criminal justice system. In K. Heilbrun, D. DeMatteo, & N. E. S. Goldstein (Eds.), *APA handbook of psychology and juvenile justice* (pp. 91–116). American Psychological Association. https://doi.org/10.1037/14643-005

Mahmoudzadeh, M., Dehaene-Lambertz, G., Fournier, M., Kongolo, G., Goudjil, S., Dubois, J., Grebe, R., & Wallois, F. (2013). Syllabic discrimination in premature human infants prior to complete formation of cortical layers. *Proceedings of the National Academy of Sciences of the United States of America*, 110(12), 4846–4851. https://doi.org/10.1073/pnas.1212220110

Michaelson, L. E., & Munakata, Y. (2016). Trust matters: Seeing how an adult treats another person influences preschoolers' willingness to delay gratification. *Developmental Science*, 19(6), 1011–1019. https://doi.org/10.1111/desc.12388

Michaelson, L. E., & Munakata, Y. (2020). Same data set, different conclusions: Preschool delay of gratification predicts later behavioral outcomes in a preregistered study. *Psychological Science*, 31(2), 193–201. https://doi.org/10.1177/0956797619896270

Mischel, W., Shoda, Y., & Rodriguez, M. I. (1989). Delay of gratification in children. *Science*, 244(4907), 933–938. https://doi.org/10.1126/science.2658056

Moffitt, T. E., Arseneault, L., Belsky, D., Dickson, N., Hancox, R. J., Harrington, H., Houts, R., Poulton, R., Roberts, B. W., Ross, S., Sears, M. R., Thomson, W. M., & Caspi, A. (2011). A gradient of childhood self-control predicts health, wealth, and public safety. *Proceedings of the National Academy of Sciences of the United States of America*, 108(7), 2693–2698. https://doi.org/10.1073/pnas.1010076108

Ó Briain, D. (2019, June 6). *Dara O Briain – Crowd Tickler – Phineas Gage* [Video]. www.youtube.com/watch?v=laBbr8ic6ZY

O'Driscoll, K., & Leach, J. P. (1998). "No longer Gage": An iron bar through the head. Early observations of personality change after injury to the prefrontal cortex. *The British Medical Journal (Clinical Research Ed.)*, 317(7174), 1673–1674. https://doi.org/10.1136/bmj.317.7174.1673a

Ordaz, S. J., Foran, W., Velanova, K., & Luna, B. (2013). Longitudinal growth curves of brain function underlying inhibitory control through adolescence. *The Journal of Neuroscience*, 33(46), 18109–18124. https://doi.org/10.1523/JNEUROSCI.1741-13.2013

Peters, S., Peper, J. S., Van Duijvenvoorde, A. C. K., Braams, B. R., & Crone, E. A. (2017). Amygdala–orbitofrontal connectivity predicts alcohol use two years later: A longitudinal neuroimaging study on alcohol use in adolescence. *Developmental Science*, 20(4), e12448. https://doi.org/10.1111/desc.12448

Pievsky, M. A., & McGrath, R. E. (2017). The neurocognitive profile of attention-deficit/hyperactivity disorder: A review of meta-analyses. *Archives of Clinical Neuropsychology*, 33(2), 143–157. https://doi.org/10.1093/arclin/acx055

Samea, F., Soluki, S., Nejati, V., Zarei, M., Cortese, S., Eickhoff, S. B., Tahmasian, M., & Eickhoff, C. R. (2019). Brain alterations in children/adolescents with ADHD revisited: A neuroimaging meta-analysis of 96 structural and functional studies. *Neuroscience & Biobehavioral Reviews*, 100, 1–8. https://doi.org/10.1016/j.neubiorev.2019.02.011

Sebastian, C., Burnett, S., & Blakemore, S.-J. (2008). Development of the self-concept during adolescence. *Trends in Cognitive Sciences*, 12(11), 441–446. https://doi.org/10.1016/j.tics.2008.07.008

Sherman, L., Rosenbaum, G. M., Smith, A. R., Botdorf, M. A., Fettich, K., Patrianakos, J. L., McCloskey, M., Steinberg, L. D., & Chein, J. M. (2019). The interactive effects of peers and alcohol on functional brain connectivity in young adults. *NeuroImage*, 197, 264–272. https://doi.org/10.1016/j.neuroimage.2019.04.003

Sherman, L., Steinberg, L., & Chein, J. (2018). Connecting brain responsivity and real-world risk taking: Strengths and limitations of current methodological approaches. *Developmental Cognitive Neuroscience*, 33, 27–41. https://doi.org/10.1016/j.dcn.2017.05.007

Steinberg, L. (2009). Adolescent development and juvenile justice. *Annual Review of Clinical Psychology*, 5, 459–485. https://doi.org/10.1146/annurev.clinpsy.032408.153603. PMID: 19327037

Steinberg, L., Albert, D., Cauffman, E., Banich, M., Graham, S., & Woolard, J. (2008). Age differences in sensation seeking and impulsivity as indexed by behavior and self-report: Evidence for a dual systems model. *Developmental Psychology*, 44(6), 1764–1778. https://doi.org/10.1037/a0012955

Sweeney, J. A., Mintun, M. A., Kwee, S., Wiseman, M. B., Brown, D. L., Rosenberg, D. R., & Carl, J. R. (1996). Positron emission tomography study of voluntary saccadic eye movements and spatial working memory. *Journal of Neurophysiology*, 75(1), 454–468. https://doi.org/10.1152/jn.1996.75.1.454

Telzer, E. H., Fuligni, A. J., Lieberman, M. D., Miernicki, M. E., & Galván, A. (2015). The quality of adolescents' peer relationships modulates neural sensitivity to risk taking. *Social Cognitive and Affective Neuroscience*, 10(3), 389–398. https://doi.org/10.1093/scan/nsu064

Tervo-Clemmens, B., Quach, A., Calabro, F. J., Foran, W., & Luna, B. (2020). Meta-analysis and review of functional neuroimaging differences underlying adolescent vulnerability to substance use. *NeuroImage*, 209, 116476. https://doi.org/10.1016/j.neuroimage.2019.116476

Thorpe, H. H. A., Hamidullah, S., Jenkins, B. W., & Khokhar, J. Y. (2020). Adolescent neurodevelopment and substance use: Receptor expression and behavioral consequences. *Pharmacology & Therapeutics*, 206, 107431. https://doi.org/10.1016/j.pharmthera.2019.107431

Tymula, A., Rosenberg Belmaker, L., Roy, A., Ruderman, L., Manson, K., Glimcher, P., & Levy, I. (2012). Adolescents' risk-taking behavior is driven by tolerance to ambiguity. *Proceedings of the National Academy of Sciences of the United States of America*, 109, 17135–17140. https://doi.org/10.1073/pnas.1207144109

van den Bos, W., Rodriguez, C. A., Schweitzer, J. B., & McClure, S. M. (2015). Adolescent impatience decreases with increased frontostriatal connectivity. *Proceedings of the National Academy of Sciences of the United States of America*, 112(29), E3765–E3774. https://doi.org/10.1073/pnas.1423095112

van Hoorn, J., Shablack, H., Lindquist, K. A., & Telzer, E. H. (2019). Incorporating the social context into neurocognitive models of adolescent decision-making: A neuroimaging meta-analysis. *Neuroscience & Biobehavioral Reviews*, 101, 129–142. https://doi.org/10.1016/j.neubiorev.2018.12.024

Van Horn, J. D., Irimia, A., Torgerson, C. M., Chambers, M. C., Kikinis, R., & Toga, A. W. (2012). Mapping connectivity damage in the case of Phineas Gage. *PloS One*, 7(5), e37454. https://doi.org/10.1371/journal.pone.0037454

Watts, T. W., Duncan, G. J., & Quan, H. (2018). Revisiting the marshmallow test: A conceptual replication investigating links between early delay of gratification and later outcomes. *Psychological Science*, 29(7), 1159–1177. https://doi.org/10.1177/0956797618761661

Whitton, A. E., Treadway, M. T., & Pizzagalli, D. A. (2015). Reward processing dysfunction in major depression, bipolar disorder and schizophrenia. *Current Opinion in Psychiatry*, 28(1), 7–12. https://doi.org/10.1097/YCO.0000000000000122

Williams, B. R., Ponesse, J. S., Schachar, R. J., Logan, G. D., & Tannock, R. (1999). Development of inhibitory control across life span. *Developmental Psychology*, 35(1), 205–213. https://doi.org/10.1037/00012-1649.25.1.205

World Health Organization. (2014). *Health for the world's adolescents: A second chance in the second decade. Summary*. World Health Organization. https://apps.who.int/iris/handle/10665/112750

Zhou, Q., Chen, S. H., & Main, A. (2012). Commonalities and differences in the research on children's effortful control and executive function: A call for an integrated model of self-regulation. *Child Development Perspectives*, 6(2), 112–121. https://doi.org/10.1111/j.1750-8606.2011.00176.x

14   Key Themes and Future Directions

In the late 1980s, the field of DCN was just a glimmer in a handful of researchers' eyes. It's exciting to see how far we've come! Through sheer curiosity, determination, and hard work, we have made great strides towards understanding how the brain changes from the prenatal period through adulthood, at both the macroscopic and microscopic levels. We've learned about some of the genetic and epigenetic processes that influence brain development, and that underpin individual differences and neurodevelopmental conditions. We've also gained insights into the neural underpinnings of the development of many different cognitive and socioemotional capacities. This research has captured the public's interest, as well as public policymakers: DCN researchers now have a seat at the table in deliberations about numerous societal issues. However, there's still much to be done on theoretical and methodological fronts – and with regard to practical application. The field is young, and we need more great researchers. Maybe you will be one of them.

14.1   Overview

There are numerous topics that require further study, and many open questions remain about how brain development relates to the emergence of cognitive abilities, as well as about the complex interactions between genes, brains, environment, and behavior. Our effort in this book has been to provide a broad overview of several central topics of interest to the field; there are many additional topics we have not been able to address. In this concluding chapter, we summarize some "big picture" take-home points and address current limitations in the field. We also outline a few cutting-edge lines of research that are developing rapidly at the time of writing. Our hope is to inspire students to pursue these exciting new directions in their own research. We end by discussing the broader impact that DCN research has had and will continue to have in years to come. Overall, these efforts will lead to better understanding of the reciprocal relationships among gene expression, brain structure and function, and contextual influences on how children develop and learn. We should note that the first half of this chapter is best suited to a more advanced audience, particularly graduate students and DCN researchers; the second half includes commentary on societal relevance that should be of interest to a broad audience.

14.1.1 The Developmental Process Is Probabilistic

A crucial point to remember is that the developmental process itself is probabilistic. Yes, the developing fetus is a product of a series of prespecified developmental events, but even these highly prespecified processes are subject to the impact of genetic variability, contextual influence, developmental noise … and random factors affecting all three. Thus, brain development can be thought of as the product of a complex series of dynamic and adaptive processes whose ultimate outcome is probabilistic. While the process is highly constrained by the genetic code, which provides the initial organizational recipe, each outcome is unique. As a result, the same genes do not yield the same person, as we see in monozygotic twins.

Brain development is generally constrained within a fixed range of possible outcomes. Many different cell types contribute to the emergence of neural structures and functions, helping brain cells organize themselves into circuits – first locally, and then at increasingly remote levels of connectivity that may span the entire brain. Because genes mediate the biochemical processes that underlie instantiation of these cellular circuits, genetic variability can (and does) have an impact on their formation. Likewise, even *in utero*, there is a measurable effect of environmental input both internal and external to the developing fetus. Sometimes the impact of this variation is easy to observe, as when a fetus exposed to environmental toxins or bearing a significant genetic mutation is born with observable phenotypic abnormalities. More often, these different sources of variability simply manifest as the vast array of individual differences we observe among humans.

This probabilistic process is constructive, and continues to shape cognition by building up mental representations of the world based on co-occurrences, contingencies, and logical inferencing (or best guesses) about what a perceptual input actually *is* in an environment in which the distal signal is often degraded or ambiguous. Memory works the same way, as do language acquisition and social learning.

We also want to underscore that, given that structural changes build on each other rapidly over the prenatal period, extreme deviations from the typical embryonic developmental trajectory are generally not compatible with life. Indeed, it is estimated that between 25 and 30 percent of all pregnancies end in spontaneous abortion, or miscarriage, defined as loss of pregnancy within 20 weeks of conception (Griebel et al., 2005; Linnakaari et al., 2019). Thus, what we know about early brain development is based on brains in bodies that have made it well past this initial filtering stage. For practical purposes, this means the norms and variability in developmental outcomes that DCN researchers study have already been through a Darwinian culling process.

14.1.2 There Are No Genes "for" Psychological and Behavioral Traits

When we observe that genes contribute to some cognitive process, we are only saying that there are genetic variants that have an impact on that process, not that there is a gene *for* that process (or resulting phenotype). This is where confounding the two meanings of gene as outlined in Chapter 3 – a unit of heredity and a means by which protein production is made possible – leads people astray in their thinking. There are situations where the meanings firmly overlap, as in the case for genes for eye color. But even eye color is not controlled (as was previously thought) in a strictly Mendelian fashion! When you get into the domain of psychological processes, you are well past the point at which genes have a one-to-one mapping to phenotypic outcomes. There is no gene for intelligence or sociability; there are genes that contribute to the construction of neural circuits that underlie intelligence or sociability. There is enormous wiggle room for variability to emerge in the complex processes underlying capacities like the development of perceptual acuity, cognitive flexibility, and interpersonal awareness.

14.1.3 Variation in Neural Circuits Contributes to Individual Differences

Neural systems have diverse functional roles, from instantiating the simplest reflexive behavior to supporting complex cognitive processes. In the cerebral cortex, the development of anatomically distributed cortical and subcortical regions underlies the emergence of functional domains that are the focus of DCN research. These include domains as diverse as visual and auditory perception, memory, social cognition, and cognitive control. The developmental organization of neural circuits is a remarkably complex process that is influenced by genetic predispositions, environmental events, neuroplastic responses to experiential demand, and the stochastic noise that is part and parcel of the developmental process itself. All these inputs impact the emerging individual by modulating connectivity and communication among neurons, both within and across individual brain regions and circuits. DCN research aims to contextualize the developmental origins of the wide array of developmental outcomes seen in humans. Critical to this enterprise is delineating how the neural circuits supporting those outcomes develop, and how those processes result in the developmental epochs we have described in this book, which vary across multiple levels of organizational change as a function of the developmental process itself.

14.2 Future Directions in Theoretical Approaches

A theoretical framework – of the kind one typically encounters in the DCN literature – is a general conceptual system. It provides building blocks, but often is too general to provide mechanistic understanding. By contrast, a theory is a scientific proposition. It may be conveyed verbally, mathematically, logically, or visually (i.e., as a set of figures introducing causal relations). Crucially, any of these forms has as its aim the description, explanation, or prediction of a set of phenomena. To move from framework to theory requires specification of mechanism, which then guides hypothesis formation. There is much to be done to move DCN from general frameworks to more theory-specific testing.

14.2.1 Interactive Specialization as a Guiding Framework

As we have outlined it in this book, DCN's focus is on how specialized and interconnected functional networks emerge in the human brain over developmental time to support a range of behaviors of interest. To frame this approach, we introduced Mark Johnson's interactive specialization hypothesis (Chapters 1 and 3), describing it as a domain-general framework to guide both the collection and interpretation of data on the relationship between human functional brain development and psychological/behavioral traits of interest (Johnson, 2011).

This take-home perspective may not have been apparent to you as you worked through the preceding chapters, given the breadth of research topics, approaches, and findings. Indeed, the mix of information may have appeared jumbled (although we hope not) – a jumbling that Johnson himself has raised as potentially problematic about the field. Where some researchers propose "local" hypotheses to motivate a given set of studies, appealing specifically to domain-specific theories (e.g., about face perception or theory of mind) to account for their data, others aim to characterize specific processes under a domain-general framework. As Johnson (2011) states, support for the interactive specialization framework will depend on our ability to relate neuroanatomical measures of connectivity change with changes in the function in question. Such an effort necessarily rests on a mechanistic understanding of the processes mediated by both individual regions and broader networks. In short, we need to move from framework to theory.

At the same time, mountains of data are being collected that suggest interesting genetic and/ or neural bases for any given typical or atypical behavior. The "bigger picture" meaning of such findings has yet to be drawn. Again, this is because many such surprising observations are made with no explanatory framework whatsoever. How can we understand such observations – much less interpret and explain them – within the broader context of the findings reviewed, which themselves reflect a multitude of methods and populations? Great question!

We suggest that, while the interactive specialization framework is the most consistent one with our aim of characterizing how specialized functional neural circuits emerge in children over developmental time, we have a long way to go towards providing explicit mechanistic accounts of how this happens. Changing brain circuits certainly contribute to children's cognitive development, but the link between neural changes and overt behavioral outcomes is still fuzzy. Moreover, given the problems inherent to cross-sectional studies (Chapter 2), direct links between behavior and test-specific hypotheses will require longitudinal task-based studies of brain development. More and more longitudinal research is being conducted – fortunately, as this is a necessary step towards continued progress in our field.

14.2.2 Making Theory Explicit

Of course, interactive specialization is not the only game in town. There are other frameworks that our field would benefit from exploring further. For example, the evolutionary principles on which DCN is based are often assumed rather than made explicit. In recent years, a theoretical framework based in evolutionary systems theory has been outlined: the hierarchically mechanistic mind (HMM; Badcock et al., 2019). While similar to interactive specialization in emphasizing networks of hierarchically embedded systems, this new framework posits that the brain is a complex adaptive system generated by hierarchical neural dynamics. As a developmental psychology-adjacent theory, HMM puts less emphasis on how these hierarchies are put into place and more on the evolutionarily instantiated mechanisms that sustain their functional structure. Indeed, if our aim is to study the mechanisms governing development of human social and cognitive competencies – including genetic and ecological ones, as well as the gene–environment interactions that adapt these competencies to specific environmental conditions – then mechanistic aspects of evolutionary theory must be part of the equation.

All too often in DCN, mechanistic status is attributed to abilities that are likely to be evolutionarily based, yet that are woefully underspecified. A good example of this is when researchers appeal to the "mirror neuron" system as their mechanistic explanation for development of various aspects of social cognition without a clear understanding of where such a system came from (or if it even exists!). Meanwhile, imitation can be (and has been) described based on basic learning processes (i.e., Hebbian or associative). By appealing to mirror neurons as an explanation for social cognition, further elucidation of its mechanistic foundations stalled for 15 years. Indeed, it was two decades ago that neuroscientists argued that mirror neurons were based in Hebbian learning processes (Keysers & Perrett, 2004). If there had been more interest early on in establishing a mechanism of action – as opposed to embracing mirror neurons as innate endowments – the conversation that is now happening about imitation (e.g., de Klerk et al., 2019) could have advanced much more quickly. Thus, a DCN approach that embraces the need for mechanistic explanation, however that effort is theoretically couched, has implications for faster scientific progress.

Better delineation is needed of many more mechanisms that underlie phenomena considered unique to humans. Continuing with the evolutionary perspective, we might focus on what changes enable seemingly human- (or hominoid) specific capacities. Maybe they are not human-specific at all! Asking the hard questions will advance our theoretical grounding in important ways.

14.2.3 Good Theory Forces Hard Questions

Hard questions abound in DCN, but good theory helps shape them into testable hypotheses. For example, a good general question is what the optimal window of development is for some particular form of learning. A better, more specific question is how the opening and closing of these windows is controlled in the first place. Just such a question has been leading to radical insights into mechanisms of plasticity. Recall the oft-repeated point that at least half of the cells in the human brain are non-neuronal glial cells. We often observe that they must be doing a lot more than we currently know (Chapters 4 and 5). Indeed, recent findings using a mouse model of visual plasticity reveal a critical role of a particular type of glial cell – astrocytes – in the development and control of critical periods (Ribot et al., 2021). The commentary accompanying the initial report of these findings (Kofuji & Araque, 2021) speculates that astrocytes likely critically influence a range of molecular and signaling pathways that support developmentally constrained, use-dependent plasticity of neural circuits.

Another hard question relates to how the brain and body interact. Despite years of calls for embodied cognition to be taken seriously (see Mahon, 2015), critiques of this approach show no signs of letting up (Goldinger et al., 2016). Yet it is abundantly clear that we can no longer afford to consider the brain in isolation from the rest of the body (Grafton, 2020). For example, the brain interacts in a bidirectional fashion with the gut: the so-called "gut–brain axis." Anomalies in the gut microbiome have been linked to mood disorders, Autism Spectrum Disorder, and Attention Deficit Hyperactivity Disorder, so much so that researchers are looking into treating the gut microbiome, even in expecting mothers, as a way to prevent or treat neurodevelopmental disorders (Larroya et al., 2021). Relatedly, there is close communication between the immune system and the nervous system, and maternal inflammation – linked to stress, asthma, metabolic syndrome, autoimmune diseases, and more – is turning out to be a key player in the development of mood disorders and other neurodevelopmental disorders (Han et al., 2021). Thus, preventing or treating inflammation in expecting mothers and in children themselves is a possible way to support healthy brain development. Finally, links between malnutrition and the microbiome are being found to impact early neurodevelopment (Coley & Hsiao, 2021).

14.2.4 Levels of Structure Inform Levels of Analysis

> According to the systemist viewpoint every mental function
> is a function of a neural system, whether permanent or
> itinerant. This hypothesis suggests looking for the smallest
> neural system capable of effectively discharging the
> function(s) concerned, and so encourages neural modeling
> as well as the design of experimental techniques, such as the
> measure of blood flow into the various subsystems as an
> indicator of their activity.
>
> (Bunge, 1980, p. 41)

What is the "right" way to study the brain, and at what level of organization of the brain? Should we be studying large-scale brain networks, or small networks of neurons, or individual neurons, or individual genes or molecules? There is no right or wrong way, regardless of what researchers wedded to a particular level of analysis might have you believe: it all depends on the phenomenon we're investigating. We will only fully understand how the brain develops – and how the developing brain gives rise to the developing mind – if we tackle it at all levels of structure, with all available methods. There is no place here for scientific chauvinism: for a truly integrative understanding of complex phenomena, we need to be open to ways of thinking and doing science that are unfamiliar to us.

Uncertainty as to which levels of analysis have the most explanatory value is evident even within human brain imaging research. Here, the pendulum has swung over the past decade from intense effort to characterize the functions of individual brain regions to efforts to understand the functions of whole brain networks. At the time of writing, there is a heavy emphasis on advanced network analyses (discussed in Chapter 2), characterizing the development of large-scale brain systems with fMRI, EEG, fNIRS, and MEG – that is, at a high level of analysis.

At the same time, fMRI studies are reaching a *more detailed* level of analysis than has previously been possible, moving beyond univariate to multivariate analyses. Univariate analyses compare trial-averaged activation between task conditions and are generally used to characterize the function of fairly large regions of interest. By contrast, multivariate fMRI analytic approaches (Haxby et al., 2014; Kriegeskorte & Diedrichsen, 2019) take a more fine-grained approach to exploring how information is represented in the brain. These types of approaches can be adopted to more carefully test for increased specificity of activation to specific types of stimuli over development – that is, increased perceptual tuning – or differences between neurotypical children and clinical populations (for early efforts on this front, see O'Hearn et al., 2020). Thus, on the one hand, network analyses provide us with a bigger picture view of brain development than when DCN began, and multivariate approaches afford a more detailed view.

Having developed tools to study both brain networks and the functions of individual regions, the challenge is to better articulate how *individual brain networks* represent and/or process information, *informed by their connections to other brain networks*. In other words, we have had a good run of research examining how regions work together in networks; it is now imperative that we go back to understanding how these individual regions function in the context of those larger networks. Danielle Bassett and colleagues (Bassett et al., 2020, p. 524) nicely describe the importance of studying both how individual regions represent information and how, and what, they communicate with other regions: "The twin paths of representation and transmission move beyond the mapping of a country's borders, to record a city's statistics and the transportation networks along which traffic flows. [...] how do we combine these twin paths to understand the transmission of representations in the network of the brain?" By extension to brain development, we can use this dual approach to investigate the interactive specialization of the brain.

14.3 Future Directions in Methodological Approaches

Science is ever-evolving. Some of the changes are trends that come and go as particular topics capture researchers' attention, or as particular methods fall in and out of favor. Underneath these fluctuations, however, is an arc that bends towards greater understanding and more rigorous scholarship over the long term. In psychology and neuroscience, more rigorous standards are emerging, with scientific best practices becoming standardized and increasingly expected. For example, we now have preregistration, replication samples, and a move towards open science, all of which put greater emphasis on transparency and replicability (Poldrack et al., 2017). We are also seeing the adoption of new methods for probing brain structure, function, and development (see Box 14.1).

These trends are evident in DCN, as are several others. For one thing, we are starting to see more and more accelerated longitudinal studies (Chapter 2), which allow us to directly measure developmental change, as opposed to the age-related differences measured in cross-sectional studies. For another, we are seeing more studies in which brain data are used to *predict* child behavioral outcomes, rather than simply establishing correlations between our dependent and independent variables. Prediction is a more powerful approach, statistically (Poldrack et al., 2020) – and it has potential practical utility, as it could support early detection of children who develop neurodevelopmental disorders or struggle in school (Gabrieli et al., 2015).

Some of the trends we're seeing in DCN seem diametrically opposed, as we shall discuss below. One set of contrasting trends relates to levels of structure under investigation, with efforts to better characterize large-scale brain organization and – at the same time – to better understand individual brain regions. A second set relates to the tension between breadth and depth in exploration: specifically, the move towards larger sample sizes, on the one hand, and deeper characterization of a small number of participants on the other. Finally, a third set of opposing trends relates to hypothesis-driven versus exploratory research.

14.3.1 Scope of Investigations

We are seeing opposing trends in DCN towards larger samples, but also deeper characterization of a smaller number of participants. We are also seeing, on the one hand, a rise in exploratory research, often assisted by powerful machine learning algorithms, that reveal unanticipated effects in complex datasets – and on the other hand, a greater commitment to principled hypothesis-testing.

With respect to participant pools, we have witnessed in recent years a move towards large sample sizes, both in studies conducted in a single lab and in collaborative projects conducted across multiple coordinating laboratories. Pooled datasets such as those in the Many Babies Project, HCP Developing Human Connectome Project, and the Adolescent Brain and Cognitive Development (ABCD) study provide, for the first time, the massive scale of data needed to answer nuanced questions. Initially, a lot of this effort has focused on the logistical issues of getting these approaches to work; these efforts are now starting to pay off. Studies are starting to include hundreds of participants – or even thousands, as in the ABCD study being conducted at 19 sites across the United States (see Chapter 4). Compare that with the two-digit number sample sizes in the early days! (In 2002, one of us was the first author of an fMRI study on the neural basis of cognitive control development, with only 16 children and 16 adults (Bunge et al., 2002). Back then, that sample size was sufficient to get it published in a top journal ... not today!)

The impetus for this upward trend in sample size is three-fold. First, large sample sizes, especially if collected across multiple sites, help ensure the robustness of the findings. Second, large samples provide more power to tease apart the contributions of many (often interacting) variables, providing a more integrative understanding of complex phenomena. Third, larger sample sizes generally mean broader sampling, which better represents the diversity present across people.

Casting a wider net in terms of sample populations makes it possible to test whether findings generalize: that is, whether they reflect universal principles of development. For example, a recent study showed that a pattern of brain connectivity that has, across multiple studies, been associated with better cognitive performance does not hold for children living below the poverty line – an understudied population; this finding highlights the point that what is adaptive for one population may not be for another (Ellwood-Lowe et al., 2021). This discrepancy was observed between populations of children living in the same country (the United States); consider, then, how different the trajectories could be across countries with vastly different cultures and resources! Taking a global perspective, we must recognize that the vast majority of studies have been conducted on WEIRD populations: that is, participants from Western, Educated, Industrialized, Rich, Democratic nations. Thus, while we can fool ourselves into thinking that any effect that replicates across multiple studies involving WEIRD samples represents a general principle of cognitive or brain development, we can't make such a claim without conducting cross-cultural research (Falk et al., 2013). Culture is important but easily taken for granted because, like the air around us, it is invisible most of the time.

For these reasons – increased robustness, statistical power, and sample diversity – the push for larger and more diverse samples is a positive development. On the other hand, the larger the sample, the harder it is to do a deep dive into the data (there are only so many hours in the day). We are also beginning to see, in DCN, a more detailed exploration of individual children's brains. This alternative approach emphasizes precise characterization of individual children – for example, painstakingly identifying specific sulci in individual participants and showing that their location in the brain can reflect functional boundaries (Natu et al., 2021) and that they can predict individual differences in behavior (Voorhies et al., 2021). "Deep phenotyping" takes this movement towards closer investigation of individual participants one step further, intensively characterizing individual brains in many ways and/or many times (Poldrack et al., 2015; Gordon et al., 2017). This, too, is a positive trend in DCN, as we have up until now ignored important variability in brain anatomy.

Another set of contrasting trends, as noted above, is between increasingly hypothesis-driven and increasingly exploratory research. Both approaches have merit. On one hand, the open science movement is prompting researchers to clearly specify – that is, "preregister" – their key predictions and planned analyses before running a study (or, in the case of existing datasets, before conducting analyses). This approach, aimed at reducing the likelihood of reporting spurious results (Kupferschmidt, 2018), encourages researchers to think ever more deeply about their hypotheses and analytic plan. This movement has been very positive for the fields of psychology and neuroscience; however, the more faithfully we stick to our prespecified set of analyses, the less likely we are to uncover something unexpected. Part of being a great researcher is being alert to new findings and to unanticipated experimental outcomes. If bacteriologist Alexander Fleming had come back from vacation and not noticed that a few of his bacteria cultures had been killed by mold, he would not have discovered penicillin.

On the other end of the spectrum, we have also seen the adoption of powerful computational algorithms that make it possible to uncover patterns in large, complex datasets that we could never have dreamed up. The human brain is, paradoxically, more complex than we can fully grasp with our limited mental capacities; thus, our theories are oversimplifications. Enter machine learning: computers can crunch through massive datasets with many variables in a way that is totally theory-free, detecting patterns that we would surely miss if we only ever looked where we expected to find something. This trend is somewhat related to the issue of sample size, as the "big data" movement lends itself to hypothesis-free exploration. The moves towards more hypothesis-driven research and more exploratory research might seem wholly incompatible, but in fact we can have our cake and eat it, too: that is, we can preregister strong predictions while also exploring our data more fully, as long as we indicate which analyses were and were not planned.

14.3.2 The Importance of Formal Modeling

We highlighted computational and other models throughout this book, but we are aware that we have underrepresented the contribution that formal modeling makes to theory development. Modeling has greatly impacted our understanding of a range of cognitive and behavioral phenomena. For one thing, it provides a means by which to address the "levels of analysis" question (Chapter 1). Moreover, the process of specifying a model forces better specification of theory. Thus, modeling presents a win-win for DCN as a field. For example, fitting models to experimental data allows researchers to better understand the parameters of the algorithms underlying the phenomenon of interest, to delineate neural correlates of computational variables worth pursuing experimentally, and to causally relate effects of genes and environment on neural development.

Earlier, we equated the idea of theory with a framework or perspective. We should be clear that a framework provides the conceptual building blocks for creating models of complex systems, and thus helps move us towards clear theory. Likewise, good modeling leads to better science by forcing us to conceptually analyze, specify, and formalize intuitions that would otherwise remain underspecified, if they are specified at all.

Box 14.1 Emerging Approaches

There have been important technical advances in systems neuroscience that are shedding light on mechanisms of brain development. First are optogenetic approaches to precisely modify neural circuit activity in awake behaving animals (Box 9.1), as well as a chemogenetic approach based on DREADS (Designer Receptors Exclusively Activated by Designer Drugs). Second, simplified neural systems called brain organoids are being used to explore how the cellular structure of the brain is built (Box 4.1). Third, several approaches have potential therapeutic applications, like critical period manipulation (Box 5.2) and modification of epigenetic markers (Chapter 3).

There are also a number of promising cognitive neuroscientific approaches that have not yet been widely adopted in DCN, some of which are outlined below.

Wireless functional near-infrared spectroscopy (fNIRS): Near-infrared spectroscopy (fNIRS) is a popular technique for use with young children, although currently available systems have relatively low spatial and temporal resolution (Chapter 2). Up-and-coming systems feature a number of improvements on currently used technology, including wireless helmets and more densely packed infrared light detectors that make it possible to pinpoint brain activity more accurately – and to assess behavior in a more naturalistic setting than methods that require participants to sit or lie still.

Magnetoencephalography (MEG): MEG provides high spatial and temporal resolution and can be used to measure brain function across the lifespan, even prenatally (Chapter 2). However, MEG systems are not widely available at this time, particularly those designed for prenatal imaging or for use in very young children. An exciting new development is that of a MEG helmet that doesn't require a magnetically shielded room, which could lead to more widespread adoption of the method – and that is wireless, making it possible to assess more naturalistic behaviors.

Advanced anatomical MRI methods: A wide array of new MRI protocols and analytic approaches are enabling richer and more precise characterization of neuroanatomical features. In particular, a number of approaches are aimed at improving our measurement of white matter. For example, MR relaxometry yields a measure called myelin water fraction. Additionally, new modeling techniques for diffusion-weighted imaging data may provide more accurate white matter fiber tracking. There are also several approaches aimed at imaging myelin and other structures more directly based on tissue composition. In particular, these recent approaches have improved the measurement of superficial white matter fibers that are not visible with traditional imaging methods.

A measure called quantitative susceptibility mapping is used to estimate iron concentration, since myelin is rich in iron (so, too, are dopaminergic neurons; therefore, this method may also be an indirect marker of dopamine). Another measure is an index of macromolecular density, based on magnetization transfer effects, as there is a high concentration of macromolecules in the myelin sheath. It is possible to validate these methods in postmortem brains by relating these MR scans to tissue histology. These approaches, called "*in vivo* histology," probe structure at a more fine-grained level than do standard MRI and diffusion tensor imaging scans (e.g., Weiskopf et al., 2015).

Transcriptomics: High throughput transcriptomic methodologies, such as microarray analysis and RNA sequencing, have been applied to postmortem human brain tissue to identify genes and their role in brain organization and development. Transcriptomic datasets include that of adult brains as well as developing brains from different stages ranging from prenatal to adolescence. Therefore, it is possible to determine which genes are essential for different stages of cortical development, and how some play a role in the arealization of the cortex (Cadwell et al., 2019; Gomez et al., 2019).

14.4 Societal Relevance

Does, could, and/or *should* DCN research impact society? If so, how? Martha Farah, a pioneering neuroscientist who helped establish the field of Neuroethics 20 years ago, has said, "Any endeavor that depends on being able to understand, assess, predict, control, or improve human behavior is, in principle, a potential application area for neuroscience" (Farah, 2012, p. 573). This is true in spades for DCN; in fact, we could (and would love to) write a whole book about this important topic. For now, let us simply point to a number of societal issues that center around brain development, with the hope that this will whet your appetite to learn more.

Perhaps the most obvious application of DCN is to clinical and educational interventions. As we have touched on throughout the book, many neurological and psychiatric disorders and intellectual disabilities are rooted in atypical brain development. These include Autism Spectrum Disorder, schizophrenia, Attention Deficit Hyperactivity Disorder, mood disorders, communication disorders, motor coordination disorders, epilepsy, and general and specific learning impairments. To the extent that we understand the root causes of these disorders and how they unfold over time, we may be able to diagnose them earlier and more reliably, and thus to treat them more effectively.

With a view towards nipping developmental problems in the bud, there currently is a major push to identify both genetic and neural biomarkers that *predict* the future onset of a disorder (Gabrieli et al., 2015). For this, we must establish a baseline: that is, we must characterize the full extent of variability in the brain and behavior across a broad pediatric population to identify what falls well outside of the norm and why. We must also better understand the time course of brain plasticity (Chapter 5): At what point(s) in development does a given neural system have the greatest potential for change? The field called educational neuroscience – or Mind, Brain, and Education, a name that acknowledges the role of behavioral research – sits at the interface between DCN and education research/practice, and concerns itself with these issues and more.

DCN is also highly relevant for public health; more broadly, basic science research is critical for the development of sound public policies and legislation. While clinicians treat individual patients and occasionally provide preventative care, public health researchers and officials focus predominantly on preemptive measures that promote health and mitigate risk at the population level. They educate communities about beneficial and risky behaviors, and help to develop policies, regulations, bills, and laws that have broad impact on societal health. As but one example, their efforts on multiple fronts have helped to slow the transmission of Covid-19, from modeling the spread of the virus to educating the public to establishing guidelines and regulations around social distancing practices and vaccination. In the right political climate, they have the opportunity to make decisions based on the best available science. In the next section, we delve into some examples of public health campaigns that are founded on findings from DCN.

14.5 Public Health

There are many arenas in which DCN research has begun to inform – or *could* inform – decision-making with regards to public health, some of which we've touched on in earlier chapters. First, there is the question of how modifiable lifestyle variables, such as diet, exercise, and sleep, affect a child's potential for learning and brain plasticity. Ongoing research on these fronts has the potential to inform public health guidelines. (At the risk of dating ourselves, we still remember when the Reagan administration decided that ketchup counted as a serving of vegetables in American public schools!) In fact, research on the behavioral and neural consequences of adolescent sleep deprivation has begun to have an impact in the United States, leading some schools and school districts to delay school start-times to accommodate adolescents' shifted biological clock. Second, we need to better understand the impact of economic inequality and systemic racism on child development (see Chapter 5) – and communicate our results. Third is the issue of the high incidence of concussions and brain injuries among children and teens who play sports (particularly football, but also soccer, volleyball, field hockey, and even cheerleading and artistic swimming). This is a rampant issue that requires the perspective of DCN researchers. Third is the thorny issue of teens' rising access to substances of abuse. As longitudinal studies settle the question of whether heavy drug use alters the trajectory of brain development, there will need to be more conversation around this topic. We will touch on a few additional topical issues below, although this is by no means an exhaustive list of topics about which developmental researchers have something to say. In short, DCN touches on a broad range of societal issues, some of which are longstanding problems and some whose implications are only just becoming apparent.

14.5.1 Public Health Mandates

As we saw with attempts to mandate simple mask wearing in response to the Covid-19 pandemic, public health mandates – no matter how seemingly benign – are not at all guaranteed to work. Here is one success story, related to the fortification of wheat products. As we have learned, formation of the neural tube is a crucial step in the formation of the embryo (Chapter 4). A deficiency in one of the B vitamins, called folic acid or folate, can cause malformations ranging from fairly minor (spina bifida) to severe, or fatal (anencephaly, in which parts of the brain and skull fail to form). It turns out that enriching wheat flour with folic acid is an easy way to redress this deficiency at a population level (just as many countries enrich milk with calcium and Vitamin D) – and there are now regulations enforcing this fortification in many parts of the world. As a result, neural tube defects have fallen dramatically (e.g., 35 percent in the United States since mandatory folic acid fortification of wheat flour was introduced in 1998 (Centers for Disease Control and Prevention, 2010)).

Also related to prenatal development is the issue of alcohol exposure in the womb. How much can you drink during pregnancy, and when? Depending on which country you live in, and which doctor you ask, you may hear that drinking in moderation is acceptable, or that you should abstain altogether. (In the United States, where this practice is discouraged, 1 in 9 women continue to drink during pregnancy (Denny et al., 2019).) Prenatal alcohol exposure is a leading cause of a particular intellectual disability, fetal alcohol syndrome (FASD). The incidence of this syndrome is around 1 in 100 live births, and the level of severity varies depending on how much, how long, and when in gestation the fetus is exposed to alcohol. So, is there a safe amount of alcohol, or a safe window during development? Elizabeth Sowell, who has documented reduced brain volumes in children with fetal alcohol syndrome (Treit et al., 2013), co-authored a commentary (Charness et al., 2016, p. 82) stating, "We believe that the message that there is no known safe level of alcohol consumption during pregnancy is crucial for society at large. FASD [...] is completely preventable with abstinence from alcohol from conception to birth." The Centers for Disease Control and Prevention in the United States concurs.

14.5.2 Pressing Public Health Issues

Public health is important, a fact made all the more salient because, as we write this final chapter, Covid-19 is still surging in many countries. In places where vaccines are readily available, this surge is fueled in part by vaccine skepticism or hesitancy resulting from mounds of misinformation. This situation lays bare the extreme challenges that public health campaigns can face – and that a lack of scientific education can foment. Going forward, public health leaders urgently need answers to questions about the impact of Covid-19 on prenatal and postnatal brain development and brain function – as well as the impact of social isolation and remote schooling. While initial findings are trickling in, it will take years of longitudinal research to fully grasp the longer-term consequences of the pandemic on the infants, children, and adolescents who have lived through it. For now, while we wait for a larger body of evidence to accumulate, policymakers must make plans by drawing on what we do already know: for example, about how viruses (including coronaviruses) on the one hand, and social isolation on the other, impact brain development.

Likewise, officials must learn from prior public health campaigns, such as those aimed at combating the misconception that vaccines routinely administered in infancy cause autism. This claim originated with a fraudulent study published in a top medical journal in 1998. Although it was retracted 12 years later, the damage was already done: the study had been picked up by the media and championed by celebrities. Its impact is still being felt today, as parents shy away from vaccinating their children (ironically, this resistance has been particularly strong in some affluent and educated communities). The fact that untruths and misinformation spread more effectively than actual research findings is an important reminder to carefully evaluate what we read before sharing it with others.

Another pressing public health issue is that of environmental toxins and air pollutants that do, or might, affect the nervous system *in utero* or during child development (Chapter 3). As but one example, a large and meticulously conducted longitudinal study by Brenda Eskenazi and her team has associated exposure *in utero* to organophosphate pesticides with increased risk of Autism Spectrum Disorder, lower intellectual functioning, and poorer executive functioning in childhood and early adolescence (e.g., Sagiv et al., 2021). The researchers also conducted an fNIRS study on adolescents in this longitudinal cohort, observing differential brain activation during performance of an executive functions task (Sagiv et al., 2019). Based on these and other findings, Eskenazi and other scientists have called for a number of policy reforms regarding pesticide usage (Hertz-Picciotto et al., 2018).

Beyond pesticides, there is an untold number of chemical substances (estimates vary wildly) used in all variety of ways, from household products and cosmetics to chemicals used in manufacturing, agriculture, energy production, and on and on. Disturbingly, very few of these chemicals have been thoroughly assessed for their safety. Given evidence that toxins can cause genetic mutations and changes in gene expression (i.e., epigenetic changes; Chapter 3), this should be setting off alarm bells. Humans often use themselves as guinea pigs (or lab rats) under the assumption of "better living through chemistry." Moreover, even those chemicals that have been shown to have harmful effects on human health and development often continue to go unregulated or underregulated, in part for political reasons.

Even once chemical safety regulations are in place, it can be difficult to eradicate existing substances from our lives and to enforce those regulations. For example, children – especially those growing up in lower-income homes – are still routinely exposed to lead, a heavy metal that has been known for decades to disturb early brain development. Approximately 6 percent of all children aged 1–2 years, and 11 percent of Black (non-Hispanic) children aged 1–5 years have blood lead levels in the toxic range (American Academy of Child and Adolescent Psychiatry, 2017). Fortunately, identifying and treating lead poisoning quickly can help prevent children from suffering permanent damage. Unfortunately, however, the children most likely to get lead poisoning also lack access to quality health care and are more likely be exposed to harmful chemicals and air pollutants. For example, in the United States, racial demographics originally were the primary basis for decisions about where hazardous waste sites were to be placed (Commission for Racial Justice, 1987).

DCN researchers have a role to play in documenting and educating others about the effects of these and other toxins on brain development. Nowhere is collaborative research more important than in the case of public health issues. Traditionally, the basic science has had to trickle up to those in a position to implement policy changes. More recently, team science efforts tackle the interwoven issues in an informed way. Such "teams" may include not only researchers from DCN, but also geneticists, neuroscientists, psychologists, statisticians, epidemiologists, and researchers from the domain of public health. Collectively, these efforts could produce bullet-proof basic science with immediate implications for public health.

14.6 Communicating the Science

The only way to achieve evidence-based legislation and practices is to communicate our findings clearly. Establishing public engagement with science relies on a foundation of clear, concise communication about that science. This is far more challenging than it may appear at first blush. Communication about research goes well beyond translating jargon into clear and comprehensible language. A range of factors need to be considered, including one's goals, what needs to be conveyed, its format, and which individuals and/or organizations are involved. In the face of these factors, there are numerous challenges to successful communication, including a lay public with the full spectrum of preparedness for understanding scientific breakthroughs and the deterioration of traditional media structures introducing a wide range of scientific proficiency in the journalists communicating the findings.

14.6.1 DCN in the News

Research on brain development has long been of interest to clinicians treating children with neurodevelopmental disorders, but it wasn't in the public eye as it is today. Now, people from all sectors of society think and talk about it. Here is just a sampling of news headlines related to brain development from the month of June, 2021:

> *"The key role of astrocytes in cognitive development"*
> *"Talking To Children Is Critical For Brain Development, No Matter What Language Is Spoken"*
> *"Nutrition's Impact on a Child's Brain Development"*
> *"Lawsuits piling up against baby food firms over potential damage to infant brain development"*
> *"Marijuana use in teen years may hinder brain development, study finds"*
> *"Lack of math education adversely affects adolescent brain and cognitive development"*

This level of interest is inspiring, as it reminds us that what we study matters (more on that below). But it also comes with a downside, which is that the catchy headlines aren't always accurate. For example, take this recent headline: *"The Internet is doing irreparable damage to our brains."* Its claim may be correct, but the article cites no evidence related to the brain whatsoever.

Or, take this memorable headline from a few years ago: *"Cell-Phone Distracted Parenting Can Have Long-Term Consequences: Study."* An eye-catching title, to be sure, but it wholly misrepresented the science behind it. The actual study (Molet et al., 2016) showed that when mother rats were given insufficient bedding to assemble an adequate nest, they provided inconsistent care to their young pups, who later exhibited behaviors that have been linked to depression in humans. At no point in the study were the mother rats given cell phones! However, the journalist extrapolated from the data in an effort to convey the idea that distracted parenting can be harmful. (This underscores the need for training in science journalism.)

Such overgeneralizations and oversimplifications are common, even among reputable science media outlets – and let's not speak of media peddling "alternative facts." Clearly, we need to be discriminating "consumers" and sharers of media coverage. And those of us who publish and/or publicize research in a professional capacity need to do so responsibly.

14.6.2 Advising Policymakers and Practitioners

The environment in which children are conceived and live has long-term consequences for their developmental outcomes. The Center on the Developing Child at Harvard University and the associated National Scientific Council on the Developing Child have made great strides in educating policymakers, practitioners, and the public about the harmful effects of poverty, toxic stress, neglect, and maltreatment on child development.

This group also had the opportunity to weigh in on an important policy matter in the recent past. Under the US Family Separation Policy from around 2017–2019, thousands of migrant children were separated from their families at the US–Mexico border and kept in prison-like conditions. The youngest of these children, Baby Constantin, was only 4 months old when he was taken from his family and placed in a foster home (Dickerson, 2019). He was reunited with his family at 9 months. The 5 months he spent institutionalized have taken their toll: at 18 months, he was developmentally delayed, unable to speak even a few words or walk unassisted.

This calamity is all too reminiscent of the institutionalization of over 170,000 young Romanian children from around 1967 to 1989, which profoundly affected child development across multiple cognitive, emotional, and social domains (Nelson et al., 2014). Drawing on these and other prior findings, Jack Shonkoff provided testimony to the US Congress about the science of early life adversity (Shonkoff, 2019). Thankfully, this inhumane family separation policy was abolished after public outcry, lawsuits, and the congressional hearings. At the time of writing, nearly 1,800 children have been reunited with their families … but over 2,100 have not yet been. The shockwaves of these early experiences will likely reverberate for decades in the absence of novel therapeutic approaches.

Another set of issues is related to heightened sensation-seeking in adolescence; as we have seen, this is a precarious time with higher rates of morbidity (medical conditions) and all-cause mortality than at other phases of life (Chapter 13). In the United States, researchers Laurence Steinberg, B. J. Casey, Beatriz Luna, and others have worked to educate legislators and the public about adolescent brain development. For example, research on the effects of peer influence on risk-taking has prompted, or at least justified, legislation in the United States prohibiting adolescents from driving with other minors in the car. Likewise, a growing body of evidence that heavy cannabis use in adolescence may alter brain development should be part of the conversation as to whether/how to restrict teen access to it. Other legal deliberations center on minimum age requirements for driving, voting, making health care decisions, purchasing a gun, joining the army, and more. By what age, generally speaking, can we be trusted to make well-reasoned decisions and exert self-control? And when are we old enough to be held criminally responsible for our actions? DCN researchers have weighed in, grappling with the question of when in development (if ever) we can say that the brain has reached maturity. The MacArthur Network on Law and Neuroscience, comprised of neuroscientists, psychologists, law professors, and judges explore these and other issues.

14.6.3 Responsible Conduct and Dissemination of Research

As research on brain development advances, it becomes more and more relevant for society. One dilemma that comes to mind is gene editing. It is theoretically possible to alter DNA sequences in human embryos, altering genes that confer risk for neurodevelopmental and other disorders. Research is moving forward, given the advent of more precise gene editing tools – in particular, CRISPR-Cas9, for which Jennifer Doudna and Emmanuelle Charpentier shared a Nobel Prize in 2020. Although this is exciting technology with a whole host of (relatively non-controversial) applications, from agriculture to medicine, the prospect that it could be used to alter humans' developmental life course gives us pause. For one thing, there are hints that – as of right now – this gene editing technology can cause chromosomal damage (Ledford, 2020), thereby potentially resulting in genetic disorders. (Famed author Kazuo Ishiguro envisions precisely this scenario in his latest novel, *Klara and the Sun*. Also a Nobel Laureate, he was inspired by a discussion with Jennifer Doudna.) Beyond the issue of possible health risks, which might be resolved with further development of the techniques, there is a broader ethical discussion to be had: depending on your point of view, the vision of eradicating disorders – neurological/psychiatric and otherwise – and elevating human potential (called "lifting" in Ishiguro's novel) is either utopian or dystopian. Is a propensity to mindwander a disorder that should be eradicated? How about an elevated probability of having poor social skills – or a propensity to question the status quo?

There are rarely easy answers to societal problems … but the more we learn, the more informed our decisions will be. Of course, policies and laws rarely, if ever, change as a result of a single study – and for good reason. It is only when we have a body of evidence that scientists can agree on that a compelling case can be made. Importantly, interdisciplinary consortia that bring policymakers and researchers – and bioethicists – together have a greater chance of effecting societal change than do scientists working alone. Although we DCN researchers are not ourselves policymakers or legislators, we can conduct societally relevant research, advise decision-makers, educate the voting public, and inspire students who have learned about brain development (you!) to be changemakers in whatever fields you choose!

And recall (Chapter 2) that the chief strength of science is not the fancy tools and instruments, or testing hypotheses. What is important about the scientific enterprise is that researchers fumble towards the truth, updating theories on the basis of evidence (McIntyre, 2019). This is of course the essence of deductive and inductive reasoning, something that we need to draw on when personal, ideological, and cognitive biases blind us to the best available evidence (Kahneman, 2011).

14.7 Wrapping Up

We hope this book has convinced you that it's important to study the developing brain for multiple reasons (not just because it may be part of a required course for your major, or because you needed the credits and that really fun course in "Monkey Behavior and Hijinks" was all booked up).

The Developmental Cognitive Neuroscience approach we have outlined here intersects with our lives and those of our friends and family in many ways. If you've ended up in a psychology class, you've probably asked yourself questions such as "Why am I the way I am? To what extent am I destined to be just like my parents?" *Foundations of Developmental Cognitive Neuroscience* provides a framework from which to answer these questions, at least in their elemental form; to design and conduct experiments, and to interpret those results.

We study DCN to satisfy our curiosity: Why do children behave and learn the way they do? How do we become our unique, fascinating, complex selves? To what extent do our earlier experiences shape our adult lives – and to what extent can those early experiences be shaped, molded, or modified to improve outcomes? (The related question of how we might overcome negative early experiences, or improve ourselves, falls within the scope of other fields, such as motivation, clinical neuroscience, and positive psychiatry.)

DCN research underpins our ability to predict the onset of neurodevelopmental disorders in individuals, and provide insights on how to treat them. In this, we can work closely with and follow the findings of geneticists and clinical researchers, and can use computational modeling to help us better understand how typically and atypically developing brains might work, both when it is ordered and disordered. All of this helps us to gain insight regarding adult brain organization and function.

Studying the developing brain also provides critical information about brain development to the broad range of people who work with or make decisions about children: parents, childcare providers, educators, clinicians, judges, parole officers, policymakers, legislators, and even the highest courts of law.

There's also the coolness factor. There are many unanswered questions in our field and advances in techniques and cutting-edge technology mean it's a field experiencing great growth, filled with the promise of discovery. It's a field that needs bright young people with new ideas, and the determination to see them through with rigorous, clever experiments. Our hope is that you, dear reader, will consider furthering your studies and joining us in this exciting field.

References

American Academy of Child and Adolescent Psychiatry. (2017). *Lead exposure in children affects brain and behavior.* www.aacap.org/AACAP/Families_and_Youth/Facts_for_Families/FFF-Guide/Lead-Exposure-In-Children-Affects-Brain-And-Behavior-045.aspx

Badcock, P. B., Friston, K. J., & Ramstead, M. J. D. (2019). The hierarchically mechanistic mind: A free-energy formulation of the human psyche. *Physics of Life Reviews*, 31, 104–121. https:/doi.org/10.1016/j.plrev.2018.10.002

Bassett, D. S., Cullen, K. E., Eickhoff, S. B., Farah, M. J., Goda, Y., Haggard, P., Hu, H., Hurd, Y. L., Josselyn, S. A., Khakh, B. S., Knoblich, J. A., Poirazi, P., Poldrack, R. A., Prinz, M., Roelfsema, P. R., Spires-Jones, T. L., Sur, M., & Ueda, H. R. (2020). Reflections on the past two decades of neuroscience. *Nature Reviews Neuroscience*, 21, 524–534. https://doi.org/10.1038/s41583-020-0363-6

Bunge, M. (1980). *The mind-body problem: A psychobiological approach.* Pergamon Press.

Bunge, S. A., Dudukovic, N. M., Thomason, M. E., Vaidya, C. J., & Gabrieli, J. D. (2002). Immature frontal lobe contributions to cognitive control in children: Evidence from fMRI. *Neuron*, 33(2), 301–311. https://doi.org/10.1016/s0896-6273(01)00583-9

Cadwell, C. R., Bhaduri, A., Mostajo-Radji, M. A., Keefe, M. G., & Nowakowski, T. J. (2019). Development and arealization of the cerebral cortex. *Neuron*, 103(6), 980–1004. https://doi.org/10.1016/j.neuron.2019.07.009

Centers for Disease Control and Prevention (CDC) (2010). CDC Grand Rounds: Additional opportunities to prevent neural tube defects with folic acid fortification. *MMWR: Morbidity and Mortality Weekly Report*, 59(31), 980–984.

Charness, M. E., Riley, E. P., & Sowell, E. R. (2016). Drinking during pregnancy and the developing brain: Is any amount safe? *Trends in Cognitive Sciences*, 20(2), 80–82. https://doi.org/10.1016/j.tics.2015.09.011

Coley, E. J. L., & Hsiao, E. Y. (2021). Malnutrition and the microbiome as modifier of early development. *Trends in Neurosciences*, 44(9), 753–764. https://doi.org/10.1016/j.tins.2021.06.004

Commission for Racial Justice. (1987). *Toxic wastes and race in the United States: A national report on the racial and socioeconomic characteristics of communities with hazardous waste sites.* Commission for Racial Justice, United Church of Christ, New York.

de Klerk, C., Lamy-Yang, I., & Southgate, V. (2019). The role of sensorimotor experience in the development of mimicry in infancy. *Developmental Science*, 22(3), e12771. https://doi.org/10.1111/desc.12771

Denny, C. H., Acero, C. S., Naimi, T. S., & Kim, S. Y. (2019). Consumption of alcohol beverages and binge drinking among pregnant women aged 18–44 years – United States, 2015–2017. *MMWR: Morbidity and Mortality Weekly Report*, 68, 365–368. http://dx.doi.org/10.15585/mmwr.mm6816a1

Dickerson, C. (2019, June 16). The youngest child separated from his family at the border was 4 months old. *New York Times*. www.nytimes.com/2019/06/16/us/baby-constantine-romania-migrants.html

Ellwood-Lowe, M. E., Whitfield-Gabrieli, S., & Bunge, S. A. (2021). What is an adaptive pattern of brain network coupling for a child? It depends on their environment. *Nature Communications*, 12. https://doi.org/10.1101/2020.05.29.124297

Falk, E. B., Hyde, L. W., Mitchell, C., Faul, J., Gonzalez, R., Heitzeg, M. M., Keating, D. P., Langa, K. M., Martz, M. E., Maslowsky, J., Morrison, F. J., Noll, D. C., Patrick, M. E., Pfeffer, F. T., Reuter-Lorenz, P. A., Thomason, M. E., Davis-Kean, P., Monk, C. S., & Schulenberg, J. (2013). What is a representative brain? Neuroscience meets population science. *Proceedings of the National Academy of Sciences of the United States of America*, 110(44), 17615–17622. https://doi.org/10.1073/pnas.1310134110

Farah, M. J. (2012). Neuroethics: The ethical, legal, and societal impact of neuroscience. *Annual Review of Psychology*, 63, 571–591. https://doi.org/10.1146/annurev.psych.093008.100438

Gabrieli, J. D. E., Ghosh, S. S., & Whitfield-Gabrieli, S. (2015). Prediction as a humanitarian and pragmatic contribution from human cognitive neuroscience. *Neuron*, 85(1), 11–26. https://doi.org/10.1016/j.neuron.2014.10.047

Goldinger, S. D., Papesh, M. H., Barnhart, A. S., Hansen, W. A., & Hout, M. C. (2016). The poverty of embodied cognition. *Psychonomic Bulletin & Review*, 23(4), 959–978. https://doi.org/10.3758/s13423-015-0860-1

Gomez, J., Zhen, Z., & Weiner, K. S. (2019). Human visual cortex is organized along two genetically opposed hierarchical gradients with unique developmental and evolutionary origins. *PLOS Biology*, 17(7), e3000362. https://doi.org/10.1371/journal.pbio.3000362

Gordon, E. M., Laumann, T. O., Gilmore, A. W., Newbold, D. J., Greene, D. J., Berg, J. J., Ortega, M., Hoyt-Drazen, C., Gratton, C., Sun, H., Hampton, J. M., Coalson, R. S., Nguyen, A. L., McDermott, K. B., Shimony, J. S., Snyder, A. Z., Schlaggar, B. L., Petersen, S. E., Nelson, S. M., & Dosenbach, N. (2017). Precision functional mapping of individual human brains. *Neuron*, 95(4), 791–807.e7. https://doi.org/10.1016/j.neuron.2017.07.011

Grafton, S. (2020). *Physical intelligence: The science of how the body and the mind guide each other through life*. Penguin-Random House.

Griebel, C. P., Halvorsen, J., Golemon, T. B., & Day, A. A. (2005). Management of spontaneous abortion. *American Family Physician*, 72(7), 1243–1250.

Han, V. X., Patel, S., Jones, H. F., & Dale, R. C. (2021). Maternal immune activation and neuroinflammation in human neurodevelopmental disorders. *Nature Reviews Neurology*, 17, 564–579. https://doi.org/10.1038/s41582-021-00530-8

Haxby, J. V., Connolly, A. C., & Guntupalli, J. S. (2014). Decoding neural representational spaces using multivariate pattern analysis. *Annual Review of Neuroscience*, 37, 435–456. https://doi.org/10.1146/annurev-neuro-062012-170325

Hertz-Picciotto, I., Sass, J. B., Engel, S., Bennett, D. H., Bradman, A., Eskenazi, B., Lanphear, B., & Whyatt, R. (2018). Organophosphate exposures during pregnancy and child neurodevelopment: Recommendations for essential policy reforms. *PLOS Medicine*, 15(10), e1002671. https://doi.org/10.1371/journal.pmed.1002671

Johnson, M. H. (2011). Interactive specialization: A domain-general framework for human functional brain development? *Developmental Cognitive Neuroscience*, 1(1), 7–21. https://doi.org/10.1016/j.dcn.2010.07.003

Kahneman, D. (2011). *Thinking, fast and slow*. Farrar, Straus & Giroux.

Keysers, C., & Perrett, D. I. (2004). Demystifying social cognition: A Hebbian perspective. *Trends in Cognitive Sciences*, 8(11), 501–507. https://doi.org/10.1016/j.tics.2004.09.005

Kofuji, P., & Araque, A. (2021). Astrocytes control the critical period of circuit wiring. *Science*, 373(6550), 29–30. https://doi.org/10.1126/science.abj6745

Kriegeskorte, N., & Diedrichsen, J. (2019). Peeling the onion of brain representations. *Annual Review of Neuroscience*, 42, 407–432. https://doi.org/10.1146/annurev-neuro-080317-061906

Kupferschmidt, K. (2018). Tide of lies. *Science*, 361(6403), 636–641. https://doi.org/10.1126/science.361.6403.636

Larroya, A., Pantoja, J., Codoñer-Franch, P., & Cenit, M. C. (2021). Towards tailored gut microbiome-based and dietary interventions for promoting the development and maintenance of a healthy brain. *Frontiers in Pediatrics*, 9, 705859. https://doi.org/10.3389/fped.2021.705859

Ledford, C. (2020). CRISPR gene editing in human embryos wreaks chromosomal mayhem. *Nature*, 583, 17–18. https://doi.org/10.1038/d41586-020-01906-4

Linnakaari, R., Helle, N., Mentula, M., Bloigu, A., Gissler, M., Heikinheimo, O., & Niinimäki, M. (2019). Trends in the incidence, rate and treatment of miscarriage: Nationwide register-study in Finland, 1998–2016. *Human Reproduction*, 34(11), 2120–2128. https://doi.org/10.1093/humrep/dez211

Mahon, B. Z. (2015). What is embodied about cognition? *Language, Cognition and Neuroscience*, 30(4), 420–429, https://doi.org/10.1080/23273798.2014.987791

McIntyre, L. (2019). *The scientific attitude*. MIT Press.

Molet, J., Heins, K., Zhuo, X., Mei, Y. T., Regev, L., Baram, T. Z., & Stern, H. (2016). Fragmentation and high entropy of neonatal experience predict adolescent emotional outcome. *Translational Psychiatry*, 6(1), e702. https://doi.org/10.1038/tp.2015.200

Natu, V. S., Arcaro, M. J., Barnett, M. A., Gomez, J., Livingstone, M., Grill-Spector, K., & Weiner, K. S. (2021). Sulcal depth in the medial ventral temporal cortex predicts the location of a place-selective region in macaques, children, and adults. *Cerebral Cortex*, 31(1), 48–61. https://doi.org/10.1093/cercor/bhaa203

Nelson, C. A., Fox, N. A., & Zeanah, C. H. (2014). *Romania's abandoned children: Deprivation, brain development, and the struggle for recovery*. Harvard University Press.

O'Hearn, K., Larsen, B., Fedor, J., Luna, B., & Lynn, A. (2020). Representational similarity analysis reveals atypical age-related changes in brain regions supporting face and car recognition in autism. *NeuroImage*, 209, 116322. https://doi.org/10.1016/j.neuroimage.2019.116322

Poldrack, R. A., Baker, C. I., Durnez, J., Gorgolewski, K. J., Matthews, P. M., Munafò, M. R., Nichols, T. E., Poline, J. B., Vul, E., & Yarkoni, T. (2017). Scanning the horizon: Towards transparent and reproducible neuroimaging research. *Nature Reviews Neuroscience*, 18(2), 115–126. https://doi .org/10.1038/nrn.2016.167

Poldrack, R. A., Huckins, G., & Varoquaux, G. (2020). Establishment of best practices for evidence for prediction: A review. *JAMA Psychiatry*, 77(5), 534–540. https://doi.org/10.1001/ jamapsychiatry.2019.3671

Poldrack, R. A., Laumann, T. O., Koyejo, O., Gregory, B., Hover, A., Chen, M. Y., Gorgolewski, K. J., Luci, J., Joo, S. J., Boyd, R. L., Hunicke-Smith, S., Simpson, Z. B., Caven, T., Sochat, V., Shine, J. M., Gordon, E., Snyder, A. Z., Adeyemo, B., Petersen, S. E., Glahn, D. C., ... Mumford, J. A. (2015). Long-term neural and physiological phenotyping of a single human. *Nature Communications*, 6, 8885. https://doi.org/10.1038/ncomms9885

Ribot, J., Breton, R., Calvo, C. F., Moulard, J., Ezan, P., Zapata, J., Samama, K., Moreau, M., Bemelmans, A. P., Sabatet, V., Dingli, F., Loew, D., Milleret, C., Billuart, P., Dallérac, G., & Rouach, N. (2021). Astrocytes close the mouse critical period for visual plasticity. *Science*, 373(6550), 77–81. https://doi.org/10.1126/science.abf5273

Sagiv, S. K., Bruno, J. L., Baker, J. M., Palzes, V., Kogut, K., Rauch, S., Gunier, R., Mora, A. M., Reiss, A. L., & Eskenazi, B. (2019). Prenatal exposure to organophosphate pesticides and functional neuroimaging in adolescents living in proximity to pesticide application. *Proceedings of the National Academy of Sciences of the United States of America*, 116(37), 18347–18356. https://doi.org/10.1073/ pnas.1903940116

Sagiv, S. K., Kogut, K., Harley, K., Bradman, A., Morga, N., & Eskenazi, B. (2021). Gestational exposure to organophosphate pesticides and longitudinally assessed behaviors related to ADHD and executive function. *American Journal of Epidemiology,* 190(11), 2420–2431. https://doi.org/10.1093/aje/ kwab173

Shonkoff, J. P. (2019, February 9). Hearing on migrant family separation policy. Migrant family separation congressional testimony, Washington, DC. https://youtu.be/uvdNRt2uavU

Treit, S., Lebel, C., Baugh, L., Rasmussen, C., Andrew, G., & Beaulieu, C. (2013). Longitudinal MRI reveals altered trajectory of brain development during childhood and adolescence in fetal alcohol spectrum disorders. *The Journal of Neuroscience*, 33(24), 10098–10109. https://doi.org/10.1523/ JNEUROSCI.5004-12.2013

Voorhies, W. I., Miller, J. A., Yao, J. K., Bunge, S. A., & Weiner, K. S. (2021). Cognitive insights from tertiary sulci in prefrontal cortex. *Nature Communications*, 12(1), 5122. https://doi.org/10.1038/ s41467-021-25162-w

Weiskopf, N., Mohammadi, S., Lutti, A., & Callaghan, M. F. (2015). Advances in MRI-based computational neuroanatomy: From morphometry to in-vivo histology. *Current Opinion in Neurology*, 28(4), 313–322. https://doi.org/10.1097/WCO.0000000000000222

Index